D0206173

A HERMAN
MELVILLE
ENCYCLOPEDIA

A
HERMAN MELVILLE
ENCYCLOPEDIA

Robert L. Gale

GREENWOOD PRESS
Westport, Connecticut • London

Library of Congress Cataloging-in-Publication Data

Gale, Robert L.
    A Herman Melville encyclopedia / Robert L. Gale.
        p.   cm.
    Includes bibliographical references and index.
    ISBN 0–313–29011–3 (alk. paper)
        1. Melville, Herman, 1819–1891—Encyclopedias. 2. Authors,
    American—19th century—Biography—Encyclopedias. I. Title.
    PS2386.G3   1995
    813'.3—dc20   94–29837

British Library Cataloguing in Publication Data is available.

Library of Congress Catalog Card Number: 94–29837
ISBN: 0–313–29011–3

First published in 1995

Greenwood Press, 88 Post Road West, Westport, CT 06881
An imprint of Greenwood Publishing Group, Inc.

Printed in the United States of America

∞

The paper used in this book complies with the
Permanent Paper Standard issued by the National
Information Standards Organization (Z39.48–1984).

10 9 8 7 6 5 4 3 2 1

For Maureen

Contents

Preface ix

Chronology xiii

Abbreviations and Short Titles xvii

The Encyclopedia 1

General Bibliography 505

Index 509

Preface

It is my hope that *A Herman Melville Encyclopedia* will be of special help to readers just beginning to appreciate Melville, who is in many ways the most unusual, challenging, disturbing, and difficult American author. My work provides an easy sorting out of plots, characters, relatives, friends, and activities. In addition, it should aid more experienced readers in college and university classes. Graduate students, seasoned teachers, and publishing scholars may also find it useful in providing an efficient review of much primary and secondary data, or at least in refreshing their memories of earlier readings.

Melville was much more than the author of *Moby-Dick,* ''Bartleby,'' ''Benito Cereno,'' *Billy Budd,* and once sensational works, notably *Typee* and *Omoo,* about South Sea cannibals. Much of his other fiction, especially but not exclusively *The Confidence-Man,* is often so bewildering in its complexity that readers may gratefully accept a little help in navigating through it. Melville was inspired to write poems about the Civil War, which were collected in *Battle-Pieces* and which have earned him tardy respect. His long narrative poem, *Clarel,* the consequence of an anguished pilgrimage to the Holy Land, is attracting more and more attention. Moreover, in leading several lives—those of sailor, author, friend of many types of people, son, brother, husband, and father—he touched the lives of many persons, dozens of whom appear in this encyclopedia. Also, critical and biographical scholarship is pouring from academic presses at such a rate that we all need help with winnowing and memory jogging. While this encyclopedia is informational and not critical, a few critical judgments are implicit here and there; and the end-of-entry bibliographies and the final, general bibliography—all of which stress post-1990 material wherever pertinent—should prove useful to the critically minded.

To aid the reader, items in *A Herman Melville Encyclopedia* are cross-referenced by being marked with an asterisk (*). All of Melville's titles and characters have individual entries, however, and are therefore not thus marked. Titles of individual pieces of writing of fewer than about 50,000 words are placed within quotation marks; longer works are italicized, for example, *White-Jacket* and ''Adieu.''

The reader will note several seeming oddities. Too often, perhaps, I quote from Melville's poetry. This is partly because in his poetry one gets a quick, concentrated, and stimulating whiff of his unique diction. Also, I stress the names and, where possible, the activities of the various nineteenth-century women whose lives—or whose men's lives—touched Melville's. This is done for two reasons: His narratives have few down-to-earth heroines (Isabel Banford, Joanna I, Yillah?; Bonny Blue, yes); and women too often played second or no fiddle at all in Melville's male-dominated era. The seeming inconsistency in the spelling of names of historical figures is—partly, at least—owing to the occasional deviation from historical acceptance by Melville, whose spellings I try to keep. Accordingly, I seldom use brackets—and never use asterisks—within plot summaries. The reader will kindly make allowances.

It is a pleasure to thank many persons for their invaluable aid and professional courtesies. My greatest debt is to Nicholas Weir-Williams, director of the Northwestern University Press, for giving me a copy of every available volume of the ongoing Northwestern-Newberry Edition of Melville's works, and even for supplying me with a working copy of its forthcoming volume of Melville's published poetry. Please note, however, that although all quotations from Melville's poetry conform to the forthcoming Northwestern-Newberry Edition, I tersely cite two currently available editions as sources of the poems individually entered below. They are *The Works of Herman Melville,* which means Raymond M. Weaver's edition (London: Constable, 1922–24, volume 16 being devoted to the poetry), and *Collected Poems of Herman Melville,* which means Howard P. Vincent's edition (Chicago: Packard and Company, 1947).

I also thank members of Mr. Weir-Williams's staff, including Kerry Costello and Heather Kenny. The numerous editors of the Northwestern-Newberry Edition also deserve monumental praise for their selfless, time-consuming, intelligent, and meticulous scholarly work. They are well known to Melvilleans but deserve to be named again. They are Harrison Hayford, Brian Higgins, Lynn Horth, Richard Colles Johnson, Alma A. MacDougall, R. D. Madison, Joel Myerson, Hershel Parker, Robert G. Ryan, G. Thomas Tanselle, and Donald Yannella. They were advised and otherwise aided by numerous associates. The following persons also answered my specific queries, provided useful information, and also helped hold my errors—now mine alone—to a minimum: Norton Andrews, Jr. (Texas Tech University), Carolyn E. Banfield (Berkshire County Historical Society, Pittsfield, Massachusetts), Alicia Mauldin (Archives, U.S. Military Academy, West Point, New York), Hershel Parker (University of Delaware), Gary Scharnhorst (University of New Mexico), James Thorpe III (Archon Books), John Wenke (Salisbury State University), and Nathalia Wright

(University of Tennessee). For kindness and encouragement of a more personal nature, I offer thanks to the following colleagues of mine at the University of Pittsburgh: H. David Brumble III, Bruce Dobler, Frederick A. Hetzel, Richard C. Tobias, and David G. Wilkins. Also I owe much to several librarians at the University of Pittsburgh (especially Laurie Cohen, Anne W. Gordon, Marcia Grodsky, and Amy E. Knapp), the Carnegie Public Library of Pittsburgh (especially Heather Brodhead and Kathryn P. Logan), and Carnegie-Mellon University. I also offer thanks to my editor, George F. Butler of Greenwood Press, for his advice, cooperation, and patience, and to Lynn E. Wheeler and Richard A. Sillett for their conscientious and intelligent copyediting and production work. A special thank-you goes to my son James D. Gale and Harriet Brumble for their skillful preparation of the Gansevoort, Melville, and Shaw family trees. Finally, once again, my love and gratitude to Maureen, who married me in war-torn London on D-Day plus 5 months. She is forever this Bridegroom-Bob's Bonny Green.

Chronology

1774	Thomas Melvill* (1751–1832), Melville's paternal grandfather, marries Priscilla Scollay (1755–1833), Melville's paternal grandmother.
1778	Peter Gansevoort (1749–1812),* Melville's maternal grandfather, marries Catherine Van Schaick (1751–1830), Melville's maternal grandmother.
1781	Lemuel Shaw* (1781–1861), Melville's father-in-law, is born.
1782	Allan Melvill* (1782–1832), Melville's father, is born.
1784	Elizabeth Knapp Shaw* (1784–1822), Melville's mother-in-law, is born.
1791	Maria Gansevoort (1791–1872), Melville's mother, is born.
1793	Hope Savage Shaw* (1793–1879), Melville's stepmother-in-law, is born.
1814	Allan Melvill marries Maria Gansevoort.
1815	Gansevoort Melville* (1815–1846), Melville's brother, is born. (The family name was spelled Melvill until 1838 or so.)
1817	Helen Maria Melville Griggs* (1817–1888), Melville's sister, is born.
1819	Herman Melville* (1819–1891) is born.
1821	Augusta Melville* (1821–1876), Melville's sister, is born.
1823	Allan Melville* (1823–1872), Melville's brother, is born.
1825	Catherine Gansevoort Melville Hoadley* (1825–1905), Melville's sister, is born. Melville attends New-York Male High School (to 1829).
1827	Frances Priscilla Melville* (1827–1885), Melville's sister, is born. Melville visits paternal grandparents in Boston (and again in 1829).

1829	Melville attends Grammar School, Columbia College, New York (to 1830).
1830	Thomas Melville* (1830–1884), Melville's brother and youngest sibling, is born. Allan Melvill fails in business and moves with family to Albany. Melville attends Albany Academy (to 1832).
1832	Allan Melvill, Melville's father, dies in Albany. Melville clerks at New York State Bank, Albany (to 1835). Melville's mother moves with family to Pittsfield, Massachusetts.
1833	Melville visits Pittsfield briefly.
1834	Works as clerk and bookkeeper in brother Gansevoort's fur and cap store, Albany (to 1835).
1835	Joins Albany Young Man's Association.
1836	Joins Ciceronian Debating Society, attends classes at Albany Classical Academy (to 1837).
1837	Gansevoort Melville's store fails. Melville manages Uncle Thomas's farm near Pittsfield, then teaches in Sikes District School, near Pittsfield, Massachusetts (to 1838).
1838	Melville's mother moves with her family to Lansingburgh, north of Albany. Melville becomes president of Philo Logos debating society, Albany. Studies surveying and engineering at Lansingburgh Academy (to 1839).
1839	Publishes ''Fragments from a Writing Desk'' pseudonymously in Lansingburgh paper; sails as crew member of the trader *St. Lawrence* New York to Liverpool and return; teaches at a school in Greenbush, near Albany (to 1840).
1840	Teaches in Brunswick, New York; visits Uncle Thomas in Galena, Illinois, with friend Eli James Murdock Fly*; travels on a Mississippi River steamboat; unsuccessfully seeks work in New York City.
1841	January, sails from Fairhaven, Massachusetts, as crew member of the American whaler *Acushnet;* March, stops at Rio de Janeiro; April, rounds Cape Horn; June, visits Santa, Peru; fall and winter, cruises through Galapagos Islands.
1842	June, in Marquesas Islands; July, with Richard Tobias Greene,* deserts the *Acushnet* and goes into the interior of Nuku Hiva; August, ships as crew member aboard the Australian whaler *Lucy Ann;* September, refuses duty near Tahiti and is imprisoned by British consul; October, escapes with John B. Troy to the island of Eimeo and works on potato farm; November, signs as crew member on the American whaler *Charles and Henry*.
1843	April, visits Lahaina, Hawaiian Islands; is discharged and works as store clerk and bowling-alley pinsetter in Honolulu; signs as ordinary seaman aboard the U.S. naval frigate *United States,* becomes friendly with John J. Chase; fall, visits Marquesas, Tahiti, Valparaiso, Callao.

1844   January, visits Lima; spring, visits Mazatlán; summer, visits Rio de Janeiro; October, is discharged in Boston and rejoins family in Lansingburgh.

1846   *Typee* is published. Gansevoort dies in London. Greene appears in Buffalo and verifies part of *Typee*.

1847   Melville tries unsuccessfully to find government work in Washington, D.C. *Omoo* is published. Melville marries Elizabeth Knapp Shaw Melville* (1822–1906) in Boston; they live in New York with his brother Allan and Allan's wife Sophia E. Thurston, and with the brothers' mother and their four single sisters. Finances are provided by Melville's father-in-law Lemuel Shaw. Melville becomes friendly with New York men of letters Evert Duyckinck* and Cornelius Mathews.*

1849   Malcolm Melville,* Melville's first son, is born. *Mardi* is published. *Redburn* is published. Melville visits England and the Continent (to 1850).

1850   August, meets Nathaniel Hawthorne*; buys a farm he names Arrowhead, outside Pittsfield; moves there with family.

1851   Stanwix Melville,* Melville's second son, is born. *Moby-Dick* is published.

1852   *Pierre* is published.

1853   Elizabeth Melville,* Melville's first daughter, is born. Family and close friends begin to worry about his financial insecurity and intermittent depression, try unsuccessfully to obtain a consular appointment for him. Melville publishes short fiction and sketches in *Putnam's Monthly Magazine** and *Harper's New Monthly Magazine** (to 1856). Catherine Melville marries John Chipman Hoadley.* Fire at Harper's destroys many of Melville's unsold books though not any stereotyped plates.

1854   *Israel Potter* is published serially in *Putnam's Monthly Magazine* (to 1855).

1855   Melville suffers from rheumatism and then sciatica. *Israel Potter* is published in book form. Frances Melville,* Melville's second daughter, is born. Oliver Wendell Holmes* examines Melville.

1856   *The Piazza Tales* are published. Travels in the British Isles, the Mediterranean region, and Asia Minor, on funds provided by father-in-law (to 1857).

1857   *The Confidence-Man* is published.

1858   Melville lectures south to Tennessee and west to Ohio.

1859   Lectures south to Baltimore and west to Wisconsin; lectures in New York and Massachusetts (to 1860).

1860   Sails to San Francisco aboard ship captained by his brother Thomas, returns via Panamanian isthmus.

1861	Visits Washington, D.C., in unsuccessful attempt to obtain consular appointment; suffering from rheumatism, spends winter in New York City with family (into 1862).
1862	Moves with family from Arrowhead into Pittsfield; is badly hurt in road accident.
1863	Moves with family to New York City.
1864	Visits Union Army camp in Virginia.
1866	Publishes five Civil War poems in *Harper's New Monthly Magazine*. *Battle-Pieces* are published in book form. Melville becomes inspector of customs at Port of New York (to 1885).
1867	Elizabeth Melville's minister and family discuss a legal separation from Melville, who they fear is insane, but decide against it. Malcolm Melville commits suicide.
1869	Stanwix Melville begins years of unstable wandering.
1872	Fire destroys Elizabeth Melville's Boston property.
1876	*Clarel* is published at uncle Peter Gansevoort's expense.
1878	Elizabeth Melville's aunt, Mrs. Martha Marett, dies and wills Elizabeth considerable money.
1880	Frances Melville marries Henry B. Thomas.
1882	Eleanor Melville Thomas, Melville's first grandchild, is born.
1886	Stanwix Melville dies in San Francisco.
1887	Melville receives final royalty statement from Harper's.
1888	Visits Bermuda, privately publishes *John Marr*.
1891	Privately publishes *Timoleon*, prepares *Weeds and Wildings*, and leaves it and *Billy Budd* in manuscript form; dies.

Abbreviations and Short Titles

Acton
Harold Acton, *The Last Bourbons of Naples (1825–1861)* (New York: St. Martin's Press, 1961).

Adler
Joyce Sparer Adler, *War in Melville's Imagination* (New York: New York University Press, 1981).

Anderson
Charles Roberts Anderson, *Melville in the South Seas* (1939; New York: Dover Publications, 1966).

Boatner
Mark Mayo Boatner III, *The Civil War Dictionary* (New York: Donald McKay, 1959).

Bryant,
Companion
John Bryant, ed., *A Companion to Melville Studies* (Westport, Conn.: Greenwood Press, 1986).

Bryant, *Repose*
John Bryant, *Melville and Repose: The Rhetoric of Humor in the American Renaissance* (New York: Oxford University Press, 1993).

Cohen, *Poems*
Hennig Cohen, ed., *Selected Poems of Herman Melville* (New York: Fordham University Press, 1991).

Cohen, *Potter*
Hennig Cohen, ed., Herman Melville, *Israel Potter: His Fifty Years of Exile* (New York: Fordham University Press, 1991).

Cohen and
Yannella
Hennig Cohen and Donald Yannella, *Herman Melville's Malcolm Letter: "Man's Final Lore"* (New York: Fordham University Press and the New York Public Library, 1992).

Davis
Merrell R. Davis, *Melville's Mardi: A Chartless Voyage* (New Haven, Conn.: Yale University Press, 1952).

Faust
Patricia L. Faust, *Historical Times Illustrated Encyclopedia of the Civil War* (New York: Harper and Row, 1986).

Finkelstein
Dorothee Metlitsky Finkelstein, *Melville's Orienda* (New Haven, Conn.: Yale University Press, 1961).

Garner   Stanton Garner, *The Civil War World of Herman Melville* (Lawrence: University Press of Kansas, 1993).

Gilman   William H. Gilman, *Melville's Early Life and Redburn* (New York: New York University Press, 1951).

Grejda   Edward S. Grejda, *The Common Continent of Men: Racial Equality in the Writings of Herman Melville* (Port Washington, N.Y.: Kennikat Press, 1974).

Howard   Leon Howard, *Herman Melville: A Biography* (Berkeley: University of California Press, 1951).

Jaffé   David Jaffé, *The Stormy Petrel [Charles Wilkes] and the Whale: Some Origins of Moby-Dick* (Baltimore: Port City Press, 1976).

Kenney   Alice P. Kenney, *The Gansevoorts of Albany: Dutch Patricians in the Upper Hudson Valley* (Syracuse, N.Y.: Syracuse University Press, 1969).

Kuykendall   Ralph S. Kuykendall, *The Hawaiian Kingdom 1778–1854: Foundation and Transformation* (Honolulu: University of Hawaii Press, 1947).

Lebowitz   Alan Lebowitz, *Progress into Silence: A Study of Melville's Heroes* (Bloomington: Indiana University Press, 1970).

Leyda   Jay Leyda, *The Melville Log: A Documentary Life of Herman Melville, 1819–1891* (2 vols., New York: Harcourt, Brace, 1951; enl. ed., 2 vols., New York: Gordian Press, 1969).

Metcalf   Eleanor Melville Metcalf, *Herman Melville: Cycle and Epicycle* (Cambridge, Mass.: Harvard University Press, 1953).

Newbury   Colin Newbury, *Tahiti Nui: Change and Survival in French Polynesia 1767–1945* (Honolulu: University Press of Hawaii, 1980).

Newman   Lea Bertani Vozar Newman, *A Reader's Guide to the Short Stories of Herman Melville* (New York: G. K. Hall, 1986).

NN (followed   *The Writings of Herman Melville,* Northwestern-Newberry Edition
by volume   (1968–).
number)

O'Reilly and   Patrick O'Reilly and Raoul Teissier, *Tahitiens: Répertoire bio-*
Teissier   *bibliographique de la Polynésie Française,* 2d ed. (Paris: Musée de l'Homme, 1975).

Sealts   Merton M. Sealts, Jr., *Pursuing Melville 1940–1980* (Madison: University of Wisconsin Press, 1982).

Shurr   William H. Shurr, *The Mystery of Iniquity: Melville as Poet, 1857–1891* (Lexington: University Press of Kentucky, 1972).

Smith   Richard Dean Smith, *Melville's Complaint: Doctors and Medicine in the Art of Herman Melville* (New York: Garland, 1991).

Stein   William Bysshe Stein, *The Poetry of Melville's Late Years: Time, History, Myth, and Religion* (Albany: State University of New York Press, 1970).

Trimpi   Helen P. Trimpi, *Melville's Confidence Men and American Politics
                    in the 1850s* (Hamden, Conn.: Archon Books, 1987).

Wallace   Robert K. Wallace, ''Melville's Prints and Engravings at the Berk-
                    shire Museum,'' *Essays in Arts and Sciences* 15 (June 1986): 58–90.

Warren   Robert Penn Warren, ed., *Selected Poems of Herman Melville: A
                    Reader's Edition* (New York: Random House, 1970).

Wilson   Edmund Wilson, *Patriotic Gore: Studies in the Literature of the
                    American Civil War* (New York: Oxford University Press, 1962).

Wright   Nathalia Wright, ed., Herman Melville, *Mardi and a Voyage Thither*
                    (Putney, Vt.: Hendricks House, 1990).

Young   Philip Young, *The Private Melville* (University Park: Pennsylvania
                    State University Press, 1993).

A

A. In *Mardi,* she is one of the three vain daughters of Nimni, on the isle of Pimminee. The other daughters are I and O.

Abdon ("The Black Jew"). In *Clarel,* he is the host of the Jerusalem inn in which Clarel stays. Earlier, Abdon went from India to Amsterdam as a trader. Now disillusioned but not bitter, he wishes in due time to be buried in Jerusalem. Abdon may be partly modeled on Hauser, a German who converted to the Jewish faith and who ran a hotel in Jerusalem, and on M. Blattner, a German-Jewish hotel proprietor in Jaffa. Melville mentions both men in his 1857 journal (6, 24 [22] January).
   Bibliography: NN 12 and 15.

Abos and Padilla, José de. In "Benito Cereno," he is the royal notary, provincial register, and notary public for the Bishop of Lima.

Abrantes, Duchess d'. In *Israel Potter,* she is an aristocratic French woman who is presumably interested in Dr. [Benjamin] Franklin's scientific experiments. The name of this probably fictitious character may have been inspired by that of Duchess d'Abrantès (1784–1838). Born Jane Permon Junot, she was the beautiful and witty wife of the Duke d'Abrantès, one of the generals of Napoleon,* and published her *Memoirs* (18 vols., 1831–1834).
   Bibliography: Cohen, *Potter.*

Abrazza, King. In *Mardi,* he is the unmarried monarch of the island of Bonovona. He pities the fallen but aids none, and he hates the sight of anything unpleasant. Babbalanja lectures him on the subject of Lombardo and *Koztanza,*

Lombardo's masterpiece. Abrazza's objection that *Koztanza* "lacks cohesion" may be Melville's criticism of his own *Mardi* for the same fault. Abrazza's name may derive from *abrazo* (Spanish, "embrace").
   Bibliography: Davis, Lebowitz, Wright.

Acarty, Marquis d'. In *White-Jacket,* he is an old Brazilian nobleman who deferentially attends Pedro II, the king of Brazil, when that monarch condescendingly visits the *Neversink.*

"The Accepted Time." Poem. *See* "Rosary Beads."

Adam. In "To Ned," Adam is a general name for a businesslike modern man.

Adams, Hannah (1755–1832). Author. Distantly related to President John Adams, she was born in Medfield, Massachusetts. She was so frail that she was taught at home by student boarders, tutored and made lace during the American Revolution, and compiled *An Alphabetical Compendium of the Various Sects Which Have Appeared from the Beginning of the Christian Aera to the Present Day* (1794). While temporarily blind, she composed *A Summary History of New England* (1799), and she later wrote *The Truth and Excellence of the Christian Religion* (1804), *History of the Jews* (1812), *Letters on the Gospels* (1826), and other works. In "On the Chinese Junk," Mrs. Hannah Adams is mentioned as the author of the *History of Religious Sects,* with comments on Junkers.
   Bibliography: Van Wyck Brooks, *The Flowering of New England, 1815–1865* (New York: E. P. Dutton, 1936).

Adeea. In *Omoo,* he is a chief on the island of Imeeo. He wonders about the ability of the natives there to resist the encroachments of the French.

"Adieu" (1947). Poem, in *Collected Poems of Herman Melville.* As the curtain falls, the poet asks us to think of him and "be happy under heaven."

Adler, George J. (1821–1868). German-American scholar and educator. He was born in Leipzig, migrated to the United States (1833), attended the University of the City of New York (now known as New York University), taught students in elective courses in German there for pay, graduated (1844), was named honorary professor of German literature, and began to teach without pay (from 1846). He was an expert on the classics, German philosophy and metaphysics, Middle-Eastern literature, and Provençal poetry, and knew several languages. Adler ruined his health while compiling a *Dictionary of the German and English Language* (1849), met Melville through their mutual friend George Duyckinck,* and sailed as a fellow passenger with Melville to England (1849). In his 1849 journal, Melville notes the following about him: "He is full of the German metaphysics, & discourses of Kant, Swedenborg &c. He has been my principal companion thus far'' (12 October). The two were together in London and later in Paris (1849), and Adler undoubtedly stimulated Melville's intellectual interests. Although the two evidently never met face to face again, Melville mentioned Adler amiably in letters to Evert Duyckinck,* who knew Adler and respected him. Adler sent Melville (1851) a copy of his translation of Johann Wolfgang von Goethe's *Iphigenia in Tauris, a Drama in Five Acts* (1850). Adler returned to New York suffering from agoraphobia, hallucinations, and paranoia (1852) and, against his will, was committed to the Bloomingdale Asylum in New York (1853–1868). He privately printed his *Letters of a Lunatic; or, A Brief Exposition of My University Life, during the Years 1853–54* (1854). Melville and Evert Duyckinck attended the unfortunate man's funeral (1868).

   Bibliography: NN 14 and 15; Sanford E. Marovitz, ''More Chartless Voyaging: Melville and Adler at Sea,'' in *Studies in the American Renaissance* (Charlottesville: University Press of Virginia, 1986), pp. 373–84; Smith.

Admiral. In ''The Temeraire.'' *See* Nelson, Horatio.

Admiral of the White, The. In ''The Admiral of the White,'' he is the admiral of the British ship who, after defeating a French enemy, stowed some surrendered French swords too near the compass. He now finds his compass needle turned and his ship sunk on jagged reefs.

Admiral of the White, The. In ''The Haglets,'' he is the admiral who after defeating the Plate Fleet of Spain orders his flagship home to report the victory. His ship sinks on treacherous reefs, however, because some sword blades clash in a case under the compass and thus turn it.

''The Admiral of the White'' (1947). Poem, in *Collected Poems of Herman Melville*. (Characters: The Admiral of the White, Captains.) The English admiral, now homeward bound, is pleased that his French enemies have surrendered their colors and swords, but he wonders why his compass needle is skipping about. It is the last Saturday of the year. His crew should celebrate. They will soon house the French flags in St. Paul's. Those swords, in a chest too near ''the needle so trembling about,'' if given up ''might yet win the day.'' Suddenly the victorious ship is dashed against rocks ashore, splits, and is ground into chips. The admiral and his men drown. This poem relates to Melville's more complex poem ''The Haglets,'' written later. He also has Agath recount the same incident in *Clarel*. Melville was inspired to write about these nautical tragedies after he had heard his captain in the harbor of Salonica, during his 1856–1857 trip to the Mediterranean area, tell how clashing swords once damaged a compass; Melville recorded the anecdote in his 1856 journal (7 and 8 December).

   Bibliography: NN 15, Shurr, Stein, Warren.

Adondo. In *Mardi,* he is a famous chief whose death is recorded in one of the chronicles recited by Mohi as Taji's party is leaving the island of Diranda. Yoomy's monody on Adondo's death may echo *Adonais* by Percy Bysshe Shelley.*

   Bibliography: Davis.

Ady. In *Mardi,* he is the lost love of Ozonna in a story which Mohi tells at Queen Hautia's isle of Flozella-a-Nina to dissuade Taji from continuing his long search for the lost Yillah. Ozonna seeks Ady in Hautia's court but finds only Rea, who resembles Ady.

"The Aeolian Harp: At the *Surf Inn*" (1888). Poem, in *John Marr.* The discordant harp in the window is less ideal than real. The poet offers an image from his memory: Men aboard the *Phocion,* bound from Alicant to Baltimore, see a dismasted, ruined lumberman, drifting unattended and dangerous to ships it might waylay. The harp wails about "lost crews never heard of!"

   Bibliography: Shurr, Stein.

"After-Piece" (1947). Poem, in *Collected Poems of Herman Melville.* The poet says that he does not relish "stupid" praise by others of valor that has proved fatal.

"After the Pleasure Party" (1891). (Full title: "After the Pleasure Party: Lines Traced under an Image of Amor Threatening.") Poem, in *Timoleon.* (Characters: Amor, Urania.) The epigraph warns virgins not to be proud of their purity but to fear slighting Amor. What follows is in the form of a dramatic monologue. The narrator-spokesman describes the setting, which involves hills, "odorous tree[s]," a house, and terraces down to the Mediterranean Sea. He explains that paradise is here and that passionate sea waves break in vain against "the iron-bound verge" of the shore. Urania, the female astronomer, then asserts that sex is an "ambuscade" and that awareness of chastity struck her sharply. The sexual drive will assert itself. She seems ashamed and stayed pure, but purity only "incense[d] the flame." Did she study astronomy only for this? Purity now seems barren. She envies a young peasant girl whom a young man likes and can surely be caught by, because "on briers her buds were strung." Members of a pleasant little party have lunch and exchange stories. The learned Urania feels that "with all my starry lore, / I'd buy the veriest wanton's rose / Would but my bee therein repose." She would like to remake herself and plunge into the mysteries of sex. Since we are "co-relatives [that] never meet / Selfhood itself seems incomplete." Sex is stronger than any love of waning stars. The narrator remarks that we do not know what happened to Urania. Perhaps the resentful Amor exacted revenge on the haughty woman, who, in any event, went to Rome, saw "an antique pagan stone / Colossal carved," grew calm, and spoke. Urania says that she became languid before "Mary's convent-shrine," half resolved to become a nun, but decided instead to ask the goddess of wisdom to arm her. She might then be ''self-reliant, strong and free.'' The narrator closes with the thought that Urania's hope is foolish, since ''Nothing may help or heal / While Amor incensed remembers wrong.'' Virgins everywhere should pray for Urania and profit by her wretched example. Urania is based partly on Maria Mitchell, America's first notable female astronomer. ''After the Pleasure Party'' is built on sudden contrasts and changes in points of view, has erotic imagery, and is shot through with irony.

Bibliography: NN 11; Vernon Shetley, '' 'After the Pleasure Party': Venus and Virgin,'' *Papers in Literature and Language* 25 (Fall 1989): 425–42; Shurr; Stein; Warren.

Agar. In *Clarel,* she is Nathan's American-Jewish wife and Ruth's mother. She did not wish to go to Jerusalem. After Nathan's murder, she and Ruth became heartbroken and soon die.

Agath (''The Timoneer''). In *Clarel,* Agath is a Greek ship pilot who is staying at Mar Saba. The old man tells about the wreck of *The Peace of God* and accompanies Clarel and the others to Bethlehem.

Agatha Story. Agatha Hatch, who lived on the Massachusetts coast, once nursed a shipwrecked sailor named Robertson back to health, married him (1807), was deserted by him, and gave birth to his daughter. Seventeen years later, he visited them when the daughter was about to be married. Agatha learned that he had a second wife who died. Agatha refused to go west with Robertson, when asked, and took no vindictive action upon learning that he had married a third time. He later died (1842). Melville found out about the uncomplaining Agatha from John Henry Clifford,* a friend of Melville's father-in-law Lemuel Shaw* (July 1852), expressed interest in her story, and received from Clifford a copy of his journal account of the unfortunate woman. Melville considered basing a story on her, later wrote to Nathaniel Hawthorne* to offer her story to him, and explained that ''in this matter you would make a better hand at it than I would'' (13 August 1852)—perhaps because Wakefield, in Hawthorne's 1835 story entitled ''Wakefield,'' deserts his wife. Hawthorne declined, since he was soon to go to Liverpool as the American consul there. Melville wrote to Hawthorne (early December 1852) that he planned to develop Agatha's story and did so (December 1852–April 1853) in a long piece of fiction. He tried to interest Harper & Brothers* in publishing it but was prevented for reasons that are still unexplained (June–November 1853). It has been conjectured that the work, now missing, was called *The Isle of the Cross.*

Bibliography: NN 14; Hershel Parker, ''Herman Melville's *The Isle of the Cross:* A Survey and a Chronology,'' *American Literature* 62 (March 1990): 1–16; Basem L. Ra'ad, '' 'The Encantadas' and 'The Isle of the Cross': Melville's Dubieties, 1853–54,'' *American Literature* 63 (June 1991): 316–23.

''The Age of the Antonines'' (1891). Poem, in *Timoleon.* (Characters: Antonine [Antoninus Pius*], Antonine [Marcus Aurelius*].) When faith in goodness is shaken by awareness of villainy in the past, let us glance back to ''[a] halcyon Age'' when ''a pagan gentleman reigned.'' Nations were at peace then, although death still stung and no postmortal paradise was envisioned. Members of society were orderly, and they avoided envy and lawsuits. In a letter to John Chipman Hoadley,* Melville sent a copy of ''The Age of the Antonines'' with the following comment: ''I remember that the lines were suggested by a passage in Gibbon (Decline & Fall) Have you a copy? Turn to *'Antonine'* &c in index. What the deuce the thing means I dont know; but here it is'' (31 March 1877).

Bibliography Anthony Birley, *Marcus Aurelius: A Biography,* rev. ed. (New Haven, Conn.: Yale University Press, 1987); Jane Donahue, ''Melville's Classicism: Law and Order in His Poetry,'' *Papers in Language and Literature* 5 (Winter 1969): 63–72; NN 11 and 14.

Agrippina [the younger]. In ''The Marquis de Grandvin: Naples in the Time of Bomba . . . ,'' she is described as a ''true'' wife exiled from Rome to Naples.

Ahab, Captain (''Old Thunder,'' ''Mogul''). In *Moby-Dick,* Ahab is the ungodly but godlike captain of the whaling vessel the *Pequod.* Ahab has been to colleges and among the cannibals. His monomaniacal hatred of Moby Dick, the white whale that deprived him of his leg, engenders a pride in him which ultimately proves fatal to him and to most of his varied crew. Valentine Pease, Jr.,* the captain of the *Acushnet,* which was the model for the *Pequod,* only superficially resembled the volcanic Ahab. A more thorough-going model was Charles Wilkes, naval officer and author of *Narrative of the U.S. Exploring Expedition during the Years 1838, 1839, 1840, 1841, 1842* (5 vols. and atlas, 1845). Both Wilkes and Ahab may be described as dangerous, eccentric, and mysterious, and both as dauntless, flawed by insolence and pride, persistent, seawise and soul-sick, and wrathful. Parallels exist in the lives of both, and their voyages were parallel at times and included similar gams.

Bibliography: Walter E. Bezanson, ''*Moby-Dick:* Document, Drama, Dream,'' pp. 169–210, in Bryant, *Companion;* Harold Bloom, ed., *Ahab* (New York: Chelsea House Publishers, 1991); NN 6; Brain Higgins and Hershel Parker, eds., *Critical Essays on Herman Melville's Moby-Dick* (New York: G. K. Hall, 1992); Jaffé; Leyda.

Aimata. In *Omoo. See* Pomare IV.

Akim. In ''Benito Cereno,'' he is an Ashantee slave who polishes hatchets during Delano's visit aboard the *San Dominick.* He is killed during the attack led by Delano's chief mate.

Alanno. In *Mardi*, he is a tall, gaunt warrior from Hio Hio. He fulminates in the Temple of Freedom in Vivenza against King Bello and Dominora. Alanno of Hio Hio is based on Senator William Allen* of Ohio.
   Bibliography: Davis.

Albert. In *Billy Budd*, he is Captain Vere's hammock-boy who is sent to bring Billy Budd to hear and respond to John Claggart's charges against him.

Aldina. In *Mardi*, he is a Mardian writer quoted by Babbalanja, who also cites Aldina's annotated transcript of Lombardo's *Koztanza* and his note in it concerning the prosodist Pollo. The name Aldina may derive from Aldine, the name of the press founded by the Venetian printer Aldus Manutius (1450–1515).

Aleema. In *Mardi*, he is an old priest from the island of Amma. He is killed by the narrator to prevent his taking Yillah as a human sacrifice to Tedaidee.

Alexander I (1777–1825). Emperor of Russia. Born in St. Petersburg, Alexander ascended the throne when his father Emperor Paul I was murdered (1801). He instituted reforms, joined a coalition against Napoleon* (1805), fought successfully against Turkey (1806–1812), helped destroy Napoleon's army during its retreat from Moscow (1812), entered Paris with his allies (1814), participated in the Congress of Vienna and formed the Holy Alliance (1815), and ruled in a reactionary manner (1820–1825). Alexander married Princess Maria Louisa (baptized Elizabeth) of Baden (1793), was amused by and tolerant of her decades-long affair with Polish Count (later Prince) Adam Jerzy Czartoryski (from 1797), had a daughter by his wife (1799), consorted with Maria Naryshkina as his mistress (from 1803), and had a daughter by her (1804). (Both daughters predeceased him.) Alexander began a friendship with the so-called prophetess Baroness von Krüdener based on mysticism (1815). Alexander and his wife enjoyed a rapproachment (1824), a year before his death, which was followed the next year by hers. In ''Poor Man's Pudding and Rich Man's Crumbs,'' Melville names Alexander of Russia as one of the aristocratic guests at the Guildhall banquet in London after the Battle of Waterloo.
   Bibliography: Henri Troyat, *Alexander of Russia: Napoleon's Conquerer*, trans. Joan Pinkham (New York: E. P. Dutton, 1982).

Alla-Malolla. In *Mardi*, he is a Mardian juridical authority who is occasionally quoted by Babbalanja. His advice is to ''club together, fellow-riddles.''

All-a-Tanto, Commander. In ''Bridegroom-Dick,'' he is an officer whom Dick remembers.

Allen, Ann Middleton (11 April 1798–1869). Illegitimate daughter of Melville's father Allan Melvill,* by Miss Martha Bent of Boston—later Martha Bent

Allen (1777–1845), wife (as of 12 December 1797) of Bethuel Allen of Canton, Massachusetts. When he was a businessman in New York, Allan Melvill had commercial relations with Ann Bent, who was his daughter Ann's aunt and foster mother, and a successful Boston businesswoman, as late as 1823, after he was married and had legitimate children, including Herman. In 1832, Ann Allen and her aunt Ann Bent called on Thomas Melvill,* Allan Melvill's father. He was not at home. Thomas Melvill, Jr.,* his son (and Allan Melvill's brother), met the two women in Boston, heard their story and their plea for money, judged them to be truthful and in need, and gave them what money he could spare. Ann Allen married Nathaniel Tracy in Boston in 1843. Melville undoubtedly was informed that he had a half-sister, and he used the revelation for dramatic purposes in *Pierre,* at the point where Pierre Glendinning learns about Isabel Banford, his half-sister.

Bibliography: Young.

Allen, Ethan (1738–1789). Soldier and diplomat. Born in Litchfield, Connecticut, Allen may have aspired to go to college; if so, his hopes were frustrated by his father's death (1755). Allen served during the French and Indian War (in 1757) and was involved (from 1769) in events transpiring in the New Hampshire Grants, which later became Vermont. As a colonel, Allen commanded the Green Mountain Boys (1770–1775) and was appointed to draw up a complaint against King George III*; however, when the American Revolution began, he participated instead in the capture of Fort Ticonderoga (1775). He was captured during the foolhardy attack on Montreal, was held prisoner on a British ship and in England and back in America (1775–1778), was paroled and exchanged, and though breveted colonel by George Washington* returned to Vermont. Allen unsuccessfully urged Vermont's claims for independence and statehood before the Continental Congress (1778), after which he entered into negotiations to attach Vermont to Great Britain—perhaps in the hope that the U.S. Congress would respond by recognizing Vermont's claims (1780–1783). Later he farmed in Burlington, where he died. Allen wrote several books, pamphlets, and newspaper articles. His two most important works are *A Narrative of Col. Ethan Allen's Captivity* (1779—valuable but partly untrue and boastful) and *Reason the Only Oracle of Man; or, A Compenduous System of Natural Religion* (1785—vituperative and partly plagiarized). Allen, a courageous, impetuous man, married Mary Bronson in 1762. The couple had one son who died young and four daughters, two of whom died young. His wife, who was a dull, illiterate, and somewhat older woman, died in 1783. A year later Allen married Frances Montresor Buchanan, and the couple had two sons and a daughter.

In *Israel Potter,* Ethan Allen is the gigantic, eloquent, brave Green Mountain Boy who is captured and humiliated by being taken in chains to Falmouth, England. Melville avoids historical truth here, since Allen was exchanged in May 1778, whereas John Paul Jones took his *Ariel* to the United States in

December 1780. Melville compares Allen, inaccurately but dramatically, to Samson in captivity.

Bibliography: Cohen, *Potter;* Charles A. Jellison, *Ethan Allen: Frontier Rebel* (Syracuse, N.Y.: Syracuse University Press, 1969); *Narrative of Ethan Allen . . .* (1779; New York: Corinth Books, 1961).

Allen, William (1803–1879). Politician. Allen was born in Edenton, North Carolina, was orphaned early, went to Chillicothe, Ohio (1819), passed the bar (1824), and entered the field of politics. He served as a Democrat in the House of Representatives (1833–1835) and the U.S. Senate (1837–1849). He favored expansionist policies, especially in Oregon and Texas, was chairman of the Committee on Foreign Relations (1843–1849), and was President James K. Polk's spokesman during the Mexican War (1846–1848). Allen enjoyed a long retirement on his Ohio fruit farm before serving as Ohio's governor (1874–1876). He is thought to have originated the slogan "Fifty-Four Forty or Fight!" Always pro-western, Allen suffered from a combination of provincialism and an absence of vision. He married Effie McArthur Coons in 1842. Allen is the partial model for Alanno of Hio Hio in *Mardi.*

Bibliography: Davis.

Alma. In *Mardi,* where he is also known as Brami and Manko, he is a great prophet. Babbalanja ponders his principles. Alma's biography, as told by Mohi, contains a story in which a man was raised from his tomb. Alma's creed of love and charity, surely parallel to that of Jesus, is the basis of the religion on the island of Serenia. Alma's name may derive from Matthew Prior's *Alma; or, the Progress of the Mind* (1718), on vanity and spiritual progress.

Bibliography: Davis; Robert A. Rees, "Melville's Alma and *The Book of Mormon,*" *Emerson Society Quarterly* 43 (Second Quarter 1966): 41–46; Wright.

Almanni. In *Mardi,* he is a stern kinsman of King Media and his regent during the king's absence.

"Always with Us!" (1924). Poem, in *Weeds and Wildings,* as part of a section entitled "The Year." The poet contends that wise guests leave in good time, because they know that "absence endears." Robin left for the South but will return in a new vest in springtime to a zestful welcome. Black Crow, however, hangs around all the time, calling "*Caw!*" in every season.

Amabilia, Miss Angelica. In *Pierre,* she is the young woman from Ambleside whose request that Pierre write a poem in her album the young man politely declines.

Ambassador, My Lord the. In "Under the Rose," he is an English ambassador, age sixty-three, to the Azem of Persia. He persuades a Greek to translate

Lugar-Lips's poem which was inspired by the Azem's amber vase and which hints that we are all death's open secret.

"The Ambuscade" (1924). Poem, in *Weeds and Wildings,* as part of a section entitled "As They Fell." The poet, in tetrameter couplets, compares a nun's white habit to a cloister not to be intruded upon. But then he changes his tone, says that her "seemly dress" resembles snow covering "love's slumbering germ," and reminds us that "frost [by melting] fed Amor's burning rose."

Amelia, Princess (1783–1810). Daughter of King George III* of England. The youngest of his fifteen children, she was his "dearest child." She and her sisters were closely supervised, but their brothers were allowed to lead freer lives. Amelia did needlework, played cards, rode, and walked a good deal; attended court and theatrical performances; accompanied her parents to Windsor Castle, other country estates, and Weymouth for boating; and fell in love with one of her father's equerries. Succumbing to a fatal cold, Amelia willed that officer her worldly possessions. In *Israel Potter,* Princess Amelia is a member of the British royal family in whose garden Sir John Millet finds temporary work for Israel Potter.
   Bibliography: John Brooke, *King George III* (New York: McGraw-Hill, 1972).

"America" (1866). Poem, in *Battle-Pieces.* Beneath maternal America's slowly undulating flag, children play in peace. But the banner streams over soldiers in cruel, desperate combat, and "the lorn Mother speechless stood." Still later, America sleeps in a "shining shroud," contorted because of the Gorgon she has seen at the "earth's foundation." Finally, she awakens, purified by pain, aware of "a shivered yoke," ready for maturity, law, and empire, but now with a "graver air." "America" is the final poem in the main body of *Battle-Pieces* and as such functions as a summary.
   Bibliography: Adler; Robert Milder, "The Rhetoric of Melville's *Battle-Pieces,*" *Nineteenth-Century Literature* 44 (September 1989): 173–200; NN 11; Shurr.

"The American Aloe on Exhibition" (1924). Poem, in *Weeds and Wildings,* as part of a section entitled "This, That and the Other." In a headnote, the poet explains the "superstition" that the aloe blooms only once a century. In the poem, he describes the public that pays 10¢ to "stare" at the blooming century plant. But at night it sighs and its "aged stem" wonders what it has to do with "joy and pride," while evanescent roses have wrongly called it a mere weed. Melville may well be indirectly complaining about the inability of the public to judge the all-time worth of his literary blossoms. In a letter sent to Evert Duyckinck* in 1850, accompanying a gift copy of *Mardi,* Melville compares his friend's library to a conservatory and his novel to a plant for it; then he adds the thought that it may "flower like the aloe, a hundred years hence—or not

flower at all, which is more likely by far, for some aloes never flower'' (2 February).
Bibliography: NN 14, Stein.

Amigo. In ''L'Envoi'' at the end of ''The Rose Farmer,'' this is the narrator's term for his addressee.

Amor. In ''After the Pleasure Party,'' he is the god of love. He warns Urania, the Mediterranean intellectual, that she can ignore him only at her grave peril.

Amoree. In *Mardi,* he is a jolly philosopher cited by Babbalanja in a rare mood of gaiety. His name may derive from *Amores,* one of Ovid's several works on love.
Bibliography: Wright.

''Amoroso'' (1924). Poem, in *Weeds and Wildings,* as part of a section entitled ''As They Fell.'' (Character: Rosamond.) The poet praises his Rosamond, ''Of roses . . . the rose,'' summer and winter. Even when ''mossed in furs,'' she is ''a ruddier star'' than Arcturus. The couple make ''a plighted pair'' and now enjoy ''wooing in the snows!''
Bibliography: Shurr, Stein.

Ampudia, Major General Pedro de (fl. 1840s). Mexican army officer. He became a general under General Antonio Lopez de Santa Anna* (1840), commanded an attack on the Texas frontier (1842), was in several skirmishes on the border between Mexico and Texas thereafter, and commanded the army during the siege of Campeche, Yucatán (December 1842). Retreating (June 1843), Ampudia withdrew to Tabasco, where he made himself reviled for the vicious execution of a general who had attacked Tabasco (1844). Although Ampudia was then dismissed from his command, he was later placed in command of the Mexican army on the Rio Grande at the beginning of the Mexican War (1846). He was active at Matamoros (April), at which point he warned General Zachary Taylor* to retire beyond the Nueces. Taylor vociferously declined to do so. Ampudia defended Monterrey for a time but then surrendered to Taylor (September). In ''Authentic Anecdotes of 'Old Zack,' '' Melville mentions Ampudia as a Mexican officer who, when he visits General Taylor, finds him letting out his coat seams.
Bibliography: K. Jack Bauer, *The Mexican War 1846–1848* (1974; Lincoln: University of Nebraska Press, 1992).

Andrea. In ''Marquis de Grandvin: Naples in the Time of Bomba . . . ,'' he is Joanna's husband, who was strangled with a cord of silk and gold. Andrea is probably Andrew of Hungary. He was the son of Charles Robert and was murdered (1345) by his wife Joanna I* (1326–1382), who was his cousin and was the Queen of Naples.

Angelico, Fra (c. 1400–1455). (Original name: Guido di Pietro; later name: Giovanni da Fiesole; nickname: Beato Angelico.) Italian Dominican friar and painter. First trained as an illuminator, he was paid as a layman for an altarpiece (1418). As early as 1423 he was being called Fra Giovanni da Fiesole. He was summoned to Rome (1445) to paint in the Vatican. He was in Orvieto briefly (1447). He died in Rome. Fra Angelico's finest paintings are of religious subjects and scenes, usually in the early Renaissance Florentine style, reflecting some classicism, showing the conventional piety of the Middle Ages, and always marked by spiritual serenity. His honorific name Angelico first appeared in 1469. In Melville's poem "Marquis de Grandvin: At the Hostelry," Fra Angelico is a painter who sympathizes with henpecked Albert Durer.

Bibliography: John Pope-Hennessy, *Fra Angelico,* 2nd ed. (London: Phaidon Press, 1974); Jacqueline Guillaud and Maurice Guillaud, *Fra Angelico: The Light of the Soul* (New York: Clarkson N. Potter, 1986).

"Angel o' the Age!" (1924). Poem, in *The Works of Herman Melville.* The poet asks the angel to harvest us as "good grain in seed," with a "drop of grace," but not "polish[ed] . . . into commonplace."

Aniello, Tommaso. In "Marquis de Grandvin: Naples in the Time of Bomba . . ." *See* Masaniello.

Anna. In "The Apple-Tree Table," she is the narrator's timid daughter. She and her sister Julia at first tearfully blame the ticking in the tree on spirits. Later they are thrilled when the bug appears. As in "I and My Chimney," the narrator's wife and two daughters here resemble Melville's wife Elizabeth Knapp Shaw Melville* and their daughters Elizabeth Melville* and Frances Melville (later Frances Melville Thomas,* wife of Henry B. Thomas).

Bibliography: Young.

Anna. In "I and My Chimney," she is one of the narrator's daughters. With her mother and sister Julia, Anna unsuccessfully tries to persuade the narrator to tear down his beloved chimney. As in "The Apple-Tree Table," the narrator's wife and two daughters resemble Melville's wife Elizabeth Knapp Shaw Melville* and their daughters Elizabeth Melville* and Frances Melville (later Frances Melville Thomas,* wife of Henry B. Thomas).

Bibliography: Young.

Annatoo. In *Mardi,* she is Samoa's shrewish, unfaithful termagant of a wife. The two are found by the narrator aboard the *Parki.* Annatoo is from an unnamed Pacific island, survives the Cholo attack on the *Parki,* troubles the nar-

rator because of her pilfering, and is washed overboard and lost during a storm. Episodes aboard the *Parki* may derive in part from F. D. Bennett's *Narrative of a Whaling Voyage* . . . (London: Richard Bentley,* 1840).
    Bibliography: Davis.

Anselm. In *Clarel,* he is a youthful monk. Derwent uses his approach as an excuse for stopping an uneasy conversation concerning faith with Clarel at Mar Saba.

Antone. In *Omoo,* he is a Portuguese sailor aboard the *Julia.* He signs the round-robin.

Antone. In *White-Jacket,* he is a Portuguese sailor who becomes involved with Peter and Mark in a fight started by John. When Antone is flogged by order of Claret, he curses and becomes desperate.

Antonine. In "The Age of the Antonines," he is a Roman emperor during a well-governed, frank era. He is better known as Antoninus Pius.*

Antonine. In "The Age of the Antonines," he is a Roman emperor during a well-governed, frank era. He is better known as Marcus Aurelius.*

Antoninus Pius (86–161). (Full name: Titus Aurelius Fulvus Boionius Arrius.) Born in Lavunium, he was proconsul in Asia, was adopted (138) by the Emperor Hadrian, and succeeded him (138). Antoninus Pius married Annia Galeria Faustina (138) and enjoyed a peaceful, prosperous reign. His daughter Faustina married his nephew Marcus Aurelius, whom he adopted and who succeeded him. He is called Antonine in Melville's poem "The Age of the Antonines."
    Bibliography: Anthony Birley, *Marcus Aurelius: A Biography,* rev. ed. (New Haven, Conn.: Yale University Press, 1987).

"Apathy and Enthusiasm (1860–1)" (1866). Poem, in *Battle-Pieces.* In November, everything is cold, seems lost, is paralyzed, and is surrounded by doubts. A mother begs her sons "[n]ot in hatred so to part." But after Easter, striplings are elated by "Sumter's cannon roar," and Michael [the archangel] seems to tower over the dwarfish "Arch-fiend." But *"every graybeard"* is aware that grief follows when *"young Indians lead the war."*
    Bibliography: Adler, Garner, NN 11, Shurr.

Ap [ap] Catesby. In "Bridegroom-Dick." *See* Jones, Thomas ap Catesby.

Apollo. In "Marquis de Grandvin: Naples in the Time of Bomba . . . ," he is a handsome but dirty-faced Neapolitan street singer.

Apostle, An. In *Pierre,* he is any of a group of artists, lawyers, and other professionals who live in rattletrap offices in the lower part of the city. Pierre joins their group.

"The Apparition (A Retrospect)" (1866). Poem, in *Battle-Pieces.* Into a lovely region of "pastoral green" erupts a dreadful convulsion, which proves that "Solidity's a crust," with fire at "[t]he core . . . below." Things "may go well" for years, but knowledge that "horrors" can happen must make us fearful. This poem was inspired by the mine explosion at Petersburg, Virginia, toward the end of the Civil War (July 1864).
    Bibliography: Adler; David Cody, " 'So, then, Solidity's a crust': Melville's 'The Apparition' and the Explosion of the Petersburg Mine," *Melville Society Extracts* 78 (September 1989): 1, 4–8; Garner; Shurr.

"The Apparition (The Parthenon Uplifted on Its Rock First Challenging the View on the Approach to Athens)" (1891). Poem, in *Timoleon.* (Characters: Emperor Constantine I, Diogenes.) Suddenly Emperor Constantine I saw in the Parthenon "the supernatural Cross . . . in [the] startled air," whereupon "his soul's allegiance" was "turned." If cynics are not converted, they are at least shaken. Diogenes, if he had seen the apparition, might not have "barked" at humankind so much.
    Bibliography: Howard, NN 11.

"The Apple-Tree Table" (1856). (Full title: "The Apple-Tree Table; or Original Spiritual Manifestations.") Short story. (Characters: Anna, Biddy, Mrs. Brown, Mrs. Democritus, Professor Johnson, Julia, Madame Pazzi.) After five years in his present city mansion, the narrator finds a key in his garden, uses it to enter his attic, and finds up there a three-legged "old escritoir" made of apple-tree wood. He takes the table downstairs and distresses his daughters with it, but his peppy wife bravely places it where breakfast and tea can be served on it. At night the narrator uses it as a reading table. One evening, while reading Cotton Mather's *Magnalia Christi Americana* and sipping hot punch, he hears an odd ticking sound, which he escapes by going to bed. The next morning his daughters are frightened when they too hear the sound. Their mother concludes that it is coming from the table, but she orders breakfast to be served on it again, anyway. Later, while the narrator is reading at the table, he notices that a shiny little worm, beetle, or bug—whatever—is emerging from a warm crack in the wood. He places a tumbler over it and retires. In the morning, he is sad to learn that the maid has tossed the insect into the fire. That evening, the four in the family set up a brave watch. A second bug appears, sparkling "like a fiery opal" in the dim room. The narrator's wife consults a celebrated naturalist, who asseverates that the bugs came from eggs laid in the living apple tree ninety years before, at a time when the tree was cut and the wood from it was made into a table; furthermore, he theorizes that the bug is sufficient proof of the glorified resurrection in store for us all.

In 1850, Melville bought and read *A History of the County of Berkshire, Massachusetts* . . . (1829), in which a chapter by the Reverend Chester Dewey contains a report that three bugs ate their way (in 1806, 1811 or 1812, and 1814, respectively) out of a table made of wood from an apple tree cut down in 1786. In *Walden* (1854), Henry David Thoreau* mentions "the story . . . of a strong and beautiful bug which came out of . . . an old table of apple-tree wood" and finds in the event "his faith in a resurrection and immortality strengthened." "The Apple-Tree Table" was published anonymously in *Putnam's Monthly Magazine** (1 May 1856). It earned Melville about $50 but was not reprinted in his lifetime.

Bibliography: Frank Davidson, "Melville, Thoreau, and 'The Apple-Tree Table,'" *American Literature* 25 (January 1954): 479–88; Leyda; Newman; Sealts.

Aquaviva, Don Hannibal Rohon Del. In *Clarel. See* Hannibal, Rohon Del Aquaviva, Don.

Aquella, Queen. In *Mardi,* she is Donjalolo's first-night queen.

Aquovi. In *Mardi,* he is a chemist and an authority on ambergris. He is cited by Mohi.

Arabella. In "Jimmy Rose," she is a charming New York lady who is graciously complimented by the indigent Jimmy Rose.

Aramboalaza, Marques de. In "Benito Cereno." *See* Joaquin, Marques de Aramboalaza, Don.

Aranda, Alexandro. In "Benito Cereno," he is the owner from Mendoza of the slaves aboard Benito Cereno's *San Dominick.* Once their revolt is successful, the slaves, who are led by Babo, murder Aranda, reduce his corpse to a skeleton, and use it as a ship's figurehead of grisly portent. Ultimately, his bones are interred at St. Bartholomew's church in Lima.

"The Archipelago" (1891). Poem, in *Timoleon.* (Character: Theseus.) The poet describes sailing through the deserted Sporads and Cyclades, and Delos. All retain their primal grace. But where is Pan now? The region is like Polynesia but "reft of palms" and lacking the balmy breezes of the Marquesas. Melville recorded in his journal his impressions of several Greek islands as he sailed the Aegean Sea (December 1856–February 1857).

Bibliography: NN 11 and 15, Shurr, Stein.

Architect of the Parthenon, The. In "Suggested by the Ruins of a Mountain-Temple in Arcadia, One Built by the Architect of the Parthenon." *See* Ictinus.

Archy. In *Moby-Dick,* he is a sailor who tells his friend Cabaco, a Cholo, that he had heard men in the after-hold. The mysterious men turn out to be Fedallah and his crew.

Archy. In "The Scout toward Aldie," Archy is a Confederate Army soldier under Mosby. Archy has been captured by the men of the Colonel during their ill-fated pursuit of John Singleton Mosby. Archy sings Pansy's song, which begins "Spring is come; she shows her pass."

Arfretee. In *Omoo,* she is the native hostess of both the narrator and Dr. Long Ghost during their stay at Partoowye. Arfretee is something over forty years of age, has been Christianized, and is the wife of Deacon Ereemear Po-Po. The couple's children are Loo, twins, and a dandified son.

Arheetoo. In *Omoo,* he is an intelligent native of the island of Motoo-Otoo. He asks the narrator to forge some papers for him.

Arhinoo. In *Mardi,* he is the husband of Nina. When he was absent, she moaned that she was a widow, according to Yoomy.

Aristippus (c. 435–366 B.C.). Greek philosopher. He left Cyrene, went to Athens, and became a pupil of Socrates, who inspired him to stress virtue and happiness, especially the latter. Founding his school of Cyrenaics back in Cyrene, Aristippus reasoned that anything maximizing pleasure is good, but he also advised using good judgment and self-control. After his death, his daughter Arete and her son Aristippus continued his school of thought. In *Clarel,* the Cypriote sings a "hymn of Aristippus." *See* "Ditty of Aristippus."

"The Armies of the Wilderness" (1866). (Full title: "The Armies of the Wilderness [1863–4].") Poem, in *Battle-Pieces.* (Characters: [General Ulysses S.] Grant, Gray-back, [General Thomas J.] Stonewall [Jackson], [General Robert E.] Lee, [General James] Longstreet, [Colonel John Singleton] Mosby.) The poet describes opposing camps on snowy Southern hills. "But for the vale's deep rent," soldiers on both sides might play football together. While Union soldiers dig trenches, they ask a prisoner to tell them about Confederate Army earthworks. He will not but does identify the states from which the various rebel elements, all loyal to Lee, have come. Our sentinel looks down from his wooded outpost on miles of enemy pickets. Along a mountain path, scarred by wagon and cannon wheels, and all through a ruined forest, lie the dead. Union soldiers "[k]indle their fires" with Virginia books and documents, and they boil water for punch in despoiled cemeteries. Grant, both meek and grim, orders his army into motion toward the Wilderness. They pass evidence of casualties on their way. They charge in the direction of volleys through "hazy groves." Eventually, "Right strove well, / And emerged from the Wilderness." The poet concludes that no one can tell the whole story, and "entangled rhyme" can provide only "hints." The dead alone can solve this "riddle." Woven throughout the narrative are four-line stanzas philosophizing chorus-like on "*this strife of brothers*" which hurls time back to "*the world's great Prime.*" Many images enriching this poem derive from Melville's visit to the Union Army camp on the Virginia front (April 1864).

Bibliography: Adler, Boatner, Faust, Garner, Howard, NN 11.

Arnaut, The ("The Epirot," "The Illyrian"). In *Clarel,* he is an Albanian soldier living at Mar Saba. He is huge, picturesque, and hearty, but also carnal.

Arrian. In *The Confidence-Man,* he is the Stoic philosopher. The metempsychotic Mark Winsome contends that he was Arrian in a previous existence.

"Art" (1891). Poem, in *Timoleon.* We falsely dream of artistic creation while "placid." In truth, Art is produced from opposites in conflict. Melville names many elements—including "pride and scorn" and "love and hate"—which "must mate," in any "wrestle" with art, to create "pulsed life."

Bibliography: NN 11, Shurr, Warren.

Asbestos. In *Pierre,* he is the publisher who, with his partners Steel and Flint, rejects Pierre's book. They intend to sue Pierre for costs and advances.

Ashby, Turner (1828–1862). Confederate soldier. Ashby was born in Fauquier City, Virginia, was taught by tutors and his widowed mother, farmed with his brothers, and achieved status as a grain dealer and local politician. After John Brown* conducted his raid on Harpers Ferry (1859), Ashby raised a cavalry company to guard Potomac River crossings against further such attacks. When Virginia seceded from the Union, Ashby joined a Virginia cavalry regiment, quickly became a colonel, and grew vengeful after the murder by a Union soldier of one of his brothers (July 1861). General Thomas J. Jackson* put Ashby in command of the Shenandoah Valley Confederate cavalry (spring 1862). He was promoted to brigadier general (May) but was killed (June) in a dismounted counterassault near Harrisonburg, Virginia. In Melville's poem "The Released Rebel Prisoner," Ashby is named as a deceased Confederate Army leader who is thought of by the released Rebel prisoner.

Bibliography: Faust.

Aspasia (470?–410 B.C.). Greek courtesan. She was the most celebrated of the Greek Hetaerae, an adventuress from Miletus, and the consort of Pericles. She may have drawn him away from an unhappy marriage. She and Pericles lived in close harmony for the last fifteen years of his life. Aspasia bore him a son named Pericles, who was initially called illegitimate but was later legitimized. The comedians satirized and ridiculed her, and she was tried as an atheist and a procuress. When Pericles pleaded for her tearfully in court, she was acquitted as a concession to him. Aspasia was feared because she was highly intelligent, educated, and amiable. She conversed with Pericles's most important Athenian associates. Their son was executed by Athenians after a naval defeat (406) toward the close of the Peloponnesian War. In "The Parthenon," Melville says that Aspasia offered to Pericles stunned praise of the beautifully completed Parthenon.

Bibliography: Donald Kagan, *Pericles of Athens and the Birth of Democracy* (New York: Free Press, 1991).

Aster, China. In *The Confidence-Man. See* China Aster.

"As They Fell" (1924). Part of *Weeds and Wildings,* containing "The Ambuscade," "Amoroso," "The Devotion of the Flowers to Their Lady," "Hearth-Roses," "L'Envoi," "The New Rosicrucians," "Rosary Beads," "The Rose Farmer," "Rose Window," "Under the Ground," "and "The Vial of Attar."

Astor, John Jacob (1763–1848). Fur trader and financier. The son of a butcher, Astor was born near Heidelberg, Germany. He migrated to the United States (1784), entered the fur trade, became prominent through shrewdness (by 1800), incorporated two fur companies (1808, 1810), and founded Astoria at the mouth of the Columbia River as his trading post but lost it to British forces (1813). Astor made enormous profits by loaning money to the U.S. government (1814), invested in New York City real estate, and monopolized the fur trade in the Mississippi Valley and the upper reaches of the Missouri River. When he sold his interests and retired (1834), he was the richest man in the United States, with an estimated worth of $20 million or more. At his death, he left $400,000 to establish the library that evolved into the New York Public Library. Astor married Sarah Todd in 1785; the couple had four sons, one of whom died as a baby and one of whom was imbecilic, and four daughters, one of whom died in infancy. Astor's curious will was published in full in the New York *Herald* (5 April 1848). His son William Backhouse Astor inherited great wealth, increased the Astor family holdings, and continued the family line. Melville satirized Astor's will in *Mardi.* In Melville's "Bartleby," Astor is the Wall Street lawyer's rich employer, who pronounced the lawyer prudent and methodical.

Bibliography: Mario L. D'Avanzo, "Melville's 'Bartleby' and John Jacob Astor," *New England Quarterly* 41 (June 1968): 259–64; Davis; John Denis Haeger, *John Jacob Astor: Business and Finance in the Early Republic* (Detroit: Wayne State University Press, 1991); Harvey O'Connor, *The Astors* (New York: Alfred A. Knopf, 1941).

Atahalpa. In *Mardi,* he is mentioned by Babbalanja as a friend, an astrologer, and an alchemist. Atahalpa has been trying to hatch a fairy by putting secret ingredients in a jar. Melville's source for this nonsense was evidently Isaac D'Israeli's *Curiosities of Literature* (five series, 1791–1834).

Bibliography: Merton M. Sealts, Jr., "Melville's 'Friend Atahalpa,' " *Notes and Queries* 194 (22 January 1949): 37–38.

Atama, Prince. In *Mardi,* he is a Juam prince who refused to become king because, if he did so, he would have to give up the pleasant sport of rowing.

Atee Poee. In *Omoo,* this is the native nickname of a pompous captain of a man-of-war. Atee Poee means "Pudding Head."

"At the Cannon's Mouth" (1866). (Full title: "At the Cannon's Mouth, Destruction of the Ram Albemarle by the Torpedo-Launch [October, 1864].") Poem, in *Battle-Pieces.* (Character: [Lieutenant William Barker] Cushing.) The poet marvels at the courage of young Cushing, who, in his "mad dash at death," drove the armed hull of his launch at the enemy vessel. Was he motivated by "martyr-passion"? Did he not realize what alluring joys he might be giving up? The successful attack occurred on 27 October 1864 in the Roanoke River. Of his fifteen-man crew, only Cushing and one other escaped death or capture. Melville revealingly links Cushing's spirit to that "which brave poets [including himself] own."

Bibliography: Boatner; Cohen, *Poems;* Faust; Garner; NN 11.

"At the Hostelry." *See* "Marquis de Grandvin: At the Hostelry."

"The Attic Landscape" (1891). Poem, in *Timoleon.* The poet advises tourists to expect nothing picturesque in the Greek scene, where clear hills face temples and thus show "Art and Nature lodged together" to form "sculptural grace."

Bibliography: NN 11, Stein.

Atufal. In "Benito Cereno," he is a gigantic African king, later a slave owned by Alexandro Aranda. Atufal helped Babo during the successful slave revolt aboard Benito Cereno's *San Dominick.* Atufal is shot and killed during the attack led by Captain Amasa Delano's chief mate.

Aunt Charity. In *Moby-Dick. See* Charity, Aunt.

"Aurora Borealis: Commemorative of the Dissolution of Armies at the Peace (May, 1865)" (1866). Poem, in *Battle-Pieces.* The poet compares the "disbanding" of the armies at the end of the Civil War to the God-decreed retreat of the "steely play" of the Northern Lights. "The million blades that glowed" have given way to "pale, meek Dawn."

Bibliography: Garner.

"Authentic Anecdotes of 'Old Zack' " (1847). (Full title: "Authentic Anecdotes of 'Old Zack' [Reported for YANKEE DOODLE by His Special Correspondent at the Seat of War].") Nine sketches. (Characters: [Major] General [Pedro de] Ampudia, P. T. "Peter Tamerlane" Barnum, Major [William Wallace Smith] Bliss, General [Braxton] Bragg, Brooks, Secretary [of War William L.] Marcy, Sambo, General Antonio Lopez de Santa Anna, a Surgeon of the Army in Mexico, General Zachary Taylor, General Tom Thumb, Yankee Doodle.) A correspondent is dispatched to the Mexican front to observe General Zachary Taylor. Reports sent to the *Yankee Doodle* magazine concern Old Zack's defusing of a Mexican mortar shell, his washing and mending his own clothes, a nail placed by a drummer boy under his saddle and probably sought by P. T. Barnum for his museum of curiosities, an eye-witness description by an army surgeon of Old Rough and Ready's personal appearance, a copy of a letter he sent to his Mexican counterpart General Santa Anna after the Battle of Buena Vista, a pie which an enemy shot caused to land on Taylor's head, Barnum's plan to exhibit Santa Anna, a rumor that Old Zack walked at one time inside the fire of a steamboat, and his aggressive eating habits.

The diary of Evert Duyckinck* reveals that Melville was the anonymous author of these "anecdotes." Although Melville failed to obtain a government job from the administration of President James K. Polk, he remained a Democrat; therefore, he hoped—though vainly—that these sketches would hurt Taylor's ambitions to be president. Melville's crack at William L. Marcy, secretary of war under Polk, was undoubtedly the result of his being rebuffed by that official when Melville applied in Washington, D.C., for work (February 1847). "Authentic Anecdotes of 'Old Zack' " appeared anonymously in seven weekly installments in *Yankee Doodle* (24 July–11 September 1847).

Bibliography: Silas Bent McKinley and Silas Bent, *Old Rough and Ready: The Life and Times of Zachary Taylor* (New York: Vanguard Press, 1946); Luther S. Mansfield, "Melville's Comic Articles on Zachary Taylor," *American Literature* 9 (January 1938): 411–18; Donald Yannella, *"Yankee Doodle,"* in *American Literary Magazines: The Eighteenth- and Nineteenth-Centuries,* ed. Edward E. Chielens (Westport, Conn.: Greenwood Press, 1986).

"The Avatar" (1924). Poem, in *Weeds and Wildings,* as part of a section entitled "This, That and the Other." Flower gods pay no attention to fancy blooms. When the god of roses visited the earth once, it took the form of "a wilding or weed."

Bibliography: Shurr, Stein.

Azem. In "Under the Rose," he is the Persian ruler whose beautiful carved amber vase sometimes contains roses that conceal relievi of angels—including an angel of death. Azem does not permit the Ambassador to talk him out of possession of his vase but does instead permit him to read Lugar-Lips's poem about it.

Azore Sailor. In *Moby-Dick,* he is a sailor aboard the *Pequod* who dances during the midnight festivities in the forecastle.

Azzageddi. In *Mardi,* he is the devilish spirit in Babbalanja, as he himself explains.

Azzolino, Queen. In *Mardi,* she is Donjalolo's second-night queen.

B

B., E. In " 'The Coming Storm': A Picture by S. R. Gifford.'' *See* Booth, Edwin Thomas.

B——. In "Bartleby," he is a lawyer who rents the vacated Wall Street offices of Bartleby's employer.

B——, Mrs. In "Shadow at the Feast: Mrs. B—— (1847),'' she is "a kinswoman,'' a young bride in May but a widow in June. She attends a Christmas dinner in a shadowy, aloof way. Melville may be reminiscing about the first Christmas after he was married. Mrs. B—— has not been identified.

Babbalanja. In *Mardi,* he is the verbose philosopher from the isle of Odo. He accompanies Taji, along with King Media of Odo, Mohi, and Yoomy, on his long and fruitless search for Yillah. Babbalanja, whose name suggests his verbosity, has long-winded opinions on astronomy, consistency, death, fame, fate, history, humankind, the imagination, immortality, literary criticism, mimickry, the moral sense, poetic inspiration, the population explosion, religion, science, war, and much else. Babbalanja is so impressed by the vision of heaven which he experiences on the isle of Serenia that he remains there. He explains that at times he is moved by the devilish spirit of Azzageddi within himself.
 Bibliography: Davis; Lebowitz; John Wenke, " 'Ontological Heroics': Melville's Philosophical Art,'' pp. 567–601 in Bryant, *Companion.*

Babo. In "Benito Cereno,'' he is the Senegalese slave, age thirty, who with the aid of Atufal and other blacks revolts successfully against his master Alexandro Aranda while they are aboard Benito Cereno's ship the *San Dominick* between

Valparaiso and Callao. He orders the atrocious murder of most of the whites aboard and later plots to commandeer the *Bachelor's Delight,* under the command of Captain Amasa Delano. When this plan fails and Babo is captured, he becomes silent, is tried, and is hanged; but in the eyes of some readers he achieves a kind of moral victory. It is possible that in naming and characterizing Babo, Melville had in mind the heroic French socialist François Noël Babeuf, who was guillotined in 1797.

Bibliography: Bernard B. Bloch, "Babo and Babeuf: Melville's 'Benito Cereno,' " *Melville Society Extracts* 96 (March 1994): 9–12; Sterling Brown, *The Negro in American Fiction* (1937; Port Washington, N.Y.: Kennikat Press, 1968).

Baby. In "The Chipmunk," it is mentioned that he leaves the poet's hearth as though startled like a chipmunk.

Bach, Old. In "The Paradise of Bachelors and the Tartarus of Maids," he is the dark-complexioned boss of the paper-making maids.

Baldy. In "Donelson," he is a newspaper worker who posts war reports on a bulletin board for the public to read.

Baldy. In *White-Jacket,* he is a likable little Scot who is captain of the mizzentop. He is one of White Jacket's messmates. Baldy falls while furling a topsail under orders to do so excessively fast and cripples himself for life by smashing through an oak platform on deck. Baldy's fall is based on an identical crippling tumble suffered (October 1843) by James Craddock aboard the *United States,* the prototype of Melville's *Neversink.*

Bibliography: NN 5.

Ballad, Ned. In *Mardi,* he is a song-singing sailor aboard the *Arcturion.*

"Ball's Bluff" (1866). (Full title: "Ball's Bluff: A Reverie [October, 1861].") Poem, in *Battle-Pieces.* "Ball's Bluff" is a poignant dramatic monologue. From his window, the poet sees young soldiers "marching lustily" off to war, cheered forward by ladies and fife music. How could these young men, feeling immortal, dream that "Death . . . / Would come to thin their shining throng?" Weeks later, the uneasy poet "mused / On those brave boys" when he heard the sound of marching feet in the street no more. On 21 October 1861, four Union regiments, having crossed the Potomac River the previous day, were ambushed by the Confederates, were pinned down near Ball's Bluff, Virginia, and suffered a thousand dead, including their colonel, Senator Edward D. Baker of Oregon, a personal friend of President Abraham Lincoln.* The battle, though of little strategic importance, hurt Union morale and caused a bitter politico-military controversy. For source material, Melville may have used *Rebellion Record: A*

Diary of American Events, with Documents, Narratives, Illustrative Incidents, Poetry, Etc., ed. Frank Moore, vol. 1, 1861.
    Bibliography: Adler, Boatner, Faust, Garner, NN 11, Warren.

Baltimore. In *Omoo,* he is the aged African-American cook aboard the *Julia.*

Bandage, Dr. In *White-Jacket,* he is the surgeon aboard the *Mohawk.* With others, he confers with Dr. Cadwallader Cuticle when that cold expert operates on the mortally wounded foretopman.

Banford, Isabel ("Bell"). In *Pierre,* she is the supposedly illegitimate daughter of Pierre Glendinning's father and hence Pierre's half-sister. For her, Pierre gives up his fiancée Lucy Tartan and argues with his haughty mother. Isabel tells a strange story about her childhood, appeals to Pierre successfully, and accompanies him to the city, where they live together (with Delly Ulver) pretending to be husband and wife. Lucy joins them and becomes the indirect cause of Pierre's killing Glendinning Stanly, after which Pierre is imprisoned for murder. Isabel reveals that she is Pierre's sister and poisons herself in prison immediately after Pierre has taken a fatal dose of poison himself. The precise nature and action of Isabel remain ambiguous. At one point, Pierre suggests that the two should pretend to be married, whereupon they "coiled . . . entangledly." Later, he embraces her and rationalizes by asking "How can one sin in a dream?" Melville never unveils anything more intimate in their conduct.
    Circumstances surrounding Isabel Banford are partly based on the fact that Melville's father Allan Melvill* had fathered and abandoned Ann Middleton Allen,* an illegitimate daughter, and that after his death she and Ann Bent, her aunt and foster mother, became claimants on his estate and were paid a sum of money by his brother Thomas Melvill, Jr.* Her shadowy French background may echo family stories of Allan Melvill's residence in Paris (1801–1802) with his brother Thomas, whose daughter Anne Marie Priscilla Melvill,* born in France, she resembles.
    Bibliography: Amy Puett Emmers, "Melville's Closet Skeleton: A New Letter about the Illegitimacy Incident in *Pierre,*" in *Studies in the American Renaissance, 1977,* ed. Joel Myerson (Boston: Twayne, 1978); Diane Long Hoeveler, "La Cenci: The Incest Motif in Hawthorne and Melville," *American Transcendental Quarterly* 44 (Fall 1979): 247–59; Paul Metcalf, ed., *Enter Isabel: The Herman Melville Correspondence of Clare Spark and Paul Metcalf* (Albuquerque: University of New Mexico Press, 1991); Henry A. Murray, *Endeavors in Psychology* (New York: Harper & Row, 1981); Henry A. Murray et al., "Allen Melville's By-Blow," *Melville Society Extracts* 61 (February 1985): 1–6; Young.

Banker, The ("Mammon," "Mynheer," "The Thessalonian"). In *Clarel,* he is a banker with a Greek and English background. He is fat, luxury loving, materialistic, and fearful of death. He and Glaucon, his prospective son-in-law, participate in the pilgrimage only from Jerusalem to the Dead Sea, where they then leave it.

Bannadonna. In "The Bell-Tower," he is the proud and accomplished caster of the enormous bell. He produces Haman, the bell striker which kills its creator at the stroke of one.

Bibliography: Darryl Hattenhauer, "The Scarlet Cipher: Bannadonna's Tower as Number One," *CEA Critic* 53 (Winter 1991): 46–53.

Bardianna. In *Mardi,* he is an ancient Mardian authority from the island of Vamba. His pithy statements are often quoted by Babbalanja, whose account of Bardianna's will echoes aspects of the much-publicized will of John Jacob Astor.*

Bibliography: Davis.

Bargas, Lorenzo. In "Benito Cereno," he is one of Alexandro Aranda's young clerks from Cadiz and a passenger on the *San Dominick.*

Barlo, Bartholomew. In "Benito Cereno," he is a Spanish sailor from the *San Dominick* who is prevented from killing a shackled black with a dagger.

Barnum, P. T. (1810–1891). (Full name: Phineas Taylor Barnum.) Impresario. Born in Bethel, Connecticut, Barnum soon disliked manual labor, held a variety of jobs, and then in 1835 saw Joyce Heth, an African-American who was exhibited as the 160-year-old nurse of George Washington.* Barnum was aware that she was a fake but, seeing possibilities, he bought her anyway, showed her off amid sensational advertisements, and even purchased supposedly relevant documents allegedly signed by Washington's father. Barnum publicized Joyce's death and burial in his family plot, and he published anonymous newspaper attacks on her authenticity to augment her notoriety. He was emboldened by awareness of public gullibility to buy Scudder's American Museum in New York (1841), called it Barnum's American Museum, and stocked it with money-making curiosities and monstrosities (to 1868). One of his greatest early coups was his quick signing of Tom Thumb,* whom he trained well and thrust into his show (1842). Barnum took his troupe on its first European tour in 1844. His wealth enabled Barnum to build a weird $150,000 mansion on the outskirts of Bridgeport, Connecticut (1848). He managed the Swedish singer Jenny Lind's American tour (1850–1852) and made her much money but made himself a veritable fortune. He went on other successful European tours (1858 and later). Barnum was elected to the Connecticut legislature (1867–1869), was mayor of Bridgeport (1875), developed a three-ring circus (from 1871), and formed the Barnum and Bailey Circus with his former rival James A. Bailey (1881). Barnum married Charity Hallett in 1829. The couple had four daughters, one of whom died in infancy. A year after Charity died (1873), he married Nancy Fish.

He evidently had an illegitimate son, born in New York between 1851 and 1855 and named Phineas Taylor, by a French circus performer active in his museum; she may have been Ernestine de Faiber.

Melville in a letter to his sister Catherine Gansevoort Melville Hoadley* reports that his wife went to Barnum's zoo at one time and met Barnum (12 April 1882). In "Authentic Anecdotes of 'Old Zack,' " Melville presents Barnum as the museum owner who seeks to exhibit the Mexican mortar shell that General [Zachary] Taylor defused, also the General's pants that were torn by a tack put in his saddle, and even his tobacco box. As Peter Tamerlane B—m, he reportedly does business with Sambo, General Taylor's servant, and is trying to purchase General [Antonio Lopez de] Santa Anna as well. In "The New Planet," a bright light hovering over the American Museum in New York is regarded as a new planet and is named the Barnum. In "On the Chinese Junk," it is said that Barnum's museum will exhibit the junk and also the Nahant sea serpent. The contents of Barnum's museum are described in "View of the Barnum Property." Some of the topical allusions in connection with Oh-Oh's museum in *Mardi* owe something to the contents of Barnum's American Museum.

Bibliography: Irving Wallace, *The Fabulous Showman: The Life and Times of P. T. Barnum* (New York: Alfred A. Knopf, 1959).

Bartleby. In "Bartleby," he is the pale, inactive, cadaverous-looking scrivener who one day tells his puzzled employer, a Wall Street lawyer, that he prefers not to copy documents any longer. Bartleby stands staring at the wall, is subsequently arrested for vagrancy, is imprisoned in the Tombs, and dies there. Bartleby may have suffered from catatonic schizophrenia. Melville's friend Eli James Murdock Fly* was a scrivener and then a confirmed invalid cared for by others; hence, he may have been a model for the character Bartleby. Melville's traveling companion George J. Adler* developed mental problems and may also have been a model.

Bibliography: Matthew C. Brennan, "Melville's Bartleby as an Archetypal Shadow," *Journal of Evolutionary Psychology* 13 (August 1992): 318–21; Fred A. Whitehead, Bruce S. Liese, and Michael L. O'Dell, "Melville's 'Bartleby the Scrivener': A Case Study," *New York State Journal of Medicine* 90 (January 1990): 17–22; Smith.

"Bartleby" (1853). (Full title: "Bartleby, the Scrivener: A Story of Wall Street.") Short story. (Characters: John Jacob Astor, B—, Bartleby, Monroe Edwards, Ginger Nut, Nippers, Turkey.) The narrator is an elderly Wall Street lawyer whose "snug" business in bonds, mortgages, and deeds does not prepare him for Bartleby. The lawyer hires this pallidly neat, forlorn young man to copy his legal documents. He allots Bartleby a section of his own private office. Still, after a while, Bartleby calmly replies to an order to proofread some items that he would "prefer not to." Soon he is neither eating nor willing to move out. His conduct outrages the lawyer's other workers; they are the scriveners Turkey (a careful copyist until noon) and Nippers (irritable until noon) and the office boy Ginger Nut. Nippers offers to throw Bartleby out bodily, and Turkey suggests punching him; but their employer delays taking any action. One Sunday morning he finds himself actually barred by Bartleby from entering his own offices. When he examines the strange man's desk later, he comes to the conclusion that the odd fellow has been camped in the office day and night, friendless, melancholy, and in solitude. Compassion sweeping over him, the employer questions Bartleby, who, however, prefers to answer nothing. The employer feels superstitious about becoming critical, soon notices that Bartleby's eyes are glazed, offers the nonworker $20, and tells him to be gone within six days. No luck. The employer blames his own plight on predestination, feels charitable, chafes when some of his professional colleagues start whispering, and decides to move out from under Bartleby and into offices nearer City Hall. The new tenant of the place where Bartleby is still camped has the landlord turn him out. Bartleby haunts the staircase and sleeps in the entryway. His former employer, feeling no conscience pangs but finding himself driving uneasily in his fine carriage, returns to his office one day—only to find a message that Bartleby is in prison and charged with vagrancy. The employer goes to the Tombs (the city prison), finds his former copyist, tries to chat with him, bribes the grub-man to provide him with some nice food, but a few days later he returns to find Bartleby dead in the prison yard. It is rumored that the poor fellow once clerked in the Dead Letter Office in Washington. The story ends thus: "Ah, Bartleby! Ah, humanity!''

"Bartleby" was published anonymously in *Putnam's Monthly Magazine** (1 November, 1 December 1853) and was reprinted in *The Piazza Tales* (1856). Melville received $55 for the November installment of "Bartleby" and $30 for the December installment in *Putnam's.* Evert Duyckinck* and his brother George Duyckinck,* editors of the New York *Literary World,* guessed in a note (3 December 1853) that Melville was the author of "Bartleby," which has some personal sources. Melville, like Bartleby, disliked reading proof and, more important, declined to "copy" what others had written, that is, write in imitation of the style of popular authors. Also, Melville resisted the efforts of his brother Allan Melville,* a Wall Street lawyer, to entice him out of his cramped writing room at Arrowhead, his home near Pittsfield, Massachusetts. Most important, both Melville and Bartleby were enamored of solitude and were suicidally inclined. Furthermore, Melville may well have regarded his novels as dead letters which never got through to their proper audience. Melville's father-in-law, the financially generous Lemuel Shaw,* also a lawyer (and a judge as well), could not understand his daughter's strange husband and repeatedly bailed him out financially. Eli James Murdock Fly,* a friend of Melville's younger years in Albany, became a scrivener and then a confirmed invalid cared for by others. Several other sources for this story have been suggested by scholars. More generally interpreted, Bartleby is "walled in" at the office and "walled away" from life, as Melville might have thought his contemporary Henry David Thoreau,* a representative transcendentalist in Melville's eyes, was at Walden Pond.

Still more generally, "Bartleby" is an enigmatic allegory depicting on one level the hero who passively declines to accept humdrum reality and on a higher level the inevitable absence of real communication among almost all people.

Bibliography: Matthew C. Brennan, "Melville's Bartleby As an Archetypal Shadow," *Journal of Evolutionary Psychology* 13 (August 1992): 318–21; Dan McCall, *The Silence of Bartleby* (Ithaca, N.Y.: Cornell University Press, 1989); Leo Marx, "Melville's Parable of the Walls," *Sewanee Review* 61 (Autumn 1953): 602–7; Thomas R. Mitchell, "Dead Letters and Dead Men: Narrative Purpose in 'Bartleby, the Scrivener,' " *Studies in Short Fiction* 27 (Summer 1990): 329–38; Newman; Douglas Robillard, "The Dead Letter Office," *Melville Society Extracts* 96 (March 1994): 8–9; Sealts.

Bartlett, William Francis (1840–1876). Union Army officer. Bartlett was born in Haverhill, Massachusetts, was a student at Harvard when the war erupted, enlisted, was commissioned captain in the 20th Massachusetts (July 1861), and recruited men in Pittsfield, Massachusetts. Bartlett fought at Ball's Bluff (21 October 1861), lost his left leg near Hampton, Virginia (24 April 1862), and was mustered out as an invalid. Rallying, however, he raised and as its colonel commanded a new regiment (the 49th) from western Massachusetts and returned to action with a wooden leg (November). He was wounded in his left wrist and right ankle at Port Hudson, Louisiana (27 May 1863), was wounded in the head in the Wilderness, in Virginia (6 May 1864), recuperated, was promoted to brigadier general, took command of a corps at Petersburg in time to charge into the crater after the explosion there, lost his artificial leg, and was captured (30 July). After some time in a prison hospital in Danville, Virginia, he was sent to Libby Prison, Richmond, from which he was exchanged (24 September), with permanent bowel ulcers. Bartlett married Mary Agnes Pomeroy, of Pittsfield (1865), and honeymooned with her in England and on the Continent (1865–1866). While in Italy, he visited Giuseppe Garibaldi,* a family friend (1866). He mustered out of the army, and he and his wife made Pittsfield their residence (from 1866). He partly owned and managed a Stockbridge ironworks (1868–1872), sought better health by vacationing in England (1870), joined the staff of the governor of Massachusetts (1872), campaigned during the unsuccessful bid of Charles Francis Adams for president (1872), and managed a Richmond, Virginia, ironworks (1872–1875). Back in Pittsfield (1875), he was too ill to accept an invitation to run for governor as a Republican. He tried to recuperate by taking another trip to England (1876), but he returned home and died. He was survived by his wife, three sons, and two daughters.

Melville saw Bartlett when he paraded his unit in Pittsfield (22 August 1863) and perhaps on other occasions. Bartlett is alluded to in Melville's poem "The College Colonel." Melville presented a copy of *Battle-Pieces* to Bartlett (1867), by which time he was a major general.

Bibliography: Garner; Leyda; NN 11; Francis Winthrop Palfrey, *Memoir of William Francis Bartlett* (Boston: Houghton, Mifflin, 1881).

Bashaw with Two Tails, The. In *Omoo,* this is the nickname given to the narrator by Dr. Long Ghost because of a turban the younger man makes out of a shirt. *See also* Typee.

Batho. In *Mardi,* he is a jealous critic who, according to Babbalanja, denounced Lombardo's *Koztanza.* Lombardo proceeded to ignore Batho. Obviously the name Batho comes from the word ''bathos.''

"The Battle for the Bay (August, 1864)" (1866). Poem, in *Battle-Pieces.* (Character: Admiral [David Glasgow] Farragut.) Melville describes in an inchoate manner how Admiral Farragut courageously and successfully attacked with a ''long fleet'' of Union vessels, including his flagship the *Hartford,* Confederate warships in the Battle of Mobile Bay. Before the battle, ''the stars withdrawn look down.'' During the encounter, Farragut, commanding while ''lashed [to the mast] . . . aloft,'' loses the ''turreted'' *Tecumseh* but captures the *Tennessee,* a Confederate ''Ram of iron and oak.'' Melville makes it clear in this poem that he favors the Union sailors when he says ''[b]ehind each . . . a holy angel stood,'' even though ''traitors have their [brief] glorying hour.'' The human cost was deadly, for ''pale on the scarred fleet's decks there lay / A silent man for every silenced gun'' and ''far below the wave'' sleep many noble sailors. Farragut's victory (5 August 1864) earned him a promotion to vice admiral. His response to a warning of ''torpedoes ahead'' was his immortal, ''Damn the torpedoes!''
Bibliography: Boatner, Faust, Garner, NN 11, Shurr.

"The Battle for the Mississippi (April, 1862)" (1866). Poem, in *Battle-Pieces.* (Character: [Admiral David Glasgow] Farragut.) Melville describes Admiral Farragut's successful ''fight by night'' up ''the powerful stream'' to silence the forts of ''the town,'' and anchor there. His ''fleet . . . [was] scarred yet firm,'' while ''[m]oody broadsides . . . / Hold the lewd mob at bay.'' Surely ''nobler worlds'' await the dead ''[w]ho nobly yield their lives in this,'' the poet concludes. The specific battle was Farragut's bombardment of Fort St. Philip and Fort Jackson (24–25 April 1862), located seventy-five miles above New Orleans and built against land assault, and his subsequent capture of New Orleans, which was abandoned by Confederate forces and which was then permanently garrisoned by Union troops under General Benjamin F. Butler (beginning 1 May 1862). The poem has brooding biblical and Miltonic overtones.
Bibliography: Boatner, Faust, Garner, NN 11, Shurr, Stein.

"Battle of Stone River, Tennessee" (1866). (Full title: ''Battle of Stone River, Tennessee: A View from Oxford Cloisters [January, 1863].'') Poem, in *Battle-Pieces.* (Characters: [General John Cabell] Breckinridge, [General William Starke] Rosecrans.) Melville immediately places the indecisive Civil War Battle of Stone River, also known as Murfreesboro, Tennessee (30 December 1862–2

January 1863), in the larger context of civil wars in general. He does so by his opening allusion to the War of the Roses: "With Tewksbury and Barnet Heath / In days to come the field shall blend." The Barnet battle occurred on 14 April 1471; that at Tewksbury, on 3 May 1471; in both engagements, the House of York defeated the Lancastrian army, after which Edward IV mounted the throne. The "rival Roses" battled for political dominance but each called it "Right." In the process, they "profaned" their lifted crucifixes by "crossing blades." Stories of such actions, however, will all end "[i]n legend." Accounts of the similar fratricidal clash of forces under Rosencrans [the Union general] and those under Breckinridge [the Confederate general, aided by General Braxton Bragg] in Tennessee also "shall fade away"; but will "North and South their rage deplore," be reunited, and "thrive . . . / Like Yorkist and Lancastrian?" The subtitle of the poem subtly implies that time may convert this Civil War battle into another legend, if seen by one located in calm and academic Oxford. In an 1857 journal entry, Melville praises Oxford as the "[m]ost interesting spot I have seen in England," calls it "[s]acred to beauty & tranquillity," and adds that it "[h]as beheld unstirred all the violence of revolutions. &c." (2 May).

Bibliography: Peter Cozzens, *No Better Place to Die: The Battle of Stones River* (Urbana: University of Illinois Press, 1990); Garner; NN 11 and 15; Warren.

"A Battle Picture" (1947). Poem, in *Collected Poems of Herman Melville.* Presented are three buglers on horseback, calling up cavalrymen, who ride forward, their sabres ringing and their plumes dancing "for joy!"

Battle-Pieces (1866). (Full title: *Battle-Pieces and Aspects of the War.*) Collection of seventy-two poems, with Notes and a Supplement. The first poem, standing separately, is "The Portent (1859)." Fifty-two poems follow. Then, under the subtitle "Verses Inscriptive and Memorial," come nineteen more. Melville's notes are mostly informational. In his prose Supplement, Melville urges Christian charity and common sense with respect to Reconstruction efforts, a wide and humane patriotism, an awareness that victory came to the North not by greater heroism but because of greater resources and population, sympathy for the liberated slaves, and decency in Congress. He concludes with a prayer that through the pity and terror generated by the Civil War we may be instructed to make progress. A major source for *Battle-Pieces* was the early volumes of *The Rebellion Record: A Diary of American Events, with Documents, Narratives, Illustrative Incidents, Poetry, Etc.,* 11 vols. and supplement (New York: G[eorge]. P[almer]. Putnam,* 1861–1868).

Bibliography: Adler; Garner; Catherine Georgoudaki, "*Battle-Pieces and Aspects of the War:* Melville's Poetic Quest for Meaning and Form in a Fallen World," *American Transcendental Quarterly,* n.s. 1 (March 1987): 21–32; Robert Milder, "The Rhetoric of Melville's *Battle-Pieces,*" *Nineteenth-Century Literature* 44 (September 1989): 173–200; NN 11.

Beadle of England. In "Falstaff's Lament over Prince Hal Become Henry V."
See Henry V, King.

Beatrice ("Bice"). In *Clarel,* she is a girl who Celio once erroneously thought
might love him.

Beauty ("Chips"). In *Omoo,* he is the ugly carpenter aboard the *Julia.* He signs
the round-robin.

Belex ("The Spahi"). In *Clarel,* he is the European Turkish leader of the six
Arab Bethlehemites who guard the pilgrims. During his service as a Turkish
cavalryman, he was nearly massacred [in 1826] by Mahmoud [II (1785–1839),
the sultan of Turkey (1808–1839)], escaped, and became a cynical toll gatherer
at the Church of the Holy Sepulcher. Belex is friendly with the nobler Djalea
and rides a fine bay named Solomon.
   Bibliography: NN 12.

Belfast Sailor. In *Moby-Dick,* he is a sailor aboard the *Pequod* who becomes
gleeful when Daggoo and the Spanish sailor begin to fight during the midnight
festivities held in the forecastle. The Belfast sailor may be based on James
Rosman, an Irish sailor aboard the *Acushnet;* he ran away at Salango, on the
Colombian coast.
   Bibliography: Leyda.

Belisent. In "The Scout toward Aldie," she is the cousin of a Confederate
soldier who is captured by the Colonel's men as they ineffectually pursue [John
Singleton] Mosby.

Bell. In *Omoo,* he is the Britisher who owns and operates the sugar plantation
at Taloo, and has a beautiful wife. He is based on a young man named Bell,
who was the real-life owner of a sugar plantation and factory in Papetoai. According to Edward T. Perkins, who later visited the islands and published *Na
Motu; or, Reef-Rovings in South Seas: A Narrative of Adventures at the
Hawaiian, Georgian, and Society Islands* (1854) about his observations there,
Bell moved with his family to the Navigator Islands, where his wife later
drowned.
   Bibliography: Anderson, NN 2.

Bell, Mrs. In *Omoo,* she is the beautiful Australian wife of the owner and
operator of the sugar plantation at Taloo. Her husband, named Bell in real life,
owned a sugar plantation and factory in Papetoai. Melville expresses the hope
that the Bells will have many little Bells to make music on Imeoo. According
to an 1848 journal kept by a naval lieutenant named Henry Augustus Wise, Mrs.
Bell had taken to drink before meeting Melville. According to Edward T. Per-

kins, who later visited the islands and published *Na Motu; or, Reef-Rovings in South Seas: A Narrative of Adventures at the Hawaiian, Georgian, and Society Islands* (1854) about his observations there, Mrs. Bell moved with her family to the Navigator Islands and later drowned.

Bibliography: Anderson, Leyda, NN 2.

Bello, King. In *Mardi,* he is a Mardian king whose warriors do a paddle chant and who is mentioned in a manuscript book of voyages in Oh-Oh's museum. Bello is the ambitious, imperialistic, but basically good king of the important island of Dominora, defeated by the brave but boastful country of Vivenza. King Bello, who put down a riot, is based on the monarch of England, who quelled a similar incident organized by the Chartists (April 1848).

Bibliography: Davis.

"The Bell-Tower" (1855). Short story. (Characters: Bannadonna, Del Fonca, Dua, Excellenza, Haman, Una.) In Italy, Bannadonna proudly builds a stone bell-and-clock tower three hundred feet in height. While its "ponderous" bell is being cast, he strikes a reluctant worker with a ladle, and a splinter from the dying man flies into the molten metal and flaws the bell. After the mechanism is hoisted into place, Bannadonna privately lifts up a cloaked statue, which appears to step into the belfry. The clock has figures personifying the hours. Garlanded "Una" stares prophetically at Bannadonna, who secretly installs the clockworks and promises the crowd that the cloaked figure, a mechanical monster devised to strike the hours, will hit at one in the afternoon. At the hour of one, a dull, mangled sound is heard. Magistrates rush up to check and find Bannadonna bleeding to death under the stroke of one, with his bell-striking automaton impending over him. Theories vary. The creature evidently destroyed its Promethean creator. During Bannadonna's funeral, the bell ringer tugs so vigorously that down comes the bell, which when examined shows a defect near its ear. A year later the tower, with a recast bell, is destroyed by an earthquake.

As manuscript adviser of *Putnam's Monthly Magazine,** George William Curtis* rejected "The Bell-Tower" on first reading it, changed his mind, and accepted it on condition that certain "erasures" be made. It was published anonymously (1 August 1855) and reprinted in *The Piazza Tales* (1856). Melville was paid $37.50 for the story. He poured details from his wide reading experience into this story, which has echoes of Benvenuto Cellini, Nathaniel Hawthorne,* Mary Wollstonecraft Shelley, Edmund Spenser, and Juanelo Torriano (an engineer in the court of Emperor Charles V).

Bibliography: Robert E. Morsberger, "Melville's 'The Bell-Tower' and Benvenuto Cellini," *American Literature* 44 (December 1972): 459–62; Newman; NN 9; Sealts.

Beltha. In *Clarel,* he is a wrinkled Bethlehemite and a member of Djalea's guard. Beltha sings a "salt-song" beside the Dead Sea.

Bembo ("The Mowree"). In *Omoo,* he is the short, shaggy-looking, tattooed savage who is second mate aboard the *Julia.* Bembo tries to run her aground, is locked up, and is not seen again. He is still in irons when the *Julia* leaves Papeetee. Bembo is based on a sailor named Benbow Byrne, aboard the *Lucy Ann.* He submitted an affidavit during an 1842 inquiry into activities aboard ship.
Bibliography: Lebowitz, Leyda, NN 2.

Ben. In *Omoo. See* Sydney Ben.

"The Bench of Boors" (1891). Poem, in *Timoleon.* While in bed, the poet muses on a picture or pictures by Teniers showing sluggish, boorish, drunken, yawning boors. They nap in their "hazy hovel," "hugg[ing]" the fire and lighted partly by their pipes. In his 1857 journal, Melville records seeing pictures by David Teniers the Younger* (1610–1690) in Turin and Amsterdam (10, 24 April). In Amsterdam, he could have seen genre paintings by Teniers of an old man having some beer and a bricklayer having a smoke.
Bibliography: NN 11 and 15, Stein.

Beneventano, Ferdinando (?–?). Opera singer. Melville twice heard Beneventano sing in Gaetano Donizetti's *Lucia di Lammermoor* in New York City (29 January, 24 December 1847). In "Cock-a-Doodle-Doo!," Beneventano is the majestic opera singer after whom the narrator names Merrymusk's noble rooster.
Bibliography: Leyda.

Benignus Muscatel. In *Clarel,* he is a friar from St. John's Convent [in Syria]. He gave Rolfe a hymnbook bound in vellum.

"Benito Cereno" (1855). Short story. It was published anonymously in *Putnam's Monthly Magazine** (1 October, 1 November, 1 December 1855) and reprinted in *The Piazza Tales* (1856). (Characters: José de Abos and Padilla, Akim, Alexandro Aranda, Atufal, Babo, Lorenzo Bargas, Bartholomew Barlo, Benito Cereno, Dago, Delano, Captain Amasa Delano, Diamelo, Francesco, Luys Galgo, Hermenegildo Gandix, Juan Bautista Gayete, Ghofan, Martinez Gola, Roderigo Hurta, Infelez, Don Joaquin Marques de Aramboalaza, José, Lecbe, Mapenda, Francisco Masa, Matinqui, Miquel, José Morairi, Mure, Nacta, Nat, Ponce, Raneds, Juan Robles, Doctor Juan Martinez de Rozas, Alonzo Sidonia, Manuel Viscaya, Yambaio, Yau, Yola.)

In 1799, Amasa Delano, captain of the *Bachelor's Delight,* a Massachusetts sealer and trading vessel, is near an island off the southern coast of Chile when he sees a Spanish merchantman, identified as the *San Dominick,* apparently in distress. He has himself rowed over in his whaler, called the *Rover,* with a few supplies. Boarding, he observes that the *San Dominick* has a cargo of slaves; he provides initial aid, orders his men to return to the *Bachelor's Delight* for water and more food, and remains by himself with her captain, a man named Benito Cereno. Delano soon encounters Babo, Cereno's ever-present Senegalese attendant. Delano quickly grows confused. Cereno seems weak and spiritless. The slaves, including females and wild little children, seem out of control. When Delano questions the other captain, he learns that the *San Dominick,* bound from Buenos Aires to Lima with fifty Spaniards and three hundred slaves, encountered storms, diseases, and accidents. These misfortunes swept all of his officers and many others, white and black, to their death. Silently critical of Cereno, Delano praises faithful Babo, promises three men to help get the *San Dominick* to Concepción, and strides confidently to the poop.

Delano soon observes many untoward incidents among the black oakum pickers and hatchet polishers. When a black lad stabs a white boy, Cereno shrugs and has a coughing fit. When a regal-looking black named Atufal reports in chains to Benito but refuses to ask his pardon, Cereno remains impassive. Delano is offended when Cereno and Babo go off whispering. Is Cereno a lunatic, an imposter, or merely a cruel adventurer? Cereno asks questions about the *Bachelor's Delight*—its cargo, crew, and arms—all of which Delano answers fearlessly. The truth surely protects the innocent, he reasons. Reassured when he sees his *Rover* approaching, Delano walks about the Spanish deck freely, observes a few other curious incidents, but accepts supplies from his men, dispatches them for more water, and plans to stay on and pilot the *San Dominick* to a near anchorage by moonlight.

Babo beseeches his master to come and be shaved in the cuddy. Delano takes delight in seeing the black so gracefully serve the white master, who, however, is nervous, shakes a bit, and hence gets cut slightly. Delano walks to the mainmast, and Babo follows, his cheek cut and whining that the captain nicked him in punishment for his carelessness. Delano concludes that slavery breeds ugly passions, gives orders in his halting Spanish to work the ship toward the harbor, and invites Cereno to board his own vessel, now nearby, for some coffee. When Cereno sullenly declines, Delano though offended hopes still to bid him a decent goodbye, but Babo stands too close; so the American steps into his *Rover,* only to be startled when Cereno leaps after him into it. Three Spanish sailors dive into the water. Babo, dagger in hand, jumps after Cereno. Are the two in league to attack Delano? A dark avalanche of slaves pours into action over the Spanish bulwarks. Delano disarms Babo and grabs the fainting Cereno, and at last—the scales falling from his eyes—the innocent American sees all. Babo, head of a slave mutiny, aimed to kill Delano. Blacks are using hatchets on the surviving whites. Spanish boys climb the riggings. Delano secures Babo, then permits his chief mate and several men to attack the Spanish vessel to recapture the revolting slaves and claim booty.

In due time, legal depositions taken at Lima tell all. Rather than storm or sickness, it was a bloodthirsty slave revolt and unmentionable atrocities that caused all the deaths; Babo was the leader, with Atufal and certain others his willing followers. When the American captain approached, the freed slaves pretended that the few whites were still their masters, and planned to kill Delano if need be. After the trial, followed by the execution of the fierce and silent Babo, the resilient Delano urges the dispirited Cereno to forget the whole unpleasant incident. But the ruined Spaniard cannot do so and soon dies.

Melville's source for the plot of ''Benito Cereno'' is Amasa Delano's *A Narrative of Voyages and Travels in the Northern and Southern Hemispheres* (Boston, 1817), which includes the real-life encounter (February 1805) of Captain Delano's *Perseverance* with the *Tryal* of Captain Don Bonito Sereno. Melville makes Benito Cereno a more elevated character and Babo more heartless; lengthens Delano's time aboard the Spanish ship; invents the oakum picking, hatchet polishing, and death of Benito; and omits having Delano argue over rescue payment. In his story, Melville presents one of his typical studies of the ambiguity of appearances, the varying responses to contact with evil, and the inscrutable power of blackness.

Bibliography: Charles Berryman, '' 'Benito Cereno' and the Black Friars,'' *Studies in American Fiction* 18 (Autumn 1990): 159–70; Robert E. Burkholder, ed., *Critical Essays on Herman Melville's ''Benito Cereno''* (New York: G. K. Hall, 1992); Gloria Horsley-Meacham, ''Bull of the Nile: Symbol, History, and Racial Myth in 'Benito Cereno,' '' *New England Quarterly* 64 (June 1991): 225–42; Sidney Kaplan, ''Herman Melville and the American National Sin: The Meaning of 'Benito Cereno,' '' *Journal of Negro History* 41 (October 1956): 311–38 and 42 (January 1957): 11–37; Newman; William D. Richardson, *Melville's ''Benito Cereno'': An Interpretation with Annotated Text and Concordance* (Durham, N.C.: Carolina Academic Press, 1987); Harold H. Scudder, ''Melville's *Benito Cereno* and Captain Delano's Voyages,'' *PMLA* 53 (June 1928): 502–32; Sealts.

Bentley, Richard (1794–1871). British publisher. Bentley was born in London, attended St. Paul's School, joined his brother Samuel Bentley in his printing establishment (1819), married (and ultimately was the father of a daughter and four sons), and became Henry Colburn's partner in a publishing firm (1829). Colburn published fashionable novels with much success. Bentley became head of the company when Colburn parted with him under unfriendly terms (1832). Bentley published such popular American authors as James Fenimore Cooper* and Henry Wadsworth Longfellow, as well as esteemed British writers such as Charles Dickens and Benjamin Disraeli. Bentley founded *Bentley's Miscellany* (1837–1868). (In one *Miscellany,* he reprinted several poems by Melville's friend Alfred Billings Street.*) Bentley also issued *Standard Novels,* a successful series ultimately numbering 127 volumes. When the London publisher John Murray* rejected Melville's *Mardi,* Bentley published it (March 1849) and also *Redburn* (September 1849). Melville met Bentley in London (November, December 1849) and arranged for him to publish *White-Jacket.* In his 1849 journal, Melville records the following: ''Last night dined with Mr Bentley, and had a very pleasant time indeed. I begin to like him much. He seems a very fine frank off-handed old gentleman'' (19 December). Bentley published the London edition of *Moby-Dick* (as *The Whale,* 1851). Trouble came early in 1852, when Bentley agreed to publish *Pierre* only if Melville would share the risks half and half, as well as the profits, if any. Bentley wrote to Melville that *Mardi, Redburn, White-Jacket,* and *The Whale* had caused him a loss of £453.4.6 (more than $2,200), added that Melville was publishing too rapidly, and criticized his style. Although Melville published *Pierre* elsewhere, Bentley late in 1852 invited him to contribute to Bentley's *Miscellany.* It is not known whether Melville ever replied. Bentley experienced financial reverses when the House of Lords nullified his claim of ownership of the British copyrights of many American books (1859). The decision cost Bentley an estimated £16,000 ($80,000). After he was hurt in an accident in a railway station (1867), he gave over considerable control of his business to his son George Bentley.

Bibliography: Royal A. Gettmann, *A Victorian Publisher: A Study of the Bentley Papers* (Cambridge, England: Cambridge University Press, 1960); Lynn Horth, ''Richard Bentley's Place in Melville's Literary Career,'' pp. 229–45 in *Studies in the American Renaissance,* ed. Joel Myerson (Charlottesville: University Press of Virginia, 1992); NN 14 and 15.

''The Berg (A Dream)'' (1888). Poem, in *John Marr.* The poet has a dream in which ''a Ship of martial build'' is steered ''as by madness mere'' into ''a stolid Iceberg.'' ''[T]he spurs of ridges'' and ''[a] prism over glass-green gorges'' in the iceberg remained unjarred as ''the stunned Ship went down.'' Seagulls in the clouds and ''[s]eals . . . on sliddery ledges'' were similarly unmoved.

Bibliography: NN 11, Shurr, Stein, Warren.

Berzelli. In *Mardi,* he is an authority on amber cited by Mohi. It has been argued that the name Berzelli is a modification of that of George Joseph Camellus (Camel, Kamel) (1661–1706), a Jesuit missionary who when assigned to the Philippine Islands studied animals, minerals, and plants there. It seems more likely that Berzelli is Melville's modification of the last name of Jöns Jakob Berzelius (1779–1848), the renowned Swedish chemist who analyzed about 2,200 compounds for their chemical composition, published an accurate table of atomic weights and combining proportions, experimented on electrolysis of solutions, theorized that compounds have positively and negatively charged components, applied his theory to both organic and inorganic compounds, discovered several elements, classified certain minerals chemically, studied several rare metallic compounds, and was enormously influential through publication of more than 250 scientific papers and *Lehr der Chemie* (in five editions, 1803–1818, 1843–1848).

Bibliography: Davis; Evan M. Melhado, *Jacob Berzelius: The Emergence of His Chemical System* (Stockholm: Almqvist & Wiksell International, 1981); Wright.

Bet. In *White-Jacket. See* Black Bet.

Bettie. In *Pierre,* she is a pretty girl in the Miss Pennies' sewing circle.

Betty. In *Moby-Dick,* she is Mrs. Hosea Hussey's chambermaid at the Try Pots Inn, on Nantucket.

Betty. In *Omoo,* she is the waitress recalled by Rope Yarn fondly.

Betty. In *Redburn,* she is a servant at Handsome Mary Danby's Baltimore Clipper in Liverpool.

Betty, Master. In "The Fiddler." *See* Betty, William Henry West.

Betty, William Henry West (1791–1874). Actor. He was born in Shrewsbury, Shropshire, England. After, as a child, he saw a performance in Belfast by the actress Sarah Kemble Siddons,* he announced that he would simply die if not allowed to become an actor (1801). Encouraged by his family, the child prodigy made a debut in Belfast, performed in Dublin, and within three months had starred in seven roles, including Romeo and Hamlet (1803). He is said to have learned Hamlet's lines in three hours. He performed in Glasgow and Birmingham, and then in Covent Garden and Drury Lane (1804). His fee rose to fifty guineas per night and then more, and troops had to be summoned to control ecstatic crowds waiting to buy tickets. After touring in the provinces, he returned to London (1805–1806). Betty expanded his repertoire, but his popularity fell off in London, though not in the provinces. His last performance as a boy actor was at Bath (1808), after which he studied at Christ's College, Cambridge (1808–1811). He returned, less successfully, as an adult actor (1812–1824) and retired in comfort, owing to a considerable fortune. He said that his early audiences had been mistaken in idolizing him. As Master Betty in Melville's "The Fiddler," he is a British child prodigy of some time ago. Standard enigmatically links his name with that of Hautboy. *See* Hautboy.
   Bibliography: Giles Playfair, *The Prodigy: A Study of the Strange Life of Master Betty* (London: Secker & Warburg, 1967).

Bey, The. In *Clarel,* he is the militant friend of the Emir in the Arnaut's song during the wine revelry at Mar Saba.

"Bice." In *Clarel. See* Beatrice.

Biddy. In "The Apple-Tree Table," she is the squeamish maid who works for the narrator, his wife, and their daughters Julia and Anna. Biddy throws the first emergent bug into the fire.

Biddy. In "I and My Chimney," she is the maid who works for the narrator and his wife.

Biddy. In "Jimmy Rose," she is the maid of the narrator William Ford and his family.

Bidi Bidie. In *Mardi,* this is the name of one of the twelve aristocratic Tapparian families on the isle of Pimminee, entertained by Nimni. Melville obviously coined the word "Tapparian" from tapa, the Polynesian cloth material.

Bidiri. In *Mardi,* he is an honest legatee mentioned in Bardianna's will.

Bildad, Captain. In *Moby-Dick,* he is a tall, pious, parsimonious, well-to-do whaleman. Once a chief mate, he is now retired and is one of the principal owners of the *Pequod.* He is a Quaker, as is Captain Peleg, another part-owner of the *Pequod.*
   Bibliography: Brian Higgins and Hershel Parker, eds., *Critical Essays on Herman Melville's Moby-Dick* (New York: G. K. Hall, 1992).

Bill. In *Israel Potter,* he is one of the two named shanghaiers of Israel Potter at Dover. The other is Jim.

Bill. In *Redburn,* he is a sailor aboard the *Highlander.* His politeness to the second mate astonishes Redburn when the lad is new to nautical etiquette.

Bill. In *White-Jacket,* he is a sailor who mistakes White Jacket aloft for the ghost of Bungs, who drowned. Bill helps lower the halyards to test White Jacket's corporeality. Later Bill smokes and discusses politics with a group in a recess between two guns.

Billson, Charles James (1858–1932). Lawyer, educator, and translator. He graduated from Oxford (1881), practiced law in Leicester, England, taught Greek to workers there, married and had three daughters, and translated Virgil's *Aeneid* (1906) and some of Pindar's works (1931). Melville received a letter from Billson from Leicester, dated 21 August 1884, asking him to fill out an enclosed incomplete list of his books. Melville answered cordially and thus began a pleasant correspondence with a sensitive British admirer. In his first letter, Melville named *White-Jacket, Battle-Pieces,* and also *Clarel,* which he said was "eminently adapted for unpopularity" (10 October 1884). Billson replied by sending Melville a copy of *Vane's Story . . .* by James Thomson, part of which Melville said "gave me more pleasure than anything of modern poetry that I have seen in a long while" and added that Billson must be happy to have known Thomson personally (1 December 1884). In return for Billson's sending him another book by Thomson—*The City of Dreadful Night . . .* —Melville gave him his "sole presentation-copy'' of *Clarel,* since Billson could not locate the rare work (22 January 1885). Evidently in reply to Billson's comment on Thomson's not becoming famous, Melville replied thus: "As to his not acheiving [*sic*] 'fame'— what of that? He is not less, but so much the more" (20 December 1885). Their correspondence continued until 1888, during which time Billson sent more books and also copies of articles he thought Melville might enjoy. When Billson learned that a book about the deceased Melville was planned, he sent Melville's daughter Elizabeth Melville* a copy of every letter he had received from Melville (1906). Billson wrote to Melville's granddaughter Eleanor Melville Metcalf on the occasion of the publication of *Herman Melville, Mariner and Mystic* by Raymond Weaver (1921). Throughout his correspondence, Billson combined personal modesty, expressions of special delight in Melville's brand of humor, and praise of *Mardi.*

   Bibliography: Metcalf, NN 14.

Billy. In *Redburn,* he is a tailor who is a steerage passenger aboard the *Highlander* from Liverpool to America. The coquettishness of his pretty wife infuriates Billy.

Billy Budd (1924). (Full title: *Billy Budd, Sailor;* also called *Billy Budd, Foretopman* and *Billy Budd, Sailor [An Inside Narrative].*) Incomplete novel. (Characters: Albert, Bristol Molly, Billy Budd, John Claggart, the Dansker, Lord Jack Denton, Donald, [Comte] de Grasse [François Joseph Paul, Marquis de Grassetilly], Captain Graveling, the Handsome Sailor, Captain Mordant, Mr. Purser, Lieutenant Ratcliffe, Red Pepper, Red Whiskers, [Admiral, Baron, George Brydges] Rodney, Squeak, Taff the Welshman, Captain the Honorable Edward Fairfax Vere, Captain Vere, Wilkes, X–.) Walking on docks, sailors will often surround their favorite shipmate, usually someone tall and handsome. Twenty-one-year-old Billy Budd is such a one. He was impressed in the late 1790s off the *Rights-of-Man.* His sweet presence had mollified and calmed the unruly crew of this oddly named merchantman, according to Graveling, her disconsolate captain. Off Billy must go. So, waving a cheerful farewell to his mates, he accompanies Lieutenant Ratcliffe aboard the H.M.S. *Bellipotent,* a seventy-four outward bound. Billy is rated an able seaman and is assigned as foretopman on the starboard watch. He looks noble but a bit adolescent, and he is a Bristol orphan, as he explains when asked about his parentage. He is also illiterate, naive, and exuberant. He has a flaw, which is a liability to stammer.

   In April 1797, a mutiny at Spithead breaks out. In May, another breaks out at the Nore. Both are suppressed after some grievances—not including impressment—are redressed. Loyalty in the marine corps and among influential sections of the crews helped as well. In the summer, when Billy boards the *Bellipotent,* she is on her way to join the Mediterranean fleet. (Melville digresses at this point to praise Admiral Horatio Nelson* for his painstaking foresight and love of glory.) The captain of the *Bellipotent* is Edward Fairfax Vere, a bachelor about forty years old. He is unselfish, strict, modest but resolute, conservatively bookish and even pedantic, unjocose, and honest and direct. Also dreamy, he is called "Starry Vere." His master-at-arms is John Claggart, about thirty-five, thin and tall, with a pale brow and dark curls, and possibly suffering from defective blood. His unknown past gives rise to rumors that he was a chevalier who avoided trouble with English law by joining the navy, which is known as a refuge for the insolvent and the immoral. Though unpopular, Claggart is promptly obeyed by his subordinates, who have built him an underground spy system aboard ship.

Life in the foretop pleases Billy, who is dutiful, especially after he once had to witness a flogging. He is troubled, however, because Claggart's police keep finding things amiss with his gear. One day he asks the Dansker for an explanation. This scarred old veteran, who likes Billy, says only that Claggart has it in for the handsome youth. The next day, the ship rolls and Billy spills his soup on the deck just as Claggart walks by, slapping his rattan. Noting the mess, he says, "Handsomely done, my lad!" Naive Billy thinks that the sarcastic words are flattering. But what ails Claggart? He is baffling, naturally depraved. He is proud, without petty sin, not mercenary or avaricious or sensual. He is a dangerous lunatic because he is inconstantly so. In short, he is evidence of "the mystery of iniquity." He both hates Billy and envies his good looks and obvious innocence. Matters are made worse when Squeak, Claggart's rat-like corporal, reports lies about Billy to the effect that Billy has applied certain critical epithets to Claggart, whose curious conscience exaggerates them and makes him decide to check up on the lad.

A few nights later, Billy is aroused from his hammock by a whisper urging him to come to the forechains. Unable to say no, he goes on deck and encounters an unknown man, also impressed into the navy, who tries to bribe Billy to help in an unspecific way. With a stammer, Billy tells him to be off. Billy is puzzled when he later sees an afterguardsman who he thinks is the man who spoke to him, because the fellow laughs and has an open manner. Billy tells part of the story to the Dansker, who says again that Claggart has it in for him. Billy does not become an informant, and he remains ignorant, simple, juvenile, and trusting. Claggart continues to speak pleasantly to him. But what about Claggart? He yearningly looks after Billy with tears in his eyes, as though he could love the lad but for fate. Meanwhile, the monomaniac feels a hidden fire eating deeper into him.

After the *Bellipotent* passes through the Straits [of Gibraltar], she is detached from the fleet on scout duty, chases an enemy ship, but loses her when she crowds sail and escapes. Immediately after this incident, Claggart requests permission to speak with Captain Vere on his quarterdeck. Vere, who barely knows his new master-at-arms, is adversely impressed and is shocked when Claggart, with a mixture of grief and determination, reports that Billy Budd during the chase of the enemy vessel behaved suspiciously and then hints that the result might become a repetition of the recent mutiny. Even though he thinks that

Claggart may be acting like a perjurer he once observed, Vere decides to investigate, calls for Billy, and orders Claggart to stand by. Billy reports to his captain. Claggart repeats his accusation. Billy turns as pale as a leper and stammers gurglingly. Vere, who has been thinking paternally of promoting the lad, tries to calm him by urging him to take his time, but Billy's huge fist shoots out like a cannon and Claggart falls dead to the floor, like a dead snake. Aghast at such an Ananias-like judgment, Vere summons the surgeon to verify the death and then—aware that Billy, though an avenging angel, must inevitably hang—convenes a drumhead court. The surgeon momentarily suspects his captain's sanity and would prefer to turn the case over to the fleet admiral.

Acting both promptly and secretly, Vere appoints three officers, holds court in the quarterdeck cabin, and describes what happened. Billy testifies that he had no malice against Claggart, did not intend to kill him, is sorry the man is dead, but felt he had to act when lied about and when his tongue failed him. Vere says that he believes Billy, who is grateful but who is removed under guard. Vere pedantically but efficiently tells the court that moral scruples vitalized by compassion are irrelevant in the face of a situation requiring military duty, and he warns the officers to ignore not only their hearts and consciences but also Billy's intent. He adds that, although God may forgive Billy, the Articles of War are clear as to the penalty for a sailor who strikes a mortal blow to anyone of superior rank. Vere calls Billy's act mutinous homicide. Vere also notes that the possible proximity of the enemy makes quick action necessary. If the death penalty does not immediately follow, the men will think that their officers are flinching. A deadly relaxation of wartime discipline will result. The court, though uneasy, sentences Billy to hang in the morning.

Vere personally reports the verdict to Billy. The exact circumstances of their final meeting are never revealed. Perhaps Vere clutched Billy to his heart as Abraham did his son. Probably Billy appreciated Vere's frank spirit. Vere tersely reports the events to his assembled crew, and soon thereafter Claggart's body is honorably buried at sea. The chaplain goes to Billy, who in sleep on the upper gun deck has a child's virgin innocence on his face. The chaplain returns, offers what spiritual comfort he can, but concludes that innocence is better to go to Judgment with, kisses Billy's rose-tan cheek, and withdraws. At four in the morning, all hands are piped on deck. Just before being run up to the mainyard, Billy in clear syllables says, "God bless Captain Vere!" The crew echoes these words. The dawn clouds are fleecy. Billy ascends in rose light, and his body does not twitch. Talking of this phenomenon later to the purser, the surgeon denies that it should be equated with euthanasia and hurries off. Billy's body is consigned to the deep. Awkward seafowl croak a requiem over the splash. Vere orders the drummer to beat to quarters.

A little later, while the *Bellipotent* is rejoining the fleet, she engages a French line-of-battle the *Atheist,* and Vere is wounded. Dying at Gibraltar, he is heard to murmur, "Billy Budd, Billy Budd," though not remorsefully. Weeks later, an authorized naval chronicle reports that Claggart discovered a mutinous plot but, before he could tell his captain, he was stabbed by William Budd, undoubtedly a foreign agent and therefore properly hanged. His shipmates, however, in time treasure bits of the spar from which he was hanged, as though they were pieces of the Cross; in addition, one tarry hand wrote a ballad called "Billy in the Darbies," which purports to be the doomed sailor's thoughts as he ponders death and dreams of falling "fathoms down" into "the oozy weeds."

At his death in 1891, Melville left *Billy Budd* as an incomplete manuscript of 351 leaves. He wrote them probably between 1886 or so and 1891, at which time he was forced to quit because of fatal illness. His numerous sources include his own experiences at sea, his ponderings while he wrote various poems in *John Marr,* his knowledge of eighteenth-century British naval law, and—closer to home—the *Somers* mutiny. The *Somers* was a U.S. naval brig, small and manned by Captain Alexander Slidell MacKenzie (1803–1848), a few junior officers, and young sailors—mostly young cadets on their first outward-bound voyage. While the *Somers* was returning from a cruise along the African coast late in 1842, a mutiny was planned by the ring leader Philip Spencer, the eighteen-year-old son of John C. Spencer, President John Tyler's secretary of war. The would-be mutineers intended to murder MacKenzie and Lieutenant Guert Gansevoort,* convert the *Somers* into a pirate vessel, and prey upon commercial shipping off the American coast. The crew of seventy-five would be required to participate or would be killed. MacKenzie was informed by a supposed conspirator. Two-thirds of the crew were involved. The officers anticipated their action and retained armed control. Three would-be mutineers—Spencer, Samuel Cromwell, and Elisha Small—were arrested, tried by drumhead court, of which Gansevoort was an appointed officer, and hanged (1 December 1842). Among Small's last words were "God bless the flag!" Gansevoort, Melville's cousin, voted that the prisoners should be put to death to make a necessary impression on the crew, but he brooded for the rest of his life over his part in the trial. The *Somers* affair caused partisan controversy and commentary for years afterward, as late—in Melville's lifetime—as 1889. In the *American Magazine* appeared "The Mutiny on the 'Somers' " (May 1888) by Lieutenant H. D. Smith; in the *Cosmopolitan,* "The Murder of Philip Spencer" (June, July, August 1889) by Gail Hamilton (Mary Abigail Dodge). Melville could have been influenced by both of these articles while he was writing *Billy Budd.* In a digression, he cites the *Somers* mutiny but "without comment." When Melville visited the Union cavalry camp of his cousin Henry Sanford Gansevoort* (April 1864), he heard about young William E. Ormsby, a hotheaded Union soldier twenty-four years of age who deserted, joined the Confederate guerrillas under John Singleton Mosby,* was captured by Union soldiers near Aldie, Virginia, and was tried by a drumhead court-martial, found guilty, and shot by a firing squad by order of his commanding officer, Colonel Charles Russell Lowell, nephew of the man-of-letters James Russell Lowell (February 1864). Several details of this incident are paralleled in Billy Budd's action, speedy trial, and quick execution.

The rich, imagistic, and allusive style of *Billy Budd* has intrigued readers, but it is the psychological nature of the three principal characters that has challenged the critics. In what ways is Billy Budd a Christ figure? What does his stammer symbolize? To what degree is Captain Vere an admirable naval officer and father figure? What is his motivation? Is Claggart an unmitigated Satan? Is *Billy Budd* to be read as Melville's testament of faith or as an ironic document concerning fallen humanity?

Bibliography: Adler; R. W. Desai, ''Truth's 'Ragged Edges': A Phenomenological Inquiry into the Captain Vere–Billy Relationship in Melville's *Billy Budd, Sailor,*'' *Studies in the Humanities* 19 (June 1992): 11–26; Garner; Harrison Hayford, ed., *The Somers Mutiny Affair* (Englewood Cliffs, N.J.: Prentice-Hall, 1959); Hershel Parker, *Reading Billy Budd* (Evanston, Ill.: Northwestern University Library, 1990); Peter Shaw, ''The Fate of a Story,'' *American Scholar* 62 (Autumn 1993): 591–600.

''Billy in the Darbies.'' Poem. *See Billy Budd.*

Bibliography: Michael C. Berthold, '' 'Billy in the Darbies,' 'Lycidas,' and Melville's Figures of Captivity,'' *American Transcendental Quarterly* n.s. 6 (June 1992): 109–19; Warren.

Bishop, The. In *Pierre,* he is the ecclesiastical superior of the Rev. Mr. Falsgrave and, four years earlier, the consecrator of his small marble church, which was financed by Mary Glendinning.

B. L. In *Clarel. See* L., B.

Black Bet. In *White-Jacket,* she is an African-American in Philadelphia. White Jacket's African-American gun captain names their gun in her honor.

Black Dan. In *Omoo,* he is a sarcastic sailor aboard the *Julia.* He signs the round-robin.

Black Guinea (''Ebony''). In *The Confidence-Man,* he is a crippled African-American beggar. His authenticity is doubted by a man with a wooden leg, but he is supported by both a Methodist army chaplain and an Episcopal clergyman. Black Guinea is surely Melville's grotesque depiction of the quintessential African-American slave.

Bibliography: Trimpi.

Black Jew. In *Clarel. See* Abdon.

Blair. In ''A Short Patent Sermon According to Blair, the Rhetorician: No. C.C.C.C.L.XXX.V.III,'' he is the rhetorician whose outline for speeches is spoofed by one in criticism of Dow Jr. A man named Hugh Blair was the author of *Lectures on Rhetoric* (1783).

Bibliography: NN 9.

Blake. In "The Scout toward Aldie," he is a Union soldier whose corpse was found earlier by [John Singleton] Mosby's* pursuers.

Bland. In *White-Jacket,* he is the sergeant-at-arms who smuggles liquor aboard the *Neversink,* sells it at high prices through his assistant Scriggs, and flogs his customers when they are found by the officers to be drunk. When he is discovered and broken to the rank of waister by Claret, Bland behaves so bravely among his enemies that he remains unharmed. He is soon restored to his former rank and position. Leggs and Pounce are among those who serve under him. In the presence of Shenly's corpse, Bland jokes about death. Bland may be based on a real-life master-at-arms known to William McNally, author of *Evils and Abuses in the Naval and Merchant Service Exposed* (1839).
   Bibliography: Howard P. Vincent, *The Tailoring of Melville's White-Jacket* (Evanston, Ill.: Northwestern University Press, 1970).

Bland, Jerry. In "To Major John Gentian, Dean of the Burgundy Club," he is a friend of the Marquis de Grandvin.

Blandmour. In "Poor Man's Pudding and Rich Man's Crumbs," he is the narrator's poet friend. He rhapsodizes on the fact that Nature bestows gifts upon the poor.

Blandmour. In "Poor Man's Pudding and Rich Man's Crumbs," he or she is any one of the the ruddy little children of Blandmour, the poet.

Blandoo. In *Mardi,* he is a dead subject whose pusillanimous discretion King Peepi has inherited.

Blink, Lieutenant. In *White-Jacket,* he is the officer whom Claret dispatches to the Peruvian sloop-of-war to arrest Jack Chase.

Bliss, William Wallace Smith (1815–1853). Soldier and administrator. His father graduated from West Point (1811) and was an army captain. Born in Whitehall, New York, young Bliss moved with his family to Lebanon, New Hampshire, and entered West Point at age fourteen. He was given the humorous nickname "Perfect Bliss" by admiring fellow cadets because of his phenomenal mental ability, which included remarkable skill in languages. (Ultimately, he could read thirteen languages and speak several of them.) Graduating from the academy (1833), Bliss was appointed second lieutenant in the infantry, served in Alabama (1833–1834) and in the Cherokee Nation (1834), taught mathematics at West Point (1834–1840), was promoted to captain and named assistant adjutant general (1839), became chief of staff to the commanding general in the Florida War (1840–1841), and served on the frontier (1842–1845). Bliss was appointed chief of staff to General Zachary Taylor* (1845–1849), with whom he attended the Grand Council involving Native Americans and held in Oklahoma (1842) and under whom he advanced in rank. Major Bliss proceeded with Taylor to the Rio Grande (January 1846). As his adjutant general, he issued his battle order to advance on Matamoras (April), and was with Taylor at Palo Alto (May) and Resaca de la Palma (May). Lieutenant Colonel Bliss fought at Buena Vista (February 1847) and was dispatched by Taylor to negotiate with Mexican officers at Agua Nueva (February). Bliss married Taylor's youngest daughter, Mary Elizabeth Taylor, in Baton Rouge (1848) and received a master's degree at Dartmouth College (1848). When Taylor became president (1849), his sparkling daughter was usually the official hostess, because of the First Lady's poor health. Bliss and his wife lived in the White House. Upon Taylor's death (1850), Bliss was assigned as adjutant general of the Western Division, with headquarters in New Orleans (1850–1853), and he continued in that capacity until he tragically died of yellow fever.

In Melville's "Authentic Anecdotes of 'Old Zack,'" Major Bliss is General Taylor's aide. He gallops away from the Mexican mortar shell which the general is eager to bet will not explode. Bliss offers a reward for the arrest of the person who put a tack in the general's saddle causing him to tear his pants. Bliss certifies as genuine the pants subsequently exhibited at Barnum's Museum (*see* Barnum, P. T.).

Bibliography: George W. Cullum, *Biographical Register of the Officers and Graduates of the U.S. Military Academy at West Point, N.Y. . . . ,* 3d ed., rev. vol. 1 (Boston: Houghton, Mifflin, 1891); Holman Hamilton, *Zachary Taylor: Soldier of the Republic,* 2 vols. (Indianapolis: Bobbs-Merrill, 1941).

Blood, Asaph. In "Daniel Orme," in one draft, this was Daniel Orme's name.

"The Blue-Bird" (1924). Poem, in *Weeds and Wildings,* as part of a section entitled "The Year." The dead bluebird lies stiff in March in his "sepulchre" in a garden beneath a fir tree but is "transfigured" in June in the azure of the larkspur. Melville may be parodying Christianity here.

Bibliography: Shurr, Stein.

Blue-Skin. In *White-Jacket,* he is a mercilessly rasping barber.

Blumacher, Tuenis Van der. In "A Dutch Christmas up the Hudson in the Time of Patroons." *See* Van der Blumacher, Tuenis.

Blunt, Bill ("Liverpool"). In *Omoo,* he is a sailor aboard the *Julia.* He signs the round-robin. *See also* William.

Blunt, Jack. In *Redburn,* he is an ugly, ill-formed, repulsive, twenty-five-year-old Irish Cockney sailor aboard the *Highlander.* He regularly consults a book about dreams, attributes the bad weather that the ship experiences on the way back to America to Mrs. O'Brien's reading the Bible to her triplet sons, and heads the group of disgruntled sailors who bid farewell to Captain Riga in an insulting manner. Blunt may be based on James Johnson, born in Ireland, a sailor at age twenty aboard the *St. Lawrence*, which Melville took to Liverpool and back (1839) and which is the model for the *Highlander*.

Bibliography: Susan VanZanten Gallagher, "Jack Blunt and His Dream Book," *American Literature* 58 (December 1986): 614–19; Gilman.

B—m, Peter Tamerlane. In "Authentic Anecdotes of 'Old Zack.'" *See* Barnum, P. T.

Boat Plug. In *White-Jacket,* he is a kind midshipman who is often blessed by the grateful sailors who serve under him. He is rebuked in class by the Professor.

Bob. In *Omoo. See* Captain Bob; Navy Bob.

Bob. In *White-Jacket,* he is a messmate with whom White Jacket tries without success to swap jackets.

Bob. In *White-Jacket,* he is a dead quarter-gunner whose boots are auctioned by the purser's steward.

Bob, Orlop. In "Bridegroom-Dick." *See* Orlop Bob.

Boddo. In *Mardi,* he is an erroneous old authority, cited by Babbalanja.

Bodisco, Waldemar de (?–1878). Diplomat. Born in Russia, Bodisco migrated to the United States at an early age with his uncle, the Russian minister to Washington, D.C. After graduating from Georgetown College, Bodisco became secretary of the Russian legation in Washington. He was twice named chargé d'affaires in Washington (1866, 1869) and was appointed Russian consul-general in New York City (1871–1878). Bodisco died in Jordan Alum Springs, Virginia. In *White-Jacket,* Melville names Baron de Bodisco as the Russian minister at whose ball, held in Washington, D.C., White Jacket meets the Commodore and chats with him.

Boldo. In *Mardi,* he is a materialistic Mardian who is mentioned by Babbalanja.

Bolton, Harry ("Bury"). In *Redburn,* he is a mysterious, dapper, effeminate little man from Bury St. Edmunds. He presumably loses much of his inheritance by gambling during a whirlwind trip with Redburn to London. Bolton then ships aboard the *Highlander* on her return trip to America. He seems to have lied about his experience as a midshipman on a vessel in the East India trade because he is unable to climb the riggings of the *Highlander*. Bolton and Redburn become fast friends. Years later, Redburn learns that Bolton was crushed to death between a whale and a vessel off Brazil.

Bomba, [King]. In Melville's poem "Pausilippo (in the Time of Bomba)," he is a monarch called Bomba and is mentioned as ruling in the region of Naples. In "Marquis de Grandvin: At the Hostelry," he is mentioned as the father and royal predecessor of King Fanny. In "Marquis de Grandvin: Naples in the Time of Bomba . . . ," he is described with a slur as "The Bomb-King." *See* Ferdinand II, King of the Two Sicilies.

"Bomb-King, The." In "Marquis of Grandvin: Naples in the Time of Bomba . . ." *See* Bomba, [King].

Bomblum. In *Mardi,* he is legatee mentioned in Bardianna's will.

Bondo. In *Mardi,* he is Noojoomo's Valapee enemy who swears, by one of his own teeth, to get revenge. His tooth becomes his "bond."

Bonja. In *Mardi,* he is a Mardian poet, according to Yoomy.

Bonny Blue ("Sweet Wrinkles"). In "Bridegroom-Dick," she is the devoted, sentimental old wife of old Bridegroom Dick. He reminisces to her about his experiences long ago at sea. She is based to a degree on Melville's long-suffering wife Elizabeth Knapp Shaw Melville.*

Boombolt. In *White-Jacket,* he is a forecastle man who, during a lively conversation as the *Neversink* nears home, vows never to go to sea again.

Boomer, Captain. In *Moby-Dick,* he is the captain of the *Samuel Enderby.* He lost his right arm while he was chasing Moby Dick with his mate Mounttop. Boomer was later attended by Dr. Jack Bunger, his surgeon.

Boone, Daniel (1734–1820). Pioneer. Born near Reading, Pennsylvania, Boone was an expert hunter and trapper by age twelve. He moved to North Carolina, where he became a blacksmith (1750), and he accompanied General William Braddock's forces during his ill-fated attempt to capture Fort Duquesne and barely escaped (1755). He married Rebeccah Bryan in 1756 (the couple had nine children, and his wife died in 1813). Boone visited Kentucky (1767, 1769–1771), led settlers there (1775), and built a fort on a site later called Boonesborough (1775). He fought Native Americans, provided meat for settlers, lived peacefully with some Shawnees, but escaped to warn Boonesborough of an attack by them (1776–1778). He held political offices in western Virginia (1781–1798) and later moved with his son Daniel Morgan Boone to Missouri, where he died. Daniel Boone was brave, strong, and accomplished in woodcraft and marksmanship. He was loyal to his friends, honest, and even-tempered. *The Discovery, Settlement, and Present State of Kentucke* by John Filson (1784), purporting to be Boone's and containing his ''Autobiography,'' began the Boone legend. In *The Confidence-Man,* Boone is mentioned in the story of Indian haters as having lost his sons to Indians.

Bibliography: Michael A. Lofaro, *The Life and Adventures of Daniel Boone* (Lexington: University Press of Kentucky, 1986).

Booth, Edwin Thomas (1833–1893). American actor. Born near Belair, Maryland, he toured with his colorful but unstable father actor Junius Brutus Booth, debuted in William Shakespeare's *Richard III* (Boston, 1849), and stood in for his father as Richard III (1851). When his father died (1852), Booth toured in California, Australia, and Hawaii. He gained celebrity as a turbulent stage personality in Sacramento, California (1856). In the East again, he was regarded as America's most distinguished actor. He comanaged the Winter Garden Theater in New York (from 1863) and performed in several Shakespearean tragedies. His actor-brother John Wilkes Booth's assassination of President Abraham Lincoln* (1865) caused Edwin Booth to retire (until 1866). The Winter Garden Theater's destruction by fire (1867) inspired him to build Booth's Theater (1869), where he scored triumphs until bad advice caused its bankruptcy (1874). He continued to do well on stage, however, in the United States, in England, and on the Continent. His farewell performance was as Hamlet at the Brooklyn Academy of Music (1891). Booth married the talented actress Mary Devlin in 1860. He persuaded her to retire from the stage, had a daughter named Edwina by her, and swore off alcohol upon Mary's death in 1863. In 1869 Booth married Mary McVicker, an ambitious but untalented actress who, after the death of their son in horrible childbirth, went insane, dying in 1881.

In '' 'The Coming Storm': A Picture by S. R. Gifford,'' Melville identifies E.B. as the owner of the painting entitled *The Coming Storm.*

Bibliography: Stephen M. Archer, *Junius Brutus Booth: Theatrical Prometheus* (Carbondale: University of Southern Illinois Press, 1992).

Boots. In *Redburn. See* Redburn, Wellingborough.

Borabolla, King. In *Mardi,* he is a fat, jolly king who is King Donjalolo's guest at a big banquet. On his island of Mondoldo, he is hospitable to Taji and his friends. He calls King Media his cousin. Borabolla's name is a modification of Borabora, an island near Tahiti.

Borhavo. In *Mardi,* he is an authority on amber cited by Mohi. Borhavo's name derives from that of Herman Boerhaave (1668–1738), the Dutch chemist, physician, and professor. After receiving degrees in philosophy and medicine, Boerhaave spent his professional life in Leyden, where he gained international renown and was revered as a teacher of chemistry and medicine. One of his principal works is *Elementa Chemiae* (1724).

Bibliography: Gerrit Arie Lindeboom, *Herman Boerhaave: The Man and His Work* (London: Methuen, 1968); Wright.

Botargo. In *Mardi,* he is a Mardian poet mentioned by Babbalanja.

Boteman. In "The Encantadas." *See* Ferryman.

Bountiful, Lord. In "The Marquis de Grandvin," this is the laudatory nickname for the Marquis de Grandvin. *See* Grandvin, the Marquis de.

Bourbon-Draco. In "Marquis de Grandvin: Naples in the Time of Bomba . . . ," he is the glittering, conceited drum major of Bomba's troops.

Bowser. In *Israel Potter,* this is a sailor's name invented by Israel Potter for himself when he is aboard the British frigate which he boards by himself from the *Ariel* during the combat engagement.

Boy. In "On the Slain Collegians," this is the general name for any brave college lad killed in battle.

Boy, The. In "At the Cannon's Mouth." *See* Cushing, William Barker.

Boy, The. In "The College Colonel." *See* the Colonel.

Brace, Ned. In *White-Jacket,* he is the after-guardsman who takes the part of Captain Spyglass in the Fourth of July theatrical put on aboard the *Neversink.*

Brade. In *The Confidence-Man,* he is the senior partner in the firm of Brade Brothers and Company. According to John Ringman, Brade introduced him to Henry Roberts.

Brade. In *The Confidence-Man,* he is the senior Brade's brother.

Bradford, Alexander Warfield (1815–1867). Lawyer. The son of the Reverend John M. Bradford, he was born in Albany, New York, graduated from Union College (1832), married Marianne Gray and was admitted to the bar (1837), and thereafter combined law practice with politics and literary endeavors. A pioneer scholar in Native-American history and culture, Bradford published *American Antiquities and Researches into the Origin and History of the Red Race* (1841). He became the corporation counsel to the city of New York (1843), coeditor of the *American Review* (1845), and surrogate for New York City and New York County (1848), and he prepared *Reports of Cases Argued and Determined in the Surrogate's Court of the County of New York* (4 vols.,

1851–1857). He retired from the bench (1858), served in the state assembly (1858–1860), resumed law practice with great monetary success, and worked to codify state laws (1857–1865). Bradford published widely and amassed a fine private library, which was catalogued and sold a year after his death. His wife died in 1875.

Bradford's father was the Melville family minister in Albany. Bradford was a classmate of Melville's brother Gansevoort Melville* at the Albany Academy and was helpful professionally to both Gansevoort (who in his journal called him "Aly") and Allan Melville,* another of Melville's brothers, in New York City. Melville prepared an article, which evidently was about *Typee* and is now not extent, and wrote to Bradford about publishing it (23 May 1846). In Melville's novel *Redburn,* the New York host and hostess who befriend Redburn shortly before he departs on the *Highlander* for Liverpool and upon his return to America are modeled after Bradford and his wife. Bradford, among others, unsuccessfully recommended Melville, in an 1861 letter to President Abraham Lincoln,* for a consular appointment.

Bibliography: Gilman, Leyda, NN 14.

Bragg, Braxton (1817–1876). Soldier. Born in Warrenton, North Carolina, Bragg graduated from West Point (1837), was appointed as a cavalry second lieutenant (1837), helped remove the Cherokees (1838), fought in the Seminole Wars (1838–1842), and was assigned to Texas (1845–1846). During the Mexican War, he served under General Zachary Taylor* (1846–1848), achieving the breveted rank of lieutenant colonel (1847). He was commissioner of public works in Louisiana (1853–1861), resigned from the army (1856) to work on his Louisiana sugar plantation, and at the onset of the Civil War joined the Confederate army. He was a brigadier general (1861), a major general (1862), and a full general (1862), at which time he succeeded General Pierre Gustave Toutant de Beauregard as commander of the Department of Mississippi. Bragg fought well at Shiloh (6–7 April 1862) and at the Battle of Stones River (30 December 1862–2 January 1863) and elsewhere. He was the subject of criticism, won at Chickamauga (19–20 September 1863), was defeated at Chattanooga and Missionary Ridge (23–25 November 1863), was relieved of his command, and became a military advisor of Jefferson Davis, president of the Confederacy (1864). He accompanied Davis in flight through Georgia, was captured with him (May 1865), but was paroled. After the war, Bragg became a civil engineer, was commissioner of public works in Alabama, and died in Galveston, Texas. Bragg married Eliza Brooks Ellis in Thibodoux, west of New Orleans, in 1849. He was an able military organizer and disciplinarian, but he was quarrelsome and erred in failing to follow up military successes.

In "Authentic Anecdotes of 'Old Zack,'" Melville identifies Bragg as a distinguished officer who certified the genuineness of General Zachary Taylor's pants, exhibited by P. T. Barnum* in his museum.

Bibliography: Grady McWhiney, *Braxton Bragg and Confederate Defeat,* vol. 1, *Field Command* (New York: Columbia University Press, 1969).

Braid-Braid. In *Mardi. See* Mohi.

Brami. In *Mardi.* The name is an alias of the prophet Alma. *See* Alma. Brami surely is meant to connote Brahma.

Brandt. In *Pierre,* he is a murderous half-breed Native American who once fought against General Pierre Glendinning but later dined with him.

Brandy-Nan. In *Redburn,* she is Mrs. Handsome Mary Danby's cook at the Baltimore Clipper in Liverpool. Brandy-Nan is Welsh.

Breckinridge, John Cabell (1821–1875). Politician and soldier. Born near Lexington, Kentucky, Breckinridge graduated from Centre College in Danbury, Connecticut (1839), studied at the College of New Jersey (now Princeton), studied law at Transylvania University in Lexington (1840–1841), and practiced law in Frankfort, Kentucky, and Burlington, Iowa. Breckinridge was a major in a Kentucky militia unit (1847), served in the Mexican War (1846–1848), was elected as a Democrat to serve in the state legislature (1849–1851) and the U.S. Congress (1851–1855), and returned to his law practice (1855–1856). He was elected to be President James Buchanan's vice president (1857–1861). In the confusion of the Democratic Party caused by the 1860 nomination of Stephen A. Douglas for president, Breckinridge was nominated by a splinter group. He became a moderate and a Unionist and presided over the Senate after Abraham Lincoln* became president (March 1861), but when military rule was established in Kentucky he escaped to the Confederacy. He was a usually effective general in its army until he was appointed by Confederate President Jefferson Davis as his secretary of war (1865). When the Confederacy was defeated, Breckinridge escaped to Cuba and England, where he lived until 1868, after which time he returned to Lexington to practice law and help develop his home state's railroad system.

In the "Battle of Stone River, Tennessee," Melville mentions Breckinridge as the Confederate commander defeated by William Starke Rosecrans at the Battle of Stone River.

Bibliography: William C. Davis, *Breckinridge: Statesman, Soldier, Symbol* (Baton Rouge: Louisiana State University Press, 1974).

Bridegroom Dick. In "Bridegroom-Dick," he is the retired sailor who reminisces to his devoted wife Bonny Blue about his experiences at sea long ago.

"Bridegroom-Dick" (1888). Poem, in *John Marr.* (Characters: Commander All-a-Tanto, Bonny Blue, Bridegroom Dick, Brown, Lieutenant Chock-a-Block, Dainty Dave, [Captain Stephen] Decatur, [Admiral David Glasgow] Farragut, the Finn, Guert Gan[sevoort], Jack Genteel, Glen, Hal, [Captain Isaac] Hull, Jewsharp Jim, [Commander Thomas] Ap [ap] Catesby [Jones], Laced Cap, Chaplain Le Fan, Lieutenant Long Lumbago, Major, Lieutenant Marrot, Orlop Bob, [Captain Oliver Hazard] Perry, Phil, [David Dixon] Porter, Rhyming Ned, Rigadoon Joe, [General Antonio Lopez de] Santa Anna, [General Winfield] Scott, Sid, Purser Smart, Starr, Starry Banner, the Surgeon, Lieutenant Tom Tight, Top-Gallant Harry, Captain Turret, Will.)

Old Dick, smoking his pipe, reminisces in the presence of his "old woman" Bonny Blue, as she drinks her "blessed Bohea" tea, about life at sea long ago aboard brave old wooden ships off Vera Cruz and later, up to the coming of ironclads during the Civil War. Dick rose in rank from the Commodore's coxswain to quartermaster. He remembers his officers and his mates. But now "they are all, all gone, I think," and his "lids . . . wink." The men are "[m]oored long in haven where the old heroes are." When the Civil War—"that wide public stress"—commenced, "the red dance began." Sailors in the North decided to "stick to the Flag," but for their Southern counterparts duty "pulled with more than one string." Meanwhile, profiteers coined "dollars in the bloody mint o' war." Bridegroom Dick remembers when the Confederate *Merrimac* sank the Union *Cumberland,* and, "dungeoned in the cockpit, the wounded go down, / And the Chaplain with them." Old Dick was also with Farragut at the Battle for the Bay. He recalls one memorable personality after another, asks his wife to kiss him, and calls himself "[a] died-down candle . . . flicker[ing] in the snuff." In "Bridegroom-Dick," Melville weaves together nostalgia, nautical camaraderie, contempt for landlubbers and religiosity, and a stoical yet genial acceptance of old age.

Bibliography: Garner, NN 11, Shurr, Stein, Warren.

Bridenstoke. In *Redburn,* he is a family friend whom Redburn fondly remembers one gloomy Sunday off Newfoundland when the *Highlander* is bound east for Liverpool.

Bridewell, Lieutenant ("First Luff"). In *White-Jacket,* he is a gray-haired first lieutenant aboard the *Neversink.* He is mentioned in an order coming from the Commander and dispatched by Adolphus Dashman. Bridewell assigns White Jacket a bewildering set of numbers—for mess, watch roll, hammock, gun, and so on. Bridewell orders his former roommate Mandeville, by this time broken in rank to common sailor, to be flogged for drinking. Bridewell fails to speak in defense of White Jacket when he comes close to being flogged.

Bridges, James. In *Israel Potter,* he is a pro-American Britisher who, with the Rev. Mr. [John] Horne Tooke and Squire John Woodcock, plots to hire Israel Potter as a courier to [Benjamin] Franklin in Paris. Later in the novel, Bridges' first name becomes John. A man named John Bridges was a neighbor of Charles

Woodcocke in New Brentford, England, and a man named John Edward Bridges was a warden of the New Brentford Chapel—both in the late eighteenth century.
   Bibliography: Cohen, *Potter.*

Bridges, Molly. In *Israel Potter,* she is mentioned as living in Bridewell and as being the only person named Bridges known by the farmer from whom Israel Potter seeks information concerning James Bridges. Her name echoes London place names and is linked with Bridewell Prison in London.
   Bibliography: Cohen, *Potter.*

Bright Future. In *The Confidence-Man,* this is an angel with a cornucopia of gold which China Aster dreams about.

Brinvilliers, The Marchioness of (c. 1630–1676). (Full name: Marquise de Brinvilliers, Marie Madeleine Marguerite d'Aubrey.) Born in Paris, she married the naive Marquis de Brinvilliers (1651), lived in Normandy with him, through him met his dashing friend Godin de Sainte-Croix, and became that fellow's mistress. When her father learned of their liaison, he had Sainte-Croix imprisoned in the Bastille for a year, after which Sainte-Croix plotted with the Marquise de Brinvilliers to poison not only her father but also her two brothers and one sister, so that the nefarious pair might eventually claim the D'Aubrey family wealth. The marquise succeeded in poisoning her father and two brothers, but while Sainte-Croix was mixing a concoction for the sister his protective mask fell off and he inhaled a fatal dose. The police discovered the plot, tortured the marquise's valet, who was an accomplice, and obtained a confession (1673). The marquise fled to a convent in Liège, was tricked into coming out, turned pseudo-pious, and remained demurely beautiful, but she was tortured nonetheless and convicted and beheaded in Paris, and her corpse was burned and its ashes scattered.
   In his poem ''The Marchioness of Brinvilliers,'' Melville implicitly contrasts her true nature with her sweet appearance and her fine eyes in a portrait.
   Bibliography: Albert Smith, *The Marchioness of Brinvilliers* (London: Richard Bentley,* 1886); Hugh Stokes, *Madame de Brinvilliers and Her Times* (New York: John Lane Company, 1912).

Bristol, The Marquis of. In *Redburn,* he is supposedly a friend of Harry Bolton, who remarks that he knows Ickworth, the marquis's county seat in Suffolk.

Bristol Molly. In *Billy Budd,* she is Billy Budd's girlfriend, according to ''Billy in the Darbies,'' a poem written by his shipmate.

Broadbit. In *White-Jacket,* he is an old sheet-anchor man. White Jacket borrows a book from him.

Brodhead, John Romeyn (1814–1873). Lawyer, diplomat, and historian. The son of a Reformed Dutch Church pastor, he was born in Philadelphia, moved with his family to New York (1826), attended the Albany Academy, graduated from Rutgers College (1831), studied law, and was admitted to the bar (1835). After practicing in New York City briefly (1835–1837), he moved to Saugerties, New York, to aid his invalid father and also to pursue literary interests. Brodhead worked in the American legation in the Netherlands (1839–1844) and was appointed (1841) by New York Governor William H. Seward as an agent to search in British, Dutch, and French archives for material to augment New York state archives. During part of his years abroad, Brodhead was secretary of legation in England (1846–1849) while the historian George Bancroft was minister there. Brodhead was named Naval Officer of the Port of New York during Franklin Pierce's presidency (1853–1857). By this time, Brodhead had assembled a vast number of historical papers, which were edited by others and became *Documents Relating to the Colonial History of the State of New York* (1856–1886). Brodhead had already published his own report, as an 1845 senate document, which he followed with *History of the State of New York*. Its first volume (1853) covers the period from 1609 to 1664; the second (1871) covers the period from 1664 to 1691. He began the third volume, to cover the years from 1691 to 1789, but never completed it. He was a member of the New York Historical Society, before which he lectured on two occasions (1864, 1866). His work is thorough and accurate. He was a trustee of the John Jacob Astor* Library (1867–1871). Brodhead was a member of the Dutch Reformed Church. He married Eugenia Bloodgood in 1856.

The Melville family knew the Brodhead family in New York, and the Melville children played with young Brodhead and his brother in the 1820s there. John Brodhead as a youth was a schoolmate of Melville's brother Gansevoort Melville* and agreed (1847) to act as Melville's literary agent in London, to secure the publication of *Omoo* there, following the death of Gansevoort. Brodhead helped Melville publish *Mardi* in London (1849), taking it to Richard Bentley* when John Murray* rejected it.

Bibliography: Davis; "John Romeyn Brodhead," *Scribner's Monthly Magazine* 13 (February 1877): 459–63; Leyda; NN 14.

Brooks. In "Authentic Anecdotes of 'Old Zack,' " he is a New York clothier. He, along with his father in the firm of Brooks & Son, might be properly asked to send General Zachary Taylor a new roundabout.

Brouwer, Adriaen (c. 1606–1638). Flemish genre and landscape painter. Born in Oudenaarde, Flanders, he was the son of a tapestry designer who taught him drawing. His father died in 1622, by which time Brouwer had studied under Frans Hals* in Haarlem. Brouwer worked in Amsterdam (1625) and Antwerp (by 1631), where he was imprisoned by the Spaniards, perhaps as a suspected spy (1633). In his best work, Brouwer depicts peasants, quack surgeons and pained patients, and vomity guzzlers and hallucinating smokers and frenzied card players in country inns and village taverns. His landscapes feature ball-players, dunes, and scrubby trees. The best of his eighty or so paintings, often undatable, include a busy *Pancake Man* (c. 1625), a dramatic *Fight over Cards* (c. 1635), *The Smokers* (c. 1636), and a complex *Tavern Scene,* which harmonizes two sloppy "lovers," three men standing and looking nearby, three indifferent conversationalists sitting down, and an onlooker with his head through a high window. The rakish, prankish, arrogant Brouwer was well known for his addiction to wine, bad tobacco, and gambling. He was indifferent to money, often in debt and slovenly, but passionately fond of his art and his friends. Rembrandt* and Peter Paul Rubens* appreciated his paintings and sought to buy them. Anthony Van Dyck* painted his portrait. David Teniers the Younger,* among other Flemish followers, was influenced by him.

In "Marquis de Grandvin: At the Hostelry," Melville names Adrian Brouwer as a wine-bibbing painter who discusses the picturesque with Carlo Dolce (*see* Dolci, Carlo), is snortingly pleased by [Paolo] Veronese, and criticizes the withdrawn posture of Michael Angelo (*see* Michelangelo). Like the good Dutch painter he is, Brouwer contends that "the sty / Is quite inodorous" so far as "Art" is concerned.

Bibliography: Gerard Knuttel, *Adriaen Brouwer: The Master and His Work* (The Hague: J. C. Boucher, 1962).

Brown. In "Bridegroom-Dick," he is the sailor commanded to tie up the Finn before his ordered flogging.

Brown, B. Hobbema. In "The Marquis de Grandvin," he is said to be a landscape painter who, though a "theoretical misanthrope," admires the Marquis de Grandvin.

Brown, John (1800–1859). Abolitionist. Brown was born in Torrington, Connecticut, moved with his parents to Hudson, Ohio (1805), and became a farmer, drover, tanner, and wool dealer. He married Diantha Lusk (1820) and had seven children by her, after which she died (1831). He then married Mary Danne Day (1832) and had thirteen more children. There was a streak of insanity and near-insanity in the Brown family, notable in his mother, his maternal grandmother, a maternal aunt, five cousins on his mother's side, and two sons by his first wife. In debt, Brown and his family moved into a community of African-Americans in North Elba, New York (1849), to Ohio, where he became an agent of the Underground Railroad (1851), and to Kansas (1855), where five of his sons were already free-soil fighters. In "Bleeding Kansas," Brown turned into a fanatic. Feeling impelled by God to destroy slavery, he was outraged by the murderous sacking of free-soil Lawrence, Kansas (21 May 1856). With seven other abolitionists, including four of his sons, he murdered five allegedly proslavery settlers at Pottawatomie Creek (24–25 May). Three hundred proslavery men attacked Osawatomie (30 August), which Brown defended and then pillaged.

Brown recruited African-Americans and other followers, and he obtained support from influential abolitionists in Boston and New York to establish a base in the mountains of Maryland and Virginia (1856–1859). Hoping to create a free state and spread slave insurrections throughout the South, Brown established a guerrilla camp near Harpers Ferry, Virginia, with twenty-one followers, including three of his sons and five African-Americans. On 16 October 1859, Brown and eighteen of his men infiltrated Harpers Ferry and occupied federal property there. When no pro-Brown uprising among local slaves followed, Brown's group seized town hostages. In the process, Brown's men killed an innocent black railroad worker. Brown and his cohorts were surrounded by several hundred local militia, and ten of his men were killed, including two of his sons. The insurrectionists were attacked and overwhelmed by U.S. Marines commanded by Robert E. Lee,* then a colonel (18 October). Brown was tried at Charles Town, Virginia (25–31 October) for murder, conspiracy to promote slave insurrection, and treason against Virginia. When convicted, he declined to plead insanity and was executed by hanging (2 December 1859). Six members of his band were also hanged (16 December 1859; 16 March 1860). Brown failed in his mission, seemed to seek his own destruction, and was reviled throughout the South and by conservatives in the North (including Nathaniel Hawthorne*), but he became a martyr in the eyes of many (for example, Ralph Waldo Emerson* and Henry David Thoreau*). ''John Brown's Body'' became a vibrant marching song for Union forces in the Civil War.

Melville alternately admired and deplored aspects of Brown's career. The man sought to end slavery but signaled the beginning of fratricidal strife. In ''The Portent (1859),'' Melville describes Brown as veiled, hanged, and portentous like a meteor.

Bibliography: Garner; Stephen B. Oates, *To Purge This Land with Blood: A Biography of John Brown* (1970; 2d ed., Amherst: University of Massachusetts Press, 1984).

Brown, Mrs. In ''The Apple-Tree Table,'' she is evidently the owner of a business establishment in which the narrator has ice cream.

Brown, Tom. In *White-Jacket,* he is a shipmate reported killed in an imaginary naval battle; however, a sailor with the same name later plays the part of Captain Bougee in a Fourth of July theatrical.

Browne, J. Ross (1821–1875). (Full name: John Ross Browne.) Author. Born in Ireland, Browne migrated to Kentucky when he was eleven, and in young adulthood he became a traveler and the author of travel books. These include *Etchings of a Whaling Cruise* (1846), which was influenced by *Two Years before the Mast* by Richard Henry Dana, Jr.,* and influenced Melville's *Moby-Dick.* Melville reviewed Browne's book on whaling. Browne went to California, was a customs inspector and an inspector of Indian affairs, and traveled in Scandinavia and Europe. He wrote about his experiences in most of these places and later became U.S. minister to China (1868–1869). Browne married Lucy Anna Mitchell in 1844 (the couple had nine children, five of whom survived him).

Bibliography: Francis John Rock, *J. Ross Browne: A Biography...* (Washington, D.C.: Catholic University of America, 1929).

Browns, Ben. In *White-Jacket,* he is mentioned in an anecdote as a painter on the Mississippi River. He painted hands on Red Hot Coal's blanket as symbols of the murderous Indian's victories.

Bruat, Armand-Joseph (1796–1855). Naval officer. Bruat was born in Colmar, France, entered naval service at an early age (1811), was in engagements in the Baltic and the Levant and off Brazil, was decorated for bravery in the Battle of Navarino (1827), and participated in the blockade of the African coast (1829– 1830), but was captured and imprisoned in Algiers (1830). His next major duty was in the Pacific region. Once France annexed the islands of the Marquesas and Tahiti (1842), Captain Bruat was appointed their governor (1843). When Abel Aubert Dupetit-Thouars* installed him, Bruat set up headquarters in Papeetee and called it his capital (1843). The British government objected to any extension of Catholicism in the Pacific but were mollified by official French pronouncements. Nonetheless, Bruat was given draconian powers, disputed with George Pritchard,* the anti-Catholic British consul to Tahiti (1844), faced a native insurrection (1844–1845), and had administrative difficulties (1846). He was made rear admiral (1846), left Tahiti (1847), became governor of the Antilles (1849), was promoted to vice admiral (1852), and was named commander-in-chief of French naval forces in the Crimea (beginning 1853). He was promoted to admiral (1855) but died of cholera on his voyage back to France. In *Omoo,* Melville defines Bruat as a hated French administrator left behind by Admiral Thouars to govern Tahiti.

Bibliography: Baron [César Lecat] de Bazancourt, *The Crimean Expedition...*, trans. Robert Howe Gould, 2 vols. (N.p. 1856); Newbury; O'Reilly and Teissier.

Brush. In *White-Jacket,* he is the captain of the paint room of the *Neversink.* On two occasions, Brush refuses to give White Jacket paint with which to waterproof his jacket.

Budd, William ("**Billy,**" "**Baby,**" "**Beauty**"). In *Billy Budd,* he is the tall, handsome, naive, stammering foretopman. He is twenty-one years old. He has been impressed from the *Rights-of-Man* to serve on the *Bellipotent,* under the command of Captain Edward Fairfax Vere. When John Claggart untruthfully reports to Vere that Billy is fomenting mutiny, Billy—unable to speak in his own defense—strikes out with his big fist and kills his accuser. Although his act was without premeditation, Billy is hanged for this capital offense. The puzzling absence of death twitches during his execution has been diagnosed as spasmodic dysphonia. His adoring mates treasure his memory. Billy is unique among Melvillean heroes because he dies in an atmosphere of love and sacrifice, not alone, not hated, not boastfully defiant.

Bibliography: Merton M. Sealts, Jr., "Innocence and Infamy: *Billy Budd, Sailor,*" pp. 407–30 in Bryant, *Companion;* Smith.

Buddha (c. 563–c. 480 B.C.). Although the term "buddha" can be applied to any person who is awakened and enlightened, the word is now mainly used to refer to the founder of Buddhism. Buddha was the sage of the Sakyas and an Indian philosopher. He was a prince in a kingdom in northern India and Nepal. His clan name was Gautama; his common name, Sakyamuni ("the quiet, wise man of the Sakya tribe"); his personal name, Siddhartha ("one who will accomplish"). Legend has it that Buddha was divinely conceived and that seven days after he was born his mother died. His father sought to keep him from becoming Buddha by exposing him only to pleasure. He married at the age of sixteen and became a father, but when he strayed outside the palace he saw human misery—pain, illness, aging, and death. Leaving home, he became ascetic, religious, and reclusive. Seeking but not finding enlightment, he decided after six years to follow a middle path between asceticism and material joys, and also to meditate until he might meet success. He evolved into the Supreme Buddha at age thirty-five, after which he preached about suffering, its causes, and its elimination through self-discipline, concentration, meditation, faith, and ultimate wisdom. Buddha welcomed lay disciples and converted companions into Buddhist monks. After a ministry of forty-five years, Buddha entered Nirvana and was cremated.

In Melville's "Buddha," the great philosopher's followers express a hope for Nirvana. In "Rammon," Buddha is the religious teacher whose beliefs the Princess of Sheba is [fictitiously] said to bring to Palestine in the time of Solomon.

Bibliography: Archie J. Bahm, *Philosophy of the Buddha* (New York: Harper, 1959); David L. Snellgrove, ed., *The Image of the Buddha* ([Toyko]: Kodansha International/ Unesco, 1978).

"Buddha" (1891). Poem, in *Timoleon.* Buddha's followers are "dumb endurers," "swim to less and less," and aspire "to nothingness." They hope that Nirvana will "absorb" and "[a]nnul" them. Melville's epigraph, from James 4:14, to the effect that life is a vapor that vanishes, in context seems sadly unchristian.

Bibliography: NN 11, Stein.

Bulkington. In *Moby-Dick,* he is a tall, broad-shouldered, big-chested seaman. He may be from Virginia. He disembarks at New Bedford from a four-year voyage aboard the *Grampus,* stays at the Spouter Inn, and in a matter of days signs aboard Ahab's *Pequod.* Bulkington is popular but aloof and seems unable to remain ashore for long. When he stands at the helm one cold winter night, Ishmael apotheosizes him inordinately for rushing back upon the ocean's depths, since "in landlessness alone resides the highest truth, shoreless, indefinite as God." Bulkington has the good qualities of the more complex Ahab.

Bibliography: Brian Higgins and Hershel Parker, eds., *Critical Essays on Herman Melville's Moby-Dick* (New York: G. K. Hall, 1992); Michael Hollister, "Melville's Gam with Poe in *Moby-Dick:* Bulkington and Pym," *Studies in the Novel* 21 (Fall 1989): 279–91.

Bunger, Dr. Jack. In *Moby-Dick,* he is the surgeon aboard the *Samuel Enderby,* whose captain, Boomer, lost his right arm while chasing Moby Dick. The two men are realistic rather than vengeful.

Bungs. In *Omoo,* he is the perpetually half-drunk old cooper aboard the *Julia.* Although he signed the round-robin, he stays aboard and therefore does not go either to the French ship or later to the Calabooza.

Bungs. In *White-Jacket,* he is a cooper with whom Scrimmage argues about buoys. Bungs later drowns, not saved by any of his leaky buoys. Bungs is based on David Black, cooper aboard the *United States,* which was the naval vessel on which Melville served (1843–1844). Black was lost overboard.

Bibliography: NN 5.

Bunk, Joe. In *White-Jacket,* he is the sailor on the launch who plays the part of the Commodore's cockswain in the Fourth of July theatrical.

Bunkum, Colonel Josiah. In "Major Gentian and Colonel J. Bunkum," he is a valiant, muscular, rash Union officer during the Civil War. He distributed spelling books throughout the South while [George B.] McClellan delayed an attack. Bunkum criticizes the Bourbons for their antidemocratic policies. In "The Cincinnati," he is a member of the Burgundy Club whose remarks on the ribbons of the Society of the Cincinnati are pleasantly queried by another club member.

Bunn, Ned. In "To Ned," he is the poet's companion in the old days. The poet remembers their adventures in the Marquesas Islands. Ned Bunn is based on Richard Tobias Greene,* Melville's companion when the two deserted the whaler *Acushnet* at Nuku Hiva, in the Marquesas Islands.

Bibliography: Shurr.

Bury. In *Redburn. See* Bolton, Harry.

Butler, Frances Anne Kemble. *See* Kemble, Frances Anne.

"Butterfly Ditty" (1924). Poem, in *Weeds and Wildings,* as part of a section entitled "The Year." When heavenly summer "comes in like a sea," butterflies "tipple the light," "rove" and "revel" idly in gardens, and lament only because "Man, Eden's Boy," cannot do so.

Bibliography: Shurr, Stein.

Buttons. In *Redburn. See* Redburn, Wellingborough.

C

C., R. F. In "The Paradise of Bachelors and the Tartarus of Maids." *See* C[ooke]., R[obert]. F[rancis].

Cabaco. In *Moby-Dick,* he is a Cholo sailor. His friend Archy tells Cabaco that he hears men in the after-hold. They turn out to be Fedallah and his crew.

Cabin Boy, The. In *Omoo. See* Guy, Captain.

Calends, Queen. In *Mardi,* she is Donjalolo's twenty-eighth-night queen.

Calvert, George, first baron Baltimore (1580?–1632). English proprietor in America. Calvert was born in Yorkshire, graduated from Trinity College, Oxford (B.A., 1597; M.A., 1605), and advanced steadily in politics. He was a member of Parliament, clerk to the Privy Council, secretary of state, a member of the council, and a diplomat on the Continent. He became a Roman Catholic (1621) and was created Baron of Baltimore in the Kingdom of Ireland (1625). He belonged to the Virginia Company (1609–1620) and the New England Company (1622). When Calvert was granted Newfoundland (1622) but objected because of its harsh climate (1629), he was granted territory in what became Maryland (1632) but died before the charter could be issued. He made three trips to America (1627, 1628, and 1629). Calvert married Anne Mynne in 1605; after giving birth to eleven children, she died (1622). He was married again (by 1628), this time to a woman named Joane. Calvert's oldest son by his first wife was Cecilius (1605–1675), who took up the Maryland grant and became governor of the province (1634–1647). In *Clarel,* it is mentioned that George Calvert was a friend of one of Ungar's ancestors, helped to settle Maryland, and married an Indian.

Bibliography: Clayton Colman Hall, *The Lords Baltimore and the Maryland Palatinate* . . . , 2d ed. (Baltimore: Nunn & Co., 1904).

"Camoens" (1924). Poem, in *The Works of Herman Melville.* It is in two parts, "Before" and "After." At first, Camoens in a restless monologue asks, "Forever must I fan this fire . . . ?" The answer is that he must, because "God demands my best." The world's beauty and people's dreams must be expressed, and they must be made to glow and ascend. But later, Camoens is dying in the hospital, and his poetry has availed him nothing. In this "[b]ase . . . world," the prudent remain strong through "wile and guile," and utilitarianism reigns.

Bibliography: Norwood Andrews, Jr., *Melville's Camões* (Bonn: Bouvier Verlag, 1989); NN 5; Shurr.

Camões, Luíz Vaz de [Luis de Camoëns] (1524–1580). Portuguese poet. Born in Lisbon or Coimbra, Camões was educated at the University of Coimbra (1539–1542) and went to Lisbon (1542), but he was banished from the court (c. 1547) because of a love affair. He lost the sight of his right eye during the campaign of John III against Morocco (1547–1549), was jailed after a street fight in Lisbon (1552–1553), became a kind of exile in the army in India, Macao, and thereabouts (1553–1569), and was imprisoned in Goa, India, because of conduct unacceptable to a ship's captain. He made his way back to Lisbon (1570) and was reinstated at the court of King Sebastian. During much of this time, Camões wrote in a variety of genres. He died of the plague. In addition to other works, Camões wrote *Os Lusíadas [The Lusiads* ("The Portuguese")], a poetic masterpiece, composed (partly in Goa) in ottava rima, treating episodes in Portuguese history—especially the voyages of Vasco da Gama—and published in 1572.

In the poem "Camoens," Melville depicts Luíz de Camões—here (and in *White-Jacket*) called Camoens—as aspiring, noble, and idealistic before embarking on his quest, but as disillusioned and critical in the hospital afterward.

Bibliography: Norwood Andrews, Jr., *Melville's Camões* (Bonn: Bouvier Verlag, 1989); C. M. Bowra, *From Virgil to Milton* (London: Macmillan, 1945); Cohen, *Poems;* A. Bartlett Giamatti, *The Earthly Paradise and the Renaissance Epic* (Princeton, N.J.: Princeton University Press, 1966); George Monteiro, "Melville and the Question of Camões," *University of Mississippi Studies in English* 8 (1990): 1–21; Shurr.

Candy. In *White-Jacket,* he is a good-natured foretopman. He correctly predicts that he will be flogged because when he was imitating Priming the captain thought he was mimicking him.

Canny, Walter. In *Moby-Dick,* he is a sailor who was lost with five others at sea from the *Eliza* in 1839. Their shipmates placed a marble in his memory in the Whaleman's Chapel in New Bedford.

"A Canticle: Significant of the National Exaltation of Enthusiasm at the Close of the War" (1866). Poem, in *Battle-Pieces*. By an extended metaphor of a cataract crashing into a dangerous pool and a rainbow rising above it, Melville suggests that the nation fell and plunged into the Civil War, then moved by an almost miraculous passage into a twining "confluence," above which "[t]he Iris half in tracelessness / Hovers faintly fair" and is "[s]table . . . [w]hen calm is in the air." We must be ever aware, however, of "[t]he Giant of the Pool" (i.e., political instability) with "his forehead white as wool," which threatens future generations.

Bibliography: Cohen, *Poems;* Garner; NN 11.

Captain. In "The Death Craft," he is the commander of the vessel that the narrator dreams about.

Captain. In "Marquis de Grandvin: Naples in the Time of Bomba . . . ," he is a fat, nervous captain of the guard in Naples. Neapolitans hate all such soldiers.

Captain. In *Moby-Dick,* he is Jonah's mercenary captain in the sermon delivered by Father Mapple at the Whaleman's Chapel in New Bedford.

Captain. In *Moby-Dick,* he is the commander of a merchant ship. He once visited Queequeg's father, the King of Kokovoko, and ignorantly washed his hands in the punch bowl, but he was not laughed at by the courteous and tolerant natives.

Captain. In *Moby-Dick,* he is the captain of the *Moss,* which carries Ishmael and Queequeg from New Bedford to Nantucket. While aboard the *Moss,* Queequeg wrestles a mimicking young bumpkin. Queequeg then saves the lad when he is knocked overboard by a swinging boom.

Captain. In *Moby-Dick,* he is the captain of the *Town-Ho* who resists the temptation to flog the mutinous Steelkilt, whereupon his mate Radney, whose jaw Steelkilt has broken, does so. Soon thereafter, Moby Dick kills Radney. In real life, Hiram Weeks was the captain of the whaler *Nassau,* aboard which a sailor named Luther Fox murdered the first officer, whose name was Jenney (April 1843).

Bibliography: Leyda.

Captain Bob. In *Omoo,* he is a fat, jolly Tahitian who acts as the easy-going guard of the white prisoners at the Calabooza. According to a journal kept by a naval lieutenant named Henry Augustus Wise, Captain Bob was dead by 1848.

Bibliography: Leyda.

Captains. In "The Admiral of the White," they are the French sea captains who surrendered their flags and swords to the Admiral of the White.

Carden, John S. (?–?). British naval officer. He is known in American naval history as the commander of the *Macedonian,* who was outmaneuvered by and after a ninety-minute battle surrendered to Stephen Decatur,* commander of the *United States,* off Madeira (October 1812), during the War of 1812. Carden was later court-martialed for poor judgment and timidity. He was branded as infamous by American authorities for forcing impressed American sailors aboard his ship to fight against a ship flying an American flag. In *White-Jacket,* Melville named Cardan as the captain of the British frigate *Macedonian.* It was said that, during the War of 1812, he ordered an impressed African-American seaman named Tawney to fire at the American man-of-war the *Neversink* and also that Cardan later surrendered to Captain Stephen Decatur, whom earlier he had known socially.

Bibliography: Captain A. T. Mahan, *Sea Power in Its Relation to the War of 1812,* 2 vols. (1905; rpt. Westport, Conn.: Greenwood Press, 1968); Theodore Roosevelt, *The War of 1812 . . .* (New York: G. P. Putnam's Sons, 1882).

Carlo. In *Redburn,* he is a Sicilian boy, aged fifteen, who comes to Liverpool and pays for his passage aboard the *Highlander* bound for America by playing his hand organ with great charm.

Carlo ("a Triton"). In "Marquis de Grandvin: Naples in the Time of Bomba . . . ," he is a Levantine youth who sings about the hubbub of Naples, partly in time with Bomba's marching troops, whom he then criticizes indiscreetly.

Carpégna, Édouard Jules Gabrielle de (1816–1883). French naval officer. He was born in Grenoble, attended a naval school (1832), and sailed around the world with Cyrille Pierre Théodore Laplace during the celebrated *Artémise* voyage (1837–1840). Assigned to the Pacific station, Carpégna served under the command of Abel Aubert Dupetit-Thouars* on the *Reine Blanche* (1841), and arrived first at Valparaiso, Chile (1842), and then at Papeete, Tahiti (1843), to serve there under Dupetit-Thouars and Armand-Joseph Bruat,* the new governor. Carpégna was in combat during the native insurrection, was awarded the Legion of Honor (1844), and was named captain of the port (1844–1845), after which he was placed in command of a schooner and returned to France (1847). Carpégna served in the Crimea (1855) and China (1858–1859) and was promoted to captain (1860). He retired (1865) and died in Paris. Carpégna married a Tahitian named Nuu Tafaratea Teina a Poroï and had a son named Adolphe Marouo Poroï, who was born in 1844 and who became a builder of transports and land structures.

In *Omoo,* Melville names Carpegna as a French assistant, along with Reine, in the service of Bruat, governor of Tahiti.

Bibliography: O'Reilly and Teissier.

Casks. In *Pierre,* he is the old Black Swan innkeeper at Saddle Meadows. Casks is sad when he learns that Pierre, whom years ago he taught to shoot, is married and is moving certain possessions out of his mother's mansion.

Catesby, Ap. In "Bridegroom-Dick." *See* Jones, Thomas ap Catesby.

Cavour, Camillo Benso (1810–1861). Italian statesman. Cavour was born in Turin, was educated at the military academy there, was a lieutenant of engineers (1826–1831), and retired to his family estate in Piedmont to divide his time between agriculture and travel (1831–1847). He cofounded *Il Risorgimento,* a periodical devoted to Italian nationalism (1847), fought against Austria (1848), represented Sardinia in the Piedmont chamber of deputies (1848), and became premier (1852–1859). To resist the incursions of Russia, Cavour allied his government with England, France, and Turkey (1854), sent Sardinian troops to the Crimea (1855), secured the admission of Sardinia to the Congress of Paris (1856) and an alliance with Napoleon III of France against Austria (1858), handled the ministry of war himself (1859) during the Italian War, and resigned once Napoleon III made peace with Austria (1859). Cavour became premier once more (1860–1861), ceded Nice and Savoy to France as a price for the unification of northern Italy, secretly supported Giuseppi Garibaldi* in Sicily (1860), ordered his forces to invade the Papal States to forestall Garibaldi's more revolutionary plans (1860), and united most of central and southern Italy under Victor Emmanuel II. Cavour's publications include his political and economic essays (1855) and his parliamentary discourses (1863–1880). In "Marquis de Grandvin: At the Hostelry," Melville describes Cavour as the crafty guard to Garibaldi's sword.

Bibliography: Action; Denis Mack Smith, *Cavour* (London: Weidenfeld and Nicolson, 1985).

Celibate, The. In *Clarel,* he is an innocent Greek monk at Mar Saba. This almoner briefly inspires Clarel to develop the will power to live ascetically.

Celio ("The Unknown"). In *Clarel,* he is a young hunchbacked Italian with a handsome face. Celio lives in the Franciscan Terra Santa monastery. A bitter, defiant, lonely Catholic doubter, he dies soon after Clarel meets and is briefly inspired by him.

Bibliography: Vincent Kenney, *Herman Melville's Clarel: A Spiritual Autobiography* (Hamden, Conn.: Archon Books, 1973).

Cereno, Benito. In "Benito Cereno," he is the Spanish captain, aged twenty-nine, of the *San Dominick.* His cargo is made up of slaves owned by his friend Alexandro Aranda. The slaves revolt somewhere between Valparaiso and Callao, murder most of the white men aboard, and unsuccessfully plot to commandeer the naive Captain Amasa Delano's sealer the *Bachelor's Delight* in the harbor of Santa Maria. Cereno is so completely and permanently unnerved by the conduct of Babo, leader of the revolt, that he dies three months after his rescue. Cereno is based on real-life Don Bonito Sereno, captain of the Spanish ship *Tryal,* boarded by Captain Amasa Delano of the sealer *Perseverance,* at the island of Santa Maria, off the coast of Chile (February 1805). In his autobiography, entitled *A Narrative of Voyages and Travels* (Boston, 1817), Delano calls the Spaniard Bonito Sereno and explains that he had taken his *Tryal* from Valparaiso two months earlier with a cargo of slaves, who had revolted. When they put into the bay of Santa Maria for water, Delano appeared and boarded the *Tryal,* only to have Bonito jump to safety, reveal the slaves' plot, and offer Delano a half share if he and his men freed the *Tryal.*

Bibliography: NN 9; Harold H. Scudder, "Melville's *Benito Cereno* and Captain Delano's Voyages," *PMLA* 32 (June 1928): 502–32.

Chang Ching. In "On the Chinese Junk," he is the father of the girl He Sing addresses in a love poem.

Chang-foue. In "On the Chinese Junk," he is a high-ranking Mandarin back home in China. He is also known as Ke-sing.

Chaplain, The. In "The Scout toward Aldie," he is the young chaplain with the Colonel's men during their ill-fated pursuit of [John Singleton] Mosby. The chaplain tends to the needs of a Confederate prisoner, evidently Mosby himself, who feigns injury from a fall. The chaplain may be based partly on Charles A. Humphreys, a Massachusetts cavalry chaplain under the command of Colonel Henry Sanford Gansevoort,* Melville's cousin whom Melville accompanied on a scout in Virginia (April 1864).

Bibliography: Garner.

Charity, Aunt. In *Moby-Dick,* she is Captain Bildad's thin old sister. She supplies the *Pequod* with ginger-jub, a mild, nonalcoholic, and hence unwanted beverage.

Charlemont. In *The Confidence-Man,* he is the hero of a story told by Francis Goodman. Charlemont, a rich man from St. Louis, hints that when he was only twenty-nine years old he ruined himself financially in order to aid a friend in need. He then supposedly made another fortune after spending nine years in Marseilles. Charlemont has been seen as a composite portrait of Melville's father Allan Melvill,* Melville's brother Gansevoort Melville,* and others.

Bibliography: Bryant, *Repose;* John Wenke, "No 'i' in Charlemont: A Cryptogrammic Name in *The Confidence-Man,*" *Essays in Literature* (Macomb, Ill.) 9 (Fall 1982): 269–78.

Charlie. In *The Confidence-Man,* this is the fictitious name taken by Egbert when he talks with Francis Goodman. *See* Egbert.

Charlton, Richard, Captain (?–?). British commercial and diplomatic agent. He was a sea captain and trader who became the first British consul to the Pacific (from 1825). The British government wanted him to encourage British trade and shipping and to persuade Hawaiian authorities to grant preference to them over other foreign groups. His commission extended to Tahiti. He opposed the work of missionaries, particularly Gerrit Parmele Judd,* and caused trouble by sending unwelcome liquor to Tahiti (1829); however, in concert with the French, he supported the rights of residence and the passage of a few Catholic priests (1836–1837). He was the object of official complaints by Judd and several Hawaiian chiefs. He claimed, perhaps fraudulently, a parcel of land in Honolulu (1840), pressed his claim, and was given possession (1847). Meanwhile, his government having lost confidence in him, Charlton was relieved of duty (1843). In Mexico, on his way back to England, he complained to Rear Admiral Richard Thomas,* commander of the British Pacific Squadron, of mistreatment of British interests by the Hawaiian government. Thomas sent Lord George Paulet* to make unfair demands of the Hawaiians, and only after much difficulty were matters straightened out.

In *Typee,* Melville depicts Captain Charlton as an abused British authority in Hawaii in 1843 and adds that he reported to Admiral Thomas at Valparaiso.

Bibliography: Gerrit P. Judd IV, *Dr. Judd: Hawaii's Friend: A Biography of Garrit Parmele Judd (1803–1873)* (Honolulu: University of Hawaii Press, 1960); Kuykendall; Ralph S. Kuykendall and A. Grove Day, *Hawaii: A History from Polynesian Kingdom to American State* (1948; rev. ed., Englewood Cliffs, N.J.: Prentice-Hall, 1961); W. P. Morrell, *Britain in the Pacific Islands* (Oxford, England: Clarendon Press, 1960).

Chartres, Louis-Philippe-Joseph, duc de. *See* Orléans, Louis-Philippe-Joseph, duc d'. In *Israel Potter,* the Duc d'Orléans, then with the title of the Duke de Chartres, is a pro-American French aristocrat. Through Chartres and [Charles Hector] the Count D'Estaing, [Benjamin] Franklin obtains a commission for John Paul Jones.

Bibliography: The Papers of Benjamin Franklin, vol. 26, *March 1 through June 30, 1778,* ed. William B. Willcox (New Haven, Conn.: Yale University Press, 1987).

Chase. In *White-Jacket,* he is Jack Chase's father. The older man sailed aboard the man-of-war *Romney* with William Julius Mickle, the translator of Camoëns's *The Lusiads.*

Chase, Jack ("Don John"). In *White-Jacket,* he is the tall, handsome, brown-bearded first captain of the top. White Jacket worships him almost as he would a god. The narrator explains that Chase lost a finger fighting for Peruvian independence and later fought under Admiral [Sir Edward] Codrington at the Battle of Navarino. Chase is well read and can recite parts of *The Lusiads* by Luíz Vas de Camões in the original Portuguese. Chase plays Percy Royal-Mast in the Fourth of July theatrical *The Old Wagon Paid Off.* He is bold enough to ask Captain Claret and the Commander for liberty to see Rio de Janeiro. He and Corporal Colbrook defend the reputation of White Jacket and protect him from an undeserved flogging. On Claret's general order, Chase reluctantly trims his fine beard. White Jacket kisses Chase's hand in Norfolk, Virginia, when the two part forever. Melville consulted his memory of Chase when he sketched the personality of Jack Roy in his poem "Jack Roy" and dedicated *Billy Budd* to "Jack Chase, Englishman, / Wherever that great heart may now be, / here on Earth or harbored in Paradise, / Captain of the Main-Top in the year 1843 / in the U.S. Frigate *United States.*" Melville's characterization of Jack Chase is based on the background and personality of John J. Chase, an Englishman and the captain of the foretop of the *United States,* which was the naval vessel on which Melville served (1843–1844). Chase was fifty-three years old when Melville first met him. He deserted his American ship the *St. Louis,* boarded the *United States* at Callao (1842), and was pardoned by American authorities when a Peruvian admiral interceded on his behalf. Chase resembles Fernão Veloso, an enlisted man in *The Lusiads,* in actions and personality.

    Bibliography: Charles R. Anderson, "A Reply to Herman Melville's *White-Jacket* by Rear-Admiral Thomas O. Selfridge, Sr.," *American Literature* 7 (May 1935): 123–44; Norwood Andrews, Jr., *Melville's Camões* (Bonn: Bouvier Verlag, 1989); NN 5.

Chase, Owen (1797–1869). Sailor. Born in Nantucket, Massachusetts, Chase was the first mate of the *Essex,* a 228-ton whaling ship out of Nantucket (1819). The *Essex* was sunk by a sperm whale (1820), west of the Galapagos and north-northeast of Henderson Island, which is not far from the Marquesas. The captain of the *Essex* was George Pollard.* Her crew of twenty men jumped into three open boats and suffered for three months thereafter. Eight men survived; some of them resorted to cannibalism of a crew member, chosen by lot along with his executioner, to do so. After being picked up at sea (February 1821), Chase and two others went to Valparaiso, Chile, and then back to Nantucket (June 1821). Chase published *Narrative of the Most Extraordinary and Distressing Shipwreck of the Whale-Ship Essex, of Nantucket* . . . (New York, 1821). Later, Chase captained two successful whaling ships, the *Winslow* (1825–1830) and the *Charles Carroll* (1833–c. 1840). He retired some time after 1840, lived in Nantucket, and died there. Chase was married four times. He married Margaret Gardner in 1818 (the couple had a son and a daughter). Margaret Chase died in 1824. In 1825 he married Nancy Joy, the widow of Matthew P. Joy, who had been the second mate of the *Essex* and the first crewmember to die after the whale attack. Chase married Eunice Chadwick in 1836. She had another man's child in 1838, when Chase had been at sea for a long time. He was granted a divorce in an uncontested case for adultery heard (1840) by Lemuel Shaw,* later Melville's father-in-law. Chase married a widow named Susan Coffin Gwinn (1840).

While Melville was a sailor aboard the whaler *Acushnet,* the second mate was John Hall, who had sailed on two three-year voyages with Chase and who spoke about him in a friendly, general way (March? 1841). Melville also talked with Chase's teenage son William Henry Chase, who was aboard a ship from Nantucket and gave Melville a copy of his father's book, which Melville read at sea (July 1841). He saw Chase himself, when the *Acushnet* met the *Charles Carroll* at sea (March? 1842), and he was impressed by Chase's appearance and manner. Melville evidently discarded or lost Chase's book, and later Lemuel Shaw found and sent him another copy (April? 1851). Melville was inspired by it when he was writing the final chapters of *Moby-Dick.*

Bibliography: Thomas Farel Heffernan, *Stove by a Whale: Owen Chase and the Essex* (Hanover, N.H.: University Press of New England, 1990).

"Chattanooga (November, 1863)" (1866). Poem, first published in *Harper's New Monthly Magazine** (June 1866) and reprinted in *Battle-Pieces.* (Character: [General Ulysses S.] Grant.) Armies fought "yester-morn" like ghosts on the misty hill, while Grant watched from a cliff and "mastered nervousness" by an outward calm. Today, though lacking reserves, Grant tells his men, whose "hearts outran their General's plan," to attack as they will. He watches them as they crawl up and in the face of cannon firing from the summit. Flags and then men "gain . . . the envied Alp"-like top, and "swarms of rebels fled"; but many victors, smiling as though they had fulfilled a dream, drop into "Death's wide-open arms."

The Battle of Chattanooga, Tennessee, was also called the Battle of Lookout Mountain–Missionary Ridge (23–25 November 1863). General Ulysses S. Grant, recently given command of the Union armies in the West, threw forces under General Joseph Hooker, General William Tecumseh Sherman,* and General George H. Thomas against Confederate General Braxton Bragg* (23 November) and forced him from Lookout Mountain; after he concentrated on Missionary Ridge, Thomas cleared all enemy units from both the ridge and the crest above (25 November). Melville's "Chattanooga" expresses his somber joy at the first success of masses of Union forces and also his admiration for Grant, whom he depicts with a cigar stump.

Bibliography: Boatner, Faust, Garner, NN 11.

Cherry. In "Hawthorne and His Mosses," she is the person who in Vermont suggests that her cousin a Virginian ought to read *Mosses from an Old Manse* by Nathaniel Hawthorne. In reality, Melville was given the book by Mary A. A. Hobart Melvill, the wife of his uncle Thomas Melvill, Jr.*

Bibliography: NN 9.

Cherry. In "Madcaps," Cherry is a child who with Lily frolics innocently in a flowery orchard.

Chew, Corporal. In "The Scout toward Aldie," he is the soldier who brings in some supposed civilians—a Southern girl and her African-American servant Garry Cuff—to his Colonel, who is vainly trying to capture [John Singleton] Mosby.

Chief. In "The Scout toward Aldie." *See* the Colonel.

Chief, The. In "Lee at the Capitol," this is the name that the Senators silently assign to Lee when they see him approach to answer their summons to testify after the end of the Civil War.

China Aster. In *The Confidence-Man,* he is a candlemaker who in Egbert's didactic story was persuaded to accept a gift which was later called a loan. With this money China Aster expanded his business, which promptly failed. He could not repay, lost everything, and died, after which his uncomplaining wife also died. Melville probably had his financially irresponsible uncle Thomas Melvill, Jr.,* in mind when he sketched China Aster's fate in *The Confidence-Man.*
   Bibliography: Cohen and Yannella; Daniel Hoffman, "Melville's Story of 'China Aster,'" *American Literature* 22 (May 1950): 137–49; Robert Sattelmeyer and James Barbour, "A Possible Source and Model for 'The Story of China Aster' in Melville's *The Confidence-Man,*" *American Literature* 48 (January 1977): 577–83.

China Sailor. In *Moby-Dick,* he is a *Pequod* sailor who is critical of the dancing during the midnight festivities in the forecastle.

"The Chipmunk" (1924). Poem, in *Weeds and Wildings,* as part of a section entitled "The Year." In autumn, the poet sees the gleeful chipmunk peeping from a beech tree. It scurries away at the slightest sound. Baby, crowing mirthfully, leaves the poet's hearth as though similarly startled—to go "whither?" Perhaps the infant had "some inkling" regarding the earth.
   Bibliography: Stein.

Chips. In *Omoo. See* Beauty.

Chock-a-Block, Lieutenant. In "Bridegroom-Dick," he is a quarterdeck officer under whom Bridegroom Dick once served at sea.

Chris, Cousin. In "A Dutch Christmas up the Hudson in the Time of Patroons," she is a girl who dances with Hans.

Christodulus. In *Clarel,* he is the authoritative, blind, sleepy old abbot of Mar Saba. He shows unctuous Derwent jeweled relics and saintly old bones.

Christopher. In *Pierre,* he is a servant of the Glendinnings who drives their vehicles and handles various odd jobs for them.

"The Cincinnati" (1924). Sketch, in *The Works of Herman Melville.* (Characters: Colonel Josiah Bunkum, Dean [Major John Gentian], Fathers, [General George] Washington.) The narrator and a philosopher, who are both members of the Burgundy Club, discuss the blue-and-white ribbon of the Society of the Cincinnati, its restricted membership, its patriotic spirit, and its archaic aspects.

Claggart, John ("Jemmy Legs"). In *Billy Budd,* he is the tall, thin, pallid master-of-arms aboard the *Bellipotent.* He is thirty-five years old. Through envy of the good looks and innocence of Billy Budd, through a strange yearning toward him, and also because of "innate depravity," Claggart falsely accuses Billy of fomenting mutiny. Unable to speak, Billy strikes out and kills Claggart without premeditation and is hanged for the capital offense. It has been suggested that the characterization of Claggart may owe something to the allegedly sadistic nature of Alexander Slidell Mackenzie, captain of the *Somers* at the time of the celebrated abortive mutiny (1842).
  Bibliography: Charles Roberts Anderson, "The Genesis of *Billy Budd,*" *American Literature* 12 (November 1940): 329–46.

Clara. In *Pierre,* she is a small, vivacious brunette with whom Glendinning Stanly is talking about statuary at his party at the time Pierre bursts in.

Clarel. In *Clarel,* he is a young American theological student. When he visits the Holy Land, he is assailed by complex religious doubts and broodingly responds in a variety of ways. On his pilgrimage, he meets and likes Nehemiah, Rolfe, Vine, Derwent, and Ungar, fellow pilgrims who he hopes will provide him spiritual guidance. He also meets Nathan and Agar and falls in love with their daughter Ruth. Clarel journeys with the other pilgrims to Jericho, the Dead Sea, Mar Saba, and Bethlehem. He is ravished by sorrow at Ruth's death, which he learns about when he returns to Jerusalem, and he is uncertain whether to become an ascetic or a defector.
  Bibliography: NN 12; Vincent Kenny, *Herman Melville's Clarel: A Spiritual Autobiography* (Hamden, Conn.: Archon Books, 1973).

Clarel (1876). (Full title: *Clarel: A Poem and Pilgrimage in the Holy Land.*) (Characters: Abdon, Agar, Agath, Anselm, the Arnaut, the Banker, Beatrice, Belex, Beltha, Benignus Muscatel, the Bey, [George] Calvert, the Celibate, Celio, Christodulus, Clarel, the Cypriote, Cyril, Derwent, Didymus, Djalea, the Dominican, the Elder, the Emir, the Emir, the Emir, Ethelward, Glaucon, Don

Graveairs, Habbibi, Hafiz, Don Hannibal Rohon Del Aquaviva, [Pasha] Ibrahim, Inez, B.L., Lazarus, the Lesbian, Max Levi, the Limeno, the Lyonese, Mahmoud [II, Sultan of Turkey], Margoth, Methodist, Mortmain, Mustapha, Nathan, Nehemiah, the Palmer, the Patriarch, Brother Placido, the Rabbi, Rolfe, Don Rovenna, the Russian, Ruth, Salvaterra, the Syrian Monk, [Count Johann Tserclaes von] Tilly, Toulib, Turbans, Ungar, Vine, a Wahabee.)

Part I. Jerusalem. In his hotel, Clarel kneels at twilight, tries to pray, and looks out over the dreary roofs of Jerusalem. He talks with Abdon, his host, goes to his room, reads, and sleeps uneasily. The [Church of the] Holy Sepulcher, other hallowed spots, and the raging, devout crusaders are described. In the morning Clarel finds the garden where Christ after the crucifixion appeared to Mary. Clarel sees exhausted pilgrims and has a sympathetic vision of Greek Christians, Levantine Moslems, Indians, and Chinese. All are pilgrims. As he leaves, he hears rival Christian liturgies. He walks through quiet streets, through the Jaffa Gate, and beyond the walls. He meets Nehemiah, a saintly old man from Rhode Island and a revered wanderer in the Holy Land. He becomes Clarel's guide. For days, they ramble about and see much. By lower Gihon they encounter three demoniacs, one of whom is Celio, a handsome but bitter hunchback doubter from Rome now living at the Franciscan convent in Jerusalem. At sundown, Celio walks along the Via Crucis, past the Ecce Homo Arch, and—thinking he resembles the Wandering Jew—out through the Gate [of St. Stephen]. Night catches him outside the locked town; so he walks through glens and past caves, weeps at the words of some Terra Santa friars, and is despondent until sunrise. At the muezzin's cry, Clarel passes through the opened gate and observes the cynical Celio.

It is Friday. Clarel and Nehemiah go to the Wailing Wall, where they see Nathan, an American, with his Eve-like daughter Ruth. As evening draws near, Nehemiah tells Clarel about Nathan. He was born in Illinois, worked as a farmer, suffered religious doubts and observed the cruelty of nature, married a Jewess named Agar, became a convert and then a Zionist, and moved to Jerusalem with Agar and Ruth—together with a younger child, who soon died. Nathan now farms at Sharon, though surrounded by hostile Arabs. That night Clarel grows restless. He goes to his roof, finds Abdon at prayer, and learns from him that a shriek they hear comes from a group watching at a deathbed. Celio has died. His body is buried in the Vale of Ashes north of town. Nehemiah accompanies Clarel there, then takes him through obscure streets where lost and forgotten people live. They stop at the old man's sparse room, to which Ruth, like a shy bird, brings some food. Nehemiah eats a little bread and then sleeps. Clarel steals away. The next morning, the two go to the home of the aloof, staring Nathan and visit with Ruth. Next day, south of town, Clarel and his guide encounter a short, rugged man—later identified as Margoth—who hammers at the rocky soil and rails when he sees that he has shocked Clarel. Next are described the stone huts of lepers inside the wall. The two visit famous regions near the Gate of Zion.

Some days pass. Clarel often calls on Agar and the lovely Ruth. Both Clarel and Ruth, depressed at being far from home, are happy to see a fellow American. One mild morning, Clarel and his guide explore the Sepulcher of Kings north of town. There they see a shy, meditative man named Vine. After visiting Moriah, Jehoshaphat, Siloam, and the Pool of Bethesda, they return with Vine toward the city. The three visit the Garden of Gethsemane, but Vine remains imperfectly communicative. At the site of the Passion, Nehemiah reads and grows dazed. Above the garden, the three encounter Rolfe, a handsome, friendly, wise, and loquacious man who, as they walk along, discourses on comparative religion. Now follows a poem about Rama, the Indian who was a god but did not know it. Perhaps someone here [Vine? Rolfe?] resembles Rama. Beside a stone where Christ sat when He predicted the fall of Jerusalem, Rolfe sits and speaks of poverty in the city. As the group tarries, he inveighs against scientific research into religions rich in legend. Then follows the story of Arculf the [very early] palmer to the Holy Land and Adamnan the abbot of Iona [off Scotland] who befriended him upon his return. Clarel, Nehemiah, Vine, and Rolfe climb a tower and from the top see the wrinkled city of Jerusalem and look [east] toward the Dead Sea. When Nehemiah, unmoved, suggests a stroll to Bethany, Rolfe gently puts him off, and the old man walks away. Rolfe tells the other two men about a sea captain rendered as meek as Nehemiah by a pair of dreadful shipwrecks. Curious now, Clarel tries without success to induce Nehemiah to talk about his past.

Clarel, who never knew his mother, finds a substitute in kind Agar and falls in love with Ruth—and she with him. He visits the grave of Celio and encounters Rolfe, who is visiting the grave of a friend named Ethelward. Clarel sees various travelers entering Jerusalem, returns to his room, and finds an enigmatic antirevolutionary poem by B.L. pasted on a wall and whitewashed over. Tidings come that hostile Arabs have killed Nathan and taken his body away. When Clarel finds that Jewish law forbids his entering a Jewish house of mourning, he sends a note and a ring to Ruth as evidence of his devotion and decides to join Vine, Rolfe, and several recently arrived pilgrims on a trip to Siddim, the Dead Sea, Mar Saba, and Bethlehem. Clarel encounters an Armenian funeral, which arouses ominous ponderings. On Candelmas morning [2 February] the travelers set out amid wrangling of their Arab guides, drivers, and guards, and under the half-cynical, half-pitying eye of Abdon the Black Jew.

Part II. The Wilderness. The cavalcade, going down Dolorosa Lane, includes the following: Derwent, an Anglican priest, benign and modern; the Elder, a Scotch Presbyterian, sour, self-reliant, and belligerent; a Greek banker, wealthy and self-pampering; Glaucon, the banker's prospective son-in-law, sweet, rakish, and light-hearted; Mortmain, gloomy and stiff; Nehemiah, on his patient ass; earnest Clarel; dapper Rolfe, riding like a Native-American scout; and Vine, lagging back alone. As the group prepares to set out, Glaucon requests that no one say the word "Death." Derwent suggests a morning canter to Clarel, but that young man is gloomily thinking of Ruth. Mortmain harangues against those who crucified the Savior. Rolfe tells Derwent about skull-capped Mortmain, details of whose life he has learned at Abdon's inn. It seems that Mortmain, an illegitimate Swede, was ignored except for money by his father, participated in revolutionary activities in France, and began to have doubts. Clarel speaks about Homer to Glaucon, but that easy-going Smyrinote has hardly heard of the poet and prefers to discuss shooting at Nazareth and then sings a love song, which annoys the Elder.

The party approaches the hamlet of Bethany, which is ugly but hallowed by the Son of God. The pilgrims' guide is Djalea the Druze, a noble, inscrutable Lebanese; the leader of their six Arab Bethlehemite guards under Djalea is Belex, a former Turkish cavalryman, rendered tough and stoical by misfortunes. While the party goes through the dangerous region of Adommin [Adummim], the Druze keeps a sharp lookout and his men scour nearby dens, while Nehemiah tells about the Good Samaritan. During a halt in a rocky place, Glaucon sings a ribald song which so offends the Elder that he departs, Djalea speaks so courteously to Vine that Rolfe concludes that the aloof American must be noble, and demented Nehemiah startles Derwent by attempting to clear the rocks in preparation for Christ's second coming. Next comes an essay in verse about the desert. It is a beautiful but horrible region, holy and yet dire. The group moves in a sullen manner, except for observant Rolfe, even-tempered Vine, and their placid escort. When some armed Turks approach on their way to Jerusalem, the wheezing banker and jolly Glaucon leave the pilgrims to join them. The diminished group proceeds to the gorge of Achor, beneath a cliff near Jericho. They pause by Elisha's fountain, when Mortmain announces that he will pass the night here alone and join the others in a day or two. By the Crusaders' Tower at Jericho the remaining pilgrims camp for the night and begin to talk about previous visitors there—biblical, military, and legendary. Rolfe speaks sympathetically to Vine and the others about the crazed Mortmain. In the middle of the night, when Rolfe gets up, Clarel avoids him and then wonders why he did so.

The next morning, Clarel, Rolfe, and Vine talk with a Syrian monk who is in the process of spending forty days on the heights of Quarantania reenacting the temptation of Christ by the Devil. The ascetic fellow tells of his vision of the Savior and His message concerning God's omnipresence, goodness, and peace that will come before death. Clarel, Rolfe, and the offended Vine see Margoth the geologist descending the mountain, in a cave which he explains has provided him with rocky specimens. The Jewish Margoth, though a member of a creditable race, outrages his auditors by suggesting that the region ought to be scientifically modernized. Started by Vine, the pilgrims have a learned discussion about Hebrews.

On the third morning, which is rainy, Djalea leads the group to the Jordan River. They cross it with seven bandit-like Arab horsemen, with whom they chat and compare arms. The pilgrims remain near the Jordan for a time. Rolfe, Clarel, and Vine sing a hymn. Nehemiah tastes the water. But Margoth calls him a fool and rushes off for some wine instead. The group encounters a Dominican friar of French background. He defends the Roman Catholic church as the only true protestant institution in the modern mad times; it is flexible, properly antiscientific, and integrally related to all other regions. When he leaves, Margoth shouts after him derisively, and Rolfe and Derwent discuss Rome's future. While the Arabs cut willows for palm leaves, Clarel approaches Vine, who grows communicative, then suddenly stops, saying to himself that the younger man must settle by himself any doubts he has.

As the pilgrims file southward toward the Dead Sea, they observe some Apples of Sodom, and a bitter mist drives at them. They talk about the biblical warning that none should traverse the desolate mountain region of Seir nearby. They see a lovely rainbow over the ugly sea. Derwent points out the location of the lost city of Petra, which Rolfe is able to describe since he is the only member of the party who has seen it. They rouse Nehemiah, who has been sleeping under a big rock, and continue their journey. On a rock face they find a chalked image of the Southern Cross and an inscription concerning science and Christ beneath it. They think that it may have been done by Mortmain offering proof that the man is alive and well. In the afternoon their Bethlehemite escort pitches camp farther south, between the Judah Mountains and the Dead Sea. Derwent starts reading placidly, to the annoyance of Rolfe, who regards the present scene to be more challenging than any book. Clarel approaches Vine at the salty marge. They are soon joined by Rolfe. He debates Margoth, who is collecting geological specimens, on the origins of the Dead Sea, a debate which Nehemiah's ass brays at, to Vine's amusement. Mortmain reappears, descending from Judah. Despite a warning "salt-song" from Beltha, one of Djalea's Bethlehemite guards, he drinks the waters of the Dead Sea. Now follows a prelusive canto on the mystery of iniquity.

That night Mortmain launches into a recital concerning the sins of which the Dead Sea seems the concentrated symbol. The other pilgrims withdraw. While Nehemiah sleeps and Margoth conducts some geological experiments, the others discuss the five sunken cities. In the night, Nehemiah dreams that the New Jerusalem has risen from the Dead Sea and is murmurously beckoning him. Walking in his sleep, he vanishes. In the morning, Vine finds Nehemiah's corpse by the shore and calls the others, and they bury his body with his book in a bone-scooped trench. Instantly comes an avalanche of flinty shards down the mountain and then a frail fog-bow over them.

Part III. Mar Saba. The pilgrims mount up, put the Dead Sea and Siddim behind them, and climb the perilous mountains of Judah toward Mar Saba. Mortmain describes God's vengefulness. To change the mood, Clarel relates a story told him by Nehemiah about a mild carpenter who once argued with his only friend and thereafter never left his home. The pilgrims discuss various conceptions of heaven. They encounter a Cypriote who has vowed to dip his mother's shroud in the Dead Sea and who is singing with incredible gaiety as he proceeds toward it, to the distress of the pilgrims when they think of Nehemiah there. They rest, and most of them talk about the dangers of the Gnostic preference of knowledge over faith and about historical cycles. Clarel admires the calm of the pipe-puffing Djalea while Vine idly crushes and tosses some porous stones. Mortmain asks Derwent to lecture them as though they needed spiritual comforting; so the cleric recommends cheerfulness and rejoicing. This does not satisfy Mortmain, who demands and gets an unpalatable exposition of influences shaping the Jewish faith. Clarel follows Vine into the crags and finds him trembling there. The group hears the distant bells of Mar Saba, see a cairn of stone piled up by Vine, ride in single file, and encounter tents of Moabites and Ammonites in a green hollow. Djalea parleys with them before the pilgrims are permitted to proceed. Several European and Middle Eastern monasteries are described; then Mar Saba, hung in the cliff clefts, looms before the pilgrims.

Clarel and the others enter Mar Saba, not from below, where the Kedron ravine is, but from the ridge above and through a wall near Mar Saba's towers. They are welcomed by the friars and assigned beds. But first they are treated to a drinking party at which they meet two persons. They are Arnaut, a huge, colorfully dressed Albanian soldier, with medals, sword, and thirst for wine, and then an aging, gay epicurean from Lesbos. The pilgrims respond to the wine differently: Derwent joins in, Djalea leaves, Rolfe offers friendship with Arnaut, aloof Mortmain soon leaves, Vine relaxes and drinks, and so does Belex. Rolfe observes a morose Greek timoneer named Agath and persuades him to tell his story. It seems that he smuggled an evil Mohammedan, who wanted to escape the plague, aboard his ship *The Peace of God* along with his sea chest. It was full of blades that turned the ship's compass and caused a wreck. Only the timoneer escaped. Later Rolfe hears that the man after his unique escape was set upon and beaten by robbers near Mar Saba. The revelry continues, with songs and recitations by the Lesbian, Derwent, Rolfe, and Agath. Praising Agar's verses, Derwent asks shy Vine for a contribution, which proves brief. The Arnaut recites a battle song. As Clarel leans from a window and broods on faith's ebb, a litany emerges from Kedron's jail. He and Rolfe walk to the ledge and see Djalea calmly smoking. To Rolfe's inquiry, he says that in his religion there is no God but God. Rolfe praises Djalea's politeness and begins to discuss Belex's position as a Turkish guard of the Holy Sepulcher and the leaping up there of fire, which Rolfe discomfits Clarel by saying strains his faith.

Dawn breaks on a holiday at Mar Saba, and four monks sing about Jeremiah, the Chaldean army, and Zedekiah. Rolfe and Derwent visit the monastery church, with its books, manuscripts, and flags. That night a torch-lit masque is performed. In it, a monk recites a monologue of the Wandering Jew, who thinks about his centuries of life, his wife Esther, and the coronation of Charlemagne which he observed, and who lurches on and on, deathless and sleepless. Hearing all of this, Mortmain shouts "Dies Irae . . ." from a peak above. The masque closes with a lyric in praise of the Golden Age. Growing anguished over his religious doubts, Clarel talks to Derwent, who appears strangely serious and touched until their conversation is interrupted by a monk named Anselm. After his breakfast, Derwent visits the porch of the minister, where he finds a marble shield depicting a fallen knight miraculously rearmed. He calls on Christodulus, the blind abbot of Mar Saba, who shows his flattering guest jeweled relics and saintly bones, then dozes off. Meanwhile, the breakfastless Clarel walks to a rocky grotto, presided over by Cyril, and containing skulls. Derwent saunters to the stables, jokes with the Lesbian, and goes with him to St. Saba's fountain in Kedron's bed and past Cyril's vault. They see an eagle drop the skullcap snatched from Mortmain, who is on a high crag, and then see Agath walking beside a chasm. At this time, Vine is reclining on a stone and singing to a palm tree in the crags to bloom bravely though high over horrors. At this moment, the Lesbian is telling Derwent about the timoneer, who was attacked once by an eagle that fell into the sea with him and bore off his hat as a prize. Derwent and the Lesbian visit a gloomy cave once occupied by the crazed Habbibi and now full of hellish inscriptions. Mortmain catches sight of Derwent and the Lesbian dancing below him, hears Cyril's cry for the password, and sees the cruciform palm which while he is thinking of his black past seems to be waving him on to Lethe. Rolfe hides on a ledge, also sees the lovely palm, and remembers when as a shipboy he deserted in Mendanna's sea [by the Marquesas Islands] and went ashore—to be greeted as a god in an Eden, but grew restless and left.

In the afternoon, Clarel thinks of Ruth again, climbs to the tree, and encounters the Celibate there. This man is a tall, pure monk who feeds his nimbus of St. Saba doves, listens as his visitor says that he misses women's domestic touch here, and responds by letting Clarel read his antifeminist tract, which also contains hymns and prayers. When Clarel looks up, the Celibate is gone; but he sees Mortmain, Vine, Rolfe, and the palm. He muses on divine and sexual love in heaven. When the pilgrims prepare to leave by the troubled light of dawn, they find Mortmain dead in the crags, his filmed eyes staring at the tree. The monks bury his corpse outside their sacred walls.

Part IV. Bethlehem. The pilgrim group, diminished by two deaths, is augmented by Agar (who rides Nehemiah's ass), the Lesbian, and a scarred, half-Indian Confederate veteran named Ungar. Like the three kings of the Orient, they head west through a region of powdery dust toward Bethlehem. The huge Arnaut accompanies them briefly and then gallops back to Mar Saba, firing his gun in farewell. The others notice a tattoo on Agath's arm of the Jerusalem ensign—crosses, palm leaves, crowns, and a star. The pilgrims persuade the old tar to tell about a certain volcanic island [Narborough, in the Galapagos] dominated by gigantic tortoises. Clarel concludes that if people cannot explain such a dreadful place, which resembles their present locale, they can hardly expect to solve the problem of the next world. An evil-looking scorpion scares Agath, whom Rolfe calls brave anyway. Watching the sailor is Ungar, who—as Djalea tells Rolfe—has drilled both Egyptian and Turkish soldiers. Ungar tells about himself: He is descended from an English Catholic who helped settle Maryland and who married a Native-American woman; after the Civil War, which ruined him financially even though he had disapproved of slavery, he became self-exiled. The pilgrims ascend a hill and see Bethlehem, with its olive orchards, vineyard, and old walls. Arriving at the Capuchin abbey, they pay and tip their guard (Belex remaining nearby), dine, and retire happily. On the terrace, Ungar greets the shining stars. Rolfe, just before falling asleep, contrasts contemporary agnostic materialism and Bethlehem's faith. Derwent rouses his friends to see dawn over the valley where the shepherds saw the Star of Bethlehem. Ungar launches into a denunciation of the materialism and hypocrisy of Anglo-Saxons, whom he calls more cruel than Turks. Before a stone monument in the valley, Derwent and Ungar debate the worldliness of modern churches. The others seem to respect Derwent when he does not argue further. For distraction, Rolfe listens to two strangers at the breakfast table as they discuss the relative merits of Turkey and Protestant Europe.

After saying goodbye to Agath, the party visits the Church of the Star, built around the site of the manger where Mary gave birth to the Christ child. The guide who points out details is Salvaterra, a hollow-cheeked Franciscan monk from Tuscany whom Rolfe regards as ardent because he is a novice but whom Derwent inwardly criticizes as effeminate. When Ungar seems sympathetic, the Franciscan suggests that the soldier's sword is a cross. Ungar retires to his thoughts, and Rolfe and Derwent debate manliness vs. Christliness. Derwent admires manliness, which Rolfe brands as sometimes carnal. As Vine breathes a few words to Clarel in praise of the monk-guide, heavenly organ music fills the church. The group leaves the grotto, finds dead Nehemiah's ass lapping from a basin of holy water, bids Salvaterra farewell, and climbs to the church roof for a view of Bethlehem which he has recommended. When Derwent mentions Naomi's Ruth, Clarel thinks of dead Nathan's Ruth, his beloved, and is tempted to go at once to Jerusalem to see her. Derwent and Rolfe discuss the survival of tradition in the Roman Catholic church. Derwent leaves, after which Rolfe and Clarel agree that Ungar is evidently a brave soldier and a sound thinker. The pilgrims visit Greek, Latin, and Armenian convents nearby, and then the Milk Grotto. Derwent, Rolfe, and Ungar debate the effectiveness of religion in today's harsh world. Up comes a stranger. He is Don Hannibal Rohon Del Aquaviva, Derwent's one-armed, one-legged friend from Mexico. He lost his limbs fighting for Mexican freedom but is now jocosely disillusioned, chats with Ungar, then leaves for a while. Ungar blasts the inefficacy of reform, adds that America will become the scene of a new Adamic fall, and hints that wickedness is an evil we have from birth. Derwent comments that the sunset is sweet. Clarel is tempted to live for his senses but then thinks of his star near the horizon. Rolfe tries to defend Ungar to Derwent.

As the group returns to town, Clarel hears an unknown voice (later identified as that of the Lyonese) singing of Inez, his love. Once in town, Derwent finds Don Hannibal sitting in a coffin and chatting with Brother Placido, a traveling Mexican funeral friar. Clarel finds that his room is to be shared for the night by the Lyonese, a sensual, effeminate singer whom he troubles with queries about Judaea. The Lyonese counters by commenting on the witchery of dark-tressed Jewesses, sings a song about Shushan [in Persia], retires, and trips out of their room early while Clarel dreams of being tugged this way and that by the lush Lyonese and the ascetic Salvaterra. Derwent startles Clarel on the parapet by praising the soft, warm form of the Lyonese, whom they watch as he leaves town. Ungar and Don Hannibal also depart. Clarel, to while away a little time before returning to Jerusalem, goes to David's Well, where he meets a Russian pilgrim who reveals that the Lyonese is Jewish but hides the fact while traveling among strangers.

On the night of Shrove Tuesday, the group leaves Bethlehem. Clarel thinks of marrying Ruth and taking her, along with her mother Agar, out of this sad land. The pilgrims pass by the Cistern of Kings, Hinnom, Zion, Rogel, Ophel, Shaveh, and Siloam, toward Jerusalem. First they stop at the Jewish cemetery, where Clarel is stunned to discover that Ruth and Agar, dead of fever and grief, are at that instant being buried under cover of darkness because of their friends' fear of the Turks. Dawn breaks on Ash Wednesday. A dirge begs death to lead Ruth gently away until her lowly lover can join her. Five days pass. Clarel sits senseless. Rolfe, Vine, and Derwent reluctantly leave him to go their necessary ways. On Palm Sunday, Clarel sees a group of cheerful Armenians who only remind him of the earlier Armenian funeral train and of death—of Nehemiah, Celio, Mortmain, Nathan, Agar, and Ruth. And now Easter Sunday—the same this year for Latin pilgrims and for the Armenians, Greeks, Syrians, and Copts. Christ is risen, yes; but where is Ruth? Clarel wonders, wanders, and is lonely in the depopulated town. On Whitsuntide, amid the train of burdened people and their beasts along the Via Crucis, is one who laments that he hears no message from a certain grave.

In an epilogue, Clarel is adjured to keep his heart, although star and clod combat each other, and to believe what faith says, that the spirit rises above the dust.

The sources of *Clarel,* an immensely complicated work, include Melville's reading in the Bible and other books both well known and recondite. Melville quotes, paraphrases, reshapes, and alludes to passages from numerous authors, including Dante, William Shakespeare, and John Milton. For geographical information, his most important source was *Sinai and Palestine in Connection with Their History* (1863) by Arthur Penrhyn Stanley; in addition, he used John Murray's *A Handbook for Travellers in Syria and Palestine* (2 vols., 1858) and three books by William Bartlett—*Forty Days in the Desert* (186-?), *The Nile Boat* (186-?), and *Walks about the City and Environs of Jerusalem* (186-?). He also uses—and sometimes names in his text—more belletristic travel writers and authors of popular nineteenth-century Eastern romances. But the document that Melville consulted the most was his own 1857 journal, at least a hundred passages from which he transfers to his poem, sometimes verbatim or nearly so. He was in the Holy Land from the day he arrived in Jaffa (6 January 1857) until the day of his departure therefrom (24 January), and he took notes ranging from terse to copious. In addition, he echoes or alludes to his own earlier publications. In indirect ways, *Clarel* is a partly autobiographical narrative of his visit to the Holy Land, complete with personalities he met. Rolfe, who combines seeking and doubting, and Ungar, a restless wanderer, have been seen as distorted self-portraits. Vine has been interpreted as containing aspects of Melville's analysis of Nathaniel Hawthorne.* To a degree, Clarel, who yearned for an immaculate friend, is to the shy and withdrawn Vine as Melville was to Hawthorne. Other characters are sketchier portraits from real life, for example, Abdon, Agar, the Banker, Glaucon, Nathan, and Nehemiah.

Melville probably began composing this long poem soon after the publication of *Battle-Pieces* and when he first worked as a New York Customs inspector (from 1866). In his spare time, he read steadily and probably added lines on a regular basis. His wife Elizabeth Knapp Shaw Melville* wrote to her stepmother Hope Savage Shaw* as follows: "Herman is . . . very busy; pray do not mention to *any one* that he is writing poetry—you know how such things spread and he would be very angry if he knew I had spoken of it—and of course I have not, except in confidence to you and the family" (9 March 1875). That August, Melville received $1,200 from Peter Gansevoort (1788–1876),* his uncle, to underwrite publication of *Clarel.* Melville's wife was glad to see it off his hands and out of the house. She reported in a letter to her cousin Catherine Gansevoort Lansing* that "this dreadful *incubus* of a *book* . . . has undermined all our happiness" (2 February 1876). *Clarel* was not well received and sold only 478 copies. Its 17,863 lines in irregularly rhyming iambic tetrameter were, as Melville himself said in a letter to his informal English correspondent Charles James Billson,* "eminently adapted for unpopularity" (10 October 1884). Its convoluted and inept syntax put generations of readers off, as did its thematic and symbolic stress on aridity, evil, death, escape, love, and the search for meaning. But the uncompromising sincerity with which Melville deals with the problem of a quest for spiritual values in the modern Waste Land of atheism and materialism has won recent converts.

Bibliography: Stan Goldman, *Melville's Protest Theism: The Hidden and Silent God in Clarel* (DeKalb: Northern Illinois University Press, 1993); Vincent Kenny, *Herman Melville's Clarel: A Spiritual Autobiography* (Hamden, Conn.: Archon Books, 1973); NN 12 and 15; Shurr; Stein; Warren.

Claret. In *White-Jacket,* he is a veteran of the Battle of Brandywine Creek [11 September 1777], the father of the former commander of the frigate the *Brandywine,* and also the father of Captain Claret of the *Neversink.*

Claret. In *White-Jacket,* he is the son of the veteran of the Battle of Brandywine Creek and the brother of Captain Claret of the *Neversink.*

Claret, Captain. In *White-Jacket,* he is the son of a veteran of the Battle of Brandywine Creek and now the large, portly captain of the American frigate the

Neversink. Captain Claret lets the crew present a Fourth of July theatrical and, at the request of Jack Chase, grants liberty to the men at Rio de Janeiro. Claret sets May-Day and Rose-Water at head-butting and then orders them flogged for fighting. He comes close to having White Jacket flogged but is dissuaded from doing so by Chase and Corporal Colbrook. Claret orders John Ushant flogged for refusing to shave his beard. Claret is based in part on James Armstrong, an officer under Charles Wilkes, naval officer and author of *Narrative of the U.S. Exploring Expedition during the Years 1838, 1839, 1840, 1841, 1842* (5 vols. and atlas, 1845), and later captain of the *United States,* the U.S. naval vessel on which the *Neversink* is modeled. Armstrong and Claret were both alcoholics.

Bibliography: Charles R. Anderson, ''A Reply to Herman Melville's *White-Jacket* by Rear-Admiral Thomas O. Selfridge, Sr.,'' *American Literature* 7 (May 1935): 123–44; Jaffé; NN 5.

Clarissa. In *Pierre,* she is Pierre's nurse, now dead and hence unfortunately not available for consultation by his biographers.

Claude. In ''I and My Chimney,'' this is the pseudonym of the writer of a note published in the local paper criticizing the narrator's chimneyed house for blemishing the view. The author of the note may be the narrator's wife.

Claude Lorrain. In ''Marquis de Grandvin: At the Hostelry.'' *See* Lorrain, Claude.

Cleothemes the Argive. In ''The Fiddler,'' he is a character in the narrator Helmstone's unwanted poetic masterpiece.

The Clerk of the Weather. In ''Pebbles,'' he represents the typically ineffectual man of science. Specifically here, he cannot predict the action of the implacable, smiling sea.

Clifford, John Henry (1809–1876). Lawyer, politician, and railroad company president. Clifford was born in Providence, Rhode Island, graduated from Brown (1827), was admitted to the bar in Massachusetts (1830), practiced law in New Bedford, and soon was renowned for professional skill and oratory. He was elected to the General Court (1835), was an aide to Governor Edward Everett (1836–1840), and became district attorney for the southern district of Massachusetts (1839–1849) and attorney general (1849–1852). He successfully prosecuted Harvard Professor John White Webster, who murdered his colleague and creditor Professor George Parkman (November 1849); the presiding judge was Melville's father-in-law Lemuel Shaw,* who sentenced Webster to be hanged (1850). Clifford was elected governor of Massachusetts (1852); after one term, he became attorney general again (to 1858), resumed private practice (1858–1867), and became president of the Boston and Providence Railway (1867–1876). Clifford married Sarah Parker Allen of New Bedford in 1832 (their son Charles W. Clifford became a distinguished Boston lawyer).

Melville met Clifford through Shaw (1852) and learned the poignant Agatha Story* from him. When Melville expressed interest, Clifford sent him a copy of his journal concerning Agatha Hatch Robertson, of Pembroke, Massachusetts. She befriended a shipwrecked British sailor named James Robertson (original name: Shinn), married him (1807), was deserted by him, and bore his daughter, Rebecca. Robertson went to Alexandria, Virginia, did well in business, and committed bigamy by marrying a second time. After seventeen years, he visited Agatha and Rebecca, on the eve of the daughter's wedding to a man named Gifford. Agatha suspected but did not know that her husband had married another woman. When that woman died, Robertson offered to take Agatha and the Giffords out west; they declined, and he went alone to Missouri and married a third time in or near St. Louis. His wife this time was Mrs. Irwin, the mother of a daughter by a previous marriage. The daughter was married to a man named Janney. After Robertson's death (c. 1840) and then that of his Missouri wife (1841), the administrator of his estate of some $20,000 found a letter from Rebecca addressing him as her father. A man named Dillingham, from Falmouth, Massachusetts, arrived in St. Louis with documents proving the existence of Agnes and the legitimacy of Rebecca A. Gifford, and laying claim to the deceased's property. Janney went to New Bedford, conferred with Clifford, and learned that Agatha had known of Robertson's third marriage but saw no reason to embarrass her legal husband by exposing him. The upshot was that Mrs. Janney seemed willing to share Robertson's estate. Intrigued by Agatha's patience and endurance, Melville discussed with Nathaniel Hawthorne* the possibility of turning her story into fiction.

Bibliography: NN 14.

Cloud, Captain. In "The Scout toward Aldie," he is a compassionate officer under the Colonel. Cloud leads his men in a vain pursuit of [John Singleton] Mosby.

"Clover" (1924). Poem, in *Weeds and Wildings,* as part of a section entitled "The Year." When "[t]he June day dawns," the sky, the fields of clover, and the robin's breast are all red. Melville may be mocking Christian asceticism here.

Bibliography: Stein.

"Clover Dedication to Winnefred." *See Weeds and Wildings.*

Cochrane, Lord. In *White-Jacket,* he is mentioned by Dr. Cadwallader Cuticle as the man who was admiral of the Brazilian fleets and under whom Cuticle served more than twenty years earlier. This Lord Thomas Cochrane is not to be confused with Lord Cochrane, Admiral Sir Alexander Forrester Inglis (1758–

1832). Cuticle's supposed friend Lord Cochrane is better known as Thomas Cochrane, 10th Earl of Dundonald.*

"Cock-a-Doodle-Doo!" (1853). (Full title: "Cock-a-Doodle-Doo! or The Crowing of the Noble Cock Beneventano.") Short Story. It was published anonymously in *Harper's New Monthly Magazine** (1 December 1853). (Characters: Beneventano, Widow Crowfoot, Jake, Merrymusk, Merrymusk, Mrs. Merrymusk, Squire Squaretoes.) The narrator has reason to feel melancholy about almost everything, including recent machinations of despots, fatal "locomotive and steamer" accidents, and debts he owes. Even nature can be disagreeable. But when he hears an unseen rooster crowing a *"Never say die!"* message, all adversities seem negligible. He would like to buy the lusty rooster; so he asks around and finally locates it at a squalid shanty occupied by Merrymusk, his wood-sawyer, and by his dying wife and four sickly children. But Trumpet, as they call the glittering creature, is not for sale at any price, since— as Merrymusk explains—its message to the Merrymusks is "Glory to God in the highest!" The narrator, renaming the musical rooster Signor Beneventano, returns some weeks later to the shanty, hears the rooster roll out its imperial music over the dead and dying Merrymusks, and sees the rooster itself fall and follow them all in death. Although the narrator buries the entire family, he is never in "the doleful dumps" when he thinks of that wonderful cock.

Melville attended an 1847 performance in New York City featuring Ferdinando Beneventano,* the celebrated operatic baritone. Calling Trumpet a "brave cock" is only the most obvious of several double entendres in this pulsing tale. In the 1850s, Melville was made gloomy by news of many disasters and political upheavals. So it is possible that Melville is satirizing overly optimistic proponents of transcendentalism by depicting a foolishly noisy barnyard fowl. After all, Merrymusk might have sold his rooster for the five hundred offered dollars and obtained some needed medical help. An anonymous reviewer, reading an early copy, identified Melville as the author of "Cock-a-Doodle-Doo!" in the New York *Literary World* (26 November 1853). Melville received about $45 in payment for the story.

Bibliography: Sidney P. Moss, " 'Cock-a-Doodle-Doo!' and Some Legends in Melville Scholarship," *American Literature* 40 (May 1968): 192–210; Newman; Egbert S. Oliver, " 'Cock-a-Doodle-Doo!' and Transcendental Hocus-Pocus," *New England Quarterly* 21 (1948): 204–16; Sealts; Young.

Cockney, The. In *Omoo. See* Shorty.

Codman, John (1814–1900). Sea captain and author. He was born in Dorchester, Massachusetts, attended Amherst for two years (1832–1834), and then began a career at sea, which took him to Brazil, the East Indies, China, the Crimea, and elsewhere. An excellent horseman, he occasionally rode from Boston to New York City; he also went to and rode in the Far West, where he owned an Idaho ranch. He argued in pamphlets in favor of free ships and free shipbuilders' materials and against subsidies for the merchant marine. His books include *Sailors' Life and Sailors' Yarns* (1847, as by Captain Ringbolt), *Ten Months in Brazil* (1867), *The Round Trip* (1879, in the West), *Winter Sketches from the Saddle* (1888), and *An American Transport in the Crimean War* (1896). Codman married Anna G. Day of New York in 1847 (the couple had a daughter). Melville reviewed Codman's *Sailors' Life and Sailors' Yarns* in an article mainly concerned with *Etchings of a Whaling Cruise . . .* by J. Ross Browne.* Evert Duyckinck* asked Melville to review both for his *Literary World* (6 March 1847).

Codrington, Sir Edward (1770–1851). British naval commander. From a Gloucestershire family, he entered the navy (1883), was promoted to lieutenant (1893), commanded the *Orion* at Trafalgar under Admiral Viscount Horatio Nelson* (1805), served under Lord Cochrane, Admiral Sir Alexander Forrester Inglis (1758–1832) on the North American station (1814), became rear admiral (1814), and was active against Washington, D.C., Baltimore, and New Orleans (1814) during the War of 1812. He was knighted (1815) and promoted to vice admiral (1821). Codrington was in command of the combined British, French, and Russian fleet when it destroyed the Turkish and Egyptian naval forces at Navarino, fought in the harbor of Navarino, now Pylos, Greece (20 October 1827); his flagship was the *Asia.* This battle was the last major fleet action involving wooden sailing vessels. Codrington was instrumental in consummating the treaty at Alexandria (1828), some time after which he was promoted to admiral (1837). He married Jane Hall of Jamaica in 1802. The couple had three sons, one of whom accidentally drowned in early life, and two daughters. One surviving son, Sir William John Codrington, became a army officer, while his other surviving son, Sir Henry John Codrington, became a naval officer. One of Sir Edward Codrington's daughters, Jane, Lady Bourchier, wrote his biography (1873). In *White-Jacket,* Codrington is said to have been the commanding officer of the British flagship the *Asia* aboard which Jack Chase was captain of one of the main-deck guns during the Battle of Navarino. Codrington published *Compressed Narrative of the Proceedings of Vice-Admiral Sir Edward Codrington, during His Command of His Majesty's Ships and Vessels on the Mediterranean Station from the 28th of February 1827, until the 22nd of August 1828* (1832), much of which concerns the events before, during, and after the Battle of Navarino.

Bibliography: Geoffrey Bennett, *Nelson the Commander* (London: B. T. Batsford, 1972); A. T. Mahan, *Types of Naval Officers Drawn from the History of the British Navy . . .* (Boston: Little, Brown, 1901); Oliver Warner, *Nelson's Battles* (Newton Abbot, England: David & Charles, 1971); C. M. Woodhouse, *The Battle of Navarino* (London: Hodder and Stoughton, 1965).

Coffee, Old. In *White-Jacket. See* Old Coffee.

Coffin. In *White-Jacket,* he is the quartermaster who plays the part of Old Luff in the Fourth of July theatrical.

Coffin, Johnny. In *Moby-Dick,* he is the younger son of Peter and Sal Coffin.

Coffin, Peter. In *Moby-Dick,* he is the landlord of the Spouter Inn, in New Bedford. He assigns Ishmael to be the roommate of Queequeg there. Coffin and his wife Sal have two sons, Sam and Johnny. Peter Coffin and Hosea Hussey are cousins.

Coffin, Sal. In *Moby-Dick,* she is Peter Coffin's wife. The Coffins have two sons, Sam and Johnny.

Coffin, Sam. In *Moby-Dick,* he is the older son of Peter and Sal Coffin.

Colbrook, Corporal. In *White-Jacket,* he is the handsome, courteous lady's man of a marine corporal. He and Jack Chase defend the reputation of White Jacket before Captain Claret and thus protect him from an unmerited flogging.

Coleman. In *White-Jacket,* he is evidently an official at the New York Astor House, where Old Coffee once worked.

Coleman, Deacon Deuteronomy. In *Moby-Dick,* he is the deacon of the First Congregational Church, on the island of Nantucket. Ishmael enigmatically tells Captain Peleg and Captain Bildad that Queequeg is a member of "the First Congregational Church"—meaning the congregation of humankind.

Coleman, John Brown, Jr. (1800–?). Whaler captain. He was born in Nova Scotia, but his Quaker family was from Nantucket. He married Susan Coffin. Coleman replaced Henry Coffin as master of the *Charles and Henry* (December 1840). The whaler was owned by Charles G. Coffin and Henry Coffin of Nantucket. Melville shipped aboard this vessel as harpooner from Eimeo (November 1842) to Lahaina, Hawaii (April 1843).
   Bibliography: Wilson L. Heflin, "Melville's Third Whaler," *Modern Language Notes* 64 (April 1949): 241–45; Helfin, "New Light on Melville's Cruise in the *Charles and Henry,*" *Historic Nantucket* 22 (October 1974): 6–27.

Coleman, Nathan. In *Moby-Dick,* he is a sailor lost with five others from the *Eliza* in 1839. Their shipmates placed a marble tablet in their memory in the Whaleman's Chapel in New Bedford.

Coleman, Nathan. In *Omoo,* he is named by Melville as the Nantucket whaling captain of the *Leviathan* who, because of an argument with some natives, vindictively introduced mosquitoes on the island of Imeeo. His name derives from that of John Brown Coleman, Jr.,* the captain of the whaler *Charles and Henry,* on which Melville shipped (November 1842–April 1843).

Coleridge, Samuel Taylor (1772–1834). English poet and critic. After an unstable youth, he married Sara Fricker (1795), published a volume of poetry (1796), published *Lyrical Ballads* (1798) with William Wordsworth, visited Germany (1798–1799), became addicted to opium (from 1803) and was irresponsible with respect to his family and friends, and published *Biographia Literaria* (1817) and *Aids to Reflection* (1825), among many other works. Coleridge advanced the cause of Romantic poetry, commented on the works of William Shakespeare, and helped introduce German idealistic philosophy to England and—indirectly—to the United States. In ''C—'s Lament,'' Melville has his persona bitterly lament the passing of youth, and by implication so does Coleridge, for whom ''C—'' undoubtedly stands. Melville began to read works by Coleridge in the late 1840s, profited from his essays on Shakespeare, was influenced by his theories as to Romantic aesthetics, and learned much about German idealism through him.

Bibliography: Walter Jackson Bate, *Coleridge* (New York: Macmillan, 1968); R. L. Brett, ed., *Coleridge* (London: G. Bell & Sons, 1971).

''The College Colonel'' (1866). Poem, in *Battle-Pieces.* (Character: The Colonel.) Back home again, the central figure, on horseback, ''brings his regiment home'' after two years of combat. His arm is in splints, and a crutch is beside his saddle. The soldiers are ''half-tattered, and battered, and worn.'' Their leader is pale and rigid. ''An Indian aloofness lones his brow.'' He remembers ''battle's pains and prayers''—including those at ''the Seven Days' Fight,'' ''the Wilderness grim,'' ''Petersburg crater,'' and ''Libby''—even while he is greeted by shouts, flags, and flowers. He does not mind a lost leg, a maimed arm, and even ''[s]elf . . . disclaimed,'' since after combat and the field hospital, ''what *truth* [came] to him.'' The colonel in this poem was William Francis Bartlett,* whom Melville saw on parade at Pittsfield, Massachusetts (22 August 1863). The poem, however, is partly fictional. When Melville saw Bartlett on horseback, his military unit had left Massachusetts only nine months earlier, had been in combat, but back home again had paraded in clean uniforms. With a different unit earlier, Captain Bartlett had lost his left leg near Hampton, Virginia (24 April 1862), had mustered out as an invalid, and therefore had not fought during the Seven Days (26 June–2 July 1862). Promoted to colonel, he raised a new regiment in western Massachusetts, returned to active duty, and was wounded again—this time at Port Hudson, Louisiana, in his left wrist and right ankle (27 May 1863). After Melville saw this unit on parade, Bartlett was wounded in the head in the Wilderness (6 May 1864), was captured following the Petersburg explosion (30 July), and was exchanged out of Libby Prison, Richmond (24 September), more than a year after the parade Melville observed.

Bibliography: Garner, NN 11, Warren.

Colonel. In "Iris (1865)," he is any one of three bearded puritans who accompany Iris (Peace) north after Sherman's March.

Colonel, The ("The Boy"). In "The College Colonel," he is the badly maimed, experienced young colonel who leads the remnant of his regiment home again after two years of combat in the Civil War. In real life, the officer was William Francis Bartlett.*

Colonel, The ("The Leader," "The Young Man," "The Youth," "Chief," "The Soldier"). In "The Scout toward Aldie," he is the recently married commanding officer of the party ordered to pursue the elusive [John Singleton] Mosby. After the Colonel is killed from ambush, his body is brought back to his bride, who has been waiting in his tent for him to return. This unfortunate officer is based on Colonel Charles Russell Lowell, who was the nephew of the author James Russell Lowell and whose bride, Josephine Shaw Lowell, was with him at his camp in Virginia not long before he was killed at the Battle of Cedar Creek, on the very day he was promoted to brigadier general (19 October 1864). Melville heard about Lowell while he was with his cousin Colonel Henry Sanford Gansevoort* in Virginia (April 1864) and not long thereafter learned of the young man's death.
Bibliography: Garner, NN 11, Warren.

" 'The Coming Storm': A Picture by S.R. Gifford" (1866). (Full title: " 'The Coming Storm': A Picture by S.R. Gifford, and owned by E.B. Included in the N.A. Exhibition, April, 1865.") Poem, in *Battle-Pieces.* (Characters: E.B. [Edwin Thomas Booth], S.R. [Robert Swain] Gifford.) In the poem, Melville suggests that the great Shakespearean actor who owned the painting—of "[a] demon-cloud" descending upon an "urned lake"—must, since he had delved to "Shakspeare's [sic] core" and found "Man's final lore" there, have somehow anticipated a personal tragedy. We "feel for him / Who felt this picture." Edwin Thomas Booth's brother, John Wilkes Booth, assassinated President Abraham Lincoln.* Robert Swain Gifford, from Massachusetts, was a popular painter and Cooper Union art teacher. Melville saw Gifford's painting at the National Academy in New York (April 1865).
Bibliography: Adler, Garner, NN 11, Shurr.

"Commemorative of a Naval Victory" (1866). Poem, in *Battle-Pieces.* These sailors are gentle, strong, good, and refined by discipline. Years later, a survivor's victory causes women to look his way and enriches "October sunsets." Yet the laureled survivor remembers casualties that "[s]leep in oblivion" beneath the gliding shark. The unnamed victor may have been Melville's cousin Guert Gansevoort* or the more renowned David Glasgow Farragut.*
Bibliography: Cohen, *Poems;* Garner; NN 11; Shurr.

Commodore. In "Donelson," he is the commander of the gunboats that are damaged during the siege of Donelson.

Commodore. In *White-Jacket,* he is the silent senior captain in command of several ships. His presence aboard Captain Claret's *Neversink* has a numbing effect on everyone. The Commodore is small, skinny, and old, and he is reputed to be virtuous. The naval career of the fictitious Commodore aboard the *Neversink* parallels to some degree the real career of Commodore Thomas ap Catesby Jones,* even though no commodore was on board while Melville served (1843–1844) on the *United States,* the *Neversink* prototype.
   Bibliography: NN 5.

Commodore, The. In *Typee,* he is the commander of the naval vessel aboard which the narrator later served when he entered the bay of Nukuheva. King Mowanna's tattooed wife comes aboard.

The Confidence-Man (1857). (Full title: *The Confidence-Man: His Masquerade.*) Novel. (Characters: Arrian, Black Guinea, Daniel Boone, Brade, Brade, Bright Future, Charlemont, China Aster, William Cream, the Deacon, Jeremy Diddler, Egbert, Mrs. Fry, Thomas Fry, Goneril, Francis Goodman, Dr. Green, Judge James Hall, General [William] Hull, the Methodist, Mocmohoc, Moredock, Moredock, Colonel John Moredock, Mrs. Moredock, Mrs. John Moredock, Charles Arnold Noble, Old Conscience, Old Honesty, Old Plain Talk, Old Prudence, Orchis, Mrs. Orchis, the Philosophical Intelligence Office Man, Pitch, John Ringman, Henry Roberts, John Truman, Weaver, Mark Winsome, Wright.)
   The reader finds himself aboard the *Fidèle,* a steamboat on the Mississippi River heading south at sunrise from St. Louis toward New Orleans, on 1 April 18—. The titular "hero," who figures in most scenes, changes appearance and also names. He is seen on the upper and lower decks, in the quarters for emigrants, on a side balcony astern, and in the ladies' saloon, the barber shop, and the cabin. He evinces extraordinary abilities. Daylight is the time of the first half of the book (Chapters 1–23); nighttime, the second (Chapters 24–45). In the first part, the confidence man adopts six or seven different disguises. At night, he is uniformly the so-called "cosmopolitan." In chapter after chapter, he talks with various passengers; in the process, he tells anecdotes and listens to anecdotes told to him about passengers. Interruptions in the narrative take the form of intercalary lectures by the author on the nature of fiction.
   In more detail . . . the "hero," stepping aboard the *Fidèle,* is in cream colors; has come from a distance; is deaf, dumb, harmless, and simple; and scribbles on a slate about charity. At an early stop, he disappears. A "negro cripple" named Black Guinea hobbles up, asks for alms and sympathy, but his disability is doubted. A widower calling himself John Ringman speaks to an apparent acquaintance, who denies knowing him. Ringman obtains money from a merchant named Henry Roberts and tries to persuade him to invest in a coal com-

pany, then criticizes a young student for reading a cynic's book. A sanctimonious-looking man in a gray coat seeks contributions to aid Seminole widows and orphans, fails to get anything, and leaves as a clergyman enters. The clergyman talks with others and voices his mistrust in general, but he donates money to a stranger in an immaculate coat for his plan for the World's Charity. A man later called John Truman asks the scholar where the widower is; when Truman says he wants to invest in the coal company, the student, eager to be duped, is allowed to purchase shares from Truman himself. Truman encounters Roberts in the gaming room, where they discuss a miser dying aboard and also Black Guinea. Roberts tells Truman what Ringman told him about his marriage to a vicious wife named Goneril who evilly influenced their daughter. Truman suggests we need to have confidence in God. (The author, in Chapter 14, digresses on the need for consistency in fictional characters, despite incongruities in nature.)

Truman descends to the emigrants' quarters and persuades a coughing miser to invest in a nostrum called the Omni-Balsamic Reinvigorator and sold by an herb doctor, who sells some to an invalid and hawks his Samaritan Pain Dissuader in an ante-cabin. When a yokel slugs him, he leaves, after which some strangers argue as to his sincerity. The herb doctor returns, questions a man on crutches, and learns he was jailed as a witness to a murder and became diseased in his legs; the murderer got off, anyway, through influential friends. When the herb doctor doubts all this, the man hobbles away, says he is a wounded Mexican War veteran, and is showered with coins by passengers. The herb doctor cannot help the miser recover his money from Truman, who disembarks. A Missouri bachelor named Pitch approaches, and he and the herb doctor discuss the subject of confidence; but Pitch harangues about natural disasters, worthless child laborers, and slaves. When the herb doctor gets off at Cape Girardeau, an agent from the Philosophical Intelligence Office enters, persuades Pitch to have more faith in lads, and leaves at Cairo. Frank Goodman, the vividly garbed ''cosmopolitan,'' tells Pitch to regard life as a picnic, and has his hand shaken for seeming to be a new Diogenes. Goodman encounters Charlie Noble, who seems to be a Mississippi operator and who relates the story of Colonel John Moredock, the Indian hater. Noble adds that Pitch is a shallow misanthrope whereas Moredock was a profound one. Noble and Goodman share some wine; praise conviviality, humor, laughter, and tobacco; wonder whether Pitch's surliness hides generosity; and argue about loaning money. (The author now digresses, in Chapter 33, to deplore some readers' demands that fiction, written only to entertain, be faithful to life.)

Goodman asks Noble if he would ignore a friend in need of money. Noble says no; listens to Goodman's story about a ''gentleman-madman'' named Charlemont, who turns ''from affable to morose'' overnight; and pleads a headache and leaves. Mark Winsome, fresh-faced and looking mystical, enters, warns Goodman about Noble, then veers into transcendental talk, whereupon Goodman avers that beauty and goodness being compatible, he does not fear the rattlesnake, which is beautiful. When a "crazy beggar . . . peddling a rhapsodical tract" and with "raven curls" comes by, Goodman purchases one; but Winsome, looking like "a cold prism," frowns him away, then explains that Noble is untrustworthy. Practical Egbert validates by experience the theoretical beliefs of his friend and mentor Winsome, who leaves. Goodman asks Egbert, to test his thoughts, whether he would loan money to a friend. Egbert replies that a loan for interest would be wrongly commercial, while giving alms would wrongly support beggars. Egbert shakes Goodman's confidence by relating the story of China Aster, a Ohio candlemaker who accepted a loan, expanded his business, failed, and died. Goodman goes to the *Fidèle* barber shop, is shaved by the barber, William Cream, is discomfited by the "No Trust" sign above the chair, and promises to pay for all deadbeats if Cream will remove the sign. When Cream agrees, Goodman walks out without paying. (In Chapter 44, the author digresses on the subject of fictional characters; they come from life but are touched by the writer's imagination.)

Goodman enters the gentlemen's cabin, finds an old man reading the Bible there, and points to a passage in the Apocrypha urging people to doubt the goodness of others. The two agree that distrusting people is tantamount to distrusting their Creator. When the old man asks for a life preserver, the cosmopolitan hands him a stool and leads him through the darkness to his stateroom.

The Confidence-Man followed Melville's unsuccessful novels *Pierre* and *Israel Potter,* his collection of attractive but ill-paying stories in *The Piazza Tales,* and other short works. *The Confidence-Man* reflects Melville's bitterness. Much in it may derive from his anguish at needing to accept charity, specifically from his father-in-law Lemuel Shaw,* whose loan enabled the author to buy Arrowhead, where he wrote *The Confidence-Man.* In it Goodman and Noble drink, smoke, and talk convivially but also hypocritically, as Melville imagined that he and Evert Duyckinck* did. The cessation of friendship between Melville and Nathaniel Hawthorne* may be echoed in the loss of intimacy between Goodman and Noble. The model for Melville's shape-shifter was "the original confidence man." The term was coined for a New York City con artist named William Thompson and also known by several aliases; his exploits were given considerable newspaper coverage (1849, 1855). Melville moved his con man to the Mississippi River, to restrict his narrative time and place to a brief voyage of a ship of faithless fools. In 1840 Melville had visited Peter Gansevoort (1788–1876),* his uncle who lived in Galena, Illinois, on the Mississippi River, and may have returned east by way of the Mississippi to Cairo, Illinois, and then up the Ohio River. In addition to using personal memories, Melville appropriated passages from James Hall's *Sketches of History, Life, and Manners, in the West* (1835) concerning John Moredock; descriptions of the Mississippi River from Timothy Flint's *A Condensed Geography and History of the Western States; or, The Mississippi Valley* (1828); perhaps descriptions and anecdotes from the sarcastic, mean-minded works of Charles Dickens, namely *American Notebooks* (1842) and *Martin Chuzzlewit* (1844); and probably other sources. Winsome may be a satirical portrait by Melville of Ralph Waldo Emerson,* while Egbert, Winsome's follower, may owe something to Henry David Thoreau.* Melville's jibes at Ringman's prickly wife Goneril may have been inspired by Melville's knowledge of gossip about the actress Frances Anne Kemble.* Edgar Allan Poe* may have been a model for the beggar with the tract. It has been suggested that, in all, the novel satirizes well over thirty prominent persons, especially politicians, of the 1850s. Melville also drew on his knowledge of contemporary writers, native malefactors and pranksters, and classical literary analogues, for example, Geoffrey Chaucer and his gallery of characters in *The Canterbury Tales.*

The Confidence-Man has the unity of time and place but hardly of action—except that the plot is a sequence of successful and failed con jobs. It is paced by the three digressions concerning truth in art; and it is livened by five little interpolated stories—about Goneril, the lame supposed soldier, Moredock, Charlemont, and China Aster. To the end of the story a puzzle remains. Was Melville's purpose in writing it to preach by allegorical satire or to mirror a fallen world by realistic character sketches? Hawthorne signed for Melville the contract with Longman, Brown, Green, Longmans, & Roberts, the London publishers of *The Confidence-Man* (20 March 1857). Does it help to know that the novel was published on April Fool's Day, 1857?

Bibliography: Warner Berthoff, *The Example of Melville* (Princeton, N.J.: Princeton University Press, 1962); John Bryant, "*The Confidence-Man:* Melville's Problem Novel," pp. 315–50 in Bryant, *Companion;* Bryant, *Repose;* John G. Cawelti, "Some Notes on the Structure of *The Confidence-Man,*" *American Literature* 29 (November 1957): 278–88; Susan Kuhlmann, *Knave, Fool, and Genius: The Confidence Man as He Appears in Nineteenth-Century American Fiction* (Chapel Hill: University of North Carolina Press, 1973); Lebowitz; NN 10; Tom Quirk, *Melville's Confidence Man: From Knave to Knight* (Columbia: University of Missouri Press, 1982); Edward H. Rosenberry, *Melville and the Comic Spirit* (Cambridge, Mass.: Harvard University Press, 1955); Lawrance Thompson, *Melville's Quarrel with God* (Princeton, N.J.: Princeton University Press, 1952); Trimpi.

"The Conflict of Convictions (1860–1)" (1866). Poem, in *Battle-Pieces.* This complex, disunified work contains seven stanzas of from two to twelve lines each in length, in roman type, alternating with six short stanzas, of from four to five lines each, in italic type, and then ending with a single six-line stanza in roman capital letters. Melville opens the poem by describing the mood just before "man's latter fall," the Civil War (but without specifying the conflict). The stanzas in roman type generally present hope, but not always. The stanzas in italic type advise a more realistic approach—that of watching, waiting, and doubting. The first long stanzas suggest that evil is skillful while purity is naively enthusiastic, but that faith can conquer "[t]he terrors of truth and dart of death." Amid these thoughts comes a call to "*Dismantle the fort*" and "*Cut down the fleet,*" though with care and patience. The first expression of doubt is followed by an italicized sneer at the thought that victory will be followed by any kind of iron-sturdy political regime. Then appears a metaphor in roman type: "I know a wind in purpose strong— / It spins *against* the way it drives." This astounding image may be meant to convey the idea that progress is inevitably countervailed by evil. Fundamental change must be preceded by exposing the "slimed foundations" of the present world. The conclusion? "Age after age shall be / As age after age has been." God lets both sides have their say but remains indifferent; therefore, both wisdom and prophecies are in vain. Melville's implicit message is that tangled theological, ethical, and political convictions are terribly dangerous.

Bibliography: Adler; Cohen, *Poems;* Garner; NN 11; Shurr; Warren.

Constable, John (1776–1837). English landscape painter. Constable was born at East Bergholt, Suffolk, attended school at Dedham, and worked at his father's water mill. After some artists recognized his ability, he studied in London (1795–1797), returned home to menial work, became a student at the Royal Academy (from 1799), exhibited his first landscape (1802), began to create realistic English landscapes and studies of rural English life (1803–1807), and improved his technique by copying portraits (1806–1809). He was poor until the death of his father (1816). Among Constable's most notable paintings are *Wivenhoe Park* (1816), *Flatford Mill* (1817), *The Hay Wain* (1821), *Salisbury Cathedral from the Bishop's Grounds* (1823), *Brighton Beach* (1824), *The Leaping Horse* (1825), *The Cornfield* (1826), *Dedham Vale* (1828), *Watermeadows near Salisbury* (1831), *Salisbury Cathedral from the Meadows* (1831), and *Arundale Mill and Castle* (1837). A few of his works won awards in France and influenced painters there (from 1824). Constable married Maria Bicknell in 1816. After she had seven children, her death at age forty (1828) profoundly depressed him. The range of Constable's paintings is usually limited to a small section of southern England; however, their veracity, atmosphere, and swirling power have the mark of admirable originality.

In Melville's collection of engravings was one of a work by Constable. In "Marquis de Grandvin: At the Hostelry," Constable is mentioned briefly by Paola of Verona [Veronese] in conversation with [Antoine] Watteau.

Bibliography: Michael Rosenthal, *Constable* ([London]: Thames and Hudson, 1987); Wallace.

Constantine I, Emperor ("The Great") (272 or 273–337). (Full name: Flavius Valerius Aurelius Constantinus.) Roman emperor. He was born in Naissus, Moesia (now Niš, in the former Yugoslavia), accompanied various leaders on expeditions to Egypt, Persia, and the West, was proclaimed successor to the throne (306), and eliminated other claimants by military victories ending in Rome— on the way to which a flaming cross together with words meaning "by this sign you will conquer" appeared in the noonday sky before him (312). Becoming emperor of the West (312), he committed himself to Christianity and extended toleration to Christians (from 313), consolidated his position and administered well (314–323), destroyed a final enemy (324), became the one and only Roman emperor, convened the Council of Nicaea, and supervised the adoption of the Nicene Creed (325). Having chosen Byzantium as his capital (323), Constantine renamed it Constantinople after himself (330). He married twice. His first wife, Minervina, was the mother of his son Flavius Julius Crispus. Constantine later married Flavia Maxima Fausta (c. 307), who after bearing him five children evidently told him that Crispus was a traitor. Constantine had him executed (326). Thereafter, he evidently learned that Crispus was innocent and had Fausta executed. Facts concerning these matters are obscure.

In "The Apparition (The Parthenon Uplifted on Its Rock First Challenging the View on the Approach to Athens)," Melville mentions Emperor Constantine as smitten by the Cross, after which he "turned his soul's allegiance there."

Bibliography: Ramsay MacMullen, *Constantine* (London: Weidenfeld and Nicolson, 1970); John Holland Smith, *Constantine the Great* (London: Hamish Hamilton, 1971).

"The Continents" (1947). Poem, in *Collected Poems of Herman Melville.* People in Stamboul praise Allah, enjoy "sherbert," and "Europe hold." Death crosses to the other side. Thus the "Bosphorous parts / Life and Death." Melville wrote ecstatically about the beauty of Constantinople and the Bosporous in his 1856 journal (16–18 December).

Bibliography: NN 15.

C[ooke]., R[obert]. F[rancis]. In "The Paradise of Bachelors and the Tartarus of Maids," a man identified only as R.F.C. is the narrator's bachelor host at the sumptuous dinner of the latter-day Templars in London. He is based on Robert Francis Cooke (1816–1891), who was the cousin and partner of John Murray,* one of Melville's British publishers. In the story, R.F.C.'s brother, the barrister William Henry Cooke, is called only "his imperial brother" and is not even given initials. Cooke was a good friend of and sometimes traveled with George Borrow, author of semiautobiographical books on Spain, including *The Bible in Spain* (1843), and much else. When he was in London, Melville met Cooke at a dinner party given by Murray. Melville recorded his impressions in his 1849 journal and described Cooke as "a round faced chap" seemingly functioning as "Murray's factotum" who pointed out portraits on the walls (23 November). Cooke later entertained Melville at dinner above his chambers in "Elm Court, Temple." In his journal, Melville called its fifth-floor dining room "The Paradise of Batchelors [*sic*]" (20 December).

Bibliography: NN 9 and 15; George Paston, *At John Murray's: Records of a Literary Circle, 1843–1892* (London: John Murray, 1932).

Coonskins. In *The Confidence-Man,* this is the nickname by which Charles Arnold Noble refers to Pitch.

Cooper, James Fenimore (1789–1851). Novelist. He was born in Burlington, New Jersey, attended Yale (1803–1805), and went to sea briefly (1806) and then again as a member of the U.S. Navy (1808–1811). His first three significant novels are *The Spy* (1821), *The Pioneers* (1823), and *The Pilot* (1823). He followed *The Pioneers,* which was the first volume of his famous Leatherstocking series, with four others over a period of years. Cooper married Susan Augusta DeLancey in 1811. The couple had five daughters (one of whom died in infancy) and two sons (one of whom died in infancy). Cooper traveled abroad with his family (1826–1833), returned home and waxed critical of his native land, and suffered a loss of popularity as a consequence. He published *The History of the Navy of the United States of America* (1839). Involving himself in the controversy surrounding the *Somers* mutiny (1842), he argued against the position of Captain Alexander Slidell Mackenzie and Melville's cousin Guert Gansevoort.* Among Cooper's dozens of novels is *The Red Rover; or, The Lost Sealers: a Tale of the Antarctic Ocean* (1828), which Melville reviewed, in an essay called "Cooper's New Novel," for the *Literary World,* edited by his friend Evert Duyckinck.* When Cooper died, Rufus Wilmot Griswold, Washington Irving,* and Fitz-Green Halleck headed a committee to hold a Cooper Demonstration in New York. Melville was invited to participate, declined, but sent a letter to Griswold in which he praised Cooper as "a great, robust-souled man" (19 December 1851). Cooper's daughter Susan Fenimore Cooper (1813–1894) published a novel entitled *Rural Hours* (1850), edited a few of Cooper's novels, and included valuable introductions.

Bibliography: Robert Emmet Long, *James Fenimore Cooper* (New York: Continuum, 1990); NN 14; Thomas Philbrick, *James Fenimore Cooper and the Development of American Sea Fiction* (Cambridge, Mass.: Harvard University Press, 1961).

"Cooper's New Novel" (1849). Review. Melville published a review of *The Red Rover; or, The Lost Sealers: a Tale of the Antarctic Ocean* (1828), by James Fenimore Cooper.* The brief essay appeared anonymously in the New York *Literary World* (28 April 1849), edited by Melville's friend Evert Duyckinck.* In it, Melville briefly praises Cooper's intriguing plot, thrilling descriptions, varied characters, and style—which he calls "singularly plain, downright, and truthful." Melville closes by calling Cooper "our National Novelist."

Corps Commander. In "On the Photograph of a Corps Commander." *See* Hancock, Winfield Scott.

Coulter, Martha. In "Poor Man's Pudding and Rich Man's Crumbs," she is William Coulter's pregnant, sick, but uncomplaining wife. She serves the narrator some Poor Man's Pudding, which is made of rice, milk, and salt.

Coulter, Martha. In "Poor Man's Pudding and Rich Man's Crumbs," she is the daughter of William and Martha Coulter. The child died in infancy.

Coulter, William. In "Poor Man's Pudding and Rich Man's Crumbs," he is the poverty-stricken woodcutter who works hard and well for Squire Teamster and whose pregnant wife Martha is weak though, like himself, uncomplaining.

Coulter, William. In "Poor Man's Pudding and Rich Man's Crumbs," he is the son of William and Martha Coulter. The boy died at the age of six.

Count. In *Pierre,* he is a rich foreign scholar who sends a package of excellent books to Plotinus Plinlimmon. Plinlimmon, however, declines to accept them and says that he would prefer a few jugs of Curaçao.

Count. In *White-Jacket,* he is a mincing little courtier who dances attendance upon Pedro II aboard the *Neversink.*

Cousin Chris. In "A Dutch Christmas up the Hudson in the Time of Patroons." *See* Chris, Cousin.

Crab, Sir. In *Clarel,* this is a name by which Rolfe refers to the Elder.

Cramer, William E. (1817–1905). Editor. Cramer knew the Melville family when his own family lived in Waterford, New York, just north of Albany. At first, he knew Melville less well than his brother Gansevoort Melville.* Though blind, Cramer established with his wife the *Wisconsin,* a daily and weekly newspaper in Milwaukee (1846). He regularly puffed Melville, his early writings, and his family. He also assisted in inviting Melville to Milwaukee to lecture on "The South Seas" (25 February 1859) and was hospitable to him at that time.
  Bibliography: Leyda; Merton M. Sealts, Jr., *Melville as Lecturer* (Cambridge, Mass.: Harvard University Press, 1957).

Cranz. In *Pierre,* he was a slave who belonged to General Pierre Glendinning, Pierre's grandfather, and was assigned to work in the stable.

Crash, Captain. In *Omoo,* he is a sailor who was convicted in a lower court at Taloo of seducing a young native woman and hence was banished.

Cream, William. In *The Confidence-Man,* he is the barber aboard the *Fidèle.* He takes down the sign reading "No Trust" when Francis Goodman guarantees him in writing against loss. Goodman then walks out owing Cream the price of a shave. Cream may be a satire of Stephen A. Douglas, the Illinois congressman and adversary of Abraham Lincoln.* Douglas and Cream have been regarded as similar with respect to physical appearance, personality, and speaking style.
  Bibliography: David R. Sewell, "Another Source for the Barber Shop Episode in *The Confidence-Man,*" *Melville Society Extracts* 60 (November 1984): 13–14; Trimpi.

Creole, The. In "The Encantadas," he is a Cuban adventurer who fought for Peruvian independence from Spain and was rewarded by being given Charles' Isle. But neither the Creole nor his dogs could hold the islanders once his deserter-recruits mutinied.

Croesus, A. In "Jack Gentian (omitted from the final sketch of him)," he is a rosy young traveler who gossips about old Gentian.

Crokarky, The Laird of. In *Israel Potter,* he is the Scottish laird whose men want to buy powder and balls from John Paul Jones. He gives them a barrel of pickles instead.

"Crossing the Tropics (from *'The Saya-y-Manto'*)" (1888). Poem, in *John Marr.* When the lonely sailor in this love lyric sees the Pole Star go down and the Southern Cross rise, he especially misses his bride of one night. He longs for her the way "[Vasco da] Gama longed for land," as the ship "swoop[s]" toward the Southern hemisphere. He feels that he has crossed beyond death. A saya-y-manto is a petticoat and mantilla, or a hood arrangement, often Peruvian.
   Bibliography: NN 11, Stein.

Crowfoot, Widow. In "Cock-a-Doodle-Doo!," she is one of the narrator's rural neighbors. She is not the owner of the lusty cock.

"C—'s Lament" (1891). Poem, in *Timoleon.* (Character: [Samuel Taylor] C[oleridge].) The persona explains that all was lovely when both "man and nature seemed divine"; everything was of value then, "[e]ven pain." But now, he says, he "wake[s] by night / With heavy heart"; so one should "lay . . . a stone" at dead youth's head. Melville began to read works by Samuel Taylor Coleridge* in the late 1840s, profited from Coleridge's criticism of William Shakespeare's works, and was influenced by Coleridge's theories as to Romantic aesthetics. "C—'s Lament," however, is less indebted to Coleridge's critical essays than to his bitter 1802 "Ode to Dejection." It should also be added that Melville deleted the name Coleridge, as well as those of Anacreon and Simonides, before calling the present poem simply "C—'s Lament."
   Bibliography: Howard, NN 11, Stein, Shurr.

"The Cuban Pirate" (1924). Poem, in *Weeds and Wildings,* as part of a section entitled "This, That and the Other." The subject is a multicolored West Indian hummingbird. "Summer is your sea," the poet notes, and it "board[s] and ravage[s]" every fair bloom savagely, with furious "passion." The poet asks it, "[A]re you Cupid in disguise / You flying spark of Paradise?"
   Bibliography: Shurr.

Cuff, Garry. In "The Scout toward Aldie," he is supposedly the young Southern woman's African-American servant. He is led by Corporal Chew to his Colonel, who is vainly trying to capture [John Singleton] Mosby. In reality, Cuff is one of Mosby's men in disguise.

"The Cumberland (March, 1862)" (1866). Poem. It was first published in *Harper's New Monthly Magazine** (March 1866) and reprinted in *Battle-Pieces.* The subject is the federal ship *Cumberland,* which "warred and sunk" off Hampton Roads, Virginia (8 March 1862), in action against the Confederate ironclad *Virginia* (formerly the U.S.S. *Merrimac*). Melville states that the noble name of the *Cumberland,* manned by a "brave crew," sounds well when "rolling on the tongue" and that her fame will "outlive the victor's name."
  Bibliography: Boatner; Faust; Leo B. Levy, "Hawthorne, Melville, and the *Monitor,*" *American Literature* 37 (March 1965): 33–40; NN 11.

Cupid. In "The Paradise of Bachelors and the Tartarus of Maids," he is the impudent lad who takes the narrator on a tour through the paper mill where the "maids" toil.

Curtis, George William (1824–1892). Editor, author, and orator. He was born in Providence, Rhode Island, attended school in Jamaica Plains, New York (to 1835), clerked in New York City, participated in the transcendentalists' Brook Farm experiment (1842–1843), and became a farmhand in Concord, Massachusetts (1844–1846). He traveled in Italy, Germany, and the Middle East as a New York *Tribune* correspondent (1846–1850), wrote about the Middle East, returned home and joined the staff of *Harper's New Monthly Magazine** (1853), and wrote its "Easy Chair" editorials (from 1859). He became an associate editor of *Putnam's Monthly Magazine** (1853); when it went bankrupt (1857), he repaid all of its debts. He edited *Harper's Weekly* (from 1863). His speech entitled "The Duties of the American Scholar to Politics and the Times" (1856) proved pivotal in his career; thereafter, he was active in many movements, including abolition, civil service reform, labor rights, and woman suffrage. His most famous lecture was "Political Infidelity," which he gave at least fifty times, from Maine to Maryland (1864–1865). Curtis lectured on English literature at Cornell (1869) and was chancellor of the University of the State of New York (1890–1892). He was a courageous idealist and a fine—if somewhat soft—stylist, once immensely popular. Curtis's books include works on travel (*Nile Notes of a Howadji* [1851], *The Howadji in Syria* [1852]), essays (*Lotus-Eating, a Summer Book* [1852], *Literary and Social Essays* [1894]), social satire (*Potiphar Papers* [1853]), and fiction (*Prue and I* [1856], *Trumps* [1861]). He also edited the historian John Lothrop Motley's correspondence (1889); Charles Eliot Norton edited Curtis's speeches (3 vols., 1893–1894). Curtis married Anna Shaw in 1856 (the couple had three children). His wife's brother was Colonel Robert Gould Shaw, the tragic Civil War hero.

As editor of *Putnam's Monthly Magazine,* Curtis accepted for publication Melville's "Bartleby," "The Bell-Tower," "Benito Cereno," "The Encanta-das," "I and My Chimney," and "The Lightning-Rod Man." In his day, his book *Nile Notes* was sometimes compared to Melville's *Typee.*

Bibliography: Hans-Joachim Lang and Benjamin Lease, "Melville and 'The Practical Disciple': George William Curtis and *The Confidence-Man,*" *Amerikastudien* 26 (1981): 181–91; Gordon Milne, *George William Curtis & the Genteel Tradition* (Bloomington: Indiana University Press, 1956).

Cushing, William Barker (1842–1874). Naval officer. Cushing was born in Delafield, Wisconsin, the youngest of four sons. After their father, a physician, died (1847), their mother moved with her children to Fredonia, New York, and set up a school which her sons helped her manage. William Cushing became a page in the U.S. House of Representatives in Washington (1856). He attended the Naval Academy (1857–1861) but resigned short of graduation to avoid being dismissed for skylarking. Soon after the Civil War began, Cushing became a master's mate (May 1861) with the North Atlantic blockading squadron, and he took an enemy tobacco schooner as a prize vessel in Hampton Roads, Virginia (May 1861). He was promoted to lieutenant (October 1862), led a daring foray into Jacksonville, Florida (November 1862), served in waters off North Carolina (December 1862), engaged Confederate forces near Norfolk, Virginia (April 1863), and participated in later actions, especially off Fort Fisher, North Carolina (August 1863). Then came the action by which he is remembered. On 27 October 1864, Cushing and fourteen other daring men sailed a small steam launch, which had a movable boom fitted with a torpedo in an iron slide, up the Roanoke River, in North Carolina. While under musket and howitzer fire, they approached the *Albemarle,* a Confederate ironclad that had damaged Union vessels and was lying at Plymouth, North Carolina. Cushing lowered the boom so as to place the torpedo under the *Albemarle* overhang, positioned it by pulling on four ropes attached to his body, exploded the torpedo under the enemy vessel's hull, and sank her just as a hundred pounds of grape fired at a ten-foot range hit the little Union launch. Cushing ordered his men to save themselves. Thirteen of the fifteen died or were captured. Cushing swam into a swamp, seized an enemy skiff, rowed into open water, and was picked up by a Union vessel the next night. He was promoted to lieutenant commander; in the winter of 1864–1865, he marked the river channel near Wilmington, North Carolina, by buoys while under fire; he was in on the assault on Fort Fisher, North Carolina (January 1865); and he was the only officer in his command to survive. After the war, Cushing had varied duty. He commanded the *Lancaster* in the Pacific squadron (1865–1867), commanded the *Maumee* in the Asiatic squadron (1868–1869), was an ordnance officer at the Boston Naval Yard (1870–1872), and was promoted to commander (1872) and granted leave because of failing health. Later he took the *Wyoming* into the harbor at Santiago, Cuba, to put a stop to the summary execution of American sailors there (1873). He developed brain fever, was placed in a government hospital for the insane in Washington, D.C. (1874), where he died. He was survived by his wife Katherine Louise Forbes, whom he married in 1870, and by their two daughters.

In Melville's poem ''At the Cannon's Mouth,'' Cushing is the death-defying Union officer who with several other men use a torpedo launch to sink the Confederate ram *Albemarle.*

Bibliography: Ralph J. Roske and Charles Van Doren, *Lincoln's Commando: The Biography of Commander W. B. Cushing, U.S.N.* (New York: Harper, 1957).

Cuticle, Dr. Cadwallader. In *White-Jacket,* he is the heartless physician of the *Neversink* and the ranking surgeon of the fleet. In the presence of Drs. Bandage, Patella, Sawyer, and Wedge, this sixty-year-old, scrawny, bewigged, false-toothed, glass-eyed butcher amputates the wounded foretopman's leg and thereby hastens the once-brawny man's death. Cuticle says that he served under Lord Thomas Cochrane, his fleet admiral more than twenty years earlier. It is possible that Melville based Dr. Cadwallader Cuticle on Dr. William Johnson, surgeon of the Pacific Fleet. But the loathsome character derives less from any real-life naval surgeon than from the Welsh surgeon Cadwallader Morgan in Tobias Smollett's nautical novel *The Adventures of Roderick Random* and from Melville's reading of medical books.

Bibliography: Anderson; Charles R. Anderson, ''A Reply to Herman Melville's *White-Jacket* by Rear-Admiral Thomas O. Selfridge, Sr.,'' *American Literature* 7 (May 1935): 123–44; Smith; Howard P. Vincent, *The Tailoring of Melville's White-Jacket* (Evanston, Ill.: Northwestern University Press, 1970).

Cylinder. In *White-Jacket,* he is a stuttering, club-footed gunner's mate.

Cypriote, The. In *Clarel,* he is a good-looking young man who meets the pilgrims between the Dead Sea and Mar Saba. He relishes wine and love songs. He plans to dip his mother's shroud in the holy Jordan River. Melville may have derived attributes of the Cypriote from Arthur Penrhyn Stanley, *Sinai and Palestine in Connection with Their History* (New York, 1863).

Bibliography: NN 12.

Cyril. In *Clarel,* he is a shrouded, ghostly figure. Formerly a soldier, he now guards a rocky grotto full of skulls at Mar Saba. Melville may have derived this demented monk's name from that of Cyril, a monk mentioned in John Murray's *A Handbook for Travellers in Syria and Palestine* (London, 1858).

Bibliography: NN 12.

D

D'Abrantes, Duchess. In *Israel Potter. See* Abrantes, Duchess D'.

Dacres, Captain Julian. In ''I and My Chimney,'' he is the rich, deceased kinsman of the narrator. Dacres was a former shipmaster and merchant in the Indian trade. The narrator momentarily thought that Dacres had hidden a treasure in the chimney of the house while he lived there.

Daggoo. In *Moby-Dick,* he is a gigantic black from Africa and then Nantucket. He is little Flask's harpooner.

Dago. In ''Benito Cereno,'' he is an intelligent slave, aged forty-six. He digs graves for the Spaniards.

Dainty Dave. In ''Bridegroom-Dick,'' he is a skinny sailing master under whom Bridegroom Dick once studied. It has been suggested that Melville had his cousin Guert Gansevoort* in mind in the characterization of both Dainty Dave and Tom Tight in this poem.
  Bibliography: Garner.

''The Dairyman's Child'' (1924). Poem, in *Weeds and Wildings,* as part of a section entitled ''The Year.'' The subject is depicted as soft as a mild morning, sweet as peach blossoms, and pure as a rosy, snowy fresco or as an opal.
  Bibliography: Shurr.

Dallabdoolmans. In *Redburn,* he is a Lascar sailor from the Indian vessel *Ir-rawaddy.* Redburn learns a great deal by talking with him on the Liverpool docks.

Dan. In *Omoo. See* Black Dan.

Dana, Richard Henry, Jr. (1815–1882). Sailor, lawyer, and author. He was born in Cambridge, Massachusetts, the son of the poet and journalist. Dana interrupted his Harvard education by going to sea and working in California for two years (1834–1836). After graduating with his Harvard class (1837) and attending its law school (1837–1840), he was admitted to the bar and began a lucrative law practice (1840). He published *Two Years before the Mast* about his experiences at sea and in California (1840). He also published *The Seaman's Friend* (1841), a handbook on the duties and rights of sailors, officers, and masters. To the displeasure of conservative Bostonians, he became involved in Free-Soil politics (late 1840s) and defended apprehended fugitive slaves (early 1850s). He vacationed in England (1856) and then in Cuba (1859), publishing *To Cuba and Back* (1859) about the latter trip. For his endangered health, he took a long trip alone around the world (July 1859–September 1860). He became U.S. District Attorney for Massachusetts (1861–1866), edited a book on international law (1866), was sued for plagiarism by the previous editor, and, after a long trial, lost the case (1879). Meanwhile, Dana served in the Massachusetts legislature (1866–1868), was nominated to be minister to England, but was rejected by the Senate (1876), and retired (1878). Dana married Sarah Watson in Hartford, Connecticut, in 1841 (the couple had six children, including Richard Henry Dana III, who married Henry Wadsworth Longfellow's daughter Edith). Toward the end of his life, he traveled abroad with his wife. He died in Rome. His private journal was first published in 1968.

Melville socialized minimally with Dana, who seems never to have sufficiently respected the obviously superior writer. In their sparse correspondence, Melville is frank, open, and detailed, while Dana is brief and sometimes stiff. Dana did help him with names on the occasion of his trip to London to sell *White-Jacket* there (1849). Melville relished *Two Years before the Mast* and notes in *White-Jacket* that Dana's "chapters describing Cape Horn must have been written with an icicle." To Dana he wrote he had thrown the original white jacket—"such a remarkable fabric"—into the Charles River (1 May 1850). In 1853 Dana recommended Melville for a consular position, but his efforts failed, as they did again in 1861. Dana in his journal defined Lemuel Shaw,* Melville's father-in-law, as "a man of intense & doting biasses" (April 1856). Melville in his "Inscription Epistolary to W.C.R.," in *John Marr,* addressed to the British nautical writer William Clark Russell,* praises Dana for knowing the sea, its waters and sailors, and details of sailing.

Bibliography: Robert L. Gale, *Richard Henry Dana, Jr.* (New York: Twayne, 1969); Leyda; NN 14.

Danby. In *Redburn,* he is the dissolute, brutal Yankee husband of Handsome Mary Danby, manageress of the Baltimore Clipper in Liverpool.

Danby, Handsome Mary. In *Redburn,* she is the attractive, forty-year-old English wife of a brutal and dissolute Yankee named Danby. She efficiently manages their Liverpool boardinghouse, called the Baltimore Clipper.

"Daniel Orme" (1924). Sketch, in *The Works of Herman Melville.* (Characters: [Jean] Lafitte, Daniel Orme.) Daniel Orme, who is a burly, reticent old sailor, once the captain of a topmast crew but now in his seventies, has retired to a rooming house ashore. He has a habit of looking at something under his darned shirt. So, one night, some curious fellow roomers drug him, examine his chest, and find the tattoo of a crucifix with a scar running through it. Was the old fellow once a buccaneer? On an Easter Day, Orme is found dead at a height overlooking the sea. He is seated and leaning against a rusty old gun. A variant title for "Daniel Orme" is "Story of Daniel Orme."
Bibliography: Frank Pisano, "Melville's 'Great Haven': A Look at Fort Tompkins," *Studies in American Fiction* 17 (Spring 1989): 111–13.

Danish Sailor. In *Moby-Dick,* he is a *Pequod* sailor who is indifferent to the approaching storm during the midnight festivities in the forecastle.

Dansker, The ("Board-Her-in-the-Smoke"). In *Billy Budd,* he is a grim, scarred old mainmastman and an *Agamemnon* veteran. He laconically tells Billy Budd that John Claggart has it in for Billy. Tragically, the Dansker never interferes and never advises, and fails to interpret or usefully react.
Bibliography: Sharon Baris, "Melville's Dansker: The Absent Daniel in *Billy Budd,*" pp. 153–73 in *The Uses of Adversity: Failure and Accommodation in Reader Response,* ed. Ellen Spolsky (Lewisburg, Pa.: Bucknell University Press, 1990).

Darby. In *Omoo,* this nickname is given by Dr. Long Ghost to an old lover on the beach at Imeeo. His wife is called Joan.

Darfi. In *Mardi,* he is Donjalolo's proud, ambitious uncle. Donjalolo decides to become king of Juam to prevent Darfi from being king.

Dash, Dick. In *White-Jacket,* he is a chivalric midshipman from Virginia. He plays the part of Gin and Sugar Sal in the Fourth of July theatrical. He is later rebuked by the Professor in class.

Dashman, Adolphus. In *White-Jacket,* he is the Commodore's urbane, polished, graceful secretary.

Dates ("Sergeant"). In *Pierre,* he is the impeccable servant of Mary Glendinning and Pierre Glendinning at Saddle Meadows.

Dave. In "Bridegroom-Dick." *See* Dainty Dave.

da Vinci, Leonardo. In "Marquis de Grandvin: At the Hostelry." *See* Leonardo da Vinci.

Deacon, The. In *The Confidence-Man,* he is the person in Francis Goodman's digression whose wife is cured of illness by getting drunk.

Deadlight, Tom. In "Tom Deadlight (1810)," he is a grizzled petty officer who, when he is dying aboard the British *Dreadnought,* says goodbye to his messmates Matt and Jock.

Dead Man, The. In *Clarel,* this is the name by which Rolfe refers to himself when he says that he would like to be buried by a grassy road in the Holy Land.

Dean. In "The Cincinnati." *See* Gentian, Major John, Dean of the Burgundy Club.

"The Death Craft" (1839). Short story attributed to Melville. It was published pseudonymously, as by Harry the Reefer, in the Lansingburgh, New York, *Democratic Press* (16 November 1839). (Characters: The Captain, Harry the Reefer, the Mate.) The narrator, Harry the Reefer, is aboard a ship in a calm so torrid that tar oozes from the ship's seams. He approaches the helmsman, only to discover a decomposing corpse. The Mate screams that they are on a Death Craft and leaps into the ocean. There are human skeletons on the yards. A violent storm suddenly lashes the vessel, and sailors rush past him as though they cannot see him. The Captain shouts orders in a frenzy. All is suddenly calm again. When Harry awakens, he is embracing his bride, whom he left a year earlier.

Bibliography: NN 9; Martin Leonard Pops, *The Melville Archetype* (Kent, Ohio: Kent State University Press, 1970).

Decatur, Stephen (1779–1820). Naval officer. Born at Sinnepuxent, Maryland, he was reared in an illustrious family in Philadelphia, attended the University of Pennsylvania briefly, and worked for a Philadelphia shipping firm. He became a midshipman on the *United States* cruising in the West Indies, was commissioned a lieutenant (1799), and began his adventurous career. He was in the Mediterranean area (1801–1805). During the war with Tripoli, his sabotage of the pirated American frigate *Philadelphia,* commanded by his friend David Porter* until her surrender, was the stuff of which legends are made (1804). Promoted to captain (1804) and home again, Decatur married Susan Walker in Norfolk, Virginia (1806). He fulfilled various official duties until the War of

1812, during which he undertook prize-seeking ventures with a squadron and then with his *United States,* which, by herself, captured the *Macedonian* near Madeira (1812) and took her to New London, Connecticut, and a hero's welcome. At sea again, Decatur was forced to surrender his *President* to British vessels off Long Island (1815—technically after peace had been declared). Lord Admiral Sir Alexander Cochrane Forrester Inglis reported that the *President* was simply overwhelmed. Decatur, in command of nine ships, went to Algiers, threatened to attack, thus pressuring Algerian authorities into paying reparations to American shipping, and did the same at Tunis and Tripoli (1815). At a victory banquet held in Norfolk, Decatur offered this celebrated toast: "Our Country! In her intercourse with foreign nations may she always be in the right; but our country, right or wrong." Prize money made Decatur and his wife wealthy. He served on the Board of Navy Commissions. He opposed the reinstatement of Captain James Barron, who challenged him to a duel and killed him. Porter was present and criticized Barron and Jesse Duncan Elliott, Decatur's rascally second. Captain Alexander Slidell Mackenzie, the officer embroiled in the 1842 *Somers* mutiny controversy, wrote a biography of his fellow officer Decatur (1846). In it Mackenzie says that Elliott, who was the second-in-command under Oliver Hazard Perry* during the battle of Lake Erie (1813), held back his *Niagara* at the beginning of that engagement in the hope that Perry and his *Lawrence* would be destroyed.

In *White-Jacket,* Captain Decatur is the former commanding officer of the fictitious American man-of-war *Neversink,* which is modeled on the aging *United States,* aboard which Melville served (1843–1844). It is mentioned that, during the War of 1812, Decatur captured the British frigate *Macedonian,* commanded by Captain Cardan (*see* Carden, John S.). In "Bridegroom-Dick," Decatur is mentioned as a famous rival officer with whom [Thomas] ap Catesby Jones served.

Bibliography: Charles Lee Lewis, *The Romantic Decatur* (Philadelphia: University of Pennsylvania Press, 1937); David F. Long, *Nothing Too Daring: A Biography of Commodore David Porter, 1780–1843* (Annapolis, Md.: United States Naval Institute, 1970).

Dedications. Melville dedicated the following books to the following persons: *Typee* to Lemuel Shaw,* his father-in-law; *Omoo* to Herman Gansevoort,* his uncle; *Mardi* to Allan Melville,* his brother; *Redburn* to Thomas Melville,* his brother; *Moby-Dick* to Nathaniel Hawthorne*; *Battle-Pieces* to the 300,000 Union soldiers who died in the Civil War; *Clarel* to Peter Gansevoort (1788–1876),* his uncle; *John Marr* to William Clark Russell,* the novelist; *Timoleon* to Elihu Vedder,* the painter; and *Weeds and Wildings* to Elizabeth Knapp Shaw Melville,* his wife. In addition, Melville dedicated *Pierre* to Greylock, "the majestic mountain" in the Berkshires near Arrowhead, and *Israel Potter* to the monument at Bunker Hill, where Israel fought.

Dedidum. In *Mardi,* this is one of the twelve aristocratic Tapparian families on the isle of Pimminee. They are entertained by Nimni there.

Deer, Derick de. In *Moby-Dick,* he is the German captain of the *Jungfrau* of Bremen. She is devoid of sperm oil.

De Grasse. In *Billy Budd. See* Grasse, François Joseph Paul, Marquis de Grasse-tilly, Comte de.

Delano. In "Benito Cereno," he is mentioned as Captain Amasa Delano's brother who died and was buried at sea.

Delano, Captain Amasa. In "Benito Cereno," he is the naive but resolute and brave captain of the *Bachelor's Delight,* a sealer and trader from Duxbury, Massachusetts. When Delano boards Benito Cereno's *San Dominick,* which is under the control of mutinous slaves, he misjudges the situation, suspects the Spaniard of inability to command and also of plotting against him, and trusts nature to reassure and guide him. As a youth, he was nicknamed Jack of the Beach.

Bibliography: William B. Dillingham, *Melville's Short Fiction 1853–1856* (Athens: University of Georgia Press, 1977); Terry J. Martin, "The Idea of Nature in *Benito Cereno,*" *Studies in Short Fiction* 30 (Spring 1993): 161–68.

Del Fonca. In "The Bell-Tower," he is the Florentine painter whose picture of Deborah is said to resemble Una's face.

Democritus, Mrs. In "The Apple-Tree Table," this is the humorous nickname which the narrator gives his wife. He has chosen it because of her energetic, level-headed practicality. These are traits that Melville's wife Elizabeth Knapp Shaw Melville* had.

Demorkriti. In *Mardi,* he is a laughing philosopher cited by Babbalanja in a rare mood of jocosity. Demorkriti is named after the Greek philosopher Democratus (c. 460–c. 370 B.C.), who laughed at humankind's limitations.

Bibliography: Wright.

de Nesle, The Sire. In "L'Envoy: The Return of the Sire de Nesle. A.D. 16—." *See* Nesle, The Sire de.

Denton, Lord Jack. In *Billy Budd,* he is a relative of Captain Edward Fairfax Vere. Denton congratulated Vere for his gallant part in the West Indian cruise under [Admiral Baron George Brydges] Rodney. Denton gave Vere the nickname "Starry."

Dermoddi, Chief. In *Mardi,* he is a Kaleedoni leader. According to King Media, when his subjects became seditious, Dermoddi fled to King Bello of Dominora for protection. The allusions are to Australia and England.
Bibliography: Davis.

De Ruyter, Mikiel Adriaanszoon (1606–1676). Dutch naval officer. He was born in Vlissingen, United Provinces (Netherlands), went to sea at the age of nine, and became a merchant captain (by 1635). He was in combat as a rear admiral in the Dutch fleet aiding Portugal against Spain (1641), returned to the merchant service (1641–1651), and often fought Barbary pirates off the northern coast of Africa. During the First Anglo-Dutch War (1652–1654), he returned to the navy, serving under Maarten Harpertszoon van Tromp, father of Cornelis Maartenszoon van Tromp.* De Ruyter was promoted to vice admiral for a victory at sea off Texel (1653). He fought with Denmark against Sweden (1659) and successfully opposed the British off Africa (1664–1665). During the Second Anglo-Dutch War (1665–1667), as lieutenant admiral he won some battles (1666, 1667) but had a dispute, caused by mutual jealousy, with Cornelis van Tromp and filed an adverse report concerning that man's alleged negligence (1666). The two later became reconciled. During the Third Anglo-Dutch War (1672–1674), De Ruyter achieved his greatest triumphs (1672, 1673). He and Tromp combined forces to defeat the Anglo-French fleet in the North Sea (1673). De Ruyter opposed the French in the Mediterranean and was killed in action off Sicily.
   In "Marquis de Grandvin: At the Hostelry," De Ruyter is mentioned as a sea captain under whom Van der [de] Velde once "cruised."
Bibliography: Charles Wilson, *Power and Profit: A Study of England and the Dutch Wars* (London: Longmans, Green, 1957).

Derwent. In *Clarel,* he is an Anglican priest who is learned, affable, and optimistic, but also professionally irresponsible in his secularism. His name probably derives from that of the Derwent River, praised in William Wordsworth's *Prelude.*
Bibliography: NN 12.

Despairer, The. In *Mardi,* he is a famous warrior of the island of Diranda. At the end of the war games held there by King Hello and King Piko, the Despairer wanders over the Field of Glory in anguish because five of his sons had been killed in such games earlier.

De Squak. In *Redburn,* she is an old black fortune-teller. According to Jack Blunt, her house in Liverpool was much frequented by sailors.

D'Estaing, Count. In *Israel Potter. See* Estaing, Charles Hector, Comte d'.

Devonshire, The Duchess of. In "Poor Man's Pudding and Rich Man's Crumbs," she is one of the aristocratic guests at the Guildhall Banquet in London following the victorious Battle of Waterloo.

"The Devotion of the Flowers to Their Lady" (1924). Poem, in *Weeds and Wildings,* as part of a section entitled "As They Fell." (Character: Clement Drouon.) The poem is attributed to Clement Drouon, an eleventh-century Provençal troubadour turned monk. Subtitled "To Our Queen," it praises the Edenic monarch, expresses regret at exile, and laments the onset of "age, decay, and . . . sorrows."

Diamelo. In "Benito Cereno," he is the calker slave Mure's slave son. He is killed during the attack on the *San Dominick* led by Captain Amasa Delano's chief mate.

Dick. In "Bridegroom-Dick." *See* Bridegroom Dick.

Dick. In *Omoo,* he is a sailor aboard the *Leviathan* at Taloo.

Dick. In *White-Jacket,* he is an assistant surgeon who witnesses Dr. Cadwallader Cuticle's amputation surgery.

Diddledee. In *Mardi,* this is the name of one of the aristocratic Tapparian families on the isle of Pimminee. They are entertained by Nimni. The name Diddledee is surely a derivation of "fiddledeedee."
   Bibliography: Wright.

Diddler, Jeremy. In *The Confidence-Man,* Pitch uses this name in conversation with Francis Goodman to refer derisively to the herb doctor, to the Philosophical Intelligence Office Man, and to Goodman himself.

Dididi. In *Mardi,* he is mentioned by Babbalanja as a digger of trenches.

Didymus. In *Clarel,* he is a person who visits Hafiz in a garden in the song sung by Derwent during the wine party at Mar Saba.

Digby, Colonel. In *Redburn,* he is a person at whose home in Liverpool Redburn's father left his card in 1808.

Diloro. In *Mardi.* he is an authority quoted once by Babbalanja.

Diogenes. In "The Apparition (The Parthenon Uplifted on Its Rock First Challenging the View on the Approach to Athens)," he is mentioned as one who would have been less cynical if he had seen the Parthenon.

"A Dirge for McPherson, Killed in front of Atlanta (July, 1864)" (1866). Poem, in *Battle-Pieces*. (Character: [General James B.] McPherson.) The poet praises this *"Sarpedon of the mighty war"* and urges that his body be accompanied by reversed arms, craped banners and white horses, muffled drums, tolling bells, and a pacing priest, as it moves through the chapel to the grave—until "a trumpet . . . shall rend / This Soldier's sleep." General James Birdseye McPherson* was an especially courageous and attractive Union officer.
   Bibliography: Boatner, Faust.

"Disinterment of the Hermes" (1891). Poem, in *Timoleon*. The message is that it is far better "[t]o dig for" divinely formed old statues "in adamant fair" than to rake for gold in "arid sands." The specific statue inspiring Melville is the Hermes of Praxiteles, discovered by the German Commission at Olympia (1877). Hermes is represented as carrying the child Dionysus on his left arm. The child is not especially well sculpted; however, the nude Hermes, strong, graceful, and healthy, is charmingly posed with his weight on the right leg (in *contropposto*) and holding a bunch of grapes in his right hand above the out-reaching child. It is the only known surviving work by Praxiteles, a few of whose other statues survive in Roman copies.
   Bibliography: NN 11, Shurr, Stein.

"Ditty of Aristippus" (1876). Poem in *Clarel*. It is a hedonistic ditty, both irresponsible and excusable, which depicts the gods as taking their ease after work and indifferent to mortals, whose prayers they might answer if they got around to it. Melville's advice for handling these gods is dour: "Ever blandly adore them; / But spare to implore them." When Edmund Clarence Stedman* asked Melville for a handwritten copy of one of his poems, he copied out the song about Aristippus* sung by the Cypriote, called it "Ditty of Aristippus," and sent it to Stedman (29 January 1888).
   Bibliography: Leyda, NN 12 and 14, Shurr.

Dives. In "The Piazza," this is the name assigned by the narrator to his neighbor who laughs at the idea of a piazza on the north side of a house.

Divino. In *Mardi,* he is a wealthy pilgrim to Ofo on the isle of Maramma. He refuses to pay Pani, the blind guide.

Djalea ("The Druze," "Lord Djalea," "The Emir"). In *Clarel,* he is a Lebanese emir's exiled son. Djalea is the guide and leader of the pilgrimage guards. He is noble, self-possessed, serene, dignified, unusually quiet, and thoughtful. He rides a beautiful mare, named Zar, expertly and without using spurs.

Dobs. In *White-Jacket,* he is a sailor who with Hodnose is accused by a Down Easter sailor of stealing his dunderfunk.

Doc. In *Pierre,* he is Glendinning's loyal African-American servant.

Doc. In "The Scout toward Aldie." *See* the Surgeon.

Doctor, The. In *Redburn. See* Thompson.

Dods, Daniel. In *Redburn,* he is an old friend of Jonathan Jones. In 1798 Dods gave Jones a copy of Adam Smith's *An Enquiry into the Nature and Causes of the Wealth of Nations,* which Jones's son gives to Redburn.

Dolci, Carlo ("Carlino") (1618–1686). Italian painter. He was born in Florence and worked there all of his life. He gained fame when only sixteen years old by painting strong, realistic portraits. Thereafter, he painted mostly religious subjects, including the excellent *Martyrdom of St. Andrew* (1646). He also produced small works, sometimes on copper. He combined languid piety, smooth, sweet surfaces with realistic details, and contrasting shades. Dolci is one of the last representatives of the Florentine baroque style. In Melville's poem "Marquis de Grandvin: At the Hostelry," Carlo Dolce, mentioned as a fastidious painter, discusses the picturesque with [Adriaen] Brouwer.
   Bibliography: George Hay, *Carlo Dolci* (New York: F. A. Stokes, 1910).

Doldrum. In *Mardi,* he is a lachrymose legatee mentioned in Bardianna's will. As his name suggests, he is in the doldrums.

Doleful Dumps. In *The Confidence-Man,* this is the nickname of Orchis before he won a large sum of money in the lottery.

Dominican, The. In *Clarel,* he is a French Catholic priest who, when the pilgrims are at the shore of the Jordan River, tells them about his religious beliefs.

Don, The. In "Marquis de Grandvin: At the Hostelry." *See* Spagnoletto.

Donald. In *Billy Budd,* he is Billy Budd's shipmate. According to another shipmate's poem, entitled "Billy in the Darbies," Donald promised Billy to stand by his plank at burial.

"Donelson (February, 1862)" (1866). Poem, in *Battle-Pieces.* (Characters: Baldy, Commodore, General [Ulysses S.] Grant, Colonel [William Ralls] Morrison, [General] Lew Wallace.) Northern civilians crowd around a rain-washed bulletin board to read reports—in italic type—of the Union siege of Confederate-held Fort Donelson. The rebels mount a sortie, then retreat to the chilly fort, where the *"ramrod bites / The lip it meets."* Union sharpshooters *"lurk / Like Indians that waylay the deer / By the wild salt-spring."* Another enemy attack is repulsed by *"a blast / Of shrapnel and quick shell."* A Union naval victory is followed by Grant's receipt of reinforcements. Wounded Union soldiers, falling in the snow, "*stiffened—perished.*" Another attack "*[v]omited out of Donelson*" like a tide; though dueled back, the rebels remained "*on conquered ground*" a while. The bulletin board resembles a "storm-beat graveyard stone." "*Storms at the West derange the wires*" until "VICTORY!" is flashed. That night, while casualties are tabulated near Donelson, some Northern civilians celebrate with undiluted punch but others scan "[t]he death-list [that] like a river flows / Down the pale sheet." The poet prays for an end to both "wail and triumph." The Union attack on Fort Donelson, which was located on the Cumberland River, Tennessee, occurred 13–16 February 1862.

Bibliography: Adler, Boatner, Faust, NN 11, Warren.

Don Hannibal Rohon Del Aquaviva. In *Clarel. See* Hannibal, Rohon Del Aquaviva, Don.

Donjalolo, King ("Fonoo"). In *Mardi,* he is the twenty-five-year-old absolutist king of the island of Juam. Though charitable, he is also effeminate, whimsical, and dissolute. His nickname "Fonoo" means "the Girl." His background suggests parallels to the reign of Kamehameha I* of Hawaii. The name Donjalolo may come from Du Djailolo, one of the islands in the Moluccas.

Bibliography: Davis.

Don Pedro. In *White-Jacket. See* Pedro II.

Don Quixote. *See* Quixote, Don.

Donna. In "Marquis de Grandvin: Naples in the Time of Bomba . . . ," she is a fictitious girl with a sweet voice in an unaging region.

Donno. In *Mardi,* he is one of Karrolono's retainers. Donno envies his master and is, in turn, envied by Flavona.

Doodle. In "On the Chinese Junk," he is identified as "king of the Yankees."

Dou, Gerard (1613–1675). (Alternate spellings: Douw, Dow; Gerrit.) Dutch genre and portrait painter. He was born in Leiden, the son of a glassmaker and engraver, who taught him as a child and apprenticed him to an engraver and then a painter on glass. Studying with the young Rembrandt* (1628–1631), Dou adopted his drawing methods and use of chiaroscuro. After painting several Rembrandt-like portraits, including one of the master's mother (c. 1630), Dou turned to domestic scenes, full of workers and edibles, with pots, pans, vegetables, cloth, shields, and skulls. Famous and sought after by the 1660s, Dou was highly paid for his glowing works, with their pure and dustless colors, meticulously smooth surfaces, subtle shadows, and narrative contents. He popularized niche pieces, i.e., scenes which both painter and viewer see through stone-framed windows or arches, and also subjects seen by candlelight. His biggest, most complex canvas is *The Quack* (1652). In it, while the artist holds his palette and looks knowingly at the viewer through an arched window, below him the central figure, a deceptive quack, is hawking his wares; some fifteen people, forming a loose triangle outside, are busy in different ways—boy tries to catch bird, woman sells pancakes, mother wipes baby's bottom, and so on—in left foreground, grotesque tree trunk; in distance, church and windmill.

In "Marquis de Grandvin: At the Hostelry," Gerard Douw is the painter who joshes Van der [de] Velde by saying that he likes old oak in furniture, not ships. Douw also describes Phillis as plucking a pheasant in a picturesque manner.

Bibliography: Svetlana Alpers, *The Art of Describing: Dutch Art in the Seventeenth Century* (Chicago: University of Chicago Press, 1983).

Dough-Boy. In *Moby-Dick,* he is the pale-faced steward of the *Pequod.* Tashtego terrifies him with a scalping knife. Dough-Boy times the spouting of whales and is rebuked for offering ginger-jub to Queequeg.

Douw. In *Pierre,* he is a stable slave of General Pierre Glendinning, Pierre's grandfather.

Dow Jr. In "A Short Patent Sermon According to Blair, the Rhetorician: No. C.C.C.C.L.XXX.V.III," he is the author of patent sermons in the Sunday Mercury of the sort satirized here in a spoof following the outline for speeches provided by Blair. The target of this satire is Elbridge G. Paige, part owner of the New York *Sunday Mercury* and author of popular "Short Patent Sermons" published in it as by Dow Jr.

Bibliography: NN 9.

Doxodox. In *Mardi,* he is a verbose, so-called sage man who inhabits an island west of Hamora. Doxodox's name comes from *doxa* (Greek for "opinion"). Melville derives Babbalanja's witty reply to Doxodox's prolixity from *Cyclopedia; or, An Universal Dictionary of Arts and Science* by Ephraim Chambers (2 vols., London, 1728).

Bibliography: Davis, Wright.

Dragoni, Prince. In *Mardi,* he is a person in a manuscript chronicle in Oh-Oh's museum.

Drinker, Tobias. In *Redburn,* this is the name on a tombstone in Liverpool. Redburn finds a drunkard asleep on it.

Drouon, Clement. In "The Devotion of the Flowers to Their Lady," he is an eleventh-century Provençal troubadour who became a monk. The poem is attributed to Drouon.

Drouth, Daniel. In "A Grave near Petersburg, Virginia," this is supposedly the name of a Confederate soldier buried near Petersburg, Virginia, by retreating soldiers. In reality, however, a heavy gun is buried beneath the headboard against a hoped-for return of the Rebels.

Druze, The. In *Clarel. See* Djalea.

Dua. In "The Bell-Tower," this is the garlanded hour of two, which holds Una's hand on the clock bell.

Duke, The. In *Redburn,* he is the white-whiskered old master of Aladdin's Palace, the opulent establishment that Redburn visits with Harry Bolton when they go to London.

Duke of Wellington, The. In *Redburn* and "Poor Man's Pudding and Rich Man's Crumbs." *See* Wellington, Arthur Wellesley, The First Duke of.

Dumdi. In *Mardi,* he is a philosopher cited by Babbalanja. Dumdi defined life as "a febral vibration of organic parts, operating on the vis inertia of unorganized matter." This theory is opposed by Babbalanja. Melville picked up Dumdi's belief from a theory espoused in David Hartley's *Observations on Man, His Frame, His Duty, and His Expectations* (London, 1749).
  Bibliography: Davis.

Dundonald, Donald. In *Pierre,* he is the chairman of the lecture committee of the Urquhartian Club for the Extension of Knowledge. When Dundonald invites Pierre to lecture on Zadockprattsville, he respectfully declines.

Dundonald, Thomas Cochrane, 10th Earl of (1775–1860). British naval officer. He was born at Annsfield, Lanarkshire. He went to sea (1793), commanded a brig (1800), captured a Spanish frigate (1801), and was audaciously vocal as a member of Parliament (1806–1809) in denouncing naval abuses. At one point, he brought accusations against an admiral, fell into disfavor with his superiors, and did not see duty again for many years. In the meantime, he began speculating in stocks, as did his dishonest uncle, who was exposed, tried, and convicted of fraud along with some of his associates. Lord Cochrane was convicted as well, was imprisoned for a year, and was expelled from Parliament. He then accepted the invitation of the government of Chile to command their navy (1817–1822) during the revolt of Chile against Spain. He captured the Spanish frigate *Esmeralda* in Callao harbor (1820). He served under Dom Pedro I of

Brazil in its rebellion against Portugal (1823–1825). After trying without notable success to serve the Greek government, he returned to England (1828), was allowed to reenter the British navy (1832), and rose to the command of the North American and West Indian station (1848–1851). This daring, resourceful, but imprudent man often busied himself with scientific inventions, ones having to do, for example, with excavating, lamps, ship propulsion, and steam engines. Cochrane secretly married Katherine Corbett Barnes of the Midlands in Annan, Scotland, in 1812. The union caused a rich uncle to disinherit him. The couple had four sons, including Thomas 11th Earl of Dundonald and Arthur Auckland Leopold Pedro, who became an admiral and the commander-in-chief in the Pacific (1873–1876). Among other works, the 10th Earl wrote *Notes on the Mineralogy, Government and Conditions of the British West India Islands* (1851), *Narrative of Services in the Liberation of Chili, Peru and Brazil* (1858), and *Autobiography of a Seaman* (2 vols., 1860–1861), which, though faulty, his son Thomas used as his main source when he coauthored a biography of his father (2 vols., 1869).

In *White-Jacket,* Melville has Dr. Cadwallader Cuticle assert that more than twenty years earlier he served under Lord Cochrane when he was admiral of the Brazilian fleets.

Bibliography: Christopher Lloyd, *Lord Cochrane: Seaman, Radical, Liberator; A Life of Thomas, Lord Cochrane, 10th Earl of Dundonald* (London: Longmans, Green, 1947).

Dunk. In *Omoo,* he is a Danish sailor aboard the *Julia.* He continues to serve aboard her.

Dunker, Mrs. In *Pierre,* she is a fictitious deceased dowager in a German prince's proclamation imagined by Pierre.

Dupetit-Thouars, Abel Aubert (1793–1864). French naval officer. Born in Turquant, France, he became a cabin boy at the age of eleven and a midshipman at fifteen. He served off Algiers (1830), was a naval commandant off Peru during its quarrel with France (1834), and was named captain of the *Vénus* for a voyage around the world (1836–1839). During this time, Dupetit-Thouars intervened to counter the success of Protestant missionaries in the Sandwich Islands by sailing into Honolulu and forcing King Kamehameha III* to decree more tolerance (July 1837). When George Pritchard,* British consul at Papeete, Tahiti, persuaded Queen Pomare (*see* Pomare IV) to expel two French Catholic missionaries (1836–1837), Dupetit-Thouars, under orders received at Valparaiso, Chili, sailed into her harbor and demanded an apology and an indemnity under threat of bombarding the island. The queen submitted and also gave the French favorable trading rights (August 1838). Dupetit-Thouars helped install Jacques-Antoine Moerenhout* as French consul in Tahiti (September) and returned to France (June 1839), which he recommended should counter British influence in

Hawaii and Tahiti by exploiting the Marquesas Islands militarily and commercially, as well as a place for deported prisoners (1839). France agreed (1841).

Dupetit-Thouars was promoted to vice admiral and placed in command of the Pacific station (1841). He arrived at Valparaiso aboard the *Reine Blanche* (March 1842), proceeded to the Marquesas Islands (April), seized a pair of islands in the group (May, June), and went back to Papeete to demand better treatment of French settlers, including Catholic ones, allegedly being mistreated in Tahiti (August). Pomare granted France, now claiming Tahiti as a protectorate, control over foreign affairs and, in return, obtained respect for her rule, native ownership of land and freedom of worship, and protection of British missionaries (September). Dupetit-Thouars, after naming Moerenhout head of an advisory council, went back to Valparaiso (October 1842), but he had to return to Tahiti yet again, this time to dispute with Queen Pomare over flag-flying, depose her, and annex Tahiti to France (November 1843). He tactlessly installed Armand-Joseph Bruat* as governor and Moerenhout as director of internal affairs. France, however, rescinded this precipitate action (February 1844). (Pritchard got himself deported [March 1844] for refusing to recognize the treaty.) By this time, Dupetit-Thouars had published his *Voyage autour du monde sur la frégate la Vénus pendant les années 1836 . . . 1839* (4 vols., 1843). He was replaced as Pacific commandant (July 1844), was promoted to vice admiral (1846), became deputy of Maire-et-Loire (1849), and was assigned to the Academy of Sciences (1855). He died in Paris. Native resistance to the French remained violent in Tahiti from the 1840s, and Anglo-Polynesian Protestantism dominated for many decades thereafter.

Melville mentions Admiral Du Petit Thouars in *Typee* and *Omoo*. He is identified in *Typee* as the commander of the French naval forces ordered to subjugate the peaceful Marquesas Islands and Queen Pomare's Tahiti. His ship is named as the *Reine Blanche*. In *Omoo*, Melville identifies him as the commander of the *Reine Blanche* in the harbor of Papeetee and adds that he has left the hated Bruat as the governor of Tahiti behind him.

Bibliography: Robert Aldrich, *The French Presence in the South Pacific, 1842–1940* (Honolulu: University of Hawaii Press, 1990); *Britain in the Pacific Islands* (Oxford, England: Clarendon Press, 1960); Newbury; O'Reilly and Teissier.

Dupont, Samuel Francis (1803–1865). (Alternate name forms: DuPont, Du Pont.) Naval officer. Dupont was born in Bergen Point, New Jersey, joined the U.S. Navy as a midshipman (1815), and slowly advanced in rank—to lieutenant (1826), commander (1843), and captain (1855). At the outbreak of the Civil War, he headed efforts to blockade the South Atlantic. His success at Port Royal, South Carolina (7 November 1861), gained him promotion to rear admiral (1862). Dupont failed, however, in later attacks against Charleston defenses (1863), was refused permission to publish an explanation that his ironclads were not impervious to shore batteries, felt censured, petitioned to be relieved of his command, and retired to his home near Wilmington, Delaware. After brief duty on a naval board in Washington, D.C., he died. He was a nephew of Eleuthére Irénée du Pont de Nemours, who founded the mighty Dupont chemical company and whose daughter, Sophie Madeleine du Pont, he married in 1833.

In Melville's poem ''Dupont's Round Fight (November, 1861),'' Samuel Francis Dupont is the Union blockade commander who sailed down a river to bomb a fort on one side, after which he returned upstream to bomb another fort on the other side. Melville finds the movement geometrically beautiful. At one point, Dupont was the immediate commanding officer of Melville's cousin Guert Gansevoort.*

Bibliography: Garner.

''Dupont's Round Fight (November, 1861)'' (1866). Poem, in *Battle-Pieces.* (Character: [Commodore Samuel Francis] Dupont.) Melville philosophizes to the effect that success in art and war is the result of following rules as enduring as geometrical and astronomical laws. ''The rebel at Port Royal'' learned this truth the hard way. The historical background is this: The Union fleet commander Samuel Francis Dupont reduced Fort Walker and Fort Beauregard (7 November 1861), two Confederate strongholds on opposite shores of Port Royal Sound, South Carolina. Dupont succeeded by steaming in a circle up the channel in two columns, the first one composed of ten vessels, including his flagship, the second with five gunboats that engaged the enemy flotilla. Then the columns went down the channel. They fired as they went. The forts surrendered. Such a surrender to naval vessels was a rarity in naval history. Exaggerated reports of Dupont's maneuver described it as being in a mathematiclly precise circle. Melville's prosody in this tidy poem is as precise as the maneuver of his subject.

Bibliography: Adler; Cohen; Garner; Charles Grobe, *Battle of Port Royal; or, The Bombardment of Forts Walker & Beauregard* (Boston, 1861); NN 11; Shurr; Warren; John K. Winkler, *The Du Pont Dynasty* (New York: Reynal & Hitchcock, 1935).

Durer, Agnes. In ''Marquis de Grandvin: At the Hostelry,'' she is Albert Durer's henpecking wife (*see* Dürer, Albrecht). She evidently dislikes gaiety.

Dürer, Albrecht (1471–1528). German artist. Born in Nuremberg, Dürer was trained in his father's goldsmith shop, after which he was apprenticed to a painter (1486–1490) who taught him painting and woodcutting. Dürer traveled to Colmar, Basel, and Strasbourg (c. 1490–1494), returned to Nuremberg, and went twice to Italy (1494–1495, 1505–1507), where he greatly respected Italy's Renaissance artists. In Nuremberg again, he gained favor in the courts of Maximilian I (1512–1520) and of Charles V (from 1520). After visiting the Low Countries (1520–1521), Dürer began to concentrate on his writings—especially those concerning anatomy and fortifications. Dürer's best works are woodcuts and wood engravings, including an Apocalypse series (1496–1498), the *Large Passion* (1498–1510) and the *Small Passion* (1509–1511) of Christ, and a *Life of the Virgin* (1501–1511). His finest engravings are *Adam and Eve* (1504),

Knight, Death and the Devil (1513), *Melancholia* (1514), and *St. Jerome in His Study* (1514). His best paintings are a phenomenal self-portrait (1500) and several altarpieces, including *Adoration of the Magi* (1504), *Feast of the Rose Garlands* (1506), and *Adoration of the Trinity* (1511). Dürer married Agnes Frey in 1494.

As Albert Durer in Melville's "Marquis de Grandvin: At the Hostelry," Dürer becomes a henpecked husband depicted as melancholy and sad in appearance.

Bibliography: Erwin Panofsky, *The Life and Art of Albrecht Dürer,* 4th ed. (Princeton, N.J.: Princeton University Press, 1955).

"The Dust-Layers" (1947). Poem, in *Collected Poems of Herman Melville.* Men walk through an Egyptian town squirting water out of "skins in bag-pipe way" to lay the dust. It seems an "indignity" to reduce to "a muddy clay" the dust around the majestic architecture of "Thotmes passed away." Here Melville contrasts past nobility and present tawdriness. Thotmes is better known as Thutmose III, who during the eighteenth Egyptian dynasty ruled efficiently and justly (1479–1426 B.C.). He is often regarded as the most enlightened monarch of ancient Egypt. The son of Thutmose II and a concubine named Isis, Thutmose III was well educated in the military arts, conquered Syria, defeated the Mitannians beyond the Euphrates River, and advanced along the Nile into the Sudan. He also encouraged Egyptian art and ordered an array of architects to design and build temples and monuments in his honor. He was buried in the Valley of the Tombs of the Kings, in western Thebes. His tomb was looted, and only a few of its contents have been recovered. His mummified remains were discovered in 1889; his mortuary temple at Dayr-al-Baḥrī, in 1962.

Bibliography: James Henry Breasted, *A History of Egypt from the Earliest Times to the Persian Conquest* (1905; rev. ed., 1912; rpt., New York: Charles Scribner's Sons, 1965); Shurr.

"A Dutch Christmas up the Hudson in the Time of Patroons" (1924). Poem, in *Weeds and Wildings,* as part of a section entitled "The Year." (Characters: Cousin Chris, Elsie, Hans, Katrina, Sharp-Eyes, Tuenis Van der Blumacher.) The poet describes a rural Christmas, with a green bough over the hearth, apples to be toasted, dancing to fiddle music, and the jingling bells of Santa Claus as he drives his sleigh through the snow toward the village. The family here should feed the livestock and scatter crumbs for the birds, but should let other chores go for now. And Katrina should welcome Tuenis Van de Blumacher, her "merry Christmas man," who is knocking at the door.

Bibliography: Stein.

Dutcher, Tom. In "Jack Gentian (omitted from the final sketch of him)," he is a Newport vacationer who gossips about old Gentian.

Dutch Sailor. In *Moby-Dick,* he is a *Pequod* sailor who sings and talks during the midnight festivities in the forecastle.

Duyckinck, Evert (1816–1878). (Full name: Evert Augustus Duyckinck). Editor, author, and bibliophile. Duyckinck was born in New York City into a prosperous and cultivated family. His father was a bookseller and publisher. His younger brother was George Duyckinck.* Evert Duyckinck graduated from Columbia College (1835) and was the sole or perhaps only the main author of the first and only issue of *The Literary: A Miscellany for the Town* (1836), a periodical featuring nearly libelous satirical verse and prose. Duyckinck was admitted to the bar (1837) but never practiced law, wrote articles and essays for several magazines, and visited the British Isles, France, and the Netherlands (1838–1839). With Cornelius Mathews,* he coedited the monthly *Arcturus: A Journal of Books and Opinion* (1840–1842), which published works by Nathaniel Hawthorne,* Henry Wadsworth Longfellow, James Russell Lowell, and others, but which Edgar Allan Poe* rightly noted was too good to enjoy great popularity. Duyckinck edited *The Library of America* (1845–1847), featuring items by Margaret Fuller, Hawthorne, Melville, Poe, William Gilmore Simms, Bayard Taylor,* and John Greenleaf Whittier, among others. At the same time, Duyckinck edited *The Library of Choice Reading* (1845–1847), featuring works by British authors. He briefly edited *The United States Magazine and Democratic Review* (1845) and published a satirical weekly called *Yankee Doodle** (1846–1847). Melville published ''Authentic Anecdotes of 'Old Zack' '' in *Yankee Doodle*; in addition, several other pieces in that weekly have been attributed to him. Duyckinck edited *Literary World: A Gazette for Authors, Readers, and Publishers* (1847), dissociated himself with it, traveled with his brother to Europe (1847), and when he returned bought and edited *Literary World,* by then subtitled *A Journal of American and Foreign Literature, Science, and Art* (1847–1853). He used this journal to encourage indigenous writings independent of Europe (mainly England), deplored the need for American authors to secure foreign copyrights ahead of American ones to avoid being pirated abroad, and published pieces by and comments on James Fenimore Cooper,* Hawthorne, Washington Irving,* Melville (including his review of *The California and Oregon Trail* by Francis Parkman, his review of *The Sea Lions* by Cooper, and his ''Hawthorne and His Mosses''), Poe, Simms, and Taylor, among others. Duyckinck and his brother bought *Holden's Dollar Magazine* but published it only in 1851.

   Then the Duyckincks issued their landmark work, the *Cyclopaedia of American Literature* (2 vols., 1855; new ed., 1856). After his brother died (1863), Evert Duyckinck prepared by himself an enlarged third edition of the *Cyclopaedia* (1866). Including entries on more than 500 U.S. authors, this massive encyclopedia is scholarly, historical, biographical, and descriptive rather than critical; it also contains authors' excerpts. Duyckinck was also an influential Wiley & Putnam editor (*see* Putnam, George Palmer). In 1860, he compiled a literary memorial to Irving, reissued Irving's *Salmagundi,* and prepared an American edition of *The Poets of the Nineteenth Century.* He wrote a history of the Civil War (3 vols., 1861–1865), *National Portrait Gallery of Eminent Americans* . . . (2 vols., 1862), pieces on Fitz-Greene Halleck (1868, 1877), a collection of biographies of the presidents from George Washington* to Ulysses S. Grant* (1873), and *Portrait Gallery of Eminent Men and Women of Europe and America* . . . (2 vols., 1873). He also helped William Cullen Bryant edit the works of William Shakespeare (3 vols., 1886–1888).

Duyckinck married Margaret Wolfe Panton in 1840. The couple had three sons; when all three died (1857, 1870, 1873), Duyckinck found solace in his Episcopalian faith. The Duyckincks' Manhattan home was an informal literary salon. Duyckinck's diaries contain a wealth of information. The two brothers amassed a library of some 17,000 volumes and in addition innumerable manuscripts, all of which were donated to the Lenox Library in New York City, which was established by John Jacob Astor* and which later became part of the New York Public Library. Evert Duyckinck introduced Melville and Hawthorne during the famous Monument Mountain picnic party in the Berkshires (5 August 1850). Later, however, Duyckinck offended both authors by partly adverse reviews of *The House of the Seven Gables* and *Moby-Dick.* Growing friendly again, Melville continued to borrow books from the Duyckincks' library. In addition, through Duyckinck, he met Bryant, Taylor, Nathaniel Parker Willis, and Charles Fenno Hoffman,* and perhaps Irving and Poe. Melville's numerous letters to Duyckinck may be dated from 1846 to 1877. Duyckinck is more important for having encouraged abler writers than for his own work, much of which, all the same, is valuable for an understanding of American literary history.

Bibliography: Perry Miller, *The Raven and the Whale: The War of Wits in the Era of Poe and Melville* (New York: Harcourt, Brace & World, 1956); NN 14; Donald Yannella, ''Evert Augustus Duyckinck,'' pp. 101–9 in *Antebellum Writers in New York and the South,* ed. Joel Myerson (Detroit: Gale Research Company, 1979).

Duyckinck, George (1823–1863). (Full name: George Long Duyckinck.) Editor and biographer. Duyckinck was the younger brother of Evert Duyckinck,* in whose shadow he lived much of the time, especially after their parents both died in the 1830s. George Duyckinck attended an academy at Geneva, New York (now Hobart College), and graduated (1843) from the University of the City of New York (now New York University). He studied law and was admitted to the bar, but he never practiced. He traveled in Europe (1847–1848, 1857) and concerned himself with literature, art, and religion. He worked with his brother on the latter's many literary and editorial projects (1848–1863). A more involved Episcopalian than his brother, George Duyckinck was elected to the executive committee of the General Protestant Episcopal Sunday School Union and Church Book Society (1855), was made its treasurer (1857), and devoted himself to promoting children's books for his church. He edited the works of William Shakespeare (8 vols., 1853) and wrote low-key but sensitive, solid biographies of four British religious figures—George Herbert (1859), Thomas Ken (1859), Jeremy Taylor (1860), and Hugh Latimer (1861). Melville knew Evert Duyckinck much better than he did George Duyckinck; he did not visit George when he was ill in a London hospital (1856), and he wrote rather few letters to him (1858–1859). He did, however, acknowledge by letter Duyckinck's generous gift to him of George Chapman's five-volume translation of Homer and other works (1858). Melville was also interested in Duyckinck's work on Herbert and Taylor.

Bibliography: Perry Miller, *The Raven and the Whale: The War of Wits in the Era of Poe and Melville* (New York: Harcourt, Brace & World, 1956); NN 14.

E

"The Eagle of the Blue" (1866). Poem, in *Battle-Pieces*. Melville uses the eagle as a symbol of Federal military strength during the Civil War. The eagle is known for its "eager calm of gaze," joy in combat, "pride of quenchless strength," and imperviousness to hurt. In a note to the poem, Melville informs the reader that many Northwestern regiments carried live eagles as "added ensign[s]" into combat and mentions one such eagle from Wisconsin. The 8th Wisconsin Volunteer Infantry safely took an eagle named "Old Abe" as its mascot through twenty battles.

Bibliography: Garner, NN 11.

Early, Jubal A. (1816–1894). (Full name: Jubal Anderson Early; nicknames: "Jube," "Jubilee," "Old Jubal," "Old Jube.") Soldier. He was born in Franklin City, Virginia, graduated from West Point (1837), served in the Seminole War in Florida, and resigned from the army to practice law at Rocky Mount, Virginia (from 1838). He served as a colonel in Virginia state forces, resigned when Virginia seceded, espoused the Confederate cause, and fought so well at First Bull Run that he was promoted to brigadier general (1861). Early was in many bloody campaigns thereafter, became a major general (1863), led his division at Gettysburg (1863) and elsewhere, and was ordered to lead a dramatic raid on Washington, D.C. (June–August 1864). He was outgeneraled in the Shenandoah Valley by William Tecumseh Sherman,* forced by Philip H. Sheridan* to retreat at Cedar Creek (October), and defeated at Waynesboro (March 1865). When the war ended, Early fled to Mexico, Cuba, and Canada. While in Canada he wrote his spicy memoirs (1866, exp. ed. publ. 1912). Returning to the practice of law, in Lynchburg, Virginia (1869), "Old Jube" remained unreconstructed to the end.

In Melville's poem "Sheridan at Cedar Creek (October, 1864)," Early is named as the Confederate general forced by the arrival of Philip Sheridan to retreat. Melville, who loved puns, labels Early "belated" here.

Bibliography: Boatner; Millard Kessler Bushong, *Old Jube: A Biography of General Jubal A. Early* (Boyce, Va.: Carr Publishing, 1961).

Eaton, Joseph Oriel (1829–1875). Portrait, landscape, and genre painter. He was born in Newark, Ohio, studied art in New York City, and worked mostly in the Middle West—in Indianapolis (1846–1848), Cincinnati (1850, 1853, 1857–1860)—but also in New Orleans (before 1857). Later, he lived in New York. He visited Europe (1873). He developed expertise in painting likenesses of sensitive children. His portrait of his fellow artist Robert Swain Gifford* and his *Landscape—View of the Hudson* (1868) are noteworthy. Eaton was an associate of the National Academy of Design and a member of the Society of Painters in Water Colors. He married Emma Jane Goodman of Cincinnati in 1855. Eaton painted portraits of Melville (1870), his brother Allan Melville,* their mother Maria Gansevoort Melville,* their sister Catherine Gansevoort Melville Hoadley,* and her husband John Chipman Hoadley.* A portrait of Melville's brother Thomas Melville* may also be by Eaton.

Bibliography: Leyda.

Ebony. In *Moby-Dick,* this is another name for the African-American cook regularly known as Fleece.

Ebony. In *The Confidence-Man,* this is a nickname of Black Guinea.

Edgar. In *Pierre,* this name is the subject of an anagram by Pierre.

Edwards, Monroe. In "Bartleby," he is a forger who died in Sing Sing. He is mentioned by the grub-man in the prison where Bartleby dies.

Egbert ("Charlie"). In *The Confidence-Man,* he is the mystical philosopher Mark Winsome's practical follower. Egbert is neat, commercial in appearance, and about thirty years old. In a dialogue with Francis Goodman, Egbert refuses him a loan on the grounds that everyone ought to be self-reliant. He also relates the illustrative story of China Aster, the man who was ruined by his friend Orchis's loan to him. Egbert's partial model is Henry David Thoreau,* while Mark Winsome is partly based on Ralph Waldo Emerson.*

Bibliography: NN 10; Egbert S. Oliver, "Melville's Picture of Emerson and Thoreau in 'The Confidence-Man,' " *College English* 8 (November 1946): 61–72; Hershel Parker, "Melville's Satire of Emerson and Thoreau: An Evaluation of the Evidence," *American Transcendental Quarterly* 7 (Summer 1970): 61–67 and 9 (Summer 1971): 70; Trimpi.

Eld. In "The New Ancient of Days," he is mentioned as the drooling companion of the cave man.

Elder, The ("Sir Crab"). In *Clarel,* he is a fiery-tongued, perpetually hatted Scotch Presbyterian. He argues intolerantly with the other pilgrims, soon turns back, and leaves them.

Eld of Mexico, The. In *Clarel. See* Hannibal, Rohon Del Aquaviva, Don.

Elijah. In *Moby-Dick,* he is a tattered prophet on the Nantucket wharf. He hints to Ishmael and Queequeg about an adverse fate in store for Captain Ahab, his crew, and the *Pequod.*

Ellery, Willis. In *Moby-Dick,* he is a sailor lost with five others from the *Eliza* in 1839. Their shipmates place a marble tablet in their memory in the Whaleman's Chapel in New Bedford.

Elsie. In "A Dutch Christmas up the Hudson in the Time of Patroons," she is a girl whom the poet asked to scatter crumbs for the birds. She evidently likes Tuenis Van der Blumacher.

Emerson, Ralph Waldo (1803–1882). Essayist, poet, and lecturer. He was born in Boston, suffered the loss of his father early (1811), attended the Boston Latin School (1813–1817), entered Harvard (1817), began his lifelong habit of keeping a journal (from 1820), graduated from Harvard (1821), and taught school and studied at the Harvard Divinity School (1821–1828). Some time after being authorized to preach as a Unitarian minister (1826), he became pastor of the Second Church, Boston, and married Ellen Louisa Tucker in 1829. She died at the age of nineteen (1831), and Emerson resigned his religious post (1832) and went to Europe, where he met Thomas Carlyle, Samuel Taylor Coleridge,* William Wordsworth, and other notables (1832–1833). Returning to the United States, Emerson moved to Concord, Massachusetts (1834) and married Lydia Jackson in 1835 (the couple had four children). Emerson participated in the Transcendental Club (1836–1843); during that time and later, he was friendly with and became the inspiration or at least the intellectual challenge of many persons, including Nathaniel Hawthorne* and Henry David Thoreau.* Emerson also wrote, lectured, and published steadily, producing *Nature* (1836), "The American Scholar" (1837), "Divinity School Address" (1838), *Essays* (1841), and *Essays, Second Series* (1844). By 1850, his writings had gained him international renown. He went to England and France (1847–1848). Returning, he published *Representative Men* (1850), *English Traits* (1856), *Conduct of Life* (1860), an oration at the funeral of Thoreau (1862), and *Society and Solitude* (1870). Though never the same after his house burned (1872), he enjoyed a final trip to Europe and went on to the Middle East (1872–1873), and returned to publish *Society and Solitude* (1870) and *Letters and Social Aims* (1876). He lapsed into passivity, marked by aphasia and senility. Several of his other works were issued posthumously.

Emerson's most popular and significant prose pieces are *Nature*; "The American Scholar" and "Divinity School Address" (both published in *Nature: Addresses, and Lectures* [1849]); "Compensation," The Over-Soul," and "Self-Reliance" (all in *Essays* [1841]); "Experience," "New England Reformers," "The Poet," and "Politics" (all in *Essays: Second Series* [1844]); "Montaigne" and "Plato" (both in *Representative Men* [1850]); "Fate" and "Illusions" (both in *The Conduct of Life* [1860]); "Thoreau" (*Lectures and Biographical Sketches* [1862]); and "Education" (*Lectures and Biographical Sketches* [1884]). Emerson published two volumes of poems—*Poems* (1847) and *May-Day and Other Pieces* (1867). His most popular poems include "Brahma," "Concord Hymn," "Days," "Each and All," "Hamatreya," "Ode Inscribed to W. H. Channing," "The Problem," "The Rhodora," "The Snow-Storm," "The Sphinx," "Terminus," "Two Rivers," and "Waldeinsamkeit."

Melville, who first came across Emerson's works and heard him lecture in 1849, wrote to his friend Evert Duyckinck,* "Say what they will, he's a great man" (24 February [1849]). He added in a later letter, however, "Nay, I do not oscillate in Emerson's rainbow, but prefer rather to hang in mine own halter than swing in any other man's swing. Yet I think Emerson is more than a brilliant fellow. Be his stuff begged, borrowed, or stolen, or of his own domestic manufacture he is an uncommon man. . . . Swear he is a humbug—then is he no common humbug." And yet he goes on thus: "I could readily see in Emerson . . . a gaping flaw. It was, the insinuation, that had he lived in those days when the world was made, he might have offered some valuable suggestions. These men are all cracked right across the brow" (3 [March 1849]). Melville satirized Emerson in the character of Mark Winsome in *The Confidence-Man.* The question of Emerson's influence on Melville is a puzzling one. He profited from thoughts concerning Platonism, aesthetics, and poetic inspiration in Emerson; however, his comments on evil Melville regarded as ludicrously simple.

Bibliography: F. O. Matthiessen, *American Renaissance: Art and Expression in the Age of Emerson and Whitman* (New York: Oxford University Press, 1941); NN 14; Egbert S. Oliver, "Melville's Picture of Emerson and Thoreau in 'The Confidence-Man,' " *College English* 8 (November 1946): 61–72; Peter Quigley, "Rethinking Resistance: Nature Opposed to Power in Emerson and Melville," *West Virginia University Philological Papers* 37 (1991): 39–51; Sealts; Trimpi; John B. Williams, *White Fire: The Influence of Emerson on Melville* (Long Beach: California State University, Long Beach, 1991).

Emir. In "In the Desert," any opponent of Napoleon in the fiercely lighted desert.

Emir, The. In *Clarel,* he is the militant Arabian friend of the Bey in the Arnaut's song sung during the wine revelry at Mar Saba.

Emir, The. In *Clarel,* he is mentioned as noble Djalea's father.

Emir, The. In *Clarel,* this is a complimentary nickname accorded Djalea.

Emmons, Pop. In "Hawthorne and His Mosses," he is the imaginary American author of an epic entitled the *Fredoniad.*

"The Encantadas" (1854). (Full title: "The Encantadas, or Enchanted Isles.") Prose sketches. "The Encantadas" was published in *Putnam's Monthly Magazine** (1 March, 1 April, 1 May 1854), as by Salvator R. Tarnmoor. (Characters: The Creole, Felipe, Juan Fernandes, Ferryman, Hunilla, Dame Nature, Oberlus, the Palmer, Captain David Porter, Truxill.)

I. "The Isles at Large." The Encantadas, also called the Galapagos, resemble a gigantic cinder pile, the world after a penal conflagration. They are uninhabitable and changeless, and their only life is hissing creatures and wiry thickets. The coasts are bound by clinkers, lashed by waves, and partly strewn with bits of decay and shipwrecks. Whalers cruised nearby until they found the tides and the winds too capricious. Grotesque tortoises crawl about looking hopeless. Even when far away, the author often thinks of those condemned creatures on the evilly bewitched isles.

II. "Two Sides of a Tortoise." You can turn a tortoise on its back and see its bright side. But because you can do so, do not deny its black side. Nor should you deny a black tortoise's bright side if you cannot turn it over. After five months at sea, the author touches the South Head of Albemarle. A shore party returns with three big tortoises, black as widows, plated with shaggy, dented, mossy shells, and slimy from sea water. They seem to have come from under the earth's foundations. They look like Coliseums or walled towns. The author examines them and later, when in his hammock, hears them resolutely but stupidly crawling on deck and pushing unavailingly against immovable objects such as the foremast. Next evening, though uneasy at the thought of the tortoises' bleak endurance, he and his mates have tortoise steaks and stews. They also carve the shells into tureens and the calipees into salvers.

III. "Rock Rodondo." The sailors see Rock Rodondo, also called Round Rock, 250 feet high, visible thirty miles at sea and resembling a distant sail. Before dawn one morning, they fish at its base. Flying sea birds make a canopy above its rocky layers. Near the bottom are penguins, pelicans, albatrosses, stormy petrels, and other birds. Through their wild din the whistle of the "boatswain's mate" may be heard. The fish, iridescent and tame, bite the hook like those who trust but do not understand human nature. At sunrise, the men climb the tall rock.

IV. "A Pisgah View from the Rock." From the top you can look south toward the Antarctic and east toward Quito 600 miles along the Equator. These islands, as well as the isles of St. Felix, St. Ambrose, Juan Fernandes, and Massafuero, act as sentinels for South America to their east. Before 1563, Spanish ships heading south from Peru to Chile often got lost because of fear of circling far west. Then Juan Fernandes (*see* Fernandez, Juan) went west beyond the trade winds and easily south; at that time, he found the island now bearing his name. About 1670 the Encantadas were come upon thus. This group includes Albemarle, Narborough, and some smaller isles.

V. "The Frigate, and Ship Flyaway." Melville discusses the action of the U.S. frigate *Essex* in these waters in 1813.

VI. "Barrington Isle and the Buccaneers." Barrington, one of the isles, used to be a West Indian buccaneers' hideaway. A minor historian once saw stone and turf seats on hillsides there. Perhaps sentimentalists, turned pirates to escape persecution back home, fashioned them and philosophized while sitting there.

VII. "Charles' Isle and the Dog-King." Southwest of Barrington is the larger Charles' Isle. A Cuban Creole was rewarded for heroic action in Peru by being given this island, which he colonized, ruled, and guarded with dogs. He turned deserters off whaling vessels into recruits. A rebellion forced him back to Peru, after which the survivors established not a democracy but a riotocracy.

VIII. "Norfolk Isle and the Chola Widow." The narrator's ship stops at Norfolk Isle, northeast of Charles' Isle, to catch tortoises. The sailors find Hunilla there. She is a Chola—that is, a half-breed Indian from Payta, Peru. Three years earlier, she and her husband, Felipe, and her only brother, Truxill, were left ashore by a French sea captain to collect tortoises and boil out and collect their oil. Although he promised to pick them up in four months, he never returned. One day the two men built a raft, went fishing, capsized, and were drowned, while Hunilla watched helplessly from a cliff. Only Felipe's body washed ashore, and she buried it reverently in the sand. Waiting for her ship to return, and then for any ship to come by, she recorded the passing days and other observations—concerning eggs, fish, tortoises, and the weather—but stopped counting after 180 days, although many more followed. The narrator's captain asks her why. She will not explain. Did whalers come by? She nearly missed seeing his ship because its crew landed on the shore opposite her hut, her husband's grave, and their dogs—now multiplied from two to ten. But something whispered to her through the enchanted air, and she climbed the rocks, saw the ship, and waved. While the men retrieve her tortoise oil, Hunilla goes to the withered cross on Felipe's sandy mound, then sets her tearless, haughty face in a gesture defying nature's torture. Taking only two dogs, since provisions aboard are limited, she must leave the others howling on the beach. The captain transports her to Tumbex, a Peruvian port, sells the oil for her there, and gives her some silver—added to by gifts from all hands. When they last see her, she is riding a gray ass into Payta.

IX. "Hood's Isle and the Hermit Oberlus." Southeast of Crossman's Isle is Hood's Isle, which has a vitreous cove called Oberlus's Landing. Fifty years ago, Oberlus, a deserter, built a den there, grew potatoes and pumpkins to sell to ships, and became sinister and debased. Once, when he tried to kidnap a black sailor put ashore to buy food, Oberlus was whipped and then released.

This humiliation made him even more misanthropic; later he kidnapped two sailors, made them slaves, and then turned them into bravoes in his pseudo-army. When a ship sent four boats ashore for provisions, Oberlus smashed three of them and escaped to Guayaquil in the fourth. His cohorts were never seen again. In Payta, Oberlus was about to persuade a tawny beauty to return with him to his island when he was jailed on suspicion of sabotage. Melville reports that one of several sources for information concerning Oberlus is Porter's *Voyages into the Pacific* [Captain David Porter,* *Journal of a Cruise Made into the Pacific Ocean,* 2 vols., 1815]. (Other sources possibly used by Melville are James Colnett, *A Voyage to the South Atlantic* . . . [1798]; James Burney, *Chronological History of the Discoveries in the South Sea or Pacific Ocean* [1803–1817]; and John M. Coulter, *Adventures in the Pacific* [1845].)

X. ''Runaways, Castaways, Solitaries, Grave-Stones, Etc.'' These islands have been populated by deserters, tortoise hunters, and victims of captains' revenge. The beaches have post offices in the form of corked and staked bottles and graves of those who died at sea but in sight of these clinkery isles. One grave is that of a man from the *Essex* killed ashore in an 1813 duel.

Although Melville used a pen name when he published ''The Encantadas,'' he was identified as the author in a notice in the New York *Evening Post* (14 February 1854); therefore, the pen name was not used when ''The Encantadas'' was reprinted, with emendations, in *The Piazza Tales* (1856). Melville received $150 for the work.

Bibliography: Newman; NN 9; Sealts; Russell Thomas, ''Melville's Use of Some Sources in *The Encantadas*,'' *American Literature* 3 (January 1932): 432–56.

Enderby, Samuel. In *Moby-Dick,* he is the merchant leader of a London family that has fitted out many whaling vessels, including one called the *Samuel Enderby,* commanded by Captain Boomer.

Bibliography: Sidney Kaplan, ''Herman Melville and the Whaling Enderbys,'' *American Literature* 24 (May 1952): 224–30.

Engihoul, The Man of the Cave of. In ''The New Ancient of Days.'' *See* Man of the Cave of Engihoul, The.

English Sailor. In *Moby-Dick,* he is a *Pequod* sailor who during the midnight festivities in the forecastle praises Captain Ahab and then insists that the fight between Daggoo and the Spanish sailor be a fair one.

''The Enthusiast'' (1891). Poem, in *Timoleon.* Melville advises the reader not to let the virtues of ''magnanimous'' youth degenerate into either personal materialism or envy of those who are successful in ''the mart.'' Never let the responsibilities of the mature adult tell ''Faith [to] abjure her skies.'' In darkness, keep ''fealty to light.'' Is Melville praising or deriding extremists here?

Bibliography: NN 11, Shurr, Stein.

"The Enviable Isles (from 'Rammon')" (1888). Poem, in *John Marr.* The poet depicts islands "drear in hue" until approached more closely. Then they become green, with murmuring surf and misty rainbows. Inland are dreamy hills, uplands, hypnotic breezes, palms and cypresses, ferns and moss, flocks unattended by "unconscious slumberers mere" with "all sorrow and all glee" lost in the "croon" of "pebbly runlets." Melville may be suggesting a Nirvana-like afterlife. "The Enviable Isles" was evidently to be part of a long work, never completed.

Bibliography: NN 11; Shurr; Stein; Eleanor M. Tilton, "Melville's 'Rammon': A Text and Commentary," *Harvard Library Bulletin* 13 (Winter 1959): 50–91.

"L'Envoi" (1924). Poem, in *Weeds and Wildings,* as part of a section entitled "As They Fell" and functioning as the conclusion of "The Rose Farmer."

Bibliography: Stein.

"L'Envoy: The Return of the Sire de Nesle. A.D. 16—" (1891). Poem, in *Timoleon.* (Character: The Sire de Nesle.) The narrator, the Sire de Nesle, is happy to have his "rovings end" and to be back in his towers. He has seen strange places and "swarm[s]" of people, and has sought much knowledge. But "thou, my stay, thy lasting love," he concludes to his beloved, would be enough. It is possible that Melville is here addressing and complimenting his wife.

Bibliography: NN 11, Stein.

Epirot, The. In *Clarel. See* the Arnaut.

"Epistle to Daniel Shepherd" (1938). Poem. It was first published in Herman Melville, *Representative Selections . . . ,* ed. Willard Thorp (New York: American Book Company, 1938.) (Character: Daniel Shepherd.) In charming quasi-pastoral lines, Melville invites his friend Daniel Shepherd, in real life a New York City lawyer and for a time his brother Allan Melville's* partner, to visit him. The poet would like Shepherd, who has "such a pastoral name," to "come and rove" with him through both the dell by the Housatonic and the one where "genial Friendship dwells." They could share some wine—"Claret and otard here I name / Because each is your favorite flame"—or perhaps "a fat black bottle or two" of bourbon. The poet would like to hear what the "Wall-Street scholar" thinks of the recent Italian rebellion against Austrian rule.

"An Epitaph" (1866). Poem, in *Battle-Pieces.* (Character: the Soldier.) When news of casualties comes one Sunday, the Soldier's widow is so "content" in her deep faith that "priest and people borrowed of her cheer."

Bibliography: NN 11.

Estaing, Charles Hector, Comte d' (1729–1794). French admiral. He was born in Ruvel, Auvergne. As a brigadier general, he accompanied Count de Lally to the East Indies (1757), was imprisoned during the siege of Madras (1759) but was soon released on parole, and got back to France (1760). He was arrested, however, by the English for breaking his parole, and was briefly jailed in Portsmouth. D'Estaing was made governor of the Antilles (1763–1766) and was promoted to vice admiral (1767). In 1778, he was placed in command of the first French fleet offering aid to the Americans in their revolution against the British, was outmaneuvered by British Admiral Richard Howe in New York Bay and off Newport, Rhode Island, and put into Boston harbor to repair storm damage to his vessels, after which he captured St. Vincent and Grenada in the West Indies. D'Estaing fought to a draw against an English fleet, advanced to attack Savannah, but was beaten back with heavy casualties (1779). At the time of peace (1783), he was in command of the entire fleet off Cadiz (1783). His undoubted energy was nullified by his inexperience in naval warfare. Elected to the Assembly of the Notables (1787), he was placed in command of the National Guard (1789) and was named admiral by the National Assembly (1793). He spoke favorably of Marie Antoinette at her trial (1793) and for doing so was executed a year later during the Reign of Terror. In *Israel Potter,* Count D'Estaing is the pro-American French aristocrat through whom, and through [Louis-Philippe-Joseph] the Duke de Chartres, [Benjamin] Franklin obtains a commission for John Paul Jones. Melville learned about D'Estaing by reading *Life and Correspondence of John Paul Jones* by Robert C. Sands (New York, 1830).

Bibliography: W. Laird Clowes, *The Royal Navy: A History from the Earliest Times to the Present* (7 vols., London: S. Low, Marston, 1897–1903); A. T. Mahan, *Types of Naval Officers Drawn from the History of the British Navy* (Boston: Little, Brown, 1901); Samuel Eliot Morison, *John Paul Jones: A Sailor's Biography* (Boston: Little, Brown, 1959).

Etchings of a Whaling Cruise, with Notes of a Sojourn on the Island of Zanzibar. To which is appended, a Brief History of the Whale Fishery; its Past and Present Condition. By J. Ross Browne.* Illustrated with numerous engravings on steel and wood. Harper & Brothers: 1846. 8 vols. *Sailors' Life and Sailors' Yarns.* By Captain Ringbolt. New York: C. S. Francis & Co., 1847. 12mo. Review. Melville reviewed these books by Browne and ''Ringbolt.'' He begins by lamenting the fact that realistic books have taken the glamour from the seaman's life, formerly portrayed in romantic fiction and poetry. He praises Browne for his fearlessly candid account, points out a cetological error or two, comments on Browne's tragicomic anecdote of a bumpkin's singing aboard a whaler, and summarizes Browne's account of his own escape. Melville warns all ''shore-disdaining, ocean-enamored youths'' who would seek adventure at sea and follows with a dramatic account of chasing, harpooning, and being towed by a whale (all prefiguring episodes in *Moby-Dick* yet to come). Melville criticizes ''Ringbolt'' for falsely insinuating that sea captains are good-natured and have been maligned. He rebukes the captain for trying to discount the criticism by Richard Henry Dana, Jr.,* of his harsh captain. Ringbolt's real name was John Codman.*

Evert Duyckinck* asked Melville to prepare this review article, which was published anonymously and without title, in the New York *Literary World* (6 March 1847), edited by Duyckinck.

Bibliography: Lisa M. Franchetti, ''Exaggeration in Melville's Review of Codman,'' *Melville Society Extracts* 56 (November 1983): 4–6; R. D. Madison, ''Melville's Review of Browne's *Etchings*,'' *Melville Society Extracts* 53 (February 1983): 11–13.

Ethelward. In *Clarel,* he is a man whom Rolfe knew long ago. Rolfe goes to Ethelward's grave when he visits the Latin and English Cemeteries at Zion hill, south of Jerusalem.

Eve. In ''The Lover and the Syringa Bush,'' she is mentioned as a truant whom the poet waits to meet.

Excellency, His. In ''Marquis de Grandvin: Naples in the Time of Bomba . . . ,'' he is a tumbler who performs in the streets of Naples.

Excellenza. In ''The Bell-Tower,'' he is the chief magistrate. He suspects that Haman is endowed with almost human powers of locomotion. After the killing of Bannadonna, Excellenza orders cloaked Haman to be sunk at sea.

F

Falcone, Aniello (1600–1656). Italian painter and church decorator. Born in Naples, Falcone was a disciple of Jusepe de Ribera* and an associate of Salvator Rosa.* Falcone painted a fine *Rest in Egypt* (1641). He gained fame and influence for popularizing pictures of battle scenes, which he depicted with restrained naturalism and precise touches. He also painted pictures of Turks and corsairs. After the abortive insurrection of Masaniello* in Naples (1647), Falcone fled for a time to France. In Melville's ''Marquis de Grandvin: Naples in the Time of Bomba . . . ,'' Agniello Falcone is mentioned as linked with patriotic Neapolitan brigands.

Falconer, William (1732–1769). Sailor and poet. Falconer was born in Edinburgh, Scotland, was poorly educated, and went to sea aboard the merchant ship *Britannia* (c. 1746). He was shipwrecked on the way from Alexandria to Venice, near Cape Colonna, on the coast of Greece, and was one of only three crew members to survive. After returning home (1751), he began to write poetry, published anonymously in the *Gentleman's Magazine* (c. 1758), and evidently returned to the sea until he published ''The Shipwreck'' (1762), his only well-known poem. Advised at this time by the Duke of York, to whom the poem is dedicated, to join the Royal Navy, Falconer served as a midshipman on the *Royal George* (1762–1763) and as a purser on the 32-gun *Glory* (1763–1769). While aboard her, he compiled a marine dictionary (published 1769). He was the purser on the frigate *Aurora* (1769) bound for India but was never seen again. An alleged survivor deposed (1773) that the *Aurora* was wrecked on rocks off Macao. Falconer married a Miss Hicks (1763 or soon thereafter). ''The Shipwreck,'' which was extravagantly praised at one time, was twice revised (1764, 1769). In three cantos, it describes marine scenes and sailors' activities, often in technical language, and sentimentally recounts the disastrous wreck. In Melville's poem "Off Cape Colonna," Falconer is mentioned as a poet whose "The Shipwreck" describes a wreck off Cape Colonna.

Bibliography: The Poetical Works of William Falconer. With a Life, by Rev. John Mitford (Boston: Little, Brown, 1854).

"The Fall of Richmond" (1866). (Full title: "The Fall of Richmond: The Tidings received in the Northern Metropolis [April, 1865].") Poem, in *Battle-Pieces.* (Character: [General Ulysses S.] Grant.) Bells, crowds, and cannon join to celebrate "a city in flames," now that "Lucifer" has been "deter[red]." Honor Grant, for "Right through might is Law." The joy of peace is undercut by the implication that evil exists and must be put down by repressive might.

Bibliography: Garner, NN 11, Shurr.

Falsgrave. In *Pierre,* he is the dainty Rev. Mr. Falsgrave's father. The man is a poor Northern farmer.

Falsgrave, Mrs. In *Pierre,* she is the dainty Rev. Mr. Falsgrave's mother. She was formerly a pretty seamstress.

Falsgrave, Rev. Mr. In *Pierre,* he is the gracious, gentlemanly leader of the Saddle Meadows congregation. His benefactress is Pierre's mother Mary Glendinning. Falsgrave may be partly based on Reverend Edward Ballard of Pittsfield, Massachusetts.

Bibliography: Leyda; Herman Melville, *Pierre,* ed. Henry A. Murray (Chicago: Hendricks House, 1949).

Falstaff, Sir John. A major character in William Shakespeare's *King Henry IV, Part I* and *King Henry IV, Part II,* and the central figure in *The Merry Wives of Windsor.* In Melville's poem "Falstaff's Lament over Prince Hal Become Henry V," Jack Falstaff, who calls himself "Fat Jack" and "Honest Jack," is depicted as sad that Hal has snubbed him. In limning the aging and deserted Falstaff, Melville may be adumbrating his own feelings as the years have passed and his wit and accomplishments seem unappreciated.

"Falstaff's Lament over Prince Hal Become Henry V" (1924). Poem, in *Weeds and Wildings.* (Characters: Jack [Sir John] Falstaff, [King] Henry V.) Falstaff remembers that he loved, nurtured, instructed, and prayed for Prince Hal. He feels that the prince is throwing away his crown as "King of good fellows" to become "Beadle of England"—all codified and moral. Nevertheless, Falstaff, sorrowful and thirsty, will drink to him.

Fanfum. In *Mardi,* he is a member of one of the twelve aristocratic Tapparian families on the isle of Pimminee. He is entertained by Nimni. His name is probably suggested by the word "fanfare."

Fanna. In *Mardi,* he is a healthy pilgrim to Ofo on the isle of Maramma. He pays Pani the blind guide before he is asked to do so.

Fanny, King. In "Marquis de Grandvin: At the Holstery." *See* Francis II, King of the Two Sicilies.

Farnoopoo ("Night," "Night-born"). In *Omoo,* she is a lovely maiden entertained by the narrator and Dr. Long Ghost on the beach at Imeeo.

Farnow. In *Omoo,* he is a retired footman serving Queen Pomaree (*see* Pomare IV). He now lives near Captain Bob in Papeetee.

Farnowar ("Morning," "Day-born"). In *Omoo,* she is a lovely maiden encountered by the narrator and Dr. Long Ghost on the beach at Imeeo.

"Far Off-Shore" (1888). Poem, in *John Marr.* The poet sees a ship with a thin signal flying. But its crew has all been swept overboard.
  Bibliography: Stein.

Farragut, David Glasgow (1801–1870). (Original name: James Glasgow Farragut.) Naval officer. He was born near Knoxville, Tennessee, moved with his family to New Orleans (1807), was adopted by the controversial naval officer David Porter* (c. 1808), became a midshipman in the navy (1810), and changed his first name to David (c. 1814) in honor of his foster father. During the War of 1812, while serving on Porter's *Essex* in the Pacific Ocean, Farragut took command of a prize vessel (1813), visited the Marquesas Islands (1813), and later was aboard the *Essex* when she was captured at Valparaiso (1814). After peace was declared, Farragut served in the Mediterranean area and studied in his spare time, partly in Tunis. He helped Porter fight pirates in the West Indies (1823). Farragut advanced slowly in rank: lieutenant (1825), commander (1841), and captain (1855). When the Civil War began, he was ordered to capture New Orleans and establish control of the Mississippi River, which he did with the support of Porter's son, the Union naval officer David Dixon Porter* (April 1862). Farragut was quickly named the navy's first rear admiral, continued blockade work (1862–1864), and captured Mobile Bay (August 1864). After a sister ship the *Tecumseh* was sunk by a Confederate mine, Farragut issued his famous "Damn the torpedoes!" command from his *Hartford* sloop and steamed ahead to victory. Farragut became the nation's first vice admiral (1864), was elevated to the position of the nation's first admiral (1866), commanded a goodwill squadron on a visit to Continental seaports (1867–1868), and died during a visit to the naval yard at Portsmouth, New Hampshire. Farragut was married twice, both times in Norfolk, Virginia. He married Susan Marchant in 1823. She died in 1840. He married Virginia Loyall in 1843 (the couple had one son).

Melville mentions Farragut in three poems. In "The Battle for the Mississippi (April, 1862)," he is the Union admiral ordered to bombard St. Philip and Jackson, two forts on the Mississippi River above New Orleans, and then to capture the city. In "The Battle for the Bay (August, 1864)," he is the Union admiral who bravely commanded from his flagship the *Hartford* during the attack on Mobile Bay. In "Bridegroom-Dick" he is mentioned as the famous officer under whom Bridegroom Dick served at Vicksburg and later in the Battle of Mobile Bay. When Farragut observed Melville's cousin Guert Gansevoort* drunk on duty in California (August 1856), he ordered him home to await further orders.

Bibliography: Garner; A. T. Mahan, *Admiral Farragut* (1892; rpt., New York: Greenwood Press, 1968).

Fathers. In "The Cincinnati," this is a general term for the founding fathers of the United States. They were mostly ex-Revolutionary Army officers and hence members of the Society of the Cincinnati.

Fat Jack. In "Falstaff's Lament over Prince Hal Become Henry V. *See* Falstaff, Sir John.

Fayaway. In *Typee,* she is the beautiful, olive-skinned native girl who evidently loves and is loved by Tommo. She is delicately tattooed, is fond of raw fish, and weeps at his departure.

Bibliography: Grejda.

Fedallah. In *Moby-Dick,* he is the Parsee whom, with four fellow Orientals, Captain Ahab secretly brings aboard his *Pequod.* At the first lowering for a whale, Fedallah and his men emerge as Ahab's "five dusky phantoms." In due time, Fedallah gives Ahab specious comfort when he prophecies equivocally; but he then precedes his master to death because of the seeming malice of Moby Dick. The name Fedallah in Arabic means "sacrifice or ransom of God." Fedallah is a diabolical, mystical infidel and an assassin offering his own life in desperate fatalism so as to destroy what he regards as the satanically proud and hate-filled Ahab. Fedallah's garb may be partly based on descriptions by Charles Wilkes in his *Narrative of the U.S. Exploring Expedition during the Years 1838, 1839, 1840, 1841, 1842* (5 vols. and atlas, 1845) of natives and mestizos in Manila, in the Philippine Islands, while Fedallah's perfidious nature may owe something to Wilkes's comments on Sulus, especially the Sultan and his son, also in the Philippines.

Bibliography: Finkelstein; Brian Higgins and Hershel Parker, eds., *Critical Essays on Herman Melville's Moby-Dick* (New York: G. K. Hall, 1992); Jaffé; Helen P. Trimpi,

"Demonology and Witchcraft in *Moby-Dick,*" *Journal of the History of Ideas* 30 (October–December 1969): 543–62.

Fee. In *Mardi,* this is one of the twelve aristocratic Tapparian families on the isle of Pimminee. They are entertained by Nimni.

Feejee Mermaid, The. In "The New Planet," she is an attraction in the American Museum.

Felipe. In "The Encantadas," he is the pure-blooded Castilian husband of Hunilla. He and his brother-in-law Truxill drowned while fishing, after which Hunilla became the wretched but uncomplaining Chola widow of Norfolk Isle.

Ferdinand II, King of the Two Sicilies (1810–1859). Italian monarch. The son of Francis I and the Spanish infanta María Isabel, he was born in Palermo, was conservatively tutored by a high-principled bishop, and suffered from epilepsy. Upon his father's death (1830), he ascended the throne as Ferdinand II. Two years later, he married María Cristina, the saintly daughter of the widowed Queen of Sardinia. She gave birth to a son, the future Francis II, and died two weeks later (1836). Ferdinand II married María Theresa, the daughter of the Archduke Charles of Austria in 1836 (the couple had eleven children). Ferdinand's reign (1830–1859), marked by a pro-Austrian tilt, was stained by conspiracies, revolts, repression, and political prosecutions. Though promising reforms, he proved to be superstitious, reactionary, dishonest, and cruel. In 1848, during the ill-fated insurrection in Sicily, he bombed Palermo, promised a constitution but broke his vow, crushed a revolt in Naples, and returned to Sicily and bombed Messina—thus earning his nicknames "King Bomba" and the "Bomb-King." He accepted the capitulation of Palermo (1849). He was denounced abroad, especially in England and France, for his despotism. He survived an assassination attempt (1856). He was such a tyrant that the Two Sicilies were not invited into the Italian unification movement until after his death. Somewhat deficient mentally, his son Francis II, King of the Two Sicilies,* succeeded him (1859) but was forced by the army of Giuseppe Garibaldi* to abdicate two years later. Melville mentions Ferdinand, as Bomba, in the poem "Pausilippo (in the Time of Bomba)" and as "the Bomb King" in "Marquis de Grandvin: Naples in the Time of Bomba . . ."

   Bibliography: Acton; Janet Penrose Trevelyan, *A Short History of the Italian People* (1920; rev. ed., London: George Allen & Unwin, 1956).

Fergus, Major. In *Omoo,* he is a Polish-born officer employed, along with Lefebre, by [Armand-Joseph] Bruat, the hated governor of Tahiti.

Fernandez, Juan (1536–1602?). Spanish navigator and discoverer. He sailed in the southern Pacific Ocean between Panama and Peruvian and Chilean settlements and discovered several islands in the process. One group which he discovered (c. 1563) was named after him. He once sailed from Callao to Chile in thirty days, by avoiding the coast and availing himself of trade winds. This unheard-of feat caused him to be arrested for sorcery. He tried unsuccessfully to colonize the island group named after him, but only goats remained and flourished. He may have sighted Easter Island. In ''The Encantadas,'' Fernandes is mentioned as the famous pilot who discovered the island now named after him, procured a deed to it, and lived there for some years.

Bibliography: Alexander Dalrymple, *An Historical Collection of the Several Voyages and Discoveries in the South Pacific Ocean* (1769–1771).

Ferryman (''Boteman''). In ''The Encantadas,'' he is the ferryman or boatman of the wretched Wandering Isles.

Fiddlefie. In *Mardi,* this is one of the twelve aristocratic Tapparian families on the isle of Pimminee. They are entertained by Nimni. The name Fiddlefie undoubtedly derives from ''fiddledeedee.''

''The Fiddler'' (1854). Short story. It was anonymously published in *Harper's New Monthly Magazine** (1 September 1854). (Characters: Master Betty, Cleothemes the Argive, Hautboy, Helmstone, [Charles and John Philip] Kemble, [Sarah Kemble] Siddons, Standard.) In New York City, Helmstone the narrator is sad because his ambitious poem has been critically blasted. A friend named Standard introduces him to the happy Hautboy, and the three go to the circus and enjoy stew and punch afterward. Hautboy's conversation is a sensible balance of feeling and thought. When Hautboy leaves briefly, Standard enigmatically links Hautboy to Master Betty, ''[t]he great English prodigy'' of years ago. Hautboy returns and takes the other two to his cozy room, where he plays his fiddle enchantingly. Later, when Standard explains that Hautboy tired of the glory of being a performing genius and now happily teaches fiddling, Helmstone decides to forego a literary career, buys a violin, and studies under the genial fiddler.

The frustrated Helmstone's rejection by the pallidly conservative literary establishment mirrors Melville's own professional fate after the failure of his *Pierre.* In real life, Master Betty was William Henry West Betty,* a British child actor who made a fortune but retired disillusioned at age thirty-three. In addition, Melville may be thinking of Joseph Burke (1815–1902), another British child prodigy whom he may have seen in Albany, where Burke eventually lived. Melville's authorship of ''The Fiddler,'' which was not reprinted in his lifetime, is established by indirect but convincing evidence. Melville was probably paid about $15 for it.

Bibliography: Gilman, Newman, NN 9, Sealts.

Fidi. In *Mardi,* he is Bardianna's body servant. He is mentioned in the philosopher's will. His fidelity is suggested by his name, which surely derives from *fidus* (Latin for "faithful").

Field, David Dudley (1781–1867). Clergyman and author. He was born in East Guilford (now Madison), Connecticut, graduated from Yale (1802), was ordained, and served as the pastor of a church in Haddam, Connecticut (1804–1819, 1837–1851) and of a Congregational one in Stockbridge, Massachusetts (1819–1837). He retired in Stockbridge. Field edited *A History of the County of Berkshire, Massachusetts* (1829—a source for Melville's *Israel Potter* and "The Apple-Tree Table"), *A History of Pittsfield, Massachusetts* (1844), and *Brief Memoirs* (1863), among other works. He married Submit Dickinson in 1803. The couple had eight sons and two daughters. Four of the sons achieved distinction: David Dudley Field, a lawyer and an author; Stephen Johnson Field, a supreme court judge; Cyrus West Field, who laid the Atlantic Ocean cable; and Henry Martyr Field, an editor, journalist, author, and publisher of a biography of his father (1898). David Dudley Field, the clergyman, was the host of the famous Berkshire picnic (5 August 1850) during which Melville met Nathaniel Hawthorne.*

"Field Asters" (1924). Poem, in *Weeds and Wildings,* as part of a section entitled "The Year." Many people see these asters, which are "namesakes" of stars; but the few who pause to look at them mostly fail to interpret their inscrutable stare.
Bibliography: Cohen, *Poems;* Shurr; Stein.

Fifth Nantucket Sailor. In *Moby-Dick,* he is a *Pequod* sailor who sees lightning during the midnight festivities in the forecastle.

"The Figure-Head" (1888). Poem, in *John Marr.* The ship is named the *Charles-and-Emma* after the owner and his bride. The figurehead at the prow is a carving of their likenesses. The ship is soon worn by sun, water, and gear, and Charles and Emma are teary-eyed, their "hug relaxed with the failing glue." One night, beams creak and ribs groan, the ship crashes, and "the pair lie prone" under dancing breakers and moaning winds. On the surface, the poem is about a shipwreck. A half-dozen or so double entendres, however, permit the interpretation that Charles and Emma lose their sexual vigor as they age.
Bibliography: Stein.

Finfi. In *Mardi,* he is a vivacious guest who tells Taji about Nimni's other Tapparian guests at the latter's party on the isle of Pimminee. Gaddi regards Finfi as a parvenu. His name may well derive from the word "fanfare."

Finn, The ("Man"). In "Bridegroom-Dick," he is a gigantic sailor who Bridegroom Dick recalled was once ordered by Captain Turret to be flogged but was then spared.

First Luff. In *White-Jacket. See* Bridewell, Lieutenant.

First Nantucket Sailor. In *Moby-Dick,* he is a *Pequod* sailor who sings during the midnight festivities in the forecastle.

Flagstaff, Lord George. In *Redburn,* he is a British officer who is said to be advertising in Liverpool to obtain a crew for his frigate *Thetis.*

Flash Jack ("Flashy"). In *Omoo,* he is a sailor aboard the *Julia.* He signs the round-robin.

Flask ("King-Post"). In *Moby-Dick,* he is the short, stout, ruddy, pugnacious third mate of the *Pequod.* He is a native of Tisbury, on Martha's Vineyard. Daggoo is his harpooner. Flask sees no symbolism in the doubloon nailed to the mainmast. The third mate of the *Acushnet,* the model for the *Pequod,* was a Portuguese named George W. Galvan, who went ashore at Payta. Melville may have had Galvan in mind when he mentions the third mate in "Charles' Isle and the Dog-King," in "The Encantadas."
  Bibliography: Leyda.

Flavona. In *Mardi,* he is one of Donno's servitors. He envies his master and is envied by Manta.

Fleece ("Ebony"). In *Moby-Dick,* he is the old African-American cook aboard the *Pequod.* He preaches to the noisy sharks as they rend and gobble whale blubber. Stubb queries Fleece on religion and lectures him on the best way to cook whale steak.

Fletz. In *Pierre,* he is a fictitious banker, partner of Flitz, in a German prince's proclamation imagined by Pierre.

Flinegan, Patrick. In *White-Jacket,* he is the captain of the head. A storm prevents his singing "The True Yankee Sailor" in costume in the Fourth of July theatrical.

Flinnigan, Patrick. In *Redburn,* he is mentioned as the Irish ostler of Redburn's uncle.

Flint. In *Pierre,* he is the publisher who, with partners Steel and Asbestos, rejects Pierre's book. They intend to sue Pierre for costs and advances.

Flitz. In *Pierre,* he is a fictitious banker, partner of Fletz, in a German prince's proclamation imagined by Pierre.

Florence, The Grand Duke of. In "Marquis de Grandvin: At the Hostelry." *See* Grand Duke of Florence, The.

Flute. In *White-Jacket,* he is a boatswain's mate who warns White Jacket that Captain Claret may flog him.

Fly, Eli James Murdock (1817–1854). Friend of Melville. The Fly family lived in Greenbush, near Lansingburgh and Albany, New York. Melville also knew Fly's sister Harriet Fly. Eli Fly was a classmate of Melville's brother Gansevoort Melville* at the Albany Academy, a law-student apprentice (c. 1835–1840) in the office of the Melville brothers' uncle Peter Gansevoort (1788–1876),* and a member with Melville of the Philo Logos Debating Society (Albany, 1838). Fly may have gone to Galena, Illinois, with Melville in search of work (spring 1840), and together the two sought work in New York City (fall 1840). Fly tried to practice law in New York and was also a scrivener (1840–1843), asked Gansevoort (1843) to recommend him for the position of New York City commissioner of deeds (1843), and got around to sending in the necessary forms (1844). Whether he was ever appointed is not known. In 1851 Melville probably accompanied Fly, then an invalid, to Springfield, Massachusetts, on his way to Brattleboro, Vermont, perhaps to a water cure there. Fly's personality figures in the characterization of Bartleby, the absurdist hero of Melville's short story "Bartleby."
  Bibliography: Leyda, NN 14, Howard, Smith.

Fofi. In *Mardi,* he is a wounded man from King Piko's island of Diranda. Nimni on the isle of Pimminee sponsors Fofi as a famous captain. According to King Media, however, he is a cunning braggart whom King Piko exiled.

Fonca, Del. In "The Bell-Tower." *See* Del Fonca.

Foni. In *Mardi,* he is an upstart rebel against the god Doleema and then is a prophet, in a story told by Mohi concerning the isle of Maramma. When Foni, once handsome, was last seen, he was old and miserable, and was eating food sacrificed to the god in his sacred forest, where he was finally killed. Foni may well be a phony.

Fonoo. In *Mardi,* this is a nickname, meaning "the Girl," of King Donjalolo.

Foofoo. In *Mardi,* this is the name of a dynasty in a manuscript chronicle in Oh-Oh's museum.

Ford, Miss. In "Jimmy Rose," either of the daughters of William Ford, the narrator.

Ford, Mrs. William. In "Jimmy Rose," she is the young and relatively less conservative wife of the narrator. She would like to modernize their New York home, which was once owned by her husband's friend James Rose.

Ford, William. In "Jimmy Rose," he is the conservative narrator who has inherited a New York home once owned by his friend James Rose. Ford tries to no avail to help Jimmy when he is swept to financial ruin.

Forgiver, The. In "The Martyr." *See* Lincoln, Abraham.

" 'Formerly a Slave': An Idealized Portrait, by E. Vedder, in the Spring Exhibition of the National Academy, 1865" (1866). Poem, in *Battle-Pieces*. (Characters: [Jane Jackson], E[lihu]. Vedder.) Melville saw the painting by Elihu Vedder* of *Jane Jackson, Formerly a Slave* at the National Academy in New York (April 1865), and was inspired by its depiction of an old African-American woman who had been a slave in the South. In his poem, Melville observes that "[t]he sufferance of her race is shown" in the painting and adds that "deliverance" for her comes "too late." Since her descendants will "know / The good withheld from her," the "sober light" of her face makes her appear "Sibylline, yet benign."
  Bibliography: Garner, NN 11, Warren.

"The Fortitude of the North under the Disaster of the Second Manassas" (1866). Poem, in *Battle-Pieces*. Melville contends that no "dark defeat" will nullify those "[w]ho fight for the Right," any more than winds, waves, and sleet, or even Antarctic storms, can destroy the cliffs of the Cape-of-Storms. In a journal entry dated 8 August 1860, Melville records his impression of an inspiring squall at sunset off a resolute Cape Horn cliff.
  Bibliography: Cohen, *Poems;* NN 11 and 15; Shurr.

Fourth Nantucket Sailor. In *Moby-Dick,* he is a *Pequod* sailor who during the midnight festivities in the forecastle reports that Captain Ahab told Starbuck to steer the ship straight into the approaching storm.

"Fragment" (1924). Essay, in *The Works of Herman Melville*. The total disappearance of glorious things surely redounds to the glory of God the omnipotent.

"Fragments from a Writing Desk" (1839). (Characters: Inamorata, M—, the Major, L.A.V., W—.) In fragment "No. 1," L.A.V. writes M— a cocky letter full of precious, mannered prose. He feels superior to most people in his "village of Lansingburgh.'' When he glitters in front of beautiful high-society ladies, many young men envy him. Three lovely girls, who attract his special attention, he describes lushly. In fragment ''No. 2,'' the narrator is resting by a river one April evening when a muffled female figure gives him a note signed Inamorata and asks him to follow the bearer. He goes along the river, through a grove, and up to a villa. He and his guide are hoisted in a basket aloft to a window. They go into a beautiful, perfumed room resembling a scene from *The Arabian Nights.* A lovely, white-robed woman is seated on an ottoman. L.A.V. kneels, utters words of love, and kisses her passionately. But then he rushes from her grasp. The ravishing creature is deaf and dumb. These two fragments were published, over the initials L.A.V., in the *Democratic Press, and Lansingburgh Advertiser,* of Lansingburgh, New York (4, 18 May 1839). The second of the three lovely girls in ''No. 1'' may be based on young Melville's friend Mary Louise Parmelee, whom Melville knew and admired in Lansingburgh before she married Anthony Augustus Peebles, the son of Maria Van Schaick Peebles,* who was a cousin of Melville's mother Maria Gansevoort Melville.*

Bibliography: Gilman; Peter A. Obuchowski, ''Melville's First Short Story: A Parody of [Edgar Allan] Poe,'' *Studies in American Fiction* 21 (Spring 1993): 97–102.

''Fragments of a Lost Gnostic Poem of the 12th Century'' (1891). Poem, in *Timoleon.* The first fragment suggests that every established family or estate will be destroyed by the brutality of matter. The second fragment suggests that since no admirably energetic endeavor—even that of ''The Good Man''—can ever purify ''the poisoned well,'' the best solution is to be indolent. Gnosticism developed at the time of early Christianity, espoused the notion of the power of evil and the limitations of good, and was in decline by the third century. Sadly, Melville probably had Christ in mind as ''The Good Man.''

Bibliography: NN 11; Shurr; Stein; Thomas Vargish, ''Gnostic *Mythos* in *Moby-Dick,''* *PMLA* 81 (June 1966): 272–77.

France, King Louis XVI. In *Israel Potter. See* Louis XVI. In *Israel Potter,* this monarch rewards John Paul Jones for his exploits, while Israel Potter receives nothing for his brave deeds.

Frances. In ''Jimmy Rose,'' she is a charming lady from New York. The indigent James (''Jimmy'') Rose praised her graciously.

Francesco. In ''Benito Cereno,'' he is a mulatto slave, about thirty-five years of age. He was Alexandro Aranda's cabin steward and became a leading plotter during the revolt of the slaves aboard Benito Cereno's *San Dominick.* Francesco wanted to poison Captain Amasa Delano during lunch.

Francis II, King of the Two Sicilies (1836–1894). (Nicknames: ''Bombino,'' ''Franceschiello,'' ''Lasa,'' ''Lasagna''). The son of Ferdinand II, King of the

Two Sicilies,* he was the last of the Bourbon kings of Naples. Born in Naples, he proved to be somewhat deficient mentally. The year 1859 was momentous for him: His father and stepmother ordered his marriage to Maria Sophia Amalia, the peppy daughter of Duke Maximilian of Bavaria and a younger sister of Empress Elizabeth of Austro-Hungary; he married Maria by proxy and gloomily met her four weeks later; he worried when Austria displeased France by invading northern Italy; he was present at his father's death; and he became king. As Francis II, he revived the constitution (1860), could neither keep Naples neutral in the war between Austria and France nor stem the tide of the freedom fighters of Giuseppe Garibaldi,* and abdicated (1861). Francis II and his wife had a daughter who lived only three months (1869). The exiled Francis II died in Austrian-held territory (later part of Italy); his wife lived until 1925. In his poem "Marquis de Grandvin: At the Hostelry," Melville nicknames Francis II "King Fanny" and identifies him as Bomba's frightened son and heir who flees Naples when he learns of Garibaldi's advance. In "Marquis de Grandvin: Naples in the Time of Bomba . . . ," Melville describes Francis II as endangered by the Red Shirt, i.e., Garibaldi.

Bibliography: Acton; Janet Penrose Trevelyan, *A Short History of the Italian People* (1920; rev. ed., London: George Allen & Unwin, 1956).

Frank. In *White-Jacket,* he is a handsome common sailor, about sixteen years of age. Because of differences in their rank, Frank avoids speaking to or even looking directly at his brother, who is an officer aboard a store ship that supplies the *Neversink* off Rio de Janeiro. Melville may have had his proscribed cousin Stanwix Gansevoort* in mind in depicting Frank. Stanwix Gansevoort was a midshipman aboard a naval store ship that supplied Melville's real-life frigate *United States* (1844), and the two cousins did not speak to each other. *See also* Jones, Frank.

Bibliography: Wilson L. Heflin, "A Man-of-War Button Divides Two Cousins," *Boston Public Library Quarterly* 3 (January 1951): 51–60; Leyda.

Franklin, Benjamin (1706–1790). Civic leader, diplomat, essayist, inventor, journalist, moralist, musician, philosopher, politician, printer, satirist, scientist, and statesman. Franklin was born in Boston, one of thirteen children. After two years of formal schooling, he was apprenticed to his printer brother, read voraciously, published some papers anonymously (1722), ran away to Philadelphia (1723), was a printer in London (1724–1726), returned to Philadelphia and bought a newspaper there (1726), renamed it the *Pennsylvania Gazette* (1729), became the printer for the Pennsylvania Assembly (1730), and published *Poor Richard's Almanac* (1733). Franklin established a fire company (1736), became postmaster of Philadelphia (1737), invented a new type of stove (1742), became first secretary of the American Philosophical Society (1744), began to study electricity (1746), let his partner manage their printing shop, cofounded the academy which became the University of Pennsylvania (1749), established a fire insurance company, and devised a lightning rod (1752). He became deputy post-master general of North America (1753–1754); proposed a plan to unite the colonies (1754); worked in England as an agent for Georgia, Massachusetts, New Jersey, and Pennsylvania in proprietary disputes (1757–1762, 1764–1775); and published *The Way to Wealth* (1758) and started his *Autobiography* (1771). Franklin represented Pennsylvania at the Second Continental Congress and became the first postmaster general under the Articles of Confederation (1775), helped write the Declaration of Independence (1776), and resided in Paris as the American minister plenipotentiary to France (1776–1785). He cosigned the Treaty of Paris (1783) and returned home to Philadelphia. Though ill by this time, he was a delegate from Pennsylvania to the Constitutional Convention (1787), and continued to add to his astonishing mass of written material, to receive many honors, and to function as a member of numerous academic, literary, political, and scientific communities and societies. Franklin married Deborah Read Rogers (1730). The couple had a son, who died as a child, and a daughter. In addition, Franklin had an illegitimate son, about whose mother there has been much speculation.

While in Paris, Franklin supported various American revolutionary efforts, working closely, for example, with John Paul Jones,* who named his *Bon Homme Richard* after Franklin's persona in *Poor Richard's Almanac.* In *Israel Potter,* Melville presents Dr. Franklin unsympathetically, as the canny American "man of wisdom" in Paris for whom Israel Potter acts as a courier; through him, Israel meets Jones; through his friends Duke de Chartres (*see* Chartres, Louis-Philippe-Joseph, duc de) and Count D'Estaing (*see* Estaing, Charles Hector, Comte d') Franklin obtains a commission for Jones. It is known that a letter dated 14 February 1777, perhaps from John Horne (i.e., John Horne Tooke*), and Charles Woodcocke (*see* Woodcock, Squire John) introduced the real-life Israel R. Potter to Franklin and solicited his help. Franklin evidently doubted the authenticity of Potter.

Bibliography: David Chacko and Alexander Kulcsar, "Israel Potter: The Genesis of a Legend," *William and Mary Quarterly* 41 (July 1984): 365–89; Ronald W. Clark, *Benjamin Franklin: A Biography* (New York: Random House, 1983); Samuel Eliot Morison, *John Paul Jones: A Sailor's Biography* (Boston: Little, Brown, 1959); William B. Willcox, ed., *Papers of Benjamin Franklin,* vol. 23 (New Haven, Conn.: Yale University Press, 1983).

Frederick William III (1770–1840). King of Prussia. The son of King Frederick William II, he was born in Potsdam, led a lonely life as a youth, became a lieutenant (1784) and later a colonel (1790) in the Prussian army. He married Louise, the daughter of Prince Charles of Mecklenburg-Strelitz (1793), and ascended the throne following the death of his father (1797). He tried to remedy his father's abusive policies, but he proved incapable and surrendered much of his realm to the demands of Napoleon* (1807). When his politically resolute wife Queen Louise died (1810), Frederick William III joined with France in a war against Russia ending in defeat (1812), after which he allied himself to Russia, reluctantly signed the Holy Alliance (1815), failed to give his people the constitution he had promised, but did try to unify Prussia. His major accomplishment in a largely repressive rule was his authorization of the customs union (1834). He entered a morganatic marriage (from 1824) with Countess Auguste von Harrach, whom he named Princess Liegnitz.

In "Poor Man's Pudding and Rich Man's Crumbs," Melville names Frederic William as one of the aristocratic guests at the Guildhall Banquet in London following the Battle of Waterloo. In doing so, Melville violates history, since the action of the second part of his story is dated 1814, whereas the Battle of Waterloo occurred a year later.

Bibliography: Hajo Holborn, *A History of Modern Germany, 1648–1840* (New York: A. A. Knopf, 1964).

French Sailor. In *Moby-Dick,* he is a *Pequod* sailor who dances during the midnight festivities in the forecastle.

"The Frenzy in the Wake: Sherman's advance through the Carolinas (February, 1865)" (1866). Poem, in *Battle-Pieces.* (Character: [General William Tecumseh] Sherman.) A Southern monologist hopes to continue the fight, wants to avenge "every woe," and curses the Northern flag. Although his skies are brassy with forest fires and enemy cavalrymen file past all day long, he vows that "even despair / Shall never our hate rescind." Melville deplored Sherman's devastation of the South.

Bibliography: Garner; R. D. Madison, "Melville's Sherman Poems: A Problem in Source Study," *Melville Society Extracts* 78 (September 1989): 8–11; NN 11; Shurr.

"The Frieze." *See* "The Parthenon."

"Fruit and Flower Painter" (1924). Poem, in *The Works of Herman Melville.* The subject is an impoverished, stoical artist woman living in a drafty, empty garret. Lacking a plum pudding, she paints a plum. She also paints roses.

"Fruit of Travel Long Ago" (1891). Subsection of *Timoleon.*

Fry, Mrs. In *The Confidence-Man,* she is a woman named by the herb doctor as a friend of his who corresponds with him on the subject of prisons. Thomas Fry denies that he has any knowledge of her.

Fry, Thomas ("Happy Tom"). In *The Confidence-Man,* he is a man on crutches. He first says that his legs were crippled because he was held in jail as an innocent witness to a murder. Later, however, he professes to be a soldier-of-fortune casualty of the Mexican War. The herb doctors tries to comfort him. Fry may be partly a caricature of George Law, a wealthy transportation magnate, expansionist, member of the Know Nothing Party, and contender for its nomination as president (1856).

Bibliography: Trimpi.

Fulvi. In *Mardi,* he is a Mardian writer quoted by Babbalanja.

G

G—, General. In ''Jimmy Rose,'' he is a hero to whom James (''Jimmy'') Rose graciously presents a brace of pistols decorated with turquoise.

Gabriel. In *Moby-Dick,* he is the mad prophet of the *Jeroboam.* He came from the Neskyeuna Shakers and predicted the death of Harry Macey when that man sought to kill Moby Dick.

Gaddi. In *Mardi,* he is an informative guest who tells Taji about Nimni's other Tapparian guests at his party on the isle of Pimminee. According to Finfi, Gaddi is a parvenu. His name must come from the word ''gad.''

Galgo, Luys. In ''Benito Cereno,'' he is a Spanish sailor, aged sixty, who attempts to warn Captain Amasa Delano but is seen by the blacks and murdered.

Gamboge. In *Omoo. See* Old Gamboge.

Gammon. In *White-Jacket,* this is the name assigned to a sailor who is impertinent to Pert.

Gandix, Hermenegildo. In ''Benito Cereno,'' he is one of Alexandro Aranda's young clerks from Cadiz and a *San Dominick* passenger. He is accidentally killed during the attack led by Captain Amasa Delano's chief mate.

Gansevoort, Catherine (''Caty'') Van Schaick (1751–1830). Melville's maternal grandmother. She was the wife of Peter Gansevoort (1749–1812).* They were married in Albany in 1778. The couple had six children, five of whom were obviously Melville's aunts and uncles, or would have been, if they had all lived to adulthood. (One of the five, Petrus Gansevoort [1786–1788], died in infancy.) The four remaining were Herman Gansevoort,* Wessel Gansevoort,* Leonard Herman Gansevoort,* and Peter Gansevoort (1788–1876).* The sixth child became Melville's mother Maria Gansevoort Melville.* Catherine and Peter Gansevoort, who were the owners of several black slaves by the 1790s, prospered in houses and lots, other land, lumber, and brewing. After her husband's death, Catherine Gansevoort managed her considerable inheritance. In later years, she worried about her health, grew depressed, but found relief in religion and in visiting her children. At her death, her estate was left in confusion and was not settled until sixteen years later—and then only with some family embarrassment. Melville's first or second extant letter is one written to Catherine Van Schaick Gansevoort (11 October 1828).

Bibliography: NN 14, Kenney.

Gansevoort, Guert (1812–1868). Melville's cousin. He was the son of Leonard Herman Gansevoort* and Mary Ann Chandonette Gansevoort.* Leonard Gansevoort was the brother of Maria Gansevoort Melville, Melville's mother. Guert Gansevoort joined the U.S. Navy as a midshipman (1823), went to sea (1824), was promoted to lieutenant (1837), served as first lieutenant aboard the brig-of-war *Somers* immediately under Captain Alexander Slidell Mackenzie during the mutiny, and was the presiding judge of the court-martial that tried and voted, because of Mackenzie's insistence, to hang the three main conspirators (1842). Gansevoort was severely depressed thereafter, although, according to a letter Mary Ann Gansevoort wrote to Peter Gansevoort (1788–1876),* the young officer felt that his tragic decision "was *approved* of God" (2 January 1843). Guert Gansevoort evidently told Hun Gansevoort,* Melville's distant cousin, and that man told Thurlow Weed,* the politician and Melville family friend, about Guert Gansevoort's reluctance to render a guilty verdict. Guert Gansevoort did heroic duty during the Mexican War (1846–1848), especially during an amphibious landing at Vera Cruz (March 1847), was promoted to commander (1855), and commanded the defensive action when 2,000 Native Americans attacked the port of Seattle in Washington Territory (January 1856). He was relieved of his post when Admiral David Glasgow Farragut* caught him drunk on duty in California (August 1856). Gansevoort was promoted to captain (1862). He was later court-martialed for negligently running the *Adirondack,* his naval sloop of war, onto a rock and wrecking her in the Bahamas, but he was found not guilty (1862). He then commanded the *Roanoke,* a steam frigate, off Hampton Roads, Virginia (1863), and had ordnance duty—as he had had earlier—in the Brooklyn naval yard (from 1864). He retired (1867), lived with his sister Catherine Gansevoort Curtis (1814–1887) in Schenectady, and died there.

Melville admired and closely followed the career of his older cousin, who, however, disapproved of Melville's going to sea in 1841. The Melville and Gansevoort families were greatly troubled by the political fallout of the *Somers*

Gansevoort Family Tree

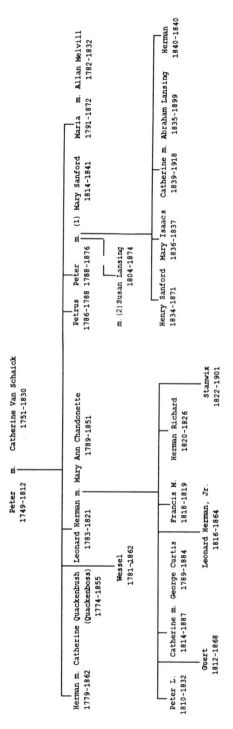

affair and Guert Gansevoort's part in the affair. Melville, in a letter to his brother Thomas Melville,* describes Guert Gansevoort as "brave as a lion, a good seaman, a natural-born officer," and adds, "I hope he will yet turn out the hero of a brilliant victory" (25 May 1862). In his poem "Commemorative of a Naval Victory," Melville may have Guert Gansevoort in mind when he limns the nature of a naval hero some years after a victory. In his poem "Bridegroom-Dick," Melville depicts "Guert Gan" as a brave naval officer whom Bridegroom Dick fondly remembers from Vera Cruz days.

   Bibliography: Harrison Hayford, ed., *The Somers Mutiny Affair* (Englewood Cliffs, N.J.: Prentice-Hall, 1959); Kenney; Leyda.

Gansevoort, Henry Sanford (1834–1871). Melville's cousin. Born in Albany, he was the son of Peter Gansevoort (1788–1876)* and Mary Sanford Gansevoort.* He did not get along with his father and disliked his stepmother. He graduated from the Albany Academy (1851) and Princeton (1855), attended Harvard Law School (1856–1858), and practiced law in Buffalo (1859) and New York City (1859–1860). He was erratic, moody, and cruel, and was able to feign illness to gain family sympathy. He preferred literature and politics to law. He vacationed in England and on the Continent (1859–1860) with his wealthy parents and his eccentric sister Catherine Gansevoort (later Catherine Gansevoort Lansing*). Becoming a Union Army artillery officer at the outbreak of the Civil War, he rose in rank (second lieutenant, 1861; first lieutenant, 1862; colonel, 1864; and brevet brigadier general, 1865). He saw service at the battles of Gainesville, Second Bull Run, South Mountain, and Antietam (1862). He captured the camp of Colonel John Singleton Mosby* (October 1864). His sporadic illnesses during these years was not improved by a bout with venereal disease (1863). After the war, Colonel Gansevoort, as he was then called, remained in his artillery regiment—until 1870, a year before he died of tuberculosis, cared for by his domineering sister.

   Henry Gansevoort knew Melville well and admired him as a writer and as a lecturer. He arranged for Melville to visit his camp at Vienna, Virginia (16–21 April 1864), and even to accompany men of his unit on a scouting expedition that resulted in capture of some Confederate soldiers. On returning home, Melville wrote him a letter of thanks and praise, ending thus: "Farewell, my hero & God bless you" (10 May 1864). Gansevoort, in letters to members of his family after the war, praised Melville's 1866 *Battle-Pieces*. He must have especially responded to "The Scout toward Aldie" since Mosby figures in it. John Chipman Hoadley,* Melville's brother-in-law, edited *Memorial of Henry Sanford Gansevoort* (1875), with the assistance of Catherine Lansing.

   Bibliography: Boatner; Faust; Garner; Kenney; Jay Leyda, "The Army of the Potomac Entertains a Poet," *Art and Action: Twice a Year* 16 (1948): 259–72; Metcalf; NN 14.

Gansevoort, Herman (1779–1862). Melville's uncle. He was the son of Peter Gansevoort (1749–1812)* and Catherine Van Schaick Gansevoort,* and was the brother of Melville's mother Maria Gansevoort Melville.* Herman Gansevoort's wife (from 1813) was the eccentric Catherine Quackenbush (or Quackenboss) (1774–1855). Herman and Catherine Gansevoort, who had no children, made their home in Gansevoort, New York, where he went when quite young to care for his father's lumber interests and later his gristmill interests. Melville was named after Herman Gansevoort. Upon her husband's death, Melville's mother was obliged to appeal to both Herman Gansevoort and their brother Peter Gansevoort (1788–1876)* for money. Peter Gansevoort was more able and more generous, partly because Herman Gansevoort was often in financial difficulty, was occasionally sued, had to be bailed out by his brother Peter, and finally went bankrupt (1847). That same year, Melville dedicated *Omoo* to Herman Gansevoort. Melville sat at the deathbed of Herman Gansevoort's wife (1855), after whose death, Melville's mother and his unmarried sisters Augusta Melville* and Frances Priscilla Melville* lived for a time with Herman Gansevoort and managed his household. He bequeathed a fine old clock to Melville, who treasured it and later gave it to his daughter Frances Melville Thomas.*

Bibliography: Kenney, Leyda, Metcalf, NN 14.

Gansevoort, Hun (1818–1843). Melville's distant cousin. His great-grandfather Johannes Gansevoort (1719–1781) was the brother of Melville's great-grandfather Harme Gansevoort (1712–1801). Hun Gansevoort's grandfather was Leonard Gansevoort, Jr. (1754–1834); that man's wife was Maria Van Rensselaer (1760–1842). The couple had nine daughters and two sons. The sons were John Gansevoort (1786–?), Hun's father, and a brother named named Rensselaer Gansevoort (1799–1839). Hun's father was an artillery lieutenant, a military agent, an unsuccessful businessman, and a police justice in Albany (1821–1825). Hun Gansevoort attended the Albany Academy. After his mother Ann Cuyler Gansevoort died (1830), his father placed his five children—Hun, John Maley Gansevoort (?–1910), and three daughters—with a married sister named Eveline in New York, and lost contact with the family. When Hun's grandmother Maria died, her will omitted all mention of her son John and his two sons. Hun, who was named after Abraham Hun (?–1812), the husband of his sister Maria Gansevoort Hun (?–1813), joined the U.S. Navy (1832), sailed as a midshipman on the *Vincennes* to the Pacific (1833–1836), attained the rank of passed midshipman, went to sea again (1837), served on the *Constitution,* but was declared by the surgeon of the U.S. frigate *Constitution* at Callao, Peru, to be unfit for duty because of venereal disease, and was sent home to Albany via Panama ill and depressed (1840). He apparently was told by Guert Gansevoort,* Melville's first cousin and a naval officer, about the court-martial aboard the *Somers* in which Guert Gansevoort had taken part (1842). (At any rate, Thurlow Weed,* New York politician, said so in his autobiography.) Hun Gansevoort advised Guert Gansevoort's younger brother, Stanwix Gansevoort,* then a teenager in the navy, to moderate his indulgence of sensual pleasure (January 1843). Hun Gansevoort evidently returned to naval duty and drowned at sea.

Bibliography: Gilman, Kenney, Leyda.

Gansevoort, Leonard Herman (1783–1821). Melville's uncle. He was the son of Peter Gansevoort (1749–1812)* and Catherine Van Schaick Gansevoort.* His siblings were Herman Gansevoort,* Wessel Gansevoort,* Peter Gansevoort (1788–1876),* and Melville's mother Maria Gansevoort Melville.* Leonard Herman Gansevoort's wife (from 1809) was Mary Ann Chandonette Gansevoort.* They had seven children, all of whom were obviously Melville's cousins. They were Peter L. Gansevoort*; Guert Gansevoort*; Catherine (''Kate'') Gansevoort Curtis (1814–1887), the wife (from 1836) of a lawyer named George Curtis (1789–1884); Leonard Herman Gansevoort, Jr.*; Francis M. Gansevoort (1818–1819); Herman Richard Gansevoort (1820–1826); and Stanwix Gansevoort.* The older Leonard Gansevoort clerked for Albany merchants, ran a store with a partner (1805–1807) until the Embargo Act of 1807 ruined them, went into the lumber business with his brother Herman (1809–1817), and became sheriff of Albany County (1820–1821), until he died of tuberculosis. Melville knew Leonard Gansevoort's widow Mary Ann, who, left in financial straits, appealed for aid to her brother-in-law Peter Gansevoort (1788–1876), and died in Brooklyn.

Bibliography: Kenney, Leyda.

Gansevoort, Leonard Herman, Jr. (1816–1864). Melville's cousin. He was the son of Leonard Herman Gansevoort* and Mary Ann Chandonette Gansevoort.* After attending the Albany Academy, as did his younger brother Stanwix Gansevoort,* he went to sea, first in the navy (1831), and then aboard the whaler *Hercules* (1835–1837) and on a packet to Liverpool and back (1837–1838). Since this last voyage took place two years before Melville's 1839 trip to Liverpool, Melville probably discussed his cousin's early experiences and also used aspects of them in *Redburn,* central episodes of which occur in Liverpool.

Bibliography: Gilman, Kenney.

Gansevoort, Mary Ann Chandonette (1789–1851). Melville's aunt. She was the wife of Leonard Gansevoort,* the brother of Melville's mother Maria Gansevoort Melville.* Mary Ann Chandonette Gansevoort and her husband had seven children, all of whom were obviously Melville's cousins. They were Peter L. Gansevoort*; Guert Gansevoort*; Catherine (Kate) Gansevoort Curtis (1814–1887), the wife (from 1836) of a lawyer named George Curtis (1789–1884); Leonard Herman Gansevoort, Jr.*; Francis M. Gansevoort (1818–1819); Herman Richard Gansevoort (1820–1826); and Stanwix Gansevoort.* Mary Ann Gansevoort was often in poor health and once temporarily lost her memory. Living in Waterford, New York, near Albany, she was friendly with Melville's mother Maria Gansevoort Melville and helped with her children early in their lives.

Some years after her husband's death in 1821 and then that of her mother-in-law Catherine Van Schaick Gansevoort* in 1830, she needed the help of her brothers-in-law Herman Gansevoort* and Peter Gansevoort (1788–1876)* to manage her financial affairs. She also occasionally appealed to old Peter for help, mainly to pay for the education of her son Stanwix when he was a teenager. She worried about her son Guert's navy career, especially after he had been involved in the *Somers* mutiny (1842). She was also troubled when Stanwix entered the navy and was adversely affected by his experiences in it.

Bibliography: Kenney, Leyda.

Gansevoort, Mary Sanford (1814–1841). Melville's aunt. She was the first wife (from 1833) of Peter Gansevoort (1788–1876),* who was the brother of Melville's mother Maria Gansevoort Melville.* Her father was Nathan Sanford (1777–1838). Having passed the bar (1799), Nathan Sanford became a Tammany Republican leader (from 1802) and a U.S. commissioner of bankruptcy (1802–1803). It is said that during his tenure as U.S. attorney for the district of New York (1803–1815) he gained as much as $100,000 a year. He was a slippery, powerful, anti–Martin Van Buren member of the assembly (1808–1809, 1811), a state senator (1812–1815), a U.S. senator (1815–1821, 1826–1831), and chancellor of New York (1823–1826). He was an unsuccessful candidate for vice president of the United States (1824—John Quincy Adams won). Sanford was an accomplished linguist and enjoyed reading Latin poets. He was married three times. His first wife was Eliza Van Horne of New York; his second, Mary Isaacs of New Haven; and his third, Mary Buchanan of Baltimore. He had one or more children by each wife. A neglected daughter of his second marriage, Mary Sanford Gansevoort had four children, all of whom were obviously Melville's cousins. They were Henry Sanford Gansevoort*; Mary Isaacs Gansevoort (1836–1837); Catherine Gansevoort Lansing,* the wife (from 1873) of Abraham Lansing*; and Herman Gansevoort (1840–1840). Mary Sanford Gansevoort cared for her tubercular father, had a near-miscarriage before the birth of her second daughter, and was injured by the difficult, premature birth of her second son. She died of tuberculosis at age twenty-seven.

Bibliography: Kenney.

Gansevoort, Peter (1749–1812). Melville's maternal grandfather. He was born in Albany. The Gansevoort family had come from Groningen, Holland. As a major in a New York regiment, Peter Gansevoort participated in the invasion of Canada (1775), was promoted to lieutenant colonel, was placed in command of Fort George, became a colonel in a New York regiment, and was put in command of Fort Stanwix (1776). This fort, at the site of present-day Rome, New York, was later called Fort Schuyler. Gansevoort and his 750 men defended the fort against 1,700 Tories and pro-British Indians commanded by General Barry St. Leger (3–22 August 1776), and by so doing prevented the British from reinforcing General John Burgoyne before the Battle of Saratoga. Next, Gansevoort was assigned a command in Albany, returned to Fort Schuyler (1878), saw action against Mohawk Indians (1879), commanded at Saratoga (1880), was active in Albany again, retired, and was commissioned brigadier general of militia (1781). He became sheriff of Albany (1790), was appointed major general of militia to fortify the frontiers in the western district (1793), was a militia agent in the northern department (1802), and was named brigadier general in the regular army (1809). Gilbert Stuart painted General Gansevoort's portrait in full uniform. At the time of his death, Peter Gansevoort was a director of the New York State Bank. His brother, Leonard Gansevoort (1751–1810), was a lawyer, politician, and judge in and near Albany.

General Peter Gansevoort, popularly known as "the hero of Fort Stanwix," married Catherine Van Schaick Gansevoort* in Albany in 1778. The couple had six children, five of whom were obviously Melville's aunts and uncles, or would have been, if they had all lived to adulthood. (One of the five, Petrus Gansevoort [1786–1788], died in infancy.) The four others were Herman Gansevoort,* Wessel Gansevoort,* Leonard Herman Gansevoort,* and Peter Gansevoort (1788–1876).* The sixth child became Melville's mother Maria Gansevoort Melville.* Herman Gansevoort's wife (from 1813) was Catherine S. Quackenbush (or Quackenboss) Gansevoort (1774–1855). Wessel Gansevoort never married. Leonard Gansevoort's wife (from 1809) was Mary Ann Chandonette Gansevoort.* The younger Peter Gansevoort's first wife (from 1833 to 1841) was Mary Sanford Gansevoort*; his second wife (from 1843) was Susan Lansing Gansevoort.* Maria Gansevoort married Allan Melvill* in 1814. They named their first son Gansevoort Melville,* using the old family name, and their second son Herman after his uncle Herman Gansevoort. Peter and Catherine Gansevoort, who were the owners of several black slaves by the 1790s, prospered in houses and lots, other land, lumber, and brewing. Melville in a letter to Evert Duyckinck* says that he and his wife will probably name their new-born son Stanwix because "this lad's great grandfather spent his summers [at Fort Stanwix] in the Revolutionary War before Saratoga came into being—I mean Saratoga Springs & Pavilions" (7 November 1851).

Melville, who never saw his illustrious maternal grandfather, grew up hearing stories about him, and in *Pierre* he modeled his hero Pierre Glendinning's deceased grandfather, General Pierre Glendinning, on him. Melville wrote to his mother to complain that people in New York City did not know that "the Gansevoort Hotel, corner of 'Little twelfth Street' and West Street" was named after "the hero of Fort Stanwix" (5 May 1870). The hotel had been built by the general's sons Herman Gansevoort and Peter Gansevoort in 1833, at a nearly ruinous cost of more than $100,000.

Bibliography: Kenney; NN 14; Amasa J. Parker, ed., *Landmarks of Albany County New York* (Syracuse, N.Y.: Mason & Co., Publishers, 1897).

Gansevoort, Peter (1788–1876). Melville's uncle. Born in Albany, Peter Gansevoort was the son of Peter Gansevoort (1749–1812)* and Catherine Van

Schaick Gansevoort.* Young Peter Gansevoort was better educated than any earlier Gansevoort or any of his siblings. His siblings were Herman Gansevoort,* Wessel Gansevoort,* Leonard Herman Gansevoort,* and Melville's mother Maria Gansevoort Melville.* Keenly intelligent, young Peter Gansevoort attended the Dutch Church Academy in Albany, became a lifelong friend of James Fenimore Cooper* while being tutored for college, attended but disliked William and Mary (1804–1805), transferred to the College of New Jersey (now Princeton—B.A. 1808, M.A. 1811), attended the Litchfield Law School (1808–1809), and was admitted to the bar (1811) and returned to Albany to practice law. He became the private secretary of Governor De Witt Clinton of New York (1817–1819) and judge advocate general of the state of New York (1819–1821). Gansevoort was politically hurt by Clinton's death (1828) but switched his allegiance to pro-Dutch Martin Van Buren and his forces. Gansevoort was a member of the state assembly (1830–1831), a state senator (1833–1836), and first judge of the court of common pleas (1843–1847). He was a director of the New York State Bank (c. 1832–1876), a trustee of the Albany Academy (1826–1876), and chairman of its board of trustees (1856–1876).

Peter Gansevoort's first wife (from 1833 to 1841) was Mary Sanford Gansevoort.* Her father, Nathan Sanford, was a slippery, powerful anti–Martin Van Buren New York City politician who became a U.S. senator and chancellor of New York. Peter and Mary Gansevoort had four children, all of whom were obviously Melville's cousins. They were Henry Sanford Gansevoort*; Mary Isaacs Gansevoort (1836–1837); Catherine Gansevoort Lansing,* the wife (from 1873) of Abraham Lansing*; and Herman Gansevoort (1840–1840). Though devastated by his wife's death, Peter Gansevoort married again. His second wife (from 1843) was Susan Lansing Gansevoort.* He was loyal and helpful to members of his extended family, some of whom were troublesome and demanding; at the same time, he dramatically displayed affection, devoutness, grief, distress, and contrariness. He and his brother Herman Gansevoort tried to cooperate during difficult times, both in commercial ventures and as family leaders, but sometimes could not do all that was begged of them.

In time, Peter Gansevoort became a major source of financial support for various family members. After the death of his brother Leonard Herman Gansevoort (1821), that man's widow, Mary Ann Chandonette Gansevoort,* appealed to him for money. When Melville's father, Allan Melvill,* fell into financial trouble (1826), he asked Peter Gansevoort to obtain a loan for him in the amount of $3,000 or $4,000. While Peter L. Gansevoort, a weak son of the deceased Leonard Herman Gansevoort, was in the U.S. Navy, he asked his uncle Peter Gansevoort to loan him $100 for winter clothes (1831). After Melville's father died (1832), Peter Gansevoort helped the young Melville get a job clerking in the New York State Bank, sent his mother what money he could spare, and let Melville's brother Allan Melville* study law with him until the two had a falling out. For years, Melville's widowed mother was obliged to appeal to both Peter Gansevoort and Herman Gansevoort for money. Peter Gansevoort was always both more able and more generous. He did, however, object once, declaring in a letter to her that he was financially pressed, was wrongly accused of a lack of affection ''because I am prevented by my pecuniary situation from anticipating your wishes,'' said that his gifts to ''you & your family'' caused him ''embarrassments,'' but enclosed $20 anyway (18 December 1839). The Panic of 1837, as well as other misfortunes, had depleted his holdings. Much later, however, he took a vacation in Europe with a lawyer friend (1853), leaving his lonely wife behind.

Melville had great affection for his Uncle Peter and wrote to him frequently and courteously. Melville's unstable friend Eli James Murdock Fly* worked in Peter Gansevoort's law office and later appealed to him for advice and assistance. Some time after his first visit to London (1849), Melville compiled a careful sightseeing list for his uncle (1853). Even in his old age, he called Melville ''Typee.'' His most generous act was sending Melville a check for $1,200 (August 1875), shortly before his death, to pay for the private publication of *Clarel,* which Melville then dedicated to him in affection and gratitude.

Bibliography: Kenney, Leyda, NN 14 and 15.

Gansevoort, Peter L. (1810–1832). Melville's cousin. He was the son of Leonard Herman Gansevoort* and Mary Ann Chandonette Gansevoort.* His father died when the boy was only eleven years of age. He was an unintelligent and unmanageable lad, twice failed the examinations for admission to West Point, joined the merchant marine (1826), and was appointed midshipman in the U.S. Navy (1831) through the influence of his uncle Peter Gansevoort (1788–1876).* While still in the service, he asked his uncle to loan him $100 for winter clothes (1831). A few months later, the young man was drowned at sea in a schooner wreck. His body was recovered and buried in Albany. Melville knew his cousin only slightly.

Bibliography: Kenney.

Gansevoort, Stanwix (1822–1901). Melville's cousin. He was the son of Leonard Herman Gansevoort* and Mary Ann Chandonette Gansevoort.* He was named after Fort Stanwix, which his grandfather Peter Gansevoort (1749–1812)* had defended against the British (1777) during the American Revolution. Stanwix Gansevoort, whose father died before the boy was born, was a problem child. He and Melville knew each other well, from 1826, when they were schoolmates at the Albany Academy, and for decades later. Stanwix's widowed mother complained to her brother-in-law Peter Gansevoort (1788–1876)* that her son was still with her at age seventeen since he lacked money and ought to ''have his little patrimony in his education'' (16 December 1839). After ineffective schooling, he went to sea as a midshipman (from 1841). He presumably merited his mother's written warning to desist from alcohol, since it has had ''the most deleterious effects upon your character'' (22 March 1844). He was in Honolulu a year and a half later. He was on active duty during part of the Mexican War

(1846–1848), and rumor had it that he fought a duel with the son of Stephen Decatur* in the South Pacific area. After resigning from the navy and moving about restlessly, he lived in lonely poverty near his sister Catherine Gansevoort Curtis in Glens Falls, New York, on small family legacies. His generous Uncle Peter willed him $1,000 (1876).

Melville may have had his proscribed cousin in mind when he has the youthful Frank in *White-Jacket* avoid catching the eye of his superior brother Guert Gansevoort* when the two sailors have a chance encounter at sea (1844).

Bibliography: Wilson L. Heflin, ''A Man-of-War Button Divides Two Cousins,'' *Boston Public Library Quarterly* 3 (January 1951): 51–60; Kenney; Leyda.

Gansevoort, Susan Lansing (1804–1874). Melville's aunt. She was the second wife (from 1843) of Peter Gansevoort (1788–1876).* She was the great-niece of John Lansing, Jr., who had been a law partner of Leonard Gansevoort (1751–1810), the brother of Peter Gansevoort (1749–1812),* Melville's grandfather. John Lansing, Jr., went on to a political career before he disappeared under mysterious circumstances, perhaps the victim of foul play. Susan Gansevoort had no children. Melville liked and often sent his love to his domestically inclined, affectionate Aunt Susan when he wrote to his uncle Peter, as he frequently did. On the day Peter Gansevoort died, Melville wrote to Abraham Lansing,* the husband of his cousin Catherine Gansevoort Lansing,* that ''the spirit of Aunt Susan'' had inspired Uncle Peter to finance the private publication of Melville's *Clarel* (4 January 1876).

Bibliography: Kenney, NN 14.

Gansevoort, Wessel (1781–1862). Melville's uncle. He was the son of Peter Gansevoort (1749–1812)* and Catherine Van Schaick Gansevoort,* and was the brother of Melville's mother Maria Gansevoort Melville.* Wessel Gansevoort attended Williams College briefly (1795–1796), served in the army under his father, studied and then sporadically practiced law, sold his interest in the lumber business of his more stable brothers Herman Gansevoort* and Leonard Herman Gansevoort* (1809), and tried being a storekeeper. Never marrying, Wessel Gansevoort turned into a clever, often charming, occasionally quarrelsome alcoholic, contracted venereal disease—perhaps while serving without distinction in the War of 1812—and by the terms of his father's will was given a small allowance on condition that he stay away from Albany. He boarded with neighbors and later died in Danbury, Vermont. Wessel Gansevoort was named— ironically, as it turned out—after the learned Dutch pre-reformation intellectual John Wessel Gansevoort.

Bibliography: Gilman, Kenney, NN 14.

''The Garden of Metrodorus'' (1891). Poem, in *Timoleon.* The poet describes an Athenian garden hidden by hedges, unapproached by any footpath, and notable for ''silence strange.'' He wonders whether ''this stillness [signifies] peace

or sin." A skeptic named Metrodorus,* as quoted by Cicero in the *Academics,* says, "We know nothing, no, not even whether we know or not."
   Bibliography: NN 11.

Gardiner. In *Moby-Dick,* he is a son of Captain Gardiner of the *Rachel.* The lad was rescued from one of the three whaleboats that pursued Moby Dick, but his twelve-year-old brother is missing in the fourth boat.

Gardiner. In *Moby-Dick,* he is the twelve-year-old son of Captain Gardiner of the *Rachel.* The boy is or was in a missing whaleboat tugged out of sight or destroyed by Moby Dick.

Gardiner, Captain. In *Moby-Dick,* he is the Nantucket commander of the *Rachel.* Captain Ahab adamantly refuses to join in the search for Gardiner's twelve-year-old son, who is or was in a missing whaleboat tugged out of sight or destroyed by Moby Dick. After the *Pequod* is sunk, Gardiner by chance sails back and rescues Ishmael.

Gardner, Augustus Kinsley (1821–1876). Physician and author. The son of a New Jersey editor, he was born in Roxbury, Massachusetts, attended Philips Academy and then Harvard (1838–1841), leaving the class of 1842 short of graduation to study for his medical degree at Harvard. He obtained it (1844) with a thesis on syphilis, and then studied obstetrics and lunacy in Paris (1844–1847). Before the outbreak of the Civil War, he worked in Massachusetts and in New York City—in hospitals and dispensaries, a poor house, an asylum, and a medical school. He eventually was professor of midwifery and of women's and children's diseases at the New York Medical College. During the war, Gardner tried without success to obtain permission to send quinine and other medicines through the Union blockade to Southern sufferers of chills and fever. He was the first to propose the installation of public drinking fountains in New York, was the first physician in New York to administer chloroform during childbirth, and imported English sparrows to eat American insect larvae. He invented and modified several surgical instruments. His published books include the following: *Old Wine in New Bottles: or, The Spare Hours of a Student in Paris* (1848), *The French Metropolis. Paris, as Seen during the Spare Hours of a Medical Student* (1850), *The Causes and Curative Treatment of Sterility* . . . (1856), *Lectures on Obstetrics* (1858), *Conjugal Sins against the Laws of Life and Health* . . . (1870), *Our Children: Their Physical and Mental Development* . . . (1872), and *The Conjugal Relationships as Regards Personal Health and Hereditary Well-Being Practically Treated* (posthumously, 1892). He also published *A Practical Treatise of the Diseases of the Sexual Organs of Women* (1861), which was his translation from the French translation of Friedrich Wilhelm Scanzoni von Litchtenfels' book on the subject. Gardner also published articles in medical journals and popular periodicals, on such subjects as gonorrhea, meat, midwifery, and swill milk. Some of his medical publications were considered controversial and daring in his day. A Unitarian, he married Anna Louise Hidden of New York in 1850 (the couple had a daughter).

Melville met Gardner through Evert Duyckinck* and George Duyckinck* (1847). Gardner gave Melville a welcome copy of his *Old Wine in New Bottles.* Melville roomed in a place in the Latin Quarter of Paris recommended by Gardner (27 November–6 December 1849). In addition, he found Gardner's book useful as a guide to Paris and its environs, especially for its comments on the Morgue, the Duypuytren museum of medical horrors, and Versailles. On his return, Melville sent a copy of *Redburn* to "Gardiner" with an accompanying letter ([4?] February 1850). When Melville and his family moved from Pittsfield back to New York City (1863), Gardner evidently became their family doctor. He was called in when Melville's son Malcolm Melville* committed suicide (1867).

Bibliography: Cohen and Yannella; Howard A. Kelly and Walter L. Burrage, *Dictionary of American Medical Biography: Lives of Eminent Physicians of the United States and Canada, from the Earliest Times* (New York: Appleton and Company, 1928); Leyda; NN 14 and 15.

Garibaldi, Giuseppe (1807–1882). Soldier and patriot. He was born in Nice, then part of France but later rejoined to the Kingdom of Piedmont-Sardinia (1814). He was a sailor in the Mediterranean and the Black Sea (1824–1833), was sentenced to death in absentia after participating in a failed mutiny in the Piedmontese navy for republicanism (1834), engaged in would-be liberating military and naval activities in and near Brazil and Uruguay (1835–1848), and returned to Italy (1848). He commanded volunteers in Milan against the Austrians (1848), sought to create a Roman republic (1849), defeated French units outside Rome (1848), retreated skillfully through central Italy to avoid French and Austrian armies, was deported from Piedmont to Tangiers (1849–1850), went to Staten Island, New York (1850–1851), and resided in Peru and sailed commercially therefrom (1851–1853). He returned to Italy (1854); bought half of the island of Caprera, north of Sardinia, for a home (1855); tried unsuccessfully to free political prisoners held by the Bourbon kings of Naples (1856); and conferred with Camillo Benso Cavour* in Piedmont concerning an anticipated war against Austria (1858). Garibaldi led Alpine volunteers well, but when his plan to invade the Papal States was rejected he retired (1859). He criticized Cavour for ceding Nice back to France, led a thousand Redshirts against the Neapolitan Bourbons in Sicily, captured Palermo and Naples, held plebiscites, presented southern Italy to Cavour, defined Victor Emmanuel as king of a united Italy, and returned to Caprera (1860). He criticized Cavour's policies and declined an offer by Abraham Lincoln* of a high command position in the Union Army (1861). Garibaldi fomented further unrest in Italy but was defeated by French and Papal forces, although he did require Austria to let Venice be included in the new Italy (1862–1867). He aided republican French forces against Germany in the Franco-Prussian War (1870–1871).

In his private life, Garibaldi was equally vigorous. In 1839 he eloped with an illiterate Brazilian woman named Anita, who was evidently married; they had a son, got married, and had more children before Anita died while he and she were with his Italian volunteers (1849). In 1860 Garibaldi married Giuseppina Raimondi of Fino, Italy (near Lake Como), but he abandoned her within hours upon being informed that she was pregnant by one of his soldiers (or perhaps by himself). Seven months later, she delivered a still-born child. In 1880 Garibaldi obtained an annulment and married Francesca Armosino, his mistress from the 1860s who had borne him several children. He had several other love affairs and at least one other child by another mistress (1859).

In "Marquis de Grandvin: At the Hostelry," Melville mentions that Garibaldi took Naples by railroad train and later compares him to the Cid. In "Marquis de Grandvin: Naples in the Time of Bomba . . . ," he is mentioned as signaling danger to Bomba's son. Garibaldi is called the Red Shirt.

Bibliography: Acton; Jasper Ridley, *Garibaldi* (New York: Viking Press, 1974).

Gayete, Juan Bautista. In "Benito Cereno," he is the carpenter on Benito Cereno's *San Dominick.* He was severely wounded during the revolt of the slaves.

Gay-Head Indian. In *Moby-Dick. See* Old Gay-Head Indian.

"The 'Gees" (1856). Sketch. It was anonymously published in *Harper's New Monthly Magazine** (March 1856). (Character: Captain Hosea Kean.) The insensitive narrator begins by telling his curious friends that the word " 'Gees" (pronounced with a hard *g*) is a corruption of "Portuguese." Three hundred years ago, Portuguese convicts were transported to colonize the Isle of Fogo off the northwest coast of Africa. The place also had "an aboriginal race of negroes," possessed of much "incivility" but short on "stature and morals." Eventually, only 'Gees remained there. Small and tough, they are clumsy sailors, are docile, reveal credulity, and display fine memories. Yankee skippers and sailors, though making racist remarks about 'Gees as morons with huge appetites, often exploit them to augment depleted crews. "The 'Gees" may be a hoax-like satire against racial prejudice. Melville received $32.50 in payment for "The 'Gees" and "Jimmy Rose" together.

Bibliography: Carolyn L. Karcher, "Melville's 'The 'Gees': A Forgotten Satire on Scientific Racism," *American Quarterly* 27 (October 1985): 421–42; Newman; Sealts.

Genteel, Jack ("Genteel Jack"). In "Bridegroom-Dick," he is a shaggy, amorous sailor whom Bridegroom Dick remembers.

Gentian. In "To Major John Gentian, Dean of the Burgundy Club," he is Major John Gentian's father, who is also a member of the Society of the Cincinnati.

Gentian, Major John ("Jack," "Milor"). In "The Marquis de Grandvin," he is mentioned as the Marquis de Grandvin's foremost disciple. In "Portrait of a Gentleman," he is described as the Dean of the Burgundians, and a gentlemanly, outspoken Northerner of South Carolinian stock who since 1865 had led a quiet life. In "To Major John Gentian, Dean of the Burgundy Club," he is defined as brave and now full of reminiscence. He lost an arm fighting in the Wilderness during the Civil War under [Ulysses S.] Grant, who later appointed him American consul in Naples. In "Jack Gentian (omitted from the final sketch of him)," he is described as becoming infirm in mind and body, but ever loving and kind. In "Major Gentian and Colonel J. Bunkum," he is said to be proud of his Cincinnati badge in his old age. In "The Cincinnati," he is mentioned as a proud member of the Society of the Cincinnati. In "Marquis de Grandvin: At the Hostelry," he is about to tell a story about an afternoon in Naples, according to the Marquis de Grandvin. In "Marquis de Grandvin: Naples in the Time of Bomba . . . ," he is the friend of the Marquis de Grandvin and describes the crowds and activities in the streets and scenes nearby, including fortresses, troops, singers, a dancing girl, Vesuvius, jugglers and tumblers, an urchin, and a canopied priest in a procession; he then thinks about Garibaldi and the future of Italy.

Geoffry. In "Under the Rose," he is the servant of My Lord the Ambassador. Geoffry narrates the events surrounding his master's coveting of the Azem's amber vase.

George the Prince Regent of England. In "Poor Man's Pudding and Rich Man's Crumbs," he is the host at the Guildhall Banquet in London following the Battle of Waterloo.

George III, King (of England, Scotland, and Ireland) (1738–1820). He was the son of the Hanoverian Frederick, Prince of Wales, who died in 1751, and the grandson of King George II, who died in 1760. George III was an impractical idealist who grew shrewd and conservative and whose early reign was marked by administrative instability until Frederick, Lord North, became prime minister (1770). North's Whig opponent, Charles James Fox, caused controversy until William Pitt the Younger became the resourceful prime minister (1783–1801). George III detested the idea that the American colonists should seek independence. The last two decades of his life were shadowed by a mysterious malady, perhaps porphyria, causing blindness and senility. Because of intermittent instability and insanity, he accepted regency rule (1811–1820) by the future George IV, who was the oldest son of fifteen children of George III and his wife Charlotte Sophia of Mecklenburg-Strelits. George III, who had married in 1761, had an interest in botany, patronized the arts, and was admired in Great Britain because of his decent personal morals, love of family, sense of duty, and concern for his people. By comparison, his son's short reign was a scandalous disaster blessedly short in duration (1820–1830).

In *Israel Potter,* George III is the British monarch in whose Kew Gardens Israel Potter works briefly. The two men talk there on one occasion.

Bibliography: John Brooke, *King George III* (New York: McGraw-Hill, 1972).

Georgiana Theresa, Lady. In *Redburn,* she is presumably an acquaintance of Harry Bolton in London. She is said to be the daughter of a certain unnamed earl.

"Gettysburg: The Check (July, 1863)" (1866). Poem, first published in *Harper's New Monthly Magazine** (July 1866) and reprinted in *Battle-Pieces.* Melville depicts the Dagon-like enemy, who "sought to blast us in his scorn, / And wither us in his ire." The rebels' three waves of advance were "foredoomed"; so "Right is a strong-hold yet." Graves of many Union dead buried there earlier were disturbed by artillery fire, but a new monument has already been begun and will soon "soar transfigured in loftier light" and with "ampler" meaning. Conventional and dramatic, Melville designed his partisan "Gettysburg" to attract a larger readership than proved to be the case.

Bibliography: Garner, NN 11, Shurr.

Ghibelli. In *Mardi,* he is a fictitious historian who writes about Ziani's pleasing the Pope by defeating Otho in a naval battle.

Ghofan. In "Benito Cereno," he is an African-born slave, a calker by trade, and is between sixty and seventy years of age.

Ghost. In *Omoo. See* Long Ghost, Dr.

Gifford, Robert Swain (1840–1905). Painter, etcher, and illustrator. Gifford was born on Nonamesset, near Naushon, an island in Buzzard's Bay, Massachusetts. His father was a sailor and a fisherman. The family moved to Fairhaven, Massachusetts, when young Gifford was two years old. He frequented the studios of two marine painters in New Bedford. One was Albert Van Beest, a skillful Dutch marine painter who encouraged Gifford to try painting; the other was William Bradford, in whose home Van Beest lived while he was in Fairhaven (1854–1857). Although Gifford had little formal art training, worked in the Fairhaven railroad yards, and often suffered from ill health, he accepted space to paint in the studio of a Fairhaven sculptor, sold some pictures, and moved to Boston (1864–1866). Going on to New York City (1866), Gifford progressed steadily, was elected to the National Academy (1867), taught art, and married Frances Eliot, one of his pupils (1873). Meanwhile, he had visited the Pacific coastal region to prepare illustrations for William Cullen Bryant's *Picturesque America* (2 vols., 1872–1874). The trip also generated some landscapes. His paintings evolved from realistic to poetically atmospheric, and are notable for their browns and dark grays and for their charming balance. Having visited England, the Continent, and the Middle East earlier (1870), he went abroad again (1874), this time studying scenery in Corsica and North Africa with his wife. Travel took him to Europe yet again (mid-1880s) and also to Alaska (1899). Later he concentrated on the Massachusetts coastal locales, where he loved to study the effects of light and air on the scenes of his youth. Gifford was best at rendering melancholy landscapes and seascapes in the style of old Dutch masters. He is superb at picturing distant objects in hazy air. His best pictures include *Cairo* (1876), *Cedars of New England* (1876), and *Near the Coast* (1885). His best etchings are frank, say much in little, show lights and shades around everyday objects, and have a touching beauty. Gifford, who designed models of yachts, owned his own yacht, the *Fawn,* which his father skippered. Gifford and his wife had seven children, five of whom survived him. His wife painted birds and landscapes and also prepared illustrations for magazines.

In his poem "The Coming Storm," Melville misidentifies R. S. Gifford as "S. R. Gifford," the painter of *The Coming Storm.* This work shows a demon-cloud bursting on a lake. Melville adds that the painting is owned by E.B., i.e., Edwin Thomas Booth.*

Bibliography: Cooper Gaw, "Robert Swain Gifford, Landscape Painter," *Brush and Pencil: An Illustrated Magazine of the Arts of To-Day* 15 (April 1905): 201–11; S. R. Koehler et al., *American Etchings. A Collection of Twenty Original Etchings, by Moran, Parrish, Ferris, Smillie, and Others. With Descriptive Texts and Biographical Matter* (1886; New York: Garland Publishing, 1978).

Ginger Nut. In "Bartleby," he is the Wall Street laywer's twelve-year-old office boy.

"Give Me the Nerve" (1924). Poem, in *The Works of Herman Melville.* The persona asks for unswerving nerve, to tempt danger and courage, and to stay calm in the face of tempests.

Glaucon ("The Smyrniote"). In *Clarel,* he is a Smyrna family scion who is traveling with the Banker and is that man's prospective son-in-law. Glaucon is irresponsible, rakish, happy-go-lucky, and irreverent. Melville probably named him after Socrates's friend Glaucon in *The Republic* of Plato. Melville's Glaucon may have been inspired by a similarly easygoing fellow named Henry whom Melville encountered in Florence, Italy, and wrote about in his journal (27 March 1857).

Bibliography: NN 12 and 15.

Gleig, Samuel. In *Moby-Dick,* he is a sailor lost along with five others from the *Eliza* in 1839. Their shipmates placed a marble tablet in their memory in the Whaleman's Chapel in New Bedford.

Glen. In "Bridegroom-Dick," he was a gun-room sailor remembered by Bridegroom Dick as liking scotch.

Glendinning. In *Pierre,* he is Pierre's great-grandfather. He was mortally wounded in an Indian battle at Saddle Meadows, the location of the Glendinning family estate.

Glendinning, Dorothea. In *Pierre,* she is the lonely, city-dwelling, unmarried sister of Pierre's deceased father. She gave Pierre, when he was fifteen years old, the smaller, more youthful portrait of his father.

Glendinning, General Pierre. In *Pierre,* he is Pierre Glendinning's huge, robust grandfather. He was a heroic Revolutionary War officr who defended a stockaded fort against Indians—including Brandt—Tories, and Regulars. He loved horses. He died in 1812. General Glendinning is closely patterned after Melville's maternal grandfather General Peter Gansevoort (1749–1812),* a robust man who defended Fort Stanwix against enemies of the colonists (1776) and died in 1812.

Glendinning, Mary. In *Pierre,* she is the mother, almost fifty years of age, of Pierre, who oddly calls her "Sister Mary." She is so proud and righteous that he cannot tell her anything about his supposed half-sister Isabel Banford. When Pierre breaks his engagement to Lucy Tartan and leaves Saddle Meadows for the city with Isabel, Mrs. Glendinning curses him, makes out her will in favor of Pierre's cousin Glendinning Stanly, goes insane, and dies.

Glendinning, Pierre. In *Pierre,* he is the younger Pierre Glendinning's well-read, gentle father, who died when the boy was twelve years old. Knowledge that the man had an illegitimate daughter, Isabel Banford, sours his son's memory of his father and ultimately destroys his life. In complex ways, young Pierre's father is partly based on Melville's own father Allan Melvill,* who had an illegitimate daughter, named Ann Middleton Allen,* family rumors about whom Melville undoubtedly heard.
   Bibliography: Young.

Glendinning, Pierre. In *Pierre,* the heroic young scion of the Glendinning family of Saddle Meadows, he is just emerging from his teens. He is engaged to Lucy Tartan until his supposed half-sister Isabel Banford turns up and appeals to him for help. He abandons Lucy, argues with his haughty mother Mary Glendinning, and goes to the city with Isabel—pretending that she is his wife—and with their servant Delly Ulver. Once there, he argues with his cousin Glendinning Stanly. This young man has inherited what would have become Pierre's estate, but Pierre's mother disinherited her son and died. Pierre also argues with Lucy's brother Frederic Tartan, kills Stanly, and poisons himself in prison to avoid death by hanging. Pierre is a partially autobiographical character. Melville undoubtedly learned that his father had an illegitimate daughter, named Ann Middleton Allen.*

   Bibliography: Young.

Gola, Martinez. In ''Benito Cereno,'' he is a Spanish sailor from the *San Dominick* who is prevented by Captain Amasa Delano from killing a shackled black slave with a razor.

Golconda, The Prince of. In ''The Marquis de Grandvin.'' This is an extravagant pseudonym for the Marquis de Grandvin.

Gold-beak. In ''Under the Rose,'' he is the Shaz at Shiraz. During a bridal festival at his palace, Lugar-Lips was inspired to write a poem about the rose-filled amber vase.

''Gold in the Mountains'' (1924). Poem, in *The Works of Herman Melville.* Heaven has no part in the search by greedy men for gold in the mountain or the glen.

Goneril. In *The Confidence-Man,* she is the straight-bodied, cactus-like, vicious wife of John Ringman. Her dreadful conduct causes him to leave her for a wandering life until he learns that she has died. The name Goneril comes from that of the hard-hearted daughter of William Shakespeare's King Lear. It may be that Melville was indirectly giving in Goneril an ugly character sketch of Frances Anne Kemble,* the renowned actress whose readings from Shakespeare Melville attended (1849) and details of whose messy divorce from Pierce Butler he followed (1849).

   Bibliography: Oliver S. Egbert, ''Melville's Goneril and Fanny Kemble,'' *New England Quarterly* 18 (December 1945): 489–500.

''The Good Craft 'Snow-Bird' '' (1888). Poem, in *John Marr.* The poet praises the brave ship ''from sunny Smyrna'' that has fought through icy head winds to bring drums of figs to Boston Bay.

Goodman, Francis (''Frank,'' ''Popinjay-of-the-world,'' ''Philanthropos''). In *The Confidence-Man,* he is the colorfully dressed, skillfully rhetorical, self-styled cosmopolitan whose conciliatory words Pitch mistakenly interprets as acceptably philanthropic. Goodman hears Charles Arnold Noble's story of the Indian-hater Colonel John Moredock, drinks convivially with Noble, and tells him about the unselfish Charlemont. Goodman talks with the mystic Mark Winsome and his practical follower Egbert. Goodman deplores Egbert's story about China Aster. Goodman agrees in writing to guarantee William Cream the barber against loss if he removes his "No Trust" sign, but then he walks out of the shop owing him for a shave. Finally, Goodman talks with an old man and then leads him to his stateroom. Many models for Goodman have been suggested, including the popular Congregationalist preacher Henry Ward Beecher and the versatile writer Bayard Taylor.* In truth, however, Goodman is a highly complex character, being a cosmopolitan con man, false wit-humorist, genial misanthrope, and satirist.

   Bibliography: Bryant, *Repose;* David R. Sewell, "Another Source for the Barber Shop Episode in *The Confidence-Man*," *Melville Society Extracts* 60 (November 1984): 13–14; Trimpi.

Goodwell. In *Redburn,* he is a kind clerk in a New York City forwarding house. Redburn, who knows him, appeals to him to help Harry Bolton find employment.

Graceman, Mark. In *Pierre,* he is a minister whose obituary Pierre writes.

"Grain by Grain." *See* "Rosary Beads."

Grand Duke of Florence, The. In "Marquis de Grandvin: At the Hostelry," he is mentioned as a gouty loser.

Grandissimo, King. In *Mardi,* he is mentioned in a manuscript memoir in Oh-Oh's museum.

Grando. In *Mardi,* he is a philosopher who hated his own body. He is cited by Babbalanja.

Grandvin, the Marquis de ("The Prince of Golconda," "Lord Bountiful"). In "The Marquis de Grandvin," he is extravagantly praised as a generous, eloquent Frenchman, a valued visitor to New York, and a member of various Fifth Avenue clubs—including the Burgundy Club. In "To Major John Gentian, Dean of the Burgundy Club," the Marquis de Grandvin is mentioned. In "Marquis de Grandvin: At the Hostelry," he is a genial Frenchman who at the hostelry speaks about Italian politics, summons shades of famous artists to debate on the nature of the picturesque, and recommends a story to be told by his friend Major John Gentian.

Grant, Ulysses S. (1822–1885). (Full name: Ulysses Simpson Grant; christened name: Hiram Ulysses Grant.) Soldier and president. He was born in Point Pleasant, Ohio, graduated from West Point (1843), served in Missouri and Louisiana and then under General Zachary Taylor* and General Winfield Scott* during the Mexican War (1846–1848). After duty in California and the Oregon Territory, he resigned his commission as captain (1854). He farmed, dealt in real estate in St. Louis, and clerked in Galena, Illinois. When the Civil War started, Grant became a colonel and then brigadier general of Illinois volunteers. His military career was remarkable. He captured Fort Henry and Fort Donelson on the Tennessee River (February 1862), suffered heavy casualties at Shiloh (April 1862), captured Vicksburg (July 1863) and Chattanooga (November 1863), was promoted to lieutenant general (March 1864) and placed in supreme command of the Union Army (March–April 1864), planned and executed an effective but bloody sequence of campaigns—the Wilderness (May 1864), Spotsylvania (May 1864), Richmond (May 1864), Cold Harbor (June 1864), and Petersburg (June–July 1864)—and accepted the surrender of General Robert E. Lee* at Appomattox Courthouse (9 April 1865). After the war, Grant had a falling out with Democratic President Andrew Johnson and was elected president on the Republican Party ticket. During his presidency (1869–1877), fiscal and civil service reforms took place, and his foreign policy was mostly noteworthy. Corruptions and scandals caused by others, however, rocked his administration. He took a world tour (1877–1880), was swept to financial ruin by the corruption of officials of a bank in which he had invested (1884), and died four days after finishing his *Personal Memoirs,* which were both a professional and a financial success (1885).

Grant married Julia Dent of the St. Louis area in 1848. They had three sons—Frederick Dent Grant, Ulysses S. (''Buck'') Grant, and Jesse Grant—and a daughter, Nellie Grant. Frederick Grant was a major general and served in the Philippines during the Spanish-American War. Frederick Grant's son, U.S. Grant III, married Edith Root, the daughter of the jurist-statesman Elihu Root, became a major general, and wrote *Ulysses S. Grant: Warrior and Statesman* (1969). Frederick Grant's daughter Julia Grant married Prince Michael Cantacuzene of Russia. Buck Grant married Fannie Josephine Chaffee, had five children by her, was widowed, and married a woman with the improbable name of America Workman Wills; the couple thus became, even more improbably, U.S. and America Grant. Jesse Grant wrote *In the Days of My Father Ulysses S. Grant* (1925).

In his poetry, Melville, who evidently met Grant briefly in Virginia (April 1864), often makes laudatory mention of him. In ''Donelson (February, 1862),'' he is the Union general who captured Donelson. In ''Chattanooga,'' he is described as watching his brave men charge in advance of his own plans to capture Chattanooga. In ''The Armies of the Wilderness,'' he is depicted as silent, meek, and grim, and is called ''the Man.'' In ''The March to the Sea,'' he is mentioned as having a Union gamecock named after him. In ''The Fall of Richmond,'' he is the three-star general praised for bravery and faith. In ''The Surrender at Appomattox,'' he is pictured as accepting Lee's sword. In ''Rebel Color-Bearers at Shiloh,'' Grant is mentioned. In ''Lee in the Capitol,'' he is the Union general remembered by Lee as victorious in Washington at the close of the Civil War; Lee is now going to the Senate to testify. In "To Major John Gentian, Dean of the Burgundy Club," Grant is mentioned as the commander during the Wilderness campaign, when Gentian lost an arm; Grant later appointed Gentian to be American consul in Naples.

Bibliography: Garner; William S. McFeely, *Grant: A Biography* (New York: Norton, 1981); James Marshall-Cornwall, *Grant as Military Commander* (New York: Van Nostrand Reinhold, 1970); Wilson.

Grasse, François Joseph Paul, Marquis de Grassetilly, Comte de (1723–1788). French naval officer. At the onset of the American Revolution, De Grasse was captain of the *Robuste,* commanded aboard her in combat off Ouessant (1778), was a squadron commodore off Fort Royal, Martinique (1779), cooperated with Charles Hector, Comte d'Estaing* in victories and defeats at Granada and Savannah, sailed to the West Indies to serve well (1780), and returned to France for promotion. In command of a large fleet, De Grasse returned to the West Indies with orders to conquer Jamaica. But his ships were met, between Dominica and islets called the Saints, by the fleet of British Admiral Baron George Brydges, Lord Rodney.* Rodney defeated De Grasse, accepted his surrender and that of the huge French flagship, almost unaccountably broke off the attack on De Grasse's half-demolished fleet (12 April 1782), and thus incurred the criticism of Sir Samuel Hood, Rodney's second-in-command. De Grasse returned via England to France, was subjected to an investigation, was exonerated, but never was in active service again. De Grasse married three times: Antoinette Rosalie Accaron in 1764 (the couple had six children); Catharine Pien Villeneuve; and, unhappily, Christine Marie Delphine Lazare de Cibon. De Grasse died before the French Revolution erupted, after which his four surviving children were driven into exile and to a grateful young United States.

In *Billy Budd,* De Grasse is named as the French naval officer whose fleet was defeated by the British fleet under the command of Admiral Rodney, after which Captain the Honorable Edward Fairfax Vere,* who served under Rodney, was promoted to post captain.

Bibliography: The Operations of the French Fleet under the Count de Grasse in 1781–1782 as Described in Two Contemporaneous Journals (1864; New York: De Capo Press, 1971); David Spinney, *Rodney* (London: Unwin, 1969).

Graveairs, Don. In *Clarel,* he is mentioned as glum in a song during the masque presented at Mar Saba.

Graveling, Captain. In *Billy Budd,* he is the obese, habitually cheerful captain of the *Rights-of-Man.* He becomes sad but is necessarily passive when Lieutenant Ratcliffe impresses Billy from her to Captain Edward Fairfax Vere's *Bellipotent.*

"A Grave near Petersburg, Virginia" (1866). Poem, in *Battle-Pieces*. (Character: Daniel Drouth.) The poet hopes that the grave of Daniel Drouth "may ... [long] be green," true-hearted rebel that he was. Full of fire, he fought and died quickly. The poet also hopes that the gun buried with him will not be unearthed. The poem has an unusually light tone. After the costly Battle of Petersburg, miles south of Richmond (15–18 June 1864), General Ulysses S. Grant* laid the town under siege for nine months.
Bibliography: Boatner, Faust, Garner.

Gray-back. In "Armies of the Wilderness," he is a Confederate prisoner who refuses to tell his Union captors what the enemy earthworks across the valley signify.

Great Duke, The. In "Under the Rose," he is the duke in whose Florentine museum My Lord the Ambassador once saw rare amber in which insects were congealed.

"The Great Pyramid" (1891). Poem, in *Timoleon*. The poet suggest that the overwhelming pyramid must not be made by man but is "some Cosmic artizan's." Its flanks are Alpine. No lichen can find a hold in its "granite-knit," weather-proof sides. Mists and birds float and skim beneath its peak. Persons who try its labyrinths emerge raving "afar on deserts dead." Its creation evokes "a blind surmise" in the observer. Melville recorded his impression of the pyramids in a journal entry partly as follows: "something vast, indefinable, incomprehensible, and awful" (3 January 1857).
Bibliography: NN 11 and 15, Shurr, Stein.

"Greek Architecture" (1891). Poem, in *Timoleon*. Greek buildings do not display magnitude, lavishness, or willful innovation, but, rather, by adapting form to site, "reverence for the Archetype."
Bibliography: NN 11, Stein.

"Greek Masonry" (1891). Poem, in *Timoleon*. Greek masonry appears to have no mortar, lines are scarcely visible, and the blocks "in symmetry congeal."
Bibliography: NN 11, Stein.

Green, Dr. In *The Confidence-Man,* he is an herb doctor mentioned by Pitch as hospitalized in spite of his herbs.

Greene, Richard Tobias ("Toby") (1819–1892). Sailor, sign painter, telegraphist, journalist, and lecturer. After being a telegraphist in Lexington, Kentucky, Greene moved to Sandusky, Ohio, published a poem in the Sandusky *Mirror* (6 November 1854), became an editor of the paper a day later, and for a time conducted a regular column in it regarding literature. One entry (2 January

1855) concerned the Galapagos Islands, which Greene said he visited in 1841 and which he described as a good place to whale from. He was local editor briefly for the Buffalo *Daily Courier* (1855) and probably returned to Ohio. Later he moved to Chicago, served in the Union Army at Vicksburg (among other places), and returned after the war to Chicago, where he died.

Toby Greene was Melville's fellow sailor aboard the *Acushnet* and then his fellow deserter at Nuku Hiva, in the Marquesas Islands (from 9 July 1842). When Greene left Melville to sign aboard another American whaler, Melville lost contact with him until, after the publication of *Typee* (1846), Greene identified himself as the narrator's real-life companion and verified details of their seemingly incredible adventures in "Toby's Own Story," Buffalo *Commercial Advertiser* (11 July 1846). The article was reprinted in newspapers in Albany and New York City. Melville and Greene soon renewed their friendship by correspondence. Greene capitalized on Melville's fame, in part by publishing pieces on his South Sea adventures in his "local" column for the Sandusky *Daily Mirror* (1854, 1855) and a piece about an *Acushnet* sailor nicknamed "Jack Nastyface" in the Sandusky *Commercial Register* (13 January 1855). Greene also gave a lecture entitled "Typee: Or Life in the South Pacific" in Elyria, Fremont, Sandusky, and Toledo, Ohio (February, March 1855); Westfield, New York; and perhaps elsewhere then and later. He called himself "Toby of Typee." *Putnam's Monthly Magazine** published an amusing note from him later (July 1857) to the effect that reviewers of *Typee* were wide of the mark in identifying him as Melville's valet and "man Friday" during their stay in the Marquesas. Greene married Mary J. Derby of Westfield and named their son, born in 1854, Herman Melville Greene. Melville received two letters (4 February 1859, 24 December 1860) from Genessee County, New York, from Oliver Russ, another ex-sailor from the *Acushnet,* in which he reported that Greene had visited his father in the area and also that Greene, an imperfect husband and father, was in Michigan. Russ also mentioned that he and his Maine-born wife named their only child Herman Melville Russ. Greene's nephew was named Richard Melville Hair. Melville wrote to Greene (probably December 1860) that he had had a spoon engraved for Greene's son and another one for Greene's nephew, Richard Melville Hair. Greene wrote to Melville from Memphis (20 October 1863) to mention his Union Army service at Vicksburg and Hair's elsewhere, and to thank Melville for three copies of *Typee*. It is thought that Greene's personal papers, perhaps including letters by Melville, were lost in the 1871 Chicago fire. It is of interest that an accomplished con man named John Wesley Greene (possibly Richard Tobias Greene's brother) impersonated "Toby" on the lecture circuit.

Bibliography: Clarence Gohdes, "Melville's Friend Toby," *Modern Language Notes* 59 (January 1944): 52–55; Kevin J. Hayes, "Toby's *Typee* Lecture," *Melville Society Extracts* 96 (March 1994): 1–4; Richard C. Johnson, Harrison Hayford, and Lynn Horth, "Bulletin: Con Man Claims to Be Toby," *Melville Society Extracts* 96 (March 1994): 4, 16; Leyda; Metcalf; NN 14.

Greenlander, The. In *Redburn,* he is a handsome lady's man of a sailor aboard the *Highlander.* He helps cure Redburn's initial bout of seasickness by giving the lad a dose of rum. The Greenlander later leads a group of sailors who extort drinking money from one of the passengers bound for Liverpool. A native and citizen of Greenland named Peter Brown was a sailor aboard the merchant ship *St. Lawrence,* on which Melville sailed to and from Liverpool (1839) and which he uses as the model for his *Highlander.* Brown is undoubtedly the model for Redburn's friend the Greenlander.

Bibliography: Gilman.

Griggs, Helen Maria Melville (1817–1888). Melville's oldest sister. Although their father Allan Melvill* paid more attention to his sons than to his daughters, she was in comfortable circumstances until he lost his business in New York City, moved with his family to Albany, and died bankrupt and insane (1832). Born lame, she was operated on (1834) to enable her to walk normally. She had probably suffered from congenital dislocation of the hip and clubfoot. She lived at home, attended the Albany Female Academy in the mid-1830s, joined the Dutch Reformed Church of Albany (1837), often visited relatives and friends (including Lemuel Shaw* and his family in Boston), and was friendly with Elizabeth Knapp Shaw [Melville]* before she married Melville. Helen became part of a large Melville household when Melville and his brother Allan Melville* married and set up housekeeping with their respective wives and also their mother and other sisters in New York (1847). She moved with Melville to Pittsfield (1850), copied the manuscript of *Pierre* for him (winter 1851–1852), and lived there until 1856 when she married George Griggs (1814 or 1815–1888). Griggs was a lawyer practicing in Brookline and Boston, Massachusetts. The two first met through Shaw, who had long known Griggs professionally. He was described as gruff and stingy. The Griggses, who made their residence in Brookline, had no children but cared for one of Melville's sons when Melville went to Europe and the Holy Land (1856–1857). Helen Griggs helped proofread *Clarel* for its demanding author (1876). She died seven months after her husband.

Bibliography: Cohen and Yannella, Leyda, Metcalf, NN 14, Smith.

Groot, Myndert Van, Judge. In "To Major John Gentian, Dean of the Burgundy Club," he is a New Yorker whom Major John Gentian knew. As a boy, Groot liked firecrackers.

"A Ground Vine Intercedes with the Queen of Flowers for the Merited Recognition of Clover" (1924). Poem, in *Weeds and Wildings,* as part of a section entitled "This, That and the Other." A lowly vine meekly asks the Rose, the Queen of Flowers, to "own . . . kin with Cousin Clover." After all, the roots of all plants interlock and each one would like to "win" more space and "balmier air."

Grummet. In *White-Jacket,* he is a tobacco-chewing quarter-gunner who refuses to bid at auction on White Jacket's jacket.

Guernseyman, The. In *Moby-Dick,* he is the ignorant chief mate of the French whaler the *Bouton de Rose.* Stubb talks him out of a precious, unsuspected treasure of ambergris inside a whale's disease-riddled corpse.

Guert Gan. In ''Bridegroom-Dick.'' *See* Gansevoort, Guert.

Guide. In ''The Scout toward Aldie,'' he is a fat, wheezing guide for the Union forces pursuing [John Singleton] Mosby. The Guide's son is fighting on Mosby's side, and his wife has also left him.

Guinea. In *The Confidence-Man. See* Black Guinea.

Guinea. In *White-Jacket,* he is the purser's Virginia slave. He ships as a seaman aboard the *Neversink* and attends his indulgent master, who even collects the black man's wages. Guinea is sleek and happy and is regularly excused from witnessing any flogging at the gangway.
   Bibliography: Grejda.

Gun-Deck. In *Redburn,* he is a little sailor aboard the *Highlander* who is full of stories.

Guy, Captain (''The Cabin Boy,'' ''Paper Jack,'' ''Miss Guy''). In *Omoo,* he is the despised, sickly captain of the *Julia.* He hands over command of his ship to John Jermin, the first mate, lounges ashore at Papeetee with his friend the consul Wilson, and leaves Tahiti when he is unable to force his rebellious sailors to continue working for him. Captain Guy is based on Henry Ventom, captain of the *Lucy Ann,* aboard which Melville sailed (1842) and which is the prototype of the *Julia.* Ventom presented an affidavit and a deposition in connection with his difficulties aboard the *Lucy Ann.*
   Bibliography: Lebowitz, Leyda, NN 2.

H

Habbibi ("Habbi"). In *Clarel,* he was a Greek monk, now long deceased, who once lived in a grotto at Mar Saba. He was obsessed by a variety of fears.

Hafiz. In *Clarel,* he is a person in a garden, visited by Didymus, in the song sung by Derwent during the wine party at Mar Saba.

"The Haglets" (1888). Poem, in *John Marr.* (Character: The Admiral of the White.) The poet asks a recumbant figure in a remote chapel to explain. The statue has swords, other trophies, and a weedy winding sheet nearby. It seems that the Admiral of the White, having defeated the Plate Fleet of Spain, leaves with his captives' humbled flags and arms in his "naval hall," and sails home-ward at the head of the captured ships. He does not notice either "the shadowing wings" of three haglets (small sea gulls) "follow[ing] fast in [his] wake" or the sharks "[s]eething" through the waters below. Earlier, the haglets followed the "quelled" Spanish "flag-ship." Soon a "favoring breeze" gives way to a storm that sends the seamen aloft to handle "shivered sails and spars." The oaken vessel meets the challenge, but "the inscrutable haglets" keep silently following. The compass needle quivers, but the helmsman "lets the trembling portent pass." It is New Year's Eve, and the sailors talk of "golden years" ahead for them. The Admiral's officers remember his prophecy—"*A tomb or a trophy*"—while the "aged" leader, alone behind his door, pays no heed to "the blades whose secret thrill / Perverts overhead the magnet's Polar will." Nor do the pursuing haglets care. Doom follows sudden warning lights, seen too late by the well-disciplined but puzzled men. The fatal reefs "deride" boats, cables, and prayers; and the haglets weave and spin through the rigging, until "[t]he weltering wreck" gurgles down into the "abysm." This poem relates to Melville's shorter poem "The Admiral of the White," written earlier. Melville also has Agath recount the same incident in *Clarel*. Melville was inspired to write about these nautical tragedies after he had heard his captain in the harbor of Salonica, during his 1856–1857 trip to the Mediterranean area, tell how clashing swords once damaged a compass; Melville recorded the anecdote in his journal (7 and 8 December 1856). "The Haglets" was published in a shorter form in the New York *Daily Tribune* and in a different form in the Boston *Herald* (both as "The Admiral of the White" and both on 17 May 1885).

   Bibliography: Cohen, *Poems;* NN 11 and 15; Shurr; Stein.

Hair-Brains. In "A Scout toward Aldie," this is the name by which one Union soldier refers to himself during the Colonel's ill-fated pursuit of [John Singleton] Mosby.

Hal. In "Bridegroom-Dick," he is a sailor recalled by Bridegroom Dick. The *Merrimac,* aboard which Hal served, sank the *Cumberland,* on which his former shipmate Will was a crew member.

Hal, Prince. In "Falstaff's Lament over Prince Hal Become Henry V." *See* Henry V, King.

Hall, James, Judge. In *The Confidence-Man,* he is Charles Arnold Noble's father's friend and the source of Noble's story about Colonel John Moredock the Indian-hater.

Hals, Frans (c. 1580? or c. 1585?–1666). Painter. The son of a Catholic cloth weaver and his Protestant wife, Hals is thought to have been born in Antwerp. In time, he joined the Calvinist church. He studied painting (c. 1603); joined the Guild of St. Luke, a Haarlem painter's association (1610); belonged to a chamber of rhetoric, which was a literary and theatrical club (1616–1625); and became a private in the civic guard of the St. George Guild, partly to advance his career as a portraitist (c. 1639). Hals was a prolific painter, often of portraits of upper-class citizens and members of the intelligentsia, civic guards, and city officials and their wives, but also of rustic people, musicians, and children. He painted René Descartes (1649). Hals was occasionally in financial trouble because of debts and also money owed him. Toward the end of his life, Haarlem officials pensioned him generously (from 1662). He was not greatly esteemed by his peers, although some praised the verisimilitude, liveliness, and novelty of many of his paintings. He grew away from the artistic tradition of his era, visualized his subjects uniquely, evolved his own style, grew somewhat more gloomy, caught fleeting expressions superbly, and was remarkable for his treatment of hands and clothing. Arnold Houbrakan's life of Hals (1718) started a probably apocryphal story that the eminent Flemish painter Anthony Van Dyck,* before his departure for England (1632), called on and praised Hals and his work. Hals married Anneke Harmens about 1610 (the couple had two sons); when she died, she was buried in a pauper's grave (1615). He married Lysbeth Reyniers in 1617 (they had ten children). His brother Dirck Hals and two of his sons, Jans Hals and Franz Hals II, were competent painters. Among Franz Hals's 145 or so preserved original works, the following are among the finest: *Banquet of the Officers of the St. George Civic Guard* (1616), *Laughing Cavalier* (1624), *Laughing Whore* (c. 1626, also called *Gipsy Girl*), *The Lute Player* (1626), *Two Singing Boys* (c. 1627), *The Merry Drinker* (c. 1629), *The Greengrocer* (1630), *Officers of a Company of the Amsterdam Crossbow Civic Guard* (1635, completed by another), *Malla Babbe* (c. 1640), *Isabella Coymans* (1648), and *Regentesses of the Old Men's Almshouse in Haarlem* (1664).

In "Marquis de Grandvin: At the Hostelry," Melville mentions Franz Hals as a painter who discusses the picturesque and also English patronage with Van Dyke.

Bibliography: Claus Grimm, *Frans Hals: The Complete Work,* trans. Jürgen Riehle (New York: Harry N. Abrams, 1989).

Haman. In "The Bell-Tower," this is the name of the grotesque monster—also called Talus. Haman was designed and constructed by Bannadonna as his mechanical slave, to act as his bell striker. Haman clubs his creator to death at— and with—the stroke of one.

Bibliography: Russ Castronovo, "Radical Configurations of History in the Era of American Slavery," *American Literature* 65 (September 1993): 523–47.

Hancock, John (1737–1793). Merchant and politician. The son of a minister, he was born in Braintree (now Quincy), Massachusetts. When his father died, young Hancock was adopted by his childless paternal uncle, graduated from Harvard (1754), entered business with his uncle, and studied business in London (1760–1761). Back home, he inherited his uncle's profitable mercantile firm (1764). Rich though he was, Hancock was soon in the thick of anti-British politics, protested the Stamp Act (1765), was caught smuggling wine off his sloop *Liberty* (1768), was elected to the state's General Court (1769–1774), and became president of the Massachusetts Provincial Congress when it replaced the General Court (1774–1775). He was a delegate to the Continental Congress (1775–1780, and president thereof 1775–1777). With a celebrated flourish, he was the first to sign the Declaration of Independence (1776) and then sought unavailingly to be the commander-in-chief of the Continental Army. He helped frame the Massachusetts constitution and was governor of Massachusetts (1780–1793), except for the time of Shays's Rebellion (1786). He announced that he would gladly be president of the United States if George Washington* declined the position. Hancock broke loose from his mistress, one Mrs. Dorcas Griffiths, to wed Dorothy Quincy of Fairfield, Connecticut, in 1775. The couple had a daughter who died in infancy and a son who died in a skating accident at age nine. Hancock was generous and ambitious, but too eager for adulation and of limited intellect and ability.

In "Major Gentian and Colonel J. Bunkum," John Hancock is mentioned as resisting the tea tax of King George III but not for the sake of democracy.

Bibliography: Herbert S. Allen, *John Hancock: Patriot in Purple* (New York: Macmillan, 1948).

Hancock, Winfield Scott (1824–1886). Army general. Hancock, named after Winfield Scott,* was born in Montgomery Square, near Norristown, Pennsylvania, to which his family moved when he was a toddler (1828). He attended the Norristown Academy and then West Point. After graduation (1844), he served in Texas (1844–1846) and with gallantry under General Scott during the Mexican War (1846–1848). During the years preceding the Civil War, Hancock gained experience by serving in Florida during the Seminole War, on the borders of Kansas, in Utah, and as a quartermaster on the Pacific coast. Then came the Civil War. On the recommendation of General George B. McClellan,* who had known him at West Point, Hancock was promoted to brigadier general (September 1861) and was placed in command of a brigade of Maine, New York, Pennsylvania, and Wisconsin regiments, which fought during the Peninsular Campaign (beginning March 1862), at Antietam (September), and elsewhere. Hancock was named major general in command of the First Division, II Army Corps (November 1862) and fought so skillfully at Fredericksburg (December) and at Chancellorsville (May 1863) that he was put in command of II Army Corps, which performed superbly at Gettysburg (July). Severely wounded, Hancock later fought in the Wilderness (May 1864) and at Spotsylvania (May), and was recalled to supervise recruiting work in Washington, D.C. (November). After the war, he was named a major general in the regular army (July 1866) and continued his distinguished military career in the West, Louisiana, and Texas. Though without any political experience, Hancock was considered as a Democratic candidate for the presidency on two occasions (1868, 1872), was nominated for president (1880), but lost to James Garfield, the Republican candidate. In his memoirs, Ulysses S. Grant* describes Hancock as unpretentiously striking in appearance and praises him as a faultless corps commander. McClellan dubbed him "The Superb." Hancock married Almira Russell of St. Louis in 1850 (the couple had a son and a daughter, both of whom predeceased their father).

In his poem "On the Photograph of a Corps Commander," Melville's persona looks at the "cheering picture" of a military figure, defines the subject, who is Hancock though unnamed, as a "manly" leader, and accords him high praise.

Bibliography: Glenn Tucker, *Hancock the Superb* (Indianapolis: Bobbs-Merrill, 1960).

Handsome Mary. In *Redburn. See* Danby, Handsome Mary.

Handsome Sailor. In *Billy Budd,* he is a typically tall and handsome sailor whose shipmates walk with him on shore. Billy Budd is described as such a type.

Hannibal, Rohon Del Aquaviva, Don ("The Eld of Mexico"). In *Clarel,* he is a one-armed and one-legged veteran fighter for Mexican freedom. Now skeptical of progress and reform, he is a friend of Derwent.

Hans. In "A Dutch Christmas up the Hudson in the Time of Patroons," he is a boy who dances with Cousin Chris.

Hanto. In *Mardi. See* Hauto.

Happy Bone-setter, The. In *The Confidence-Man. See* the Happy Man.

"The Happy Failure" (1854). (Full title: "The Happy Failure, a Story of the River Hudson.") Short story. (Character: Yorpy.) The narrator, a young lad, meets his uncle by the Hudson River. With the help of the aged man's faithful old African-American servant, they load a heavy box onto a skiff and row it to an island upstream. The box contains the uncle's arduously constructed invention of pipes and syringes by which the fellow plans to drain swamps and thereby gain riches and plaudits. Warning his companions to be on the lookout for spies, the uncle uncrates and experiments with his contraption. It fails totally. He gripes but soon regains his composure and advises his nephew "never [to] try to invent anything—but happiness." They plan to sell the useless metal for scrap. The experience renders the nephew wiser. The uncle becomes a good old fellow and, when dying, seems to be devout in praise of God for his failure. The depiction of an old man and his old black servant may owe something to Legrand and Jupiter in "The Gold Bug" by Edgar Allan Poe.* The notion of serenity, even joy, owing to failure comes more directly from Melville's observations of a pair of serenely unsuccessful uncles and also his own growing stoicism during the mid-1850s when he philosophically faced the indifference of his readers to his literary inventiveness. Melville's authorship of this story, anonymously published in *Harper's New Monthly Magazine** (1 July 1854) and probably earning him about $15, is established by indirect but convincing evidence.

Bibliography: John M. J. Gretchko, "An Incisive Analogue to 'The Happy Failure,' " *Melville Society Extracts* 86 (September 1991): 9; Newman; NN 9; Sealts.

Happy Man, The ("The Happy Bone-setter," "Mr. Palaverer"). In *The Confidence-Man,* this is the reported nickname of the herb doctor. He sells Omni-Balsamic Reinvigorator and Samaritan Pain Dissuader to a sick man, a cripple named Thomas Fry, and a senile miser. However, a shaggy backwoodsman refuses to buy any of his nostrums and instead slugs him. Nor does Pitch buy any.

Happy Tom. In *The Confidence-Man. See* Fry, Thomas.

Hardy, Ezekiel, Captain. In *Moby-Dick.* He is a whaling captain killed by a sperm whale off the coast of Japan in 1833. His widow erected a tablet in his memory in the Whaleman's Chapel in New Bedford.

Hardy, Joe. in *White-Jacket,* he is a shipmate reported killed in an imaginary sea fight.

Hardy, Lem ("Hardee-Hardee"). In *Omoo,* he is an English-born deserter turned "renegado from Christendom" at Hannamanoo who, after ten years ashore, has become the military leader and a war god of the island. He even married into the royal family. Hardy evidently gave Melville erroneous information about tattooing on the island of Hivarhoo.
   Bibliography: Anderson.

Hardy, Mrs. Ezekiel. In *Moby-Dick,* she is Captain Ezekiel Hardy's widow. She erected a tablet in his memory in the Whaleman's Chapel in New Bedford.

Harper & Brothers. Publishers. The brothers, James Harper (1795–1869), John Harper (1797–1875), Joseph Wesley Harper (1801–1870), and Fletcher Harper (1806–1877), came from an honorable, religious, well-read farm family living in Newtown, Long Island, until they moved to New York City (1816). Earlier, James Harper had so admired the autobiography of Benjamin Franklin* that he decided to become a printer himself, was apprenticed in New York, and lived there (from 1811). One of his fellow printers was Thurlow Weed,* later famous in editorial work and politics. John Harper was apprenticed to a printer in New York (1812), and the two brothers started their own printing business there (1817). They issued 200 books as J. & J. Harper. In came Wesley Harper (1823), and then Fletcher Harper (1825). The firm changed its name to Harper & Brothers (1833), with the disarming explanation that any brother was the first-named "Harper." The brothers dipped into a common financial pool as each needed cash for business and personal expenses. They gradually developed specialties: James Harper was pressman; John Harper, compositor; Wesley Harper, literary expert; and Fletcher Harper, go-getter. They pioneered with steam presses and big-volume electrotyping. For several years (before 1853), the firm printed twenty-five books a minute during each ten-hour workday. James Harper suggested *Harper's New Monthly Magazine** (1850), but Fletcher Harper managed it and also started *Harper's Weekly* (1857) and *Harper's Bazar* (1867). He also allowed Thomas Nast free rein even though his cartoons for *Harper's Weekly,* blasting the Tweed Ring for corruption in Albany and New York, jeopardized the Harper brothers' lucrative schoolbook business throughout the state. Fletcher Harper often went abroad on business. James Harper was elected mayor of New York City on a reform ticket (1844); he sought reelection but was too honest to succeed. He was killed in a horse-carriage accident (1869). For decades, Harper & Brothers was the most successful publishing firm in the United States and perhaps in the entire world. The numerous authors, both American and foreign, published by the firm include Richard Henry Dana, Jr.,* Charles Dickens, Hamlin Garland, Thomas Hardy, William Dean Howells, Henry James, Sarah Orne Jewett, Theodore Roosevelt, William Makepeace Thackeray, Anthony Trollope, Mark Twain, and Owen Wister. Their best illustrators include Edwin Austin Abbey, Winslow Homer, and Howard Pyle.

The Harpers, as they were usually called, rejected Melville's *Typee,* on the grounds that the narrative could not be true (1845); however, they subsequently published his *Omoo, Mardi, Redburn, White-Jacket, Moby-Dick, Pierre,* and *Battle-Pieces* and later obtained the American publishing rights to *Typee* (1849). They suffered a devastating fire when a can of fluid used for cleaning plates was accidentally ignited (10 December 1853). All six houses of the firm on Cliff Street and going back to Pearl Street were destroyed, along with nineteen power presses, adjacent hand presses, and plates. The loss of buildings and contents was reckoned at $600,000; the plates, another $400,000. The brothers, who had some insurance and much money in reserve, were back in business soon (summer 1855).

Melville's works were so unpopular by this time that the firm did not reissue them. Melville was actually in debt to the firm, especially after the financial failures of *Pierre* and *Battle-Pieces,* until 1878. Thereafter, slightly better sales permitted the firm to send Melville a check for $223.72 (1884) and then a final one for $50.02 (1887). Incidentally, Melville's friend Dana declined the Harpers' tentative offer of a 10 percent royalty after the first 1,000 copies of his *Two Years before the Mast* would be sold; instead, he accepted $250 plus 24 copies for all rights (1840). By the time the original copyright had run out (1869), Dana estimated Harper profits on his book at about $50,000.

Bibliography: Eugene Exman, *The Brothers Harper: A Unique Publishing Partnership and Its Impact upon the Cultural Life of America from 1817 to 1853* (New York: Harper & Row, 1965); Exman, *The House of Harper: One Hundred and Fifty Years of Publishing* (New York: Harper & Row, 1967); Leyda; NN 14; John Tebbel, *A History of Book Publishing in the United States,* vol. 1, *The Creation of an Industry 1630–1865* (New York: R. R. Bowker, 1972).

Harper's New Monthly Magazine. Magazine. It was founded and published by Harper & Brothers,* mainly by Fletcher Harper, in 1850. It ran until 1900, changed its name to *Harper's Monthly Magazine* and then *Harper's Magazine,* and is still being published. In 144 double-columned pages and with sparse woodcuts, it started with a bang—by pirating and serializing the best of British novelists, and at first without paying any nonrequired royalties. It also included biographical sketches, essays on science, and travel pieces. The artwork soon became superb, and American authors were given space, mostly for short works. For example, Melville published "Cock-a-Doodle-Doo!", "The Fiddler," "The 'Gees," "The Happy Failure," "Jimmy Rose," "The Paradise of Bachelors and the Tartarus of Maids," and "Poor Man's Pudding and Rich Man's Crumbs" in *Harper's,* which also printed "The Town-Ho's Story" from *Moby-Dick* (1 October 1851). Columns devoted to humor were added, and "The Editor's Easy Chair" became a fine feature of the magazine (from 1851), especially when George William Curtis* handled it (1859–1892). At the beginning of the Civil War, *Harper's* enjoyed a circulation of 200,000, but its early attempts to be fair to the South cut temporarily into sales figures. Later, Henry Mills Alden ably edited *Harper's* (from 1869 to 1919) and brought it to unusual distinction.

Bibliography: Frank Luther Mott, *A History of American Magazines, 1850–1865* (Cambridge, Mass.: Belknap Press of Harvard University Press, 1957).

Harry. In *Moby-Dick,* he is a sailor who, with Jack and Joe, is suspicious of Jonah in Father Mapple's sermon at the Whaleman's Chapel in New Bedford.

Harry the Reefer. In "The Death Craft," he is the narrator, a sailor who dreams that he is aboard an imperiled craft and then awakens—to embrace his wife.

Harry, Top-Gallant. In "Bridegroom-Dick." *See* Top-Gallant Harry.

Hat, The. In *Clarel,* this is a name for Nehemiah, used because he is hatted among turbaned Turks in Jerusalem.

Hautboy. In "The Fiddler," he is the titular hero, a short, fat, ruddy-faced fiddler about forty years of age. His emotional and intellectual balance is something the narrator Helmstone admires. Hautboy is a former touted child prodigy. It has been suggested that the depiction of Hautboy may be Melville's mild caricature of Cornelius Mathews.*

Bibliography: Donald Yannella, "Writing the 'Other Way,'" pp. 63–81 in Bryant, *Companion.*

Hautia, Queen. In *Mardi,* she is the luscious queen of Flozella-a-Nina. As an incognita, she stares at Yillah on the isle of Odo and evidently spirits her away, perhaps to a watery death. Hautia sends flower-bearing messengers to follow Taji on his quest for Yillah, and finally though only temporarily woos him on her delightful island, which he visits in the hope of gaining news about Yillah. Hautia is a combination, common in romantic literature, of glittering serpent and seductive enchantress ruling an island paradise. The name Hautia may come from a hibiscus of that name which is native to the South Seas and which is mentioned by Frederick Debell Bennett in his *Narrative of a Whaling Voyage round the Globe, from the Year 1833 to 1836* (2 vols., 1840), a possible source

for Melville's *Mardi.* Hautia was also the name of an early nineteenth-century prime minister of Huahine Island, in the Society Islands.
Bibliography: Davis, Lebowitz, Wright.

Hauto. In *Mardi,* he is a reader who told Lombardo that his *Koztanza* was rather good, according to Babbalanja. Hauto's name is spelled ''Hanto'' in some editions of *Mardi.* The name Hauto, however, suggests haughtiness.
Bibliography: NN 3, Wright.

Hawthorne, Nathaniel (1804–1864). Author. He was born in Salem, Massachusetts. His father was a sea captain, who died of yellow fever in Surinam, Dutch Guiana (1808). Young Hawthorne injured his foot (1813), read a great deal indoors, and was tutored at home. He moved with his mother and two sisters to Maine and attended school in Portland (1818–1819). He graduated from Bowdoin College (1825), with Henry Wadsworth Longfellow, the future poet, and Franklin Pierce, the future president, as classmates. Hawthorne resided in his mother's Salem home for years (1825–1838). During this time, he published his first novel, *Fanshawe* (1828), at his own expense, edited *The American Magazine of Useful and Entertaining Knowledge* for almost no pay in Boston (1836), and edited *Peter Parley's Universal History on the Basis of Geography* (1837). He also published *Twice-Told Tales,* a collection of short stories (1837); it included such classics as ''The Gentle Boy,'' ''The Gray Champion,'' ''The May-Pole of Merry Mount,'' ''The Minister's Black Veil,'' and ''Wakefield.'' He took a job as a measurer of salt and coal in the Boston Custom House (1839–1840), and wrote little during this time; published *Grandfather's Chair, Famous Old People,* and *Liberty Tree,* three collections of historical essays in fictional frames (1841); and lived at the Brook Farm utopian community at Roxbury, then just outside Boston (1841). He published an expanded edition of *Twice-Told Tales* (1842), adding ''The Ambitious Guest'' and ''Endicott and the Red Cross,'' among other pieces. Hawthorne married Sophia Amelia Peabody in 1842 (the couple had three children). While the Hawthornes were living at the Old Manse, Concord, Massachusetts (1842–1845), Hawthorne associated with numerous proponents of transcendentalism, including Ralph Waldo Emerson* and Henry David Thoreau.* Hawthorne and his family moved into his mother's home (1845–1847). He published *Mosses from an Old Manse,* another collection of stories (2 vols., 1846); it features ''The Artist of the Beautiful,'' ''The Birth-Mark,'' ''The Celestial Railroad,'' ''Drowne's Wooden Image,'' ''Earth's Holocaust,'' ''Egotism; or, the Bosom Friend'' (later called ''Egotism; or, The Bosom Serpent''), ''Rappaccini's Daughter,'' ''Roger Malvin's Burial,'' and ''Young Goodman Brown,'' among other stories. Hawthorne took a job as a surveyor in the Salem Custom House (1846); but when the Whigs under President Zachary Taylor* gained power, most Democrats, including Hawthorne, were swept from their politically appointed positions (1849). Hawthorne was forced to accept financial assistance from friends for a while.

After publishing *The Scarlet Letter* (1850), Hawthorne moved with his family to Lenox, Massachusetts (1850–1851), where Frances Anne Kemble* and Melville were neighbors and Oliver Wendell Holmes* was a summer resident. In 1851 Hawthorne published *The House of the Seven Gables* and *The Snow-Image, and Other Twice-Told Tales*; the latter includes ''Ethan Brand,'' ''The Great Stone Face,'' and ''The Snow-Image: A Childish Miracle,'' as well as a republication of his 1832 ''My Kinsman, Major Molineux'' (later called ''Major Molineux''). The Hawthornes resided in West Newton, Massachusetts (1851–1852). In 1852, Hawthorne purchased a house called the Hillside in Concord, Massachusetts, from Bronson Alcott, renamed it the Wayside, lived there with his family (until 1853), and published *The Blithedale Romance, A Wonder-Book for Girls and Boys,* and *Life of Franklin Pierce.* Then, after publishing *Tanglewood Tales, for Girls and Boys* (1853), he became U.S. consul in Liverpool, England, where he went with his family and served until 1857. Instead of returning to America, he vacationed with his family in England, France, and Italy (1857–1860). The literary fruits of these years were *The Marble Faun* (1860) and several notebooks (published posthumously). Hawthorne resumed residence at the Wayside, hoping to continue writing; however, depression over the Civil War and poor health caused a decline in productivity. He did publish *Our Old Home* (1862), a travel book about England, but soon died, leaving a mass of literary fragments.

Hawthorne knew many of the leading men and women of letters of his time, including George William Curtis,* Evert Duyckinck* and George Duyckinck,* Emerson, Holmes, Longfellow, the educator Horace Mann (his wife's brother-in-law), Melville, the reform-publisher Elizabeth Peabody (his sister-in-law), and Thoreau. While in Italy, Hawthorne socialized with literary and artistic expatriates, both American and British.

Melville and Hawthorne first met on 5 August 1850 during a sociable literary outing at Stockbridge, Massachusetts, near Pittsfield, where the Melvilles were living. Present also at the gathering were Evert Duyckinck, George Duyckinck, Holmes, Cornelius Mathews,* and several others. While there, Melville denied Holmes's contention that English writers were better than American writers. Evert Duyckinck later wrote to his wife that Hawthorne merely looked on. Melville wrote ''Hawthorne and His Mosses'' either just before the outing or just after their meeting. A little later, Melville, Duyckinck, and Mathews called on Hawthorne and enjoyed sampling some of his champagne. Hawthorne wrote to Duyckinck (29 August 1850) to praise the author of ''Hawthorne and His Mosses,'' which Melville had just published in Duyckinck's *Literary World.* Coincidentally, Hawthorne in the letter praised Melville's writings, especially *Redburn* and *White-Jacket;* he also said he liked *Mardi*—but with reservations. Melville visited the Hawthornes in Lenox (3–7 September 1850) and delighted the whole family. Melville wrote to Duyckinck again, to praise Hawthorne for ''evincing a quality of genius, immensely loftier, & more profound, too, than any other American has shown hitherto in the printed form'' ([12 February 1851]). When Hawthorne sent him a copy of *The House of the Seven Gables,*

Melville replied in part thus: "There is the grand truth about Nathaniel Hawthorne. He says NO! in thunder; but the Devil himself cannot make him say *yes*" ([16 April? 1851]). Melville probably revised much of *Moby-Dick,* which he dedicated to Hawthorne, because of his evolving influence. The two saw one another later in 1851 and continued to correspond. Hawthorne sent Melville a letter, which is now lost but which evidently praised *Moby-Dick.* To it, Melville replied in part: "A sense of unspeakable security is in me this moment, on account of your having understood the book. . . . I shall leave the world, I feel, with more satisfaction for having come to know you. Knowing you persuades me more than the Bible of our immortality" ([17? November 1851]). Melville wrote to Hawthorne's wife about *Moby-Dick* thus: "I had some vague idea while writing it, that the whole book was susceptible of an allegoric construction, & also that *parts* of it were—but the speciality of many of the particular subordinate allegories, were first revealed to me, after reading Mr Hawthorne's letter, which . . . intimated the part-&-parcel allegoricalness of the whole" (8 January 1852). Melville wrote to Hawthorne at least three times in 1852 (beginning in August) to discuss the so-called Agatha Story.*

When Franklin Pierce was elected president and asked Hawthorne to become American consul to Liverpool (December 1852), Melville hoped for a diplomatic post himself. Hawthorne met in New York with his brother Allan Melville,* who assembled letters of recommendation and sent them to Washington, D.C., where Hawthorne, then conferring with Pierce about his own mission, tried unsuccessfully to help Melville. On his way to the Holy Land, Melville spent a few days with Hawthorne in and around Liverpool (10–14 November 1856). Hawthorne signed for Melville the contract with Longman, Brown, Green, Longmans, & Roberts, the London publishers of *The Confidence-Man* (20 March 1857). Later, Melville and Hawthorne drifted apart. Melville's portrayal of Vine, the gifted, reclusive character in *Clarel,* may owe much to the friendship of the two writers. In "To Major John Gentian, Dean of the Burgundy Club," Melville mentions Hawthorne as a person who appreciates the past. In his 1891 poem "Monody," Melville may well be thinking of Hawthorne when he writes of loving someone but being estranged—"[a]nd neither in the wrong."

Hawthorne's son Julian Hawthorne wrote *Nathaniel Hawthorne and His Wife: A Biography* (1884) and *Hawthorne and His Circle* (1903). While preparing the first book, he wrote to Melville to ask for letters from Hawthorne to Melville but was told that they had been destroyed. The second book contains a description of Melville as furtive, nervous, and aimless, which caused Melville's widow Elizabeth Knapp Shaw Melville* to write the author to object; Julian Hawthorne evidently never replied.

Bibliography: NN 14; James C. Wilson, ed., *The Hawthorne and Melville Friendship: An Annotated Bibliography, Biographical and Critical Essays, and Correspondence between the Two* (Jefferson, N.C.: McFarland, 1991).

"Hawthorne and His Mosses" (1850). (Full title: "Hawthorne and His Mosses: By a Virginian Spending July in Vermont.") Essay. It was anonymously published in the New York *Literary World* (17, 24 August 1850). (Characters: Cherry, Pop Emmons, Nathaniel Hawthorne, Tompkins, a Virginian.) A Virginian spending July in Vermont explains that his country cousin Cherry gave him a copy of *Mosses from an Old Manse* by Nathaniel Hawthorne. The narrator, who says that he does not know Hawthorne, took the book to the hay barn, lay down in "new mown clover," and read it in ecstasy. "The soft ravishments of the man spun me round about in a web of dreams." The narrator especially liked "Buds and Bird-Voices" and "Fire-Worship." "The Old Apple Dealer" he found suffused with "the subtlest spirit of sadness." "Monsieur du Miroir" was "charming"; "Earth's Holocaust," appalling. "The Christmas Banquet" and "The Bosom Serpent" would challenge "curious and elaborate analysis." The narrator confesses that "it is that blackness in Hawthorne . . . that so fixes and fascinates me," partly because it is also against such blackness that "Shakespeare plays his grandest conceits." Shakespeare may be too unconditionally adored. America can produce Shakespeares too. The narrator qualifies: "Now, I do not say that Nathaniel of Salem is a greater than William of Avon. But the difference between the two men is by no means immeasurable." The narrator urges Americans to "prize and cherish" their own writers. After naming a few, Melville praises *Twice-Told Tales* and *The Scarlet Letter* and then, concentrating on *Mosses from an Old Manse* a final time, discusses "Young Goodman Brown," which he calls "deep as Dante," and "A Select Party," which he much prefers to *The Faerie Queene* by Edmund Spenser. He concludes that Hawthorne has "the largest brain with the largest heart" of any writer America has thus far produced.

Whether Melville wrote this essay before or after he met Hawthorne is still in dispute. Evert Duyckinck,* editor of *Literary World,* made changes in the manuscript.

Bibliography: NN 9.

Hay-Seed. In *Moby-Dick,* he is a typical green bumpkin who comes to New Bedford to ship aboard a whaler.

"Hearth-Roses" (1924). Poem, in *Weeds and Wildings,* as part of a section entitled "As They Fell." (Character: Love.) The sugar maple is rose-like— musky, red, and mortal. The poet expresses the hope to Love that when they die their dust will smell sweet like that of hearth roses.

Bibliography: Stein.

"Hearts-of-Gold" (1924). Poem, in *The Works of Herman Melville.* When he is "snug in . . . bed," the poet dreams of Hafiz, Horace, and Beranger [Pierre Jean de Béranger], all of whom are wine-loving, "hearts-of-gold" eluders of "the Fall."

Bibliography: Shurr, Stein.

Heath, Joyce. In "The New Planet," she is described as the former nurse of General [George] Washington. Now 104 years of age, she is a feature of the American Museum. P. T. Barnum* exhibited her, as Joyce Heth, in his museum.

Hello, King. In *Mardi*, he is the convivial ruler with King Piko of the island of Diranda. The two reduce their exploding population by holding gory war games on the Field of Glory. Hello's name may be a polite form of "Hell." Melville may have been inspired to satirize war in this manner by reading Thomas Robert Malthus's *Essay on the Principle of Population* (1798, rev. 1803).

Helmstone. In "The Fiddler," he is the narrator. Helmstone is an unsuccessful poet whose moroseness Hautboy the fiddler succeeds in dissipating.

Henro. In *Mardi*, he is King Bello's father, who seized control of Kaleedoni, according to King Media. Bello has been identified as a satirical portrait of the King of England and Kaleedoni as Scotland. Henry VIII of England defeated the forces of James IV of Scotland and killed him (1513).

Henry V, King. A major character in William Shakespeare's *King Henry IV, Part I*, and *King Henry IV, Part II*, and the central figure in his *King Henry V.* In "Falstaff's Lament over Prince Hal Become Henry V," he is the monarch whose royal snub of him Jack [Sir John] Falstaff laments; Falstaff calls Henry V the "Beadle of England."

Her. In "Lyon," she would seem to be the wife of Lyon. Melville says, "he [General Nathaniel Lyon] wrote the will, / And left his all / to Her for whom 'twas not enough to fall." Next morning, Lyon leads his troops to his death. (It should be noted, however, that Lyon never married and that he bequeathed most of his $30,000 estate to the Union government.)

"Herba Santa" (1891). Poem, in *Timoleon*. The persona suggests that smoking tobacco—"Pacific Herb," "ruffled fag," "weed"—can provide peace and comfort more successfully than even a "supper divine," which results in "bickerings" and "feuds." The poem explicitly praises the Indian peace pipe and implicitly criticizes hypocrisy in some Christians. Melville was blissfully addicted to nicotine.
    Bibliography: Cohen, *Poems;* NN 11; Shurr; Stein.

He Sing. In "On the Chinese Junk," he is a Mandarin who addresses a love poem to the daughter of Chang Ching. (He is also called Hesing.)

Hevaneva. In *Mardi*, he is a materialistic carver of religious icons and canoes on the isle of Maramma. The name Hevaneva most likely derives from that of

Hevaheva, who was a priest of the war god of Hawaiian chieftain Kamehameha I* (sometimes spelled Tamehameha) and who is mentioned in William Ellis's *Polynesian Researches* (4 vols., London, 1833). The name is usually given as Hewahewa.
   Bibliography: Davis, Wright.

High-Chief, A. In *Moby-Dick,* he is the King of Kokovoko and is Queequeg's father.

High Priest, A. In *Moby-Dick,* he is Queequeg's noble uncle and the brother of the King of Kokovoko, Queequeg's father.

Hilary. In "Inscription Epistolary to W.C.R.," preceding *John Marr,* he is the poet's fictitious friend, a Manhattan optician who theorizes that William Clark Russell* reveals his New-World birth in his writings, even though his parents were English and he was reared in England. Calling the insight "moonshine," the poet goes on to praise Russell's novel *The Wreck of the Grosvenor.*

Hill, Ambrose Powell (1825–1865). Confederate Army officer. He was born in Culpepper County, Virginia, graduated from West Point (1847), served during the Mexican War (1846–1848), fought against the Seminole Indians (1849–1850, 1853–1855), and resigned his captaincy to defend his native state (1861). Rising to the rank of lieutenant general in the Confederate Army, Hill served in numerous engagements against Union forces: the First Battle of Bull Run (July 1861), Williamsburg (May 1862), the Seven Days' Fight (June–July), the Second Battle of Bull Run (August), Antietam (September), Fredericksburg (December), Chancellorsville (where he was wounded, May 1863), Gettysburg (July), the Wilderness (May 1864), and Cold Harbor (June). He was twice on sick leave (May 1864 and March 1865). Returning to his troops at the siege of Petersburg, he was shot and killed by Union soldiers (2 April 1865). Hill married Kitty Grosh Morgan, the sister of the future Confederate General John H. Morgan, in 1859. Hill was regarded as brave, aggressive, and unusually willing to sustain heavy losses; but he was also psychosomatically ill on occasion and was never distinguished. In Melville's poem "The Released Rebel Prisoner," Hill is mentioned as a dead Confederate leader thought of by the released prisoner.
   Bibliography: Boatner, Faust.

Hiram [I], King. In "Rammon," he is the king of Tyre. He has a commercial alliance with Solomon that survives both monarchs and makes possible Zardi's visit with Prince Rammon. Rammon knows that Hiram's sailors often tell about the Enviable Isles.

[. . .] Hivohitee MDCCCXLVIII. In *Mardi,* he is the present pontiff, a feared oracle, of the isle of Maramma. He is the product of no less than 1,847 successive incestuous unions. During the lifetime of any Hivohitee pontiff, his name may not be spoken. This ban results in linguistic confusion on Maramma. Yoomy interviews him and finds him to be a hermit living in darkness.

Hoadley, Catherine ("Kate") Gansevoort Melville (1825–1905). Melville's sister. Although her father Allan Melvill* paid more attention to his sons than to his daughters, she was in comfortable circumstances as a child until he lost his business in New York City, moved with his family to Albany, and died bankrupt and insane (1832). When her brother Gansevoort Melville* seemed to be recouping the family's fortunes, she attended the Albany Female Academy with her sisters. These girls were more often with their mother Maria Gansevoort Melville,* who wrote to her brother Peter Gansevoort (1788–1876)* back in 1829 that Catherine was her most rebellious, ungovernable child. She joined the Presbyterian Church (1843). When Melville got married (1847), he and his brother Allan Melville,* also recently married, set up housekeeping in New York City with their respective wives, and their sisters, including Catherine Melville. When Melville and his family moved to Arrowhead, near Pittsfield, Massachusetts (1850), the sisters accompanied them. Catherine Melville married John Chipman Hoadley* in Pittsfield, in 1853, and lived with him in Lawrence, Massachusetts. The couple had two daughters, Maria Gansevoort Hoadley Mackintosh (1855–1904, Mrs. William H. Mackintosh) and Charlotte Elizabeth Hoadley (1859–1946), and one son, Francis Washburn Hoadley (1865–1930—he married Frances A. Swift).

   Bibliography: Gilman, Leyda, Metcalf, NN 14.

Hoadley, John Chipman (1818–1886). Civil and mechanical engineer, engineering designer, and manufacturer. Hoadley was born in Martinsburg, New York. His father, a farmer, moved with his family to Utica (1824). After public schooling, young Hoadley spent two years in a Utica machine and pattern shop and a few months with a surveying team along the Utica and Binghamton railroad, and studied a year at the Utica Academy. In 1836 he aided engineers surveying for an Erie Canal enlargement, advanced from rodman to surveyor, was put in charge of the Utica-to-Rome section, and was praised for his accuracy. In 1844 Hoadley became a civil engineer at a textile plant in Lancaster, Massachusetts, in charge of building and installing equipment in new mills. In 1848 he and the inventor and industrialist Gordon McKay established a firm in Pittsfield, Massachusetts, to construct mill machinery, steam engines, and waterwheels. Hoadley became supervisor of a machine shop in Lawrence, Massachusetts (1852–1857), which built textile and paper-mill machinery, waterwheels, steam engines, and locomotives. After the Lawrence shop failed (1857), he constructed and improved portable steam engines by himself (1857–1877). He served a term as a Massachusetts state representative (1858) and went to England during the Civil War as a state-militia captain to report on harbor ordnance so as to improve such defenses back home (1862). He was a charter member of the American Society of Mechanical Engineers. From 1873, he acted mostly as a consultant and as an expert witness in patent and damage lawsuits. He suffered financial reverses (1877) but retained his poise and good temper. He lectured on water meters, engine pressures, and engine temperatures, and published in his field, his leading works being *The Portable Steam Engine* (1863) and *Steam Engine Practice in the United States* (1884). He was a member of the State Board of Health, Lunacy, and Charity (1873–1882); was a staunch abolitionist and a devout Episcopalian; and enjoyed literature, could read French, German, Greek, and Latin, and occasionally wrote poetry.

Hoadley married Charlotte Sophia Kimball, the daughter of a friend of Lemuel Shaw,* at Needham, Massachusetts, in 1847; she died the following year. Hoadley married Catherine Gansevoort Melville, Melville's sister, at Pittsfield, in 1853 and thus became Melville's brother-in law; the couple had three children. (*See* Hoadley, Catherine Gansevoort Melville.) According to family tradition, Melville did not approve of the marriage but soon got along well with Hoadley, partly because of their common literary interests but largely because of Hoadley's sympathy, generosity, and keen intelligence. When Melville gave him a copy of *Moby-Dick,* his inscription called Hoadley a friend "closer than a brother" (6 January 1853 [1854]). In a letter to Hoadley, Melville acknowledged receipt of Hoadley's poem about Marco Polo, sent him a copy of his own poem "The Age of the Antonines," and wrote as follows: "I remember that the lines were suggested by a passage in Gibbon (Decline & Fall) Have you a copy? Turn to '*Antonine*' &c in index. What the deuce the thing means I dont know; but here it is" ([31 March] 1877).

Bibliography: Leyda, NN 14.

Hodnose. In *White-Jacket,* he is a sailor who with Dobs is accused by a Down Easter sailor of stealing his dunderfunk.

Hoffman, Charles Fenno (1806–1884). Author and editor. Hoffman was born in New York City, went to a harsh school in Poughkeepsie, returned home to be tutored, and suffered an accident requiring the amputation of his right leg (1817). He studied at Columbia (1821–1824) but failed courses and did not graduate (honorary M.A. 1837). He studied law in Albany, was admitted to the bar (1827), practiced in a dilatory way until 1830, by which year he was already a successful author of newspaper articles. Hoffman was coeditor of the New York *American* (1830), edited the new *Knickerbocker Magazine* (1833), traveled through the Northwest Territory on horseback, and returned to edit the *American Monthly Magazine* (1835–1836). He edited the New York *Mirror* and worked with Horace Greeley on the *New Yorker.* He was clerk for the surveyor of the Port of New York (1841), was deputy surveyor (1843–1844), and was terminated only for political reasons. Returning to journalism, he worked for the *Evening Gazette* and became editor of the New York *Literary World,* associating with Melville's friend Evert Duyckinck* (1847). Hoffman clerked briefly for the State Department in Washington, D.C., suffered a severe mental disorder, grew worse (1849), and in 1850 was committed to a hospital in Harrisburg, Pennsylvania, where he remained insane until his death. Hoffman wrote nonfictional prose, novels, and poetry, the best in each genre, respectively, being *Wild Scenes in the Forest and Prairie* (1839), *Greyslaer: A Romance of the Mohawk* (1840; dramatized anonymously [1840]), and *The Vigil of Faith and Other Poems* (1842). Hoffman's misfortunes included the accidental burning by a servant of the unique manuscript of his novel *The Red Spur of Ramapo* (1842), which he never rewrote.

Through Duyckinck, Melville met Hoffman in New York City (1847). Hoffman reviewed *Typee* favorably in the *Gazette and Times* (28 March 1846). When Melville heard of Hoffman's mental condition, he wrote Duyckinck a letter, part of which reads thus: ''he was just the man to go mad—imaginative, voluptuously inclined, poor, unemployed, in the race of life distanced by his inferiors, unmarried,—without a port or haven in the universe to make.'' Melville continues, ''[I]n all of us lodges the same fuel to light the same fire. And he who has never felt, momentarily, what madness is has but a mouthful of brains'' (5 April 1849). Melville was thrilled by Hoffman's stirring military poem ''Monterey'' (1856). In ''To Major John Gentian, ᴺean of the Burgundy Club,'' Melville notes that John Gentian knew Charlie Fenno Hoffman personally.

Bibliography: NN 14.

Hohori. In *Mardi,* he is King Media's attendant whose faultlessly beautiful teeth King Peepi of Valapee and the beggar Jiji of Padulla unsuccessfully covet.

Holmes, Oliver Wendell (1809–1894). Physician, professor of anatomy, and man of letters. Born in Cambridge, Massachusetts, Holmes graduated from Harvard (1829), studied medicine in Paris (1833–1835), and earned a medical degree at Harvard (1836). He taught at Dartmouth (1838–1840) and, after private practice, at Harvard (1847–1882). Holmes found time to publish in a variety of genres. His several collections of poems begin with *Poems* (1836). His *Homeopathy and Its Kindred Delusions* (1842) stirred up a professional controversy. His books of essays include *The Autocrat of the Breakfast-Table* (1858), *The Professor at the Breakfast-Table* (1860), *The Poet at the Breakfast-Table* (1872), and *Over the Teacups* (1872). His novels are *Elsie Venner* (1861), *The Guardian Angel* (1867), and *A Mortal Antipathy* (1885)—called ''medicated novels'' because they dramatize aspects of Holmes's forward-looking psychoanalytical theories. In 1840 Holmes married Amelia Lee Jackson, the daughter of a Massachusetts Supreme Court justice in Boston. The couple had two sons and a daughter. Oliver Wendell Holmes, Jr. (1841–1935), was a Union Army officer during the Civil War, then an attorney, and finally a brilliant justice of the U.S. Supreme Court.

Oliver Wendell Holmes knew all of the literati in the Boston-Cambridge area. The Holmes family vacationed in Pittsfield, Massachusetts, at their summer residence just north of the Melvilles' Arrowhead (1849–1856). Holmes and Melville met at the famous Berkshires picnic (5 August 1850), which was also attended by Evert Duyckinck,* Nathaniel Hawthorne,* and Cornelius Mathews,* among others. On this occasion, Melville opposed Holmes's theory that British literature was superior to American literature. In June 1855, Holmes, summering at Pittsfield, treated Melville for spinal rheumatism, sciatica, and perhaps depression. Melville, who later saw Holmes socially, must have relished three of Holmes's most celebrated poems: "Old Ironsides" (1830), "The Last Leaf" (1831), and "The Deacon's Masterpiece; or, The Wonderful 'One-Hoss Shay' " (1858). The first poem praises a venerable warship; the second concerns Major Thomas Melvill,* Melville's grandfather; and the third satirizes Calvinism. When Melville says in "I and My Chimney" that Hiram Scribe, the master mason, examined the narrator's chimney, he is thought to be alluding to Holmes's examination of Melville himself.

Bibliography: Howard; Leyda; Metcalf; Sealts; Miriam Rossiter Small, *Oliver Wendell Holmes* (New York: Twayne, 1962).

Holy Joe. In "Tom Deadlight," he is evidently the chaplain aboard the British *Dreadnought.*

Honest Jack. In "Falstaff's Lament over Prince Hal Become Henry V." *See* Falstaff, Sir John.

"Honor" (1924). Poem, in *The Works of Herman Melville.* (Character: The King of India.) The King of India orders a lavish parade, replete with elephants, grandees, trumpets, banners, and soldiers—all to see "the Diamond of Golconda." But what about "the Litle Pearl of Price"?

Horror, A. In *Clarel. See* Toulib.

"The House-top: A Night Piece (July, 1863)" (1866). Poem, in *Battle-Pieces.* This harsh work was inspired by the New York drafts riots (13–16 July 1863), during which mobs ranged through the streets looting, committing arson, and lynching scapegoat blacks. Mobs also sacked the draft headquarters at Third Avenue and 46th Street. The riots were in protest against the First Conscription Act (3 March 1863). Aiming to gather more soldiers for the Union Army, it made all men from twenty to forty-five years of age liable to military service but exempted those able to purchase immunity for $300 or to buy a three-year substitute. The first draft drawings had ignited riots in New York City working-class neighborhoods. Peace was restored when militia regiments arrived and the draft law was suspended. Writing in sinewy blank verse, Melville's narrator positions himself safely above lowly roof tops, in the sultry night air, reports hearing the "muffled sound" of the approaching rioters, and observes fires leaping up and glaring. The town is like a ship taken over by rats. The behavior of the populace, thrown "whole aeons back in nature," illustrates the soundness of "Calvin's creed"—especially concerning innate depravity—and the "cynic tyrannies of honest kings." When the Draconian authorities call out the artillery, the "redeemed" town gives pious thanks but fails to note that the policy negates the notion that "Man is naturally good" and undeserving of the scourge.

Bibliography: Boatner; Cohen, *Poems;* Faust; Garner; NN 11; Shurr; Warren.

Howe, William Howe, 5th Viscount (1729–1814). British army officer. An illegitimate descendant of King George I, Howe was active in North America during part of the French and Indian War (1754–1763), became a Whig member of Parliament (from 1758), and opposed his country's harsh treatment of the American colonists, but he obeyed the order of King George III* to return to America. He helped defeat the colonists at Bunker Hill (1775) and was elevated (1776) to the position of supreme commander of the British forces. Knighted (1776), he captured and occupied New York City (1776–1777); defeated Americans at White Plains, the Brandywine, and Germantown (1777); and occupied Philadelphia (1777–1778). His failure to rout the troops of George Washington* at Valley Forge led indirectly to the British defeat at Saratoga (1778). Both Howe and his brother Admiral Lord Richard Howe may have secretly sympathized with the American cause. William Howe resigned (1778), returned to England, took up commands there, was promoted to general (1793), and on the death of his brother gained the Irish title of Viscount Howe (1799). He was a fine tactician, a poor strategist, and a popular officer. In *Israel Potter,* Lord General Howe is the British commander in America whose very name Ethan Allen reviles during his disgraceful captivity in Falmouth, England.

Bibliography: Ira D. Gruber, *The Howe Brothers and the American Revolution* (New York: Atheneum, 1972).

Hugh. In "Running the Batteries," Hugh is a Union sailor aboard a ship with Ned and Lot running past the Confederate batteries at Vicksburg.

Hughes, Sir Edward (c. 1720–1794). English naval officer. Born in Hertford, he joined the Royal Navy (1735), saw action at Porto Cabello (1739), was promoted to lieutenant (1740), and served in engagements at or near Cartegena (1741), Toulon (1744), Louisbourg (1758), and Quebec (1759). He returned to England (1763) and as a commodore became commander-in-chief of forces in the East Indies (1773–1777). Promoted to rear admiral and knighted (1778), he resumed the position of commander-in-chief of the East Indies (1779–1783) with a six-ship squadron, including the flagship *Superb.* He destroyed the fleet at Mangalore of Haider (also spelled Hyder) Ali, the cruel ruler of Mysore and an ally of France (1780). As vice admiral, he took a large force back into the East and was reinforced by three additional vessels—the *Hero,* the *Isis,* and the *Monmouth.* Hughes helped take Negapatam despite Dutch defense forces (1781) and returned to defend Madras against anticipated French forces. He fought five gory but indecisive battles between Madras and Tricomalee against a French squadron commanded by Admiral Pierre André de Suffren de Saint Tropez* (1782–1783), during which Hughes retook Tricomalee (1783). When peace was declared (1783), he returned to England and was later designated Admiral of the Blue (1793). Hughes enriched himself in India to the amount of £40,000 per year. He married Ruth Ball, had no children, and willed his fortune to her son by a previous marriage. That ne'er-do-well married a Spanish dancer and wasted his inheritance by gambling and dissipation.

In *Israel Potter,* Melville names Sir Edward Hughes, calling him "Hughs," as the commander of the fleet including the *Unconquerable,* the *Undaunted,* and the *Unprincipled* and heading for East Indian waters. It is aboard the *Unprincipled* that Israel Potter is impressed from Dover; she is sailing to join the other two vessels when Potter is sent from her to become part of the depleted crew of a revenue cutter.

Bibliography: C. E. Buckland, *Dictionary of Indian Biography* (1906; New York: Haskell House, 1968); James Ralfe, *The Naval Biography of Great Britain . . . during the Reign of His Majesty George III* (London: Whitmore & Penn, 1828).

Hull, Isaac (1773–1843). American naval officer. He was born in Derby, Connecticut. His father, an army officer during the American Revolution, was captured by the British and spent a year in a filthy prison ship (1777–1778); later he was a whaleboat flotillaman. Young Hull, who was adopted by William Hull,* his uncle and the illustrious American Revolutionary War veteran, became a cabin boy at age fourteen, grew experienced at sea, and was a ship master by age nineteen. Commissioned lieutenant aboard the *Constitution* (1798), he fought in the Tripolitan War on ships he commanded (1801–1805) and was promoted to commander (1804) and captain (1806). After shore duty back home, he commanded the *Constitution* (1810–1812), and during the War of 1812 wrecked, captured, and burned the British frigate *Guerrière* 700 miles east of Boston (1812). His victorious ship was dubbed "Old Ironsides," later immortalized in the poem "Old Ironsides" by Oliver Wendell Holmes.* Hull had responsible shore assignments, between which as a commodore (from 1824) he commanded a Pacific squadron (1824–1827)—partly on the frigate *United States* off Callao and Valparaiso—and a Mediterranean squadron, with headquarters at Minorca (1839–1841). He finally made his home in Philadelphia (from 1841). Hull married Anna McCurdy Hart of Saybrook, Massachusetts, in 1813. The couple had no children. He distressed his crew by taking his wife and her unmarried sister aboard with him to Callao and Minorca. He was twice charged with financial irregularities but exonerated (1822, 1833). Hull was able, courageous, and impatient. In "Bridegroom-Dick," Hull is mentioned as a famous naval officer with whom [Thomas] ap Catesby [Jones] served.

Bibliography: Bruce Grant, *Isaac Hull[,] Captain of Old Ironsides: The Life and Fighting Times of Isaac Hull and the U.S. Frigate Constitution* (Chicago: Pellegrini and Cudahy, 1947); Louis B. Wright and Julia H. Macleod, *The First Americans in North*

Africa: William Eaton's Struggle for a Victorious Policy against the Barbary Pirates, 1799–1805 (Princeton, N.J.: Princeton University Press, 1945).

Hull, William (1753–1825). Soldier. Born in Derby, Connecticut, Hull worked on his grandfather's farm, graduated from Yale (1772), taught for a year, studied divinity briefly at Yale, read for the law in Litchfield, Connecticut, and passed the bar (1775). Elected captain of a Derby company of soldiers, Hull joined George Washington* at Cambridge, Massachusetts, rose in the ranks—from captain (1776) to major (1777) and lieutenant colonel (1779)—and participated in battle after battle, before and after arduous winterings north of New York City—at White Plains, Trenton, Princeton, Saratoga, Monmouth, Stony Point, and Morrisania (October 1776–January 1781). After leaving the army (1784), he returned to his law practice in Newton, Massachusetts, headed diplomatic missions to Canada (1784, 1793), helped suppress Shays's Rebellion (1786), and visited England and France (1798). President Thomas Jefferson appointed Hull governor of the Michigan Territory (1805). When the War of 1812 began, he reluctantly accepted a commission as brigadier general, commanded inadequate army and Ohio militia forces—many of whom deserted—and also lacked proper support from Major General Henry Dearborn, his superior in the Niagara River–New England theater. Hull's enemies in the field included the Shawnee chief Tecumseh's ruthless warriors as well as British army regulars, who controlled Lake Erie. He was therefore unable either to attack British forces north of Detroit effectively or to defend the American fort there. To prevent a threatened massacre of civilians, including part of his own family, Hull surrendered Fort Detroit (August 1812). He was court-martialed (1814), largely as a scapegoat in a trial presided over by Dearborn, who had been replaced as Niagara commander for incompetence (1813). Hull was acquitted of treason but was convicted of cowardice and neglect of duty, and he was sentenced to be shot. President James Madison approved the sentence but remitted the punishment because of Hull's Revolutionary War record and because of his age. Cashiered, Hull returned to Newton.

Hull married Sarah Fuller of Newton in 1781. The couple's son was killed in action (1814) during the War of 1812. The Hulls also adopted Isaac Hull,* the future naval hero. William Hull published a defense of his 1812 actions (1814) and then his memoirs (1824). His daughter Maria Hull Campbell and his grandson James Freeman Clarke, the Kentucky clergyman and transcendental friend of Ralph Waldo Emerson* and Nathaniel Hawthorne,* published Hull's biography (1848).

In *The Confidence-Man,* General Hull is identified as an army officer whose act of apparent cowardice was such that it caused brave Colonel John Moredock to refuse to sleep in a bed once slept in by Hull.

Bibliography: Henry Adams, *History of the United States of America during the First Administration of James Madison* (New York: Charles Scribner's Sons, 1890); Charles H. Weygant, *The Hull Family in America* (Pittsfield, Mass.: Sun Printing Company, 1913).

Hummee Hum. In *Mardi,* this is one of the twelve aristocratic Tapparian families on the isle of Pimminee, entertained by Nimni. A hum is a hoax; to hum is to humbug.
   Bibliography: Wright.

Hunilla. In ''The Encantadas,'' she is the tragic Chola widow. A half-breed Indian from Payta, Peru, she went with her husband Felipe and her brother Truxill to collect tortoise oil on Norfolk Isle. Through terrible adversity, Hunilla was left there alone for three horrible years.
   Bibliography: Bryan C. Short, *Cast by Means of Figures: Herman Melville's Rhetorical Development* (Amherst: University of Massachusetts Press, 1992).

Hurta, Roderigo. In ''Benito Cereno,'' he is a boatswain's mate who is thrown overboard alive with Manuel Viscaya from the *San Dominick* during the slave revolt.

Hussey, Hosea. In *Moby-Dick,* he is the proprietor of the Try-Pots on the island of Nantucket. Ishmael and Queequeg stop there before signing aboard Captain Ahab's *Pequod.* Hussey and Peter Coffin are cousins.

Hussey, Mrs. Hosea. In *Moby-Dick,* she is the wife of the proprietor of the Try Pots on the island of Nantucket. She is famous for her clam chowder, which Ishmael and Queequeg enjoy.

Huysum, Jan van (1682–1749). Dutch painter. The son and older brother of painters, he was born in Amsterdam. He painted detailed and brightly colored flower-and-fruit still lifes, in the baroque style. He occasionally included elegantly drawn insects. Two of his notable works are *Flowers* (1706) and *Bouquet of Flowers* (1726). He pioneered in using light backgrounds. His landscapes are less esteemed. In ''Marquis de Grandvin: At the Hostelry,'' Huysum is a flower painter mentioned by Dolce (*see* Dolci, Carlo).
   Bibliography: Maurice Harold Grant, *Jan van Huysum, 1682–1749, Including a Catalogue Raisonné of the Artist's Fruit and Flower Paintings* (Leigh-on-Sea, England: F. Lewis, 1954).

I. In *Mardi,* she is one of the three vain daughters of Nimni, on the isle of Pimminee. The others are A and O.

"I and My Chimney" (1856). Sketch. (Characters: Anna, Biddy, Claude, Captain Julian Dacres, Julia, Hiram Scribe, Deacon White.) The narrator smokes his pipe constantly in his old farmhouse whose enormous, pyramidal chimney, some twelve feet wide at its base, is also an inveterate smoker. The narrator's wife complains that the chimney takes up too much of the ground floor. Fireplaces let into the chimney, floor after floor, also make the upper rooms small and inconvenient. But the narrator relishes his spine-like chimney and the stairs spiraling around it, and he wants the old structure—and his Montaigne, cheese, wine, chairs, and even neighbors—to remain unchanged. Supported by their two daughters, his wife is addicted to newness, has wanted for some time to tunnel through the chimney to the awkward dining room, and even hires an architect to draw up plans to eliminate the chimney. The narrator resists and refuses to surrender even though the architect asserts that the chimney has a secret compartment with a hidden treasure. To his wife's complaint that the house is settling because of the chimney's weight, the narrator replies that he and his chimney can sink together—as in a feather bed. He bribes the architect to declare in writing that there is no hidden chamber in the chimney. Despite various threats, the narrator, not having left his chimneyed realm for seven years now, stands guard; as he grimly concludes, "I and my chimney will never surrender."

"I and My Chimney," which was anonymously published in *Putnam's Monthly Magazine** (1 March 1856) and was not reprinted in Melville's lifetime, has personal overtones. The farmhouse, its chimney, and its locale all resemble his 1850–1863 residence at Arrowhead, near Pittsfield, Massachusetts. Melville was afflicted with spinal rheumatism and sciatica so severe that Oliver Wendell Holmes* ministered to him (June 1855). Melville describes his narrator as somewhat similarly crippled. The narrator's wife may be humorously patterned on Melville's wife Elizabeth Knapp Shaw Melville,* who, however, once noted that Melville's mother Maria Gansevoort Melville* was a more likely model. The nonpareil nagging wife, however, is that of Rip Van Winkle, created by Washington Irving,* whose works Melville enjoyed. The master mason who examines the narrator's chimney is an indirect picture of Holmes. Melville also agreed with his friend and neighbor Nathaniel Hawthorne* in praise, amounting almost to worship, of the domestic fireplace.

Bibliography: Newman, Sealts, Young.

Ibrahim Pasha (1789–1848). Egyptian general and viceroy under Ottoman rule. He was born in Kavalla, Rumelia, the eldest son of Muhammad Ali, an Egyptian ruler who had seventeen sons and thirteen daughters (by one wife and eight or more concubines). Ibrahim Pasha joined his father in Egypt (1805), became governor of Cairo, defeated rebels in Arabia (1816–1818), and held others at bay in Greece (1824) until British, French, and Russian forces caused his retreat. He was victorious against Syrian forces beyond Palestine (1831–1832). When Syria and Adana were ceded to Egypt, Ibrahim Pasha became governor of both provinces. His rule was enlightened but severe. His defeat of an Ottoman army invading Syria (1839) frightened European powers into negotiating a treaty in London (1840) whereby Muhammad Ali forfeited Syria and Adana so as to be allowed to continue to rule Egypt. When the old man became deranged by illness (1848), Ibrahim Pasha was named viceroy but soon died, a few months before his father. In *Clarel,* Ibrahim Pasha is mentioned as the tough military leader under whom Belex fought at one time in Lebanon.

Bibliography: Afaf Lutfi Al-Sayyid Marsot, *Egypt in the Reign of Muhammad Ali* (Cambridge, England: Cambridge University Press, 1984).

Iceland Sailor. In *Moby-Dick,* he is a *Pequod* sailor who refuses to dance during the midnight festivities in the forecastle.

Ictinus (also spelled Iktinos) (fl. 5th century B.C.). A Greek architect, Ictinus designed and built the Parthenon at Athens (447–431 B.C.), with the help of Callicrates (a fellow architect and a possible professional rival) and with the encouragement of the statesman Pericles* and the sculptor Phidias. Ictinus also helped build the Hall of the Mysteries, Eleusis (c. 440 B.C.). Pausanius in his *Description of Greece* (1st century B.C.) identifies Ictinus as the architect of the Temple of Apollo Epicurius at Bassae, in Arcadia, near Phigalia (c. 420 B.C.). In ''The Parthenon,'' Melville names Ictinus as the reputed architect of the Parthenon, while in ''Suggested by the Ruins of a Mountain-Temple in Arcadia,

One Built by the Architect of the Parthenon," he is the Architect of the Parthenon.

Bibliography: R. A. Tomlinson, *Greek Sanctuaries* (New York: St. Martin's Press, 1976).

Ideea. In *Omoo,* she is the backsliding and only partly Christianized daughter of Farnow, in Tahiti.

Ides, Queen. In *Mardi,* she is Donjalalo's thirtieth-night queen.

Illyrian, The. In *Clarel. See* the Arnaut.

"Immolated" (1924). Poem, in *The Works of Herman Melville.* The poet, who once lived with hope, decided to destroy his "Children," namely, his poems, to prevent their being mistreated by the insincere and mediocre public. They now sleep safely in darkness. Melville probably wrote a good deal of poetry at Arrowhead, near Pittsfield, Massachusetts (1850–1863). Before he and his family moved back to New York City, he must have discarded much of it because he wrote to his brother Thomas Melville* about his "doggerel" thus: "I have disposed of a lot of it at a great bargain. In fact, a trunk-maker took the whole stock off my hands at ten cents the pound" to use for lining (25 May 1862).

Bibliography: Cohen, *Poems;* NN 14; Warren.

"In a Bye Canal" (1891). Poem, in *Timoleon.* The persona describes a canal at sleepy noon. When the oar of his "indolent gondolier" scrapes against "a palace hoar," enticing female eyes peer through window lattices in a "mute summoning." He has known "calms far off Peru," whales, sharks, and envy and slander in "[t]he enemy's desert." But this? He thinks of Jael. He urges his gondolier to take him away fast, feeling as wise as Ulysses to flee such latter-day sirens. The poem is dotted with sexual puns: "Bye Canal" may mean "buy a canal," "hoar" may mean "whore," and the sirens here are called "waylayers." Melville's 1857 journal has two pertinent entries. Melville describes women peeping out "from "[l]attice-work of . . . projecting windows" in Cairo (3 January); and later he records looking "up and down G. Canal" in Venice and seeing "beautiful women," one of them at "the window at end of a long, narrow passage" there (5 April).

Bibliography: Cohen, *Poems;* NN 11 and 15; Shurr; Stein; Warren.

"In a Church of Padua" (1891). Poem, in *Timoleon.* In the church is a boxlike confessional, with holes punctured in a "silver panel square" through which the sinner's voice is "sieved" and heard by the "immured" priest. The confessional is compared to a diving bell by means of which the priest descends into "consciences / Where more is hid than found." While in Italy, Melville made a brief journal record of his visit to Padua's "Church of St. Anthony & Shrine. Supurb [*sic*]" (1 April 1857).

   Bibliography: Cohen, *Poems;* NN 11 and 15; Shurr; Stein.

"In a Garret" (1891). Poem, in *Timoleon.* The poet will let others collect gems; he wants "to grapple from Art's deep / One dripping trophy!" "Grapple" is a powerfully suggestive verb here. Melville first gave "In a Garret" the title "Ambition," then "Schiller's Ambition," and penultimately "The Spirit of Schiller."

   Bibliography: Cohen, *Poems;* NN 11; Shurr; Stein.

Inamorata. In "Fragments from a Writing Desk," she is the beauty who writes to L.A.V. asking him to come to her. He does so, only to retreat upon discovering that she is deaf and dumb.

"In a Nutshell" (1947). Poem, in *Collected Poems of Herman Melville.* Those who think they are wise should realize that knaves will trick, fools will kick, and grief will pick joy's pocket.

Income for Melville. When Melville married Elizabeth Knapp Shaw Melville* in 1847, it is alleged that her father Lemuel Shaw* settled a $3,000 trust fund on the couple. By April 1851, sales in the United States and England of *Typee, Omoo, Mardi, Redburn,* and *White-Jacket* and English sales of *Moby-Dick* earned Melville $8,069. At that time, however, he owed Harper & Brothers* $696 and his father-in-law, Lemuel Shaw, $5,000 or so. The Harpers advanced Melville a total of $800 in 1852 and 1853. Royalties offset part of this debt until February 1864, at which time Melville paid them $200, following which royalties from Harpers were little until 1887, after which records are lacking. Meanwhile, Melville earned income by publishing elsewhere. *Israel Potter,* short prose works, and poetry gained him $725 or so by 1856. Lecturing from 1857 to 1860 paid him $1,274 before expenses. In 1860 Shaw forgave Melville all debts in return for the Arrowhead property, which he then transferred to Melville's wife. Upon Shaw's death in 1851, his will bequeathed $15,114 to her. In 1862 Melville received a $900 legacy from Priscilla Melvill,* his aunt. In 1866 he became a New York district inspector of customs at about $1,250 per annum minus political party assessments. In 1876 Peter Gansevoort (1788–1876),* Melville's uncle, gave Melville $1,200 to print *Clarel* and a year later bequeathed him another $500. In 1884 Lemuel Shaw, Jr.,* died and willed his sister (Melville's wife) $37,949, of which $33,517 was paid to her before Melville's death. In 1885 Melville's sister Frances Priscilla Melville* died, leaving Melville $4,240, gradually paid from 1886 to 1889. At his death, Melville's estate was appraised at $13,261. In 1906, when his widow died, her estate was appraised at $170,370. In sum, Melville was at first a financial success as a writer (1846–1851), paid no rent (from 1851), then averaged about $228 a year by writing (1851–1866), worked as a customs inspector (1866–1885), and enjoyed the fruits of legacies totaling $63,370.

   Bibliography: William Charvat, ''Melville's Income,'' pp. 190–203 in *The Profession of Authorship in America 1800–1870,* ed. Matthew J. Bruccoli (New York: Columbia University Press, 1992).

India, The King of. In ''Honor,'' he is the selfish monarch who orders the jeweled welcoming procession.

Inez. In *Clarel,* she is the object of the Lyonese's love song, which is overheard by the lonely Clarel at Bethlehem.

Infelez. In ''Benito Cereno,'' he is the Peruvian monk who attends the litter-borne Benito Cereno during the trial of Babo at Lima.

''Inscription'' (1924). Poem, from *Weeds and Wildings,* as part of the section entitled ''This, That and the Other.'' A prose epigraph explains that the poem is for a boulder marking where the last ''hardhack'' (i.e., a rusty, hairy shrub of the rose family) was cut out by the new proprietor of Arrowhead. The poem admits that the shrub is a useless, ugly weed but says that heaven permitted it to live and ''idle . . . in the sun.''

   Bibliography: Stein.

''Inscription Epistolary to W.C.R.'' *See John Marr.*

''Inscription for the Graves at Pea Ridge, Arkansas'' (1866). Poem, in *Battle-Pieces.* A soldier speaks. We preferred combat to tranquillity, since we fought for human rights against ''traitor[s]'' and ''fell—victorious!'' The Battle of Pea Ridge (Elkhorn Tavern), Arkansas (6–8 March 1862) pitted pro-Union Missourians under Major General Samuel R. Curtis, one of whose scouts was ''Wild Bill'' Hickok, against pro-Confederate Missourians under Major General Earl Van Dorn, who was ill at the time and whose command included three Cherokee Indian regiments under Stand Watie. Curtis's costly victory brought Missouri over to the Union side for the next two years and more. Casualty figures differ, but the Union suffered at least 1,380 in killed, wounded, and missing, compared to 800 or more on the Confederate side.

   Bibliography: Boatner, Faust, NN 11.

''Inscription for Marye's Heights, Fredericksburg'' (1866). Poem, in *Battle-Pieces.* The poet offers a stone to those who, with their eyes on ''the heavenly flag,'' crossed the river, climbed the hill, and died. The marker would memorialize more than a victory. Union General Ambrose E. Burnside on 13 December 1862 used poor judgment when, though having superior numbers, he crossed the Rappanhannock River and—among other misguided maneuvers—attacked

Marye's Height, well defended by General James Longstreet,* near Fredericksburg, Maryland, which was firmly held by General Robert E. Lee.* During the entire Battle of Fredericksburg, Burnside lost 12,650 in killed, wounded, and missing, to the Confederates' 5,310. He grew distraught, was persuaded to revoke his order for a renewed attack, and withdrew across the river (15 December).

Bibliography: Boatner, Faust, Garner, NN 11, Warren.

"Inscription for the Dead at Fredericksburgh [*sic*]" (1864). Poem, first published in *Autograph Leaves of Our Country's Authors,* edited by Alexander Bliss and John P. Kennedy (New York, 1864). The "patriot" soldiers, to whom "Death's a starry night," are now glorified and transfigured, and "their vale of death" should be strewn with palms. Union General Ambrose E. Burnside swiftly attacked Fredericksburg, Maryland, several times, against units under General Robert E. Lee* which were inferior in numbers but well positioned. Burnside lost heavily, withdrew (15 December 1862), and was replaced by General Joseph Hooker (25 January 1863). Although Melville did not include this poem in his *Battle-Pieces,* it was reprinted, as "Inscription for the Slain at Fredericksburgh [*sic*]," in *The Battle-Pieces of Herman Melville,* ed. Hennig Cohen (New York: Thomas Yoseloff, 1963).

Bibliography: Boatner, Faust, Garner, NN 11.

"In Shards the Sylvan Vases Lie" (1924). Poem, in *The Works of Herman Melville.* The vase is in pieces. Brambles, weeds, and spider webs cover it. And bits of Apollo's bust are converted to "lime for Mammon's tower."

"In the Desert" (1891). Poem, in *Timoleon.* (Characters: Emir, Napoleon.) The poet suggests that light from the flaming desert sun is more trying than "Pharoah's Night," "[u]ndulates" like a "blank ocean in blue calm," and is called "[i]mmaterial incandescence" and "the effluence of the essence" of God. Napoleon might defeat emirs here, but his gunners were struck down by the sun's bayonets. In his 1857 journal, Melville records his impression of the desert—"more fearful . . . than ocean"—surrounding the Egyptian pyramids (3 January).

Bibliography: Cohen, *Poems;* NN 11 and 15; Shurr; Stein.

"In the Hall of Marbles (Lines Recalled from a Destroyed Poem)" (1924). Poem, in *The Works of Herman Melville.* Melville asserts that modern man "flouts the aims" of Greek sculptors and has devolved into something richer, yes, but "narrower" too. The poem concludes memorably: "Man fell from Eden, fall [*sic*] from Athens too."

Bibliography: Shurr, Stein.

"In the Jovial Age of Old" (1924). Poem, in *The Works of Herman Melville.* In former jovial times, instead of gold, such as was showered on Danaë, silvery blossoms from "love's bower" fell on brides.

"In the Old Farm-House: The Ghost" (1924). Poem, in *The Works of Herman Melville.* In "the dead of night," the poet sits with "the dead," who laughs and reminds him of Shakespeare and [Sir John] Falstaff.

"In the Pauper's Turnip-Field" (1924). Poem, in *Weeds and Wildings,* as part of the section entitled "The Year." The impoverished narrator asks why the crow is preaching to him from a dead hemlock. A heavy hoe bends the man and "foreshow[s]" a heavier implement, that is, a mattock. Is the heavier tool that of a gravedigger?
Bibliography: Stein.

"In the Prison Pen (1864)" (1866). Poem, in *Battle-Pieces.* Here is a picture of a prisoner of war, under the "smiting sun," hemmed in by palisades and glared at by sentries, with nothing to do—until he drops and is carried out, "[d]ead in his meagreness." This poem was triggered by Melville's awareness of the ghastly treatment of Union Army prisoners by their Confederate captors and probably also by his recollection that the Union Army hero William Francis Bartlett* had been such a prisoner.
Bibliography: Garner, NN 11.

"In the Turret (March, 1862)" (1866). Poem, in *Battle-Pieces.* (Character: [Lieutenant John Lorimer] Worden.) Melville offers enormous praise to Worden, who "bore the first iron battle's burden / Sealed as in a diving-bell." He was as brave as Alcides (i.e., Hercules), who challenged Hell to bring back the bride of King Admetus. Worden defied a deriding spirit whose voice says, "I have thee now" in a "goblin-snare." Worden did his duty, first, next, and last, and survived "in life and story" both. The Confederate ironclad *Virginia* (formerly the U.S.S. *Merrimac*) sank the wooden Union man-of-war *Cumberland* and burned the *Congress* off Hampton Roads (8 March 1862). The next day, the Union ironclad *Monitor,* under the command of Lieutenant John Lorimer Worden,* who had himself confined in a revolving turret amidships, engaged the *Virginia* in an indecisive but valiant four-hour exchange—the first such battle in naval history. During the fight, Worden sustained severe eye injuries.
Bibliography: Cohen, *Poems*; Garner; NN 11; Shurr.

Invader, The. In "Lee in the Capitol." *See* Lee, Robert E.

Iris. In "Iris (1865)," she is a flower-like post-bellum belle from Savannah or perhaps a flower personifying both peace and immortal nature.
Bibliography: Stein.

"Iris (1865)" (1924). Poem, in *Weeds and Wildings,* as part of the section entitled "This, That and the Other." (Characters: Colonel, Iris, [General William Tecumseh] Sherman.) In June, after Sherman's victorious "March," Iris captivates three bearded colonels who recently were busy freeing slaves. She rails and rallies, but "a minor tone" lurks in her merry voice. Her future is dark. When her ravisher wins, the rainbow appears—but soon leaves. Over her tomb, cypress covers palm leaves. This enigmatic poem concerns war and peace, womanhood, and nature's cycle of death and renewed life. It was evidently written as a memorial following the death in June 1874 of Rachel Turner Pond, whom Melville evidently knew.

   Bibliography: Garner, Leyda, Stein.

Irving, Washington (1783–1859). Author. Born in New York City, he was the last of eleven children of a well-to-do Scottish immigrant whose main business was in hardware. Although he passed the bar (1804), Irving practiced little. He visited Europe (1804–1806), became an inactive partner in his brothers' import firm based in Liverpool and New York (1810), saw service during the War of 1812 (1813–1814), and went abroad again (1815–1832). During this period, he tried in Liverpool to help his brothers' failing business (until it went bankrupt [1818]), traveled on the Continent and in the British Isles, met John Jacob Astor* and Sir Walter Scott, became a translator on the staff of the American embassy in Madrid (1826–1829), and was secretary of the American legation in London (1829–1832). By the time he returned to New York, Irving was an internationally revered American author and celebrity. He bought a Dutch house (1835), which he named Sunnyside, on his beloved Hudson River near Terrytown, and retired and welcomed visitors and relatives there. He signed a contract with the *Knickerbocker Magazine* (1839) for $2,000 a year and provided an essay every three weeks for two years. He returned to Europe as minister to Spain (1842–1846). Home again for good, he was a pallbearer at Astor's funeral (1848) and an executor of his will.

   Irving, whose fiancée died in 1809, never married. During the 1850s, he was active in trying to secure changes in copyright laws. His works include *A History of New York from the Beginning of the World to the End of the Dutch Dynasty . . . by Diedrich Knickerbocker* (1809), *The Sketch Book of Geoffrey Crayon, Gent.* (1819–1820), *Bracebridge Hall; or, The Humorists* (1822), *Tales of a Traveller* (1824), *A Chronicle of the Conquest of Granada* (1829), *The Alhambra* (1832), *A Tour of the Prairies* (1835), *Astoria* (1836, coauthored by Irving's nephew Pierre Irving; about Astor's frontier enterprises in Astoria, Oregon), and *Wolfert's Roost and Other Papers* (1855, mostly old *Knickerbocker* essays). In addition, Irving wrote biographical studies of Christopher Columbus and some of his companions (1828, 1831), Oliver Goldsmith (1840), Mahomet and his successors (1850), and George Washington* (5 vols., 1855–1859). Irving's best writings combine a charming style, deft humor, mild romanticism, and native American material. He is now best loved for his satirical *History of New York* and for such short stories as "Rip Van Winkle," "The Legend of Sleepy Hollow," and "Adventure of the German Student."

While Melville's brother Gansevoort Melville* was secretary to the American legation in England, Irving visited London from his diplomatic post in Madrid. The two men met (1846) when Gansevoort was reading proofs for *Typee,* which was about to be published in London by the British publisher John Murray.* Irving read most of the proofs, praised the work, predicted success for it, and commended Melville to Murray. In his poem "Rip Van Winkle's Lilac," Melville mentions that Irving is the author of the original "Rip Van Winkle." More privately, Melville in a letter to Evert Duyckinck,* in which he praises Nathaniel Hawthorne,* comments that "Irving is a grasshopper to him—putting the *souls* of the two men together, I mean" ([12 February] 1851).

Bibliography: NN 14; Edward Wagenknecht, *Washington Irving: Moderation Displayed* (New York: Oxford University Press, 1962).

Ishmael. In *Moby-Dick,* he is the narrator and possibly the hero. After four voyages in the merchant service, Ishmael signs aboard the *Pequod,* Captain Ahab's whaling vessel, becomes the bosom friend of the harpooner Queequeg, vows with the others to pursue Moby Dick, and uniquely escapes the resulting wreck. He is called Skrimshander by Peter Coffin.

Bibliography: David Scott Arnold, *Liminal Readings: Forms of Otherness in Melville, Joyce and Murdoch* (New York: St. Martin's Press, 1993); Brian Higgins and Hershel Parker, eds., *Critical Essays on Herman Melville's Moby-Dick* (New York: G. K. Hall, 1992); Robert Zoellner, *The Salt-Sea Mastodon: A Reading of Moby-Dick* (Berkeley: University of California Press, 1973).

Isleman, The. In *Clarel. See* the Lesbian.

Israel Potter (1855). (Full title: *Israel Potter: His Fifty Years of Exile.* The original magazine title, *Israel Potter: His Fifty Years of Exile. A Fourth of July Story* was soon shortened to *Israel Potter: His Fifty Years of Exile.*) Novel. (Characters: Duchess D'Abrantes, Colonel Ethan Allen, Princess Amelia, Bill, James Bridges, Molly Bridges, [Louis-Philippe-Joseph] Duke de Chartres, the Laird of Crokarky, [Charles Hector] Count D'Estaing, Dr. [Benjamin] Franklin, George III King of England, Lord General [Sir William] Howe, Sir Edward Hughs [Hughes], Jack Jewboy, Jim, Colonel Guy Johnson, Captain John Paul Jones, [Louis XVI] King of France, Kniphausen, Colonel McCloud, Captain Martindale, Mungo Maxwell, Sir John Millet, Captain Parker, General John Patterson [Paterson], Captain [Richard] Pearson, Phil, Potter, Potter, Israel Potter, Mrs. Potter, Mrs. Israel Potter, [General Israel] Putnam, the Countess of Selkirk, the Earl of Selkirk, Rev. Mr. Shirrer, Jenny Singles, Sergeant Singles, Admiral [Pierre André de] Suffrien [Suffren Saint Tropaz], Tidds, Rev. Mr. [John] Horne Tooke, General [George] Washington, Lieutenant Williamson, Mrs. Woodcock, Squire John Woodcock.)

Israel Potter appeared anonymously as a serial in *Putnam's Monthly Magazine** (July 1854–March 1855), published by George Palmer Putnam,* and then as a book in 1855. Melville was identified, in a New York City newspaper review, as the author as soon as the first *Putnam* installment of the serial appeared. *Israel Potter* is based on the real-life activities of Israel R. Potter (1744?–1826), the American Revolutionary War hero, prisoner of the British, and longtime impoverished resident of England.

At the age of eighteen, Israel, born and reared in the eastern part of Berkshire, Massachusetts—"in sight of the sparkling Housatonic"—falls in love with an "amiable" but "weak" girl named Jenny, leaves the region when his father is vehement in his disapproval, traps and also trades among the Indians, becomes a sailor on "barbarous waters," and returns home to find Jenny married to a man named Singles. Israel becomes a farmer until the American Revolution. He fights at Bunker Hill (April 1755); is wounded in the arm, chest, hip, and ankle; recovers in time to join a ship blockading Boston; is captured by the British and is taken by prison ship to Spithead; but immediately escapes his drunken guards.

It is now the spring of 1776. Israel makes his way toward London; is caught but escapes again; finds employment at an estate near Brentford, in Princess Amelia's garden, in "magnanimous" King George III's Kew Gardens, and finally with some farmers. Soon Israel is commissioned by a squire named John Woodcock, the politician Horne Tooke, and other "friends to America" to go to Paris with some secret papers for the illustrious Dr. Franklin, who feeds and lectures him, wines him on water, and assigns him a room. After meeting the "tawny," restless Captain John Paul Jones, who wants Franklin to assign him a combat ship, Israel is sent back with secret dispatches to Woodcock. After three days and nights hidden by his host, who is in danger himself because of his "clandestine proceedings," in a tiny "coffin-cell" behind a chimney, Israel emerges in desperation—to find Woodcock's room draped in black. His host has died.

Israel filches some fine clothes from Woodcock's closet, gets back to Dover, learns that a diplomatic blockade makes his return to Franklin in Paris impossible, accepts drinks from "a pleasant-looking, cousinly stranger" at an inn, but is then shanghaied into the royal navy and assigned to a revenue cutter, which John Paul Jones soon chases in his *Ranger*. Israel knocks his British captain "over the taffrail into the sea," is taken by Jones aboard his vessel, and becomes his quartermaster. Jones explains that Franklin has commissioned him to menace enemy shipping in any way he can. In a short time, Jones—"a knave or a hero, or a union of both"—captures a vessel off Dublin; bombards another off southern Scotland; sinks a coaster and accomplishes some sabotage with a landing party including Israel in and near Whitehaven on the Solway Firth; unsuccessfully attempts to kidnap the Earl of Selkirk, whose residence is on St. Mary's Isle nearby; and sails to Carrickfergus, lures the British twenty-gun *Drake* out of the harbor there, engages her in a running fight, captures her, and takes her to Brest. Jones is honored by the King of France, who sends him ''a sword and a medal.'' Israel gains nothing.

During three months of ''half-disciplined chaos,'' Jones assembles a fleet of nine ragtag ships, including his *Duras,* aboard which Israel is posted on to the poop with a spyglass. He suggests renaming her the *Poor Richard,* which Jones translates into the *Bon Homme Richard.* Off Flamborough Head, Jones engages the fifty-gun *Serapis* (23 September 1779). Though deserted by most of his consorts, the *Richard*—with armament roughly equaling that of a thirty-two-gun frigate—defeats the enemy, partly because Israel drops a hand grenade into the enemy's main hatchway and kills twenty British tars in one explosion of heaped cartridges. Jones boards the shattered *Serapis* as his own vessel, ''gorged with slaughter,'' sinks, ''like Gomorrah, out of sight.'' After much inactivity, Jones and Israel head for America aboard the *Ariel.* During an engagement with a British frigate, Israel answers a boarding order, swings alone by the spanker boom onto the enemy craft, and when the attack is broken off escapes detection by pretending to be an able if demented British sailor. When his new ship docks at Falmouth, he goes ashore and sees at Pendennis Castle the noble Yankee Ethan Allen, hero of Ticonderoga but captured at Montreal and now in British chains. Israel would try to help this ''Samson among the Philistines,'' but he is recognized and innocently identified by another American prisoner—none other than Sergeant Singles, Jenny's husband. Israel must escape again, this time toward crowded London.

For thirteen weeks, Israel works just outside London as a brick maker in a slimy, gravelike pit, saves a few coppers, and walks on to London. Forty-five wretched years now pass in that grimy Dis where belching smoke eclipses the sun and where not marble nor flesh nor the sad spirit of man can remain white. Israel works as a warehouse porter, a chair bottomer, and a park attendant. He saves money for passage home but squanders it to marry a bakery-shop girl who nursed him back to health after he was run over. They produce eleven children. Ten of them die, as does their mother in due time. In 1793 the French war makes employment easier in London, but then the peace of 1817 discharges work-hungry hordes back from Waterloo. Israel has been half demented ever since a rotten beam in a hovel fell on him. He vaguely recalls the waving fields of his youth and tells his lone son about his home in New England. The boy circulates the story until it is believed; in 1826, with aid from the American consul, father and son leave Moorfields and embark for Boston. Home again, Israel Potter wanders with his son to the Housatonic region, finds almost everything changed, but he locates his parental hearthstone—disturbed by a stranger's plow—and sits out his remaining days, without medals and forgotten.

Shortly before sailing for England in 1849, Melville bought Henry Trumbull's *Life and Remarkable Adventures of Israel R. Potter* (Providence, 1824). After *Pierre* failed and while his short fiction was encountering an indifferent public, Melville sought to recoup by writing up the stirring true story of Potter, a common soldier, sailor, and victim of fate. Putnam agreed to pay Melville a handsome $5 per page for serial rights to *Israel Potter,* was happy with the generally complimentary reviews, negotiated with Melville's brother Allan Melville* about book publication, and advertised the book conscientiously. *Israel Potter* in serial form earned Melville $421.50; thereafter, its three quick printings as a book in some 3,700 copies gained him $197.27 more within four months. In addition, he must have felt complimented—if unreimbursed—when the literary pirate George Routledge in London produced a popular shilling edition there. Aside from Trumbull's life of Potter, Melville used or may have used the following sources: *A Narrative of Colonel Ethan Allen's Captivity* (1779), by Allen; *The Life and Character of Chevalier John Paul Jones* (1825), by John Henry Sherburne; *Life and Correspondence of John Paul Jones . . .* (1830), by Robert Charles Sands; and *A History of the Navy of the United States* (1839), by James Fenimore Cooper.* *Israel Potter* was reviewed favorably in America but unfavorably in England. The astute French critic Émile Montégut published a review of it in fifty-two pages, most of which was a condensed translation, in the *Revue des Deux Mondes* (July–September 1855). Thereafter, it was largely neglected by critics and readers alike until the 1920s. Putnam sold the plates of *Israel Potter* for $218.66 (1857) to a Philadelphia publisher named T. B. Peterson, who with his brothers legally reissued the novel but with *The Refugee* as its new title (1865). Melville was annoyed, sent Peterson a complaint to no avail, and criticized him in a letter to the New York *World. Israel Potter* was not fully translated into any foreign language until a German version appeared in 1946. Modern critics and subsequent translations, however, have more than made up for earlier neglect.

Bibliography: Lawrence Buell, "Melville and the Question of American Decolonialization," *American Literature* 64 (June 1992): 215–37; Cohen, *Potter;* Lebowitz; NN 8; Arnold Rampersad, *Melville's Israel Potter: A Pilgrimage and a Progress* (Bowling Green, Ohio: Bowling Green University Popular Press, 1969); Reino Virtanen, "Émile Montégut as a Critic of American Literature," *PMLA* 63 (December 1948): 1265–75.

Jack. In *Moby-Dick,* he is a sailor who, with Joe and Harry, is suspicious of Jonah in Father Mapple's sermon at the Whaleman's Chapel in New Bedford.

Jack. In *Omoo,* he is a Hawaiian sailor whom the narrator takes along to interpret for him when he attends the missionary cathedral of Papoar, near the Calabooza.

Jack. In *Omoo,* this is the name, perhaps only generically used, of a white man-of-war's man who acts as the barber of a Tonga Island king.

Jack. In *Omoo. See* Flash Jack.

Jack. In *Redburn. See* Redburn, Wellingborough.

Jack. In *White-Jacket. See* Mad Jack, Lieutenant; Paper Jack.

"Jack Gentian (omitted from the final sketch of him)" (1924). Sketch, in *The Works of Herman Melville.* (Character: A Croesus, Tom Dutcher, Major Jack [John] Gentian, Mrs. Jones.) This sketch, a kind of postscript to "To Major John Gentian, Dean of the Burgundy Club," is a summary of the gossip that Jack Gentian, though ever humane and loving, is becoming infirm in mind and body.

Jack Jewboy. In *Israel Potter. See* Jewboy, Jack.

Jack of the Beach. In "Benito Cereno." *See* Delano, Captain Amasa.

"Jack Roy" (1888). Poem, in *John Marr.* (Characters: Larry o' the Cannakin, Jack Roy.) The poet fondly remembers Jack Roy, the maintop captain of the *Splendid,* and so does his messmate Larry o' the Cannakin. Jack regarded caring for "the Starry Flag" high on the mast as a challenge. If a shot splintered any wood, he would thank the enemy for providing toothpicks. He was gallant while "on liberty . . . in escapade" and regarded joys as toys. The prototype of Jack Roy is clearly Jack Chase,* whom Melville knew when both were sailors aboard the U.S. naval frigate *United States* (1843–1844) and to whom he dedicated *Billy Budd.*
   Bibliography: Cohen, *Poems;* NN 11; Shurr; Stein; Warren.

Jackson. In *Redburn,* he is a physically weak, psychologically dominating, misanthropic, irreligious, seemingly cursed sailor aboard the *Highlander.* He is anywhere between thirty and fifty years old. He bullies the crew and hates Wellingborough Redburn, in particular, because the lad is young and handsome. On the return voyage, Jackson grows desperately ill, coughs up blood while reefing a sail, and plummets overboard to his death. Jackson is based to a degree on Robert Jackson, from New York City and aged thirty-one, a sailor aboard the *St. Lawrence,* on which Melville sailed to Liverpool and back and which is the model for the *Highlander.*
   Bibliography: Gilman, Lebowitz.

Jackson, Jane. Former slave. This old African-American woman had been a slave in the South, had had a son fighting in the Union Army, and after the Civil War sold peanuts on Broadway, in New York City. Her combination of meekness, patience, resignation, and endurance inspired the painter Elihu Vedder,* whose studio was nearby. He persuaded her to sit for him, and he also caused her to be photographed. The result was his painting *Jane Jackson, Formerly a Slave,* exhibited at the National Academy in New York. When Melville saw the painting, he was inspired to write his poem entitled " 'Formerly a Slave': An Idealized Portrait, by E. Vedder." *The Cumean Sibyl* (1876), another of Vedder's works, was also inspired by Jane Jackson.

Jackson, Thomas J. (1824–1863). (Full name: Thomas Jonathan Jackson; nickname: "Stonewall.") Confederate Army officer. He was born in Clarksburg, Virginia (now West Virginia). When his father died, the boy was reared by an uncle. Though ill-prepared, Jackson studied hard and graduated from West Point (1846). For brave service during the Mexican War (1846–1848), he was praised by General Winfield Scott* and breveted major. After service in New York and Florida, he taught artillery and natural philosophy at the Virginia Military Institute, at Lexington (1851–1861). He commanded a cadet corps from his institute at the hanging of John Brown* (2 December 1859). At the outbreak of the Civil War, Jackson was a Virginia militia major and joined the Confederate Army. He went from colonel to brigadier general and, after distinguishing himself at the First Battle of Bull Run (July 1861), to major general (October). He assumed command of the Shenandoah Valley (November), was involved in a dispute with a fellow general (January 1862), was defeated at Kernstown, Virginia (March 1862), and worked well with General Robert E. Lee* (from April). Jackson was dazzlingly brilliant in the Valley Campaign (May), was ineffective in the Seven Days' Campaign (June), followed up well at and after the Second Battle of Bull Run (August), took 12,520 Union prisoners at Harpers Ferry (September), supported Lee well at Antietam (September), was promoted to lieutenant general (October), and fought victoriously at Fredericksburg (December). He executed a superb flank march near Chancellorsville (May 1863), but tragedy was its aftermath. By mistake, his own men fatally wounded him. Jackson, an austere, abstemious, and devout Presbyterian, married twice. He wed Elinor Junkin in 1853. She died giving birth to a stillborn infant (1854). He married Mary Anna Morrison in 1857 (the couple had a daughter). His widow published *Memoirs of Stonewall Jackson* (1895).

Melville mentions Jackson in several poems. In ''The Victor of Antietam (1862),'' he identifies Stonewall Jackson as the Confederate general under Lee who was defeated at Antietam by [George B.] McClellan. In ''Stonewall Jackson Mortally Wounded at Chancellorsville (May, 1863),'' he is praised as a fierce, earnest, true, and relentless enemy leader. In ''Stonewall Jackson (Ascribed to a Virginian),'' he is depicted as a calm, stoical, iron-willed, fatalistic warrior. In ''The Armies of the Wilderness,'' he is mentioned as having led a charge in this area earlier. In ''Rebel Color-Bearers at Shiloh,'' he is mentioned. And in ''Lee in the Capitol,'' he is limned as the dead Confederate general remembered by Lee as the latter approaches the Capitol.

Bibliography: Byron Farwell, *Stonewall: A Biography of General Thomas J. Jackson* (New York: W. W. Norton, 1992).

Jacobi, Cranz. In *Pierre,* this is a fictitious name in a German prince's proclamation imagined by Pierre Glendinning.

Jake. In ''Cock-a-Doodle-Doo!,'' he is the narrator's servant boy.

Jan o' the Inn. In ''Marquis de Grandvin: At the Hostelry.'' *See* Steen, Jan Havickszoon.

Jarl (''The Viking,'' ''The Skyeman''). In *Mardi,* he is the brawny sailor who deserts the *Arcturion* with the narrator. He becomes the narrator's faithful follower as far as the island of Moldoldo, where the narrator abruptly leaves him with King Borabolla as a remembrance. While at the island of Maramma, the narrator receives a message from Borabolla that Jarl has been killed by arrows, probably shot by Aleema's vengeful sons. A jarl was an earl or a chief in old Scandinavia. Jarl's background and character may have been suggested to Melville by his reading of *Fingal* by James MacPherson (1762 edition) and *Frithiof's Saga* by Esais Tégner (1835, 1838 editions).

Bibliography: Davis, Wright.

Jarmi. In *Mardi,* he is a Mardian minstrel about whom Yoomy tells an anecdote.

Jefferson, Joseph (1829–1905). (Stage name: Joe Jefferson.) Actor. He was born in Philadelphia, appeared on stage at the age of three, and toured with his theatrical family (1837–1842). When his father died of yellow fever in Mobile, Alabama (1842), Jefferson became the head of the family and began barnstorming through the South (to 1848). He succeeded in New York City, Philadelphia, Baltimore, and the South again with his own company (from 1849). He went to London and Paris to attend theaters and improve his acting (1856), and returned to New York to join the company of the actress-manager Laura Keene (1856). Although they often argued, he was a hit in several plays, especially as the titular hero in Tom Taylor's *Our American Cousin* (1858–1859), in Charles Dickens's *The Cricket on the Hearth* as dramatized by Dion Boucicault (1859), and in Boucicault's *The Octoroon; or, Life in Louisiana* (1859). Then came *Rip Van Winkle.* The story "Rip Van Winkle" by Washington Irving* was published in 1819 and was often adapted for the stage, once by Jefferson's half-brother Charles Burke (1850). Jefferson modified earlier texts for a new stage version, but with no great success (Washington, D.C., 1859). He went to California (1860) and Australia (1861–1865). He did not appear in *Our American Cousin* when President Abraham Lincoln* attended the play on the night of his assassination. In London (1865), Jefferson met and persuaded Boucicault to write a peppier version of *Rip Van Winkle.* It became an enormous hit; and Jefferson starred in the title role in London (1865, 170 nights), New York (1866), and elsewhere around the world for thirty-odd years. He returned in triumph to the British Isles and Paris (1875–1877). From 1880, he alternated his Rip (until 1904) with performances in Richard Brinsley Sheridan's *The Rivals.* Jefferson developed the practice of taking his whole cast on tour, and not simply the stars, instead of relying on local stock companies and other personnel to fill supporting roles. He was president of the Players' Club (1893–1905). This talented and revered actor appeared in more than a hundred roles, over a period of seventy-one years. Jefferson married the actress Margaret Clements Lockyer in 1850 (the couple had five children). His wife's death in 1861 impelled Jefferson to go to Australia. He married Sarah Warren in 1867 (the couple had two children, and Sarah Jefferson died in 1894). *The Autobiography of Joseph Jefferson* (1895) is a valuable document for historians of the American stage. In his "Rip Van Winkle," Melville mentions Jefferson as the star actor in a dramatic version of Irving's story.

Bibliography: Gladys Malvern, *Good Troupers All: The Story of Joseph Jefferson* (Philadelphia: Macrae Smith Company, 1945).

Jehu. In "Poor Man's Pudding and Rich Man's Crumbs," he is the London hack driver who takes the narrator from the Guildhall back to his rooms.

Jemmy Legs. In *Billy Budd. See* Claggart, John.

Jennie. In *Pierre,* she is the attractive young woman in the Miss Pennies' sewing circle.

Jennings, Betsy. In *Redburn,* she is the starving woman who dies with her three children in the wretched cellar of a Liverpool warehouse, in spite of Redburn's efforts to help the hopeless family.

Jenny. In *Moby-Dick,* this is a name in a song partly recited by Pip in front of the doubloon nailed to the mainmast.

Jermin, John. In *Omoo,* he is the short, thickset, curly-haired first officer of the *Julia,* whose command he has taken from Captain Guy by default. Jermin, who is often intoxicated, is an eager fighter and is respected by his men for his expert seamanship. When the *Julia* leaves Papeetee, Jermin is virtually in charge again. Jermin is based in part on John (sometimes recorded as James) German, the mate in 1842 of the *Lucy Ann,* which was the prototype of Melville's *Julia.* German offered an affidavit against the mutineers in 1842.
   Bibliography: Anderson, Leyda, NN 2.

Jeroboam. In "Rammon," he is a courageous and mighty but penitent man who unsuccessfully offers his allegiance to the recently crowned, disdainful King Rehoboam.

Jethro. In "Rammon," he is mentioned [erroneously] as the father of Solomon.

Jewboy, Jack. In *Israel Potter,* he is a sailor aboard the British frigate which Israel Potter boards alone off the *Ariel.*

Jewel, Jack. In *White-Jacket,* he is a shipmate, reported to have been killed in an imaginary sea fight.

Jewsharp Jim. In "Bridegroom-Dick," he is a sailor remembered by Bridegroom Dick.

Jiji. In *Mardi,* he is a hungry miser on the isle of Padulla. He collects monetary teeth in pelican pouches but is obliged to beg for food.

Jim. In *Israel Potter,* he is one of the two named shanghaiers of Israel Potter at Dover. The other is Bill.

Jim. In *Omoo,* he is the rich and officious but capable native pilot who takes the *Julia* into the harbor at Papeetee.

Jim. In *Omoo. See* Long Jim.

Jim. In *White-Jacket,* he is a sailor who is rebuked for putting his foot on a mess cloth in Mess No. 15.

Jim, Jewsharp. In "Bridegroom-Dick." *See* Jewsharp Jim.

Jimmy. In *Typee,* he is the irresponsible, tabooed old sailor in the household of King Mowanna of Nukuheva. Jimmy helps Toby escape from Nukuheva but is unable, or unwilling, to try to manage the release of Tommo from Typee.

Jimmy Dux. In *Redburn. See* Redburn, Wellingborough.

"Jimmy Rose" (1855). Short story. (Characters: Arabella, Biddy, Miss Ford, Mrs. William Ford, William Ford, Frances, General G—, James Rose.) The narrator is an old man with a youngish wife, two daughters, and a maid. He inherits an old house on a narrow street in New York City. Like the street, the house has fallen into decay. The rooms are big and impressive, but the French wallpaper of peacocks and roses in the parlor has been stained by a leak from the eaves. A former proprietor of the house was James Rose. Jimmy, as he was called, was once well to do, handsome, eloquent, and wondrously hospitable; however, after suffering financial ruin when two of his vessels from China sank off Sandy Hook, he disappeared. The narrator, wanting to help, located Jimmy Rose in a house on C— Street but was refused admittance. Twenty-five years elapsed. Then the narrator saw Jimmy Rose again and learned that he had been receiving $70 a year, lived meagerly off its interest, visited friends at teatime, and decorously wolfed down bread while regaling them with stories of Europe and literature. His cheeks remained rosy, his smile fabulously rich, his manners proudly courteous, and his compliments charming "alms to the rich"—all this although his worn and mended cuffs revealed his penury. When Jimmy Rose lay dying, he was tended to by an "opulent" alderman's "sweet" daughter. To this day, the narrator is lovingly reminded of Jimmy when he looks at his wallpaper of peacocks and roses.

There are several autobiographical touches in "Jimmy Rose." C— Street may be Courtlandt Street, in New York City, where Melville lived in a big old house as a child; interior details of the Rose house may owe something to other houses of Melville family members. Melville's father Allan Melvill* went bankrupt, as Rose did. Major Thomas Melvill,* Melville's grandfather, became an anachronism, as Jimmy Rose did, and was celebrated as such in "The Last Leaf," the 1831 poem by Oliver Wendell Holmes.* "Jimmy Rose" was anonymously published in *Harper's New Monthly Magazine** (1 November 1855). Melville received $32.50 in payment for it and ''The 'Gees'' together.

Bibliography: James W. Gargano, ''Melville's 'Jimmy Rose,' '' *Western Humanities Review* 16 (Summer 1962): 276–80; Newman; Sealts.

Jingling Joe. In *Omoo,* he is a sailor aboard the *Julia* who, in the presence of Dr. Johnson, pretends to be sick. Jingling Joe signs the round-robin.

Jiromo. In *Mardi,* he is a rebellious plotter against King Media, who orders him to be beheaded.

Joan. In *Omoo,* this is the nickname given by Dr. Long Ghost to an old woman who is cozily amorous with her Darby on the beach at Imeeo.

Joanna I (1326–1382). Countess of Provençe and Queen of Naples. Born in Lucania, she was the daughter of Duke Charles of Calabria. She succeeded her grandfather King Robert I to the throne, thus becoming Joanna I (1343). Her alleged complicity in the 1345 murder of her husband Andrew, who was also her cousin, triggered the hatred of Andrew's brother, King Louis I of Hungary. Joanna was forced out of Naples (1348), returned when Pope Innocent VI intervened on her behalf (1352), but reigned only with difficulty. She weakened her position by political intrigues and three miserable marriages (to Louis of Taranto, to King James III of Majorca, and to Otto of Brunswick), paid homage to the antipope Clement VII, and was deposed by Pope Urban VI at the behest of Charles of Durazzo (1380), after which he seized Naples, occupied the throne as Charles III (1381), and ordered her murder a year later. Joanna was attractive and intelligent, and she patronized poets and scholars. In ''Marquis de Grandvin: Naples in the Time of Bomba . . . ,'' Melville describes Joanna as joking with her husband Andrea about strangling him. That night he is hanged by a cord of silk and gold.

Bibliography: Benedetto Croce, *History of the Kingdom of Naples,* trans. Frances Frenaye (Chicago: University of Chicago Press, 1970).

Joaquin, Marques de Aramboalaza, Don. In ''Benito Cereno,'' he is a *San Dominick* passenger, lately from Spain. He is accidentally killed during the attack led by Captain Amasa Delano's chief mate. On Don Joaquin's body is found a jewel meant for the shrine of Our Lady of Mercy in Lima.

Jock. In ''Tom Deadlight (1810),'' he is one of the dying Tom Deadlight's messmates.

Joe. In *Moby-Dick,* he is a sailor who, with Jack and Harry, is suspicious of Jonah in Father Mapple's sermon at the Whaleman's Chapel in New Bedford.

Joe. In *Omoo,* he is a wooden-legged Portuguese violinist who is part of the foreign rabble around King Tammahamaha III of Hawaii (*See* Kamehameha III).

Joe, Holy. In "Tom Deadlight (1810)." *See* Holy Joe.

Joe, Jingling. In *Omoo. See* Jingling Joe.

Joe, Rigadoon. In "Bridegroom-Dick." *See* Rigadoon Joe.

John. In *White-Jacket,* he is a bully who starts a fight with Peter, Mark, and Antone, is flogged by order of Captain Claret, but only leers under the cat.

John VI (1769–1826). King of Portugal. Born in Lisbon, he was the son of Peter III and Maria I. Soon after his father's death (1786), he commenced his long political career. He received the title of Prince of Brazil (1788), assumed control of Portugal when his mother went insane (1792), became regent (1799), and escaped during the Napoleonic wars to Brazil (1807). He became John VI, king of Portugal, upon his mother's death (1816) but remained for some years in Brazil, did not object when the Portuguese instituted a constitutional government (1820), left Brazil to his son Pedro I and returned to Portugal (1822), swore to uphold its new form of government, suppressed and banished his rebellious younger son Miguel (1824), recognized the independence of Brazil (1825), and supported the Portuguese monarchy of his granddaughter Maria II* (sister of Pedro II*) until his death in Lisbon. In *White-Jacket,* Melville mentions John VI as the former King of Portugal and the grandfather of Pedro II, the present king of Brazil, and of Maria, the present queen of Portugal.
   Bibliography: H. V. Livermore, *A New History of Portugal* (Cambridge, England: Cambridge University Press, 1967).

"John Marr" (1888). Poem, in *John Marr.* (Characters: Marr, John Marr, Mrs. John Marr.) After an introduction in prose, John Marr's life and reminiscences are presented in a poem. While a sailor, Marr was badly wounded by pirates off the Keys; so he retired, about 1838, to the frontier in the prairies and married, only to lose both his wife and their child to fevers. Unappreciated by his hardworking, successful farmer neighbors, "this kinless man" thinks about his old shipmates and wonders at their present silence. Never "holding unto life too dearly," those daring sailors bravely skimmed whole oceans and enjoyed "larks ashore" together; however, they are now separated, like sundered logs of a raft. Memories of their "shadowy fellowship" wash about John Marr at "eve's decline." Melville felt as isolated from those who could appreciate him as John Marr does among well-to-do farmers on the prairie.
   Bibliography: Stein, Warren.

John Marr (1888). (Full title: *John Marr and Other Sailors.*) Collection of poems. Preceding the poems are "Author's Note" and "Inscription Epistolary to W.C.R." In the note, Melville explains that sailors' profanity, having lost its original meaning, is mere sinless "percussion of the air." In the inscription, the poet says that his friend Hilary thinks that William Clark Russell,* though born to English parents and reared in England, reveals his New World birth in his nautical novels. Doubting this insight, the poet praises Russell's novel *The Wreck of the Grosvenor.* The poems then follow and are "The Aeolian Harp: At the *Surf Inn*," "The Berg (A Dream)," "Bridegroom-Dick," "Crossing the Tropics," "The Enviable Isles," "Far Off-Shore," "The Figure-Head," "The Good Craft 'Snow-Bird,' " "The Haglets," "Jack Roy," "John Marr" (partly in prose), "The Maldive Shark," "The Man-of-War Hawk," "Old Counsel," "Pebbles," Tom Deadlight (1810)," "To Ned," "To the Master of the *Meteor,*" and "The Tuft of Kelp."

Johnson, Cave (1793–1866). Politician. He was born near Springfield, in Robinson County, Tennessee. His father was a Tennessee politician and militia general. Young Johnson entered Cumberland College, in Nashville (1808), and attended classes until he was expelled for refusing to study such required subjects as Greek and Latin (1811). His reading for the bar (1811–1814) was interrupted by service as a first lieutenant with his father, under the command of General Andrew Jackson, in a campaign against Creek Indians (1813–1814). Johnson practiced law at Yellow Creek (from 1815), was elected a district solicitor general and moved to Clarksville (1817), and served as a U.S. congressman (1829–1837, 1839–1845)—filling that hiatus by resuming his law practice back in Clarksville. Johnson supported James K. Polk, who when elected president (1844) appointed Johnson to be his postmaster general (1845–1849). Johnson systematized the mail service, lowered rates, required the sender to pay postage, and introduced postage stamps (beginning July 1845). He had a dispute with Cornelius Vanderbilt,* when that corrupt man sought to raise his annual fee from $6,000 to $8,000 for carrying mail between New York and New Haven on his steamboats. When Johnson asked railroaders to carry the mail from New York instead, he encountered a pro-Vanderbilt conspiracy; he arranged for horse-drawn vehicles to do the job (1847). He also negotiated foreign-mail deliveries between the United States and France and Germany (1847), and Great Britain (1848), and after the Mexican War (1846–1848) between the eastern part of the United States and California and Oregon. Johnson practiced law at home again (1849–1853), was appointed circuit judge (1853), and became president of the State Bank of Tennessee (1853–1859). His support of James Buchanan's successful campaign to be president (1856) resulted in his appointment as a commissioner to settle claims of Americans against both the government and the Paraguay Navigation Company (1860). Johnson spoke in favor of unionism before the Civil War, but once it started he was loyal to the Confederate side. He was heartbroken when, after being elected in peacetime to the Tennessee

Senate (1866), he was not allowed to serve, because of his former Confederate sympathies. He was honest, energetic, and efficient, but not brilliant. In 1838, Johnson married Elizabeth Dortch Brunson, a widow with three children; the couple had three sons of their own, all of whom served with the Confederate forces during the Civil War.

In Melville's "On the Sea Serpent" and "On the Chinese Junk," Johnson is identified as the postmaster general who has novel plans for distributing the mails. In the former article, it is hinted that Johnson owes Vanderbilt money.

Bibliography: Clement Lyndon Grant, *The Public Career of Cave Johnson . . .* (Nashville, Tenn.: The Joint University Libraries, 1952).

Johnson, Dr. In *Omoo,* he is the resident British physician of Papeetee. He is friendly with Captain Guy of the *Julia* and interviews the supposedly sick members of her crew both aboard ship and in the Calabooza. All of the men despise him. Johnson is based on a real-life Dr. Francis Johnstone, who was living in Tahiti in 1842.

Bibliography: Anderson, Leyda, NN 2.

Johnson, Guy (c.1740–1788). Superintendent of Indian affairs and loyalist. Johnson was born in Ireland, migrated to America at an early age, and was living in the Mohawk Valley of New York by 1756. He served in the French and Indian War (1756–1763), as the secretary of Sir William Johnson, to whom he may have been related, and as a New York ranger under General Sir Jeffrey Amherst (1759–1760). After the war, Guy Johnson was an officer in the New York militia and then was appointed a deputy of Indian affairs (from 1762). He married Sir William Johnson's daughter Mary (1763). Guy Johnson and his wife lived in Guy Park, near Amsterdam, New York, and he served in the New York Assembly (1773–1775). When the American Revolution seemed imminent, he stirred up Native Americans against the colonists, went to Montreal with several Native Americans and a large contingent of rangers (1775), wintered in England (1775–1776), proceeded toward Quebec (1778), wintered in Halifax, arrived in Quebec (July 1779), aided the British at a battle near Newtown, New York (August), and headquartered in Niagara (1779–1781)—all the while urging Native Americans to murder remote colonists. After the war, Johnson went to London, where he died. In *Israel Potter,* Guy Johnson is identified as a Tory who sailed to England on the same ship that bore the long-suffering Ethan Allen there as a prisoner.

Bibliography: Cohen, *Potter;* James Sullivan et al., eds., *The Papers of Sir William Johnson* (14 vols., Albany: University of the State of New York Press, 1921–1965).

Johnson, Professor. In "The Apple-Tree Table," he is the cool, long-winded naturalist who explains to the narrator and his family that the emergent bug probably came from an egg laid in the living wood of the apple tree 170 years ago.

Jonah. In *Moby-Dick,* he is the living hero of Father Mapple's stirring sermon at the Whaleman's Chapel in New Bedford.

Jonathan. In "On the Chinese Junk," he is a typical American who talks to Ke-sing.

Jonathan. In *White-Jacket,* he is a New England sailor who from the temporary security of the main-royal-yard of the *Neversink* flings insults down at Pedro II on deck until Jack Chase urges him to desist.

Jones. In *Redburn,* he is the New York City friend of Redburn's older brother. Jones, who is about twenty-five years of age, and his wife befriend Redburn, and Jones introduces him to Captain Riga of the *Highlander* and thus starts the lad on his first voyage. The real-life model for the fictitious Jones couple could be any of several couples that Melville's brothers Allan Melville* and Gansevoort Melville* knew in New York City.

Jones, Frank. In *White-Jacket,* he is the sailor who plays the part of Toddy Moll in the Fourth of July theatrical. *See also* Frank.

Jones, John Paul. (1747–1792). (Original name: John Paul.) American sailor and naval officer. Born in Kirkcudbrightshire, Scotland, he was apprenticed at age twelve to a merchant shipper and soon visited his older brother, a tailor in Fredericksburg, Virginia. He went into the slave trade (1766–1768); commanded the *John,* his own merchant vessel (from 1769); and was responsible for the death of his ship's carpenter (1770); however, he was cleared of murder by a Scottish court. While commanding a vessel in the West Indies trade, he put down a mutiny by killing its leader (1773), returned to Fredericksburg, and began to call himself John Paul Jones. He went to Philadelphia and became a senior lieutenant in the Continental Navy (1775), distinguished himself in Bahamian waters, commanded the sloop *Providence,* was promoted to captain (1776), in six weeks destroyed eight British ships and captured eight others, commanded the *Alfred* skillfully (1776), and was ordered to France on the *Ranger* (1777) to pick up the French-built *Indien,* only to be frustrated when she was sold to the French government. He continued to command the *Ranger* in British waters (February–May 1778), executing shore raids and capturing a British sloop. Jones reported by letter (1 June 1778) to Benjamin Franklin,* then in France to advance the American revolutionary cause, that Louis-Philippe-Joseph, duc de Chartres* had expressed an inclination to help Jones obtain a ship recently built in Amsterdam. Instead, he was given command (August 1779) of a refitted merchant ship which he renamed the *Bon Homme Richard,* as a tribute to Franklin's *Poor Richard's Almanac.* Chancing upon the British trading-fleet escorts *Countess of Scarborough* and *Serapis* (September 1779), he attacked the latter and after one of the goriest fights in naval history captured her, transferred his men, and let his own horribly damaged ship sink. After sailing on the *Alliance* (to 1780), he was feted in Paris, borrowed the French ship *Ariel,* and returned to America. After the American Revolution ended, Jones negotiated payments for prize ships held in France and Denmark (1783, 1788), revisited America and received honors there (1787), served as a rear admiral in the Russian navy (1788–1789), retired to Paris, and died there.

In *Israel Potter,* Melville portrays Jones as a daring, tawny-colored, tattooed naval officer famed for terrorizing British waters in his *Ranger, Bon Homme Richard,* and *Ariel.* Jones reveres Israel Potter, calls him ''Yellow-hair,'' and appoints him to be his quartermaster.

Bibliography: Lebowitz; Samuel Eliot Morison, *John Paul Jones, a Sailor's Biography* (1959; rev. ed., New York: Time Inc., 1964); *The Papers of Benjamin Franklin,* vol. 26, *March 1 through June 30, 1778,* ed. William B. Willcox (New Haven, Conn.: Yale University Press, 1987).

Jones, Jonathan. In *Redburn,* he is the father of Redburn's friend in New York City.

Jones, Mrs. In ''Jack Gentian (omitted from the final sketch of him),'' she is the hostess at a dinner where old Gentian was the subject of gossip.

Jones, Mrs. In *Redburn,* she is the kind and hospitable wife of the friend of Redburn's older brother. She feeds the lad well during his brief stay in New York.

Jones, Thomas ap Catesby (1790–1858). Naval officer. He was born in Westmoreland County, Virginia, was orphaned early in his life, and was taken by an uncle to Richmond and placed in school there. He became a midshipman (1805), served under Isaac Hull* and Stephen Decatur* at Norfolk and David Porter,* among others, at New Orleans. After participating in the suppression of the slave trade, smuggling, and piracy, and enforcing neutrality laws in the Gulf of Mexico (1808–1812), Jones was promoted to lieutenant, performed gallantly in an attack on pirates at Barataria, Louisiana (1814), and was wounded defending New Orleans against British Admiral Alexander Forrester Inglis Cochrane until obliged to surrender (1814). After three years' duty in the Mediterranean area and five as an ordnance inspector at the Washington Navy Yard—meanwhile being promoted to commander (1820)—Jones was given command of the Pacific Squadron (1825) and touched at the Sandwich Islands. While there (1826), he supported Americans in their dispute with the British consul Richard Charlton,* who sought sovereignty for his government over the islands. Jones drew up ''articles of arrangement'' with King Kamehameha III* for amicable relations between Americans and Hawaiians with respect to navigation and commerce. Though never ratified, this rough treaty was long respected by both countries. Promoted to captain (1829), Jones was again made ordnance inspector (1831–

1836). A disagreement with Mahlon Dickerson, President Martin Van Buren's secretary of the navy, caused Jones to resign the command of a surveying and exploring expedition to the South Seas (1837). After prolonged inactivity, Jones was assigned command of the Pacific Squadron, consisting of five ships, including the frigate *United States* (December 1841). Acting on verbal orders only, he received reports that French naval vessels were leaving Peru (May 1842) and that British Admiral Richard Thomas* was heading a three-vessel squadron in the region (September 1842). Jones was mistakenly informed that war had broken out between the United States and Mexico, assumed that the British had seized California, and promptly captured Monterrey himself (May 1842). Although he apologized and returned the city to Mexican authorities, he was relieved of his duties. He was never censured and later regained command of his squadron (1848). At the close of the Mexican War (1846–1848), Jones levied military contributions at Mazatlán (1848) and used some of the funds to transport refugees from Lower California, but he was accused of using the balance improperly. He was court-martialed (1850), suspended with some loss of pay (1850–1855), and placed on reserve. Jones married Mary Walker Carter in Richmond in 1823 and was survived by four children.

The naval career of the fictitious Commodore who is on board the *Neversink* in Melville's *White-Jacket* parallels to some degree the real career of Commodore Jones, even though no commodore was on board while Melville served on the *United States* (1843–1844), the prototype of his *Neversink*. While being called simply Ap Catesby in "Bridegroom-Dick," Jones is said in that poem to have been a famous naval officer under whom Bridegroom Dick evidently once sailed; it is added that Ap Catesby served with Decatur, Hull, [Oliver Hazard] Perry, and Porter.

Bibliography: James High, "Jones at Monterey, 1842," pp. 88–100 in *The Mexican War: Changing Interpretations,* ed. Odie B. Faulk and Joseph A. Stout, Jr. (Chicago: Swallow Press, 1973); Kuykendall; NN 5; Robin Reilly, *The British at the Gates: The New Orleans Campaign in the War of 1812* (New York: G. P. Putnam's Sons, 1974).

Jones Three. In "The New Ancient of Days," he is a common man, dethroned by the new ancient.

Jos. In "The New Ancient of Days," he is a common man, opposed by the new ancient.

José. In "Benito Cereno," he is a Spanish-speaking slave, about eighteen years of age, owned by Alexandro Aranda. José spies on Aranda for Babo.

Josy. In *Omoo,* he is Old Mother Tot's "man."

Juan Fernandes. In "The Encantadas." *See* Fernandez, Juan.

Judd, Gerrit Parmele (1803–1873). Missionary and statesman. Judd was born in Paris, Oneida County, New York, the oldest son of a physician. Young Judd studied in his father's office, attended a medical school at Fairfield, New York, obtained his degree (1825), and decided to engage in missionary work. He accepted an appointment as physician to the Sandwich Islands Mission of the American Board of Commissioners for Foreign Missions (1827), married Laura Fish of Plainfield, New York (1827), and went with her to Honolulu (1828). Judd earned the respect of Kamehameha III,* the king of Hawaii, and of his chiefs; admired the natives, their customs, and their thoughts; learned the Hawaiian language thoroughly; and was the official governmental interpreter and translator (from 1833). Discontinuing his missionary duties (1842) to work exclusively for the king, he became a member of the treasury board and the governmental recorder (1842). He advocated cooperation between natives and foreigners so as to make constitutional independence of the islands possible and to limit the influx of aliens. This plan was impeded by foreigners—Americans, Britishers, and the French—interested in advancing their own competing commercial, political, and religious interests. Especially troublesome were Captain Richard Charlton,* first British consul to the Pacific (from 1825); Jacques-Antoine Moerenhout,* French consul in Tahiti; Lord George Paulet,* his replacement; his superior Admiral Frederick J. Thomas; and Abel Aubert Dupetit-Thouars,* a militant French admiral. Judd became minister of foreign affairs (1843–1845), minister of the interior (1845–1846), and minister of finance (1846–1853)—all the while serving as de facto prime minister.

Accompanied by the king's nephew Prince Alexander Liholiho (later King Kamehameha IV [1854–1863]) and the king's brother Prince Lot Kamehameha (later King Kamehameha V [1863–1872]), Judd took a diplomatic contingent abroad (1849–1850), not merely to seek reparations from the French government for hostile acts by the French consul and the French admiral, but also to modify treaties with England, France, and the United States. Judd returned to assist the king and a committee in the preparation of the liberal 1852 constitution. A year later, however, Judd was forced out of government office by antimonarchical political factions. He practiced medicine again, improved agricultural procedures on the islands, and advocated measures for the moral and spiritual improvement of the populace. He became a member of the legislature (1858) and a member of the constitutional convention (1864), during which time he sought to limit the power of Kamehameha V. Judd served on the Hawaiian Evangelical Association from its inception (1863) until his death. He was the object of much criticism by the American commissioner and the British consul general (1844–1853). Judd's widow Laura Fish Judd reported his major accomplishments in *Honolulu . . . from 1828 to 1861* (1880).

Melville, who was in the Pacific region in 1842 and 1843, makes mention in *Typee* of Captain Charlton, Admiral Du Petit-Thouars, Dr. Judd, and Lord George Paulet. He defines Dr. Judd as ''a sanctimonious apothecary-adventurer'' and reports that in 1843 Judd irresponsibly advised the half-civilized king of

Hawaii, King Kammahamaha III, and refused to cooperate with either Captain Charlton or Lord George Paulet.

Bibliography: Gerrit P. Judd IV, *Dr. Judd: Hawaii's Friend: A Biography of Gerrit Parmele Judd (1803–1873)* (Honolulu: University of Hawaii Press, 1960); Kuykendall; Ralph S. Kuykendall and A. Grove Day, *Hawaii: A History from Polynesian Kingdom to American State* (1948; rev. ed., Englewood Cliffs, N.J.: Prentice-Hall, 1961); W. P. Morrell, *Britain in the Pacific Islands* (Oxford, England: Clarendon Press, 1960).

Judy. In *Redburn,* she is a servant girl at Handsome Mary Danby's Baltimore Clipper in Liverpool.

Julia. In ''The Apple-Tree Table,'' she is the narrator's timid daughter. At first, she fearfully blames the ticking in the table on spirits but later sees in the emergence of the bug from it a proof of humankind's ultimate spiritual resurrection. She is Anna's sister. As in ''I and My Chimney,'' the narrator's wife and two daughters here resemble Melville's wife Elizabeth Knapp Shaw Melville* and their daughters Elizabeth Melville* and Frances Melville (later Frances Melville Thomas,* wife of Henry B. Thomas).

Bibliography: Young.

Julia. In ''I and My Chimney,'' she is one of the narrator's daughters. With her mother and her sister Anna, Julia unsuccessfully tries to persuade the narrator to tear down his beloved chimney. As in ''The Apple-Tree Table,'' the narrator's wife and two daughters here resemble Melville's wife Elizabeth Knapp Shaw Melville* and their daughters Elizabeth Melville* and Frances Melville (later Frances Melville Thomas,* wife of Henry B. Thomas).

Bibliography: Young.

K

Kaahumanu (c. 1768–1832). Hawaiian queen. She was the daughter of Keeaumoku, a warrior and counselor of King Kamehameha I.* While in her early teens, she became another of Kamehameha's wives and in time his favorite wife. The explorer Captain George Vancouver called her beautiful, and according to certain native standards, so she was. When fully mature, she was six feet tall and weighed 300 pounds. She encouraged her husband to unify the islands under his absolute rule. After his death (1819), she became coruler with his son Kamehameha II.* She helped persuade that man to improve the standing of Hawaiian women by taking the unprecedented step of eating in public with some of them. Thereafter, Hawaiian religions could be more quickly replaced by Christianity, once American Protestant missionaries began to appear (1820). Officially cool toward them at first, she did permit them to pray for her recovery from a grave illness (1821). When Kamehameha II went to England (1823), where he soon died (1824), Kaahumanu became regent for Kamehameha III.* She took an entourage of a thousand through the islands, met people, and quelled incipient rebellions (1822). The missionaries taught her to read and write in a matter of days, after which she promoted both Christianity and education throughout the islands; the missionaries also helped her develop Hawaii's first legal code (1824), baptized her and named her Elizabeth (1825), and were pleased by her anti-Catholicism (from 1827). She informally treatied with Thomas ap Catesby Jones* regarding American deserters and also debts owed by Hawaiians to American traders (1826). She named her brother Kuakini governor of Oahu (1829); he was already governor of Hawaii. Kaahumanu had an interesting marital history. She married Kaumualii, the king of Kauai, in 1821 and a little later married his son Kealiiahonui, whom she was persuaded by her missionaries to discard. Kaumualii died in 1824. Kaahumanu had no children.

In *Typee,* Melville identifies Queen Kaahumanu as the 400-pound dowager queen of Hawaii who used to lift up offending men and break their spines.

Bibliography: Kathleen Mellen, *The Magnificent Monarch: Kaahumanu, Queen of Hawaii* (New York: Hastings, 1952).

Kalow. In *Typee,* he is a Typee chief who attended the probably cannibalistic feast from which Tommo is excluded.

Kamehameha I (c. 1758–1819). Hawaiian king. During his reign (1795–1819), he visited the ships of Captain James Cook (1778), gained control of the northern part of Hawaii (1782), and gradually, because of superior vessels and weapons, conquered other Hawaiian islands (1785–1810). Under his rule, government was organized, crime was suppressed, foreign traders were permitted to settle, and native religion was made less severe. His favorite queen was the childless Kaahumanu.* At his death, his son Kamehameha II* became king. When that man died (1824), Kamehameha III,* another son of Kamehameha I, became king.

In *Typee* Melville mentions Kamehameha I (whose name he spells Kammahammaha) as the renowned conqueror and king of the Hawaiian Islands.

Bibliography: Kuykendall; Anne H. Spoehr, *The Royal Lineages of Hawai'i* (Honolulu: Bishop Museum Press, 1989).

Kamehameha II (1797–1824). (Alternate name: Liholiho.) Hawaiian king. After the death of his father, Kamehameha I,* he became king and ruled until his death. He admitted New England missionaries (1820) but declined to become a Christian because of his desire to retain five wives and also because of his fondness for rum. He and his favorite wife, Kamamalu, sailed for England (1823); but, not long after their arrival he died in London of measles. Upon his death, his brother Kamehameha III* became king.

Bibliography: Kuykendall.

Kamehameha III (1814–1854). (Alternate name: Kauikeaouli.) Hawaiian king. Soon after the death in London of his brother Kamehameha II,* Kamehameha III became king and ruled until his death. At first, however, he was placed under the regency of Kaahumanu,* who was the favorite wife of Kamehameha I.* When Kaahumanu died (1832), Kamehameha I's daughter Kinau became regent, until Kamehameha III, her half-brother, became the full-fledged king (1833)— and a licentious and dissipated one, at that. A little later, however, he did promulgate several exemplary measures, including the Declaration of Rights (1839), the Edict of Toleration (1839), and Hawaii's first constitution (1840). Under this last document, he established a legislature of elected representatives and a supreme court. He also achieved diplomatic recognition of the independence of his island nation by the United States (1842), England (1843), and France (1843).

In *Typee,* Melville describes King Kamehameha III (whose name he spells Kammahammaha) as the half-civilized, fat, lazy, and alcoholic king of Hawaii in 1843. Melville adds that the king was foolishly persuaded by Dr. [Gerrit Parmele] Judd to surrender Hawaii to the British. Admiral [Richard] Thomas returned the islands to their king. In *Omoo,* Melville describes Kamehameha III (whose name he spells Tammahamaha) as the present king of Hawaii and adds that the king was a mere lad in 1835 but now expansively keeps at his court a rabble of foreigners, including Billy Loon, Joe, and Mordecai.

Bibliography: Kuykendall.

Kammahammaha, King. In *Typee. See* Kamehameha I.

Kammahammaha III. In *Typee. See* Kamehameha III.

Kandidee, King of. In *Mardi,* he is a person whose name appears in a manuscript chronicle in Oh-Oh's museum.

Kannakoko, King. In *Mardi,* he is the fictitious king of New Zealand.

Karakoee. In *Typee,* he is a tall, tabooed renegade shanghaier from Oahu. Because of Karakoee's efforts, along with those of Marnoo, Tommo is able to leave the Marquesas Islands aboard the *Julia.*

Karhownoo. In *Mardi,* he is one of King Borabolla's sea divers. He fractures his skull against a coral reef. Despite Samoa's skillful brain surgery, Karhownoo dies. He was Roi Mori's younger son.

Bibliography: Merton M. Sealts, Jr., ''Melville's 'Friend Atahalpa,' '' *Notes and Queries* 194 (22 January 1949): 37–38.

Karkeke. In *Mardi,* he is the man whose spirit after death misplaced its head in heaven, according to a story by Babbalanja.

Karkie. In *Mardi,* this is one of the twelve aristocratic Tapparian families on the isle of Pimminee, entertained by Nimni.

Karky. In *Typee,* he is the master tattooer of Typee. Tommo resists his arts.

Karluna. In *Typee,* he is mentioned as a native whose property, like that of other Typees, is respected by everyone.

Karnoonoo. In *Typee,* he is a Typee native whose javelin handle Tommo carves.

Karolus [I], King. In *Mardi,* he is the beheaded king of Dominora, according to the anonymous manuscript read in north Vivenza. Since Dominora is a satirical representation of England, this Karolus is obviously an allusion to King Charles I of England (1600–1649).

Karolus [II], King. In *Mardi,* he is the second monarch named Karolus, who "returned in good time" and reigned in Dominora after King Karolus I had been beheaded there. Since Dominora is a satirical representation of England, this Karolus is obviously an allusion to King Charles II of England (1630–1685). During Oliver Cromwell's rule, Charles II spent much time in France.

Karrolono. In *Mardi,* he is one of Uhia's chieftains. He envies his monarch and is envied by Donno.

Katrina. In "A Dutch Christmas up the Hudson in the Time of Patroons," she is a girl working in the kitchen. Her boyfriend is Tuenis Van der Blumacher.

Kean, Hosea, Captain. In "The 'Gees," he is a sea captain from Nantucket who examines 'Gees on the isle of Fogo before hiring them as seamen aboard his ship. He does this instead of relying on false descriptions of them from middlemen.

Keekee. In *Omoo. See* Zeke.

Kekuanoa, General. In *Typee,* he is the immoral governor of Oahu in 1843. He profiteers from prostitution.

Kemble, Charles (1775–1854). Actor and theater manager. His parents, Roger and Sarah Ward Kemble, formed a traveling company in which some of their twelve children acted. Charles Kemble was born in Brecknock, Brecknockshire, Wales. His siblings included the actor John Philip Kemble* and the actress Sarah Kemble Siddons.* Charles Kemble first appeared notably on the stage as a teenager (1792 or 1793) and then in London with John Philip Kemble in *Macbeth* (1794). Charles Kemble, with his wife, Maria Theresa de Camp Kemble, acted in comedies. He performed at the Drury Lane and Covent Garden theaters, the latter of which he also managed, but he did poorly until his daughter Frances Anne Kemble* made her popular debut there (1829). He toured the United States with her (1832, 1834). Deafness forced his retirement from the stage (1836), after which he became a government examiner of plays. In "The Fiddler," Charles Kemble is one of the famous Drury Lane acting troupe reputedly ousted from the public eye by Master Betty (*see* Betty, William Henry West).
    Bibliography: Jane Williamson, *Charles Kemble: Man of the Theatre* (Lincoln: University of Nebraska Press, 1970).

Kemble, Frances Anne ("Fanny") (1809–1893). Actress and authoress. She was born in London into a celebrated theatrical family. Her father was Charles

Kemble,* whose siblings included the actor John Philip Kemble* and the actress Sarah Kemble Siddons.* Fanny Kemble and her father went to New York, where they began a tour (1832, 1834). She married a slave-owning Southerner named Pierce Butler, in Philadelphia (1834). They bought a house in Lenox, Massachusetts; however, she soon returned to London without him (1835), published a popular work called *Journal of Frances Kemble Butler* (2 vols., 1835), gave dramatic Shakespeare readings, and was divorced for desertion (1849). Butler obtained custody of their two daughters. Thereafter, Fanny Kemble lived in the United States intermittently (1849–1877), published *Journal of a Residence on a Georgia Plantation in 1838–1839* (1863), continued to offer readings in America and England, summered in Switzerland, and made her final home in London. Celebrated as a hostess, she wrote several more books of reminiscence and one of travel in Italy. Her daughter, Sarah Butler Wister, was the mother of Owen Wister, author of the popular and influential Western novel *The Virginian*. Melville, who lived at Arrowhead, near Pittsfield and Lenox, followed the details of the Frances and Pierce Butler divorce proceedings and sympathized with the husband. When Melville heard Fanny Kemble read from *Macbeth* and *Othello* in Boston, he wrote the following comment in 1849 to Evert Duyckinck*: ''She makes a glorious Lady Macbeth, but her Desdemona seems like a boarding school miss.—She's so unfemininely masculine that had she not, on unimpeachable authority, borne children, I should be curious to learn the result of a surgical examination of her person in private. The Lord help Butler . . . I marvel not he seeks being amputated off from his matrimonial half'' (24 February). Melville may have partly patterned the unpleasant Goneril in *The Confidence-Man* after Fanny Kemble.

Bibliography: Oliver S. Egbert, ''Melville's Goneril and Fanny Kemble,'' *New England Quarterly* 18 (December 1945): 489–500; J. C. Furnas, *Fanny Kemble: Leading Lady of the Nineteenth-Century Stage* (New York: Dial Press, 1982); NN 14.

Kemble, John Philip (1757–1823). Actor and theatrical manager. His parents, Roger and Sarah Ward Kemble, formed a traveling company in which some of their twelve children acted. John Philip Kemble was born in Prescot, Lancashire, England. His siblings included the actor Charles Kemble* and the actress Sarah Kemble Siddons.* After preliminary training for the priesthood in France, John Philip Kemble returned to England to take up a theatrical career (from 1776). Always austere and stiff on stage, he was successful only after playing Macbeth opposite his sister Sarah Siddons (from 1795). He managed the Drury Lane theater for a while (from 1788) and then Covent Garden (from 1803), but a fire in the latter (1808) hurt him financially. He retired to the Continent. In ''The Fiddler,'' John Philip Kemble is one of the famous Drury Lane acting troupe reputedly ousted from the public eye by Master Betty (*see* Betty, William Henry West).

Bibliography: Linda Kelly, *The Kemble Era: John Philip Kemble, Sarah Siddons and the London Stage* (New York: Random House, 1980).

Ke-sing. In "On the Chinese Junk." *See* Chang-foue.

Keying. In "On the Chinese Junk," he is the Chinese commissioner who allows the British to build a church. Yankee Doodle thinks that Christianity might be better served if the British spiked the guns they have in China.

Killett, Capt[ain]. In "On the Chinese Junk," he is the junk captain whose Chinese crew go on strike but are jailed for smoking opium.

Kilpatrick, Judson (1836–1881). (Full name: Hugh Judson Kilpatrick.) Union general. Kilpatrick, who was from New Jersey, dropped his first name upon entering West point, from which he graduated (1861). He became an artillery and cavalry second lieutenant, was promoted to captain three days later, and was the first regular army officer to be wounded in the Civil War. The event occurred during the first land battle of the war, at Big Bethel, Virginia (10 June 1861). As a cavalry lieutenant colonel, Kilpatrick helped defend Washington, D.C. (1861–1862), was also in Kansas (1861–1862), returned to Virginia, and saw action up to and including Second Bull Run (August 1862). Promoted to brigadier general, he fought on to and including Gettysburg (July 1863), where he issued at least one ill-conceived order. He was sent to Virginia (1864), at which time General William Tecumseh Sherman* requested his services in the West, knowing that he was foolhardy and wanting him for precisely that reason. Kilpatrick was in the cavalry corps of the Army of the Cumberland (April–October) and was wounded again (October) shortly before the Atlanta campaign, during which he was cavalry division commander under Sherman (October 1864–June 1865). He participated in the March to the Sea (November–December 1864). After the war ended, he was promoted to major general (June 1865), became minister to Chile (1865–1868), ran unsuccessfully for Congress (1880), and returned to his ambassadorial duties in Chile, where he died. Kilpatrick was a small, restless, and wiry womanizer, used influential friends to get ahead professionally, was nicknamed "Kill Cavalry" because of his reckless daring, and was so unprincipled and rapacious that he often demoralized his troops. In "The March to the Sea," Melville mentions Kilpatrick as the commander of some of Sherman's perplexing outriders.
  Bibliography: Boatner, Faust.

King. In "Time's Betrayal," he is the poet and King of his maple orchard.

King of India, The. In "Honor." *See* India, The King of.

King of France, The. In *Israel Potter. See* Louis XVI.

King-Post. In *Moby-Dick,* this is Stubb's nickname for Flask.

Kit. In *Pierre,* he is a stable slave of General Pierre Glendinning, Pierre's grand-father.

Kitoti. In *Omoo,* he is one of the four recreant chiefs whom the French governor [Armand-Joseph] Bruat puts in charge of the four sections into which he divides Tahiti. The others are Tati, Utamai, and Paraita.

Klanko, King. In *Mardi,* he is the slave-driving monarch of the dreary, gloomy land between Bobovona and Serenia. King Media insists upon avoiding King Klanko's region of volcanic mines. The name Klanko suggests the sound of clanking chains.

Kniphausen. In *Israel Potter. See* Knyphausen, Wilhelm von.

Knowles, Ned. In *White-Jacket,* he was Jack Chase's first loader at a main-deck gun of Admiral [Sir Edward] Codrington's flagship the *Asia.* Knowles was said to have been killed during the Battle of Navarino (20 October 1827). Codrington was in command of the combined British, French, and Russian fleet when it destroyed the Turkish and Egyptian naval forces at Navarino, during an en-gagement in the harbor of Navarino, now Pylos, Greece (20 October 1827). This battle was the last major fleet action involving wooden sailing vessels.

Knyphausen, Wilhelm von (1716–1800). (Full name: Baron Wilhelm von Knyphausen.) German soldier. He was born in Lützberg, entered the Prussian army (1734), became a general in the army of Frederick the Great (1775), and was ordered to the American colonies as second in command (under General Le-opold Philip de Heister) of 12,000 Hessians. Knyphausen sailed in a fleet with 6,000 soldiers from Bremen and landed on Staten Island after a twenty-week voyage (October 1775). He was involved in the battles of Long Island (August 1776), White Plains (October), and Fort Washington (November). After Fort Washington, New York, was captured, it was briefly renamed Fort Knyphausen. When General Sir William Howe* disputed with Heister, the latter was recalled and Knyphausen was placed in command of all Hessians, with the rank of lieu-tenant general (June 1777). He fought in the battles of the Brandywine (Septem-ber) and Monmouth (June 1778). He occupied the northern part of Manhattan Island and part of the time was in command of the entire city (1780). In due time, the gallant old soldier grew infirm and in addition was blind in one eye; he finally retired (1782) in disappointment over his ultimate lack of accomplishment in the New World. He was named governor of Kassel, where he died. Knyphausen's main professional complaints were that most of his troops came from work-houses or were impressed, that their shipboard drilling was inadequate, and that their casualty figures were swelled by desertion more than by combat.

In *Israel Potter,* Melville names Kniphausen as the Hessian commander in America whom Ethan Allen reviles during his captivity in Falmouth, England.

In his narrative, Allen lumps "Howe, [General John] Burgoyne, and Knyphausen" together as enemy generals who were vicious and conceited after the British capture of Fort Ticonderoga (July 1777).

Bibliography: Rodney Atwood, *The Hessians: Mercenaries from Hessen-Kassel in the American Revolution* (Cambridge, England: Cambridge University Press, 1980); R. Ernest Dupuy, Gay Hammerman, and Grace P. Hayes, *The American Revolution: A Global War* (New York: David McKay, 1977).

Ko-ka-poo. In "On the Chinese Junk," he was a Chinese who built the first ship 5,000 years ago. After he died, his spirit sat on his mainmast and bent it into the crooked shape followed by shipbuilders to this day.

Kokovoko, The King of. In *Moby-Dick,* he is Queequeg's Polynesian father, a high chief. He may be dead by the time Ishmael and Queequeg meet and become friends.

Kolor. In *Typee. See* Kolory.

Kolory ("Lord Primate"). In *Typee,* he is a Typee soldier-priest. He cuffs Moa Artua, his religious doll, into providing acceptable answers to questions he whispers to it. He is also called Kolor.

Konno. In *Mardi,* he is an ingenious man of Kaleedoni, who "lately died in Verdanna." According to Babbalanja, Konno cured the evils of his land by building a fire under a huge cauldron and thus making the people regard him as quite busy. Konno is based on Daniel O'Connell,* the recently deceased Irish patriot. Melville thus adverts to O'Connell's agitation for Catholic emancipation in Ireland and freedom of Ireland from Great Britain.

Bibliography: Davis.

Kooloo. In *Omoo,* he is a Tahitian native who adopts the narrator as his friend only to spurn him later for another. Poky, the narrator's other native friend, is more loyal.

Kory-Kory. In *Typee,* he is the tall, athletic, happy son of Marheyo and Tinor. Kory-Kory, about twenty-five years of age, carries Tommo about on his back, bathes him, explains various aspects of native life (for example, burial platforms, dancing, and polygamy), and ministers to his needs as well as he can. When Melville's British publisher John Murray* said that the reading public would welcome proof of the veracity of parts of *Typee,* Melville replied that he lamented his inability "to subpoena . . . Kory-Kory who I'll be bound is this blessed day taking his noon nap somewhere in the flowery vale of Typee" (2 September 1846).

Bibliography: Anderson, Davis, NN 14.

Krako. In *Mardi,* he is Bardianna's disciple, mentioned in the philosopher's will.

Kravi. In *Mardi,* he is a cunning man whose finger bones, fashioned into a fishhook, are in Oh-Oh's museum. His name suggests craving.

Kroko, King. In *Mardi,* he is a character in a manuscript ballad in Oh-Oh's museum.

Kubla. In *Mardi,* he is a priest who gives King Donjalolo the royal girdle that makes him king of Juam. The name Kubla was undoubtedly suggested to Melville by his reading of ''Kubla Khan'' by Samuel Taylor Coleridge,* the subject of which is the Mongolian ruler Kublai Khan (1215?–1294).

L

L., B. In *Clarel,* he is a devout pilgrim from St. Mary's Hall, Oxford. Some time earlier, he left an enigmatic antirevolutionary poem on a wall in Clarel's room at the inn in Jerusalem.

L—, Miss. In *Redburn,* she is a woman to whom Redburn's father presented a letter in Liverpool in 1808.

Lacedaemonian Jim. In *Omoo. See* Long Jim.

Laced Cap. In "Bridegroom-Dick," this is a general term used by Bridegroom Dick to refer to any fancy naval officer.

Laffite, Jean (1780?–1825? or 1849?). (Alternate spellings: Lafite, Lafitte.) Privateer, smuggler, and soldier. Laffite may have been born in Bordeaux, France, and served under Napoleon.* He and his brother Pierre may have established a New Orleans blacksmith shop used as a front for smuggling slaves and merchandise. Jean Laffite evidently built up a colony of ruffians on Grand Terre Island, in Barataria Bay south of the city. He obtained a privateer commission from Cartagena (now part of Colombia), which had revolted against Spanish rule. He was thus licensed to plunder Spanish shipping, and what he seized he fenced through mainland merchants. When the British planned an assault on Mobile during the War of 1812, they hired Laffite as a naval captain and gave him $30,000 for his loyalty, whereupon he warned Louisiana Governor William C. C. Claiborne, who doubted his report and ordered Laffite's Baratarian holdings attacked and his men jailed (1814). General Andrew Jackson obtained a pardon for Laffite, assigned him and his Baratarians army combat roles, and commended their accomplishments during the Battle of New Orleans (1814–1815). Laffite resumed his corsair career, established a colony called Campeche (1817, near present-day Galveston), called himself its governor (1819), and again preyed upon Spanish shipping. He and his followers attacked American vessels (1820), were resisted, and burned a nearby town. He disappeared from reliable history with a crew aboard his favorite *Pride*. His marital life is also obscure: He may have married Christina Levine about 1800, and had two sons and a daughter with her; she may have died about 1803. He may have married Emma Hortense Mortimore in 1832 and had two sons with her.

In "Daniel Orme," Lafitte is mentioned as a buccaneer reputed to have been Daniel Orme's leader at one time.

Bibliography: The Journals of Jean Laffite: The Privateer Patriot's Own Story (New York: Vantage Press, 1958); Frank Richard Prassel, *The Great American Outlaw: A Legacy of Fact and Fiction* (Norman: University of Oklahoma Press, 1993).

Lais. In "The Parthenon," Lais, who was a priestess of Venus in Corinth, is described as a beautiful Greek courtesan. Melville adds that [Baruch] Spinoza thinks of her beauty when he thinks of the beauty of the Parthenon. In ancient history, there were two women named Lais. One Lais was a notorious Greek courtesan who served the Corinthian cult of Aphrodite and was allegedly the mistress of Aristippus.* A second Lais was a similarly notorious mistress of Alcibiades.

Bibliography: Gail H. Coffler, *Melville's Classical Allusions: A Comprehensive Index and Glossary* (Westport, Conn.: Greenwood Press, 1985); NN 11.

"The Lake: Pontoosuce." *See* "Pontoosuce."

Lakreemo. In *Mardi,* he is a legatee who is mentioned in Bardianna's will. Bardianna, when ill, was pleased that Lakreemo "made tearful inquiries" about his health (and was therefore lachrymose).

Lamia. In mythology, Lamia was a vampire who tempted young men and sucked their blood. In Melville's poem "Lamia's Song," she is a singer who urges the mountaineer to "come" down from his cold heights to her "valley."

Bibliography: Stein.

"Lamia's Song" (1891). Poem, in *Timoleon.* (Character: Lamia.) The singer urges the mountaineer to descend from the wintry-looking heights to May flowers. The cataracts will provide a hymn as he approaches his reward—of "more than a wreath."

Bibliography: Shurr, Stein.

Lanbranka Hohinna. In *Mardi,* she is a spinster legatee who is mentioned in Bardianna's will.

Landless ("Happy Jack"). In *White-Jacket,* he is a foretopman with ten years of service in the U.S. Navy. He is a typically stupid, immature, happy-go-lucky sailor, who is often flogged and cares for nothing but rum and tobacco. He advises Shippy.

Langford, Joseph Munt (1809–1884). Editor and drama critic. He was in charge of the London office of Blackwood & Sons (1845–1881) and was drama critic of the London *Observer.* He knew many of England's leading writers, including Charles Dickens, George Eliot, and William Makepeace Thackeray. With a friend, Langford translated a French play and saw it on stage as *Like and Unlike* (1856). Melville met Langford in London, was taken by him to see William Charles Macready* in *Othello,* was entertained by him at dinner in his home, and was introduced to several pleasant fellow guests (November 1849).
   Bibliography: NN 14 and 15.

Langsdorff, Georg Heinrich von, Baron (1774–1852). German scientist and explorer. Born in Wöllstein, he went as a physician to Lisbon (1787) and as a naturalist to Siberia (1803), and continued to travel. He sailed widely in the South Seas, during which time he spent ten days on Nukuhiva, in the Marquesas Islands (1804), where he found two white deserters. Langsdorff lived in Brazil (1821–1829) and for a time was the Russian consul there. His major publication was *Voyages and Travels in Various Parts of the World, during the Years 1803, 1804, 1805, 1806, and 1807* (2 vols., 1813). In 1805, Langsdorff met Captain John D'Wolf II (1779–1872), the husband of Melville's aunt Mary Melvill D'Wolf (1778–1859), the sister of Melville's father Allan Melvill.* Langsdorff and D'Wolf became close friends and traveled together (1805–1806), partly on a vessel commanded by D'Wolf, who named his only son John Langsdorff D'Wolf (1817–1886). Melville may have read Langsdorff's *Voyages and Travels* and used parts of it when he composed *Typee.* In *Redburn,* "Captain" Langsdorff is mentioned as a friend of Redburn's old sea-captain uncle. Redburn reports that his uncle was later lost at sea; in reality, D'Wolf retired from the sea (1827), resided in Massachusetts, and died near Boston forty-five years later. Melville must have talked as a child with his uncle and perhaps heard from him about Langsdorff.
   Bibliography: Anderson, Metcalf, NN 14.

Lansing, Abraham ("Abe") (1835–1899). Lawyer. He was born in Albany into an illustrious old family of Dutch extraction. He attended the Albany Academy and then graduated from Williams College (1855). He studied law in his father's office in Albany and graduated from the Albany Law School (1857). He practiced law in Albany, suffered for a year in bed with inflammatory rheumatism, resumed his practice, became the city attorney of Albany (1868), was the first supreme court reporter (1869), became the acting state treasurer (1874–1876) and the corporation counsel for Albany (1876–1882), and was elected state senator to represent Albany County (1882). Lansing held several other professional and civic offices. In 1873, after an eleven-year, off-and-on engagement, he married Catherine ("Kate," "Kitty") Gansevoort, the daughter of Peter Gansevoort (1788–1876),* Melville's uncle. (The couple had no children.) Catherine was also Melville's aunt Susan Lansing Gansevoort's stepdaughter. Thus, Lansing became Melville's amiable cousin-in-law. The two men shared a love of the poetry of Pierre Jean de Béranger. During the Civil War, Lansing associated with Henry Sanford Gansevoort,* the war hero and the brother of his wife-to-be. Melville knew Lansing's sister Anna Lansing and his brothers John Lansing, William Lansing, and Edwin Yates Lansing—all younger than Abraham Lansing. Edwin Lansing, whom Melville knew well, saw action during the Civil War; once, as a Union cavalry captain, he came close to capturing the elusive Colonel John Singleton Mosby* (1864). Abraham Lansing was the executor of the estate of Melville's sister Frances Priscilla Melville.* Robert Lansing, a distant cousin of Abraham Lansing, was President Woodrow Wilson's secretary of state (1915–1920).

Bibliography: Kenney; Leyda; NN 14; Amasa J. Parker, ed., *Landmarks of Albany County New York* (Syracuse, N.Y.: Mason & Co., Publishers, 1897).

Lansing, Catherine ("Kate," "Kitty") Gansevoort (1839–1918). Melville's cousin. She was the daughter of Peter Gansevoort (1888–1876),* who was the brother of Melville's mother Maria Gansevoort Melville,* and the sister of Henry Sanford Gansevoort.* She argued with her brother but wrote to him regularly—especially when he was on active duty during the Civil War—went to Nassau, in the Bahamas, to help him get home during his convalescence there, and mourned him hysterically when he died (1870) and self-humiliatingly afterward. With the assistance of John Chipman Hoadley,* Melville's brother-in-law, she edited her brother's letters (1875). Earlier, after an eleven-year, off-and-on engagement, she married Abraham Lansing* in 1873 (the couple had no children). After the death of Melville's brother Allan Melville* (1872), Catherine Lansing was kind to and corresponded with his widow for several years. After her father's death (1876), Catherine Lansing offered Melville money, which he refused; later the two quarreled (1879), after which their relationship was strained. She founded the Gansevoort chapter of the Daughters of the Revolution (1895). She became eccentric after her husband died of cancer (1899). At her death, executors found the Gansevoort family estate to be worth $350,000.

Bibliography: Kenney, NN 14.

Larfee. In *Mardi,* she is a witch in Mohi's story. She falsely condemns the questing lover Ozonna for supposedly killing Rea, a maiden in Queen Hautia's court of the isle of Flozella-a-Nina. Mohi relates the story in an effort to dissuade Taji from continuing his search for Yillah.

Larry. In *Redburn,* he is a sailor aboard the *Highlander.* He speaks of his experiences as a whaler and rails against "snivilization."

Larry o' the Cannakin. In "Jack Roy," he is a jovial singer of the praises of his mate Jack Roy.

Lascar Sailor. In *Moby-Dick,* he is a *Pequod* sailor who interrupts the dancing during the midnight festivities in the forecastle by announcing the approach of a storm.

"The Last Tile." *See* "The Parthenon."

Lathers, Richard (1820–1903). Melville family friend. In 1846 Lathers married Abby Pitman Thurston, a sister of Sophia Thurston, who was the wife of Allan Melville,* Melville's brother. Melville, who became friendly with Lathers through his brother and Evert Duyckinck,* often visited Winyah, the Lathers' book-filled estate outside New Rochelle, New York. Lathers gave Melville a welcome set of the works of Washington Irving* (1853). Melville and his brother sought Lathers's influence in obtaining passes to visit Henry Sanford Gansevoort,* their cousin, who was serving with the Union Army in Virginia (1864). Lathers, president of the Atlantic & Great Western Insurance Marine Company in New York, in 1866 employed Melville's son Malcolm Melville,* who was still working for the firm at the time of his suicide (1867). Lathers and his wife, who often visited the Melvilles at Arrowhead, near Pittsfield, Massachusetts, bought property, built close by, and moved there (1869). *Reminiscences of Richard Lathers: Sixty Years of a Busy Life in South Carolina, Massachusetts and New York,* appearing posthumously (1907), mentions Melville with affection.
   Bibliography: Cohen and Yannella, Leyda, Metcalf, NN 14.

L.A.V. In "Fragments from a Writing Desk." *See* V., L. A.

Lavender. In *Redburn,* he is the handsome mulatto steward of the *Highlander.* A former Broadway barber, he likes Liverpool because he can step along freely there.
   Bibliography: Grejda.

Lazarus. In *Clarel,* this is the name taken by a count turned monk who came to Mar Saba and set up a carved marble shield in a porch of the minister there.

Lazarus. In *Moby-Dick,* this is the name Ishmael assigns to a shivering beggar who is sleeping on the curb outside Peter Coffin's Spouter-Inn at New Bedford.

Leader, The. In "The Scout toward Aldie." *See* the Colonel.

Lecbe. In "Benito Cereno," he is a vicious Ashantee slave. He polishes hatchets during Captain Amasa Delano's visit aboard the *San Dominick.* Lecbe helped Matinqui mortally mutilate Alexandro Aranda and also helped kill Francisco Masa.

Lee, Robert E. (1807–1870). (Full name: Robert Edward Lee.) Soldier. The son of Henry ("Light-Horse Harry") Lee of American Revolutionary War fame, Lee was born in Westmoreland County, Virginia. Not long after his father's death (1818), Lee entered West Point, graduating second in his class and without demerits (1829). He commenced a distinguished military career, serving as an engineer in Georgia, Virginia, Washington, D.C., Missouri, and New York state. Daring and competent during the Mexican War, he fought at Vera Cruz under General Winfield Scott* (March 1847), at Cerro Gordo (April 1847, alongside George B. McClellan*), and at Chapultepec (September 1847), where he was wounded. After being breveted lieutenant colonel, Lee was stationed in Baltimore (1848–1852), served as superintendent at West Point (1852–1855), and—aided by Jefferson Davis, then secretary of war in President Franklin Pierce's cabinet—began to serve in the field with a cavalry unit (1855–1859), partly in Texas. While on leave in Washington, Lee was ordered to counter the attack by John Brown* at Harpers Ferry (1859), and he executed his assignment smoothly.

Lee, a Unionist, did not own slaves in 1861 and did not favor secession; however, he felt more loyal to Virginia than to the United States. Scott made him colonel of the First Cavalry (16 March), and President Abraham Lincoln* offered him the field command of all U.S. Army units (18 April). Instead, Lee submitted his resignation (20 April), and—though having hoped to stay out of the war—agreed to command Virginia's forces (23 April), was made a general in the Confederate Army (reactive to June), and was appointed by Davis as his military adviser (August 1861–June 1862). Lee commanded the Army of Northern Virginia, prevented the capture of Richmond, won many victories—and made Union forces pay heavily for theirs—during the Seven Days' Campaign (June–July, over General McClellan), at Second Bull Run (August), at Fredericksburg (December), and at Chancellorsville (May 1863). The tide turned against Lee at Gettysburg (July 1863), after which General Ulysses S. Grant* wore him down by attrition and superior numbers, especially in the Wilderness (May 1864), at Spottsylvania (May), at Cold Harbor (June), and at Petersburg (winter 1864–1865). Lee, whose best subordinate generals had been Thomas J. Jackson,* James Longstreet,* and James E. B. Stuart,* surrendered at Appomattox (9 April 1865). Afterward, Lee became president of Washington College (1865–1870), where he improved its curriculum and established the first departments of commerce and journalism in the United States. Lee married Mary Ann Randolph Custis, the great-granddaughter of Martha Washington, the wife of George Washington,* in 1831 (the couple had seven children). Lee was a military genius with respect to field fortifications, the ability to read his opponents' minds, and seizing strategic initiatives by aggressiveness. He was less admirable regarding supply work, and to his detriment he sometimes left tactical field details to subordinates. His men revered him and followed him loyally. After his death, Washington College became Washington and Lee University.

Melville treats Lee in many poems. In "The Victor of Antietam (1862)," he is named as the Confederate general defeated by McClellan. In "The Armies of the Wilderness," Lee is lauded by a Confederate prisoner. In "The March to the Sea," he has a Union gamecock named after him. In "The Surrender at Appomattox," he presents his sword to Grant. In "Rebel Color-Bearers at Shiloh," Lee is mentioned. In "Presentation to the Authorities," he is mentioned as surrendering. In "The Scout toward Aldie," he is mentioned. In "Lee in the Capitol," Lee (called "The Chief" and "The Invader") is described as testifying after the Civil War before the U.S. Senate and is imagined as urging a policy of understanding and a renewal of harmony under reestablished laws. In "To Major John Gentian, Dean of the Burgundy Club," he is mentioned. Melville admired Lee tremendously.

Bibliography: Douglas Southall Freeman, *Lee's Lieutenants: A Study in Command,* 3 vols. (New York: C. Scribner's Sons, 1942–1944); Garner; Wilson.

"Lee in the Capitol" (1866). Poem, in *Battle-Pieces.* (Characters: [General Ulysses S.] Grant, [General Thomas J.] Stonewall Jackson, [General Robert E.] Lee, [General John] Pope, [General William Tecumseh] Sherman, [General James E. B.] Stuart.) Approaching the U.S. Senate when summoned, Lee reminisces about his fallen comrades. He has accepted "[h]is doom . . . / And acquiesces in asserted laws." When, at the close of his testimony, he is asked if he has anything to add, Lee is imagined as speaking "for the brave / Who else no voice or proxy have." He urges the senators to believe that the South wants to enjoy "peace . . . [under] quiet law," desires that the Northern triumph not be pushed too far, is of the opinion "that North and South were driven / By Fate to arms," and that Southerners naturally fought to defend their region of the country. Melville concludes by suggesting that the senators were "[m]oved, but not swayed" by Lee, and yet "Faith in America never dies." In a long note to the poem, Melville justifies his giving Lee an imagined speech by saying classical historians and Shakespeare have exercised similar license.

Bibliography: Garner, NN 11, Shurr, Warren.

Le Fan, Chaplain. In "Bridegroom-Dick," he is the religious man whom Bridegroom Dick in his reminiscences contrasts with Tom Tight.

Lefevre. In *Omoo,* he is a spy and a scoundrel employed, along with Major Fergus, by [Armand-Joseph] Bruat, the hated French governor of Tahiti.

Legare, Tom. In *Redburn,* he is the treasurer of the Juvenile Temperance Society, of which Redburn is a member.

Leggs. In *White-Jacket,* he is, with Pounce, one of the two ship's corporals under Bland. Leggs, formerly a prison turnkey in New York City, ferrets out illicit gamblers aboard the *Neversink.*

Lemsford. In *White-Jacket,* he is a nervous poet, whose acquaintance aboard the *Neversink* White Jacket cherishes. Lemsford conceals his poetry in a casket-like box. He wants to draw up the playbill for the Fourth of July theatrical and reveres the sea, at least in his conversation. Lemsford may be partly based on George W. Wallace and Ephraim Curtiss Hines, both of whom were poets and sailors with Melville aboard the *United States* (1843–1844), the prototype of the *Neversink.*
    Bibliography: Anderson; Harrison Hayford, ''The Sailor-Poet of *White-Jacket,*'' *Boston Public Library Quarterly* 3 (January 1951): 221–28; NN 5.

''L'Envoi.'' *See* ''L'Envoi'' (under E).

''L'Envoy: The Return of the Sire de Nesle. A.D. 16—.'' *See* ''L'Envoy: The Return of the Sire de Nesle. A.D. 16—'' (under E).

Leonardo da Vinci (1452–1519). Italian architect, author, engineer, painter, scientist, and sculptor. He was born near Vinci, close to Florence, to which he later moved (1466). Once there, he was apprenticed to a sculptor (c. 1466–c. 1476), where he was well trained, and began to paint (to 1481). He worked in Milan as an artist and adviser to architects and civil and military engineers (c. 1482), and went on to Pavia (1490) and Mantua and Venice (1500) before returning to Florence and its environs (1500–1506). He began the cartoons for his ambitious but aborted *Battle of Anghiari* (1503). He worked in Milan and Florence (to 1513). He went to Rome (1513–1516), during which time he was briefly in Parma (1514). He went to the court of Francis I in France as painter and architectural adviser. Leonardo died at Cloux, near Amboise, in France. His sponsors included Lorenzo the Magnificent, Lodovico Sforza, Cesare Borgia, and Louis XII and Francis I of France. Leonardo da Vinci, one of the greatest and most restless geniuses in the history of the world, studied aeronautics, anatomy, biology, cartography, geology, mathematics, painting, physics (including light and optics), and sculpture. He was often too frenziedly occupied with research projects to finish them. He pushed his unique intellect to incredible limits. His notebooks reveal that he was the most creative mind and ingenious researcher that the Renaissance produced. He is best known for his paintings. His most striking early picture is *Ginevra de' Benci* (1474); two middle-phase works are *The Virgin of the Rocks* (1483) and *The Last Supper* (1497); his last works include a red-chalk self-portrait (c. 1512), *Mona Lisa* (1503), and *St. John the Baptist* (c. 1515).
    When Melville saw Leonardo's *Last Supper* in Milan, he penned the following terse comment in his 1857 journal: ''Significance of the Last Supper. The

joys of the banquet soon depart. One shall betray me, one of you—man so false—the glow of sociality so evanescent, selfishness so lasting'' (7 April). In his poem ''Marquis de Grandvin: At the Hostelry,'' Melville depicts Leonardo as ''lost in dream,'' with his ''subtle brain, convolved in snare, / Inferring and over-refining there.''

   Bibliography: Kenneth Clark, *Leonardo da Vinci: An Account of His Development as an Artist* (1939; rev. ed., Harmondsworth, England: Penguin Books, 1967); Robert Wallace et al., *The World of Leonardo, 1452–1519* (New York: Time-Life Books, 1967).

Lesbia. In ''The Vial of Attar,'' she is depicted as having a lover who is sad at her death.

Lesbian, The (''The Lesbos,'' ''The Mytilene,'' ''The Isleman''). In *Clarel,* he is a middle-aged salesman from Mytilene, on the island of Lesbos, who does business at Mar Saba. He is an easy-going believer only in the happy here and now.

Lesbos. In *Clarel. See* the Lesbian.

Levi, Max. In *Clarel,* he is a friend of Margoth, who says that Levi traversed the traditionally impassable Seir, which is a region near the Dead Sea.

Lewis, Jack. In *Typee,* he is a sailor aboard the *Dolly* whose ability to steer is unfairly criticized by Captain Vangs.

Lewis, Morgan. In ''Report of the Committee on Agriculture,'' he is the president of the Berkshire Agricultural Society and as such is the recipient of the long-winded report.

''The Lightning-Rod Man'' (1854). Short story. (Character: Jupiter Tonans.) The narrator explains that at the very moment a storm of lightning and thunder is breaking over his house a stranger comes clattering at his door. The fellow is thin and gloomy and has ''pitfalls of eyes . . . ringed by indigo halos.'' Dripping wet, he strides to the center of the room. He flourishes a wooden staff attached to which is a copper rod, with two glass balls ringed by copper bands. Calling him Jupiter Tonans, the narrator thanks him for evoking the storm. The stranger counters with a lecture on the dangers of lightning hereabouts, warns the narrator against standing by the hearth or near the walls, and offers to sell him a lightning rod. Feeling confident, however, the narrator rebukes him as a peddler of indulgences from divine ordinations, adds that he will stand at ease in the hands of his God, and observes not only that his house is unharmed but also that a rainbow is now appearing. In a black rage, the salesman attacks his host with his rod. The narrator seizes it, breaks it, and tosses the fellow out. All the same, this man is still profiting from "the fears of man," especially "in storm-time."

This tale, for which Melville received $18, was anonymously published in *Putnam's Monthly Magazine** (August 1854) and was reprinted in *The Piazza Tales* (1856) and in William E. Burton's *Cyclopaedia of Wit and Humor . . .* (1858). Satirizing lightning-rod salesmen in particular, Melville is more generally sneering at proponents of the stern religious notion that God can strike sinners out of stormy clouds.

Bibliography: Newman, Sealts, Young.

Lily. In "Madcaps," Lily is a child who with Cherry frolics innocently in a flowery orchard.

Limeno, The. In *Clarel,* he is a close Peruvian friend of the Lyonese, who mentions him with a sigh.

Lincoln, Abraham (1809–1865). (Nicknames: "Honest Abe," "Old Abe," "The Rail-Splitter.") President. Lincoln was born near Hidgenville, Kentucky, moved with his family to Indiana and then Illinois, had little formal education but read profoundly, and was admitted to the bar (1836). He served in the Illinois legislature (1834–1841) and—as a Whig—in the U.S. House of Representatives (1847–1849). Though opposed to the Mexican War (1846–1848), he supported its hero Zachary Taylor* for president (1848). Lincoln returned to private practice (to 1855), at which time he unsuccessfully opposed Stephen A. Douglas for senator from Illinois. Lincoln joined the new Republican Party (1856), again ran against Douglas, and challenged him to a series of debates (21 August–15 October 1858), which, although they did not win him a senatorial seat, catapulted him to national prominence. In a brilliant speech at Cooper Union, New York City (27 February 1860), Lincoln criticized Douglas's doctrine of popular sovereignty and appealed for understanding among inflamed sections of the country. He was nominated for president at his party's Chicago convention (May 1860), and stated in his inaugural address his willingness to let slavery remain in Southern states but opposed its extension (March 1861). When Fort Sumter, in Charleston, South Carolina, was fired on (12 April), the Civil War began. Although Lincoln assumed extraordinary executive powers, the war did not go well for him during the first years. He issued the Emancipation Proclamation (January 1863) to preserve the union, rallied proponents of popular government with his Gettysburg Address (November 1863), placed Ulysses S. Grant* as lieutenant general in command of all Union land forces (March 1864), defeated George B. McClellan* for president (November 1864), appealed in his second inaugural address (March 1865)—"with malice toward none, with charity for all"—to the nation to proceed to victory, rejoiced at the surrender of Robert E. Lee* (April 1865), but was assassinated days later.

Lincoln married Mary Todd in 1842. The couple had four sons, but only one survived his parents. He was Robert Todd Lincoln (1844–1926), a member of General Grant's staff briefly (1865), secretary of war (1881–1885) in the cabinets of presidents James Garfield and Chester Arthur, minister to England (1889–1893), and president of the Pullman company (1897–1911).

Melville in his poem "The Martyr" praises Lincoln, whom he calls "the Forgiver," as a kind, calm, clement leader. But the poet predicts that Lincoln's assassination will cause the avenger to replace the forgiver.

Bibliography: Garner; Mark E. Neely, Jr., *The Last Best Hope of Earth: Abraham Lincoln and the Promise of America* (Cambridge, Mass.: Harvard University Press, 1993); Wilson.

Lippi, Fra Filippo (or Lippo) (c. 1406–1469). Italian painter. He was born in Florence, was orphaned early, was reared by an aunt, became a Carmelite monk (1421), and painted Carmine Chapel frescoes. He left Florence (1432), lived in Padua (1434), and returned to Florence (1437) when he was sponsored by the Medici family to decorate convents and churches there. Lippi became the rector of the Saint Quirico church at Legnaia (1442). Leading a vivid life, he was convicted of forgery (1455), abducted a nun named Lucrezia Buti (1456), but then received papal permission to marry her. The couple had a son, the future painter Filippino Lippi, and also a daughter. After working in Florence and Prato, the elder Lippi moved to Spoleto (1466), commissioned by the Medicis to beautify the cathedral choir there. Influenced at first by Masaccio and Fra Angelico,* he evolved his own style and painted religious works making superb use of color, balance, perspective, and realistic—and even homely—details. His human figures are gentle and graceful, and they often convey a kind of narrative message. In "Marquis de Grandvin: At the Hostelry," Melville depicts Frater Lippi as a wicked-eyed monk turned painter who discusses the picturesque with other artists.

Bibliography: Gloria Fossi, *Filippo Lippi* (New York: Riverside, 1989).

"The Little Good Fellows" (1924). Poem, in *Weeds and Wildings,* as part of the section entitled "The Year." The robins tell people to move aside and let them cover any dead and deserted humans "with buds and leaves"; they will also urge little animals to avoid molesting the corpses. Further, the robins adjure "maids and men" to nullify the effects of winter by being "[a]live to the bridal-favors when / They blossom your orchards every Spring." Though more overtly optimistic, this poem may have been influenced by the dreadful dirge, which begins "Call for the robin-red-breast, and the wren," in *The White Devil* by the Elizabeth dramatist John Webster, whose works Melville asked Evert Duyckinck* to loan him (1862).

Bibliography: NN 14, Shurr, Stein.

Livella. In *Mardi,* he is a Mardian historian, some of whose books have been lost. Livella is mentioned by Babbalanja. When he named Livella, Melville was

undoubtedly thinking of the Roman historian Livy (59 B.C.–A.D. 17), 107 of whose 142 books have been lost.
   Bibliography: Wright.

Liverpool. In *Omoo. See* Blunt, Bill.

Llanyllan, Mrs. In *Pierre,* she is Lucy Tartan's childless and widowed aunt. Lucy visits her in the village of Saddle Meadows and thus can be near Pierre.

Logodora. In *Mardi,* he is an aloof Mardian mentioned by Babbalanja.

"The Loiterer" (1924). Poem, in *Weeds and Wildings,* as part of the section entitled "The Year." The poet adjures his audience to believe that "[s]he [the spring] will come tho' she loiter." We wait while snow is under the fir, log embers doze in the moonlight, and the caged bird is warmed by a thin sun, until she appears at the door. Golly, then tears come to our eyes when she says, "Old folks, aren't ye glad to see *me!*" Melville tentatively entitled this poem "The Late-Comer" and reworked it extensively in draft form.
   Bibliography: Stein.

Lol Lol. In *Mardi,* this is one of the twelve aristocratic Tapparian families on the isle of Pimminee, entertained by Nimni.

Lombardo. In *Mardi,* he is the independent, financially pinched, long-suffering literary genius who wrote *Koztanza,* an ancient Mardian masterpiece. This work is revered by Babbalanja, who discusses Lombardo's career; it is also much read by King Media, known by Yoomy, and criticized by King Abrazza. Lombardo is clearly a partial self-portrait by Melville as of the time he was writing *Mardi,* which itself bears comparison with Lombardo's *Koztanza.*

"Lone Founts" (1891). Poem, in *Timoleon.* Melville advises us to eschew both youthful optimism and worldliness, be steadfast, guard against being surprised, "[s]tand" with "the Ancients," and drink "the never-varying lore" from their "lone founts" to gain permanent wisdom. Melville considered calling this nine-line poem "Counsels" and also "Giordano Bruno," after the excommunicated sixteenth-century Italian philosopher of disillusionment.
   Bibliography: Cohen, *Poems;* Howard; NN 11; Shurr; Stein.

Long, Robert. In *Moby-Dick,* he is a sailor lost with five others from the *Eliza* in 1839. Their shipmates placed a marble tablet in their memory in the Whaleman's Chapel in New Bedford.

Long Ghost, Dr. ("The Long Doctor"). In *Omoo,* he is a tall, lazy, colorless, fair-haired, gray-eyed ship's physician. He shares all of the narrator's adventures as the two rebel against Captain Guy of the *Julia,* go to the Calabooza at Papeetee, and wander to Martair, Tamai, Imeeo, Loohooloo, Partoowye, and Taloo. At one point, Long Ghost calls himself Peter and the narrator Paul. The original of the mysterious Dr. Long Ghost was John B. Troy, steward of the *Lucy Ann,* prototype of the *Julia.* As steward, he was in charge of and dispensed medical supplies and therefore might have been regarded as something of a doctor and might have been one. Henry Ventom, captain of the *Lucy Ann* and model for Guy, and his friend Dr. Francis Johnstone of Papeete, model for the despised Dr. Johnson, deposed against Troy for embezzlement as well as for refusing duty.

Bibliography: Anderson, Lebowitz, NN 2.

Long Island Sailor. In *Moby-Dick,* he is a *Pequod* sailor who dances during the midnight festivities in the forecastle.

Long Jim ("Lacedaemonian Jim"). In *Omoo,* he is an eloquent, belligerent sailor aboard the *Julia.* He signs the round-robin.

Long-locks. In *White-Jacket,* he is the afterguardsman who plays the part of Mrs. Lovelorn in the Fourth of July theatrical.

Long Lumbago, Lieutenant. In "Bridegroom-Dick," he is an officer remembered by Bridegroom Dick as a crabbed, severe person aboard Captain Turret's ship.

Longstreet, James (1821–1904). Confederate Army officer. He was born in Edgefield District, South Carolina, moved with his parents to Alabama (1831), graduated from West Point (1842), and served as a second lieutenant in Missouri, Louisiana, and Florida. He fought courageously during the Mexican War (1846–1848) under General Zachary Taylor* and General Winfield Scott.* He was wounded at Chapultepec (September 1847) and breveted major. Soon after the outbreak of the Civil War, he resigned from the Union Army (June 1861) to join the Confederate forces. As a brigadier general, he fought well at the First Battle of Bull Run (July 1861), was promoted to major general (October), and was courageous at Williamsburg (May 1862) but ineffective at Seven Pines (May). He redeemed himself during the Seven Days (June–July), provided slow aid to General Thomas J. Jackson* before and during the Second Battle of Bull Run (August), was skillful at Antietam (September), was promoted to lieutenant general (October), maneuvered well but sustained heavy casualties at Fredericksburg (December), and was assigned to guard Richmond (February 1863). After Jackson's death (May 1863), General Robert E. Lee* made Longstreet— and called him—his "Old War Horse." Longstreet fought tentatively and at great cost at Gettysburg (July), saw action at Chickamauga (September) and Knoxville (November), and fought well in the Wilderness, where, however, his own men accidentally wounded him (May 1864). Returning to action, he defended Richmond (November 1864–April 1865). Longstreet deeply disliked his fellow Confederate General Jubal A. Early.* A persistent legend has it that Longstreet cost Lee the victory at Gettysburg. After the Civil War, Longstreet held a variety of jobs—in insurance work, the cotton business, the lottery, and, as a Republican and therefore despised by most Southerners, at the federal level. Late in life he joined the Catholic church, was troubled by his war wound, and suffered the loss of vision in one eye. His autobiography, *From Manassas to Appomattox* (1896), is a combination of inaccurate reminiscence and rationalizing. Longstreet, perhaps the most controversial Confederate general, was a brave combat officer but a poor independent strategist.

Longstreet married Mary Louise Garland in Lynchburg, Virginia, in 1848. The couple had ten children, three of whom died of smallpox in a matter of days in 1862. Mary Longstreet died (1889), and Longstreet married Helen Dortch (1897). In 1905, she privately published *Lee and Longstreet at High Tide: Gettysburg in the Light of the Official Records,* a chaotic but touching defense of his generalship.

In "The Armies of the Wilderness," Melville describes Longstreet as slanting through the Wilderness.

Bibliography: Glenn Tucker, *Lee and Gettysburg* (Indianapolis: Bobbs-Merrill, 1968); Jeffrey D. Wert, *General James Longstreet* (New York: Simon & Schuster, 1994).

Loo. In *Omoo,* she is the voluptuous but chilly daughter of Deacon Ereemear Po-Po and Arfretee. Loo is fourteen years old. When Dr. Long Ghost becomes incipiently amorous, she quietly stabs him with a thorn.

"Look-out Mountain: The Night Fight (November, 1863)" (1866). Poem, in *Battle-Pieces.* At night, the mountain is luridly lighted and thunderous. An epic battle rages there between "Wrong and Right." When Dawn blessedly comes, "Anarch" flees. This dramatic monologue is loaded with irony. During the Battle of Lookout Mountain (23–25 November 1863), Union troops under generals Joseph Hooker, William Tecumseh Sherman,* and George Henry Thomas forced Confederate troops under General Braxton Bragg* from Lookout Mountain, some 1,100 feet above the Tennessee River, and from the knolls southeast of Chattanooga, Tennessee. The Union side suffered losses of about 5,820 in killed, wounded, and missing, to the Confederate losses of about 6,670. The result was the horizontal bisecting of the Confederacy.

Bibliography: Boatner, Faust, Garner, NN 11.

Loon, Billy. In *Omoo,* he is a shabbily dressed black man who is part of the rabble around King Tammahamaha III (*see* Kamehameha III) of Hawaii.

Looney. In "On the Sea Serpent," he is a dock fisherman who thinks he has caught the Nahant sea serpent.

Lord Bountiful. In "The Marquis de Grandvin," this is a laudatory nickname for the Marquis de Grandvin.

Lord Mayor of London, The. In "Poor Man's Pudding and Rich Man's Crumbs," he is a host of the Guildhall Banquet in London following the Battle of Waterloo.

Lorrain, Claude (1600–1682). (Alternate spelling: Lorraine; original name: Claude Gellée or Gelée de Lorrain.) French landscape painter. Born in Chamagne, in Lorraine, in poverty, he was poorly schooled and orphaned at the age of twelve. He went to Rome, where he studied landscape painting, and to Naples, where he learned perspective and painted scenes of mountains and valleys, harbors, and coastal sea-and-land views. His pictures often feature people and buildings dwarfed by natural scenery. Lorrain may have returned to Nancy, France (c. 1625), but, if so, soon thereafter lived permanently back in Rome (from c. 1627). Though never married, he fathered and cared for a daughter, who was a member of his large, unprepossessing household. His first influential patrons were Pope Urban VIII and King Philip IV of Spain (c. 1635). Though friendly with his fellow artist Nicolas Poussin,* Lorrain remained rather aloof, worked steadily, amassed a fortune, and—to prevent forgery—kept sketches of his authentic works in a set of volumes called *Liber Veritatis* (from c. 1634). Lorrain's corpus evolved from animated, quaint paintings and more formal, classical works to heroic, poetic monumentalism. His finest paintings include *The Mill* (1631), *Pastoral Landscape* (1647), *Landscape: The Marriage of Isaac and Rebekah* (1648), *Seaport: The Embarkation of the Queen of Sheba* (1648), and *The Rest in the Flight to Egypt* (1661). His style influenced the styles of several seventeenth-century Dutch painters and a few nineteenth-century English landscapists.

Melville owned prints of Claude Lorrain, one of his favorite painters. In "Marquis de Grandvin: At the Hostelry," he mentions Lorrain as a mild painter from Lorraine. Lost in "theory's wildering maze," Lorrain declines to discuss the picturesque with other artists.

Bibliography: Helen Langdon, *Claude Lorrain* (Oxford, England: Phaidon, 1989); Frank Jewett Mather, Jr., "Herman Melville," *New York Review* 1 (16 August 1919): 298–301.

Lot. In "Running the Batteries," he is a Union soldier aboard a ship with Ned and Hugh running past the Confederate batteries at Vicksburg.

Louis-Philippe (1773–1850). Last king of France. Born in Paris, he was the oldest son of Louis-Philippe, Duke of Chartres. When the French Revolution began (1789), the young man joined nobles supporting the revolutionary government, joined the Jacobin Club (1790) and was named lieutenant general in the war against Austria (1792); but he deserted to the Austrians (1793), escaped to Switzerland, and became Duke of Orleans when his father was executed (1793). He lived in the United States (1797–1800) and England (1800–1809), and supported Louis XVIII, Bourbon king of France who reigned from 1814 to 1824. Louis-Philippe joined the royal Bourbon family in Sicily and married Marie-Amélie, daughter of King Ferdinand IV of Naples (1809). The couple, who eventually had five surviving sons and three surviving daughters, returned to France (1814) but soon fled to England (1815), from which Louis-Philippe opposed Louis XVIII. When Charles X, who reigned from 1824 to 1830, was forced to abdicate, Louis-Philippe became ''King of the French'' (1830). Pro-British and anti-Dutch, he was threatened by a proletarian insurrection and abdicated (1848), went to England, and died there.

In *Omoo,* Melville mentions that Louis Philippe was the French monarch to whom Queen Pomaree (*see* Pomare IV) appealed in an effort to effect the recall of the hated Merenhout (*see* Moerenhout, Jacques-Antoine). To honor Louis-Philippe, Pomare IV of Tahiti named one of her sons Prince Joinville, after the king's third son, François, Prince of Joinville.

Bibliography: T.E.B. Howarth, *Citizen King: The Life of Louis-Philippe King of the French* (London: Eyre & Spottiswoode, 1961).

Louis XVI (1754–1793). King of France. He was born at Versailles, became heir to the throne upon the death of the dauphin Louis (1765), married Marie-Antoinette (1770), and ascended the throne upon the death of his grandfather Louis XV (1774). Louis XVI was amiable to the people; however, his weak character and his irresolution, as well as the reactionary behavior of the aristocracy and the clergy, prevented his establishing even a limited constitutional monarchy. This led to the revolution. Louis XVI declined to sanction reforms, ignored sound advice, tried to flee from Paris, was arrested (1791), was ill-advised by the queen, tried to circumvent the 1791 constitution he had sworn to implement, and vainly hoped for foreign powers to come to his aid. The people rose again (1792), and he was soon executed. In *Israel Potter,* he is the monarch who rewards John Paul Jones for his exploits.

Bibliography: John Hardman, *Louis XVI* (New Haven, Conn.: Yale University Press, 1993).

Love. In ''Hearth-Roses,'' she is the poet's faithful love.

Lovely, Lord. In *Redburn,* he is a doll-like, glossy, tiny aristocratic friend whom Harry Bolton avoids while in Liverpool.

''The Lover and the Syringa Bush'' (1924). Poem, in *Weeds and Wildings,* as part of the section entitled ''The Year.'' As the persona awaits his ''truant Eve'' by the syringa, its blooms, because of the ''heightening power . . . [of] love,'' seem like a lighted Christmas, a grotto, coral in the sea, and a starry sky.

Bibliography: Stein.

Lucree. In *Mardi,* he is a reader who asked Lombardo how much money he would make by his *Koztanza*—this according to Babbalanja. Lucree's name suggests a love of lucre.

Ludwig the Debonnaire, King. In *Mardi,* he is one of several Ludwigs of Franko mentioned by Babbalanja at King Abrazza's banquet. King Ludwig the Debonnaire is based on King Louis (Ludwig) I, the Debonair, le Debonnaire, Holy Roman emperor (778–840). He was also called the Pious, le Pieux. Melville implies that King Ludwig the Debonnaire and King Ludwig the Pious are two separate Franko kings.

Ludwig the Do-Nothing, King. In *Mardi,* he is one of several Ludwigs of Franko mentioned by Babbalanja at King Abrazza's banquet. King Ludwig the Do-Nothing is based on King Louis V, the Sluggard, le Fainéant, of France (967–987).

Ludwig the Fat, King. In *Mardi,* he is one of several Ludwigs of Franko mentioned by Babbalanja at King Abrazza's banquet. King Ludwig the Fat is based on King Louis VI, the Fat, le Gros, of France (1081–1137).

Ludwig the Great, King. In *Mardi,* he is one of several Ludwigs of Franko mentioned by Babbalanja at King Abrazza's banquet. King Ludwig is based on King Louis XIV, the Great, le Grand Monarque, of France (1638–1715).

Ludwig the Juvenile, King. In *Mardi,* he is one of several Ludwigs of Franko mentioned by Babbalanja at King Abrazza's banquet. King Ludwig the Juvenile is based on King Louis VII, the Young, le Jeune, of France (1121?–1180).

Ludwig the Pious, King. In *Mardi,* he is one of several Ludwigs of Franko mentioned by Babbalanja at King Abrazza's banquet. King Ludwig the Pious is based on Louis (Ludwig) I, the Pious, Holy Roman emperor (778–840). He was also called le Debonnaire. Melville implies that King Ludwig the Debonnaire and King Ludwig the Pious are two separate Franko kings.

Ludwig the Quarreler, King. In *Mardi,* he is one of several Ludwigs of Franko mentioned by Babbalanja at King Abrazza's banquet. King Ludwig the Quarreler is based on King Louis X, the Quarreler, le Hutin, of France (1289–1316).

Ludwig the Stammerer, King. In *Mardi,* he is one of several Ludwigs of Franko mentioned by Babbalanja at King Abrazza's banquet. King Ludwig the Stammerer is based on King Louis II, the Stammerer, le Bègue, of France (846–879).

Luff. In *Omoo,* this is the nickname bestowed by the crew of the *Julia* on Wymontoo-Hee.

Lugar-Lips. In "Under the Rose," he is the great Persian poet who was so inspired while attending a bridal festival at the palace of the Shaz Gold-beak at Shiraz that he wrote a poem about the rose-filled amber vase, now owned by the Azem. A Greek renegade translates the poem for My Lord the Ambassador from England. Lugar-Lips may be a misprint for Sugar-Lips.

Luke. In "The Scout toward Aldie," he was evidently a Union soldier concealed in the yard of a deserted house during the ill-fated pursuit of [John Singleton] Mosby.

Lullee. In *Omoo,* she is a native girl at Taloo. She is loved vainly and from a distance by William, a ship's carpenter who has run away. A law forbids whites and natives to marry. In real life, William eventually married Lullee, according to Edward T. Perkins, who later visited the islands and published *Na Motu; or Reef-Rovings in the South Seas: A Narrative of Adventures at the Hawaiian, Georgian, and Society Islands* (1854) about his observations there. He noted that Lullee's left eye was missing.
   Bibliography: Anderson.

Lumbago, Long, Lieutenant. In "Bridegroom-Dick." *See* Long Lumbago, Lieutenant.

"Lyon" (1866). (Full title: "Lyon: Battle of Springfield, Missouri [August, 1861].") Poem, in *Battle-Pieces.* (Characters: Her, [General Nathaniel] Lyon, Corporal Tryon.) The speaker, a survivor of General Nathaniel Lyon's troops, praises his leader, who, knowing that he was doomed to die, displayed steadfast courage in the face of superior numbers, including "Texans and Indians." He wrote out his will, advanced, had his horse Orion shot under him, led the charge, was wounded, continued to lead, and died. "Lyon" is an awkward poem weakened by Melville's using nine different rhymes with "Lyon." The bloody Springfield engagement is now usually known as the Battle at Wilson's Creek. (Lyon, whose will Melville says he made out to "Her," never married.)
   Bibliography: Boatner, Faust, Garner, NN 11.

Lyon, Nathaniel (1818–1861). Union Army officer. Born in Ashford, Connecticut, Lyon endured a Puritanical upbringing, graduated from West Point (1841), served in the Seminole War and the Mexican War, and was a captain during the 1850s, much of that time at Fort Riley, Kansas. His observations in Kansas made him detest the institution of slavery. When he was transferred to St. Louis (1861), he supported the pro-Union Missouri legislature and opposed the pro-secessionist actions of Governor Claiborne F. Jackson. Lyon disguised himself as a farm woman and spied on Jackson's maneuvering of the state militia, which he proceeded to capture with his own federal troops on the grounds that it was about to seize the federal arsenal. When Jackson declared for the Confederacy, Lyon, promoted to brigadier general (May 1861), sought to drive him out of the state. Confederate units under General Ben McCulloch were waiting for Lyon and his troops at Wilson's Creek, at Oak Hills, near Springfield. Without allowing the enemy time to attack, Lyon ordered and led a surprise assault, before dawn, against superior numbers, during which he was killed (10 August). The 10,000 Confederates suffered about 1,200 casualties; however, the 5,500 Union forces suffered about 1,300 casualties. Lyon was hotheaded and treated his men with contempt; nonetheless, they respected his ability and courage. Never married, he willed most of his $30,000 estate to the Union war effort. He was considered an early martyr in the cause of unionism. *The Last Political Writings of Gen. Nathaniel Lyon* soon appeared (1861). In his poem "Lyon," Melville, calling him "the Leader," identifies Lyon as a brave Union officer killed leading his men at the Battle of Springfield, Missouri, in August 1861.

Bibliography: Christopher Phillips, *Damned Yankee: The Life of General Nathaniel Lyon* (Columbia: University of Missouri Press, 1990).

Lyonese, The ("The Prodigal"). In *Clarel,* he is a happy, sensual French Jewish salesman of French luxuries. He has traveled from Jaffa to Bethlehem for the purpose of flirting. He spends a night at the Bethlehem inn with the unquiet Clarel. He presents a somewhat effeminate appearance, and ignores and even hides his Jewish heritage.

M

M—. In ''Fragments from a Writing Desk,'' he is the recipient of a letter from L.A.V., of Lansingsburgh. It describes three lovely girls.

McClellan, George B. (1826–1885). (Full name: George Brinton McClellan; nicknames: ''Little Mac,'' ''Little Napoleon.'') U.S. Army officer. He was born in Philadelphia, attended the University of Pennsylvania (1840–1842), attended West Point, and graduated second in his class (1846). He served well under General Winfield Scott* during the Mexican War (1846–1848), taught military engineering at West Point (1848–1851), was an army engineer in Arkansas and Texas, went to Santo Domingo to ascertain its naval value (1854), and observed European armies in action (1855–1857, partly in the Crimea). Resigning his captaincy (1857), he became a railroad executive (1857–1860), finally residing in Cincinnati. When the Civil War began, he was appointed major general of Ohio volunteers, performed commendably before the First Battle of Bull Run (July 1861), was placed in command of the Army of the Potomac at once, and replaced General Winfield Scott as general-in-chief (November). Then began McClellan's controversial Civil War career. He upgraded the army well but, being anti-Republican, feuded with the administration, delayed, was ordered by President Abraham Lincoln* into speedier action (January 1862), moved 118,000 men to Fort Monroe (March), was harassed by smaller Confederate units, won at Williamsburg (May) and Malvern Hill (July), but then retreated (July). Lincoln turned McClellan's army over to General John Pope*; however, when Pope was defeated at the Second Battle of Bull Run (August), Lincoln returned it to McClellan (August). He fought to a draw at Antietam (September), failed to pursue General Robert E. Lee,* but did hold him out of Maryland. McClellan dallied until Lincoln placed him on leave, whereupon he ran against

Lincoln for president as a peace candidate but lost (November 1864). McClellan traveled abroad (1865–1868), engaged in business ventures, was governor of New Jersey (1878–1881), and published a self-justifying autobiography entitled *McClellan's Own Story* (1887). McClellan was commendable at organizing, equipping, training, and caring for his admiring troops; however, he was also chronically cautious, inaccurate in judging his superiors and the strength of the enemy, and too eager for excess reserves and supplies. He married Ellen Mary Marcy in 1860 (the couple had a son and a daughter).

Melville mentions McClellan in several poems in *Battle-Pieces.* In ''Malvern Hill (July, 1862),'' he is identified as the Union commander at Malvern Hill, the final engagement of the Seven Days' Battle. In ''The Victor of Antietam (1862),'' he is defined as the Union commander who after the Seven Days' Battle was discarded, only to be recalled to improve the army after Pope, to rout Lee, to force [Thomas J.] Stonewall Jackson's retreat, and to win at Antietam. In ''Rebel Color-Bearers at Shiloh,'' McClellan is mentioned. In ''Major Gentian and Colonel J. Bunkum,'' he is mentioned as delaying.

Bibliography: Boatner; Faust; Garner; Howard M. Hensel, *The Anatomy of Failure: The Case of Major General George B. McClellan and the Peninsular Campaign* (Montgomery, Ala.: Air Command and Staff College, 1985).

McCloud, Colonel. In *Israel Potter,* he is the British commander at Montreal who mistreats his prisoner Ethan Allen there. Melville erred in giving this person the name Colonel McCloud. In *A Narrative of Colonel Allen's Captivity,* one of Melville's sources for *Israel Potter,* Allen mentions ''M'Cloud of the British'' on two occasions and describes him as generous and helpful. The real-life bad-tempered British officer was Colonel Richard Prescott.

Bibliography: Cohen, *Potter;* NN 8.

Macey, Harry. In *Moby-Dick,* he is the chief mate of the *Jeroboam,* the commander of which is Captain Mayhew. Macey defies the prediction of the mad prophet Gabriel and pursues Moby Dick, which finally kills him.

Macey, Mrs. Harry. In *Moby-Dick,* she is the woman whose letter via the *Pequod* reaches the *Jeroboam* too late. Her husband was chief mate of the *Jeroboam* until Moby Dick killed him.

McGee. In *Omoo,* he is an ugly sailor aboard the *Julia.* He was born in Ireland but, according to rumor, was transported to Australia. He signs the round-robin. Father [James] Murphy at Papeetee refuses to have anything to do with him.

Mack (''Commodore''). In *Omoo,* he is a Scotsman who leads a gang of beachcombers at Papeetee.

McPherson, James Birdseye (1828–1864). Soldier. Born near Clyde, Ohio, McPherson was reared in poverty, graduated from West Point (1853), taught engineering there for a while, and became a captain of engineers (1861). McPherson was an aide, as lieutenant colonel, to the chief engineer for Major General Ulysses S. Grant,* was promoted to colonel during the Fort Donelson campaign (February 1862), became a brigadier general (August 1862), a major general (October 1862), and a corps commander under Grant (1863). McPherson's intrepidity, skill, and decency were legendary. Assigned under General William Tecumseh Sherman* (1864), McPherson made a flanking movement against Confederate soldiers, who spotted him on horseback and killed him. McPherson, the highest-ranking Union casualty, was a brilliant officer, a soldiers' soldier, and a splendid gentleman. In his poem ''A Dirge for McPherson, Killed in front of Atlanta,'' Melville calls McPherson ''Sarpedon,'' laments his being killed in July 1864, solemnly extols him, and implies a sense of personal loss.

Bibliography: Boatner, Faust, Garner.

Macready, William Charles (1793–1873). English actor. He was born in London and educated at Rugby. His debut was in Birmingham (1810), after which he acted in London (1816), the United States (1826), and Paris (1828). He managed Covent Garden (1837–1839) and Drury Lane theaters (1841–1843). He performed again in the United States (1843–1844, 1849), where he met many important Americans, including George William Curtis* and Ralph Waldo Emerson.* Macready's last visit was disastrously marred by a riot (10 May 1849) outside the Astor Opera House in New York City. The incident was caused by professional rivalry involving the popular American actor Edwin Forrest. Ordinary American playgoers preferred Forrest's style, whereas more aristocratic audiences preferred Macready's sophistication. When from 10,000 to 15,000 people surrounded the theater in which Macready was performing and began shouting ''Down with the English hog,'' military forces were summoned to control the mob, charged it, were repulsed and injured by flying bricks, and in turn shot and killed twenty-two people. Macready escaped the theater in disguise, went to Curtis's home in Boston, and returned to England. More than sixty rioters were arrested; ten were tried, and a few were convicted. Macready's final stage appearance was as Macbeth (Drury Lane, 1851). He married Catherine Francis Atkins in 1823 (the couple had many children, but only two survived their parents). His wife died in 1852, and Macready in 1860 married Cecile Louise Frederica Spencer, thirty-four years his junior (the couple had one child). The old actor's memoirs are contained in *Macready's Reminiscences, and Selections from His Diaries and Letters* (1875).

A few days before the Astor Place riot, Melville, Evert Duyckinck,* Washington Irving,* and several other prominent New Yorkers signed a petition urging Macready to continue his acting engagement despite Forrest's rival performance. When Melville was in London later in 1849, he attended a performance of Shakespeare's *Othello,* and in his journal jotted the following: "Mcready painted hideously. Did'nt [*sic*] like him very much upon the whole— bad voice, it seemed" (19 November). In "The Two Temples," the narrator attends a play in London and calls Macready's performance in it as Cardinal Richelieu almost priest-like. (The play would have had to be Edward Bulwer-Lytton's *Richelieu; or, The Conspiracy.*)

Bibliography: Alan S. Downer, *The Eminent Tragedian William Charles Macready* (Cambridge, Mass.: Harvard University Press, 1966); Leyda; NN 15.

Macy, Seth. In *Moby-Dick,* he was a sailor lost with five others from the *Eliza* in 1839. Their shipmates placed a marble tablet in their memory in the Whaleman's Chapel in New Bedford.

"Madam Mirror" (1947). Poem, in *Collected Poems of Herman Melville.* The mirror explains that, relegated to a garret now, she reflects on memories deeper than faces. Everyone has confided in her—maidens, betrayers, beauties. Like a priest, she keeps the secrets of those who confess here—those in pain after pleasure and smiles, those who weep, and those who sense "old age drawing near." In the garret, she is now content to avoid both reality and appearance. This poem should be paired with Melville's "The Wise Virgins to Madam Mirror." Both owe their inspiration in part to "Monsieur Miroir," by Nathaniel Hawthorne,* which also puns on the word "reflection."

Bibliography: Shurr, Stein.

"Madcaps" (1924). Poem, in *Weeds and Wildings,* as part of the section entitled "The Year." (Characters: Cherry, Lily.) The poem watches two children, Cherry and Lily, frolicking in a flowery orchard with madcap butterflies for companions.

Bibliography: Stein.

Mad Jack, Lieutenant. In *White-Jacket,* he is a tyrannical, lovable, alcoholic, bellicose quarterdeck officer. He is contrasted with Lieutenant Selvagee. Mad Jack's bravery, in the face of Captain Claret's ineptness, saves the *Neversink* during a storm off Cape Horn. By off-handed geniality, Mad Jack later stops an incipient mutiny of the crew over Claret's stupid order that all beards be trimmed. Mad Jack, who was Melville's idea of a perfect sea officer, was based partly on Lieutenant Latham B. Avery, who served on the *United States* while Melville was aboard (1843–1844).

Bibliography: Anderson; NN 5; Howard Vincent, *The Tailoring of Melville's White-Jacket* (Evanston, Ill.: Northwestern University Press, 1970).

Madonna of the Trefoil. In "Clover Dedication to Winnefred," in *Weeds and Wildings. See* Winnefred.

"Magian Wine" (1891). Poem, in *Timoleon.* (Characters: Miriam, Solomon.) Rays lighting this wine gleam like a "liquid mirage" to Miriam and turn Solomon's "Syrian charms" opaline. Through its waves come anthems, sighs, and ambiguous prophecies. This confusing poem may be Melville's uncertain response to Christian ritual.
   Bibliography: NN 11, Stein.

"Magnanimity Baffled" (1866). Poem, in *Battle-Pieces.* (Character: The Victor.) The Victor speaks generously to his defeated foe (lying on a cot with his back turned), offers to shake his hand, but generates no response. On grabbing the "stubborn hand" anyway, he finds the foe dead.

Mahinee. In *Omoo,* he is an old Tahitian chief with whom John Jermin leaves the sea chests of the rebellious sailors from the *Julia.* In real life, a man named Mahine, the son of a hereditary king known as Tetuaveroa, was a chief of the islands of Raiatea and Huahine in the Tahitian group. Historical records of Mahine go back to the 1820s. (This Mahine is said to have died in 1838, before Melville's sojourn in Tahiti.)
   Bibliography: Newbury; George Pritchard, *The Aggression of the French at Tahiti and Other Islands in the Pacific,* ed. Paul De Deckker (Auckland, New Zealand: Auckland University Press, 1983).

Mahmoud. In *Clarel. See* Mahmud II.

Mahmud II (1785–1839). (Also spelled Mahmut.) Sultan of the Ottoman Empire. During his rule (1808–1839), he initiated reforms despite early failures to modernize the army, which was dominated by an elite corps of Turkish troops (called Janissaries). Mahmud ordered their massacre (1826), after which he made improvements in administration, education, health, the military, the postal service, and the tax system. When he lost the Battle of Navarino (10 October 1827) and the Russo-Turkish War (1828–1829), he was obliged to recognize the independence of Greece (1830). He broke his promise to reward Muhammed Ali of Egypt, his anti-Greek ally, by giving him Syria. For this reason, Egypt attacked him (1831–1833), during which time Constantinople was saved only with Russian help (and without help from England or pro-Egyptian France). Vengeful Mahmud attacked Egyptian forces in Syria but lost again (1839), after which he died. Wars hurt Mahmud and cost him territory, but he did begin invaluable Western-style administrative, social, and other reforms. In *Clarel,* Mahmoud is mentioned as ordering the massacre of the Spahis (the Turkish cavalry), one of whom, Belex, escaped.
   Bibliography: M. Philips Price, *A History of Turkey from Empire to Republic* (London: George Allen & Unwin, 1956).

Mahone. In "The New Ancient of Days," he is a common man, opposed by the new ancient.

Mai-Mai. In *Omoo,* he is a fat old native at Taloo. He is a drinking companion of the captain of the *Leviathan.*

Major. In "Bridegroom-Dick," he is the commanding officer of the marines who is ordered by Captain Turret to supervise the flogging of the Finn, according to Bridegroom Dick's reminiscence.

Major, The. In "Fragments from a Writing Desk," he is L.A.V.'s friend, who has courteously attended to a request.

Major, The ("The Senior"). In "A Scout toward Aldie," he is a grizzled, experienced officer under the young Colonel. The Major survives [John Singleton] Mosby's ambush of the Colonel and his men.

"Major Gentian and Colonel J. Bunkum" (1924). Sketch, in *The Works of Herman Melville.* (Characters: Colonel Josiah Bunkum, Major [John] Gentian, John Hancock, [General George B.] McClellan.) In this curious work, purportedly a newspaper clipping, are discussed the pride of Major Gentian in his Society of the Cincinnati ribbon, the bravery of its wearers, and Colonel Josiah Bunkum's valorous but senseless scheme to distribute spelling books throughout the South—because the Bible says "My people perish through ignorance."

"The Maldive Shark" (1888). Poem, in *John Marr.* Pilot-fish, "sleek little" creatures, attend the "phlegmatical" shark. They glide beside "his ghastly flank" or in front of "his Gorgonian head," guide him to his prey, and retreat "when peril's abroad" to the "asylum" of his tooth-filled "charnel of maw" in perfect safety. The Maldive Islands, an archipelago of coral atolls, are located west of Sri Lanka in the Indian Ocean. This poem is a masterly depiction of symbiosis.
    Bibliography: Cohen, *Poems;* NN 11; Shurr.

Maltese Sailor. In *Moby-Dick,* he is a *Pequod* sailor who speaks erotically while his mates dance during the midnight festivities in the forecastle.

"Malvern Hill (July, 1862)" (1866). Poem, in *Battle-Pieces.* (Character: [General George B.] McClellan.) Do the elms on Malvern Hill remember McClellan's brave men as they fought, many dying, near Richmond, and then retreated after paying a terrible price? Yes, the elms reply; we remember, but regardless of human activity, sap must flow into twigs and leaves *"must be green in Spring."* The Battle of Malvern Hill (1 July 1862) helped improve the position and reputation of General George B. McClellan* after the failure of his Peninsula Campaign against Richmond (from 11 March 1862), which included the Seven Days' Battles (26 June–2 July), mentioned in the poem.

Bibliography: Cohen, *Poems;* Garner; NN 11; Warren.

Mammon. In *Clarel,* this is a name by which Rolfe refers to the Banker.

Man. In "Bridegroom-Dick," this is the name by which Captain Turret addresses the Finn.

Man, The. In "The Armies of the Wilderness." *See* Grant, Ulysses S.

Mandeville. In *White-Jacket,* he is a rakish-looking officer who after being broken in rank for excessive drinking is transferred aboard the *Neversink.* Within a week he is found drunk and is ordered flogged by Lieutenant Bridewell, who was his former roommate aboard the *Macedonian.*

Manko. In *Mardi,* this is an alias of the prophet Alma. In using the name Manko, Melville may have had in mind Manco Capac, supposedly a child of the sun and the founder of the Peruvian Inca dynasty.

Bibliography: Wright.

Man of the Cave of Engihoul, The. In "The New Ancient of Days," he is a cave man whose skeleton when discovered upset traditions. The anatomist and paleontologist Philippe Charles Schmerling found human skull and skeletal remains, along with cavebear, elephant, hyena, and rhinoceros bones from the Quaternary Period, in the ossiferous Engis and Engihoul caves along the Meuse River, near Liège, Belgium (1832, 1835). The Engis skull presented evidence of intellectual development both high (very large brain cavity) and low (narrow, low forehead), which caused confusion among opposing schools of anthropology.

Bibliography: P. C. Schmerling, *Recherches sur les ossemens fossiles, découverts dans les cavernes de la province Liège* (2 vols. in 1, 1833); Richard Dean Smith, *Melville's Science: "Devilish Tantalization of the Gods!"* (New York: Garland, 1993).

Man of Mosses, The. In "Hawthorne and His Mosses." *See* Hawthorne, Nathaniel.

"The Man-of-War Hawk" (1888). Poem, in *John Marr.* The black man-of-war hawk placidly flies above the black ship, with its sky-sail white in the sun; "we low-flyers" cannot attain such a height, nor can arrows or thoughts.

Bibliography: Stein.

Manta. In *Mardi,* he is a bedridden person in Ohonoo who envies gadabout beggars and who, in turn, is envied by Uhia for being able to die unmolested.

Manxman, The ("The Old Manx Sailor"). In *Moby-Dick,* he is an old nautical seer who, the first time he observes Captain Ahab, surmises that the stricken man must be scarred from crown to toe. The old sailor is wearily critical of the wild *Pequod* crew during the midnight festivities in the forecastle.

Mapenda. In "Benito Cereno," he is an Ashantee slave who polishes hatchets during Captain Amasa Delano's visit aboard the *San Dominick.* Mapenda is killed during the attack led by Delano's chief mate.

Mapple, Father. In *Moby-Dick,* he is the rugged, venerable preacher at the Whaleman's Chapel in New Bedford. Since he was once a sailor, his salty sermon on the subject of Jonah moves Ishmael and the other sailors who hear it.
  Bibliography: W. H. Auden, *The Enchafèd Flood, or The Romantic Iconography of the Sea* (New York: Random House, 1964).

Marbonna. In *Omoo,* he is a big, muscular, proud Nukuhevan who is the guardian of Queen Pomaree's children at Taloo (*see* Pomare IV). He escorts the narrator and Dr. Long Ghost into the queen's court.

"The March into Virginia" (1866). (Full title: "The March into Virginia: Ending in the First Manassas [July, 1861]"). Poem, in *Battle-Pieces.* These soldiers would not be cheerful and trusting, ardent and joyful, if they were not "ignorant" before battle. "No berrying party . . . [e]ver went less loth than they" through those "leafy" woods. They chatted, laughed, and hoped for glory. Some of them will be "enlightened in the vollied glare" and die, while others will stonily survive. Melville tried several last lines: "Manassas's second throe and deadlier share"; "Thy second shock, Manassas, share"; "The throe of second Manassas share." The standard text now reads "Thy after shock, Manassas, share." At Bull Run, near Manassas Junction, Virginia (21 July 1861), Union soldiers under General Irvin McDowell were defeated by outnumbered Confederates commanded by General P.G.T. Beauregard and General Joseph E. Johnston.
  Bibliography: Adler; Cohen, *Poems;* Garner; NN 11; Shurr; Warren.

Marchioness of Brinvilliers, The. In "The Marchioness of Brinvilliers." *See* Brinvilliers, The Marchioness of.

"The Marchioness of Brinvilliers" (1891). Poem, in *Timoleon.* (Character: The Marchioness of Brinvilliers.) The poet notes that the titular figure is depicted in a painting as "sprightly," "meek," candid, mysterious, sweet, and with "fathomless mild eyes." In reality, Marie Marguerite d'Aubray, Marquise de Brinvilliers (c. 1630–1676), poisoned her father and two brothers, and was tried and executed in Paris for doing so. Melville thus implicitly contrasts her mild appearance and her diabolical nature, and thus issues a general warning that

appearances can be deceptive. Melville owned a copy of *The Letters of Madame de Sévigné,* in which the authoress describes witnessing the marquise's execution by beheading, the burning of her remains, and the scattering of her ashes. It has been said and denied that Melville may have been thinking of a picture of the marchioness by Charles le Brun (1619–1690), painter in the court of Louis XIV.
  Bibliography: NN 11, Shurr, Stein.

"The March to the Sea" (1866). (Full title: "The March to the Sea [December, 1864].") Poem, first published anonymously in *Harper's New Monthly Magazine** (February 1866) and reprinted in *Battle-Pieces.* (Characters: [General Ulysses S.] Grant, [General Judson] Kilpatrick, [General Robert E.] Lee, [General William Tecumseh] Sherman.) Nothing could stop the "glorious glad marching." Columns moved like flowing rivers. Their advance was like a bull through gnats. Outriders were perplexing. Flankers brought in livestock. Banners attracted runaway slaves. Foragers helped themselves freely. Soldiers trampled crops, burned buildings, and left famine and "wailing" in their wake. Whether it was "havoc" or "retribution," Sherman will long be remembered. General William Tecumseh Sherman* commanded a march of Union forces (November–December 1864) to wreak devastation, invest Savannah, demoralize the Confederacy, and thus help end the Civil War. Melville's main source for this poem was *The Story of the Great March* by Major George Ward Nichols (1865).
  Bibliography: Cohen, *Poems;* Frank L. Day, "Melville and Sherman March to the Sea," *American Notes & Queries* 2 (May 1964): 134–36; Garner; NN 11; Warren.

Marcus Aurelius (121–180). (Original name: Marcus Annius Verus; later name: Marcus Aelius Aurelius Antoninus). Born in Rome, he was the nephew of Antoninus Pius,* who adopted him (138) and whose daughter Faustina II (Annia Galeria) he married (145). The couple had at least fourteen children before her death (175). Marcus Aurelius was privately tutored (mainly in rhetoric and poetry), was made consul (140), held various public offices (to 161), and became emperor (161–180). He was much occupied in defending his empire from military and political attacks. He and his troops won many victories. He was an eminent, learned Stoic philosopher, knew of and condoned the persecution of Christians, and wrote his *Meditations* in Greek. In his poem "The Age of the Antonines," Melville calls him Antonine and praises him.
  Bibliography: Anthony Birley, *Marcus Aurelius: A Biography,* rev. ed. (New Haven, Conn.: Yale University Press, 1987).

Marcy, William L. (1786–1857). (Full name: William Learned Marcy.) Statesman. Marcy was born in Southbridge, Massachusetts, graduated from Brown (1808), and practiced law in Troy, New York (1811–1812, 1815, 1816–1823). He was a captain during the War of 1812 (1812, 1814). Entering politics, Marcy was a New York state comptroller (1823–1829), New York supreme court justice (1829–1831), U.S. senator (1831–1832), and New York governor (1833–

1839). He was U.S. secretary of war (1845–1849) in the cabinet of President James Polk and then became secretary of state (1853–1857) under President Franklin Pierce. While Marcy was secretary of state, he secured the negotiation of the Gadsden Treaty (1853), which adjusted the border of Mexico and the United States and added area to the United States. He was involved in the formulation of the Ostend Manifesto (1854); but when the ill-fated effort to take Cuba by dollar diplomacy or gunboat aggression backfired, he disavowed the document. Marcy was married twice. He married Dolly Newell in 1812. (The couple had two sons, and his wife died in 1821.) He married Cornelia Knower in 1824. (The couple had two daughters, one of whom died in early childhood, and one son.)

Bibliography: Ivor Debenham Spencer, *The Victor and the Spoils: A Life of William L. Marcy* (Providence, R.I.: Brown University Press, 1959).

Mardi (1849). (Full title: *Mardi: And a Voyage Thither.*) Novel. (Characters: A, King Abrazza, Adondo, Ady, Alanno, Aldina, Aleema, Alla-Malolla, Alma, Almanni, Amoree, Annatoo, Queen Aquella, Aquovi, Arhinoo, Atahalpa, Prince Atama, Azzageddi, Queen Azzolino, Babbalanja, Ned Ballad, Bardianna, Batho, King Bello, Berzelli, Bidi Bidie, Bidiri, Blandoo, Boddo, Boldo, Bomblum, Bondo, Bonja, King Borabolla, Borhavo, Botargo, Queen Calends, Darfi, De-didum, Demorkriti, Chief Dermoddi, the Despairer, Diddledee, Dididi, Diloro, Divino, Doldrum, King Donjalolo, Donno, Doxodox, Prince Dragoni, Dumdi, Fanfum, Fanna, Fee, Fiddlefie, Fidi, Finfi, Flavona, Fofi, Foni, Foofoo, Fulvi, Gaddi, Ghibelli, King Grandissimo, Grando, Hanto, Queen Hautia, King Hello, Henro, Hevaneva, [. . .] Hivohitee MDCCCXLVIII, Hohori, Hummee Hum, I, Queen Ides, Jarl, Jarmi, Jiji, Jiromo, King of Kandidee, King Kannakoko, Kar-hownoo, Karkeke, Karkie, King Karolus [I], King Karolus [II], Karrolono, King Klanko, Konno, Krako, Kravi, King Kroko, Kubla, Lakreemo, Lanbranka Hoh-inna, Larfee, Livella, Logodora, Lol Lol, Lombardo, Lucree, King Ludwig the Debonnaire, King Ludwig the Do-Nothing, King Ludwig the Fat, King Ludwig the Great, King Ludwig the Juvenile, King Ludwig the Pious, King Ludwig the Quarreler, King Ludwig the Stammerer, Manta, Prince Mardonna, King Marjora, Mark, Marko, Marmonora, Bill Marvel, King Media, King Media, Midni, Minta the Cynic, Mohi, Mondi, Nimni, Nina, Queen Nones, Nonno, Noojoomo, King Normo, Nulli, O, Ohiro Moldona Fivona, Oh-Oh, Ononna, Oram, Otho, Prince Ottimo, Ozonna, Paivai, Pani, Parki, Peenee, King Peepi, Pendiddi, Pesti, Philo, Phipora, King Piko, Pollo, Pondo, Lord Primo, Quiddi, Rabeelee, Prince Rani, Ravoo, Raymonda, Rea, Ridendiabola, Roddi, Roe, Roi Mori, King Rondo the Round, Roo, Roonoonoo, Rotato, Samoa, Saturnina, Sober Sides, Solo, Taji, Talara, King Tammaro, King Taquinoo, King Teei, Titonti, Tongatona, Tooboi, Tooroorooloo, Topo, Torf-Egill, Prince Tribonnora, King Uhia, Vangi, Varnopi, Vavona, Vee-Vee, Queen Velluvi, Verbi, Vivo, Voluto, Vondendo, Voyo, Willi, Wynodo, Xiki, Yamjamma, Yamoyamee, Yillah, King Yoky, Yoomy, Zenzi, Zenzori, Ziani, Queen Zmiglandi, Znobbi, Zonoree, Zooperbi, Zozo, Zuma.)

After three years of unsuccessful whaling aboard the *Arcturion,* the narrator, an American sailor, deserts by taking the ship's bow-boat west of the Gallipagos, with a dull Skyeman named Jarl as his companion. They head for the Kingsmill Islands far to the west. After sixteen days, they sight and board a brigantine. Tattooed Samoa and his ugly wife Annatoo descend from the sails and explain in broken English that their ship, the *Parki,* from Lahina off the coast of Mowee sought pearls and shells but was attacked by Cholos, who murdered the whole crew. Samoa and Annatoo escaped by hiding. The narrator takes command of their ship and heads west, but she is sunk by a Pacific storm. Annatoo is washed overboard and perishes. The narrator, Jarl, and Samoa launch a lifeboat. Nine days later, they are attacked by natives in a double canoe. The narrator kills Aleema, the enemy priest on the canoe; rescues the beautiful, fair Yillah from it; and persuades her to come with him, and with Jarl and Samoa as well. Yillah explains that she was reared by Aleema on the Island of Delights and would have been sacrificed by him in a vortex near Tedaidee but for the narrator's intervention. The narrator tells her untruthfully that he knew her as a child. They fall in love, drift to the Mardi Islands, approach one of them, and are carried ashore by natives who say he resembles Taji, a god of theirs long absent. The narrator asserts that he is a god.

King Media invites "Taji" and his party to the isle of Odo. His guests begin a lush life but are disturbed by Media's pitiless rule. Taji and Yillah live in bliss until she disappears. He searches for her among the islands, accompanied by Media, his historian Mohi, the mystic Babbalanja, a minstrel named Yoomy, Vee-Vee the dwarf, and others. They visit Valapee, pass a rock called Pella, are warned by enigmatic flower messages from Queen Hautia, and sail on to Juam, ruled by the sensualist Donjalolo. Afloat again, the party is regaled by Mohi's accounts of invisible spirits called the Plujii and of the soporific island of Nora-Bamma. Hautia's flower-bearers reappear, again with a cautionary message about love, death, and joy. Taji and his friends land at Ohonoo, settled by exiles and ruled by the ambitious King Uhia. On to Mondoldo, whose king is jolly Borabolla. While there, Samoa performs unsuccessful brain surgery on a sea diver. Three of murdered Aleema's sons turn up, raving for revenge against Taji, who perjures himself by swearing that their story is untrue. Hautia's messengers send him another gloomy message.

Leaving Jarl and Samoa behind, Taji, with Babbalanja, Media, Vee-Vee, and Yoomy, continues his quest; they land on Maramma, and climb Ofo, its peak, with a group of pilgrims. Babbalanja lectures on troubles and uncertainties. The group goes to an island in search of a shy pontiff named Hivohitee, whom Yoomy finds in a pagoda. Hautia's messengers tell Taji that Jarl is dead. Media cheers Taji with pipes and tobacco, after which the group heads for Padulla, with its museum of relics presided over by an antiquarian named Oh-Oh who delights Babbalanja by showing him a nonreligious tract promoting goodness. Babbalanja lectures on the accident of fame and the permanence of merit; Yoomy sings love songs; and the party sails off to Pimminee, whose snobbish residents pride themselves on showy clothes. While the group is sailing away, three arrows hiss by and inspire Taji to confess that he killed Aleema, some of whose fourteen sons are pursuing him. Babbalanja discourses on fatalism, man's irresponsibility, and the joys of righteous living. They observe corulers Hello and Piko on the island of Diranda, where war games systematically reduce its exploding population.

As Taji and his friends sail on, Media explains that the island of Dominora is ruled by ambitious King Bello of the Hump, who covets Porpheero, a neighboring island, as well as other islands. Bello used to shanghai canoers from Vivenza into his own navy but was defeated in a war with Vivenza. Yillah is nowhere to be found in Dominora, which, though beautiful, is filled with poor people. The party sails to Kaleedoni, called Bello's stepchild island and full of brave, devout, and friendly people. They visit Verdanna and Franko. Babbalanja lectures further, and Yoomy sings again, as the party approaches Kolumbo, containing Kanneeda in the north and Vivenza in the south. Media dislikes hearing that Vivenza boasts of freedom and equality. In Vivenza, Taji and the others visit the Temple of Freedom, observe drinkers, attend political rallies, observe Saturnia, go south and see serfs and overlords, and hear fiery-eyed Nulli there. Yillah is not in Vivenza. The party goes south to Kolumbo, where Media and Babbalanja debate on the advisability of tyranny there. The group rounds a cape and heads north to gold fields, which Babbalanja says could never lure Yillah. They sail to Orienda, where song and science dawned. As they proceed to Hamora they encounter a storm, and Taji confesses that he has no sailing chart but prefers shipwreck to quitting. When they visit an island inhabited by reputedly wise Doxodox, Babbalanja finds his match in the verbose fellow.

On and on for weeks they sail. Taji defeats a would-be assassin. Hautia sends another flower message. They land on the island of Hooloomooloo, filled with cripples. Babbalanja harangues on unknowables in the cosmos and the unimportance of everything, including Mardi citizens. Once past a death cloud, they visit the island of Bonovona, presided over by King Abrazza, a bachelor demigod full of pity but uncharitable. Babbalanja lectures him on *Koztanza,* the immortal writing of Lombardo, the independent, long-suffering Mardian genius. Abrazza hosts a lavish supper, with much wine. Taji and his followers sail on, to the isle of Serenia, where an old man tells them about the religion taught to the people there by Alma—a religion based on love, charity, and little government. Babbalanja, Media, Mohi, and Yoomy are impressed. Babbalanja plans to remain in Serenia, but Taji and the others press on in their quest. Hautia's messengers tell Taji that through their queen he may find Yillah. The group hastens to Hautia's nymph-filled isle, called Flozella-a-Nina. Taji sees Hautia, resists her poisonous advances for a while, but succumbs to her flowers and wine. He feels that by surrendering he may learn about Yillah. Mohi tells him about a young man named Ozonna who sought Ady, his lost love, was told that she was hiding among Hautia's maidens, who all looked alike, but never found her. Hautia urges Taji to stay and sin with her. When he notices that she is holding Yillah's rose pearl, he rushes to a cavern, sees a vision in its waters, and dives in—but to no avail. Mohi and Yoomy beseech Taji to make his home in Serenia, but he launches his boat yet again—toward the deeps. Three armed specters are in pursuit. Arcturus the red star looks down.

Melville began to write *Mardi* in New York City shortly after his marriage (August 1847). The novel began as a nautical sequel to *Omoo,* evolved into something more complex, and was finished nine months later. His wife and a sister or two laboriously completed a copy of it a month after that. Melville offered it to John Murray,* the publisher who had issued *Typee* and *Omoo* in London. When he refused, Melville sold *Mardi* to the London publisher Richard Bentley,* who paid him 200 guineas outright (March 1849). Melville's friend John Romeyn Brodhead,* secretary of the American legation in London, made arrangements with Bentley. When *Mardi* was published in New York (April) by Harper & Brothers,* who had published the American edition of *Omoo,* Melville received $500 in advance and a promise of half the profits, and retained the copyright. British reviewers were often partially laudatory—especially with respect to the depiction of adventure in the early parts—but were sometimes viciously critical. American reviewers offered more general praise, were sometimes critical because they were bewildered, but avoided the animosity demonstrated in England; Evert Duyckinck* and his brother George Duyckinck* both praised it in their *Literary World.* Melville's wife wrote to her stepmother Hope Savage Shaw* thus: "I suppose by this time you are deep in the 'fogs' of 'Mardi'—if the mist ever does clear away, I should like to know what it reveals to *you*" (30 April 1849).

In his preface to *Mardi,* Melville says that since the public read his autobiographical *Typee* and *Omoo* as fiction, he wonders if fictitious *Mardi* will be taken as fact. Instead, reviewers not simply indifferent to his latest work were critical of it, the public was puzzled, and sales were poor. Melville was paid about $750 for it in the United States and £210 in England. He made up for this failure by quickly writing *Redburn* (1849) and *White-Jacket* (1850), both of which were popular; but then he puzzled his readers anew with *Moby-Dick* (1851). Sales of *Mardi* were poor—under 3,000 in the United States and so few in England (about 1,000) that the publisher lost money and paid Melville nothing beyond the advance. The Harpers' fire (December 1853) destroyed most of the unsold copies. More were printed (1855, 1864) but did not sell well. The American edition brought Melville $741 (by 1887). Bentley, the British publisher, never recouped his costs. In a letter to Evert Duyckinck, Bentley imaged *Mardi* as a plant that "may possibly . . . flower like the aloe, a hundred years hence" (2 February 1850).

Mostly misunderstood or ignored well into the twentieth century, *Mardi* is now seen as a challenging combination of quest narrative, lush description and travelogue, poetic prose, digressive essays, literary allusions, disguised partial autobiography, satire, and allegory. Hautia derives from Duessa in Edmund Spenser's *Faerie Queene.* Melville also makes abundant use of substantive and stylistic elements from other favorite authors of his, including Sir Thomas Browne, Richard Burton, François Rabelais, William Shakespeare, and Jonathan Swift, and from many books about exploration and travel in the Pacific area. Dominora is to be identified with Great Britain, Franko with France, Hamora with Africa, Hapzaboro with Austria, Hooloomooloo with Hawaii (and Ohonoo with Oahu, and Donjalolo with the Hawaiian King Kamehameha II*), Ibeerea with Spain, Jutland with Denmark, Kaleedoni with Scotland, Kanneeda with Canada, Kolumbo with North America and South America, Latianna with Italy, Luzianna with Portugal, Muzkovi with Russia, Orienda with Asia, Porpheero with Europe, Romara with Rome, Tutoni with Germany, Vatikanna with the Vatican, Verdanna with Ireland, and Zandanavia with Scandanavia. The "British" king's hump symbolizes England's national debt. Vivenza stands for the United States, and in the chapters devoted to it Melville makes oblique comments on nationalism, slavery, mistreatment of Native Americans, the Mexican War, and many controversial figures. The Temple of Freedom is to be equated with the U.S. Senate, Nulli with John C. Calhoun, Saturnia with Daniel Webster, and so on. In Oh-Oh Melville lampoons P. T. Barnum.* Isles of Palms and of Myrrh refer to the South Sea islands Melville knew and loved as a youth. More generally, Yillah represents beauty, happiness, and truth, whereas Hautia partially represents evil, falsehood, lust, sadness, pride, and ugliness. The doctrines of Alma are to be equated with those of Christ. Serenia is a region of secularized Christianity, with high principles but no pomp. Taji does not aim to abandon the serene Christian way of life permanently; instead, he wants to find truth through Yillah—truth encompassing but not bound by formal religion. Melville implies that Taji will never fully succeed. The literary work called *Koztanza* is described by its author Lombardo as incoherent and episodic, which may be Melville's indirect way of describing *Mardi* itself. Dozens of references to flowers have enhanced meanings because of Melville's knowledge of flower symbolism.

In addition to sources in the realm of imaginative literature, Melville ransacked many books of travel. The most notable sources are Frederick Debell Bennett, *Narrative of a Whaling Voyage Round the Globe, from the Year 1833 to 1836. Comprising Sketches of Polynesia, California, and the Indian Archipelago, etc. with an Account of Southern Whales, the Sperm Whale Industry, and the Natural History of the Climates Visited* (2 vols., 1840); William Ellis, *Polynesian Researches, during a Residence of Nearly Six Years in the Pacific Sea Islands, Including Descriptions of the Natural History and Scenery of the Islands—with Remarks on the History, Mythology, Traditions, Government, Arts, Manners, and Customs of the Inhabitants* (2 vols., 1829; 4 vols., 1833); *Journals of Voyages and Travels by the Rev. Daniel Tyerman and George Bennet, Esq.* (2 vols., 1831); and Charles Wilkes, *Narrative of the United States Exploring Expedition. During the Years 1838, 1839, 1840, 1842* (5 vols. and atlas, 1845). Melville also read in philosophy and science. Between the time he published *Omoo* and the time he finished *Mardi,* his mind expanded exponentially and *Mardi* became a partly inchoate, mixed masterpiece but more importantly a rehearsal for *Moby-Dick.*

Bibliography: Michael C. Berthold, " 'born-free-and-equal': Benign Cliché and Narrative Imperialism in Melville's *Mardi,*" *Studies in the Novel* 25 (Spring 1993): 16–27; Davis; Wai-chee Dimock, *Empire for Liberty: Melville and the Poetics of Individualism* (Princeton, N.J.: Princeton University Press, 1989); Lebowitz; Leyda; NN 3; Sealts; Cindy Weinstein, "The Calm before the Storm: Laboring through *Mardi,*" *American Literature* 65 (June 1993): 239–53; Wright.

Mardonna, Prince. In *Mardi,* he is a Juam prince who refused to become king because he would have had to give up roving.

Margoth. In *Clarel,* he is a short, powerfully built, materialistic, and atheistic Jewish geologist. Nothing but scientific and commercial, he would like to see a telegraph installed on Olivet and a railroad station built at Gethsemane. He prefers a Sodom apple to a palm leaf.

Margrave, The. In "The Margrave's Birth Night," the Margrave (i.e., prince) is the owner of the castle. The peasants mechanically gather to celebrate his birth night. The absent host is to be equated with Christ; the season, with Christmas.

"The Margrave's Birth Night" (1891). Poem, in *Timoleon.* (Character: The Margrave.) Peasants laboriously come up from valleys and down from uplands, on sledges drawn by tired horses, to the Margrave's castle. They celebrate his "birth-night, in mid-winter, . . . year after year." Inside are tables, a festive board, holly berries, stewards, and minstrels. The debased guests evince little concern that there is "no host." This is all an "[o]ld observance." Would it not be wondrous if "toil and travail" were rewarded by water turned to wine and bread from black to white? The host is implicitly Christ; the season, Christmas.

Bibliography: Cohen, *Poems;* NN 11; Shurr; Stein.

Marhar-Rarrar ("The Wakeful," "Bright-Eyed"). In *Omoo,* she is a lovely maiden encountered by the smitten narrator and by Dr. Long Ghost on the beach at Imeeo.

Marharvai. In *Omoo,* he is the old chief who is the host of the narrator and Dr. Long Ghost at Loohooloo.

Marheyo. in *Typee,* he is Kory-Kory's father. It is in Marheyo's hut that Tommo stayed during his captivity among the Typees. Marheyo is senile, spends much time tinkering with the construction of a shed, but understands his unhappy guest's desire to return home.

Maria II (1819–1853). (Full name: Maria da Gloria.) Queen of Portugal. She was born in Brazil, the granddaughter of King John VI of Portugal and the daughter of Dom Pedro I, emperor of Brazil. When John VI died (1826), his son declined to leave Brazil, handed over the throne of Portugal to Maria instead, then abdicated in Brazil in favor of his son Pedro II* (1831) in order to return to Portugal and fight for Maria's right to the throne there. Maria became queen of Portugal (1826–1828) with the understanding that she would marry her paternal uncle, Dom Miguel. He reneged, however, usurped the throne, and became the reactionary king (1828–1834). The British and French governments forced him out, and Maria resumed her moderate reign (1834–1853). She sought to establish a constitutional monarchy and in the process mediated between conservative and liberal factions. She married Duke Augustus of Leuchtenberg in 1834, but he died four months later. She married Duke Ferdinand of Saxe-Coburg in 1836, had eleven children, and died in childbirth at age thirty-four. The Portuguese throne was then occupied by her sons Peter V (1853–1861) and Louis I (1861–1889). Under Louis I, slavery was abolished in all Portuguese colonies (1869). In *White-Jacket,* Melville mentions that Maria is the present queen of Portugal and the sister of Pedro II, king of Brazil.

Bibliography: H. V. Livermore, *A New History of Portugal* (Cambridge, England: University Press, 1967).

Marianna. In "The Piazza," she is the lonely young woman who lives with her hard-working brother in the mountain-side cottage. The romantic narrator thinks that their cottage is theatrically attractive. Marianna in turn thinks that his house resembles marble and must be the abode of a happy man. The resignedly dignified Marianna owes something to Marianna in Shakespeare's *Measure for Measure,* in Alfred, Lord Tennyson's "Marianna" and "Marianna in the South," and in the painter John Everett Millais's *Marianna.*

Bibliography: Nancy Fredricks, "Melville and the Woman's Story," *Studies in American Fiction* 19 (Spring 1991): 41–54; John M. J. Gretchko, "A Pre-Raphaelite Marianna and a Question of Liberty," *Melville Society Extracts* 82 (September 1990): 9–11.

Marie. In *Pierre,* she is a pretty young lady in the Miss Pennies' sewing circle.

Marjora, King. In *Mardi,* he is the brother of King Teei of the island of Juam. Marjora killed his brother and set up his own residence at Willamilla.

Mark. In *Mardi,* he is a harpooner aboard the *Arcturion.*

Mark. In *White-Jacket,* he is a sailor suffering from a pulmonary complaint. When he becomes involved with Peter and Antone in a fight started by John, Mark is flogged by order of Captain Claret, after which he becomes sullen.

Marko. In *Mardi,* he is Bardianna's scribe and is mentioned in the philosopher's will. As a scribe, Marko made many marks.

Marmonora. In *Mardi,* he is a rich Tapparian guest of Nimni on the isle of Pimminee. According to Gaddi, Marmonora is heartless.

Marnoo. In *Typee,* he is the handsome, curly-haired native of Pueearka who is permitted to wander inviolate through all of the valleys. When Marnoo speaks English, Tommo decides to beg him—to no avail—to lead him back to Nukuheva. Later, however, Marnoo is instrumental in aiding Karakoee's management of Tommo's escape.

Marquis. In *White-Jacket,* he is a beribboned courtier who dances attendance upon Don Pedro II aboard the *Neversink.*

"The Marquis de Grandvin" (1924). Sketch, in *The Works of Herman Melville.* (Characters: B. Hobbema Brown, Major John Gentian, the Marquis de Grandvin.) Melville praises the Marquis de Grandvin, who is visiting America from France. He is an popular honorary member of several New York clubs. He has a genial temper, is liked by the ladies, and forms democratic friendships. The author would like to immortalize the magnetic man in a lovely, lasting book.

"Marquis de Grandvin: At the Hostelry" (1924). Poem, in *The Works of Herman Melville.* (Characters: Fra Angelico, [King] Bomba [Ferdinand II, King of the Two Sicilies], Adrian [Adriaen] Brouwer, [Camillo Benso] Cavour, [John] Constable, [Mikiel Adriaanszoon] De Ruyter, Carlo Dolce [Dolci], Gerard Douw [Dou], Agnes Durer, Albert Durer [Albrecht Dürer], King Fanny [Francis II, King of the Two Sicilies], [Giuseppe] Garibaldi, [Major John] Jack Gentian, the Grand Duke of Florence, the Marquis de Grandvin, Franz [Frans] Hals, [Jan van] Huysum, Leonardo [da Vinci], Frater [Fra Filippo] Lippi, Claude [Lorrain], Frater Michael Angelo [Michelangelo], Phillis, Pope [Pius IX], [Nicolas] Poussin, Raphael, Rembrandt, Salvator Rosa, Sir Peter Paul [Rubens], Spagnoletto, Jan [Havickszoon] Steen, [Herman van] Swanevelt, [David the Younger?] Teniers, Tintoretto, [Cornelis Maartenszoon] van Tromp (also Trump), [Willem I?] Van der [de] Velde, [Anthony] Vandyke [Van Dyck], [Diego Rodriguez de Silva y] Velasques [Velazquez], Paola of Verona [Veronese], [Antoine] Watteau.)

In a general Preface which precedes "At the Hostelry" and "Naples in the Time of Bomba" and which was published in *The Works of Herman Melville* (1924), it is explained that the Marquis narrates "At the Hostelry" (first entitled "At Delmonico's") and that the Marquis's friend Jack Gentian narrates "Naples in the Time of Bomba" (first entitled "A Morning in Naples").

In "At the Hostelry," in which short prose prefaces introduce and reinforce eight poetic sections, followed by a "Sequel," the Marquis de Grandvin, who is a genial Frenchman, speaks about Italian politics; summons up the spirits of many famous old Dutch, French, German, and Italian artists, who conduct a lengthy symposium on the nature of the picturesque; and recommends a story to be told by his friend Jack Gentian. Some of the local color in this poem evolved from the journal Melville kept while he was in Naples (18–24 February 1857).

Bibliography: Dennis Berthold, ''Melville and Dutch Genre Painting,'' pp. 218–45, in Savage Eye: Melville and the Visual Arts, ed. Christopher Sten (Kent, Ohio: Kent State University Press, 1991); NN 15; Shurr; Stein.

''Marquis de Grandvin: Naples in the Time of Bomba . . .'' (1924). Poem, in The Works of Herman Melville. (Characters: Agrippina [the younger], Andrea, Apollo, [King] Bomba [Ferdinand II, King of the Two Sicilies], Bourbon-Draco, Captain, Carlo, Donna, His Excellency, [Aniello] Falcone, [Francis II, King of the Two Sicilies], [Giuseppe] Garibaldi, Major [John] Jack Gentian, Queen Joanna [I], Masaniello, Merry Andrews, Nestors, a Peri, Punchinello, Salvator Rosa.)

This work has nine poetic sections, most with short prose prefaces, and closes with an ''After-Piece.'' In the work, Major Jack Gentian, a lover of democracy, expresses his displeasure that Naples is ruled by fear and tyranny. He describes the colorfully festive Neapolitan street crowds, the intimidating fortresses and the frightful troops there, a charming singer, a dancing flower girl—she gives Jack a rose that slowly fades—smoking Vesuvius, entertainers—including beach jugglers, tumblers, and singers—an urchin named Carlo who criticizes Bomba's soldiers in a daring song, a canopied priest with hidden host, and finally the deliverer of Naples—Garibaldi—who is yet to come. Much of the local color in this poem evolved from the journal Melville kept while he was in Naples (18–24 February 1857).

Bibliography: NN 15, Shurr, Stein.

Marr. In ''John Marr,'' he or she was the child of John Marr and died with the mother of a fever in the prairies.

Marr, John. In ''John Marr,'' he is a retired sailor. He was wounded by pirates off the Keys, and settled about 1838 on the frontier in the prairies. He married, had a child, and then lost both wife and child to death. Not especially esteemed, or even understood, by his farmer neighbors, John Marr apostrophizes his old shipmates in a poignant manner.

Marr, Mrs. John. In ''John Marr,'' she was John Marr's prairie wife, who died of fever with their child.

Marrot, Lieutenant. In ''Bridegroom-Dick,'' he is the officer remembered by Bridegroom Dick as ordering the constables to imprison the drunken Finn.

Marten. In *Pierre,* he is the servant of Pierre Glendinning's aunt Dorothea Glendinning. Pierre remembers that Marten once served him some fruitcake.

Martha. In *Pierre,* she is a pretty young lady in the Miss Pennies' sewing circle.

Martha. In *Pierre,* she is Lucy Tartan's chambermaid, who tends the stricken Lucy after Pierre Glendinning falsely tells her that he is married.

Martindale, Captain. In *Israel Potter,* he is the officer in command of the brigantine *Washington,* from which Potter is taken captive by men on the British ship *Foy.*

"The Martyr" (1866). (Full title: "The Martyr: Indicative of the passion of the people on the 15th of April, 1865"). Poem, in *Battle-Pieces.* Melville predicts that after he (Abraham Lincoln) was "killed . . . from behind" because of "madness" and "blindness" in "the evil-willed," his spirit of kindness and forgiveness will be replaced by a desire for vengeance. "Beware the People weeping / When they bare the iron hand."
Bibliography: Garner, NN 11.

Marvel, Bill. In *Mardi,* he is a yarn-spinning sailor aboard the *Arcturion.*

Mary. In *Redburn,* she is the imagined girlfriend of a typical Canadian soldier on cold sentry duty in Quebec.

Masa, Francisco. In "Benito Cereno," he is Alexandro Aranda's middle-aged cousin from Mendoza. He was wounded by Lecbe and thrown overboard alive off the *San Dominick.*

Masaniello (1622–1647). (Real name: Tommaso Aniello.) He was an Amalfi fisherman who led the 1647 revolt in Naples against Spanish rule. A fruit tax added by the oppressive government caused a riot which resulted in an agreement signed by the Neapolitan viceroy and Masaniello, by which the rebels were pardoned and the tax removed. A few days later, however, Masaniello was murdered by the viceroy's thugs while he was addressing a mob. In "Marquis de Grandvin: Naples at the Time of Bomba . . . ," he is mentioned as a bridegroom, the darling of the Neapolitan mob, and a beheaded patriot-martyr.
Bibliography: Acton.

Master. In "Old Counsel," he is the master of a wrecked clipper ship who warns sailors to beware when they are rounding the Horn out of the Golden Gate.

Master. In "Under the Ground," he is the boyish gardener's master. He orders roses to be entombed.

Master Betty. In "The Fiddler." *See* Betty, William Henry West.

Mate, The. In "The Death Craft," he is the officer of the Death Craft in Harry the Reefer's dream. He throws himself overboard.

Mathews, Cornelius (1817–1889). Author and editor. He was born in West Jefferson, New York. After studying at Columbia (1830–1832), he transferred to the University of the City of New York (now New York University), and was a member of the first graduating class there (1834). He studied law and was admitted to the bar (1837), but although he practiced until about 1850, his real love was literary writing and editing. After placing some minor prose and poetry in American magazines, he published in a versatile manner. His many works include tales and sketches (*A Motley Book: A Series of Tales and Sketches* [1838], *The Indian Fairy Book: From the Original Legends* [1856, retitled *The Enchanted Moccasins,* 1869]); novels (*Behemoth: A Legend of the Mound-builders* [1839], *The Career of Puffer Hopkins* [1842, about New York politics], *Big Abel and the Little Manhattan* [1845, about a descendant of Native Americans who sold Manhattan Island to the Dutch], *Moneypenny; or, The Heart of the World. A Romance of the Present Day* [1849], *Chanticleer: A Thanksgiving Story of the Peabody Family* [1850]); poetry (*Wakondah: The Master of Life. A Poem* [1841, lamenting the passing of Native Americans from materialistic America], *Poems on Man in His Various Aspects under the American Republic* [1843]); and plays (*The Politicians* [1840, critical of New York politics, unproduced], *Witchcraft; or, The Martyrs of Salem* [1846, internationally popular, translated into French], *Jacob Leisler, the Patriotic Hero; or, New York in 1690* [1848, concerning an early New York governor], *False Pretences; or, Both Sides of Good Society* [1855, satirizing parvenus], *Calmstorm, the Reformer: A Dramatic Comment* [1853, critical of American injustice]). Of more significance was Mathews's editorial work. Mathews and his close friend Evert Duyckinck* cofounded *Arcturus: A Journal of Books and Opinion* (1840–1842). Mathews was editor of the short-lived weekly *Yankee Doodle** (1847) where Melville published "Authentic Anecdotes of 'Old Zack,' " and perhaps items attributed to him, in it. During the 1880s, Mathews edited the New York *Dramatic Mirror.* He supported American literary efforts and fought for an international copyright law. He never married.

Bibliography: Perry Miller, *The Raven and the Whale: The War of Wits in the Era of Poe and Melville* (New York: Harcourt, Brace & World, 1956); Allen F. Stein, *Cornelius Mathews* (New York: Twayne, 1974).

Matilda. In *Redburn,* she is one of the three charming girls who live with their parents in a cottage outside Liverpool. Redburn has tea and buttered muffins with them one memorable afternoon.

Matinqui. In ''Benito Cereno,'' he is an Ashantee slave who polishes hatchets during Captain Amasa Delano's visit aboard the *San Dominick*. He helped Lecbe mortally mutilate Alexandro Aranda and is killed during the attack led by Delano's chief mate.

Matt. In ''Tom Deadlight,'' he is one of the dying Tom Deadlight's messmates. Matt fans his friend with a sou'wester.

Max the Dutchman (''Red Max''). In *Redburn,* he is a good-natured, red-haired sailor aboard the *Highlander*. He has a wife named Meg in New York and another wife named Sally in Liverpool. Max tosses Mrs. O'Brien's Bible overboard during the return voyage of the *Highlander* to America.

Maxwell, Mungo. In *Israel Potter,* he is a mutinous sailor reportedly flogged to death by Captain John Paul Jones. Jones denies the charge.

May. In ''Stockings in the Farm-House Chimney,'' she is depicted as waiting for Santa Claus.

May-Day. In *White-Jacket,* he is an enormous African-American sailor aboard the *Neversink*. He assists Old Coffee, the ship's cook. May-Day is good at the sport of head-butting, but after thus fighting Rose-Water he is flogged by Captain Claret.
  Bibliography: Grejda.

Mayhew, Captain. In *Moby-Dick,* he is the commander of the whaler *Jeroboam,* which has the mad Shaker prophet Gabriel aboard. The ship recently lost her chief mate to Moby Dick and is now swept by a malignant epidemic.

Mayor of London, The. In ''Poor Man's Pudding and Rich Man's Crumbs.'' *See* Lord Mayor of London, The.

May Queen. In *The Confidence-Man,* this is the name assigned by the herb doctor to the Creole or Comanche child who accompanies her shaggy, backwoodsman father. His mysterious pain impels him to hit the herb doctor.

''The Medallion in Villa Albina &c'' (1924). Poem, in *The Works of Herman Melville*. Since the basic expression of a face, turned serious after all smiles cease, reveals ''the inmost self,'' why should anyone object when ageless verses become endowed ''[w]ith reveries'' and ''candor grave'' more profound than any glosses?

Media, King. In *Mardi,* he is the father of Taji's friend King Media of Odo.

Media, King. In *Mardi,* he is the intially materialistic monarch of the isle of Odo. He professes to be a demigod and acts as judge and jury of his realm. Ordering Babbalanja, Mohi, and Yoomy to come along, King Media accompanies Taji on his search for Yillah as far as Serenia. The religion of Serenia moves him, causes his conversion, and inspires him to quit professing to be a demigod. Later, he returns to his kingdom and remains there to try to quell sedition. Melville may have obtained the names Media and also Mardi from Charles Anton's 1845 *Classical Dictionary,* in which Media is a country in Upper Asia and Mardi a people of Asia.
Bibliography: Davis.

"A Meditation Attributed to a Northerner after attending the last of two funerals from the same homestead—those of a National and a Confederate officer (brothers), his kinsmen, who had died from the effects of wounds received in the closing battles" (1866). Poem, in *Battle-Pieces.* When at the close of a military siege, soldiers see that enemy ranks include relatives and friends, thoughts of enmity conflict with those of brotherhood, and feelings of love "curse . . . the cause of war." "Can Africa pay back this blood / Spilt on Potomac's shore?" During lulls in combat, enemies talked about fighting alongside each other during the Mexican War, praised one another's bravery, tossed biscuits across the lines, and saved one another's wounded comrades. We should remember that opposing generals trained together at West Point. It would be pharisaical of the North if it called the South a sinner now. Remember that when Confederates marched out of Vicksburg in surrender, "[s]ilent the victors stood, scorning to raise a shout."
Bibliography: Garner, NN 11, Warren.

Meg. In *Redburn,* she is the New York wife of Max the Dutchman, who also has a wife named Sally in Liverpool.

Mehevi. In *Typee,* he is the brave, noble-looking chief of the Typees among whom Tommo lives for about four months. He does not want Tommo to leave. Mehevi's damsel is Moonoony, but the fellow is also flirtatious elsewhere.
Bibliography: Anderson.

Melvill, Allan (1782–1832). Melville's father. Born into a Unitarian family in Boston, he was the son of Major Thomas Melvill* and Priscilla Scollay Melvill, the younger brother of Thomas Melvill, Jr.,* Mary Melvill D'Wolf, and Nancy Wroe Melvill,* and the older brother of Priscilla Melvill,* Robert Melvill, Jean Melvill Wright, John Scollay Melvill, Lucy Melvill (who died as an infant), Lucy Melvill Clark Nourse,* and Helen Melvill Souther. On 11 April 1798, Allan Melvill's illegitimate daughter, Ann Middleton Allen,* was born. The mother was Martha Bent of Boston—later Martha Bent Allen, wife (as of 12 December 1797) of Bethuel Allen of Canton, Massachusetts. Allan Melvill en-

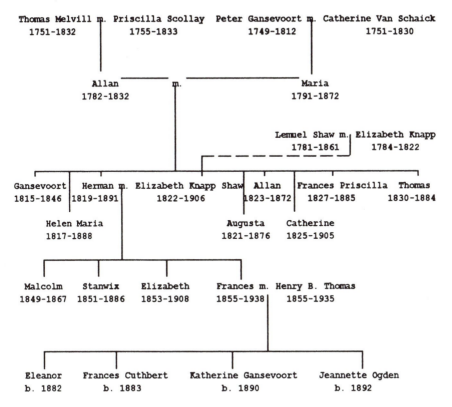

Melville Family Tree

tered the import business (1807), visited his brother Thomas in Paris, had an
ineptly managed affair abroad, and married Maria Gansevoort of Albany (1814).
He lived for years with his Dutch Reformed in-laws, traveled to Liverpool,
elsewhere in England, and Paris (1818), and set up his import business in New
York (1818). He and Maria Gansevoort Melville* eventually had eight children.
They were Gansevoort Melville,* Helen Maria Melville Griggs,* Herman Melville,* Augusta Melville,* Allan Melville,* Catherine Gansevoort Melville
Hoadley,* Frances Priscilla Melville,* and Thomas Melville.* For years, Allan
Melvill was well-to-do; however, after the depression of 1830, his business
began to fail. He borrowed heavily from his brother-in-law Peter Gansevoort
(1788–1876),* moved with his family to Albany, joined a fur company there,
and borrowed from his father. He grew ill, fell into nervous delirium and perhaps
insanity, and died $26,000 in debt. The cause of death may have been enceph-
alitis or fever-induced metabolic derangement. Gansevoort Melville and Herman
Melville were taken out of school. While Herman began clerking in a bank,
Gansevoort managed their father's business. Allan Melvill may be defined as
dandified, overly optimistic, dependent on others, harsh and capricious with his
children, sanctimonious, and hypocritical.

Melville made use of his father's early travel to Liverpool in *Redburn* and his illegitimate daughter in *Pierre*. In many of his other works, he develops the theme of a searcher—often for a new and better father figure.

Bibliography: Newton Arvin, *Herman Melville* ([New York]: William Sloan Associates, 1950); Cohen and Yannella; Howard; Leyda; Metcalf; Smith; Young.

Melvill, Anne Marie Priscilla (1810–1858). Melville's cousin. She was the daughter of Melville's uncle Thomas Melvill, Jr.,* and his first wife, Françoise Raymonde Eulogie Marie des Douleurs Lamé-Fleury Melvill.* Priscilla, as she was called, was born in France. A discarded critical theory once had it that Priscilla was the daughter of Melville's father Allan Melvill* by Françoise Fleury Melvill, the first wife of his brother Thomas Melvill, Jr. This man moved his family from France (c. 1812) to Pittsfield, Massachusetts. Priscilla, who inherited a little French property after her mother died in Pittsfield (1814), lived with Melville's brother Allan Melville* and his family in New York City (by 1824). She was back in Pittsfield (by 1846), moved to Canandaigua, New York, to work mainly as a seamstress in a girls' school run by friends there (1848–1853), perhaps overstayed her welcome at Melville's Arrowhead home (winter 1853–1854), and advertised to make wardrobe articles and do fine embroidery (1855). This sad woman died in Pittsfield of tuberculosis. She resembles Isabel Banford, the dark heroine of *Pierre*.

Bibliography: Metcalf, Young.

Melvill, Françoise ("Fanny") Raymonde Eulogie Marie des Douleurs Lamé-Fleury (1781–1814). Melville's aunt. This French woman was born in Spain and married Melville's uncle, Thomas Melvill, Jr.,* in Paris in 1802. The couple had six children between 1804 and 1814. Thomas Melvill, Jr., appealed to his father for money and moved himself and his family to Pittsfield, Massachusetts (c. 1812), where his wife soon died.

Bibliography: Metcalf, Young.

Melvill, George Raleigh ("Rolly") (1826–1899). Melville's cousin. He was the son of Melville's uncle Thomas Melvill, Jr.,* and of his second wife, Mary Ann Augusta Hobart Melvill.* As a teenager in Galena, Illinois, George Melvill worked in the mining industry (1845), became a steamboat clerk on the Mississippi River between Galena and Saint Paul, Minnesota (1852), owned a river steamboat (by 1854), and married Mary French in 1854. For some time, his brother Robert Melvill* was his steamboat captain.

Bibliography: Leyda.

Melvill, Helen Jean (1829–1905). Melville's cousin. She was the daughter of Melville's uncle Thomas Melvill, Jr.,* and his second wife, Mary Ann Augusta Hobart Melvill.* She lived in Galena, Illinois, and after Herman Melville's death remained in correspondence with his widow Elizabeth Knapp Shaw Melville* (at least into 1892).

Melvill, Henry Dearborn (1812–1896). Melville's cousin. He was the son of Melville's uncle Thomas Melvill, Jr.,* and his first wife, Françoise Raymonde Eulogie Marie des Douleurs Lamé-Fleury Melvill.* He suffered right-side paralysis as a child, could read but not retain what he had read, and was later judged to be insane. His father advised with Lemuel Shaw* in order to obtain a power of attorney to investigate the possibility of his receiving French property or money left him by his deceased mother (1845). His estate was sold in Pittsfield, Massachusetts (1850), where he evidently died later.

Bibliography: Leyda, Young.

Melvill, Julia Marie (1820–1846). Melville's cousin. She was the daughter of Melville's uncle Thomas Melvill, Jr.,* and his second wife, Mary Ann Augusta Hobart Melvill.* In 1841, Edward Ballard, the Melville family minister in Pittsfield, Massachusetts, wrote to Lemuel Shaw* to inform him that sickness had rendered her almost blind. She died five years later, evidently of consumption.

Bibliography: Leyda.

Melvill, Mary Ann Augusta Hobart (1796–1884). Melville's aunt. She was the second wife of Melville's uncle, Thomas Melvill, Jr.* Married in 1815, the couple had eight children between 1817 and 1833. Widowed in Galena, Illinois, in 1845, Mary Melvill wrote to Lemuel Shaw* about creditors and debtors. She also reported later family activities to him. Most significantly, she gave her nephew Melville a copy of *Mosses from an Old Manse* by Nathaniel Hawthorne* (July 1850). *See* Cherry in ''Hawthorne and His Mosses.''

Bibliography: Leyda.

Melvill, Nancy Wroe (1780–1813). Sister of Melville's father Allan Melvill.* She was engaged to marry Lemuel Shaw* but died before a wedding could take place. Although in time he had two other wives, Shaw carried two letters from Nancy in his wallet thereafter.

Bibliography: Young.

Melvill, Pierre (1806–1844). *See* Melvill, Thomas Wilson.

Melvill, Priscilla (1784–1862). Melville's aunt. She was the sister of Melville's father Allan Melvill.* She never married and suffered an attack of rheumatic fever (1824). She was proud of Melville's literary accomplishments and willed Melville $900 upon her death in Boston.

Bibliography: Leyda.

Melvill, Robert (1817–1881). Melville's cousin. He was the son of Melville's uncle Thomas Melvill, Jr.,* and his second wife, Mary Ann Augusta Hobart Melvill.* He married Susan Bates in Pittsfield in 1838 (the couple had two sons, one of whom died as a child, and also one daughter). He inherited Broadhall, his father's dilapidated residence in Pittsfield, Massachusetts (1845), reluctantly farmed there, answered a letter from Lemuel Shaw* to report the names and ages of his siblings (1845), welcomed Melville and his family for a visit to his farm and inn (July–September 1850), and took him on a days-long wagon tour of Berkshire County (July). Melville bought an adjoining farm and called it Arrowhead (September). A month later, he ghost-wrote all or part of ''Report of the Committee on Agriculture'' for Robert Melvill. Within a couple of years, Robert Melvill moved to Galena, Illinois, where his mother lived, to work irregularly there. One job he had (beginning in 1854) was commanding a steamboat owned by his brother George Raleigh Melvill.* He died in Davenport, Iowa.

Bibliography: Leyda.

Melvill, Thomas (1751–1832). Melville's grandfather. In 1774 he married Priscilla Scollay (1755–1833) and had eleven children with her. They were Thomas Melvill, Jr.,* Mary Melvill D'Wolf (1778–1859), Nancy Wroe Melvill,* Allan Melvill* (Melville's father), Priscilla Melvill,* Robert Melvill (1786–1795), Jean Melvill Wright (1788–1866), John Scollay Melvill (1790–1815), Lucy Melvill (1793–1794), Lucy Melvill Clark Nourse,* and Helen Melvill Souther (1798–1864). Thomas Melvill achieved fame during the American Revolution by being part of the Boston Tea Party (1773), was a major in the Continental Army, and was thereafter called Major Melvill. He was appointed by President George Washington* to be collector of the Port of Boston (1789), bought property called Broadhall in Pittsfield, Massachusetts (1816), and held his easy job in Boston until Andrew Jackson became president (1829) shortly before the old man's death. Meanwhile, the codger had gained fame by being the subject of ''The Last Leaf,'' the 1831 poem by Oliver Wendell Holmes.* The practical major felt chronically obliged to answer the pleas of his sons Thomas Melvill, Jr., and Allan Melvill for money when they were imprudent in their commercial dealings and personal lives. Allan Melvill died in January 1832; his father, that September.

Bibliography: Leyda, Metcalf.

Melvill, Thomas, Jr. (1776–1845). Melville's uncle. He was the son of Thomas Melvill* and his wife Priscilla Scollay Melvill, and the brother of Mary Melvill De Wolf (1778–1859), Nancy Wroe Melvill,* Allan Melvill* (Melville's father), Priscilla Melvill,* Robert Melvill (1786–1795), Jean Melvill Wright (1788–1866), John Scollay Melvill (1790–1815), Lucy Melvill (1793–1794), Lucy Melvill Clark Nourse,* and Helen Melvill Souther (1798–1864). Thomas Melvill, Jr., married twice. By his first wife, Françoise Raymonde Eulogie Marie des Douleurs Lamé-Fleury Melvill,* who was born in Spain and whom he married in Paris in 1802, he had six children. They were Françoise Marie Raymonde Priscilla Melvill (1804–1821), Pierre François Henry Thomas Wilson Melvill (*see* Melvill, Thomas Wilson), Napoléon Alexander (''Allan'') Melvill (1808–

1814), Anne Marie Priscilla Melvill,* Henry Dearborn Melvill,* and Peter Francis Melvill (1814–1814). By his second wife, Mary Ann Augusta Hobart Melvill,* who was the granddaughter of a friend of his father's and whom he married in 1815, Thomas Melvill, Jr., had eight more children. They are Robert Melvill* (married Susan Bates), Mary Anne Sophia Melvill (1818–1882, married John Dean), Julia Marie Melvill,* Allan Cargill Melvill (1823–1832), John Scollay Melvill (1825–1862, married Catherine Ryan), George Raleigh Melvill* (married Mary French), Helen Jean Melvill,* and another Allan Cargill Melvill (1833–1882, married Florinda Drum). Thomas Melvill, Jr., went to France (c. 1895), associated with American expatriates, grew wealthy by negotiating French government bonds and in commercial ventures, and dabbled in diplomacy and literature. His marriage enabled him to advance in the French banking world because his wife's uncle (and adoptive father) was a leading Parisian banker. After making but then losing a great deal of money in the banking business in France, Thomas Melvill, Jr., appealed to his father to send him a substantial sum by which to get himself and his family to the United States (1812). He opened a commissary to serve a new army cantonment in Pittsfield, Massachusetts, and at first did well financially (1812–1815). His father bought a mansion in Pittsfield (1816), and Thomas Melvill, Jr., and his children moved into it. He tried farming, did poorly, and was imprisoned for debt (1821, 1835). He evidently gave Ann Middleton Allen,* Melville's illegitimate half-sister, some spare money out of pity and to buy her silence (1832). He moved to Galena, Illinois (1837), where—calling himself Major Melvill—he seemed out of place with his Frenchified manners and clothes, worked in a friend's store, became a chamber of commerce officer (1840), embezzled from his partner, but was not prosecuted. He died in Galena. Many letters have survived which he wrote to Lemuel Shaw,* long a family friend, and which deal with family, financial, agricultural, and political matters.

Melville, who liked both his uncle Thomas and Thomas's young second wife, visited them at their Pittsfield farm (mid-1830s) and in Galena (1840); may have had his charming, elegant, eccentric failure of an uncle in mind when he sketched the hero manqué of the short story "Jimmy Rose"; and wrote an unsigned, and inaccurate, memoir of his uncle, entitled "Sketch of Major Thomas Melville Junior, by a Nephew," for *The History of Pittsfield (Berkshire County) Massachusetts, from the Year 1800 to the Year 1876,* edited by Joseph Edward Adams Smith* (2 vols., 1876).

Bibliography: Cohen and Yannella; Stanton Garner, "The Picaresque Career of Thomas Melvill, Junior," *Melville Society Extracts* 60 (November 1984): 1–10, and 62 (May 1985): 1, 4–10; Gilman; Leyda; Young.

Melvill, Thomas Wilson (1806–1844). (Formal name: Pierre François Henry Thomas Wilson Melvill.) Melville's cousin. The son of Thomas Melvill, Jr.,* and his first wife, Françoise Raymonde Eulogie Marie des Douleurs Lamé-Fleury Melvill.* Born in Paris, he became a midshipman out of Boston in the

U.S. Navy headed for the Pacific (1826), was aboard a ship off Callao (1829), arrived back in New York (1830), was suspended from duty for fighting at sea in the West Indies (1831), was court-martialed but acquitted (May 1832), was ill with Asiatic cholera in New Orleans (July? 1832), resigned from the navy (1834), sailed aboard American whalers (1835–1841), and suffered from scurvy off Australia (1840). Thomas Melvill communicated with his father repentantly after nine years of silence (1841), reported to the family that he had conquered his drinking habit (1844), but soon died at sea in the Pacific and was buried in Lahaina, in the Hawaiian Islands.

Bibliography: Leyda.

Melville, Allan (1823–1872). Melville's brother. Allan Melville was the fifth child of Allan Melvill* and Maria Gansevoort Melville.* When his father died in Albany, young Allan was a pupil at the academy there and remained there for some years. In 1837 he was placed in the law office of his uncle Peter Gansevoort (1788–1876).* He left that office after a quarrel possibly provoked by his uncle (1839), went to New York City to be with his brother Gansevoort Melville,* but returned to Albany to work in a law firm there (1839). By 1842, Allan Melville was reading law in and doing legal work for a firm back in New York. Partly through his brother's contacts, Herman Melville began his association with Evert Duyckinck.* Allan Melville rose steadily in his profession, and six weeks after Melville was married (1847), he married Sophia Eliza Thurston (1827–1858). The two couples set up housekeeping together at 103 Fourth Avenue, in New York, with the brothers' mother and their four sisters—Helen Maria Melville (later Helen Maria Melville Griggs*), Augusta Melville,* Catherine Melville (later Catherine Gansevoort Melville Hoadley*), and Frances Priscilla Melville.* This arrangement was partly financed by Herman Melville's generous father-in-law Lemuel Shaw.* Allan Melville and his wife eventually had five daughters. They were Maria Gansevoort Melville Morewood (1849–1935), Florence ("Flossie") Melville (1850–1919), Katherine ("Kate," "Kitty") Gansevoort Melville (1852–1939), Julia Melville (1854–1854), and Lucy Melville (1856–1885).

Melville dedicated *Mardi* to his brother Allan Melville (1849). Herman Melville moved himself and his growing family out of Manhattan to Pittsfield, Massachusetts (1850), but the brothers continued their close relationship. Allan Melville was Melville's attorney and business adviser, handling contracts with, advances, payments, and royalties from, and sums owed to publishers (from 1846). He transferred funds sent to him by Shaw for Melville's use. At one time, Daniel Shepherd* was Allan Melville's partner and became Melville's friend. The two brothers and members of their families enjoyed a mountain climb and picnic in the Berkshires with Evert Duyckinck and his brother George Duyckinck,* among others (August 1851). The event was organized and also attended by Sarah Huyler Morewood* and her husband John Rowland Morewood,* Melville's Pittsfield neighbors and the parents of William Barlow Morewood (1847–1923), who in 1874 married Allan Melville's daughter Maria. When Allan Melville was in London, he dined with Melville's publisher, John Murray*—a fellow guest was John Gibson Lockhart (fall 1851). Allan Melville and his family summered at Pittsfield (1852). Aspects of Allan Melville and his law office may be reflected in Melville's "Bartleby" (1853). With Nathaniel Hawthorne,* Allan Melville tried hard though unavailingly through friends to get Melville a consular appointment to Antwerp or Honolulu (1853). In 1860, some eighteen months after the death of his young wife Sophia, Allan Melville married Jane W. Dempsey (?–1890). He tried again, this time with Shaw, but again failed to obtain a consular appointment for Melville, this time to Florence (1861).

Melville and his family moved back to New York and bought Allan Melville's house, now called 104 East 26th Street, with cash and the Arrowhead deed, and by assuming the mortgage held by the deceased Sophia Melville's mother (1863). Thereafter, Allan Melville and his family maintained a home on 35th Street, New York, even while summering at Arrowhead and welcoming Melville there for visits. Through his contacts in Washington, D.C., Allan Melville was able to obtain a pass for Melville and for himself to visit the war front in Virginia (1864). Allan Melville and his wife Jane toured abroad, including Egypt, among other countries (1866). Allan Melville helped his brother Thomas Melville* secure the position of governor of the Sailors' Snug Harbor, on Staten Island (1867). Allan Melville died suddenly of chronic tuberculosis and lung collapse.

Bibliography: Howard, Leyda, NN 14.

Melville, Augusta ("Gus") (1821–1876). Melville's sister. Augusta was the fourth daughter of Allan Melvill* and Maria Gansevoort Melville* Although her father Allan Melvill paid more attention to his sons than to his daughters, she was in comfortable circumstances until he lost his business in New York City, moved with his family to Albany, and died bankrupt and insane (1832). When her brother Gansevoort Melville* seemed to be recouping the family's fortunes, she attended the Albany Female Academy with her sisters. Their mother Maria Gansevoort Melville wrote to her brother Peter Gansevoort (1788–1876)* back in 1828 that Augusta was learning to dance gracefully and lightly. She won an award at the academy (1836), joined the Reformed Dutch Church in Albany (1838), was intensely religious, saw life as a vale of tears, and had literary tendencies. She moved with her sisters into the New York City home of her married brothers Herman Melville and Allan Melville* (1847) and helped Melville by copying manuscripts and reading proofs of his writing, for example, *Mardi,* which she called "My own Koztanza! child of many prayers" in a letter to Melville's wife (27 January 1849). She also handled some of his correspondence—for example, to Evert Duyckinck.* She was with Melville and his family during most of their time at Arrowhead (1850–1863). While there, she made the acquaintance of Nathaniel Hawthorne* and his wife Sophia. Melville esteemed his sister, gave her books, and took her on short visits and vacations,

sometimes so that she could help with his children. Sarah Huyler Morewood*
wrote to George Duyckinck* from Pittsfield, Massachusetts, that she found Augusta "a pleasanter companion than any of her sisters are" (27 October 1851).
Hope Savage Shaw,* the stepmother of Melville's wife, also praised Augusta
for being considerate during a visit by the Shaws to Arrowhead (1855). Augusta
may have counseled with Melville during the composition (1856) of *The Confidence-Man*. She encouraged Peter Gansevoort to use his influence to help Melville obtain an appointment in the New York customhouse (1857). When
Melville moved with his family back to New York, Augusta accompanied them
and then lived part of the time with them (from 1863). She urged family members to regard the suicide of Melville's son Malcolm Melville* as an accident
(1867). While Melville was pushing *Clarel* through the press (1876), his wife
urged Augusta not to proceed from Albany, where she was staying, and visit
them in New York but instead to visit their brother Thomas Melville,* then
living at the Sailors' Snug Harbor, on Staten Island. She did so and died suddenly there, of a cold and internal hemorrhaging. She was Melville's favorite
sister, and her death affected him deeply.
   Bibliography: Gilman, Leyda, NN 14.

Melville, Catherine ("Kate") Gansevoort (1825–1905). Melville's sister. She
married John Chipman Hoadley* in 1853. *See* Hoadley, Catherine Gansevoort
Melville.

Melville, Catherine ("Kate," "Katie") Eliza Bogart (1842–1928). Melville's
sister-in-law. She was the wife of Thomas Melville.* They married in New
Rochelle, New York, in 1868, soon after he had become governor of the Sailors'
Snug Harbor, Staten Island. She was the daughter of S.V.R. Bogart, resident
physician at the Snug Harbor. Melville often socialized with his brother and
sister-in-law. Widowed from 1884, she attended Melville's funeral.
   Bibliography: Leyda, NN 14.

Melville, Elizabeth ("Bess," "Bessie") (1853–1908). Melville's older daughter. She was born in Pittsfield, Massachusetts. In the 1870s, she developed rheumatism which left her crippled, although she was able to help keep house for
her parents. She and her sister Frances Melville were closely supervised by their
mother until Frances married (1880) and became Frances Melville Thomas.*
Bessie continued to make her residence with her parents. She and her mother
both suffered from hay fever; so they often took summer vacations out of town.
After Melville's death, Bessie and her mother sold their home on 26th Street
and lived in an apartment at 105 East 18th Street, New York. When her mother
died (1906), Bessie was asked by the critic Edmund Clarence Stedman* to
provide biographical materials about her father. Instead, she kept the now-
famous tin breadbox crammed with Melville's manuscripts to herself and at her
death left them to her sister Frances Thomas, whose daughter Eleanor Melville

Thomas Metcalf preserved them, donated them to Harvard University (1942), and made scholarly use of them herself (1953).
   Bibliography: Metcalf, NN 14.

Melville, Elizabeth ("Lizzie") Knapp Shaw (1822–1906). Melville's wife. She was the daughter of Lemuel Shaw* and Elizabeth Knapp Shaw,* his first wife. Shaw's second wife, Hope Savage Shaw,* became Lizzie's affectionate stepmother (from 1827). Soon after returning from sea (1844), Melville met Lizzie, who knew his sister Helen (later Helen Maria Melville Griggs*) in Boston and Lansingburgh. After he wrote *Typee* in New York, dedicated it to Judge Shaw, and saw to its publication (1846), Melville visited the Shaws in Boston, where Helen was a guest of Lizzie, who soon paid the Melvilles in Lansingburgh—now including the attractive young novelist—a two-months' visit later the same year. Melville, who quickly published *Omoo* (1847), and Lizzie were married in Boston (4 August 1847), honeymooned in New England and Canada, and set up housekeeping with his brother Allan Melville* and his wife Sophia Eliza Thurston Melville in a house at 103 Fourth Avenue, in New York City. Also with them were the brothers' mother, Maria Gansevoort Melville,* and their four sisters—Helen, Augusta Melville,* Catherine Melville (later Catherine Gansevoort Melville Hoadley*), and Frances Priscilla Melville.* The house was partly financed by Lizzie's father.
   Living as a new husband in New York, Melville wrote steadily while his wife grew bored and listless in the process of playing second fiddle to her live-in mother-in-law. Lizzie copied *Mardi,* which Melville proofed and added to, in 1848. She visited her father and his family in Boston (1848). Melville and Lizzie became parents of their first child, Malcolm Melville* (1849). When *Mardi* fared badly with the public and the critics, Melville wrote *Redburn* and *White-Jacket* (1849) and went to England, on business, and then to the Continent, while his wife and son returned to Boston (October 1849–February 1850). Melville and his family, accompanied by Lizzie's female in-laws, moved to Pittsfield, Massachusetts (1850), where they bought Arrowhead by borrowing money from Shaw against Lizzie's inheritance. During the Melvilles' thirteen-year stay there, Lizzie gave birth to another son and two daughters. They were Stanwix Melville,* Elizabeth Melville,* and Frances Melville Thomas.* Lizzie liked the Berkshires and relished local friendships, not least that of Nathaniel Hawthorne* and his family, in nearby Lenox; delighted in visits from and to members of the Shaw family, traditionally to Boston for weeks around Thanksgiving; but was oppressed by and critical of her husband's regimen of scribbling and reading. She became what may be described as an ineffectual, overly protective mother. The failure of *Pierre* (1852) caused Lizzie and her family to renew efforts to obtain a consular position for Melville, but without success (1853). Melville's "I and My Chimney" (1856) contains veiled expressions of his resentment at feeling henpecked. It was probably Lizzie who persuaded her father to stake Melville to a second trip abroad, to the tune of at least $1,400 (1856–1857).

When sporadic lecturing failed to provide him with much income (1857–1859), Melville tried writing poetry, left a batch for Lizzie and his brother Allan Melville to try to publish, and sailed for California, feeling out of sorts (1860). Meanwhile, Shaw canceled most of his son-in-law's notes, accepted Pittsfield property deeds instead, and made that property over to Lizzie. Upon Melville's return, Lizzie's father tried unavailingly to get Melville a consular appointment (1861). Shaw died (1861).

The Melvilles put Arrowhead up for sale, moved to a rented house in Pittsfield (1862), and then returned to New York (1863), where they bought the New York house, now called 104 East 26th Street, then owned by Allan Melville, by giving him cash and the Arrowhead property (now Lizzie's), and by assuming the mortgage held by Allan's deceased wife's mother. Despite having income from Boston property and investments, Lizzie must have been happy when Melville was hired as a New York customs inspector (1866). Even so, he continued to be such a distressing husband that Lizzie considered visiting her brothers in Boston and not returning home, and even having Melville declared mentally unstable (spring 1867). There is some slight evidence that Melville may have physically and emotionally abused Lizzie. Then came the tragedy of their son Malcolm's suicide (September 1867). They mended, but slowly. It is possible that the tragedy brought his wife closer to Melville. She disliked what writing *Clarel* did to him and was glad when the "incubus," as she called the book, was out of the house (1876). She surely took muted pleasure in Melville's "Bridegroom-Dick" (1876), which contains personal hints of old-age marital joys, and in poems he wrote later that focus on roses and shyly express his autumnal love for her. They rejoiced in the marriage of their daughter Frances (1880) and the birth of their first grandchildren.

Lizzie and their daughter Elizabeth, who always lived at home, left Melville in town while they avoided it by going into New England and upstate New York during hay-fever time (1880s). Not long after the death of her stepmother Hope Shaw (1879), Lizzie as a residual legatee of her father's estate began to receive regular payments (from 1884). Once Melville resigned from the customhouse (1885), Lizzie developed the habit of silently giving him $25 a month to buy books and prints with. Only then did she look fondly on his resumption of a writing career—mostly revising old poems and composing new ones. The death of their younger son Stanwix (1886) disturbed Lizzie more than it did the stoical Melville. Late in their marriage, they came into a great deal of money. Melville made out a will leaving everything to Lizzie (1888). The will of her aunt, Martha Bird Knapp Marett (1796–1878), when tardily probated, gave Lizzie $2,471 (1889), to add to $15,000 Mrs. Marett's daughter Ellen Marett Gifford had willed to Lizzie and $8,000 she had willed to Melville. Some time after the death of Lizzie's stepbrother Lemuel Shaw, Jr.,* her $33,516 share of his residual bequest was paid (1889). Lizzie helped Melville prepare *Timoleon* for publication (1891). He planned to dedicate to her a collection of poems, entitled *Weeds and Wildings, with a Rose or Two* but died before putting it through the press. She sold her home on 26th Street and moved with her daughter Elizabeth to an apartment at 105 East 18th Street, New York, where she died. Elizabeth then took control of Melville's box of manuscripts.

Bibliography: Cohen and Yannella; Howard; Leyda; NN 14; Elizabeth Renker, "Herman Melville, Wife Beating, and the Written Page," *American Literature* 66 (March 1994): 123–50.

Melville, Frances ("Fanny") (1855–1938). Melville's younger daughter. She married Henry Besson Thomas (1855–1935) in 1880. *See* Thomas, Frances Melville.

Melville, Frances ("Fanny") Priscilla (1827–1885). Melville's sister. Frances was the seventh child of Allan Melvill* and Maria Gansevoort Melville.* Although her father paid more attention to his sons than to his daughters, she was in comfortable circumstances until he lost his business in New York City, moved with his family to Albany, and died bankrupt and insane (1832). When her brother Gansevoort Melville* seemed to be recouping the family's fortunes, she attended the Albany Female Academy with her sisters. When Melville and his brother Allan Melville* married (1847), the Melville women became part of a large housekeeping unit in New York City. They went with Melville and his wife to Pittsfield, Massachusetts, and socialized pleasantly there (1850–1863). Upon the death (1855) of the wife of Herman Gansevoort* in Gansevoort, New York, Frances, his niece, remained there with her mother, at first to keep house for the grieving man (1855); and she continued to live there after his death (1862). During Melville's early time as a New York customs inspector (from 1866), his mother and his sister Frances often paid his household long visits. Frances also paid occasional visits to their brother Thomas Melville* on Staten Island and to their married sisters, Catherine Gansevoort Melville Hoadley* and Helen Maria Melville Griggs,* in their homes. Melville's whereabouts are often traceable because of the assiduity of Frances Melville's correspondence to family members over the years. This gentle, considerate, conservative woman died in her sister Helen's home in Brookline, Massachusetts.

Bibliography: Leyda, Metcalf.

Melville, Gansevoort (1815–1846). Melville's brother. Gansevoort was the first child of Allan Melvill* and Maria Gansevoort Melville.* As the favored firstborn and always his mother's darling, Gansevoort enjoyed the advantages of a well-appointed home and good schooling. After his father had business reverses in New York (1826) and moved with his family to Albany (1830), Gansevoort was placed in the Albany Academy but had to be withdrawn when his father died bankrupt and insane (1832). As the new head of the family, young Gansevoort hoped to do well in his father's fur and cap business, partly financed by his mother's inheritance from the Gansevoort family. The store survived for a few years. It was damaged by fire (1834). Herman Melville clerked in it for a time (1835), and it expanded (1836). But it went bankrupt during the Panic of 1837, and Peter Gansevoort (1788–1876),* Maria Melville's brother, reimbursed his nephew Gansevoort's creditors. The bankruptcy ate up all of Maria Melville's holdings.

After lying abed for many months recovering from an ankle injury (1838–1839), Gansevoort Melville began to live in New York, helped get his brother Herman a berth on a merchant ship bound for Liverpool (1839), studied to become a lawyer, took a cruise down to the Caribbean and the Gulf of Mexico (January 1841), and stumped with fiery oratory through parts of Tennessee, Kentucky, Ohio, and New York state on behalf of James K. Polk during his successful bid for the presidency (1844). Though losing money and clients the while, Gansevoort gained popularity by bellowing "Fifty-four forty or fight!" during the Oregon crisis. Failing to obtain the position of first marshal of New York, he was appointed secretary of the American legation in England, and set sail (July 1845) with most of the manuscript of *Typee* in his luggage, intent upon securing an English copyright for his brother's novel when complete. He showed parts of it to John Murray,* the London publisher (October 1845), sold publication rights to him (December), and as soon as he had the finished draft in hand concluded generous arrangements (January 1846). Gansevoort combined work at the embassy with heroic proofreading. He showed part of *Typee* to Washington Irving,* who happened to be spending some time in London away from his ambassadorial assignment in Madrid. He praised the work highly (January) and persuasively recommended it to George Palmer Putnam,* who was a partner of Wiley and Putnam, his American publishers, and with whom Gansevoort concluded terms (January). Although he completed his proofreading job well (February), he was less successful as a diplomat and proved to be embarrassing to his superiors (partly because of the old Oregon controversy). He prevented his being relieved of his duties by dying of cerebral anemia (12 May).

Most poignantly, Melville wrote to Gansevoort seventeen days later, not yet knowing of his death. His passing caused Melville to become the head of his widowed mother's children. Ironically, some of the anti-imperialism evident in *Mardi* (1849) is owing to Melville's distress at Gansevoort's expansionist political philosophy and rhetoric. When Melville was in London for the first time, he penned an 1849 journal entry indicating his eerie awareness that a few years earlier his brother, now dead, "was writing here in London, about the same hour as this—alone in his chamber, in profound silence—as I am now" (24 November). It may be that all his life Melville harbored resentment that his mother had initially favored Gansevoort over him and had praised Gansevoort more. Late in his life, Melville wrote "Timoleon (394 B.C.)," a poem in which, among much else, a mother prefers her older, flashier son over her younger, more reliable one.

Bibliography: Janet Galligani Casey, "New Letters of Gansevoort Melville: 1845–1846," pp. 141–50 in *Studies in the American Renaissance,* ed. Joel Myerson (Charlottesville: University Press of Virginia, 1991); "Gansevoort Melville's 1846 London

Journal,'' ed. Hershel Parker, *Bulletin of the New York Public Library* 69 (December 1965): 633–54, 70 (January, February 1966): 36–49, 113–31; Howard; Kenney; Leyda; NN 1 and 15.

Melville, Helen Maria (1817–1888). Melville's sister. She married George Griggs (1814 or 1815–1888) in 1854. *See* Griggs, Helen Maria Melville.

Melville, Herman (1819–1891). The salient facts of Melville's life are as follows. Herman Melville was born in New York City. His father, Allan Melvill,* was an importer and a merchant; his mother, Maria Gansevoort Melville,* from a well-to-do Albany family, was the daughter of an American Revolutionary War hero. Melville's parents had seven other children. They were Gansevoort Melville,* Helen Maria Melville Griggs,* Augusta Melville,* Allan Melville,* Catherine Gansevoort Melville Hoadley,* Frances Priscilla Melville,* and Thomas Melville.* After going to school in New York (1825–1830), Melville moved with his family to Albany when his father's business collapsed (1830). Melville attended school in Albany (1830–1831). Fellow students at the academy included his cousins Hun Gansevoort,* Leonard Herman Gansevoort, Jr.,* and Stanwix Gansevoort.* When his father died bankrupt and insane (1832), Melville took various jobs, in Albany and near Pittsfield, Massachusetts (to 1838), and also studied the classics in Albany and surveying in Lansingburgh, New York (1835–1838). After publishing a few sketches, he became a common seaman on a trading vessel to Liverpool and back (1839). He taught school in New York state (1839–1840) and signed aboard the whaler *Acushnet* (1841–1842). He deserted in the Marquesas, lived briefly in the Taipi Valley of Nukuhiva, shipped aboard an Australian whaler, deserted and was imprisoned briefly at Tahiti, escaped, and worked on a potato farm there (1842). He signed aboard a Nantucket whaler (1842–1843), was discharged in the Sandwich Islands, and worked in Honolulu (1843). He joined the American navy on the frigate *United States* (Honolulu to Boston, 1843–1844).

Melville then began his literary life. In Lansingburgh again, he wrote *Typee* (published 1846, first in London through the efforts of his brother Gansevoort, secretary of the American legation, then in New York) and *Omoo* (1847). He married Elizabeth Knapp Shaw (Melville*), daughter of Lemuel Shaw,* Chief Justice of the Massachusetts Supreme Court, in 1847, and moved with her to New York. (The Melvilles ultimately had four children—Malcolm Melville,* Stanwix Melville,* Elizabeth Melville,* and Frances Melville Thomas.*) Melville published short pieces (1847–1850), the most significant of which was ''Hawthorne and His Mosses'' (1850), even while he also wrote and published *Mardi* and then *Redburn* (both 1849). He wrote a pair of anonymous reviews. The first review was of *The California and Oregon Trail* by Francis Parkman. This review was published in the New York *Literary World* (31 March 1849). The second review was of *The Sea Lions* by James Fenimore Cooper* (*Literary World,* 28 April 1849). The *Literary World* was owned and edited by Melville's friends Evert Duyckinck* and his brother George Duyckinck.* After a trip to London to see publishers and to go on to the Continent (1849–1850), Melville published *White-Jacket* (1850), met and admired Nathaniel Hawthorne,* borrowed money from his wife's father and bought a farm he named Arrowhead near Pittsfield, Massachusetts, and moved there with his family (1850). He published *Moby-Dick* (1851) and *Pierre* (1852). His professional life took a turn for the worse when *Mardi, Moby-Dick,* and *Pierre* failed to win wide approval.

Melville tried without success to obtain a consular appointment (1853), was oppressed by financial worries and depression, but managed to publish more than a dozen stories and sketches in *Harper's New Monthly Magazine** and *Putnam's Monthly Magazine** (1853–1856). He serialized *Israel Potter* (1854) and republished it in book form a year later. ''Bartleby,'' ''The Bell-Tower,'' ''Benito Cereno,'' ''The Encantadas,'' and ''The Lightning-Rod Man'' he collected in *The Piazza Tales* (1856), for which he wrote ''The Piazza'' as an introductory sketch. Pieces not collected and reprinted in Melville's lifetime include ''Cock-a-Doodle-Doo!,'' ''Poor Man's Pudding and Rich Man's Crumbs,'' ''The Happy Failure,'' ''The Fiddler,'' ''The Paradise of Bachelors and Tartarus of Maids,'' ''Jimmy Rose,'' ''I and My Chimney,'' ''The 'Gees,'' and ''The Apple-Tree Table.'' (Melville's short story ''The Two Temples'' could not find any publisher in his lifetime.) Minor items and attributed pieces swell the total of prose writings slightly. Melville again went abroad (1856–1857), this time to Glasgow, Liverpool (where he rendezvoused with Hawthorne), the Holy Land, Greece, and Italy; he then returned home via England. *The Confidence-Man* (1857) followed, but it was such a popular and critical failure that Melville's professional writing career came to an end at this point. His eight major books sold roughly 35,000 copies and earned about $10,400 up to the time of his death in 1891.

Melville lectured for three winter seasons, on ''Statues in Rome'' (1857–1858), ''The South Seas'' (1858–1859), and ''Traveling: Its Pleasures, Pains, and Profits'' (1859–1860). Audience responses were mixed, and Melville netted rather little money—$400 during the first season, just over $500 for the second season, and just over $100 for the brief third season. Melville never published his lectures, and no manuscripts of them have survived. He restlessly traveled again, this time on the clipper ship captained by his brother Thomas, to San Francisco, returning via the Panama isthmus (1860). Melville failed again in his efforts to obtain a consular position (1861). Following Judge Shaw's death (1861), the Melvilles moved to New York and into Melville's brother Allan's house in Manhattan. Not long after visiting a Union army camp in Virginia following a Civil War military engagement nearby (1864), Melville published *Battle-Pieces* (1866). It includes ''The Portent (1859),'' written in 1859 after the ominous hanging of John Brown,* and ''Misgivings'' (1860), with these chilling lines—''I muse upon my country's ills— / The tempest bursting from the waste of Time / On the world's fairest hope linked with man's foulest crime.'' Other major titles include ''The College Colonel,'' ''The House-top: A

Night Piece (July, 1863)," "Malvern Hill (July, 1862)," "The March into Virginia," "Sheridan at Cedar Creek (October, 1864)," and "Shiloh: A Requiem (April, 1862)." After the war, Melville became an outdoor deputy customs inspector at the port of New York (1866–1885). Suspicion of insanity in Melville resulted in abortive talk of a marital separation (1867); later the same year, his older son Malcolm Melville committed suicide. Melville published *Clarel* (1876). His younger son died friendless in San Francisco (1886). Melville collected most of his sea poetry in *John Marr* (1888) and *Timoleon* (1891), and at his death he left more poems and *Billy Budd.*

Melville is one of America's most stirring authors. His early novels are delightfully romantic but are darkened with touches of dualism, as he contrasts primitivism and Christian morality, mindless pleasure and calculated cruelty. With *Mardi,* he grew more serious but then reverted to somewhat simpler narratives, until the time of his masterpiece, *Moby-Dick,* which mixes symbolism and ambiguity with factual details, autobiographical touches, and tingling adventure, all of which perplexed his first readers. With *Pierre* came permanent trouble, and not even the best of *The Piazza Tales* could revive interest in "that man who had lived among cannibals." After the complex and satirical ironies of *The Confidence-Man* failed to attract many readers in the generally optimistic reading public of the 1850s, Melville was aware that neither popular nor critical success could be his during his lifetime, if ever. The Civil War further depressed him, although it inspired him to write uniquely moving war poetry. He might have scored an autumnal success if he had chosen to polish and publish *Billy Budd.* Instead, he lapsed into near-silence in the 1870s and 1880s, apart from his exceedingly long religious poem *Clarel,* and it remained for the twentieth century to discover and laud his unique powers. It was not until the 1920s that his true worth began to be thoroughly understood.

Bibliography: Howard, Leyda.

Melville, Malcolm ("Barny," "Mackie," "Macky") (1849–1867). Melville's older son. He was born in Boston, in the home of Lemuel Shaw,* the father of Malcolm's mother Elizabeth Knapp Shaw Melville.* She made the boy her special pet. Not long after Melville's return from England (1850), Malcolm moved with his parents to Pittsfield, Massachusetts (1850). Soon he had a brother, Stanwix Melville,* and two sisters, Elizabeth Melville* and Frances Melville (later Frances Melville Thomas*). Malcolm attended a school (beginning summer 1853) in the vacation home of Oliver Wendell Holmes.* His mother often took her children to visit relatives in Boston and Gansevoort, New York. Upon the Melvilles' return to New York City (1863), Malcolm went to a boarding school outside Boston. He worked for a marine insurance company for $200 a year (beginning 1866). He joined an infantry unit of the New York State National Guard (c. 1867), was proud of his uniform, and had a pistol. On the night of 10–11 September 1867 he stayed out late with friends, returned home at 3:00 A.M., was mildly criticized by his mother, who then kissed him goodnight (Melville had retired). He was found the next day in his room dead of a self-inflicted gunshot wound in the head.

Bibliography: Cohen and Yannella; Leyda; Edwin E. Schneidman, ''Some Psychological Reflections on the Death of Malcolm Melville,'' *Suicide and Life-Threatening Behavior* 6 (Winter 1976): 231–42.

Melville, Maria Gansevoort (1791–1872). Melville's mother. She was the sixth and last child—and the only daughter—of Peter Gansevoort (1749–1812)* and Catherine Van Schaick Gansevoort.* In 1814 in Boston, she married Allan Melvill* and began to live with him comfortably in New York City. The couple had four sons and four daughters. They were Gansevoort Melville,* Helen Maria Melville Griggs,* Herman Melville,* Augusta Melville,* Allan Melville,* Catherine Gansevoort Melville Hoadley,* Frances Priscilla Melville,* and Thomas Melville.* When her husband, who moved his failing commercial interests to Albany, died bankrupt and insane there (1832), Maria Melville hoped that her son Gansevoort would salvage his father's fur and cap business. When it failed (1837), she moved with her family up the Hudson River to Lansingburgh to economize; she also had to rely on the charity of her brothers, mainly Peter Gansevoort (1788–1876),* other relatives, and also Lemuel Shaw,* a family friend and later Melville's father-in-law. When Gansevoort, her favorite son, died in London (1846), her next son, Herman, back from the sea and starting a literary career, became the head of the family; but she remained the critical, willful, perfection-demanding matriarch. His marriage (1847) resulted in crowded living arrangements: His mother and four sisters moved in with him, and with his recently married brother Allan and his wife, in a house in New York City, financed partly by Shaw and partly by Allan's in-laws (1847–1850).

Allan's mother approved of his sensible career as a lawyer. But when Melville moved with his family to Pittsfield, Massachusetts, his mother and sisters went along (1850–1863). She occasionally paid visits to relatives in the Albany area, taking her four daughters along, until two of them got married, after which she visited their new households. In *Pierre* (1852), Melville depicts his young hero's mother as matriarchal, as his own mother was, but initially more coy and capricious than the dour Maria. None of Melville's letters written to his mother during his trips to England, the Continent, the Holy Land, and California (1849–1850, 1856–1857, 1860) have survived; nor have any others written to her—with one exception (that of 5 May 1870). She sent some of these letters to her brother Peter and to other family members for their information, and they were undoubtedly discarded. When Melville and his family left Pittsfield and began their residence in New York again (from 1863), his mother established her own home in Gansevoort, New York, but for ten years she was a frequent visitor in various relatives' homes. For example, she was part of a family reunion on the occasion of Thomas Melville's marriage (1868), and she relished a Christmas reunion at his home later that year. She wrote to her brother Peter: ''I have seen my thirteen children & grandchildren they are all well & seemed to enjoy the

Christmas & New Years holidays. . . . On Christmas Day the whole family dined here'' (25 December 1868). She remained another six weeks, visited Melville and his family, and then returned home (April 1869). Her "successful" son Allan's death (1872) hastened her own seven weeks later. Maria Gansevoort Melville has been variously analyzed by biographical scholars. She came from a respected family. She had well-to-do relatives. Her husband's personality, behavior, and fate caused her emotional and financial distress. She was a possessive, humorless, domineering woman.

Bibliography: Cohen and Yannella; Howard; Leyda; Paul Metcalf, ed., *Enter Isabel: The Herman Melville Correspondence of Clare Spark and Paul Metcalf* (Albuquerque: University of New Mexico Press, 1991); Young.

Melville, Stanwix ("Stanny") (1851–1886). Melville's younger son. He was born in Pittsfield, Massachusetts, four days following the publication of *Moby-Dick*. He was named after the American Revolutionary War Fort Stanwix, defended by his maternal great-grandfather Peter Gansevoort (1749–1812)* and after Stanwix Gansevoort,* a grandson of old Peter Gansevoort. Young Stanwix and his brother Malcolm Melville* accompanied their parents on visits to relatives and were sometimes left with relatives, often in Gansevoort, New York— for example, when Melville journeyed to Europe and the Holy Land (1856– 1857). Stanwix Melville was evidently a sickly, troublesome lad. The suicide of his brother Malcolm (1867) damaged his spirits dreadfully. Stanwix worked as a clerk in the law office of his uncle Allan Melville,* quit because of deafness, went to sea as a passenger on a ship heading for China and captained by a friend of his seafaring uncle Thomas Melville* (April 1869), got to Shanghai (September), wrote home from London (January 1870), returned home (July), considered working with machinery for Melville's brother-in-law John Chipman Hoadley,* went instead to Kansas (May 1871) but returned home for Christmas, and trained to become a dentist but headed west again (1872). After he tried Kansas once more (April), he may have gone to New Orleans, and then surely proceeded to Cuba and a few Central American countries, including Costa Rica and Nicaragua. He suffered from shipwreck, fever, and loss of his possessions, but he got home again (February 1873) to resume dental training. When he decided that his nearsightedness would prevent his being a dentist, he took ship for San Francisco (April) and worked on a California sheep ranch. He returned home (June 1874), worked as a dental assistant again, fell ill (1875), returned to San Francisco, and worked as a wholesale-house clerk (November 1876). He wrote to his mother's brother Lemuel Shaw, Jr.* (December) of his plan to mine in the Black Hills and obtained funds from him to do so (January 1877). Whether he went into mining is uncertain. He received a $4,000 bequest upon the death of Martha Bird Knapp Marett (September 1878), who was his mother's aunt and the mother of Ellen Marett Gifford. At this time, Stanwix was in the San Francisco area, ill with pulmonary problems, but working as a canvasser. He moved to the San Rafael area for his health (1885). Melville sent him a power of attorney so that Melville could collect his son's share of the estate of Frances Priscilla Melville,* Stanwix's aunt; Stanwix signed it, returned it (14 February 1886), and died eleven days later of tuberculosis in a San Francisco hospital. Melville collected money due his dead son from his aunt (1886) and later from Ellen Gifford (1890).

   Bibliography: Howard, Leyda.

Melville, Thomas ("Tom") (1830–1884). Melville's brother. Thomas was the eighth and last child of Allan Melvill* and Maria Gansevoort Melville.* After the death of Gansevoort Melville,* Allan Melville* and Thomas were Melville's two surviving brothers. Melville's return after four years at sea (1844) undoubtedly fired young Tom's ambition to get away from home in Lansingburgh, New York, which was dominated by his mother and four sisters, and to try the manly nautical life himself. As soon as he turned sixteen, he joined a whaler out of Westport, Connecticut (1846), which freed a room for Melville to write *Omoo* in. Tom rejoined the family in New York City (1848), vainly sought work on land, and took to the sea again—this time on a commercial vessel to the Far East (1848). Melville dedicated *Redburn* to "Thomas Melville, Now a Sailor on a Voyage to China" (1849). Tom returned home via London (1850). He was chief mate on a vessel in the Australia-China trade (1852), docked in Boston off another vessel as second mate (1854), sailed as first mate aboard the clipper ship *Meteor* (launched in South Boston, 1852) bound for San Francisco and the East Indies (1855), sent word home from Hong Kong (1857), returned from Manila and Calcutta to Boston as the *Meteor*'s master (January 1859), visited happy family members, set sail for San Francisco (March 1859), and returned to Boston (April 1860). Melville accompanied Tom on the *Meteor,* her captain, from Boston to San Francisco (May–August 1860). Melville wrote to Evert Duyckinck* of the trip thus: "A noble ship and a nobler Captain—& he my brother" ([29] May 1860). Melville had planned to go around the world, but he abandoned the idea and returned home via Panama. Tom, with orders changed, sailed for England rather than for Manila, sold the *Meteor* in Calcutta, and returned home via California (January 1862). He made a final commercial voyage as captain of the *Bengal* (1862–1864), again including the Orient. Tom visited Melville in New York, took little trips with him, and attended the theater with him. Tom and their sister Catherine's husband John Chipman Hoadley* speculated successfully in oil and West Virginia land (1865). Supported by letters of recommendation from influential family friends, mainly Allan's, Tom was elected governor of the opulently appointed Sailors' Snug Harbor, on the northwest tip of Staten Island, New York (1867), at a salary of $2,000 per year, which was expected to be doubled a year later. Tom and his ultra-religious wife Catherine Eliza Bogart Melville,* whom he had married in 1868, had no children. During their eighteen years of marriage, Tom welcomed visits, long or otherwise, by various family members. Ultimately, his aging mother and unmarried sisters moved to Staten Island. Tom and his wife hosted huge dinners during the Christmas season (for example, 1871 and 1878). Throughout their adult lives, Tom was Melville's favorite brother and after Gansevoort's death became their mother's favorite son. Tom helped Stanwix Melville,* Melville's younger son, get passage for his first sea voyage (1869). Augusta Melville,* their sister, died in Tom's home (1876). Thomas Melville died suddenly of heart disease.

Bibliography: Gilman, Leyda, NN 14 and 15, Young.

Merenhout. In *Omoo. See* Moerenhout, Jacques-Antoine.

Merry Andrews. In "Marquis de Grandvin: Naples in the Time of Bomba . . .," they are happy people on the beach in Naples.

"Merry Ditty of the Sad Man" (1924). Poem, in *The Works of Herman Melville.* Nothing is so effective as singing to drive away the "blue-devils" of sorrow.

Merrymusk. In "Cock-a-Doodle-Doo!," he is the indigent wood-sawyer who owns the noble rooster called Trumpet, which he refuses to sell to the narrator or anyone else. Merrymusk is a Marylander and a former sailor. He, his wife, and their four children all finally die. So does Trumpet, who is also called Beneventano, Dr. Cock, and Shanghai.

Merrymusk. In "Cook-a-Doodle-Doo!," they are any of the ailing children of the Merrymusks. All die.

Merrymusk, Mrs. In "Cook-a-Doodle-Doo!," she is the mortally ill but uncomplaining wife of the indigent wood-sawyer and the mother of his four ailing children. The entire family dies.

Methodist. In *Clarel,* he is the chaplain of the ship *Apostles.* According to Agath, he composed a poem about the evening star, which was steadfast even in times of war.

Methodist, The. In *The Confidence-Man,* he is a tall army chaplain born in Tennessee. He saw service in the Mexican War and supports Black Guinea when he begs on the deck of the *Fidèle.*

Metrodorus. This was the name of five ancient philosophers. Metrodorus of Athens was a philosopher and painter. Metrodorus of Chios was a member of the Atomistic School. One Metrodorus of Lampsacus was a disciple of Epicurus; another was a pupil of Anaxagorus and an interpreter of works by Homer. And Metrodorus of Stratonice studied under Apollodorus and Carneades. A pupil of Nessus or perhaps of Democritus himself, this Metrodorus accepted Democritus's theory of atoms and the void and of the plurality of worlds. He also separately theorized that the stars were formed day after day by moisture in the air heated by the sun. He is quoted by Cicero in the *Academics* to the effect that "We know nothing, no, not even whether we know or not!" He further asserted that everything is to anyone only what it seems to be to that unique individual. In his poem entitled "The Garden of Metrodorus," Melville probably is referring to Metrodorus of Chios when he assigns the name Metrodorus to the owner of an Athenian garden. What may be found in that garden?— sadness, happiness, peace, sin?

Michelangelo (1475–1564). (Full name: Michelangelo [Michelagniolo] di Ludovico Buonarroti-Simone.) Italian painter, sculptor, architect, and writer. Michelangelo was born in Caprese, near Arezzo, into a fine Florentine family. His mother died when he was six years old. He was trained in painting (from 1488) and in sculpture (from 1489). He had the educative advantages of being patronized by Lorenzo de'Medici. He sought to balance and fuse rational classicism and Christian faith. Working in Rome (1496–1501), he created marble statues of *Bacchus* (1497) and *Pietà* (1500). His return in Florence (1501–1505) was marked by his *David* (1504). He was recalled to Rome by Pope Julius II (1505) to design and decorate his tomb, for which the artist's *Moses* (c.1515) was to be a part. Michenangelo turned to embellishing the Sistine Chapel in the Vatican (1508–1512). In its ceiling frescoes he illustrates the biblical history of humankind. Thereafter he lived in Florence (1516–1532) and Rome (1532–1545). Political changes in the Roman Catholic church caused Michelangelo to become disillusioned, although his statues in the Florentine Medici Chapel celebrate eternal beauty and dignity, if also suffering, in all people (1519–1534). His last period of creativity, mostly spent in Rome, is especially notable for his Sistine Chapel *Last Judgment* painting (1541) and for architectural contributions to the Farnese Palace (finished 1550), the Campidoglio and the Capitoline Hill, and Saint Peter's Basilica. His last fine sculpture, a Deposition often called the *Florentine Pietà* (c.1555), planned for his tomb, combines physical resignation and spiritual hope. His writings present a religious autobiography and include more than 300 sonnets.

In "Marquis de Grandvin: At the Hostelry," Michael Angelo is presented as an artist sitting in a withdrawn manner. [Adriaen] Brouwer is critical of him in conversation with [Fra Filippo] Lippi.

Bibliography: Ludwig Goldscheider, *Michelangelo: Paintings, Sculptures, Architecture* (Greenwich, Conn.: Phaidon Publishers, 1953); Robert S. Liebert, *Michelangelo: A Psychoanalytic Study of His Life and Images* (New Haven, Conn.: Yale University Press, 1983).

Mickle, William Julius (1735–1788). Man of letters, translator, and sailor. Mickle was born in Langholm, Dumfriesshire, Scotland, the son of a parish minister. After schooling in Langholm and Edinburgh, Mickle at age fifteen began to work in a brewery purchased by his father, inherited it when his father died (1757), ran it into debt, and moved to London to become a writer (1763). Having already published some poetry, he worked for the Clarendon Press in Oxford (1765) and published a translation of the *Lusiads* by Luíz Vaz de Camões* (1775). This translation (reprinted 1778, 1798, and 1807) was a free one but was true to the spirit of the original, had independent poetic merit, and earned Mickle £1,000. Still, he lacked steady work, wrote a poetic tragedy that no one produced, and was appointed to be Commodore George Johnstone's secretary aboard a ship heading for Portugal, where Mickle was honored by members of the royalty and where he wrote a poetic epistle about Lisbon (1781). Returning to England, he became an agent to dispose of naval prizes and grew rich in the process. He paid off his brewery debts, married an heiress named Mary Tomkins in 1781, settled near Oxford, and continued his literary career. A posthumous edition of his poems appeared in 1794, the proceeds from which benefited a surviving son.

In *White-Jacket,* Mickle is named as the translator of Camoens's *Lusiads* and as a fellow sailor with Jack Chase's father when both were aboard the man-of-war *Romney.*

Bibliography: Robert F. A. Fabel, *Bombast and Broadsides: The Lives of George Johnstone* (Tuscaloosa: University of Alabama Press, 1987).

Midni. In *Mardi,* he is an ontologist and entomologist, cited by Babbalanja.

"Milan Cathedral" (1891). Poem, in *Timoleon.* The poet sees, beyond the gardens of Lombardy and through "light green haze," the miraculous pinacles and spires of the cathedral. By placing "synodic hierarchies" of saints' statues in concourses high in the air, the builder must have intended "to signify the host of heaven." After seeing the vast cathedral, Melville appreciatively described it in his 1857 journal (7 April).

Bibliography: Cohen, *Poems;* NN 11 and 15; Shurr.

Milk-and-Water. In *White-Jacket,* this is a nickname for Pert.

Millet, Sir John. He was a farmer in Ealing in the late eighteenth century. In *Israel Potter,* he is a kindly Britisher who befriends Potter, even though he is aware that the wretched man is an escaped American. Millet employs him as his gardener at Brentford for six months. In Henry Trumbull's *Life and Remarkable Adventures of Israel R. Potter* (1824), Melville's principal source for his novel, Millet is called Sir John Millet, Sir John, Mr. Millet, and Mr. M.

Bibliography: Cohen, *Potter.*

Millthorpe. In *Pierre,* he is Charles ("Charlie") Millthorpe's deceased father. He was once a handsome, though also a poverty-stricken and melancholy, old farmer who lived on a small plot of Glendinning land.

Millthorpe, Charles ("Charlie"). In *Pierre,* he is the refined, sweet-tempered son of tenant farmers on a small plot of Glendinning land. He is twenty-two years of age. As a boy, he played with Pierre Glendinning. Shortly after his father's death, Millthorpe sold out and took his mother and sisters to the city and supported them by law and authorship among the Apostles. He helps Pierre in the city and offers to introduce him to Plotinus Plinlimmon. He tries to help Pierre in prison but arrives just after the fated youth has taken poison.

Millthorpe, Miss. In *Pierre,* she is any one of Charles Millthorpe's inquisitive, hopeless, and half-envious sisters.

Millthorpe, Mrs. In *Pierre,* she is Charles Millthorpe's gentle, thin, and retiring widowed mother. Pierre Glendinning remembers her well.

Milor. In "Marquis de Grandvin: Naples in the Time of Bomba . . . ," this is the term of respect which His Excellency the Neapolitan tumbler might have used in addressing Major John Gentian.

Mink. In "The Scout toward Aldie," he is a Union soldier wounded during the ambush set by [John Singleton] Mosby for the Colonel and his men.

Minta the Cynic. In *Mardi,* he is a legatee mentioned in Bardianna's will.

Miquel. In "Benito Cereno," he is a black slave assigned the task of striking the hours aboard Benito Cereno's *San Dominick.*

Miriam. In "Magian Wine," she is mentioned as one who prizes certain amulets.
Bibliography: NN 11.

"Misgivings (1860)" (1866). Poem, in *Battle-Pieces.* The poet watches an autumn storm fill "the sodden valley" with "horror" as a spire in town falls with a crash. Even while nature is revealing its "dark side," a storm is forming behind this one. The poet ponders his "country's ills." A tempest is about to break "[o]n the world's fairest hope," namely, America, which is "linked with man's foulest crime," in other words, slavery, disunion, fratricide.
Bibliography: Adler, Garner, NN 11, Shurr.

Miss Guy. In *Omoo,* this is a derogatory term for Captain Guy.

Moby-Dick (1851). (Full title: *Moby-Dick; or, the Whale;* title of first British edition: *The Whale* [1851].) Novel. (Characters: Captain Ahab, Archy, Azore Sailor, Belfast Sailor, Betty, Captain Bildad, Captain Boomer, Bulkington, Dr. Jack Bunger, Cabaco, Walter Canny, Captain, Captain, Captain, Captain, Aunt Charity, China Sailor, Johnny Coffin, Peter Coffin, Sal Coffin, Sam Coffin,

Deacon Deuteronomy Coleman, Nathan Coleman, Daggoo, Danish Sailor, Derick de Deer, Dough-Boy, Dutch Sailor, Elijah, Willis Ellery, Samuel Enderby, English Sailor, Fedallah, Fifth Nantucket Sailor, First Nantucket Sailor, Flask, Fleece, Fourth Nantucket Sailor, French Sailor, Gabriel, Gardiner, Gardiner, Captain Gardiner, Samuel Gleig, the Guernseyman, Captain Ezekiel Hardy, Mrs. Ezekiel Hardy, Harry, Hay-Seed, a High-Chief, a High Priest, Hosea Hussey, Mrs. Hosea Hussey, Iceland Sailor, Ishmael, Jack, Jenny, Joe, Jonah, The King of Kokovoko, Lascar Sailor, Lazarus, Robert Long, Long Island Sailor, Harry Macey, Mrs. Harry Macey, Seth Macy, Maltese Sailor, the Manxman, Father Mapple, Captain Mayhew, Mounttop, Old Gay-Head Indian, Don Pedro, Captain Peleg, Perth, Perth, Mrs. Perth, Pip, Portuguese Sailor, Queequeg, Radney, Mrs. Radney, St. Jago's Sailor, Don Sebastian, Second Nantucket Sailor, Sicilian Sailor, Snarles, Dr. Snodhead, Spanish Sailor, Starbuck, Starbuck, Starbuck, Starbuck, Mary Starbuck, Steelkilt, Stiggs, Stubb, Sub-Sub, Nathan Swain, Tahitian Sailor, John Talbot, Miss Talbot, Tashtego, Third Nantucket Sailor, Tistig, Tranquo, Usher.)

The narrator begins his account with the words "Call me Ishmael." He leaves Manhattan for New Bedford to seek work on a whaler. At an inn he meets Queequeg, a friendly Polynesian sailor. In the morning he attends Father Mapple's Whaleman's Chapel. Ishmael and Queequeg take a schooner to Nantucket and sign for duty aboard the *Pequod,* the captain of which is Ahab, who lost a leg to a monstrous whale and has only half recovered. Elijah, a pock-marked prophet, warns them about serving Ahab. Ishmael and Queequeg fancy that they see four or five shadowy figures dart onto the *Pequod,* which on Christmas Day "blindly plunged like fate into the lone Atlantic." Starbuck, a married Quaker, is first mate and wants Queequeg as his harpooner. Happy-go-lucky, cool Stubb from Cape Cod, the second mate, wants Tashtego, a noble Gay Head Indian, for his harpooner. The third mate, pugnacious Flask of Martha's Vineyard, selects an enormous African-American named Daggoo for his harpooner. Finally "moody stricken Ahab," the *Pequod*'s captain, appears on the quarterdeck and soon tosses his pleasureless pipe over the side in the bright springtime. At the masthead one day, Ishmael lets dangerous pantheistic thoughts interfere with his looking out for whales. Ahab assembles the crew, nails a gold coin to the mast, and promises to give it to the first man to sight Moby Dick, the white, wrinkle-browed, crooked-jawed whale with punctures in his left fluke. When Ahab says that that whale "dismasted" him, the crew voices loyalty. Starbuck complains that the voyage is for profit and not revenge on a dumb brute, but Ahab overmans him by defining Moby Dick as inscrutable malice.

Ishmael records that the huge Moby Dick seems possessed of an "unexampled, intelligent malignity" and that its weirdly white color may represent "a dumb blankness," the "indefiniteness" of which "shadows forth the heartless voids and immensities of the universe." Ahab heads for the southern tip of Africa so as to make for the equatorial hunting grounds of the Pacific Ocean. One sultry day while Ishmael is weaving a mat and pondering necessity, free will, and chance, Tashtego sights a sperm whale. Five dusky phantoms emerge on deck. They are Ahab's prophetic friend Fedallah and that Parsee's crew of tiger-yellow Orientals. The *Pequod*'s first chase after a whale ends in failure. When southeast of the Cape of Good Hope, her crew hails the *Goney* but learns nothing about Moby Dick's whereabouts. Then the *Pequod* gams with the *Town-Ho* and hears about Steelkilt, a Lakeman who, when provoked, struck his officer Radney, was flogged, and planned to kill Radney; but he was spared the trouble when Moby Dick chewed Radney to bits. Steelkilt escaped to Tahiti and beyond. Daggoo mistakes a squid for the white whale. In the Indian Ocean, Stubb lowers for a whale, kills it in a gory way, and dines on whale steak while sharks thrash the sea and tear off pieces of whale meat at the water level. Next day is the Sabbath, broken by topside butchery as the crew cuts strips of blubber and tries out innumerable barrels of oil. The men learn from the *Jeroboam* that Moby Dick has just killed her chief mate and therefore Ahab cannot deliver a letter to him. When the *Pequod* hangs the heads of a right whale and a sperm whale on opposite yardarms, Ishmael contrasts them as Stoical and Kantean. Queequeg rescues Tashtego when the noble fellow falls into the sperm whale's head and into the sea with it; Queequeg's sword thus resembles an obstetrician's scalpel.

The *Pequod* meets the *Jungfrau,* sadly devoid of sperm oil. Daggoo, Queequeg, and Tashtego kill a sick whale, which promptly sinks from sight. Ahab steers between Sumatra and Java, aiming for the Philippines and the coastal waters of Japan. Ishmael and his friends see an armada of whales, some dallying amorously. Weeks later, Stubb talks an ignorant crew aboard the *Bouton de Rose* into giving him precious ambergris inside a diseased whale's corpse. Pip, the little black cabin boy from Alabama, falls into the water and is demented when rescued. Thereafter, Pip is tenderly treated by Ahab. One day Ahab explicates the image of three mountains on his nailed coin in such a way as to reflect credit upon himself. Starbuck interprets the mountains as the Trinity. Stubb takes note of the zodiacal arch over the peaks. Flask sees nothing of symbolic value. The *Pequod* encounters the *Samuel Enderby,* whose captain lost an arm to Moby Dick but regards the whale as displaying ''awkwardness'' not ''malice.'' Admitting that ''an accursed thing is not always what least allures,'' Ahab rushes away, wrenches his ivory leg, and orders his carpenter to make him a new one. Queequeg inspects leaky oil casks in the hold, catches a chill which turns to a deadly fever, and orders the carpenter to make him a coffin; but he recovers. When his ship enters the vast Pacific, Ahab orders his blacksmith to fashion a special harpoon barb, which he tempers blasphemously in heathen blood from Daggoo, Queequeg, and Tashtego, saying ''Ego non baptizo te in nomine patris, sed in nomine diaboli!'' The *Bachelor* sails by, loaded with sperm oil and bound for home in Nantucket. Ahab watches a whale swing its head toward the setting sun and die. Fedallah predicts that Ahab will have neither hearse nor coffin, that he will see two hearses, that Fedallah will precede his captain to death, and that only hemp can kill Ahab.

Ahab discards his quadrant, plows through a typhoon, addresses fiery corposants on his yardarms, replaces a lightning-turned compass with one of his own devising, and loses his log and log line. When a man falls overboard and sinks along with a buoy hurled after him, Queequeg has his coffin lidded and caulked as a kind of buoy. Ahab refuses to aid the *Rachel,* outfought by Moby Dick, in a search for her missing sailors. Ahab seeks only his enemy. The *Delight* rolls by, in a shambles after the white whale attacked her. Ahab reminisces gently in Starbuck's presence, "dropped a tear in the sea," but resumes the pursuit. They sight Moby Dick, and three days of attack follow. On the first day, Moby Dick bites Ahab's small boat in two. On the second day, after Moby Dick smashes three boats pursuing him, Ahab's ivory leg and Fedallah are missing. On the third day, Ahab chases the white whale, on whose back fouled lines have tangled Fedallah, who thus points his captain the way to death. The whale is the prophet's hearse. Moby Dick smashes the small boat and kills all in it but one tossed free, then butts a fatal hole in the *Pequod* herself. Ahab recognizes her as the second hearse. When Moby Dick turns back toward Ahab, the fated man lances his monster, but a harpoon line loops around the man and he is carried to his doom. The *Pequod* sinks. The lone survivor, Ishmael, floats on Queequeg's coffin and is plucked from the shroud-like sea by the *Rachel.*

Moby-Dick is enormous, with a prefatory "Etymology" and "Extracts" (i.e., quotations about whales), 135 chapters, and an "Epilogue." In more than forty chapters, Melville has Ishmael suspend his narrative to offer cetological information, beginning with Chapters 24 and 25, "The Advocate" and "Postscript," in which he discusses the goriness of whaling, the uses of whale oil, and the predominance of Americans in the whaling industry. Other cetological digressions concern types of whales, specific functions of men involved in whaling, the dangers and seeming fatalism of hunting specific whales, pictures of whales, the food of whales, the harpoon and its accoutrements, cutting up the blubber, the whale's anatomy, "The Glory and Honor of Whaling" (Chapter 82), schools of whales as "The Grand Armada" (Chapter 87), whales as lovers, symbolism in "Fast-Fish and Loose-Fish" (Chapter 89, the former being hooked, the latter wounded but free), ambergris, and finally "Does the Whale's Magnitude Diminish?—Will He Perish?" (Chapter 105). "The Gam" (Chapter 53) defines the meeting at sea of whaling vessels; nine irregularly spaced chapters (Chapters 52, 54, 71, 81, 91, 100, 115, 128, 131) are devoted to gams of the *Pequod* and other whalers. Beginning with "Enter Ahab; to him, Stubb" (Chapter 29), there are eleven chapters (continuing with Chapters 36–40, 108, 120–122, and 127) cast in the form of mini-dramas with stage directions, soliloquies, and dialogue.

Moby-Dick, though written and rewritten in several stages and not perfectly assembled, is one of the greatest novels in world literature. Sadly, Melville was right when he complained in a letter to his friend Nathaniel Hawthorne* ([1 June? 1851]): "The calm, the coolness, the silent grass-growing mood in which a man *ought* always to compose,—that, I fear, can seldom be mine. Dollars damn me; and the malicious Devil is forever grinning in upon me, holding the door ajar." Melville added this: "What I feel most moved to write, that is banned,—it will not pay. Yet, altogether, write the *other* way I cannot. So the product is a final hash, and all my books are botches.'' *Moby-Dick,* though imperfect, is anything but a botch. It appeals to readers on several levels. Young readers like its wild adventure. Older readers find its varied style most appealing. And all readers should be challenged by ''moody, stricken'' Ahab, who is partly Promethean but also partly Satanic. He seeks monomaniacally to destroy the seemingly ubiquitous, omniscient, omnipotent white whale, which he perceives as hugely malevolent. Yet his desire for revenge on what Starbuck calls ''a dumb brute'' is insane, if not, as Starbuck adds, ''blasphemous,'' and that desire ruins the innocent.

In writing *Moby-Dick,* Melville drew upon his personal experiences aboard whale ships, especially the *Acushnet,* as well as sailors' yarns told there and elsewhere, for details of the whaling fishery. Aboard the *Acushnet,* the following sailors may have provided details of characterization, thus: John Backus, for Pip; Martin Brown and Joseph Luis (called Jo Portuguese), for the Portuguese sailor; George W. Galvan, for Flask; John Hall, for Stubb; Valentine Pease, Jr., for Ahab; Frederick R. Raymond, for Starbuck; James Rosman, for the Belfast sailor; and Ephraim Walcott, for Perth. In addition, Melville read the following books for background material: Thomas Beale, *The Natural History of the Sperm Whale to Which Is Added a Sketch of a South-Sea Whaling Voyage in Which the Author Was Personally Engaged* (London, 1839); Frederick Debell Bennett, *Narrative of a Whaling Voyage round the Globe, from the 1833 to 1836...* (London, 1840); J. Ross Browne,* *Etchings of a Whaling Cruise...* (1846); Owen Chase,* *Narrative of the Most Extraordinary and Distressing Shipwreck of the Whale-Ship Essex, of Nantucket; Which Was Attacked and Finally Destroyed by a Large Spermaceti-Whale in the Pacific Ocean...* (New York, 1821); Henry T. Cheever, *The Whale and His Captors; or, the Whaleman's Adventures, and the Whale's Biography...* (New York, 1849); Richard Henry Dana, Jr.,* *Two Years Before the Mast* (New York, 1840); Jeremiah N. Reynolds,* ''Mocha Dick: or the White Whale of the Pacific: A Leaf from a Manuscript Journal'' (*Knickerbocker,* May 1839); William Scoresby, Jr., *An Account of the Arctic Regions, with a History and Description of the Northern Whale Fishery* (Edinburgh, 1820); Scoresby's *Journal of a Voyage to the Northern Whale-Fishery; Including Researches and Discoveries on the Eastern Coast of West Greenland... in... 1822* (Edinburgh, 1823); Charles Wilkes, *United States Exploring Expedition...* (Philadelphia, 1844–1846); and much else. Melville's manner of plundering his autobiographical, historical, literary, and scientific sources is complicated almost beyond analysis.

When it was first published, *Moby-Dick* attracted many reviews both in the United States and in England. Some reviewers admired the narrative, the descriptive passages, the humor, the philosophy, and the unusual literary form. Others objected to the form, the impiety, and the interjected cetological material. *Moby-Dick* sold about 2,000 copies in the United States in its first few months but in the following third of a century considerably under 2,000 more. Genuinely perceptive criticism and valuable scholarship on *Moby-Dick* did not commence until well into the twentieth century.

Bibliography: Walter E. Bezanson, ''*Moby-Dick:* Document, Drama, Dream,'' pp. 169–210 in Bryant, *Companion;* Brian Higgins and Hershel Parker, eds., *Critical Essays on Herman Melville's Moby-Dick* (New York: G. K. Hall, 1992); NN 6.

Mocmohoc. In *The Confidence-Man,* he is mentioned as a perfidious Native American. He treacherously killed the Wrights and the Weavers, who were migrants from Virginia to Kentucky.

Moerenhout, Jacques-Antoine (1796–1879). French diplomat. He was born in Ekeren, Belgium, at a time when the region was occupied by French revolutionary army forces. He served in the French army (1812–1814), went into business in Antwerp, and was hired to become the private secretary of the Dutch consul in Chile (1826–1829). On his way to Valparaiso, he spent fourteen months in Tahiti (1828–1829) after the vessel to take him the rest of his way had sunk by accident. While in Tahiti, he looked into the commercial possibilities of the pearl and pearl-shell trade, became a planter in Papeete, reported to Valparaiso, and returned to Papeete as a commercial negotiator. Back in Valparaiso again, he married a Chilean named Petronila Garcia y la Guerta (1833) and established a home with her in Papeete (1834). After a mysterious voyage taking him to the United States and France, he returned to Tahiti as U.S. consul there (1836) and had an audience with Queen Pomare IV* (1836). Having given support and asylum to a few Catholic missionaries from France, he was relieved as U.S. consul (1837) and became French consul (1838), whereupon he criticized the American position and also that of England being voiced by George Pritchard,* his commercial rival and the British consul in Tahiti as well. Moerenhout and his wife were attacked by a half-Indian and half-black sailor from Mexico. Moerenhout was injured and his wife was mortally wounded; the murderer was apprehended and executed (1838). Abel Aubert Dupetit-Thouars,* the French naval commander in the area, presented Moerenhout as French consul to Queen Pomare (1838, confirmed 1839) and as commissioner of the king of France (1839). When Armand-Joseph Bruat,* the French governor of Tahiti (as of 1843), replaced him, Moerenhout became director of native affairs and helped Bruat (1843). Moerenhout painted an attractive watercolor portrait of Queen Pomare. After disputes involving British vessels, he was sent as French consul to Monterey, California (1845–1848, 1852–1859), and became consul to Los Angeles (1859–1879), where he died. His detailed *Voyages aux îles du Grand Océan . . .* (2 vols., 1837) contains a moving passage in which he deplores the forcing of European commercial, political, religious, social, and other habits on the Polynesian natives, to their detriment.

In *Omoo,* Melville calls Merenhout the hated commissioner royal under the hated French governor Bruat of Tahiti.

Bibliography: J. A. Moerenhout, *Travels to the Islands of the Pacific Ocean* (Lanham, Md.: University Press of America, 1992); Newbury; O'Reilly and Teissier; George Pritchard, *The Aggressions of the French at Tahiti and Other Islands in the Pacific,* ed. Paul De Deckker (Auckland University Press, 1983).

Mogul. In *Moby-Dick,* this is the crew's nickname for Captain Ahab.

Mohi ("Braid-Beard," "Champollion Mohi"). In *Mardi,* he is the bearded historian from the isle of Odo. He accompanies Taji, along with King Media of Odo, Babbalanja, and Yoomy, on Taji's long and fruitless search for Yillah. Mohi and Yoomy leave Taji on the isle of Flozella-a-Nina but return from Odo to try to rescue him from Queen Hautia of Flozella. The narrator calls Mohi "Champollion Mohi" when he is able to decipher an inscription on a Vivenza statue. He becomes a convert in the haven of Serenia. The name Mohi may be Melville's variation on the name of Muhji ed-Din ibn 'Ali ed-Dīn al-Jamāli, a sixteenth-century Turkish historian, or Melville's variation on the name of Mohijeddin Al-Arabi, a mystic sheikh of Islam.

Bibliography: Davis, Finkelstein.

Moll. In *Omoo. See* Mother Moll.

Molly. In *Billy Budd. See* Bristol Molly.

Molly. In *Redburn,* she is a servant girl at Handsome Mary Danby's Baltimore Clipper in Liverpool.

Mondi. In *Mardi,* he is a neighbor of Bardianna and is mentioned in the philosopher's will.

Monee. In *Omoo,* he is the grinning, paunchy, bald old man who acts as a cook and butler for Deacon Ereemear Po-Po at Partoowye.

"Monody" (1891). Poem, in *Timoleon.* The poet laments the death of one whom he "loved . . . / After loneness" but was then "estranged" from—and with "neither in the wrong." Now his grave is draped by icy snow, as a shy grape might be hidden by a "cloistral vine." Melville may have had his dear but "estranged" friend Nathaniel Hawthorne* in mind here. Evidence is not limited to but includes the poet's use of the word "vine." Vine, the sensitive, withdrawn, highly moral character in *Clarel,* may be Melville's sketch of Hawthorne.

Bibliography: Cohen, *Poems;* Harrison Hayford, *Melville's "Monody": Really for Hawthorne?* (Evanston, Ill.: Northwestern University Press, 1990); NN 11 and 12; Shurr; Stein; Warren.

Monoo. In *Typee,* he is a Typee chief and warrior of long ago. According to Kory-Kory, Monoo built the foundation of the sacred Hoolah Hoolah ground in a single day.

Montaigne, Michel Eyquem de (1533–1592). French essayist. He was born in his well-to-do family's chateau outside Bordeaux, studied classical humanism from the age of six, and studied law, probably at Toulouse (1546–1550). He succeeded his father as counselor of the Bordeaux parliament (1557–1570), was elected mayor of Bordeaux (1581–1585), and thereafter lived in considerable seclusion in the Montaigne chateau, where he read, studied, and wrote. His first published work was a translation of *Theologia naturalis* (1569), by Raymond Sebond, a Catalan theologian. Montaigne's essays—he invented the form and gave it respectability—are his legacy (3 vols., 1580, 1580, 1588). Varying in length and mood, the best are solid discussions of profound topics such as aging, conversation, death, disillusionment, education, experience, foolishness, friendship, illness, inconsistency, pain, repentance, sex, and virtue. Montaigne married Françoise de la Chassaigne in 1565, was not happy with her, had several children, and lost all of them in their infancy except a daughter, of whom he was not fond. Montaigne adopted Marie de Gourney, who edited his works.

Melville admired Montaigne because his works revealed an honest, inconsistent, modest, paradoxical, and skeptical mind. In Melville's poem ''Montaigne and His Kitten,'' Montaigne speaks about immortality to Blanche, his kitten.

Bibliography: Gorman Beauchamp, ''Melville, Montaigne and the Cannibals,'' *Arizona Quarterly* 37 (Winter 1981): 293–309; Elizabeth De Mijolla, *Autobiographical Quests: Augustine, Montaigne, Rousseau, and Wordsworth* (Charlottesville: University Press of Virginia, 1994); Patrick Henry, ed., *Approaches to Teaching Montaigne's Essays* (New York: Modern Language Association of America, 1994).

''Montaigne and His Kitten'' (1924). Poem, in *The Works of Herman Melville.* (Character: [Michel Eyquem de] Montaigne.) Montaigne explains to Blanche, his kitten, that the two of them avoid ambitious activity, since it seldom alleviates ''life's pain.'' Around the kitten's neck he ties a ribbon given to him by the King. He asks Blanche if she wants the ''grandiose eternity'' reserved for humankind to include her. It is wrong to exclude animals. Anyway, Montaigne concludes, let's frolic and let serious thinkers ''fool it while they may!'' Charles IX, of the House of Valois, was the king of France when in 1571 Montaigne was decorated by the Order of St. Michael.

Bibliography: Cohen, *Poems;* Shurr.

Montgomery. In *White-Jacket,* he is the midshipman who is ordered by his lieutenant to break open a chest mailed by the sergeant-at-arms Bland to the purser. The chest contains contraband liquor.

Moonoony. In *Typee,* she is the damsel of Mehevi, who also shares her affections with a fifteen-year-old lad.

Morairi, José. In "Benito Cereno," he is one of Alexandro Aranda's young clerks. He is from Cadiz and was a passenger aboard the *San Dominick.*

Mordant, Captain. In *Billy Budd,* he is Captain Edward Fairfax Vere's captain of marines. He is a good-natured, obese, brave officer. He serves on the drumhead court and reluctantly votes to condemn Billy Budd to death.

Mordecai. In *Omoo,* he is a villainous-looking juggler who is part of the rabble around King Tammahamaha III of Hawaii (*see* Kamehameha III).

Moredock. In *The Confidence-Man,* this is the name of the family of Moredock Hall, in Northamptonshire, England, mentioned by Francis Goodman but not related to Colonel John Moredock.

Moredock. In *The Confidence-Man,* he was Colonel John Moredock's father, massacred by Indians.

Moredock, Colonel John. In *The Confidence-Man,* he is the celebrated Indian-hater whose life Francis Goodman summarizes in conversation with Charles Noble. In real life, John Moredock was habitually a decent husband and family man, until he was off on one or another of his killing expeditions. Melville's major source was *Sketches of History, Life, and Manners, in the West* (2 vols., 1835), by James Hall. In Part IV, Chapter VI, entitled "Indian hating—Some of the Sources of this Animosity—Brief Account of Col. Moredock"—Hall tells about the massacre by Indians of Moredock's mother's sequence of husbands and of his own siblings, about his woodsmanship, and about his cunning in vengefully stalking and killing Indians. Hall goes on to detail Moredock's being an early settler in Illinois territory, "a ranging officer during the war of 1813–14," a territorial legislator, and a militia officer. Hall adds that Moredock helped form the Illinois state government, respectfully declined to be a candidate for governor, and died of old age (c.1831). Hall also discusses the Treaty of Fort Stanwix (1768).

   Bibliography: Joyce Sparer Adler, "Melville on the White Man's War against the American Indian," *Science and Society* 36 (Winter 1972): 417–42; Richard Drinnon, *Facing West: The Metaphysics of Indian-Hating and Empire-Building* (Minneapolis: University of Minnesota Press, 1980).

Moredock, Mrs. In *The Confidence-Man,* she is Colonel John Moredock's mother. Her three husbands and eight of her nine children were massacred by Indians, thus causing her one surviving child to become a ruthless Indian-hater.

Moredock, Mrs. John. In *The Confidence-Man,* she is Colonel John More-dock's wife, for whom the Indian-hater provided well.

Morewood, John Rowland (1821–1903). Melville's friend. Morewood and his wife Sarah Huyler Morewood* returned from Europe and for $6,500 bought the Melvill family homestead, called Broadhall, just outside Pittsfield, Massachusetts (1850). In anticipation of the sale, Melville bought the adjoining farm, soon called Arrowhead (1850). Thus began a mutually fruitful association with Melville and his family, once they moved into the area from New York City. Morewood cosigned the contract Melville agreed to (1851) for the publication by Richard Bentley* in London of *The Whale,* later entitled *Moby-Dick.* Melville was encouraged to borrow books from the Morewood library. Morewood honored Colonel William Francis Bartlett,* the heroic subject of Melville's poem "The College Colonel," when he led his regiment back to Pittsfield (1863). Morewood felt even closer to Melville when in 1876 the widowed man's son William Barlow Morewood married Maria Gansevoort Melville, the oldest daughter of Allan Melville,* Melville's brother. One of Morewood's Pittsfield friends was the journalist Joseph Edward Adams Smith.*

Bibliography: Garner, Leyda, NN 14.

Morewood, Sarah Huyler (1824–1863). Melville's friend. She was from the well-to-do Huyler family of Passaic, New Jersey. She and her husband John Rowland Morewood* returned from Europe, settled in Pittsfield (1850), and became friendly with Melville and his family there. Mrs. Morewood was a bright, lively, and charming woman who organized parties, picnics, and little trips in the Berkshires, in which all sorts of cultured people—for example, Evert Duyckinck* and his brother George Duyckinck,* Nathaniel Hawthorne* and his wife Sophia, Oliver Wendell Holmes,* Cornelius Mathews,* and the Melvilles—gratefully participated. Mathews wrote up one such excursion. In an essay entitled "Several Days in the Berkshire" (*Literary World* [24 August 1850]), he disguises references to Mrs. Morewood by calling her "Fairy Belt." Evert Duyckinck wrote letters to his wife about another such venture, which Mrs. Morewood organized to climb nearby Greylock Mountain (August 1851). Melville wrote to her to advise her not to read his "forthcoming" *Moby-Dick* ([12 or 19? September 1851]). After Mrs. Morewood went at one time with the Melvilles to Lake Pontoosuc, she wrote to George Duyckinck about Melville's increasing delight in the place (8 October 1851). On another occasion, she wrote to Duyckinck to praise Augusta Melville* as the finest of Melville's sisters (27 October 1851). Mrs. Morewood came to like Melville more and more, but she disliked his "irreverent language," as she put it in a letter to Duyckinck after a big Christmas dinner the Melvilles attended at the Morewood home (28 December 1851); she added that she felt "strangely attached" to Melville's wife Elizabeth Knapp Shaw Melville.* Mrs. Morewood in a letter to Duyckinck expressed disapproval of Melville's brother Allan Melville* for remarrying, saying "he is now only an acquaintance of the past" (9 April 1860). In another letter to Duyckinck, she voiced disapproval of *Elsie Venner,* the novel by her summer neighbor Oliver Wendell Holmes*: "He has created a Storm in many quarters" (20 March 1861); it has been suggested that Holmes's heroine is based partly on Sarah Morewood. One of Mrs. Morewood's Pittsfield friends was the journalist Joseph Edward Adams Smith.* She contributed to Smith's *Taghconic; or, Letters and Legends about Our Summer Home* (1852). During the Civil War, she was kind to wounded and ill soldiers in a hospital near her residence. She died of tuberculosis. Thirteen years later, in 1876, Maria Gansevoort Melville, the oldest daughter of Allan Melville, married the Morewoods' son William Barlow Morewood.

Bibliography: Garner; Leyda; NN 14; Hershel Parker, with Edward Daunais, "Sarah Morewood's Last Drive, as Told in Caroline S. Whitmarsh's 'A Representative Woman,' " *Melville Society Extracts* 93 (June 1993): 1–4.

Morille. In *Redburn,* he is a person whom Redburn's father called upon in Liverpool in 1808.

Morn, Captain. In "The Scout toward Aldie," he is the officer ordered by the Colonel to picket the roads and stop all travelers, during their ill-fated pursuit of [John Singleton] Mosby.

Morrison, William Ralls (1824?–1909). Soldier and politician. Morrison was born in Monroe County, Illinois. His mother died early, and his father remarried and managed an inn in Waterloo, Illinois, where the boy overheard much political talk. He became a deputy sheriff at age twenty-two, fought during the Mexican War under General Zachary Taylor* at Buena Vista (1847), sought gold in California (1849), and returned home to attend McKendree College (1850–1852). He became a clerk in the Waterloo circuit court (1852–1854), and while serving in the state legislature (1854–1860) he studied law and passed the bar. At the onset of the Civil War, Morrison organized an Illinois infantry regiment, became its colonel, and was wounded during the siege of Fort Donelson (February 1862). While in command in the field, he was elected to the U.S. Congress as a Democrat and served (1863–1865). He was returned to the state legislature (1871–1872) and to congress (1873–1887). He was a member of the Interstate Commerce Commission (1887–1897), after which he went home again to Waterloo to practice law and to farm. Morrison married Mary Jane Drury in 1852, fathered two sons who died young, was widowed, married his deceased wife's half-sister Eleanora Horine, and had another child who died in infancy.

Melville's poem "Donelson (February, 1862)" has the following erroneous couplet: "We mourn the loss of Colonel Morrison, / Killed while cheering his regiment on."

Bibliography: James J. Hamilton, *The Battle of Fort Donelson* (South Brunswick, N.J.: Thomas Yoseloff, 1968).

Mortmain ("The Swede"). In *Clarel,* he is an illegitimate Swede, unloved by both parents. He was a revolutionary leader in Paris and a wanderer, and he is now a politically, philosophically, and spiritually desperate masochist. His name means "dead hand," and he wears a black skullcap. He dies of psychic exhaustion high up in the rocks at Mar Saba. Mortmain shares traits with both Captain Ahab of *Moby-Dick* and Bartleby of "Bartleby."

Bibliography: NN 12.

Mosby, John Singleton (1833–1916). Confederate officer. He was born near Richmond, Virginia, attended the University of Virginia, shot and wounded a fellow student, and was jailed for a time. He studied law, passed the bar (1855), and was practicing law in Bristol, Virginia, when the Civil War began. Mosby joined a cavalry unit, fought at the First Battle of Bull Run (July 1861), was commissioned first lieutenant (February 1862), became a scout for General James E. B. Stuart,* and at the time of the Seven Days' Battle (July) developed the strategy of riding around the army ineptly commanded by Union General George B. McClellan.* Stuart gave Mosby permission to organize and lead the Partisan Rangers (January 1863). His group captured a Union general, many of his men, and their mounts, at Fairfax Court House, Virginia (March). Mosby's rangers were independent until mustered into the regular Confederate army (June). They harassed Union forces in northern Virginia, an area sometimes called "Mosby's Confederacy," so exasperatingly that General Ulysses S. Grant* ordered that Mosby be summarily hanged if captured. When Union forces caught and hanged seven of his rangers, Mosby hanged an equal number of enemy prisoners, wrote to General Philip H. Sheridan* to explain and to express the hope that this kind of conduct need not be repeated, and thus put a stop to it (November 1864). Mosby advanced in rank, from captain (March 1863) to major (April) to lieutenant colonel (February 1864) to colonel (December). He controlled up to 800 highly disciplined men, split into parties of from 20 to 80 men. Wounded seven times, he was physically slight, aggressive and determined, but never cruel. Mosby contended that he prevented as many as 30,000 enemy troops from getting into front-line combat engagements. General Robert E. Lee* mentioned him in dispatches, orders, and reports more often than he did any other Confederate officer. After the war, Mosby practiced law in Warrenton, Virginia, supported Grant for president, was U.S. consul in Hong Kong (1878–1885), practiced law in California, and served as an attorney in the U.S. Justice Department (1904–1910). He published *Mosby's War Reminiscences, and Stuart's Cavalry Campaign* (1887) and *Stuart's Cavalry in the Gettysburg Campaign* (1908). Mosby married Pauline Clarke of Kentucky in 1855 and was survived by three daughters and one son.

Melville's cousin Henry Sanford Gansevoort,* a Union officer, tried unsuccessfully to capture Mosby, whom Melville mentions in two poems in *Battle-Pieces.* In "The Armies of the Wilderness," Mosby is described as having his men on the prowl. In "The Scout toward Aldie," he is the elusive partisan leader who outwits his Union pursuers near Aldie. He may be the Confederate prisoner who, after attempting to escape, feigns injury from a fall. *See also* Slyboots, Sir.

Bibliography: Jeffry D. Wert, *Mosby's Rangers* (New York: Simon and Schuster, 1990); Wilson.

Moss-Rose. In "Amoroso." *See* Rosamond.

Mossy Man, The. In "Hawthorne and His Mosses." *See* Hawthorne, Nathaniel.

Mother Moll. In *Omoo,* she is an expert at making muffins and is fondly remembered by Rope Yarn.

"The Mound by the Lake" (1866). Poem, in *Battle-Pieces.* The grass will remember the grave of that single woman who set a "wayside table" for the weary soldiers as they painfully made their way home. Childless and unwed, she comforted them "like a mother." In this poem, Melville is implicitly eulogizing a woman named Mrs. Deacon Curtis T. Fenn, who cared for sick and wounded Union soldiers resting in Pittsfield, Massachusetts. Sarah Huyler Morewood* and Melville's wife Elizabeth Knapp Shaw Melville,* among other Pittsfield women, helped Mrs. Fenn in her selfless work.

Bibliography: Garner.

Mounttop. In *Moby-Dick,* he is the first mate of the *Samuel Enderby,* whose captain, Boomer, lost his right arm while chasing Moby Dick.

Mowanna, King. In *Typee,* he is the ruler of Nukuheva. He is encouraged by the French to foment trouble involving Nukuheva, the Typees, and the Happers. Mowanna has a tattooed wife.

Mow Mow. In *Typee,* he is the fierce, one-eyed Typee chief who is wounded in a victorious engagement with a group of Happars. He later opposes Tommo's successful effort to escape to the Australian vessel in the harbor. (His name is also given as Mow-Mow.)

Mowree, The. In *Omoo. See* Bembo.

Moyar. In *Pierre,* he is the loyal African-American servant of General Pierre Glendinning, Pierre's grandfather.

"Mr. Parkman's Tour" (1849). Review. Melville's review of *The California and Oregon Trail* by Francis Parkman was published in the *Literary World* (31 March 1849), edited by Melville's friends Evert Duyckinck* and his brother George Duyckinck.* Melville calls the work entertaining, straightforward, "simple,'' and unpretentious. He criticizes the title, notes that most books about Indians are poor, and dislikes Parkman's demeaning of Indians as brutes. Then comes the praise. Parkman valuably shares his knowledge with us and engagingly depicts his companion Quincy A. Shaw and the hunter Henry Chatillon. The book has ''the true wild-game flavor.''

Bibliography: Thomas L. Altherr, ''Drunk with the Chase: The Influence of Francis Parkman's *The California and Oregon Trail* on Herman Melville's *Moby-Dick, or The Whale*,'' *Journal of the American Studies Association of Texas* 21 (October 1990): 1–14.

Mungo. In *Typee,* he is the African-American cook aboard the *Dolly.*

Mure. In ''Benito Cereno,'' he is an African-born slave and a calker by trade. He is between sixty and seventy years of age. He and his son are killed during the attack on the *San Dominick* led by Captain Amasa Delano's chief mate.

Murphy, James (1806–1844?). Missionary. Murphy, who was called Father Columba (also Columban) Murphy, was born in Dundalk, County Meath, Ireland, was apprenticed to a carpenter, became a choir brother in the Society of Picpus (1828, a Congregation of the Sacred Hearts of Jesus and Mary), and with a British passport left Bordeaux, France (1833), for Valparaiso and the Gambiers Islands (1834). Seeking to learn whether French Catholic missionaries could succeed in Tahiti, he arrived there (1835) only to encounter difficulties with George Pritchard,* the British consul at Papeete. Murphy went on to Honolulu to try to reopen Catholic establishments there (1835). He spent some time in Monterey (then part of Mexico, now part of California, 1836) and back perhaps in the Gambier Islands and certainly in Tahiti (1836). Expelled almost immediately from Tahiti, he surfaced in Valparaiso (1837) and the Gambiers Islands, where he was ordained a priest (1837) and from which he went to Honolulu (1837–1839). Father Murphy returned to the Gambiers Islands (1840) and was sent to the Marquesas Islands (1840) and Papeete (1841), where he clashed with Jacques-Antoine Moerenhout,* who dominated Queen Pomare IV* (1841). Melville met Father Murphy at Papeete (September–October 1842). Evidently, the man was recalled to France (1843), soon thereafter to leave his congregation and return to Ireland.

In *Omoo,* Melville describes Father Murphy as a ''hale and fifty'' Irish-born, French-trained priest. (He was actually forty-two.) He visits the rebellious crew members when they are in the Calabooza. He ignores McGee but befriends Pat and the other prisoners. Melville esteems him as a person but harbors some doubts about his spiritual profundity.

Bibliography: Anderson; Robert S. Forsythe, ''Herman Melville's Father Murphy,'' *Notes & Queries* 177 (April 1937): 254–58, 272–76; O'Reilly and Teissier; George Pritchard, *The Aggressions of the French at Tahiti and Other Islands in the Pacific,* ed. Paul De Deckker (Auckland, New Zealand: Auckland University Press, 1983).

Murray, John (1808–1892). Publisher. The son and grandson of publishers of that name, John Murray III was born in London, was sent to the Charterhouse for schooling, studied mainly science at the University of Edinburgh, graduated from there (1827), went to the Continent for pleasure and to learn a few foreign languages, and assembled notes on how to travel efficiently. He returned to London and published the first of many "Murray's Handbooks" (1836), the initial one being on Belgium, northern Germany, and the Netherlands. Murray faithfully aided his father, who was the founder of the influential Tory *Quarterly Review* (1809) and was a publisher of the best writers, including Jane Austen, Lord Byron, and Sir Walter Scott, but who is now notorious for destroying the manuscript of Byron's memoirs (1824). After his father's death (1843), Murray continued the tradition of the publishing house. He planned his inexpensive "Home and Colonial Library," began the series with Robert Southey's biography of Horatio, Lord Nelson* (1843) and *The Bible in Spain* by George Borrow (1843). Continuing his father's late-life ban, Murray published almost no fiction or poetry; instead, among his successes were Charles Lyell's *Geology* and Charles Darwin's *Origin of Species,* and books by Paul Du Chaillu, William Ewart Gladstone, George Grote, David Livingstone, and Arthur P. Stanley, among others, and also a collection of Byron's unpublished letters. Murray lived over the offices of his firm until his mother's death (1846), after which he married Marion Smith, the daughter of an Edinburgh banker (1847). The best man was Robert Francis Cooke,* his cousin and partner. The Murrays had three sons and one daughter. The first son, also named John Murray, together with his brother Alexander Henry Hallam Murray, continued the work of the firm.

Melville's brother Gansevoort Melville* was responsible for obtaining John Murray's interest in publishing *Typee* (1846), once Murray was assured that the narrative was not fictional. He also published *Omoo* but none of Melville's later works. Still, when Melville visited London, he was invited to dine at the illustrious Murray home; he did so but in his 1849 journal deplored the "miserable stiffness, reserve, & absurd formality" of the affair (24 November). Melville had more fun with Cooke, who invited him to dinner and who became the model for R.F.C. in Melville's short story "The Paradise of Bachelors and the Tartarus of Maids." Murray tried to help Melville find a publisher of *White-Jacket,* the manuscript of which Melville had taken to London. During his travels in the Old World, Melville consulted many of Murray's guidebooks to Egypt, France, Germany, Greece, Italy, London, Palestine, the Papal States, Spain, Syria, and Turkey.

Bibliography: NN 15; George Paston, *At John Murray's: Records of a Literary Circle, 1843–1892* (London: John Murray, 1932).

Mustapha. In *Clarel,* he is the old muezzin who is tardy in crying from the Omar minaret to announce the coming of dawn.

"The Muster: Suggested by the Two Days' Review at Washington (May, 1865)" (1866). Poem, in *Battle-Pieces.* Melville exultantly compares the two-day marching of victorious Union troops past reviewing stands in Washington, D.C., to an "Abrahamic river" into which flow streams, torrents, rapids, and freshets. It includes "Eastern warriors, Western braves." It is a veritable "Milky Way of armies." On 23 May 1865, General George Meade's vast Army of the Potomac marched past throngs of spectators in Washington, D.C., with flags at full staff for the first time since the assassination of President Abraham Lincoln.* Meade's soldiers were polished and precise. On 24 May 1865, the legions under the command of General William Tecumseh Sherman* marched through Washington's streets. They were noticeably casual in attire and discipline.

Bibliography: John S. Bowman, ed., *The Civil War Almanac* (New York: Facts on File, 1982); NN 11.

"My Jacket Old" (1924). Poem, in *The Works of Herman Melville.* When work is finished, the poet dusts his old jacket and dreams about Asia, where "other garbs prevail." More "Edenic," they attest to a freer time, before work became necessary. The jacket is supposedly the one Melville wore while he was a New York customs inspector outdoors.

Bibliography: Shurr.

My Lady. In "Under the Rose." *See* Ambassador, My Lord the.

My Lord the Ambassador. In "Under the Rose." *See* Ambassador, My Lord the.

Mynheer. In *Clarel,* this is a name by which Glaucon addresses the Banker.

Mytilene, The. In *Clarel. See* the Lesbian.

Nacta. In "Benito Cereno," he is a calker by trade, aboard Benito Cereno's *San Dominick.* Nacta was born in Africa and is now between sixty and seventy years of age.

Nan. In *Redburn. See* Brandy-Nan.

"Naples in the Time of Bomba." *See* "Marquis de Grandvin: Naples in the Time of Bomba . . ."

Napoleon (1769–1821). Napoleon Bonaparte, Emperor of France. Born in Ajaccio, Corsica, Napoleon attended French military schools (1779–1785) and worked his way up in the army until after the French Revolution he became commander of the Army of the Interior (1795). Then began his meteoric rise and fall. His career may be divided into three periods. First (1796–1805), his Italian and Egyptian campaigns were climaxed by his coronation as emperor and his assumption of the title of king of Italy. Second (1805–1814), he gained control of most of the Continent, was denied sea supremacy by Horatio Nelson* at Trafalgar, built military and commercial strongholds throughout Europe and into Russia, was defeated by the Allies, abdicated, and was exiled to Elba. Third (1815–1821), he left Elba, raised fresh armies in France, fought well until his defeat at Waterloo forced his surrender, and was taken to the island of St. Helena, where he died. Napoleon was a military and administrative genius but also a self-aggrandizing exploiter. He married Joséphine de Beauharnais in 1796, divorced her in 1809, married the Austrian Archduchess Maria Luisa in 1810 and, by her, had one son—François Charles Joseph Bonaparte. In the poem "In the Desert," Melville mentions Napoleon as having soldiers who defeated the Emirs but lost to the bayonet-like sun of the desert.

Bibliography: Corelli Barnett, *Bonaparte* (New York: Hill and Wang, 1978); Owen Connelly, *Blundering to Glory: Napoleon's Military Campaigns* (Wilmington, Del.: Scholarly Resources, 1987).

Narmo-Nana Po-Po. In *Omoo. See* Po-Po, Deacon Ereemear.

Narmonee. In *Typee,* he is a brave warrior in an engagement with the Happars. The contest yields three Happar corpses for what is probably a cannibal feast.

Narnee. In *Typee,* he is a clownish man but is also an expert at climbing coconut trees.

Nat. In "Benito Cereno," he is a cousin with whom Captain Amasa Delano recalls going berry hunting on the beach when both were children.

Nathan. In *Clarel,* he is the husband of an American Jewess named Agar and the father of Ruth. Nathan, an American born in New Hampshire, moved from puritanism to doubt to deism to pantheism and, through marriage, to an espousal of the Jewish faith and Zionism. He takes his family to Jerusalem, farms outside the walls, and is murdered by hostile Arabs. Nathan may owe something to Warder Cresson, a Philadelphian turned Jew, about whom Melville made a terse note in his 1857 journal, calling him "Crisson" (26 January).

Bibliography: Isidor S. Meyer, ed., *The Early History of Zionism in America* (New York: American Jewish Historical Society, 1945); NN 12 and 15.

Nature, Dame. In "The Encantadas," she is the creator of the ugly island tortoises.

Navy Bob. In *Omoo,* he is a sleepy old sailor aboard the *Julia.* He signs the round-robin.

"The Nearer View." *See* "The Parthenon."

Ned. In *Pierre,* he is one of Mrs. Mary Glendinning's servants. Although he is a husband and father, he has evidently seduced Delly Ulver, another servant, and must therefore be dismissed.

Ned. In *Redburn,* he is a sailor aboard the *Highlander.* He offers cigars all around, shortly after the ship leaves New York for Liverpool.

Ned. In "Running the Batteries," he is a Union sailor aboard a ship with Hugh and Lot running past the Confederate batteries at Vicksburg.

Ned. In "To Ned." *See* Bunn, Ned.

Ned. In *Typee,* he is a sailor aboard the *Dolly.* He points to the valley of Typee as the locale of cannibals.

Ned, Rhyming. In "Bridegroom-Dick." *See* Rhyming Ned.

Nehemiah ("the Hat"). In *Clarel,* he is a gentle old American millennialist who quotes the Bible and never has doubts. Nehemiah talks with Clarel, takes him to the home of Nathan and Agar, and introduces him to their daughter Ruth. Nehemiah accompanies the other pilgrims on their journey at Clarel's expense, rides along on a patient ass, drowns in the Dead Sea, and is buried with his Bible. Nehemiah is partly based on a Holy Land wanderer from Connecticut on whom Melville comments in his 1857 journal (26 January).
   Bibliography: NN 12 and 15.

Nellie. In *Pierre,* she is a pretty girl in the Miss Pennies' sewing circle.

Nellie. In "Stockings in the Farm-House Chimney," she is a little girl depicted as waiting for Santa Claus.

Nelson, Horatio (1758–1805). (Full name: Viscount Horatio Nelson.) British naval officer. He was born in Norfolk, was minimally schooled, and started his career under the auspices of a sea-going uncle. Nelson saw active service in the British navy in the West Indies off Nicaragua (1780), was given command of his own vessel in those waters (1784), and was in action against revolutionary France (1793–1800). He was blinded in his right eye in combat off Corsica (1794), participated in a mission at Elba, and was part of the British naval defeat, off Cape St. Vincent, of French and Spanish naval adversaries (1797), after which he was promoted from commodore (as of 1796) to rear admiral (1797). At the time of the Great Mutiny (1797), most dramatic at Spithead, in the English Channel, and at the Nore, at the mouth of the Thames River, Nelson helped blockade Cadiz, Spain (1797). During unsuccessful action as captain of the *Agamemnon* off Santa Cruz de Tenerife, he was so grievously wounded that his right arm had to be amputated quickly and in the dark (1797). After a painful recovery in England, Nelson commanded the *Vanguard,* was detached from the main British fleet off Cadiz, pursued the French fleet, and was victorious even while receiving a head wound in the battle of the Nile, east of Alexandria (1798). (During this battle, Nelson captured the French *Téméraire,* later refitted by the British and placed in service at the Battle of Trafalgar.) From Sicily Nelson ordered the blockade of Jacobin-held Malta and Naples until both surrendered and he could controversially restore members of Neapolitan royalty to their thrones (1799). As vice admiral (from 1801), he attacked Copenhagen and was made viscount (1801). When war resumed against France, he was placed in command in the Mediterranean (1803), blockaded Toulon, pursued French naval elements to the West Indies (1805) and back to Spain, skillfully maneuvered his flagship *Victory* during the battle of Trafalgar, off Cape Trafalgar between Cadiz and Gibraltar (1805), but at his most triumphant moment was killed by a French sharpshooter perched in the mizzenmast of the *Redoutable*. This battle ended French naval pretensions and established England as mistress of the seas for the rest of the century.

While in the West Indies, Nelson met and married the young and widowed Frances Nisbet (1787), separated from her (1801), and continued a sensational relationship with the married Lady Emma Hamilton, whom he had met in Naples (1793). Nelson glowed with the inner fire of patriotism, was a uniquely skillful mariner, was vain, and rejoiced in braving danger. In his poem "The Temeraire," Melville offers praise of old wooden warships such as the *Téméraire* and also the *Victory,* whose captain "[s]hone in the globe of the battle glow— / The angel in that sun." In *Billy Budd,* Melville quotes praise of Nelson as "the greatest sailor since our world began," from Alfred, Lord Tennyson's "Ode on the Death of the Duke of Wellington."

Bibliography: Russell Grenfell, *Horatio Nelson: A Short Biography,* 2d ed., rev. (London: Faber and Faber, 1952); David Howarth, *Sovereign of the Seas: The Story of Britain and the Sea* (New York: Atheneum, 1974); Ralph W. Willett, "Nelson and Vere: Hero and Victim in *Billy Budd, Sailor,*" *PMLA* 82 (October 1967): 370–76.

Nesle, The Sire de. In "L'Envoy: The Return of the Sire de Nesle. A.D. 16—," he is described as glad to end his rovings and to return to his towers and his good love. Although the Nesle family was a well-known French one, it appears that Melville had no particular historical Nesle in mind as a model for his Sire de Nesle.

Bibliography: NN 11.

Nestors. In "Marquis de Grandvin: Naples in the Time of Bomba . . . ," this is the name assigned by the beach juggler to thralls.

"The New Ancient of Days" (1924). (Full title: "The New Ancient of Days: The Man of the Cave of Engihoul.") Poem, in *The Works of Herman Melville.* (Characters: Eld, Jones Three, Jos, Mahone, the Man of the Cave of Engihoul, the Pope, Joe Smith, the King of Thule.) The poet reports a discovery: the bones of a cave man—older than "Culver's mastodon" and almost as old as the sea itself. The bony man confounds "old Chronos" himself. He is part of a veritable "Barnum-show"—"Megalosaurus, . . . Glyphæcon," and so on. He demonstrates that Adam's "gran'ther's a crab, d'y'see!" and our kinsmen are apes whose scratching we emulate. Going back to the time of Chaos, Chance, and Anarch, this "ogre of bone" gleefully throws "his fossiliffer's stone" at common people and impishly threatens to "rule." Melville read *The Geological Evidence of the Antiquity of Man* (1863) by Sir Charles Lyell and *The Descent* *of Man and Selection in Relation to Sex* (1871) by Charles Darwin, was much troubled by the theory of evolution, and in this rollicking spoof appears to accept its upsetting implications. The scientific background of the poem is the following: Philippe Charles Schmerling, a paleontologist and anatomist, found parts of human skulls in the Grotte d'Engis and human bones in the Engihoul cavern, by the Meuse River, near Liège, Belgium (1832, 1835). The so-called Engis skull and certain Neanderthal fossils found later (1856) contributed to the "missing link" theory. In his poem, Melville alludes to "[a] wizard" (perhaps Lyell), professes to laugh at Mosaic geology, and mentions "[i]ndus" (a form of limestone discussed by Lyell) and the "Carisbrook well" (on the Isle of Wight and functional since the Middle Ages). In his *Principles of Geology* (1833), Lyell discusses Schmerling's findings in the Engis and Engihoul caves. Melville's title, from Daniel 7:9—"I beheld till the thrones were cast down, and the Ancient of days did sit"—suggests that innovative science is the present-day divinity.

Bibliography: Stephen Jay Gould, *Time's Arrow, Time's Cycle: Myth and Metaphor in the Discovery of Geological Time* (Cambridge, Mass.: Harvard University Press, 1987); Thomas H. Huxley, "Some Fossil Remains of Man" (1863), in *Man's Place in Nature and Other Anthropological Essays* (New York: D. Appleton and Company, 1896); P. C. Schmerling, *Recherches sur les ossemens fossiles, découverts dans les cavernes de la province Liège* (2 vols. in 1, 1833); Shurr; Richard Dean Smith, *Melville's Science: "Devilish Tantalization of the Gods!"* (New York: Garland, 1993).

"The New Planet" (1847). Article attributed to Melville, published anonymously in *Yankee Doodle** (24 July 1847). (Characters: [P. T.] Barnum, the Feejee Mermaid, Joyce Heath, General Tom Thumb.) A professor of astronomy and celestial trigonometry from Columbia College in New York writes to Yankee Doodle, Esq., to report his observation of a strange light in the southwestern sky and asking for information. Yankee Doodle replies that he has received several reports of such sightings, theorizes that the light must be coming from a new planet called the Barnum hovering over the American Museum, and adds that it presided over the birth of old Mrs. Joyce Heath, General [George] Washington's nurse, and over the birth of the Feejee Mermaid, controls the fates of General Tom Thumb and Mr. Barnum himself, and seems to influence certain city politicians.

"The New Rosicrucians" (1924). Poem, in *Weeds and Wildings,* as part of the section entitled "As They Fell." Melville jibes at his era's optimists through a hedonistic persona who says that, having enjoyed life's pleasures heedless of any preaching about "mortal sin," he and his fellows now "recline," let "life's billows toss" them, and plan to avoid sorrow by twining their rose vine around the cross of orthodox Christianity.

Bibliography: Shurr, Stein.

"The New Zealot to the Sun" (1891). Poem, in *Timoleon.* From the East came religion, which requires adulation, abasement, and adherence to rites. This leads to militaristic "incursive horde[s]" but can also inspire "delirious screeds" and "myths and creeds," including "Calvin's last extreme." So Science comes along, more powerful than religion, and promises to rout all darkness and "[e]lucidate" all mysteries, including religion itself.

Bibliography: Shurr, Stein.

"The Night-March" (1891). Poem, in *Timoleon.* Melville depicts a well-ordered army, its weapons lighting the darkness, "stream[ing] and gleam[ing]" through "boundless plains," but with no visible "Chief." Legends contend that "he lonely wends" and signals "[h]is mandate" back to "that shining host." Interpretations vary. Is the unseen leader Christ? Abraham Lincoln*? Some other religious or political chief, or perhaps some philosophical or artistic force?

Bibliography: Shurr, Stein.

Nimni. In *Mardi,* he is the leading Tapparian of the isle of Pimminee, is married to Ohiro Moldona Fivona, and is the father by her of three daughters, named A, I, and O. He holds open house for Taji and his friends so as to show them the well-dressed Tapparian aristocracy.

Nina. In *Mardi,* she is Arhinoo's young wife. When her husband was away, Nina moaned that she was a widow, according to Yoomy.

Nippers. In "Bartleby," he is the Wall Street lawyer's scrivener, aged twenty-five. Nippers is bewhiskered, sallow, impatient, possessed of a poor stomach, and—unlike his fellow-worker Turkey—irritable only until noon.

Noble, Charles Arnold ("Charlie"). In *The Confidence-Man,* he is the stranger who tells Francis Goodman about Colonel John Moredock, the Indian-hater. Over wine, Noble and Goodman indulge in a curious conversation about misanthropy and generosity. Mark Winsome calls Noble a Mississippi operator and warns Goodman about him. Noble may be in part a caricature of William Lowndes Yancey (1814–1863), the fiery Alabama orator, lawyer, editor, and congressman who favored slavery and states' rights.

Bibliography: Trimpi.

Nones, Queen. In *Mardi,* she is Donjalolo's twenty-ninth-night queen.

Nonno. In *Mardi,* he is a "sour, saturnine" Tapparian guest at Nimni's party on the isle of Pimminee. He probably says "No no" to everybody.

Noojoomo. In *Mardi,* he is a Valapee enemy of Bondo, who swears by his teeth to be avenged.

Noomai. In *Omoo*, he is the King of Hannamanoo and is a friend of Lem Hardy.

Nord. In *White-Jacket,* he is a tall, thin, erect, aloof after-guardsman. White Jacket becomes friendly with him through their shared interest in books. Nord is a saturnine hermit aboard the *Neversink* and refuses to be friendly with Williams. When the crew disembarks at Norfolk, Nord stalks off into the woods alone. He is partly based on Oliver Russ, who called himself Edward Norton, shipped on the *United States* with Melville (1843–1844), and so admired Melville that he later named his son Herman Melville Russ.

Bibliography: Harrison Hayford, "The Sailor Poet of *White-Jacket,*" *Boston Public Library Quarterly* 3 (July 1951): 221–22; NN 5.

Normo, King. In *Mardi,* he is a king in a story told by Babbalanja. Normo ordered his fool Willi to go to a tree. Willi had to do so, although whether by walking on his feet or on his hands he was free to decide for himself. Normo may stand for the normal person.

Nourse, Lucy Melvill Clark (1795–1877). Melville's aunt. She was a sister of Allan Melvill,* Melville's father. Lucy Melvill married Justin Wright Clark in 1828. After his death (1833), she married Dr. Amos Nourse (1794–1877), of Hollowell, Maine. He had a medical degree from Harvard (as of 1817), was an obstetrician, taught at Bowdoin, and was active in politics. The Nourses lived in Hallowell and vacationed in Bath, Maine, on the coast to the south. The first or second extant letter Melville ever wrote was addressed to this aunt ([by 11 October 1828]). Lucy Nourse gave Melville's wife Elizabeth Knapp Shaw Melville* a Bible as a wedding present (1847) and was always solicitous of her health. Dr. Nourse occasionally sent letters to Lemuel Shaw,* his friend and Melville's father-in-law, about the Melvilles. He praised *Redburn,* reported on Elizabeth's health after the birth of her son Stanwix Melville,* and at least once expressed concern that Melville was writing too unremittingly: "Her husband [Melville] I fear is devoting himself to writing with an assiduity that will cost him dear by & by" (1 March 1852). Dr. Nourse had influential friends in Washington, D.C, whom he tried unsuccessfully to persuade to help Melville obtain a consular appointment. At this time, Melville wrote to his wife that Nourse was "as facetious as ever," was applying for office himself, but was likely to fail ([24, 25 March 1861]). Dr. Nourse died in Bath, six months before his widow died there.

Bibliography: Leyda, NN 14.

Nulli. In *Mardi,* he is the bright-eyed, gray-haired, cadaverous-looking advocate of slavery in southern Vivenza. Nulli is a satirical portrait of John C. Calhoun, whose nullification, proslavery position Melville also satirized, though more indirectly, in *The Confidence-Man.*

Bibliography: Davis, Trimpi, Wright.

O

O. In *Mardi,* she is one of the three vain daughters of Nimni, on the isle of Pimminee. The others are A and I.

Oberlus. In "The Encantadas," he is a Caliban-like farmer on Hood's Isle. He used to sell his potatoes and pumpkins to crews of passing ships. When discomfited in a kidnapping attempt, Oberlus became misanthropic and criminal, escaped to Payta, Peru, and was jailed.

O'Brien. In *Redburn,* any one of Mrs. O'Brien's mild triplet sons.

O'Brien, Mrs. In *Redburn,* she is a widowed Irish woman who is a passenger, along with her mild triplet sons, aboard the *Highlander* bound for America. Her widowed sister, Mrs. O'Regan, and her wild triplet sons are also aboard.

O'Connell, Daniel (1775–1847). Irish political leader. He was born near Cahirciveen, County Kerry, Ireland. After the outbreak of the French Revolution forced him to leave his studies at the Catholic College in Douai, France, O'Connell studied in London, joined the Irish Union (1797), and passed the bar in Ireland (1798). When the British Parliament abolished the Irish Parliament (1800), he argued that the British must therefore repeal various anti-Catholic laws. He disputed against the proposal for Catholic relief on the grounds that the British government retained veto rights over Catholic bishopric appointments in England and Ireland (1813). He defied the law against the establishment of permanent Catholic political organizations by convening meetings to draft various petitions. He cofounded the Catholic Association (1823) and helped it grow beyond the ability of the British government to suppress it. It became the New

Catholic Association (1826) and successfully lobbied against the policies of British landowners in Ireland. O'Connell as a Catholic was ineligible to sit in the House of Commons, but he ran anyway and defeated his opponent (1828). After the Emancipation Act of 1829, he was reelected, uncontested, and was permitted to sit. Aiding in the overthrow of the Conservative Party of Sir Robert Peel, O'Connell promised to assure calm in Ireland if the government developed reform policies there (1835). So little was accomplished, however, by the Whigs in power that O'Connell established the Repeal Association to nullify Anglo-Irish legislative cooperation (1839). He was imprisoned on a charge of seditious conspiracy (1844), was released, grew physically weak, and died in Italy. O'Connell married Mary O'Connell (a third cousin once removed) in Dublin in 1802 (the couple had ten children, seven of whom survived infancy). O'Connell is remembered for developing the first democratic political movement in Roman Catholic Ireland. After his death, Irish constitutional nationalism temporarily foundered. Melville satirizes O'Connell in his characterization of Konno in *Mardi*.

Bibliography: Davis; Oliver MacDonagh, *The Emancipist: Daniel O'Connell 1830–1847* (New York: St. Martin's Press, 1989).

"Off Cape Colonna" (1891). Poem, in *Timoleon*. (Character: [William] Falconer.) The columns "crown the foreland" and compose "[a] god-like group." They serenely watch when storms destroy shipping, including the "hull of Falconer," in the seas below them. Cape Colonna, called Sounion, ancient Sunium Promontorium, is a landmark watched for by uneasy sailors approaching Athens. The Scottish poet-sailor William Falconer* barely survived death in those waters and wrote "The Shipwreck" (1762) about the catastrophe.

Bibliography: Cohen, *Poems;* Shurr; Stein.

Ohiro Moldona Fivona. In *Mardi,* she is the wife of Nimni, the leading Tapparian on the isle of Pimminee.

Oh-Oh. In *Mardi,* he is a hump-backed, large-nosed antiquarian on the isle of Padulla. The manuscripts in his museum intrigue Babbalanja. Some of the topical allusions in connection with Oh-Oh's museum owe something to the contents of the American Museum of P. T. Barnum,* whom Melville also satirizes elsewhere.

Bibliography: Davis, Wright.

"Old Age in Its Dreaming" (1924). Poem, in *The Works of Herman Melville.* An old man may rail and scorn at dreamy youth, but at the same time he hopes to avoid "waxing so grave / As, reduced to skimmed milk, to slander the cream."

Bibliography: Shurr.

Old Bach. In "The Paradise of Bachelors and the Tartarus of Maids." *See* Bach, Old.

Old Coffee. In *White-Jacket,* he is the ship's cook. Old Coffee is a dignified African-American who claims to have worked at the New York Astor House. His assistants are May-Day, Rose-Water, and Sunshine.
   Bibliography: Grejda.

Old Combustibles. In *White-Jacket,* he is a short, grim, grizzled gunner. He has a frightful scar on his forehead and left cheek. Old Combustibles may be partly based on Asa Curtis, the gunner on the *United States* at the time of Melville's naval duty aboard her (1843–1844). The *United States* was the prototype of Melville's *Neversink.*
   Bibliography: NN 5.

Old Conscience. In *The Confidence-Man,* he is a friend, as are Old Plain Talk and Old Prudence, of China Aster's now deceased father.

"Old Counsel" (1888). (Full title: "Old Counsel of the Young Master of a Wrecked California Clipper.") Poem, in *John Marr.* (Character: Master.) The Master says that sailors should take care when rounding the Horn out of the Golden Gate and thus avoid being awakened by the cry *"All hands save ship!"*
   Bibliography: NN 11, Stein.

"The Old Fashion" (1924). Poem, in *Weeds and Wildings,* as part of the section entitled "The Year." (Character: Ver.) Ver is always youthful, and "her bobolinks" pour out songs of "juvenile cheer." Ver is also "[o]ld-fashioned," and her young bobolinks remain true to the old ways.
   Bibliography: Stein.

Old Gamboge. In *Omoo,* he is a lieutenant aboard the French frigate in the harbor at Pateetee. He is old, bald, and all moustache and stick-thin little legs.

Old Gay-Head Indian. In *Moby-Dick,* he is a member of the *Pequod* crew. He explains that Ahab lost his leg off the coast of Japan.

Old Hemlock. In "Bridegroom-Dick." *See* Turret, Captain.

Old Honesty. In *The Confidence-Man,* he is China Aster's indigent father, now deceased.

Old Manx Sailor. In *Moby-Dick. See* the Manxman.

Old Mother Tot. In *Omoo,* she is a notorious English woman. She runs one disreputable house after another all over the South Seas. Her "man" is Josy. When Old Mother Tot is ferreted out by Wilson in Tahiti, she spits on him.

Old Plain Talk. In *The Confidence-Man,* he is a friend of China Aster's father.

Old Prudence. In *The Confidence-Man,* he is another friend of China Aster's father.

Old Revolver. In *White-Jacket,* he is the tiny, bespectacled arms yeoman of the *Neversink.* He tries unsuccessfully to make White Jacket his subaltern.

Old Rough and Ready. In "Authentic Anecdotes of 'Old Zack.' " *See* Taylor, Zachary.

"The Old Shipmaster and His Crazy Barn" (1924). Poem, in *The Works of Herman Melville.* This dramatic monologue is spoken by a retired sea captain whose barn has wrinkled shingles, lichen-covered boards, a settling sill, creaky timbers, and moldy corn. But it is inhabited by a clinging spirit with a friendlier voice than any he ever heard at sea. So the cranky old man will not raze his old barn and build a new one.
   Bibliography: Shurr.

Old Thunder. In *Moby-Dick,* this is the name that the mad prophet gives Captain Ahab.

Old Yarn ("Pipes," "Yarn"). In *White-Jacket,* he is the boatswain who is an expert smuggler of liquor. He is once robbed of some brandy but flogs the culprit when the thief is discovered intoxicated. Old Yarn may be partly based on William Hoff, an alcoholic sailor aboard the naval vessel *United States,* on which Melville sailed (1843–1844) and which is the prototype of his *Neversink.*
   Bibliography: NN 5.

Old Zack. In "Authentic Anecdotes of 'Old Zack.' " *See* Taylor, Zachary.

Omoo (1847). (Full title: *Omoo: A Narrative of Adventures in the South Seas.*) Novel. (Characters: Adeea, Antone, Arrfetee, Atee Poee, Baltimore, Beauty, Bell, Mrs. Bell, Bembo, Betty, Black Dan, Bill Blunt, [Armand-Joseph] Bruat, Bungs, Captain Bob, Carpegna, Nathan Coleman, Captain Crash, Darby, Dick, Dunk, Admiral [Abel Aubert] Du Petit Thouars, Farnoopoo, Farnow, Farnowar, Major Fergus, Flash Jack, Captain Guy, Lem Hardy, Ideea, Jack, Jack, John Jermin, Jim, Jingling Joe, Joan, Joe, Dr. Johnson, Josy, Kitoti, Kooloo, Lefevre, Dr. Long Ghost, Long Jim, Loo, Billy Loon, [King] Louis Philippe, Lullee,

McGee, Mack, Mahinee, Mai-Mai, Marbonna, Marhar-Rarrar, Marharvai, [Jacques-Antoine] Merenhout, Monee, Mordecai, Mother Moll, Father [James] Murphy, Navy Bob, Noomai, Old Gamboge, Old Mother Tot, Paraita, Pat, Poky, Pomaree [I], Pomaree II, Pomaree III, Queen Pomaree Vahinee I [Pomare IV], Poofai, Deacon Ereemear Po-Po, Pot Belly, [George] Pritchard, Rartoo, Reine, Robins, Rope Yarn, Salem, Shorty, Stubbs, Sydney Ben, the King of Tahar, King Tamatoy, Tammahamaha III, Tanee, Tati, Tonoi, Tooboi, Typee, Utamai, Van, Varvy, Victor, the Vineyarder, William, William, Wilson, [Charles Burnett] Wilson, Wymontoo-Hee, Zeke.)

In midafternoon, the narrator, who has a limp, signs aboard the *Julia*, a Yankee-built Australian whaler, and thereby escapes from the natives of Typee. His native costume prompts questions from the crew, some of whom he recognizes from previous voyages. Sickly young Captain Guy, treated disrespectfully by his men, leaves nautical decisions and actions to his mate, the rough-and-ready, sharkish little John Jermin, who is half-drunk all the time but knows his seamanship well. Dr. Long Ghost, the tall, bony, wandering ship's surgeon (retired from duty after arguing with Guy), a vicious New Zealand harpooner named Bembo, and an ugly carpenter (called Beauty and Chips) are also aboard the leaky, bouncy barque. Crew members are few, and supplies are worse. A couple of days after leaving Nukuheva, the *Julia* anchors at the island of St. Christina (Hytyhoo), where the native rulers declare her taboo, to keep native girls from boarding and causing disorder. Several crew members temporarily desert the first night. Then the *Julia* sails north to the island of Dominica (Hivarhoo), where Captain Guy looks for more deserters and just for fun fires his pistol at some natives. At a bay called Hannamanoo they encounter a white renegade named Lem Hardy. He has a blue shark tattoo and a colossal local reputation. The narrator offers a digression on Hivarhoo tattooing.

The *Julia* sails west into strange waters, with her sick crew, but encounters no whales. Jermin conceals their position, and Guy remains out of sight. The narrator, still an invalid, plays chess with Long Ghost, reads the man's books, and becomes familiar with the forecastle—and its cockroaches and tame rats. Levity is momentarily stopped by the death of two ill shipmates. They are buried at sea, and the crew turns superstitious, especially Van the Finn, who predicts that soon not a quarter of the crew will still be aboard. The captain grows sicker, and Jermin veers off for Tahiti. The crew continues to plague Rope Yarn, a former baker's apprentice from London and later Australia. Beauty the carpenter, with his cohort Bungs the cooper, steals liquor from a hatchway cask. The *Julia* rides through a gale east of Tahiti, but waves break the cookhouse of Baltimore, the African-American cook, loose from its moorings. While drunk, Jermin shoots the sun with a rusty quadrant and checks the time with a broken chronometer. They sail past the beautiful coral island of Pomatu. The narrator discusses coral, the aroma of the sweet islands, coconut oil, and pearls. Next morning they make shimmering, lush Tahiti. But the men must remain aboard ship, because Guy, on a stretcher attended by Jermin, orders himself taken ashore and the ship under Bembo to put to sea.

The men are so angry that Long Ghost and the narrator are hard put to restrain them from mutiny. The narrator suggests a round-robin, or a petition, which sixteen of the men sign and send to Wilson, the British consul ashore. When that functionary appears onboard, he proves to be unsympathetic, questions the men about Jermin and their food in a prejudiced manner, and orders the ship to prepare for a three-months' voyage for whales. The narrator hopes to persuade the crew to refuse duty but not to mutiny. They get drunk instead and listen indecisively to Jermin's suggestion that they go whaling and drinking, perhaps never to return for Guy. Bembo and Sydney Ben, an ex-convict from Australia, get into a fight. Next morning the men discover sullen Bembo sailing the *Julia* straight for a coral reef. They turn her in the nick of time, jump on Bembo, and would kill him except that Jermin locks him in a scuttle. Jermin grows impatient and takes the *Julia* into the risky harbor of Papeetee, aided by Jim, the native pilot. Wilson climbs on board, blusters, and transfers under arrest the rebellious seamen—including the narrator and Long Ghost—to the *Reine Blanche,* a magnificent French man-of-war full of dainty, unprofessional sailors. For five days and nights, the prisoners remain on board, fed badly.

The rebellious men are taken ashore, quizzed by Wilson, and upon refusing to return to duty are marched along a beautiful road under the careless eye of Captain Bob, the native guard, to the Calabooza Beretanee, in other words, the British jail. They are placed in stocks made of two logs but are soon given more freedom by Bob, who trades sea biscuits brought along by Rope Yarn for breadfruit. He lets them go into nearby orange groves to pick baskets of the fruit. The narrator digresses on the villainous French at Tahiti, British connivance with them there, Polynesian elephantiasis, and the beauty of Tahitian girls. Dr. Johnson, Wilson's crony, visits the calabooza, listens to the complaints of the prisoners, and sends them some medicine—including a little laudanum. After a few weeks in jail, the men are hauled before Wilson again. He reads trumped-up depositions designed, without success, to frighten them into agreeing to sail on the *Julia.* Back in the calabooza they are visited by three French-trained priests, one of whom, Father Murphy, sends them clothes and bread. Long Ghost and the narrator share a little French brandy with the priest and hence will always think fondly of him. After three more weeks, Guy and Jermin collect a new crew and sail off without the rebels, who conclude that the consul hopes that they will disperse without further ado. They pick up their chests, which Jermin kindly left behind with a native friend, and begin to enlarge the circle of their activities.

To each white sailor a native pal attaches himself loyally. The idle crew members jovially pilfer from ships in the harbor and have moonlight picnics with the proceeds. They debate the virtues of missionaries. The narrator bows to a bevy of white ladies on the road and almost causes some fainting. The men attend worship in a native Christian church, which features an anti-French, pro-

British sermon and much noise. The narrator digresses on the easy hypocrisy of the natives in matters of religion, their mode of dressing, missionaries in Tahiti, segregation of white children and Hawaiian children, indolence and white men's diseases in Tahiti, and rampant evil and hopelessness there. Melville quotes many authorities and presents anecdotes of his own.

When Dr. Johnson calls at the calabooza again, Long Ghost throws a fit in order to be assigned to more comfortable quarters; however, when his new digs lack extra food he returns to the jail. One day three weeks after the departure of the *Julia,* the men crowd after Wilson and force him to feed them properly. His behavior convinces the narrator and Long Ghost that they should accept employment as hands for some white farmers in the valley of Martair on nearby Imeeo island. After bidding their cronies goodbye, off they go and soon are helping a Yankee named Zeke and a Cockney named Shorty cultivate sweet potatoes, turnips, yams, and sugar cane. Most of the time, however, they are off in the hills with their friendly hosts looking at curious trees and flowers and a weed-grown cemetery, hunting wild bullocks and boars, and indulging in nocturnal feasts. The occasional hoeing and weeding, however, still prove too arduous; so, after Zeke sells some potatoes to a passing ship, the narrator and Long Ghost bid their saddened employers farewell and head for the village of Tamai, where they enjoy witnessing a native dance in the moonlight. After a few days, they learn that authorities are on the lookout for white vagrants; so they return to Martair for a hearty supper and proceed to Taloo—by easy stages along the beach. They stop for refreshments at the hut of a loving old pair, dubbed Darby and Joan, and are saluted by three pretty maidens who escort them to the village of Loohooloo. Marharvai, its chief, welcomes them to his dwelling and offers them rolls, fish, poee, fruit, and relishes. The narrator strolls through a grove of coco palms, which are the blessed trees of many uses. He and Long Ghost enjoy themselves; so they stay a few days before bidding a touching adieu to the bright-eyed girls (notably lovely Marhar-Rarrar) and go by canoe toward Taloo, examining coral reefs as they do so. After about ten days from the time they left Zeke and Shorty, they find themselves close to Taloo, near which they spend the night in the bamboo coop of Varny, a dealer in contraband liquor, which he makes by boiling and fermenting a yam-like root. Long Ghost becomes tipsy, has a hangover the next morning, and is missing his boots. Varny cannot seem to locate them anywhere.

The two companions hike barefooted over a hot, sandy tract to Partoowye, a hospitable village near the harbor of Taloo. They are welcomed by a kind, Christianized native named Ereemear (Jeremiah) Po-Po, who provides for his friendly wife Arfretee, a beautiful but frigid young daughter called Loo, a dandified son, twins, and other persons in his home of cane and palmetto leaves. The white men eat well, remain several days, and enjoy rambling through the eighty-house settlement, at the end of which is the residence of Queen Pomaree Vahinee I. When Long Ghost grows too amorous at one point with cool Loo, she quietly stabs him with a thorn. The visitors inspect a sugar plantation run

by a white man named Bell, whose wife is surpassingly beautiful. The visitors
attend the Taloo chapel, where Po-Po is a deacon, and witness a native criminal
court proceeding against a fellow named Captain Crash. They push their way
into the presence of Queen Pomaree but are dismissed.

Unable to persuade the queen to commission them in her navy, Long Ghost
and Typee decide to leave. They have spent about five weeks in Partoowye. The
narrator wants to ship aboard a whaler called the *Leviathan.* He likes everything
about her—its appearance, crew, and food. So he asks the captain, a tall, robust
man from Martha's Vineyard, who over a bottle agrees to take him on but not
Long Ghost. That individual, when told everything, commends the Vineyarder's
powers of analysis. Before he ships out, the narrator bids a boozy bye-bye to
Po-Po, Arfretee, Loo, and his lanky whilom confrere. The Pacific Ocean looms
ahead. (In an aside, Melville explains that the term ''omoo'' means ''rover.'')

Omoo was designed by Melville from the start as a continuation of *Typee*
(1846). Both are based on his experiences at sea and on South Sea islands
(1842–1843). His fictional *Julia* is based on the Sydney whaler *Lucy Ann,* on
which he escaped from Nukuheva; the *Leviathan,* on the *Charles and Henry,*
which was out of Nantucket and which took him to Lahaina, in the Sandwich
Islands. The French warship *La Reine Blanche* was real. Many characters and
episodes in *Omoo* are loosely based on acquaintances of Melville's and events
that occurred during this time. In addition to his own experiences, Melville used
two source books, also used for *Typee.* They are *Voyages and Travels in Various
Parts of the World . . . 1803–1807* (1813), by Georg Heinrich von Langsdorff,*
and *A Visit to the South Seas, in the U.S. Ship Vincennes, during the Years
1829 and 1830* (1831), by Charles S. Stewart. Melville also profitably read
Polynesian Researches (1833), by William Ellis; *Historical Account of the Circumnavigation of the Globe, and of the Progress of Discovery in the Pacific
Ocean,* anonymously published (1837); *Polynesia* (1843), by Michael Russell;
and *Narrative of the United States Exploring Expedition* (1845), by Charles
Wilkes. The authenticity of many details in Melville's account, doubted at first
by publishers, critics, and ordinary readers, was verified by Lieutenant (Henry
Augustus) Wise's subsequent *Los Gringos; or, An Inside View of . . . Polynesia*
(New York, 1849). Melville plays fast and loose with the time line in *Omoo,*
as he had done, only more so, in *Typee.* In truth, Melville signed aboard the
Lucy Ann 9 August 1842, in Tahiti refused duty 24 September, ''escaped'' to
Eimeo in October, and signed aboard the *Charles and Henry* in early November.
In *Omoo,* these scant three months become a good four. Melville dedicated
Omoo to his uncle Herman Gansevoort.*

Melville corresponded about *Omoo* with John Murray,* who had published
Typee in London and who Melville hoped would publish *Omoo;* sent proof
sheets prepared by Harper & Brothers,* destined to be Melville's American
publishers for some time, to London via his friend John Romeyn Brodhead,*
who had replaced Melville's deceased brother Gansevoort Melville* as legation
secretary in London; and accepted Murray's terms. *Omoo* was published in

London (27 March 1847), and Melville was paid £144.3.4 via Brodhead. *Omoo* appeared in England ahead of the American edition, to ensure British copyright. The Harper edition then appeared (c.1 May). *Omoo* was more widely reviewed than any other book by Melville. It was generally liked, but Melville's veracity was questioned and his criticism of missionaries deplored. All of this was so good for sales that Melville soon received $718.79 (including an advance of $400) from sales of the American edition of just over 3,600 copies (as of 31 July). Murray's *Omoo* lost money until year's end but turned a £96 profit by mid-1848. For the remainder of Melville's life, *Omoo* sold moderately well. Murray and Harper printings to the year 1900 totaled more than 15,000 copies. A compliment to *Omoo* was an 1850 pirated edition by the London publisher George Routledge. Appearing soon also were translations in Dutch and German, and others followed later. Sophia Hawthorne, wife of Nathaniel Hawthorne,* called Melville "Mr. Omoo."

   Bibliography: NN 2; Lieutenant (Henry Augustus) Wise, *Los Gringos; or, An Inside View of . . . Polynesia* (New York, 1849).

"On a Natural Monument in a Field of Georgia" (1866). Poem, in *Battle-Pieces.* Only an "unhewn" rock stands where certain "nameless brave" are buried. The poet praises these soldiers over whom "fell disease did gloat," far from home and in anguish, unsung, and with their deeds unrecorded. Enduring, they were sure only of "[t]his healing sleep." In a note, Melville explains that he wrote this poem before the establishment of the National Cemetery at Andersonville, where, he adds, several hundred Union soldiers were reinterred without identification, near some 15,000 known and identified ones.

   Bibliography: Garner; MacKinlay Kantor, *Andersonville* (Cleveland, Ohio: World, 1955); NN 11.

Ononna. In *Mardi,* he is a valiant warrior begotten through the efficacy of the marzilla wine treasured by King Donjalolo of the island of Juam.

"On Sherman's men who fell in the Assault of Kenesaw Mountain, Georgia" (1866). Poem, in *Battle-Pieces.* (Character: [General William Tecumseh] Sherman.) Melville says that this battle gives the lie to the notion that fame, duty, and glory are no more. Here "gentler hearts are bared to deadlier war" than mailed knights ever experienced. During his march through Georgia, General William T. Sherman was frustrated by Confederate General Joseph E. Johnston's retreat maneuvers and decided to attack at Kenesaw Mountain, west of the Chattahoochee River, in Georgia (27 June 1864). Sherman ordered a diversionary movement on Johnston's lower flank. When it succeeded and a foothold was retained, Sherman attacked Johnston's center and right, but his men stalled, suffered casualties, and were pinned down. Advances up dangerous slopes faltered, and the Union effort failed. Union casualties were almost 3,000 in dead and wounded, compared to about 750 Confederate casualties.

Bibliography: Boatner, Faust, Garner.

"On the Chinese Junk" (1847). Article attributed to Melville, published anonymously in *Yankee Doodle** (17, 24, 31 July; 21 August; 4, 11, 18 September 1847). (Characters: Hannah Adams, [P. T.] Barnum, Chang Ching, Chang-foue, Doodle, He Sing, Cave Johnson, Jonathan, Keying, Capt[ain] Killett, Ko-ka-poo, Plunkett, Cap[tain] Stockton, Wang Taou, Yankee Doodle.) Yankee Doodle offers thirteen reports. 1. "Curious Exhibition": Barnum will display a Chinese junk and the sea serpent in a tank of water. 2. "Being the Current News with Yankee Doodle's Comments": Keying, the Chinese commissioner, suggests that to advance the cause of Christianity the British should spike not Chinese guns but their own. 3. "Yankee Doodle's Visit": Yankee, with some friends, boards the Chinese junk, off the Battery, inspects her parts, and talks with her British captain and a Chinese named Chang-foue. 4. "The Chinese Junk": A cartoon of Chinese sailors hauling up the stern boat by pulling on their queues. 5. "Being the Current News with Yankee Doodle's Comments": Reports that the American *Sea Witch,* though less graceful, beat the junk *Keying* from China to the United States; that *The Stranger's Grave* by Grattan is attracting readers; and that it would be pleasant to ask one of those planet-disturbing rockets seen off Boston about celestial navigation. 6. "Being the Current News with Yankee Doodle's Comments": Expresses fear that since the French are exporting alcoholic beverages and fancy clothes to the Society Islands, there soon may be no Tahitians left to dress; and quotes He Sing's love poem to Chang Ching's daughter. 7. "The Junk Is Genuine": Chinese Emperor Wang Taou reports to Doodle, king of the Yankees, that documents have been found proving that the Chinese junk is authentic. 8. "Farewell": Goodbye poem to the guest junk, the contents of which Neptune would not swallow even though they have "bamboozled" the Yankees. 9. "Mr. Cave Johnson's New Method of Distributing the Mails": The postmaster general, having failed to contract for mail delivery via a telegraph company and then via the junk, plans to do so via "the 'big shooter' of Cap. STOCKTON." 10. "The Opium War Revived": Junk sailors aboard attacked Capt. Killett for higher wages but were imprisoned for excessive use of opium. 11. "Being the Current News with Yankee Doodle's Comments": When a man called the junk sailors "strangers grave" and praised their "tails," Plunkett mistakenly thought that he was praising Plunkett's "tale" entitled "The Stranger's Grave." 12. "Error Corrected": The Junk people are not Junkers, do not worship dogs, but do eat them. 13. "Will You Go, or Won't You?": Since we have said goodbye to the Junk, why will she not sail off?

Henry Willoughby Grattan Plunkett, writing as H. P. Grattan, probably wrote *The Stranger's Grave: A Tale of the Seventeenth Century* (1823); Melville puns on "grave strangers" and also named Plunkett as the author.

Bibliography: D. J. Donoghue, *The Poets of Ireland: A Biographical and Bibliograph-*

ical Dictionary of Irish Writers of English Verse (1912; Detroit: Gale Research Company, 1968); NN 9.

"On the Grave of a young Cavalry Officer killed in the Valley of Virginia"

(1866). Poem, in *Battle-Pieces*. Melville says that the soldier lying here has a "happier fortune in this mound" than in his beauty, youth, "manners sweet," friends, money, and education.

Bibliography: Garner, NN 11.

"On the Home Guards who perished in the Defense of Lexington, Missouri"

(1866). Poem, in *Battle-Pieces*. Melville says that these young men though defeated "fortified / The Cause" and provided an example for future soldiers "sore beset." Confederate Major General Sterling Price after his victory at Wilson's Creek, during which Union Brigadier General Nathaniel Lyon* was killed, aimed to sweep Union sympathizers from Missouri. He and some 7,000 Confederate state guardsmen besieged Lexington, which was defended by Colonel James A. Mulligan and 2,800 troopers (12 September 1861). Each side waited for support; when none arrived, Price cut off the town's water supply (18 September). Mulligan surrendered (20 September). In reality, Mulligan's Home Guard, which sustained 159 casualties, fought ineptly; for example, they used the strategically important brick rampants only as a hospital, which was soon overrun.

Bibliography: Faust, Garner.

"On the Men of Maine killed in the Victory of Baton Rouge, Louisiana"

(1866). Poem, in *Battle-Pieces*. Melville explains that many men from Maine, with its cold groves of pine trees, died here in a different climate, where "fig and orange, cane and lime" grow. Yet it was one country, and "in youth they died for her." Their example should encourage valorous faith in the republic. The Battle of Baton Rouge (5 August 1862) came about thus: When Union forces failed to take Vicksburg by naval and land attack, Admiral David Glasgow Farragut* transported some 3,200 troops, many ill with fever, back to Baton Rouge. Confederate Major General John Cabell Breckinridge* attacked the city with 4,000 men, many also feverish. The Union defender was Brigadier General Thomas Williams. His regiments, including those from Maine, Massachusetts, and Michigan, were pushed back. The *Arkansas,* a Confederate vessel, could not provide support when she lost an engine and was scuttled. During combat in a fog, the Confederates were forced back. Union casualties were 84 killed, including Williams, and 299 wounded and missing; of the killed, 40 percent were Maine men, and of the wounded, 25 percent. The Confederate losses were 84 killed and 372 wounded and missing.

Bibliography: Boatner, Faust, Garner, NN 11.

"On the Photograph of a Corps Commander" (1866). Poem, in *Battle-Pieces*. (Character: [General Winfield Scott Hancock].) Melville praises the leader for aspects of his posture, his "eagle mien," and, "lighting all, the soul that led / In Spottsylvania's charge to victory." His ancestors include fighters at Agincourt, Norman knights, and Templars. Christ's humbling example is so remote that one finds it easier to identify with "manly greatness." The brave II Corps commander was General Winfield Scott Hancock* at Spotsylvania, Virginia, when during the Wilderness campaign he captured part of a Confederate brigade by breaking through the center of the line formed by General Robert E. Lee* (12 May 1864). When he visited the military camp of his cousin Henry Sanford Gansevoort* in Virginia (April 1864), Melville may have seen and been impressed by Hancock.

Bibliography: Boatner; Cohen, *Poems;* Faust; Garner; Warren.

"On the Sea Serpent" (1847). Article attributed to Melville, published anonymously in *Yankee Doodle** (19 June 1847). (Characters: [Cave] Johnson, Looney, Teg, [Cornelius] Vanderbilt.) In the first section, entitled "Piscatory Sports at the Docks" (not attributable to Melville), Teg tells fellow fisherman Looney that he has caught the slippery sea serpent. In the second section, entitled "$1,000 Reward," it is announced that Johnson, the postmaster general, proposes a thousand-dollar reward to anyone who can get him an interview with the Nahant sea serpent, with a view toward having it carry the mail from Boston to Halifax. No engineer who has worked on explosion-prone steamboats and railroads, such as Vanderbilt owns, need apply.

Bibliography: NN 9.

"On the Slain at Chickamauga" (1866). Poem, in *Battle-Pieces*. Melville says that soldiers deserve praise who survive "long wars . . . unscarred," with limbs as well as "honor . . . unmarred," and so do soldiers who are defeated but with their "will" and "aim" unhurt. The Battle of Chickamauga (19–20 September 1863) was this: Union Major General William Starke Rosecrans* placed several divisions of his Army of the Cumberland, including that of Major General George Henry Thomas, against Confederate General Braxton Bragg* and his Confederate divisions, reinforced by Lieutenant General James Longstreet.* Longstreet broke Rosecrans's lines and caused a massive Union retreat, with the exception of Thomas and his men. They rallied and held for a time, then gathered with their confreres in Chattanooga, where they were besieged. This was Bragg's greatest victory but one which he unaccountably failed to follow up. Casualties were 1,657 killed, 9,756 wounded, and 4,567 missing on the Union side; 2,312 dead, 14,674 wounded, and 1,468 missing on the Confederate side. Historians reckon casualties at 28 percent on each side during this dreadful battle.

Bibliography: Boatner, Faust, Garner, NN 11.

"On the Slain Collegians" (1866). Poem, in *Battle-Pieces.* (Character: Boy.) War appeals to young men, and women and "duty" incite their "ardor, uncooled by . . . wisdom or . . . gain." And therefore sweet, gentle, sunny-faced boys from the North and from the South honorably take their vows, kisses, and blessings to "a bloody bed." "Warred one for Right, and one for Wrong? / So put it; but they both were young— / Each grape to his cluster clung, / All their elegies are sung." Their mothers seek "balm divine," but "the striplings" died before knowing the "care or cloy" of life, and they resemble "plants that flower ere comes the leaf" and are mowed down "in their flush of bloom."

Bibliography: Cohen, *Poems;* Garner; NN 11; Warren.

Oram. In *Mardi,* he is Bardianna's servant, mentioned in the philosopher's will.

Orchis ("Doleful Dumps"). In *The Confidence-Man,* he is China Aster's friend. After winning a large sum in a lottery, Orchis induced China Aster to accept a thousand dollars, married, then called the gift a loan, and demanded repayment. The act resulted in China Aster's financial ruin and death.

Orchis, Mrs. In *The Confidence-Man,* she is the wife of Orchis, who after marrying her changed his formerly generous ways.

O'Regan, Mike. In *Redburn,* he is one of the wild triplet sons of the widowed Mrs. O'Regan.

O'Regan, Mrs. In *Redburn,* she is the widowed Irish woman who is a passenger, along with her wild triplet sons, Mike, Pat, and Teddy, aboard the *Highlander* bound for America. Her widowed sister, Mrs. O'Brien, and her mild triplet sons are also aboard.

O'Regan, Pat. In *Redburn,* he is another of the wild triplet sons of the widowed Mrs. O'Regan.

O'Regan, Teddy. In *Redburn,* he is the third of the wild triplet sons of the widowed Mrs. O'Regan.

Orléans, Louis-Philippe-Joseph, duc d' (1747–1793). French military and naval officer and statesman. He was born in St. Cloud, France, as Duc de Montpensier, became Duc de Chartres (1752), and was appointed a colonel in the Chartres regiment (1765). In 1769 he married fifteen-year-old Louise-Marie-Adélaïde, the daughter of the wealthy Duc de Bourbon-Penthièvre. Chartres had three sons and two daughters by his wife, even though he also had a mistress, Comtesse de Genlis. Appointed as an officer in the navy, he served dishonorably at the battle of Ouessant against the English (July 1778) and was thereafter given a sinecure in the army. When his father died (1785), he inherited the title of Duc d'Orléans. He entrusted his sons' education to Comtesse de Genlis, fell out with his wife, emerged as a politician, sided with the common people during the French Revolution, called himself Égalité, voted for the execution of King Louis XVI (January 1793), and was himself executed for complicity in treason (November 1793). His oldest son, after narrow escapes and a long exile, became Louis-Philippe,* "King of the French." In Melville's *Israel Potter,* the duc d'Orléans, as Duke de Chartres, helps John Paul Jones.

Bibliography: T.E.B. Howarth, *Citizen-King: The Life of Louis-Philippe King of the French* (London: Eyre & Spottiswoode, 1961).

Orlop Bob. In "Bridegroom-Dick," he is a sailor remembered by Bridegroom Dick.

Orm (also Orrm, Orrmin). English writer, perhaps of the thirteenth century. His one known work is the *Ormulum.* Orm may have been an Augustinian canon of Scandinavian descent, living at the Elsham Priory, in North Lincolnshire; or he may have been Orm, the brother of William, an Augustinian prior at Carlisle (1150–1170). The unique manuscript of the *Ormulum* is to be dated c. 1210. What has survived is a collection, in 20,512 short lines, of homilies designed to be read aloud in church as a series of sermons. In his dedication, Orm reveals that he plans to present an English version of the Gospels for the entire year, with each section including an interpretation with application. His table of contents lists 242 homilies. Only numbers 1–31 are preserved, plus a fragment of number 32. The poems lack rhyme and alliteration. Each line has fifteen syllables, with monotonous rhythm. The clear, dull content is often derivative and repetitious. In his poem "Pebbles," Melville may be referring to Orm when he says that "Orm from the schools to the beaches strays," to learn the truth by "reverent[ly]" putting a seashell to his ear. However, Orm in "Pebbles" may be a variant spelling of Orme. *See* Orme, Daniel.

Bibliography: Bruce Dickins and R. M. Wilson, eds., *Early Middle English Texts* (New York: W. W. Norton, 1951).

Orme, Daniel. In "Daniel Orme," he is a burly, reticent old sailor. He has a tattoo of a crucifix. Once captain of a maintop crew, he has retired to a rooming house ashore and then dies one fine Easter Day on an armed height overlooking the sea. Melville may be referring to this Orme or to the medieval poet Orm when in the poem "Pebbles" he describes Orm as leaving his schools to seek the truth from a seashell's message. *See* Orm. In one draft, Daniel Orme is called Asaph Blood.

Bibliography: Cohen, *Poems;* Young.

Osceola (c. 1804–1838). (Alternate name: Billy Powell.) Native-American leader. He was born near what is now Tuskegee, Alabama, the only child of

William Powell, an Englishmen, and Polly Copinger, his second Indian wife. A treaty in 1832 persuaded some Florida Seminoles to submit to relocation in what is now Oklahoma. Although he was a Creek and not a Seminole, and was never a chief, Osceola gathered a small band and resisted, and they murdered not only a chief preparing to move to Oklahoma but also a U.S. Indian agent at Fort King (1835). President Andrew Jackson dispatched army units to the region. Osceola attacked them, fell back, and attacked again. Then, probably ill with malaria (from 1836), he accepted a truce-flag invitation to parlay at Saint Augustine (1837). The American offer was dishonorable, and Osceola was captured and imprisoned at Fort Moultrie, Charleston, South Carolina, where he died of quinsy. The Seminole War continued intermittently until 1842. In *White-Jacket,* Chief Osceola is named as a Florida Indian against whom a marine now aboard the *Neversink* once fought—or so he boasts, from daybreak to breakfast.

Bibliography: Patricia R. Wickman, *Osceola's Legacy* (Tuscaloosa: University of Alabama Press, 1991).

Otho. In *Mardi,* he is Barbarossa's fictitious son who, according to the historian Ghibelli, was defeated by Ziani in a naval battle.

Bibliography: Wright.

Otoo. In *Omoo,* this is the original name of Pomaree [I].

Ottimo, Prince. In *Mardi,* he is a foolish man, thirsting for fame, in one of Mohi's stories.

Ozonna. In *Mardi,* he is a young lover in a story told by Mohi. Ozonna sought his lost Ady in Queen Hautia's court and thought he found her, but she turned out to be Rea. Ozonna's fate parallels that of Taji with his lost Yillah.

P

Paivai. In *Mardi,* he is a Tapparian on the isle of Pimminee who ignored the family tree and put his faith, instead, only in his tailor.

Palaverer, Mr. In *The Confidence-Man,* this is the sarcastic name that Pitch uses to address the herb doctor, who calls himself "The Happy Man."

Palmer, The. In "The Encantadas," he is a palmer who observes the island monsters.

Palmer, The. In *Clarel,* he is a pilgrim who in a song read by Clarel in Abdon's hotel tells about roaming over Judaea.

Pani. In *Mardi,* he is the blind, white-haired, materialistic guide on the island of Maramma. Pani loudly warns pilgrims who try to ascend the peak of Ofo without his aid. At the same time, he privately admits doubts as to his own ability.

Pansy. In "The Scout toward Aldie," he is evidently a dead Confederate soldier who wrote a song beginning with this line: "Spring is come; she shows her pass." Pansy's friend, Archy, a soldier under [John Singleton] Mosby, sings it when he is captured by the Colonel's men during his ill-fated pursuit of Mosby.

Paola of Verona. In "Marquis de Grandvin: At the Hostelry." *See* Veronese, Paolo.

Paper Jack. In *Omoo. See* Guy, Captain.

Paper Jack. In *White-Jacket,* this is a general term for any incompetent commander.

"The Paradise of Bachelors and the Tartarus of Maids" (1855). Short story. It was anonymously published in *Harper's New Monthly Magazine** 1 April 1855). (Characters: Old Bach, R.F.C. [Robert Francis Cooke], Cupid, Socrates.) I. The narrator is invited one evening in May to a banquet for nine persons at the Templars' cloisters in London, a place filled with snug old furniture and happy, unmarried lawyers. The head waiter, with a Socrates-like head, supervises the serving of dinner of oxtail soup, turbot, beef and other meats, claret and other drinks, tarts and puddings, and cheese and crackers. The carefree men eat well, share pleasant anecdotes, take their snuff with joy, and depart. The narrator tells his host, R.F.C., that the place is a veritable Paradise of Bachelors. II. On a winter day, the same narrator, in the seed business, takes his horse and buggy to a New England paper mill near Woedolor Mountain beyond a pass called the Mad Maid's Bellows-pipe and a gorge called the Black Notch. He wishes to buy an enormous quantity of envelopes in which to distribute seeds. He locates the mill beside Blood River, which furnishes the power, in a hollow called the Devil's Dungeon. Nearby dormitories house the pale girls employed at the mill. Inside the mill, the narrator observes blank-looking girls operating huge machines. The boss, a dark man known as Old Bach, notes the narrator's frozen cheeks, which seem bitten by Actæon's hounds, and rubs them with snow. The visitor is then led on a factory tour by Cupid, a dimpled lad. They observe the workers at a $12,000 machine chopping dusty rags, converting the pieces into an "albuminous" pulp, and moving it through a sequence of cylinders. Out comes perfect foolscap in nine minutes. The process is fascinating but repulsive. (Clearly, Melville is flirting here with gestation symbolism.) Pale female faces gleam all about. Old Bach explains that the company employs only maidens, because married women are not "steady." Back again at the Black Notch, the narrator pauses to contrast the Paradise of Bachelors and this veritable Tartarus of Maids.

While Melville was in London, Robert Francis Cooke,* the cousin and partner of John Murray,* one of Melville's British publishers, entertained Melville at dinner above his chambers in "Elm Court, Temple." In his 1849 journal, Melville called its fifth-floor dining room "The Paradise of Batchelors [*sic*]" (20 December). "The Paradise of Bachelors and the Tartarus of Maids," for which Melville was probably paid $40, is in two sadly contrasting parts and hence resembles two other stories that Melville also wrote: "Poor Man's Pudding and Rich Man's Crumbs" and "The Two Temples."

Bibliography: Newman, NN 15, Sealts, Young.

Paraita. In *Omoo,* he is one of the four recreant chiefs whom the French governor [Armand-Joseph] Bruat places in charge of the four sections into which he had divided Tahiti. The others are Kitoti, Tati, and Utamai.

Parker, Captain. In *Israel Potter,* this is the fictitious name used by the captain of the British frigate during its attack by John Paul Jones and his *Ariel.*

Parki. In *Mardi,* he is the tall, handsome Hawaiian chief after whom the ship *Parki* was named. In naming Parki, Melville may have had in mind a famous early nineteenth-century Honolulu chief named Paki, notable for his fine bearing.
   Bibliography: Wright.

Parkins. In *Redburn,* he is the part-owner of the Parkins & Woods warehouse in Liverpool, where Betsy Jennings and her three children starve to death.

Parsee, The. In *Moby-Dick. See* Fedallah.

Parsee, The. In ''The Rose Farmer,'' he is the Persian's slender neighbor, who chops up roses to make attar.

''The Parthenon'' (1891). Poem, in *Timoleon.* (Characters: Aspasia, Ictinus, Lais, Pericles, [Baruch] Spinoza.) ''The Parthenon'' contains four brief numbered and titled parts. In ''Seen Aloft from Afar,'' the Parthenon resembles a ''sun-cloud'' at noon, enchanting in the ''long after-shine'' of Art. ''Nearer Viewed,'' its beauty inspired Spinoza to imagine ''that one architect designed / Lais—and you!'' ''The Frieze'' aesthetically combines gay horses, grave riders, and meek, pitcher-bearing virgins. When ''The Last Tile'' was laid, the architect Ictinus rested, and Pericles heard his mistress Aspasia's stunned praise of the work. Melville recorded his observation of the Parthenon in his 1857 journal (8 February).
   Bibliography: Cohen, *Poems;* NN 11 and 15; Shurr; Stein.

[Pasha], Ibrahim. In *Clarel. See* Ibrahim Pasha.

Pat. In *Omoo,* he is an Irish-born sailor, sixteen years of age, aboard the *Julia.* He signs the round-robin and is befriended by Irish-born Father [James] Murphy in the Calabooza.

Pat. In *Redburn,* he is an Irish fisherman who cleverly steals fifteen fathoms of rope from the *Highlander* when she is just off the coast of Ireland.

Pat. In *Redburn,* he is an Irish steerage passenger aboard the *Highlander* on her way back to the United States. When he is caught stealing food, he is punished by being forced to wear a wooden tub.

Patella, Dr. In *White-Jacket,* he is the *Algerine* surgeon, who with others confers with Dr. Cadwallader Cuticle, when that expert operates on the fatally wounded foretopman.

Paterson, John (1744–1808). Army officer. Born in Wethersfield (now New Britain), Connecticut, Paterson graduated from Yale (1762), taught school back home for several years, and then practiced law. Moving to Lenox, Massachusetts, with his family (1774), he entered Berkshire County politics on the side of revolution, raised a militia regiment, was a member of the Massachusetts Provisional Congress (1774–1775), joined his well-equipped unit to revolutionary forces following the battles of Lexington and Concord (April 1775), and was commissioned colonel of what was called for a time the Paterson regiment (May 1775). It was held in reserve during the battle of Bunker Hill (June 1775), and was reinforced and became a regular Continental Army regiment (January 1776). Paterson went with the army to Canada, fought at the Cedars, west of Montreal (May 1776), and retreated with General Benedict Arnold to the colonies (July 1776). Paterson saw action at Fort Ticonderoga, near the Delaware River, at Trenton, and at Princeton. He was promoted to brigadier general (1777), was ineffective at Ticonderoga and Saratoga, wintered at Valley Forge, and saw his last action at Monmouth (June–July 1778). Paterson was a member of the court-martial that condemned Major John André to death as a British spy (October 1780). Promoted to major general (September 1783), Paterson left the army two months later, resumed his law practice in Lenox, helped suppress Shays's Rebellion (1786), moved to Boston (1791), served in the Massachusetts legislature (1792–1793) and the U.S. Congress (1803–1805), and became a two-county Massachusetts judge. Paterson married Elizabeth Lee of Farmington, Connecticut, in 1766. The couple had five daughters and two sons, and his widow lived until 1841. Their house, together with his personal papers, burned shortly after his death.

In *Israel Potter,* General John Patterson [*sic*] is identified as the officer—at that time a colonel—in whose Lenox regiment Israel Potter enrolls in 1774.

Bibliography: Mark Mayo Boatner III, *Encyclopedia of the American Revolution* (New York: David McKay, 1966); David H. Murdoch, ed., *Rebellion in America: A Contemporary British Viewpoint, 1765–1783* (Santa Barbara, Calif.: Clio Books, 1979).

Patriarch, The. In *Clarel,* he is the patriarch who by letter authorizes the entrance of visitors into Mar Saba.

Patterson, General John. In *Israel Potter. See* Paterson, John.

Paul. In *Omoo,* this is the name given to the narrator by Dr. Long Ghost, who calls himself Peter, when the two men work for Zeke and Shorty, and also during their subsequent wandering toward and around Taloo. Paul is also called Typee.

Paulet, George (1803–1879). British naval officer. A member of an illustrious English family named after the parish of Pawlett, in Somerset, Paulet studied at the Royal College (from 1817), became a midshipman (1819), and earned promotions up to that of captain (1833). In command of the *Carysfort* (1841), Lord

Captain Paulet was ordered to Honolulu (February 1843) by Rear Admiral Richard Thomas,* commander of the British Pacific Squadron, to protect British interests which Captain Richard Charlton,* the previous British consul there, had wrongly complained to Thomas were being violated. Paulet presented an ultimatum to King Kamehameha III,* declined to negotiate through the king's interpreter Gerrit Parmele Judd,* issued harsh demands, and required the king to cede the island to England (February). In letters to the governments of the United States and France, the British government disavowed Paulet's actions. Thomas arrived, returned the islands to native rule (July), and endeared himself to the people. The British government refused to indemnify Hawaii for Paulet's actions. During his time in the area, Jacques-Antoine Moerenhout* regularly opposed him. Paulet went to Tahiti (July 1844), took Queen Pomare IV* to Eimeo (July), and soon returned to Hawaii, which in time he left to return to England (1845). He died in London.

In *Typee,* Melville calls Lord George Paulet a responsible British authority in Hawaii in 1843.

Bibliography: Kuykendall; W. P. Morrell, *Britain in the Pacific Islands* (Oxford, England: Clarendon Press, 1960); O'Reilly and Teissier.

Paul Pry. In "To Ned," this is a general name for the modern maritime materialist.

"Pausilippo (in the time of Bomba)" (1891). Poem, in *Timoleon.* (Characters: Bomba [King Ferdinand II of the Two Sicilies], Silvio [Pellico].) There is a view from a Neapolitan hill called Pausilippo so beautiful that simply being there is supposed to cause "easement unto pain." But the poet from his landeau sees old Silvio there, attended by a little girl; he childishly strums "a homely harp" while she sings. Silvio, long ago imprisoned for writing "a patriotic ode/ Construed as treason," then released all "bleached" and "bowed," is past improvement by any scenery or even "silver doled . . . silent[ly]" by passersby. Meanwhile, "the bland untroubled heaven / Looked down." Melville's portrayal of Pellico here is not accurate in the least.

Bibliography: NN 11, Shurr, Stein.

Pazzi, Madame. In "The Apple-Tree Table," she is a celebrated conjuress whom Julia and Anna would like to consult for an explanation of the emergence of bugs from the table.

Pearson, Sir Richard (1731–1806). British naval officer. Born in Lanton Hall, near Appleby, Westmoreland, Pearson entered the navy (1745), served three years in the Mediterranean and elsewhere, worked for the East India Company (1750–1755), and returned to varied naval duies (1755–1762), finally as a first lieutenant. After time spent in England, Pearson sailed to Jamaica (1769), commanded a sloop (1770–1773), was present at a royal review at Spithead (1773), and served at and near Quebec (1776–1778). He was placed in command of the *Serapis* (1778), which John Paul Jones,* commander of the *Bon Homme Richard,* captured and boarded after one of the fiercest fights in naval history (23 September 1779), a few hours after which Jones's *Bon Homme Richard* sank. It was said that Jones's sharpshooters spared Pearson because of his gallantry on deck. Back in England, he was court-martialed but acquitted (1780). When Jones learned that his adversary had been knighted, he offered to meet him again and ''make a lord of him.'' Pearson held other commands, retired to the Greenwich Hospital (1790), and became lieutenant governor there (1800–1806). Pearson married Margaret Harrison of Appleby and with her had four sons and two daughters.

In *Israel Potter,* Captain Pearson is named as the commander of the British *Serapis* whose surrender to Captain John Paul Jones and his *Bon Homme Richard* is honorable under all of the unusual circumstances.

Bibliography: Wm. Laird Clowes, *The Royal Navy: A History from the Earliest Times to the Present,* vol. 4 (London: Sampson, Low, Marston and Company, 1899).

Pease, Valentine, Jr. (c. 1798–1870). Ship's captain. His residence was in Edgartown, Massachusetts. He was part-owner and master of the *Acushnet,* of Fairhaven, Massachusetts. The *Acushnet* was built in 1840, had two decks and three masts, was 104 feet, 8¼ inches long; 27 feet, 10 inches broad; 13 feet, 11 inches deep; and it measured 358 and 71/95 tons. Pease's reports home and his legal depositions provide information on details of the voyage of the *Acushnet* from the time Melville was first aboard (January 1841) until his desertion (July 1842). By 1850, Pease had retired and was living on Martha's Vineyard. He died in Edgartown. Pease bore only a superficial resemblance to the volcanic Ahab, captain in *Moby-Dick* of the *Pequod,* which was modeled to a degree after the *Acushnet.* Melville may have had Pease in mind when he mentions the captain in ''Charles' Isle and the Dog King,'' in ''The Encantadas.''

Bibliography: Leyda.

''Pebbles'' (1888). Poem, in seven parts, in *John Marr.* (Characters: the Clerk of the Weather, Orm.) The weatherman may predict, but the winds blow where they please. Orm leaves his books, goes to the beach, and listens to the unvarying, echoless truth from a seashell. Wrecks of fleets cause the sea merely to smile, ''[p]leased, not appeased.'' The poet finishes by ''laud[ing] the inhuman Sea'' and its ''pitiless breath / Distilled in wholesome dew named rosmarine,'' which is healing.

Bibliography: Cohen, *Poems;* Stanton Garner, ''Rosmarine: Melville's 'Pebbles' and Ben Jonson's *Masque of Blackness,''* *Melville Society Extracts* 41 (February 1979): 13–14; NN 11; Shurr; Stein.

Pedro, Don. In *Moby-Dick,* he is a Spanish friend of Ishmael's who with Don Sebastian heard Ishmael tell at the Golden Inn in Lima the thrilling story of Steelkilt and Radney of the *Town-Ho.*

Pedro II (1825–1891). (Full name: Pedro de Alcântara). Second and last emperor of Brazil. A scion of the House of Coburg-Braganza, he was born in Rio de Janeiro. When his father, Pedro I, abdicated and departed for Portugal (1831) to help his daughter Maria II* regain the throne there, Pedro II was designated the constitutional emperor of Brazil. After a regency period, he was declared of age (1840) and was crowned (1841), but he was inattentive to provincial revolts (1841–1845) and squabbled with countries along his border (to 1870). Pedro II, however, was enlightened with respect to public improvements, education, and the arts and sciences. Brazil ended the importation of slaves (1850), abolished slavery of newborns (1871), emancipated slaves over sixty-five years of age (1885), and finally freed all slaves (1888). After military and republican leaders overthrew Pedro II (1889), he went to Europe and died in Paris. Remembered as artistic, learned, literary, religious, and temperate, he disliked being the emperor of Brazil and would have preferred being its president. He agreed to an arranged marriage with the Neapolitan princess Teresa Cristina (1843) and by her had two sons, who died in early childhood, and two daughters, who survived him. He was less fond of his wife than of the Countess de Barral, his longtime mistress (from 1856).

Melville in *White-Jacket* identifies Don Pedro II as the overdressed, corpulent, pleasant-looking, easygoing young Brazilian emperor and describes his condescending visit to the *Neversink* when she was at anchor off Rio de Janeiro. Calling him Most Noble Marquis of Silva, Melville mentions that Pedro II was the grandson of King John VI of Portugal and the brother of Maria, now queen of Portugal.

Bibliography: Harry Bernstein, *Dom Pedro II* (New York: Twayne, 1973).

Peebles, Maria Van Schaick (1782–1865). Relative of Melville. A daughter of John Gerritse Van Schaick, she was a niece of his sister Catherine Van Schaick Gansevoort,* who was the wife of Peter Gansevoort (1749–1812).* Peter Gansevoort was the father of Melville's mother Maria Gansevoort Melville,* who was hence Maria Peebles's cousin and was her neighbor in Lansingburgh. Maria Peebles was kind and generous to Melville's mother, and Melville knew Mrs. Peebles's son Anthony Augustus Peebles (1822–1905). Melville also knew and tenderly admired Peebles's wife Mary Louise Parmelee before her marriage to Anthony Peebles; Melville perhaps used her as the model for the second of the three lovely ladies he describes in "Fragments from a Writing Desk."

Bibliography: Gilman, Leyda, Metcalf, NN 14.

Peenee. In *Mardi,* this is one of the twelve aristocratic Tapparian families on the isle of Pimminee, entertained by Nimni.

Peepi, King. In *Mardi,* he is the ten-year-old king of Valapee. He has inherited the diverse spiritual qualities of sundry intestate dead. Before naming Peepi, Melville may have read about Peepe, the daughter of a South Sea Island chief, in *Scenes, Incidents, and Adventures in the Pacific Ocean* . . . , by Thomas Jefferson Jacobs (1844); furthermore, *Pi* in Tahitian means young or immature. But Melville may have named Peepi as he did to chortle at incontinence in some teeny-weeny members of royalty. He is surely satirizing the notion of the divine right of kings.

Bibliography: Davis, Leyda, Wright.

Peggy. In *Redburn,* she is one of the waitresses at the Baltimore Clipper, which is managed by Handsome Mary Danby in Liverpool.

Peleg, Captain. In *Moby-Dick,* he was formerly the chief mate under Captain Ahab of the *Pequod* and is now one of her principal owners. Like Captain Bildad, another part-owner, he is a Quaker. After interviewing Ishmael in a blustering manner, Peleg signs him aboard and argues with the stingy Bildad about Ishmael's pay.

Bibliography: Brian Higgins and Hershel Parker, eds., *Critical Essays on Herman Melville's Moby-Dick* (New York: G. K. Hall, 1992).

Pelican, The. In *White-Jacket,* he is the skinny, knock-kneed, sour-looking assistant surgeon. He once examines White Jacket and strangely asks him whether he is pious. His nickname is owing to his chop-fallen expression.

Pellico, Silvio (1789–1854). Italian patriot and writer. He was born in Saluzzo, then in the Kingdom of Sardinia but now part of Italy. He was educated at Turin, lived in Lyons, France (1805–1809), returned to Italy, and resided in Milan. His tragedy *Francesca da Rimini* was an enormous hit on stage (1815), and other plays followed. As part of a revolutionary movement, Pellico co-founded and edited *Il Conciliatore* (1818), a liberal, anti-Austrian newspaper. When it was suppressed by the Austrian police (1819), Pellico wrote a farce for an actress he loved. His family's disapproval impelled him to join the secret society of Carbonari. He was arrested after authorities found damaging evidence against him in a colleague's correspondence, was convicted of treason (1820), and was condemned to death (1822). His sentence was commuted to fifteen years in prison. After serving a total of ten years in three dreadful prisons, he was released (1830). Although he wrote much else, including a quickly suppressed play (1831), *Le mie Prigioni* (1832) remains his masterpiece. It describes his specific sufferings but mainly presents Pellico as a man hurt in his physical nature but converted by the spirit of Christian forgiveness and now favoring charitable thoughts and actions toward all. Many of his former colleagues deplored his new pacifism and meek tolerance and made him a prisoner of loneliness. He appreciated the friendship, generosity, and hospitality of the Marchese Carlo Tancredi di Barolo and his reform-minded wife Juliet Colbert. She pensioned him and welcomed him into her home (from 1838). The sketch of "Silvio'' in Melville's narrative poem ''Pausilippo (in the Time of Bomba)'' is totally fictional.

Bibliography: I. G. Capaldi, ''Introduction'' to Silvio Pellico, *My Prisons: Le mie Prigioni,* trans. I. G. Capaldi (1963; Westport, Conn.: Greenwood Press, 1978).

Pence, Peter. In *Pierre,* he is a fawning book designer who offers his services to Pierre Glendinning—strictly for cash.

Pendiddi. In *Mardi,* he is a neighbor of Bardianna's and is mentioned in the philosopher's will.

Pennie, Miss. In *Pierre,* she is either of the two deaf, pious, benevolent, gossipy friends of Mrs. Mary Glendinning.

Peri, A. In ''Marquis de Grandvin: Naples in the Time of Bomba . . . ,'' this is the complimentary designation of a girl in Naples who lightly pins a red rose to the poet's lapel, accepts a tip, dances off, and is gone.

Pericles (c. 495–429 B.C.). Athenian military leader and statesman. Pericles began his career by opposing Cimon (463), the aristocratic Athenian statesman and general who fell out of favor with his allies, who were the Spartan opponents of the Helots. Pericles instituted democratic reforms, fought Sparta (446–445), increased his control over the empire, defeated rebels, established a democracy, colonized strategic regions, and collected tribute. He allied Athens with Corfu, knowing that thereby he would provoke Corinth, Sparta's ally. He refused Sparta's request to open his harbors, outraged Sparta and its ally the Peloponnesians, and triggered the Peloponnesian War (431–404). Pericles was successful in supporting the arts and in initiating a memorable public building program, which, among much else, produced the matchless Parthenon. Being a better admiral than a general, he controlled waterways and harbors and attacked enemy shipping and coastal towns, but abandoned his own countryside to Spartan predators even as he herded the Athenian populace into Athens proper. Overcrowding led to a plague and his ouster. Though reelected (429), Pericles had no time to establish new policies before he succumbed to the plague. Pericles married, had two sons, Xanthippus and Paralus, and obtained a divorce after ten years of marriage. During his last fifteen or so years, he lived with the attractive courtesan Aspasia,* had a son, also named Pericles, by her, and after the death by plague of his first two sons legitimized young Pericles, who became a general but was executed by Athenians after a naval defeat (406).

In his poem ''The Parthenon,'' Melville mentions both Pericles, the Athenian statesman, and his mistress Aspasia.

Bibliography: Donald Kagan, *Pericles of Athens and the Birth of Democracy* (New York: Free Press, 1991).

Pericles. In ''Syra (A Transmitted Reminiscence),'' he is an innkeeper in Syra who sells wine.

Perkins, Peter. In *Israel Potter,* this is the pseudonym Israel Potter uses to avoid detection aboard the British frigate which he boards during an abortive attack on her by Captain John Paul Jones and his *Ariel.*

Perry, Oliver Hazard (1785–1843). Naval officer. The son of a U.S. Navy officer, he was born in South Kensington, Rhode Island. He had four brothers, all of whom also became naval officers, including Matthew Calbraith Perry, whose gunboat diplomacy opened Japan to the West (1854). Oliver Hazard Perry learned navigation at a Newport school, became a midshipman in the U.S. Navy (1799), served aboard a vessel captained by his father in West Indian waters during difficulties with France (1799–1800), and was active in two campaigns against Tripoli (1802–1803, 1804–1806). Perry commanded a schooner (1809) and recovered an American ship flying a British flag (1810). During the War of 1812, he commanded naval forces on Lake Erie (1813), built a ten-vessel fleet, and helped capture Fort George on Lake Ontario. Then came his time of glory. He engaged the British squadron on Lake Erie, directed the attack aboard the *Lawrence* until she was shot to pieces, transferred to the *Niagara,* and took over from her commander, James Duncan Elliott, who though Perry's second-in-command had held back from the battle for some hours. Perry forced the capitulation of all six of the enemy's ships (10 September 1813). ''We have met the enemy, and they are ours'' was his famous report. Elliott involved Perry later in an argument over credits for the victory. When Perry was court-martialed for quarreling with a marine officer and the matter ended with reprimands (1816), Elliott egged the marine into challenging Perry to a duel ending without bloodshed—to Elliott's frustration. After service in the Mediterrean region (1816–1817), Perry was dispatched to Venezuela and Buenos Aires to urge a discontinuance of South American raids on U.S. commercial vessels (1819); however, he contracted yellow fever and died on a schooner off Port of Spain, Trinidad. Upon his death, the Argentine mission was aborted. Perry married Elizabeth Champlin Mason of Newport in 1811. The couple had three sons and a daughter; one son served in the navy, another in the army.

In ''Bridegroom-Dick,'' Melville names Perry as a famous naval officer with whom [Thomas] Ap Catesby [Jones] served.

Bibliography: Richard Dillon, *We Have Met the Enemy: Oliver Hazard Perry, Wilderness Commodore* (New York: McGraw-Hill, 1978).

Persian, The. In ''The Rose Farmer,'' he is a prosperous rose farmer who advises the poet to treasure his evanescent roses and not distill them into attar for a profit.

Pert ("Milk-and-Water"). In *White-Jacket,* he is a midshipman who runs errands aboard the *Neversink.* Pert is disliked by the sailors, and his cockiness earns him a rebuke from the Professor in class.

Perth. In *Moby-Dick,* he is the limping, bearded blacksmith of the *Pequod.* When he was about sixty years old, he was driven to sea by liquor and the wretched death of his long-suffering wife and their three children. Captain Ahab orders Perth to forge a special harpoon with which he hopes to kill Moby Dick. The blacksmith aboard the *Acushnet,* which was the partial model for Melville's *Pequod,* was a man named Ephraim Walcott; he reportedly ran away to San Francisco.
   Bibliography: Leyda; John Satterfield, ''Perth: An Organic Digression in *Moby-Dick,*'' *Modern Language Notes* 74 (February 1959): 106–7.

Perth. In *Moby-Dick,* he or she is any one of Perth's children, all of whom died.

Perth, Mrs. In *Moby-Dick,* she was the long-suffering and now deceased wife of Perth the alcoholic blacksmith aboard the *Pequod.*

Pesti. In *Mardi,* she is a woman whose love for Bardianna was unrequited. The philosopher, who may have regarded her as a pest, mentions her unflatteringly in his will.

Peter. In *Omoo. See* Long Ghost, Dr.

Peter. In *White-Jacket,* he is the handsome mizzen-top lad, about nineteen years old, who was involved with Mark and Antone in a fight started by John. When flogged on orders from Captain Claret, Peter cries and loses all spirit.

Peter Paul, Sir. In ''Marquis de Grandvin: At the Hostelry.'' *See* Rubens, Peter Paul.

Peter the Wild Boy. In *White-Jacket,* he is a young Down Easter with thick, inflexible yellow hair.

Petit-Thouars, Abel Aubert du. *See* Dupetit-Thouars, Abel Aubert.

Phil. In ''Bridegroom-Dick,'' he is a flaxen-haired sailor who is remembered by Bridegroom Dick.

Phil. In *Israel Potter,* he is one of Potter's drunken guards during his first unsuccessful attempt to escape while he was between Spithead and London.

Philanthropos. In *The Confidence-Man,* this is a nickname that Francis Goodman gives himself when he is talking with Willim Cream.

"Philip" (1866). Poem, first published in *Harper's New Monthly Magazine**
(April 1866) and reprinted in *Battle-Pieces* as "Sheridan at Cedar Creek (October, 1864)."

Phillis. In "Marquis de Grandvin: At the Hostelry," she is a kitchen maid
described by Douw as plucking a pheasant in a picturesque manner.

Philo. In *Mardi,* he is a philanthropist in a manuscript memoir of Oh-Oh's
museum.

Philosophical Intelligence Office Man, The ("Praise-God-Barebones"). In
The Confidence-Man, he is the stooped little fellow in a cheap suit and with a
brass plate that says P.I.O. man suspended from his neck. He reasons Pitch out
of his animus against boy workers and for three dollars agrees to send him a
splendidly industrious lad in two weeks.

Phipora. In *Mardi,* he is an ancestor of King Abrazza, according to Mohi.

Phocian (c. 402–318 B.C.). Athenian soldier and statesman. He studied under
Plato* and associated with Xenocrates, the Platonic philosopher. Phocian fought
for Persia as a mercenary, helped Athens remain independent, and aided Athenian military units when they attacked Philip II (348). After supporting allies
against the Macedonians, Phocian tried diplomacy to avoid conflict with them
(323). He represented Athens at a peace conference, modified Athenian indem-
nities, but agreed to let Macedonia occupy the Athenian port of Piraeus (322).
Following the death of the regent Antipater (319), Phocian allied himself with
Cassander and ruled Athens well; but when the democratic forces regained
power, he was deposed for permitting the Piraeus occupation, was convicted of
treason, and was forced to drink hemlock. Later, repentent Athenians reburied
his corpse and erected a statue in his honor. In "Timoleon (394 B.C.)," Melville
mentions Phocian as an Athenian general.
   Bibliography: Lawrence A. Tritle, *Phocian the Good* (London: Croom Helm, 1988).

"The Piazza" (1856). Sketch. It serves as the title tale for *The Piazza Tales.*
(Characters: Dives, Marianna.) The narrator tells about his solid old farmhouse,
south of Greylock. He builds a piazza, looks out from it at nature all about him,
reads there, gets sick, and recovers. One day he decides to ride over to see who
lives in the pretty house with a golden-glowing window far to the northwest.
Coming closer, he finds the place to be a gray cottage and in it a pale seamstress
named Marianna. She points out to him a marble abode—his house—and wonders aloud what happy being lives there. He cannot say. The narrator's farm-

house is based on Melville's farmhouse, called Arrowhead, in the Berkshires of western Massachusetts. When Melville wrote "The Piazza," which is a poetic description of his residence, as a preface to a book reprinting several stories, he was following a device that Nathaniel Hawthorne* had used in his collection of reprinted stories, *Mosses from an Old Manse* (1846), which has as its preface "The Old Manse," describing his residence. Melville received no money for "The Piazza."

Bibliography: Newman; Sealts; Mark Z. Slouka, "Herman Melville's Journey to 'The Piazza,'" *American Transcendental Quarterly* 61 (October 1986): 3–14.

The Piazza Tales (1856). Collection of five short stories, published by Dix & Edwards, in New York. Melville's name is on the title page, thus first acknowledging his authorship of the tales. The five stories, preceded by an introduction called "The Piazza," are "Bartleby," "Benito Cereno," "The Lightning-Rod Man," "The Encantadas," and "The Bell-Tower." Sales were so poor that Melville earned no royalties, and the firm that published the collection soon went bankrupt, after which the plates were sold at auction. *The Piazza Tales* were not reprinted in Melville's lifetime.

Bibliography: Louise K. Barnett, " 'Truth Is Voiceless': Speech and Silence in Melville's *Piazza Tales,*" *Papers on Language and Literature* 25 (Winter 1989): 59–66; Newman; Mary-Madeleine Gina Riddle, *Herman Melville's Piazza Tales: A Prophetic Vision* (Göteborg, Sweden: Acta Universitatis Gothoburgensis, 1985).

Pierre. In *Pierre. See* Glendinning, Pierre.

Pierre. In *White Jacket,* he is the "chummy" of the mortally ill Shenly. Pierre tenderly adjusts the corpse's clothing before the burial at sea.

Pierre (1852). (Full title: *Pierre; or, The Ambiguities.*) Novel. (Characters: Miss Angelica Amabilia, an Apostle, Asbestos, Isabel Banford, Bettie, the Bishop, Brandt, Casks, Christopher, Clara, Clarissa, Count, Cranz, Dates, Doc, Douw, Donald Dundonald, Mrs. Dunker, Edgar, Falsgrave, Mrs. Falsgrave, Rev. Mr. Falsgrave, Fletz, Flint, Flitz, Glendinning, Dorothea Glendinning, General Pierre Glendinning, Mary Glendinning, Pierre Glendinning, Pierre Glendinning, Mark Graceman, Crantz Jacobi, Kit, Mrs. Llanyllan, Marie, Marten, Martha, Martha, Millthorpe, Charles Millthorpe, Miss Millthorpe, Mrs. Millthorpe, Moyar, Ned, Nellie, Peter Pence, Miss Pennie, Plotinus Plinlimmon, Rowland, Glendinning Stanly, Steel, Susan, Tartan, Tartan, Frederic Tartan, Lucy Tartan, Mrs. Tartan, Delly Ulver, Mrs. Walter Ulver, Walter Ulver, Mrs. Van Lord, Vivia, Professor Monsieur Volvoon, Wen, Ralph Winwood, Wonder.)

Pierre Glendinning, just outgrowing his teens, is the only son of the rich, conceited, widowed Mary Glendinning. They live in a mansion called Saddle Meadows, in a town of the same name. Both of his parents are descended from heroic military officers. After a jolly breakfast, Pierre kisses his mother, whom he calls Sister Mary, and drives by phaeton to visit Lucy Tartan, his docile fiancée. Lucy, whose rich and widowed mother approves the match, as does Mrs. Glendinning, is visiting her aunt in a nearby cottage. But Pierre has been dreaming about a certain dark face. When Lucy asks about the dream, he grows so angry that she weeps. He amiably fetches a portfolio of Lucy's sketches from her snowy-white bedroom and leaves to ponder grief in a nearby grove. He recalls first seeing that mysterious face at a sewing-circle meeting attended by his mother, who, when queried, told him to think only of Lucy. Returning home, he is reassured when his mother urges him to marry Lucy soon. But that night, just as he is about to visit Lucy, a stranger delivers a letter from a nearby girl named Isabel Banford, who says she is his father's unacknowledged daughter.

Quickly vowing to defend Isabel, who is living out of town near the lake, Pierre recalls a family story about how his father's artist cousin dashed off a portrait of the man while he was visiting a mysterious French emigrant, about Mrs. Glendinning's preference for a portrait of her husband as an older man, about her refusal to discuss her husband's early life, and about that dying man's delirious talk of a daughter. Pierre will see Isabel despite family opposition. He writes to Lucy to tell her that he must be away for a while. He shares breakfast with his mother, to whom he will say nothing untoward, and with the Rev. Mr. Falsgrave, her admiring local clergyman. When Falsgrave chances to discuss a manservant who has a wife, a child, and a pregnant girlfriend named Delly Ulver, Pierre asks whether the man's two children should love or avoid one another. Mrs. Glendinning takes a righteous line, whereas her clergyman contends that different circumstances require different solutions. That evening Pierre visits Isabel, who is living with Delly and her father. The siblings kiss. Isabel spills out a dreamy story of her childhood and youth, perhaps in France. She lived with different people, was visited by her father, who rumor later said was dead, did different chores, learned to play the guitar enchantingly, and now works for the Ulvers. Pierre, moved by her music, promises to return the next evening.

Pondering all day, Pierre goes back to Isabel, who says that she had a handkerchief labeled ''Glendinning'' from their father and that the guitar, perhaps her mother's, came from the Glendinning house and was labeled ''Isabel.'' The girl moved ever closer to Saddle Meadows through chore work, caught sight of Pierre, and decided to write to him although she does not wish to disturb his mother. She says that Delly's baby was born but soon died. Pierre vows to help the shamed girl. He goes to Falsgrave, learns that he and Mrs. Glendinning plan to order Delly from the region, and rebukes the supposed Christian. When alone, Pierre wallows in his problems: He must protect his sister, preserve his mother's ignorance, and shield his dishonored father's name. Feeling inspired by an ''unsuppressible and unmistakable cry of the godhead'' to pretend that Isabel is his wife, Pierre rushes to Lucy's room and tells the girl that he is married. She faints, revives, and orders him away. He tells his mother the same story, even though he is sure the irate woman will disinherit him. She suspects that he has married the "slut" he saw at the sewing circle, even though Falsgrave tells Mrs. Glendinning that he did not marry Pierre to any woman. Pierre goes to an inn to order rooms for himself and his "wife." His mother sends him a chest of his possessions. In it, he finds no gold, only his father's smirking portrait—which he burns.

Pierre talks with Isabel but conceals the extent of his sacrifice. Leaving Saddle Meadows by coach forever, the couple go with Delly to the city. On the way, he reads a pamphlet called "Chronometricals and Horologicals," which contrasts chronometrical time for ideal Christians and horological time for contemporary practical people. He asks his cousin Glendinning Stanly for the use of his town house, but Glen orders him away. Through a childhood friend named Charles Millthorpe, son of a Saddle Meadows farmer, Pierre, with Isabel and Delly, finds three bare rooms in a building which is behind the Church of the Apostles and which has rattletrap offices for unsuccessful professionals who call themselves the Apostles. Charlie Millthorpe, who does law work and writing to support his widowed mother and three sisters, is a happy transcendental Apostle. Pierre, who wrote some acceptable little things back home, determines to write a treatise on neglected truth, based on much reading and original thought, and thus earn some money. He is interrupted by horrible news: His mother has willed everything to Glen, gone insane, and died; also, Glen is courting Lucy, now back in town with her mother. Pierre writes on and on, until it is winter. In one of his works, he castigates current popular writing in America.

Lucy sends him a letter professing her continued love and expressing her intention to live as a sister with him and with his companion. On learning this, dark Isabel says that she has dreamed of fair Lucy but agrees to be Pierre's bad angel and welcome the girl. Although all secrets will be kept, Pierre feels that Lucy has guessed Isabel is not his wife; still, he tells the troubled Delly that Lucy, his *cousin*, will now be with Isabel, his *wife*. Charlie helps deliver Lucy's easel and trunks. When Glen and also Fred Tartan, Lucy's older brother, a naval officer, try to stop Lucy from moving in, Pierre outfaces the two men, whom a few Apostles then drag away. Lucy's mother curses her daughter, who is sustained by love. Isabel serves the girl and plans to give guitar lessons. Lucy will sell sketches. Pierre and Lucy are never alone, but when he and Isabel are alone, they feel embarrassed. Pierre worries about Glen and Fred, who may seek revenge but whom he vows to kill in his own defense. He scribbles on and on, like a proud ship heading for a wreck.

When his eyes trouble him, Pierre takes a walk, faints, and has a vision of a peak back home named the Mount of Titans. The fierce outcropping resembles Enceladus, the Titan, struggling out of the ground to defy the heavens. Pierre recalls that Enceladus was the son and grandson of incest and rightly sought to regain his birthright by force. Pierre and his two female companions visit an art gallery, where they observe two paintings. One is a copy of Guido's *Cenci;* the other, called *The Stranger,* Pierre and Isabel regard as a portrait of their father. Pierre wonders if enigmatic Isabel is really his sister. The three young people take a boat ride out into the Atlantic Ocean. Feeling unwanted, Isabel tries to drown herself but is saved. Home again, Pierre finds two letters. One letter is from his publishers, who regard his treatise as so blasphemous that they threaten a lawsuit to recover costs and payments advanced to him. The other letter is from Glen, who brands him "a villainous and perjured liar." Thus challenged, Pierre obtains two pistols from an Apostle and seeks out Fred and Glen. When Glen cowhides him across the face, Pierre shoots and kills him.

Pierre, who calls himself "the fool of Truth, the fool of Virtue, the fool of Fate," is imprisoned and sentenced to execution for murder. Isabel and Lucy visit him in his cell. When Isabel, who has brought a vial of poison, identifies herself as Pierre's sister, Lucy shrinks "like a scroll" and drops dead. Fred and Charlie enter later and find Pierre dead of poison. Isabel remarks that "All's o'er, and ye know him not," drops her empty vial, and falls dead on Pierre.

Melville began writing *Pierre* late in 1851, after *Moby-Dick* had been published, changed his tentative plans for *Pierre,* added much to it, and produced a puzzling, partly inchoate novel combining a somewhat autobiographical hero, a Gothic plot, curious Elizabethan and Jacobean dialogue, humorous satire of various literary devices, and much else. Melville's family and an old family home in the Berkshires figure in the people and environs of Saddle Meadows. Melville's father Allen Melvill* had an illegitimate daughter in Boston named Ann Middleton Allen,* who tried to claim part of his estate (1832). Melville's beloved uncle, Thomas Melvill, Jr.,* had an attractive French wife named Françoise Raymonde Eulogie Marie des Douleurs Lamé-Fleury Melvill,* who died five years before Melville was born. Melville considered publishing *Pierre* anonymously, probably to avoid family embarrassment. The Ulver cottage may owe something to the cottage of Nathaniel Hawthorne* in Lenox, Massachusetts, in which the Hawthornes lived (1850–1851) and which Melville visited. Melville, like Pierre, was criticized by editors for trying to write too unconventionally; Melville even transforms one such editor, Evert Duyckinck,* into a superficial friend of Pierre's. Such unity as *Pierre* has may have been inspired in part by the unity of *Eureka: A Prose Poem* (1848), by Edgar Allan Poe.* Melville's motives in writing *Pierre* are puzzling. Melville desired both to exemplify and to satirize various orotund styles. In a pre-Freudian way he also sought to probe dreams, incest, and murder (including suicide) sympathetically and against a social background of hypocritical Christianity. *Pierre* is a huge critical challenge because of its technical, even modernist, virtuosity and its controversial themes. Since it was ahead of its time, it sold badly and was a critical failure. Thereafter, Melville turned to writing short works, including those republished in *The Piazza Tales* (1856), published *The Confidence-Man* (1857), his final unsuccessful novel, and never again sought professional recognition as a writer.

Bibliography: Richard D. Birdsall, *Berkshire County: A Cultural History* (New Haven, Conn.: Yale University Press, 1959); James Creech, *Closet Writing/Gay Reading: The Case of Melville's Pierre* (Chicago: University of Chicago Press, 1993); Brian Higgins and

Hershel Parker, "Reading *Pierre*," pp. 211–39 in Bryant, *Companion;* Lebowitz; Samuel Otter, "The Eden of Saddle Meadows: Landscape and Ideology in *Pierre*," *American Literature* 66 (March 1994): 55–81; Hershel Parker, "Why *Pierre* Went Wrong," *Studies in the Novel* 8 (Spring 1976): 7–23; Smith; Young; Tomoyuki Zettsu, "*Pierre* and Pierre Bayle on Androgyny," *Melville Society Extracts* 97 (June 1994): 1–4.

Piko, King. In *Mardi,* he is the convivial ruler with King Hello of the island of Diranda. The two reduce their exploding population by holding gory war games on the Field of Glory. Melville may have chosen the name Piko because it echoes the name of the pointed weapon called a pike. He may also have been inspired to satirize war as he did by reading Thomas Robert Malthus's *Essay on the Principle of Population* (1798, rev. 1803).

Pillgarlic. In *Redburn. See* Redburn, Wellingborough.

Pills. In *White-Jacket,* he is Dr. Cadwallader Cuticle's pale, hollow-eyed, cadaverous-looking young steward. Pills assists at the amputation operation performed on the fatally wounded topman and later dispenses vile-tasting medicines to White Jacket.

Pip ("Pippin"). In *Moby-Dick,* he is a little African-American lad from Alabama. He is a castaway during a chase for a whale and goes insane, after which Captain Ahab befriends him in a touching manner. Pip may be based to a degree on John Backus, described as a little black person aboard the *Acushnet,* which was the partial model of the *Pequod.*
   Bibliography: Brian Higgins and Hershel Parker, eds., *Critical Essays on Herman Melville's Moby-Dick* (New York: G. K. Hall, 1992); Leyda.

Pipes. In *White-Jacket,* this is another name for Old Yarn, the whistling boatswain.

Pippin. In *Moby-Dick. See* Pip.

"Pisa's Leaning Tower" (1891). Poem, in *Timoleon.* The Leaning Tower, with its "trunk of rounded colonnades," wonders whether it should tilt itself over but then draws back. Melville pondered in front of the famous Leaning Tower of Pisa and then described it in his 1857 journal as "like pine poised just ere snapping. You wait to hear crash. . . . [I]t will move all together if it move at all, for Pillars all lean with it" (23 March).
   Bibliography: NN 11 and 15, Stein.

Pitch ("Coonskins"). In *The Confidence-Man,* he is the Missouri backwoodsman in a bear's-skin jacket who has no confidence in nature and therefore none in the nostrums of the herb doctor. Pitch does succumb, however, to the analogical reasoning of the Philosophical Intelligence Office Man; therefore, instead of wanting any longer to invest in machines to replace boy workers, Pitch pays him three dollars to have an industrious boy—his thirtieth—sent to him. In some ways, Pitch may be a satirical portrait of Thomas Hart Benton, the forthright, pugnacious, antislavery, long-term Jacksonian-Democrat senator from Missouri.

Bibliography: Bryant, *Repose;* Trimpi.

Pius IX, Pope (1792–1878). (Informal name: Pio Nono.) Longest-reigning Roman Catholic pope. He was born Giovanni Maria Mastai-Ferretti, in Sinigaglia, into a noble family. He studied in Volterra and then Rome, was ordained there (1819), served at a Roman orphanage (1819–1823), was apostolic delegate to Chile and Peru (1823–1825), and returned to Italy and became archbishop of Spoleto (1827), bishop of Imola (1832), cardinal (1839), and—succeeding Pope Gregory XVI—Pope Pius IX (1846). He issued a general political amnesty (1846), began to reform the Papal States, and granted a constitution for them (March 1848), but grew conservative and fled from Rome to Gaeta because of mob action during the Italian Revolution (1848). Not long after the French army had restored papal authority (1849), Pope Pius IX returned to Rome (1850), grew bitter, and did not restore the papal constitution. After the Franco-Sardinian War against Austria (1859), the Papal States joined the Kingdom of Sardinia-Piedmont (1860); so, to protect much-reduced papal holdings, Napoleon III garrisoned Rome for a decade (1860–1870), until the Franco-Prussian War required French troops back home. Thereafter, the Italian army occupied Rome (from 1870) and Rome joined the Kingdom of Italy as its capital. Pope Pius IX refused to accept laws defining Italian-Vatican relations, despite an offer (1871) of an indemnity if he would disavow his temporal authority; instead, he called himself a prisoner of the Vatican. Among his theological accomplishments are the proclamation of the dogma of the Immaculate Conception of Mary (1854), condemnation of secular and anticlerical aspects of modern thought (1864), the First Vatican Council endorsement of papal infallibility (1870), and the consolidation of papal authority in a centralized Vatican bureaucracy.

According to an 1857 journal entry, Melville while in Rome caught a glimpse of Pope Pius IX (6 March). In Melville's poem "Marquis de Grandvin: At the Hostelry," this Pope is mentioned as nominally supported by [Giuseppe] Garibaldi.

Bibliography: Acton; Frank J. Coppa, *Pope Pius IX: Crusader in a Secular Age* (Boston: Twayne Publishers, 1979); NN 15.

Placido, Brother. In *Clarel,* he is a funeral friar from Mexico with whom Don Hannibal Rohon Del Aquaviva stays while he is in Bethlehem.

Plato (427–347 B.C.). Greek philosopher. Plato was born in Athens to Athenian aristocrats. His stepfather knew Pericles.* Plato was a pupil and admirer of Socrates, whose execution (399) contributed to Plato's turning from political ambitions and to retirement in Megara. Plato founded the Academy in Athens (387), which he directed and in which he taught while doing research in philosophy and science. He visited Sicily on three occasions (387, 367–365, 361), finally to try, to no avail, to tutor Dionysius the Younger to become an enlightened republican king there. Plato resumed his teaching and writing in Athens, where he died. Plato wrote twenty-six philosophical dialogues—all extant. The early ones, usually in dramatic dialectal form, work out definitions of abstractions, memorialize Socrates, and relate to his trial. Plato's middle-period dialogues, which date after the founding of the Academy, concern ideal forms, being and understanding, and beauty, goodness, and love, and include his *Republic.* After his last return from Syracuse, a person from Elea replaces Socrates as the central spokesman in the final dialogues, which are about appearances, being and non-being, specifics, and ideal forms; Plato also ponders the origin, evolution, and nature of the universe, and the part that pleasure plays in the good life. Plato had faith that reason can make permanent sense out of mutable reality, and that therefore education, recollection of pre-incarnated human life, and properly phrased thought will generate virtuous living both for the individual and for all citizens in a harmonious governmental structure. And this because humankind must emulate in its ephemeral world divine, permanent ideas and forms.

In *Moby-Dick,* Ishmael warns the reader to beware of the "sunken-eyed young Platonist" who will never bring home any whale oil. About 1860, Melville discarded a poem in which he calls Plato's utopian Republic reasonable but impracticable. In "Timoleon (394 B.C.)," Melville mentions Plato as exerting an influence on the times while Timoleon is still in Corinth.

Bibliography: Richard Kraut, ed., *The Cambridge Companion to Plato* (n.p.: Cambridge University Press, 1992); Leyda.

Platoff the Hetman. In "Poor Man's Pudding and Rich Man's Crumbs," he is a Cossack guest at the Guildhall Banquet in London following the Battle of Waterloo.

Plinlimmon, Plotinus. In *Pierre,* he is the mystical author of the pamphlet entitled "Chronometricals and Horologicals," which Pierre finds and reads while he is in the coach taking him forever away from Saddle Meadows. Charles Millthorpe points out Plinlimmon to Pierre in the city as the Grand Master of the Apostles. Plinlimmon, a combination of Apollo and Saturn, is cheerful and yet nonbenevolent and inscrutable.

Bibliography: Nathan Cervo, "Melville's PIERRE," *Explicator* 51 (Summer 1993): 223–24.

Plunkett. In "On the Chinese Junk," he is a man aboard the junk who leaves in confusion when he is mistakenly thought to be the author of *The Stranger's*

Grave (1823). The work was probably written by Henry Willoughby Grattan Plunkett, who wrote as H. P. Grattan.

Poe, Edgar Allan (1809–1849). Fiction writer, poet, and critic. Poe was born in Boston. After his father's disappearance (1810) and his actress mother's death (1811), Poe was taken into the Richmond, Virginia, home of John Allan, a merchant, and his wife, but was never adopted. Poe accompanied the Allans to England and attended school there (1815–1820), returned with them to Richmond and went to school there (1821–1825), used Allan as his middle name (after 1824), attended the University of Virginia (1826), quarreled with Allan over money, went to Boston, published his first poetry (1827), entered the U.S. Army as Edgar A. Perry (1827–1829), attended the U.S. Military Academy at West Point briefly (1830–1831), and published his first short stories (1832). Next, Poe did editorial work in Richmond (1835–1837), New York (1837–1838, 1844–1849), and Philadelphia (1838–1844). He was brilliant, prolific, and versatile, but also doomed by instability and alcoholism. His poetry, usually concerning beauty, stressing melancholy, and displaying technical skill, includes *Tamerlane and Other Poems* (1827), *Al Aaraaf, Tamerlane and Minor Poems* (1829), *Poems* (1831), and *The Raven and Other Poems* (1845). His fiction, usually about horror and the processes of ratiocination, includes *The Narrative of Arthur Gordon Pym of Nantucket* (1838), *Tales of the Grotesque and Arabesque* (1840), *Prose Romances of Edgar A. Poe* (1843), and *Tales* (1845). His criticism, often stressing structural unity and the need for single effects, and deploring didacticism and jingoism, includes reviews of Henry Wadsworth Longfellow (1842) and Nathaniel Hawthorne* (1842, 1847), an article about "The Raven" entitled "The Philosophy of Composition" (*Graham's Magazine,* April 1846), and an essay called "The Poetic Principle" (*New York Home Journal,* 31 August 1850). Poe married his fourteen-year-old cousin Virginia Clemm in 1836. She died in 1847, after which Poe fought alcoholism with little success, attempted suicide (1848), initiated relations with a few women, lectured well (1849), and died in Baltimore under mysterious circumstances.

A few contemporary reviewers of Melville noted Poesque elements in some of his works, especially "Bartleby," "The Bell-Tower," "Benito Cereno," "The Encantadas," *Israel Potter,* and *Pierre.* The unity of Poe's *Eureka: A Prose Poem* may have influenced unity in *Pierre.* Melville may have had Poe in mind as a target for satire when he presents a demented peddler hawking "a rhapsodical tract" in *The Confidence-Man.* The tract itself has been compared to *Eureka,* which George Palmer Putnam,* Melville's publisher, bought and issued.

Bibliography: Harrison Hayford, "Poe in *The Confidence-Man," Nineteenth-Century Fiction* 14 (December 1959): 207–18; Michael Hollister, "Melville's Gam with Poe in *Moby-Dick:* Bulkington and Pym," *Studies in the Novel* 21 (Fall 1989): 279–91; Jeffrey Meyers, *Edgar Allan Poe: His Life and Legacy* (New York: Charles Scribner's Sons, 1992); Trimpi; James D. Wallace, "*Pierre en regarde:* Apocalyptic Unity in Melville's *Pierre,*" *American Transcendental Quarterly* n.s. 4 (March 1990): 49–55.

Poky. In *Omoo,* he is a Tahitian native who adopts the narrator as his friend, finds shells for him, introduces him here and there, and proves to be more loyal to him than the narrator's other native friend, Kooloo.

Pollard, George (1789–1870). Sailor. He was the captain of the *Essex,* a 228-ton whale ship out of Nantucket, Massachusetts (1819). The first mate was Owen Chase.* The *Essex* was sunk by a sperm whale (20 November 1820), west of the Galapagos and north-northeast of Henderson Island, not far from the Marquesas. Her crew of twenty men jumped into three open boats and struggled for some three months. Eight men survived, some resorting to cannibalism of a crew member, chosen by lot, as was the executioner, to do so. After being picked up at sea (23 February 1821), Pollard and one other man went to Valparaiso and Nantucket (11 June 1821). Pollard commanded another whaleship, *Two Brothers* (12 November 1821), was wrecked on a coral reef (April 1822), took to an open boat, and was rescued. While a passenger aboard a brig, Pollard stopped at Raiatea, near Tahiti (16 April 1823), met two British traveling missionaries named George Bennet and Daniel Tyerman, and told them the story of the *Essex* disaster. They published it in their *Journal of Voyages and Travels* (2 vols., London, 1831; 3 vols., Boston, 1832). They include Pollard's account of how the men in his lifeboat off the *Essex* drew lots, shot the loser, their cabin boy Owen Coffin, and survived by eating his corpse. Pollard made his way back to Nantucket (1825), retired from the sea, and became a watchman and an admired citizen.

Melville writes about Captain Pollard and his *Essex* disaster in *Moby-Dick.* While vacationing at Nantucket, Melville and his father-in-law Lemuel Shaw* called on Pollard (July 1852). Melville was impressed by his unassuming manner, remembered him, and described him in *Clarel* as a meek and patient night watchman, without naming him.

Bibliography: Thomas Farel Heffernan, *Stove by a Whale: Owen Chase and the Essex* (Hanover, N.H.: University Press of New England, 1990); Wilson Heflin, ''Melville and Nantucket,'' pp. 165–179 in *Moby-Dick Centennial Essays,* ed. Tyrus Hillway and Luther S. Mansfield (Dallas, Texas: Southern Methodist University Press, 1953); Leyda.

Pollo. In *Mardi,* he is a supercilious prosodist reader of Lombardo's *Koztanza.* Pollo suggests improvements in it, according to Babbalanja.

Pomare I (1743?–1803). King of Tahiti. He was the son of Teu and his wife Tetupaia, was called Tu at first, and was identified as Otoo (also spelled Otou, Otu) by the English explorer Captain James Cook during his second and third voyages. Pomare I (as of 1791) was the first Pomare monarch and started the Pomare succession. His son was Pomare II.* Melville in *Omoo* reports that Pomaree was the ruler of Tahiti during the time of Captain Cook and that ever since he changed his name to Otoo the royal patronymic has been Pomaree. Melville also mentions Pomaree as "the first Tahitian," in *Mardi.*

Bibliography: Newbury, Wright.

Pomare II (1774?–1821). King of Tahiti. The son of Pomare I* and his wife Itia, Pomare II (named Tu at first) became king in 1803, and rose to secular and religious ascendancy by winning in tribal warfare. Tahiti was converted to Christianity by British missionaries (officially in 1815). Pomare II, who became literate and canny, was baptized in 1819 and built a 700-foot chapel, but he had a drinking problem and kept an entourage of homosexual servants. His family enjoyed success by monopolizing trade and weapons, developing agriculture, and accepting aid from friendly Europeans, including deserters from European vessels. His only son was Pomare III.* In *Omoo,* Melville identifies Pomaree II as Pomaree I's famous but debauched son and the king of Tahiti, and adds that he died in 1821.

Bibliography: Newbury.

Pomare III (1820–1827). King of Tahiti. He was the son of Pomare II* and his wife Teremoemoe. Cared for by British missionaries to the time of his father's death (1821), he was nominally crowned in 1824 but died of dysentery three years later at the age of seven. His half-sister Pomare IV* then became queen. In *Omoo,* Melville identifies Pomaree III as Pomaree II's son who became king of Tahiti, died in 1827, and passed the crown to his oldest sister, Aimata, the present queen, who is called Pomaree Vahinee I.

Bibliography: Newbury.

Pomare IV (1813–1877). (Full name: Pomare Vahine IV). Queen of Tahiti. Named Aimata at first, she was the illegitimate daughter of Pomare II* and was the half-sister of Pomare III.* She was inattentive at the missionary schools to which she was sent. In 1824, she married Tapoa II, the sixteen-year-old sovereign of Bora Bora, one of the Tahitian Islands. She assumed the throne in 1827 when her half-brother died. Her early rule was weak and irresponsible, and her chiefs had to guard against apostasy and sedition. She repudiated her husband when he proved sterile (1829). Under disputed circumstances, which caused temporary rebellion and bloodshed, she married youthful Tenania, of the island of Raiatea, in 1832. Political, commercial, and religious problems developed. George Pritchard,* the British consul at Papeete, Tahiti, persuaded Queen Pomare to expel two French Catholic missionaries. Abel Aubert Dupetit-Thouars* responded by taking a gunboat into her harbor and demanding an apology and an indemnity under threat of bombing the island. The queen submitted, gave the French favorable trading rights, and granted France control over foreign affairs in return for promising respect for her rule, native ownership of land and freedom of worship, and protection of British missionaries (1838). Dupetit-Thouars later returned to Tahiti, disputed with Queen Pomare over flag-flying, deposed her, and annexed Tahiti to France (1843). Armand-Joseph Bruat* was installed as governor (1843–1844), during which time there was native armed resistance. Several British men-of-war appeared, one of which transported Pomare IV to the Leeward Islands for her safety (1844). Pritchard refused to recognize the treaty and was deported (1844), and the British naval officers saluted the flag of the French protectorate (1845). France modified the results of Dupetit-Thouars's action (1845), unrest diminished, and Pomare IV returned (1847). Under Bruat's successors, relations involving Tahitians, the French, and the British were more peaceful (from 1847); however, Pomare IV still had to contend with problems of administration, agriculture, commerce, international politics, and conflicting religious practices. She and her second husband had eight children. Two of them died as infants. A son named Ariiaue died of syphilis at the age of twenty (1855), whereupon the next son, Teratane, took Ariiaue's name and, when their mother Pomare IV died (1877), became Pomare V. (He had led a dissolute life beginning in the 1860s, was diseased and alcoholic, agreed to a marriage arranged for political purposes by his mother [1875], was unfaithful, and was divorced.) Teariimaevarua, the daughter of Pomare IV, was adopted by her ex-husband Tapoa II and upon his death became Queen of Bora Bora (1860). The last three children of Pomare IV, all sons, distinguished themselves: Tamatoa became King of Raiatea, his father's home island; Teriitapunui became a local chief; and Teriitua studied in France, returned to Tahiti, became a local chief, and was christened Prince Joinville in honor of a son of Louis-Philippe* of France.

In *Typee,* Melville mentions that Pomare is the queen of Tahiti and that she was forced to flee from Papeete to Emio by canoe to escape Admiral Du Petit Thouars's attack. In *Omoo,* Melville calls her Pomaree Vahinee I and Aimata, and identifies her as the monarch of Tahiti and the Society Islands in general. He adds that she is over thirty years of age, looks forty, and has been married twice—first to Pot Belly, a son of the King of Tahar, and then to the henpecked but occasionally rebellious Tanee of Imeeo. The narrator and Dr. Long Ghost try without success to obtain an audience with her in an effort to be appointed officers in her navy, but they do see her briefly. Melville probably had his moment with the queen on about 10 January 1843.

Bibliography: Robert Aldrich, *The French Presence in the South Pacific, 1842–1940* (Honolulu: University of Hawaii Press, 1990); Anderson; W. P. Morrell, *Britain in the Pacific Islands* (Oxford, England: Clarendon Press, 1960); Newbury; George Pritchard, *The Aggressions of the French at Tahiti and Other Islands in the Pacific,* ed. Paul De Deckker (Auckland, New Zealand: Auckland University Press, 1983); O'Reilly and Teissier. (These authorities use different spellings and titles for many of the Tahitian leaders.)

Pomaree-Tanee. In *Omoo. See* Tanee.

Ponce. In ''Benito Cereno,'' he is the Spanish servant of Don Joaquin Marques de Aramboalaza.

Pondo. In *Mardi,* he is a materialistic friend of Bardianna. The philosopher leaves Pondo nothing in his will.

"Pontoosuce" (1924). Poem, in *The Works of Herman Melville* (as "The Lake"). The poet begins by depicting a lovely autumnal scene, with orderly pine trees crowning a bluff over a gleaming lake, "pastoral fields" and "[l]onely roads," distant neighborhoods, corn, and orchards. "Nature," her labor completed, "reclined / In kinship with man's meditative mind." Now comes the "counter thought": "All dies!"—trees, grass, people, noble deeds, and even "[t]he poet's forms of beauty." Today's nature puts moss on "ruins of . . . aeons . . . ago." But wait. A female spirit, rosy and adorned with a combination of lively sprigs and "humid . . . mould," offers a final message: Yes, death is inevitable, but "[t]he grass . . . dies and it lives again." All things in God's cycles "wax and wane," "ever end, and begin again . . . forever." Do not cry for what "waneth here below. / Let go, let go!" She kisses the poet and leaves him both warmed and chilled with "wedded life and death." Pontoosuc Lake, which Melville dearly loved, is a few miles north of where he lived at Arrowhead, near Pittsfield, Massachusetts. (Pontoosuc is now spelled without the terminal "e.")

Bibliography: Shurr, Warren.

Poofai. In *Omoo,* he is a descendant of the kings of Taiarboo. Poofai is bold and accomplished, hates the missionaries, and opposes Queen Pomaree Vahinee I (*see* Pomare IV).

"Poor Man's Pudding and Rich Man's Crumbs" (1854). Short story. (Characters: Alexander [I] of Russia, Blandmour, Blandmour, Martha Coulter, Martha Coulter, William Coulter, William Coulter, the Duchess of Devonshire, Frederic[k] William [III] King of Prussia, George [III] the Prince Regent of England, Jehu, the Lord Mayor of London, Platoff the Hetman, Squire Teamster, [Arthur Wellesley] the [First] Duke of Wellington.) The narrator listens as his poetic friend Blandmour discusses Poor Man's Manure (snow, poor farmer's fertilizer), Poor Man's Eye-water (melted snow for sick eyes), Poor Man's Egg (cup of rain water), Poor Man's Plaster (medicine made of cheap natural elements), and Poor Man's Pudding. The narrator tests this last item by visiting a woodcutter's damp old house. His sick wife offers what hospitality she can. Their meal includes a pudding made of cheap rice, milk, and rancid salt. That night, the narrator and Blandmour share a nice cup of tea before a pleasant fire, and the narrator speaks threateningly of the rich. During the following summer (1814), the narrator visits the scene of a guildhall banquet given the previous day by the Prime Regent of England to honor some princes after the Battle of Waterloo. Hungry people who have blue tickets are allowed to enter the hall and eat the remains of the feast. The narrator is almost crushed by the frenzied mob. His guide remarks on the good fortune of those permitted to lap up the leavings of aristocrats. The narrator prays that he may be saved from poor people's pudding and rich people's crumbs.

This story was anonymously published in *Harper's New Monthly Magazine** (1 June 1854). Melville was probably paid $30. It was not reprinted in his lifetime. It is in two sadly contrasting parts and thus resembles two other stories that Melville also wrote: "The Paradise of Bachelors and Tartarus of Maids" and "The Two Temples." Melville chose 1814 as the date of the guildhall banquet, whereas the Battle of Waterloo, for which it was given, did not occur until June 1815.

Bibliography: James Duban, "Transatlantic Counterparts: The Diptych and Social Inquiry in Melville's 'Poor Man's Pudding and Rich Man's Crumbs,' " *New England Quarterly* 66 (June 1993): 274–86; Newman; NN 9; Beryl Rowland, "Melville's Waterloo in 'Rich Man's Crumbs,' " *Nineteenth-Century Fiction* 25 (September 1970): 216–21; Sealts.

Pope. In "Marquis de Grandvin: At the Hostelry." *See* Pius IX, Pope.

Pope, John (1822–1892). Army officer. Pope was born in Louisville, Kentucky, but grew up in Kaskaskia, Illinois. Upon graduating from West Point (1842), he was a topographical and surveying engineer, served under General Zachary Taylor* during the Mexican War (1846–1848), resumed surveying work, and was assigned to lighthouse duty (1859–1861). After service as a mustering officer in Chicago (early 1861), Pope fought for the Union cause but was embroiled in controversy during the early days of the Civil War. He was a brigadier general under General John C. Frémont in Missouri (July 1861), was with the Army of the Mississippi (March–April 1862), participated in the opening of the Mississippi River down to Memphis, and was promoted to major general of volunteers (March). He fought alongside General Ulysses S. Grant* (June 1862) and organized the Army of Virginia to protect Washington, D.C., and to support General George B. McClellan* during the Peninsular campaign; when McClellan failed (July), his troops were transferred to Pope's army. Pope was tactless in the face of challenging missions and unable to deflect attacks by Confederate generals Thomas J. Jackson,* Robert E. Lee,* and James Longstreet.* Pope was ineffective during the Second Battle of Bull Run (August), retreated toward Washington, and was relieved of his command (September). He blamed General Fitz John Porter, who was tried, dismissed from the Army, but later reinstated. Meanwhile, Pope was assigned to the Northwest to fight Native Americans. He was given command of the Division of the Missouri (January 1865). He held postbellum commands until his retirement (1886). Pope married Clara Pomeroy Horton of Pomeroy, Ohio, in 1859. The couple had two sons and two daughters. One of his daughters died in infancy in 1862; his wife, in 1888. Pope published his *Campaign in Virginia* (1863).

Melville mentions Pope in two poems. In "The Victor of Antietam (1862)," he is named as the Union general whose failures McClellan must rectify. In

"Lee in the Capitol," Lee as he is about to testify before the Senate remembers Pope as the Union general who retreated from the Capitol.

Bibliography: Wallace J. Schutz and Walter N. Trenerry, *Abandoned by Lincoln: A Military Biography of General John Pope* (Urbana: University of Illinois Press, 1990).

Pope, The. In "The New Ancient of Days," he is the Pontiff urged to beat down the new ancient.

Popinjay-of-the-world. In *The Confidence-Man,* this is the name by which Pitch first addresses Francis Goodman.

Po-Po, Deacon Ereemear ("Narmo-Nana Po-Po" ['The Darer-of-Devils-by Night'], "Jeremiah," "Jeremiah-in-the-Dark"). In *Omoo,* he is the Partoowye host of the narrator and Dr. Long Ghost. Po-Po is a kind, Christianized native, the husband of Arfretee, the father of Loo and a dandified son and twins, and the employer of Monee.

"The Portent (1859)" (1866). Poem, in *Battle-Pieces.* (Character: John Brown.) John Brown, called *"Weird"* here, is depicted as hanging, swaying, and casting a shadow on the green valley of Shenandoah. His cap hides *"the anguish none can draw."* Shenandoah's future is similarly obscure. But Brown's beard is the visible *"meteor of the war."* The poem is a masterpiece of Melvillean metrics.

Bibliography: Adler, Garner, NN 11, Shurr, Warren.

Porter, David (1780–1843). Naval officer. He was born in Boston, the son of an American Revolutionary War commander of privateersmen and later a sailing master. Young Porter accompanied his father to Haiti (1796), went to the West Indies twice again, became a midshipman in the U.S. Navy (1798), was promoted to lieutenant (1799), saw action off Tripoli, fought ashore and was wounded and captured (1803–1805), and was made commandant of the New Orleans naval station (1808–1810). Being given command of the famous *Essex* (1811), he protected merchantmen along the Atlantic coast, was promoted to captain (1812), and captured nine prizes, including the sloop *Alert,* the first prize taken during the War of 1812. He sailed the *Essex* around Cape Horn, and his was the first naval vessel to show the American flag in the Pacific Ocean (1813). Headquartered at the Galapagos Islands, Porter captured twelve British whalers and thus crippled the British whaling industry for decades. To combat a British fleet thought to be in the region, Porter refitted his *Essex* in the Marquesas Islands, renamed Nukuhiva Madison Island, fortified it, and sought to Americanize the natives. He sailed to Valparaiso, was blockaded there by British warships, and fought well, but he surrendered after sustaining severe casualties (1814). He was paroled and later fought on the Potomac (1814), bought property north of the White House (1815), and became commissioner of the Navy Board as well as a lavish host in Washington, D.C. (1815–1823). A friend of Stephen Decatur,* he was present at Decatur's fatal duel (1820), and he was openly critical of James Barron, who killed Decatur, and of Jesse Duncan Elliott, Decatur's second. Porter became commander-in-chief of the West Indies Squadron ordered to suppress piracy—which he did (1823–1825). In retaliation for the mistreatment of one of his officers, he intemperately raided a fort in Puerto Rico, demanded and received an apology, but was court-martialed back in Washington, D.C. Barron presided at the trial, and Elliott was on the court. Porter was convicted, was only slightly punished (1825), but resigned his commission (1826), went to Mexico, and was named commander-in-chief of the Mexican Navy (1826–1829). He modernized it, was nearly assassinated on two occasions by anti-American elements, and was never paid. He was appointed American consul general to the Barbary States but was unable to land in Algiers because of the French occupation there (1830), became chargé d'affaires to the Ottoman Empire (1831), went to Constantinople in that capacity and as minister to Turkey (1831–1843), and died there.

Porter married Evelina Anderson of Chester, Pennsylvania, in 1806. The couple had six sons and four daughters, and in addition adopted David Glasgow Farragut,* later a naval hero. The Porters' marriage collapsed into disaster. He trusted his unstable wife to guard a box of secret papers (1830) which he said validated his claim to hundreds of thousands of dollars owed him by Mexico and Spain. When the papers were later missing (1838), he accused her—as well as their ne'er-do-well oldest son (1840), whom he reviled and disowned—of the theft, and in addition accused his wife of infidelity (for good reason) and threatened to put her in a mental institution. One of his sons died of yellow fever (1828); another was the first American officer killed in the Mexican War (1846); another was court-martialed by the navy for drunkenness, insubordination, and quarreling, was acquitted (1842), fought and was captured during the Civil War, survived imprisonment, and lived until 1872. Porter was proud of one son—David Dixon Porter,* later an admiral. Two of Porter's daughters evidently died in infancy. Porter wrote *Journal of a Cruise Made to the Pacific Ocean* . . . (2 vols., 1815) and *Constantinople and Its Environs* . . . (2 vols., 1835). He was sharply intelligent, fearless, and politically farsighted, but also conceited, impetuous, choleric, and vindictive.

In "The Encantadas," Melville identifies David Porter as the commander of the *Essex,* which during the War of 1812 touched at the Enchanted Isles and unsuccessfully pursued an elusive enemy "flyaway" ship in their waters in 1813. Porter's *Essex* book, which Melville calls Porter's *Voyages into the Pacific,* was a source for some of the sketches in "The Encantadas." In his poem "Running the Batteries," Melville alludes to Porter as the father of the Union commander of the fleet that runs the Vicksburg batteries.

Bibliography: Anderson; David F. Long, *Nothing Too Daring: A Biography of Commander David Porter* (Annapolis, Md.: United States Naval Institution, 1970).

Porter, David Dixon (1813–1891). Naval officer. He was born in Chester, Pennsylvania, the son of David Porter.* Young Porter went with his father to the West Indies (1823), attended school in Mexico City while his father was commander-in-chief of the Mexican navy, entered the Mexican navy as a midshipman (1826–1829), and was captured by the Spanish and imprisoned in Havana, Cuba (1829). Released, he became a midshipman in the U.S. Navy and served in the Mediterranean area (1829–1831). During Porter's second tour of duty there, this time on the frigate *United States* (1833–1835), his commanding officer was Commodore Daniel Todd Patterson. Also aboard was Patterson's daughter George Ann, whom Porter married in 1839. (The couple had four sons and four daughters. One son later joined the navy; another, the marines.) Promoted to lieutenant (1841), Porter did Coastal Survey and Naval Observatory work (to 1846) and was in combat during the bombardment of Veracruz and Tabasco (1847) during the Mexican War. He grew impatient with desk and survey assignments in peacetime, entered the merchant service, and sailed in Caribbean, Pacific, and Australian waters (1849–1855). Rejoining the navy, he went twice to the Mediterranean region to buy camels for army use as pack animals in the Southwest (1855–1857). Tiring of naval-yard and more surveying assignments (1857–1861), he planned to go to California, but the Civil War gave him more vigorous challenges. He did blockade work off Florida and Alabama, hunted Confederate commercial raiders in Caribbean and South American waters, and was promoted to commander (1861). He commanded a mortar flotilla in support of his stepbrother David Glasgow Farragut* near New Orleans (April 1862), commanded the Mississippi Squadron (October), joined land forces in the capture of Arkansas Post (January 1863), and participated in the battle of Grand Gulf (May) and in the reduction of Vicksburg (July). He was promoted to rear admiral (July). His naval unit supported the army's Red River Expedition (spring 1864). He bombarded Fort Fisher, Wilmington, North Carolina, with sixty vessels, the largest single U.S. fleet to that time (January 1865). After the war, Porter was commandant of the Naval Academy at Annapolis (1865–1869). President Ulysses S. Grant* made him an adviser to his secretary of the navy (1869–1870). Porter, an admiral (from 1870), commanded a fleet out of Key West to settle the *Virginius* incident without further bloodshed. (Cuban authorities had intercepted and executed many Americans flying the American flag and trying to run guns to rebels against Spanish rule [1873].) Porter's final years were spent heading the U.S. Naval Board of Inspections (1877–1891). Late in life, Porter wrote *The Naval History of the Civil War* (1890).

In "Bridegroom-Dick," Porter is mentioned as a famous naval officer with whom [Thomas] Ap Catesby [Jones] served. In "Running the Batteries," Porter is identified as the Union commander of a fleet of gunboats running past the Confederate batteries at Vicksburg.

Bibliography: John D. Milligan, *Gunboats down the Mississippi* (Annapolis, Md.: United States Naval Institute, 1965).

"Portrait of a Gentleman" (1924). Sketch, in *The Works of Herman Melville.* (Character: Major John Gentian.) This essay describes Major John Gentian as a gentlemanly, outspoken Northerner of South Carolinian background; since 1865, he has been quite calm. However, he can still swear like a trooper.

Portuguese Sailor. In *Moby-Dick,* he is a *Pequod* sailor who interrupts his mates' dancing during the midnight festivities in the forecastle by reporting the advent of a storm. There were Portuguese sailors aboard the *Acushnet,* which was the partial model for the *Pequod.* Among them were Martin Brown, a boatsteerer who ran away to or was killed at one of the Marquesas, and Joseph Luis, called Jo Portuguese, who returned home; in addition, the third mate, George W. Galvan, was Portuguese.
Bibliography: Leyda.

Pot Belly. In *Omoo,* this is, according to Melville, the native nickname of the first husband of Queen Pomaree Vahinee I, who divorced him in spite of his being the son of the King of Tahar (Tahaa, just southeast of Bora Bora). In reality, Pomare IV,* Queen of Tahiti, was known as Aimata when in 1824, at the age of eleven, she married Tapoa II, then sixteen. He was the son of Tapua I and by this time was sovereign of Bora Bora, one of the Tahitian Islands. When her half-brother died in 1827, she assumed the throne and became Pomare IV. She repudiated her husband when he proved sterile (1829). She remarried and had eight children.
Bibliography: Newbury.

Potter. In *Israel Potter,* he is Potter's farmer father, who opposes his son's love affair with Jenny.

Potter. In *Israel Potter,* he is the only surviving child of Israel Potter and his wife. The boy grows up in London, repeats his father's story until people believe it, and accompanies the old man to America.

Potter, Israel ("Yellow-hair," "Yellow-mane," "Peter Perkins," "Bowser," "Rowser," "Snowser," "Towser"). In *Israel Potter,* he is a Berkshire farm boy who runs away from home at the age of eighteen when his love for Jenny is unrequited. He goes to sea, is wounded and captured at Bunker Hill, escapes to London, and becomes a courier for Dr. [Benjamin] Franklin in Paris. Potter joins Captain John Paul Jones on the *Ranger,* the *Bon Homme Richard,* and the *Ariel,* and then boards a British frigate at sea during a brief naval engagement.

He endures a forty-five-year exile in and near London, returns to America with his son, and dies in his beloved Berkshires.
   Bibliography: Lebowitz, NN 8.

Potter, Mrs. In *Israel Potter,* she is Israel Potter's farm-wife mother.

Potter, Mrs. Israel. In *Israel Potter,* she is a London bakery-shop woman who befriends Israel Potter when he is run over. The two marry. They have eleven children, but only one, a son, lives to maturity. She dies in England before Potter's return with their son to America.

Pounce. In *White-Jacket,* with Leggs, he is one of the two ship's corporals under Bland. Pounce, formerly a Liverpool policeman, ferrets out illicit gamblers aboard the *Neversink.*

Poussin, Nicolas (1594–1665). French painter. Poussin was born near Les Andelys, on the Seine in Normandy. While in school (1600–1609), he showed skill in drawing, studied in Paris (1612–1621), painted frescoes there for a Jesuit church (1622, the work now lost) and a picture of the Virgin for Notre Dame (1623, lost), and went to Rome (1624). During his first Roman period (to 1640), he was inspired by themes from classical mythology, was commissioned to paint religious works, was ill (1629), and married Anne-Marie Dughet, a Roman landscapist's sister (1633). Studying aesthetics, literature, mathematics, and optics to deepen his creativity (1630s), Poussin grew famous in Italy and Spain and was commissioned by King Louis XIII of France to supervise the decorations of the royal palace (1638). Returning to Paris, Poussin met Cardinal Richelieu, was presented to the king, and grew arrogant in the company of other artists. He was commissioned to decorate the Grand Gallery of the Louvre and to do other court work in and near Paris (1641), but he did not succeed with big palace designs and returned to Rome (1642) to begin his second Roman period (to 1658). Many of his works in the 1640s include heroic landscapes, formally structured, dramatic, but severely controlled, for example, the austere *Holy Family on the Steps* (1648) and *Landscape with the Body of Phocian Carried from Athens* (1648). Among his works in the 1650s are *Assumption of the Virgin* (1650), *Christ Healing the Blind Men of Jericho* (1651), an intelligent self-portrait (1650), and *Annunciation of the Virgin* (1657, with dark tones, subdued colors, Virgin and Gabriel in static postures). Poussin's final phase (1658–1664) is marked by moody, introspective work, his wife's death (1664), and his own paralysis (1665). Poussin and the Dutch landscape painter Herman van Swanevelt* may have influenced each other. Poussin, a baroque, pictorial classicist, believed that order must control vitality and movement, and that art should lead the viewer to make rational, moral choices. His followers favored mind-appealing drawing over eye-appealing color.
   Melville accompanied his friend George J. Adler* to the Dulwich Gallery,

south of London, and records in his 1849 journal (17 November) that he enjoyed seeing several paintings there, including an "Assumption," which is probably Poussin's *Assumption of the Virgin* (c. 1626). In "Marquis de Grandvin: At the Hostelry," Melville describes Poussin as a painter with an antique air about him. In Melville's collection of engravings were six of works by Poussin.

Bibliography: Walter Friedlaender, *Nicolas Poussin: A New Approach* (New York: Harry N. Abrams, 1964); NN 14 and 15; Wallace.

Praise-God-Barebones. In *The Confidence-Man,* this is the nickname assigned by Pitch to the Philosophical Intelligence Office Man.

Prescott, Colonel Richard. In *Israel Potter. See* McCloud, Colonel.

"Presentation to the Authorities" (1866). (Full title: "Presentation to the Authorities by Privates, of Colors captured in Battles Ending in the Surrender of Lee.") Poem, in *Battle-Pieces.* (Character: [Robert E.] Lee.) Melville says that the flags captured by the victors are here properly laid at the altar of our "sovereign" country. We would have laid down our "precious" lives "as freely." Many comrades now "lie low," with "dear" wives left behind. Let us return "[t]o waiting homes with vindicated laws." The specific event may be fictional.

Bibliography: Garner.

Priming. In *White-Jacket,* he is a nasal-voiced, harelipped gunner's mate. He belongs to Jack Chase's mess but does not share its tolerant philosophy. Priming, because of his bile and superstition, calls White Jacket a Jonah—the thirteenth of their mess—and blames him for Baldy's accident, the death of the foretopman after his leg is amputated, and Shenly's mortal illness.

Primo, Lord. In *Mardi,* he is a typical feudal lord in Dominora for whom hungry farmers toil. Such a person thinks of himself as of primary importance in the political and social scheme of things.

Prince —. In "Rammon," he is mentioned as having wonderful philosophical conceptions.

Prince of Golconda, The. In "The Marquis de Grandvin," this is an extravagant pseudonym for the Marquis de Grandvin.

Pritchard, George (1796–1883). British missionary. Born in Birmingham, he was ordained in the Congregational church (1824), married Eliza Aillen, and left with her almost at once to become a Protestant missionary in Tahiti (1824). Pritchard was in charge of Christian religious life at Papeete (1825), developed commercial interests in the islands, considered moving his Protestant community to the Marquesas (1827), and appealed vainly to his government to be named

British consul at Tahiti. Then trouble began: Queen Pomare IV* refused admittance to two French priests to her dominions (1836); Jacques-Antoine Moerenhout* was named American consul there (1836); and this caused Pritchard to be appointed English consul (1837), on condition that he stop his missionary work. He agreed but kept on mixing business and religion anyway. He aided Moerenhout and his Chilean wife at a time of native unrest, during which Moerenhout was wounded and his wife murdered (1838). Pritchard still felt bothered by increasingly pro-French Tahitian authorities, even as Moerenhout feared a concentration in Pritchard of too much religious, political, and commercial power. Conflicts among British, French, and American forces in Hawaii (from 1840) exacerbated the situation, until the islands were placed under French protection (1842). Pritchard meanwhile returned to England to report adverse conditions in the South Pacific generally (1841–1843). His book entitled *The Missionary's Reward; or, The Success of the Gospel in the Pacific* was published in London (1844) after his return to Tahiti, where, ill-armed with new powers, he was seized by the French, charged with fomenting trouble among the natives, and expelled (1844). Home a final time, he sought compensation for £4,000 in property damage. Queen Victoria decreed that the matter had been settled satisfactorily (1845). Pritchard also wrote but never published *The Aggressions of the French at Tahiti and Other Islands in the Pacific.* He enjoyed a lengthy retirement and was survived by his widow and several children.

In *Typee,* Melville describes Pritchard as the famous British missionary consul at Papeete, Tahiti. He adds that Mrs. Pritchard refuses to be intimidated by the French under Admiral [Abel Aubert] Du Petit Thouars. In *Omoo,* Pritchard, while he is absent back in England, leaves Wilson in his place.

Bibliography: Anderson; O'Reilly and Teissier; George Pritchard, *The Aggressions of the French at Tahiti and Other Islands in the Pacific,* ed. Paul de Deckker (Auckland, New Zealand: Auckland University Press, 1983).

Pritchard, Mrs. In *Typee,* she is the brave wife of the British consul at Papeete, Tahiti. She defends her flag when the French under Admiral [Abel Aubert] Du Petit Thouars want it taken down.

Prodigal, The. In *Clarel. See* the Lyonese.

Professor, The. In *White-Jacket,* he is an erudite, gentlemanly noncombatant aboard the *Neversink.* About forty years of age, he instructs the midshipmen every afternoon in ballistics, mathematics, naval tactics, and navigation. The Professor rebukes Boat Plug, Pert, Dick Dash, and Slim. This tall, skinny pedant was once a West Point cadet but became disqualified because of weak eyes. The Professor is based on Henry Hayes Lockwood, a graduate of West Point who served aboard the *United States,* the naval vessel on which Melville sailed (1843–1844) and which is the model of his *Neversink.*

Bibliography: NN 5.

"Profundity and Levity" (1924). Poem, with an introduction in prose, in *Weeds and Wildings,* as part of the section entitled "This, That and the Other." Melville explains that an owl, disturbed by a meadowlark's morning song, responds poetically thus: The lark leaves "wisdom behind," and instead goes "curving and singing . . . in the sun," while I cudgel my wits "in wood" and ask, since I "blink . . . at strong light" and "wander . . . in night like a dream," whether life is worth living.

Bibliography: Shurr, Stein.

Punchinello. In "Marquis de Grandvin: Naples in the Time of Bomba . . . ," he is a member of the jolly Neapolitan crowd.

Purser, Mr. In *Billy Budd,* he is Captain Vere's purser. He tells the ship's surgeon that he was surprised to note that Billy Budd displayed no death spasm when he was hanged.

Putnam, George Palmer (1814–1872). Publisher. He was born in Brunswick, Maine. His father was chronically ill, and his mother largely supported the family by managing a coeducational school. After minimal formal education there, Putnam was apprenticed to his father's sister's husband, who was a Boston carpet merchant (1825). Putnam escaped to New York (1829), worked in a bookstore and for the publishing firm of Wiley & Long (1833–1840). Putnam educated himself by a rigorous program of after-hours reading. He compiled a popular *Chronology; or, an Introduction and Index to Universal History* (1833 and later). He became a partner of John Wiley and George Long (1838 or 1840). When the firm became Wiley & Putnam, Putnam was placed in charge of the London branch office (1837–1847). He started an American literary agency not only in England but also in Belgium, France, Germany, and Italy, to exchange American and foreign books (c. 1838). He wrote and published *The Tourist in Europe* (1838). Returning home briefly (1841), Putnam married Victorine Haven, one of his mother's former pupils. The bride, age sixteen, accompanied him back to London, where he solidified his relationship with the British book industry, of importance to his own publishing interests. To correct British misconceptions about Americans, especially after Charles Dickens published his *American Notes,* Putnam published *American Facts* (1845). He was London correspondent for three American newspapers. When he, his wife, and their growing family returned to the United States, he broke up his partnership with Wiley (1847) and established his own firm (from 1848). Putnam quickly obtained rights to publish significant American authors.

When Charles Frederick Briggs sought a publisher for a magazine he had in mind, Putnam agreed to publish what became *Putnam's Magazine** (1853–1857). He sold it to the New York publishing firm of Dix and Edwards (c. 1855). Coedited part of the time by George William Curtis* and Parke Godwin, it suspended independent publication because of financial shortages caused by dishonest associates and also the Panic of 1857. It resumed under the editorship of Putnam and Briggs (1868) but soon merged with *Scribner's Monthly* (1870). During and after the Civil War, Putnam coedited *The Rebellion Record* (11 vols. and supplement, 1861–1868) and consigned his publishing efforts to another firm (1862–1868). He renamed his publishing firm G. P. Putnam and Son (1866–1871) and G. P. Putnam and Sons (from 1871). He died at work in his office.

From 1837 Putnam fought for a sensible, ethical international copyright law. He always favored American material over foreign reprints and early and late published works by the following Americans, among others: Louis Agassiz, William Cullen Bryant, James Fenimore Cooper,* Nathaniel Hawthorne* and his wife Sophia (Putnam was Sophia Hawthorne's cousin), Washington Irving,* Henry Wadsworth Longfellow, James Russell Lowell, Edgar Allan Poe,* Bayard Taylor,* Henry David Thoreau,* and Melville. Three of Putnam's eleven children were especially noteworthy: George Haven Putnam was a Union Army major and a prisoner of war during the Civil War, became president of his father's publishing house (1872–1930), and was the author of miscellaneous works, including *A Memoir of George Palmer Putnam* (2 vols., 1907); Ruth Putnam was a biographer and historian; and Mary Corinna Putnam Jacobi was a physician, author, and educator.

Melville's relationship with Putnam began when Irving introduced Melville's brother Gansevoort Melville* to Putnam in London (1846) and Putnam accepted *Typee* for American publication. He was involved in publishing the following other works by Melville: "The Apple-Tree Table," "The Bell-Tower," "Benito Cereno," *Clarel,* "The Encantadas," "I and My Chimney," *Israel Potter* in serial form, and "The Lightning-Rod Man." Putnam and Briggs rejected Melville's "The Two Temples" in 1854. Melville was upset when in 1857 Putnam sold the plates of *Israel Potter* to the Philadelphia publisher T. B. Peterson of Philadelphia, who published the novel as *The Refugee* (1865). In "A Thought on Book-Binding," Melville expresses the wish that Putnam, who published *The Red Rover,* by Cooper, had bound it more appropriately—in cloth the color of flame, blood, or jet.

Bibliography: Miriam N. Kotzin, "George Palmer Putnam," pp. 300–3 in *Dictionary of Literary Biography,* vol. 3, *Antebellum Writers in New York and the South,* ed. Joel Myerson (Detroit: Gale Research Company, 1979).

Putnam, Israel (1718–1790). Army officer. He was born in Salem Village (now Danvers), Massachusetts. He was so poorly educated that his adult writing is practically illiterate. He built a house on land given him by his father (1738), married Hannah Pope (1739), and soon moved with her to the part of Pomfret that later was designated as Brooklyn, Connecticut, where he prospered. When the French and Indian War erupted (1754), he became a second lieutenant in the Connecticut volunteers, was promoted to captain (1755), fought under the command of General William Johnson, and was promoted to major (1758) and lieutenant colonel (1759)—seeing much action around Lake Champlain and

Lake George. Putnam was part of a group seeking to capture Havana, only to be shipwrecked and decimated by drowning and sickness and hunger ashore (1762). After being in combat against Pontiac and his men (1764), Putnam suffered the death of his wife (1765), who had given birth to four sons and six daughters. He settled into pre-Revolutionary politics and married Deborah Lothrop Avery Gardiner, the widow of the prosperous, socially important John Gardiner (1767). Putnam ran a tavern while he continued in local politics. When he heard that the British government was to cede land in Florida to veterans, he traveled in the Caribbean and up the Mississippi River but got no land (1772–1773). A colonel in the Connecticut militia (from 1774), he joined revolutionary forces after the battle of Lexington, became a brigadier general in Connecticut and a major general in the Continental Army (1775), and was conspicuous—not always admirably—throughout the American Revolution. Though not in supreme command, he bustled bravely during the battle of Bunker Hill (June 1775), commanded in New York City, participated in the disastrous battle of Long Island (August 1776), and commanded in Philadelphia. He earned the disapproval of General George Washington* when he was tardy in advancing to Princeton as ordered (January 1777), was relegated to a command in the Hudson River highlands, disobeyed another order from Washington, was rebuked, was ordered to do recruiting work—performed unsatisfactorily—and was sent to insignificant posts. After sustaining a paralytic stroke (1779), Putnam was mustered out. His cockiness and popularity earned him assignments above his ability. Legends have multiplied about his undoubted but foolhardy courage.

In *Israel Potter,* General Putnam is identified as the commanding officer of the rebellious American soldiers at Bunker Hill, to which hill Melville dedicates his novel.

Bibliography: Fredrike Shumway Smith, *Old Put: The Story of Major General Israel Putnam* ([Chicago]: Rand McNally, 1967).

Putnam's Monthly Magazine. (Original full title: *Putnam's Monthly Magazine of American Literature, Science, and Art.*) Magazine. It was founded in 1853, evidently at the instigation of Charles Frederick Briggs. Through George William Curtis,* Briggs obtained an entree to George Palmer Putnam,* who agreed to publish the planned magazine, hired Curtis and Parke Godwin as assistant editors, and helped solicit material from many established American authors. They include—in addition to Melville—Louis Agassiz, William Cullen Bryant, James Fenimore Cooper,* Horace Greeley, Nathaniel Hawthorne* and his wife Sophia, Washington Irving,* Henry Wadsworth Longfellow, James Russell Lowell, Edgar Allan Poe,* Bayard Taylor,* and Henry David Thoreau,* as well as many biographers, critics, historians, humorists, political commentators, scientists, and travel writers. Putnam sold his magazine to the New York publishing firm of Dix and Edwards (c. 1855). After *Putnam's Magazine* suffered financial reverses because of the Panic of 1857 and also because dishonest associates mishandled dwindling funds, it merged with *Emerson's United States Magazine*

(1857)—Emerson being the publisher Jesse Milton Emerson. *Putnam's Monthly Magazine: Original Papers on Literature, Science, Art, and National Interests* was revived by Putnam and Briggs as a separate entity (1868), did well, and merged with *Scribner's Monthly* (1870). A new *Putnam's* began again (1906) but merged with the *Atlantic Monthly* (1910).

The original *Putnam's Monthly Magazine* published the following works by Melville: "The Apple-Tree Table," "The Bell-Tower," "Benito Cereno," "The Encantadas," "I and My Chimney," *Israel Potter* in serial form, and "The Lightning-Rod Man." Putnam and Briggs rejected Melville's "The Two Temples" (1854). *Putnam's* published a letter from Richard Tobias Greene* (July 1857) supporting the veracity of statements about him in *Typee,* which novel George Palmer Putnam had published.

Bibliography: Edward E. Chielens, ed., *American Literary Magazines: The Eighteenth and Nineteenth Centuries* (Westport, Conn.: Greenwood Press, 1986); Leyda; NN 14.

"Puzzlement as to a Figure Left Solitary on a Unique Fragment of Greek Basso-Relievo" (1947). Poem, in *Collected Poems of Herman Melville.* The poet is puzzled on seeing a carved figure of the goddess Artemis looking Eve-like, flirtatious, and hence human. Is a boyfriend nearby but out of sight?

Bibliography: Stein.

Q

Queen of Sheba, The. In "Rammon." *See* Sheba, the Princess of.

Queequeg. In *Moby-Dick,* he is Ishmael's bosom friend, a tattooed Polynesian prince whose father was king of the island of Kokovoko. Queequeg is assigned to be Starbuck's harpooner, rescues Tashtego from a sinking whale head, becomes ill after working in the damp hold, and orders the carpenter to make him a coffin. When Queequeg recovers his health, he uses the coffin for a sea chest. After the *Pequod* sinks, the coffin pops up from the depths and saves Ishmael's life. Captain Peleg calls Queequeg Quohog. Queequeg's background, appearance, artifacts, character, and behavior may owe something to the detailed comments on an amiable New Zealand chief named Ko-towatowa, of Kororarika, by Charles Wilkes in his *Narrative of the U.S. Exploring Expedition during the Years 1838, 1839, 1849, 1841, 1842* (5 vols. and atlas, 1845).

Bibliography: Brian Higgins and Hershel Parker, eds., *Critical Essays on Herman Melville's Moby-Dick* (New York: G. K. Hall, 1992); Jaffé; Robert Martin, "Sleeping with a Savage: Deculturation in *Moby-Dick,*" American Transcendental Quarterly n.s. 5 (September 1991): 195–203; Helen P. Trimpi, "Melville's Use of Demonology and Witchcraft in *Moby-Dick,*" *History of Ideas* 30 (October–December 1969): 543–62.

Quiddi. In *Mardi,* he is an improvisator, cited by Babbalanja. His name may echo the word *quiddity.*

Quixote, Don. The hero of *Don Quixote de la Mancha,* by Miguel de Cervantes Saavedra. Don Quixote is unhinged mentally because of a diet of chivalric romances, gets himself into a suit of rusty armor and a cardboard helmet, and becomes his notion of a knight errant. He intends to go far and wide, righting wrongs. There are times when he is sane enough, for example, when toward the end an enemy defeats him and forces him to discontinue his self-imposed mission. Thereafter, he goes home, repents, and dies. The narrator of ''The Piazza'' calls Don Quixote the ''sagest sage that ever lived.'' In ''The Rusty Man (by a Soured One),'' Melville accords the unnamed Don a sardonic accolade for his outmoded chivalry.

Bibliography: E. C. Riley, *Don Quixote* (London: Allen & Unwin, 1986).

Quohog. In *Moby-Dick,* this is Captain Peleg's mispronunciation of the name Queequeg.

Quoin. In *White-Jacket,* he is a bitter, whimsical old quarter-gunner whom Lemsford mistakenly suspects of destroying his poems.

R

Rabbi, The ("Rabboni"). In *Clarel,* he is a rabbi who visits Nathan, Agar, and Ruth. The rabbi gazes coldly on Clarel, who has been brought by Nehemiah.

Rabboni. In *Clarel.* This is the nickname for the Rabbi.

Rabeelee. In *Mardi,* he is a laughing philosopher cited by Babbalanja in a rare mood of humor. The name Rabeelee obviously echoes that of François Rabelais (c. 1495–1553), the French physician and ribald writer.

Radney ("Rad"). In *Moby-Dick,* he is the ugly Vineyarder mate of the *Town-Ho.* Radney offended Steelkilt, one of his men, and threatened him with a hammer. Steelkilt crushed his jaw for his pains. Radney then tied and flogged Steelkilt, who would have murdered him but for the timely appearance of Moby Dick, which both men chased and which savagely killed Radney. Radney may be modeled in part on a man named Jenney, the first officer of the *Nassau,* a whaleship out of New Bedford. He argued with a crew member named Luther Fox, who severely cut Jenney's leg with a mincing knife. Jenney bled to death (April 1843). Fox was handed over to American consular authorities in Honolulu (June).
  Bibliography: Leyda.

Radney, Mrs. In *Moby-Dick,* she is the wife of the *Town-Ho* mate. She dreams in Nantucket of the white whale that killed her husband.

"A Rail Road Cutting near Alexandria in 1855" (1947). Poem, in *Collected Poems of Herman Melville.* The poet deplores the Egyptian engine, inspired by the acclaimed ''Watts his name,'' as it rolls through ''tomb and catacomb,'' makes a pyramid slip, and uproots glorious objects of former veneration. In an 1857 journal entry, Melville, who traveled from Alexandria to Cairo by the recently constructed railroad, records seeing a macadamized road in Alexandria which he sadly thought was made ''with the pulverised ruins of thousand cities'' (3 January).

Bibliography: NN 15; Shurr.

''Rammon'' (1947). Prose and poetic piece, in *Collected Poems of Herman Melville.* (Characters: Buddha, King Hiram [I], Jeroboam, Jethro, Prince —, Prince Rammon, King Rehoboam, the Princess of Sheba, Solomon, Zardi.) When Soloman's haughty and disdainful son Rehoboam is crowned, penitent Jeroboam offers a pledge of allegiance but is spurned. This action further saddens Rammon, a precocious son of Solomon and Rehoboam's half-brother. Rammon has been thinking of the novel doctrine of immortality promulgated by Buddha. The princess of Sheba has brought Buddha's teachings to Jerusalem. Rammon turns to Zardi, a pleasant Tyrian improvisator, in quest for an explanation of this doctrine. It is not long, however, before Rammon notes the shallowness of Zardi, who sings for him a song of ''The Enviable Isles,'' which is a place where both sorrow and glee are lulled. *See also* ''The Enviable Isles.''

Bibliography: Eleanor M. Tilton, ''Melville's 'Rammon': A Text and Commentary,'' *Harvard Library Bulletin* 13 (Winter 1959): 50–91.

Rammon, Prince. In ''Rammon,'' he is identified as a precocious, isolated, not robust son of Solomon's old age. Rammon is concerned with the doctrine of immortality, does not wish to have eternal life, and is rendered uneasy when he studies Buddha.

Raneds. In ''Benito Cereno,'' he is the mate of Benito Cereno's *San Dominick.* Raneds, a good navigator, was senselessly killed by the rebellious slaves simply for making a seemingly suspicious gesture with his quadrant.

Rani, Prince. In *Mardi,* he is a Juam prince who refused to become king because, if he had done so, he would have had to give up roving.

Raphael (1483–1520). (Full name: Raphael Sanzio.) Italian painter. Raphael was born in Urbino, the son of a palace painter and chronicler. Raphael studied under his father and Perugino (by about 1494) and then went to Florence (1504–1508), where he profited by analyzing works by several masters, including Leonardo* da Vinci. Raphael was summoned to Rome by Pope Julius II to decorate part of the Vatican Palace (1508–1513), at a time when Michelangelo* was working on the Sistine Chapel ceiling. Pope Leo X ordered Raphael to do other decorative work (from 1513). His many oil, fresco, and tempera paintings include alterpieces, portraits, and mythological, historical, and religious works.

He made skillful drawings and sketches, and was an architect, papal archaeologist, and tentative sculptor. Three of Raphael's most exquisite palace paintings are *Parnassus* (c. 1511), *School of Athens* (c. 1512), and *Deliverance of St. Peter from Prison* (c. 1513). Among his other great paintings are *St. George* (c. 1505), *La Belle Jardinière* (1507), *The Sistine Madonna* (c. 1514), *The Fornarina* (c. 1518), and *The Transfiguration* (1520). His best portraits include those of Julius II (c. 1512), Baldassare Castiglione (c. 1515), and Leo X with the cardinals Giulio de' Medici and Luigi de' Rossi (1518). Raphael died of fever in Rome and is buried in the Pantheon.

When Melville was in Rome, he saw several of Raphael's works and also items once attributed to Raphael, and Melville's journal has brief references to them (March 1857). In "Marquis de Grandvin: At the Hostelry," Melville mentions Raphael in a headnote as worried about Dante's melancholy.

Bibliography: Roger Jones and Nicholas Penny, *Raphael* (New Haven, Conn.: Yale University Press, 1983).

Rartoo. In *Omoo,* he is an old chief in whose house the narrator and Dr. Long Ghost stay while passing through Tamai.

Rash, Captain. In *White-Jacket,* he is an imaginary captain, typical of mariners who rashly try to round treacherous Cape Horn under too much sail.

Ratcliffe, Lieutenant. In *Billy Budd,* he is the officer from the *Bellipotent* who boards the *Rights-of-Man.*

"The Ravaged Villa" (1891). Poem, in *Timoleon.* Broken "sylvan vases" are covered with brambles. The fountain is choked. Spiders are in the laurels. Weeds drive the flowers away. And a bust of Apollo is converted to "lime for Mammon's tower." Here Melville voices his disgust that classical beauty and lore have surrendered to materialism. In Naples, Melville saw, as he puts it in his 1857 journal, "remains of school of Virgil and other ruins of villas" (20 February).

Bibliography: Cohen, NN 11 and 15, Stein, Warren.

Raveling. In *White-Jacket,* this is the name of any stingy sailor who refuses to give a needy shipmate even a needleful of thread.

Ravoo. In *Mardi,* he is the fleet-footed messenger of Hivohitee MDCCCXLVIII on the isle of Maramma.

Raymonda. In *Mardi,* she is a deceased subject whose simplicity King Peepi inherited.

Rea. In *Mardi,* she is a maiden in Queen Hautia's court on the isle of Flozella-a-Nina. According to Mohi's story, Rea resembles the lost Ady, whom Ady's lover Ozonna vainly seeks. Mohi tells the story hoping to dissuade Taji from continuing his search for his lost Yillah.

"A Reasonable Constitution" (1947). Poem, in *Collected Poems of Herman Melville.* It does not matter that "Reason forged your scheme." After all, "Reason dreamed the Utopia's dream." It is silly to think that reason can govern man, that "reasoning creature."
   Bibliography: Shurr.

Reb. In "The Scout toward Aldie," he is a Confederate prisoner of the Colonel's men. They offer him a drink.

"Rebel Color-Bearers at Shiloh" (1866). (Full title: "Rebel Color-Bearers at Shiloh: A plea against the vindictive cry raised by civilians shortly after the Surrender at Appomattox.") Poem, in *Battle-Pieces.* (Characters: [General Ulysses S.] Grant, [General Thomas J.] Stonewall [Jackson], [General Robert E.] Lee, [General George B.] McClellan.) Melville praises the courage and pride of the Confederate color bearers, who were virtual "martyrs" at Shiloh, and says, "Perish their Cause! but mark the men," as their admiring opponents did. Events at Shiloh, Chickamauga, and the Wilderness "have passed away," and treason is dying out. Let us be noble, not spiteful, and remember how "Grant met Lee." In a note, Melville explains that the incident inspiring his poem was reported in *The Rebellion Record.* During the first day of the battle of Shiloh (April 1862), the Confederate color bearers displayed such audacity that Union sharpshooters were ordered not to kill them.
   Bibliography: Cohen, Garner, NN 11.

Redburn. In *Redburn,* he is Wellingborough Redburn's brother, eight years older than the sailor. He gives his younger brother a letter to a friend named Jones. This letter aids Redburn in finding a berth on Captain Riga's *Highlander.* This older brother is partly based on Melville's older brother Gansevoort Melville.*

Redburn. In *Redburn,* he is Wellingborough Redburn's infant brother.

Redburn (1849). (Full title: *Redburn: His First Voyage, Being the Sailor-boy Confessions and Reminiscences of the Son-of-a-Gentleman, in the Merchant Service.*) Novel. (Characters: Betty, Bill, Billy, Jack Blunt, Harry Bolton, Brandy-Nan, Bridenstoke, the Marquis of Bristol, Carlo, Dallabdoolmans, Danby, Mrs. Handsome Mary Danby, De Squak, Colonel Digby, Daniel Dods, Tobias Drinker, the Duke, the Duke [of Wellington], Lord George Flagstaff, Patrick Flinnigan, Lady Georgina Theresa, Goodwell, the Greenlander, Gun-Deck, Jackson, Betsy Jennings, Jones, Jonathan Jones, Mrs. Jones, Judy, Miss L—, Captain [Baron Georg Heinrich von] Langsdorff, Larry, Lavender, Tom Legare, Lord Lovely, Mary, Matilda, Max the Dutchman, Meg, Molly, Morille, Ned, O'Brien, Mrs. O'Brien, Mike O'Regan, Mrs. O'Regan, Pat O'Regan, Teddy O'Regan, Parkins, Pat, Pat, Peggy, Redburn, Redburn, Jane Redburn, Martha Redburn, Mary Redburn, Mrs. Walter Redburn, Walter Redburn, Wellingborough Redburn, Captain Riga, Rigs, [William] Roscoe, Sally, Sampson, Miguel Saveda, Bob Still, Sweeny, Thompson, the Marquis of Waterford, Senator Wellingborough, Wilt, Wood.)

The young narrator is Wellingborough Redburn, the son of a New York importer, once rich, then bankrupt, and now dead. Long dreaming of going to sea, Redburn says goodbye to his mother and sisters one June day, accepts a gun from his sick and officious older brother to sell, sails 180 miles down the Hudson River to Manhattan, visits the home of a college friend of his brother's, and signs aboard the *Highlander,* commanded by deceptively jolly Captain Riga. Redburn conquers hunger, homesickness, and seasickness; follows orders ignorantly; accepts rum from a fellow sailor despite his temperance pledge but declines to smoke; argues with his mates when a drunken sailor pitches himself overboard to his death; and is frightened by the "starved tiger" eye of a venomous little bully named Jackson.

Redburn takes note of his fellow sailors and is befriended by a few. The *Highlander* passes a Hamburg vessel sailing west; rams another during the night; sees a few whales (too small to swallow Jonah, Redburn thinks); and passes the Grand Banks, off which the men observe a ruined vessel with greenish corpses lashed to her rails. Redburn grows nimble in following orders but finds nautical terms puzzling, is not allowed to stand at the helm, and observes the passengers, including twenty or so in steerage. The crew welcomes a six-year-old stowaway returning to England following the death of his father in America. After thirty days, the *Highlander* passes Ireland and Wales and docks at Liverpool. Redburn is surprised when a sailor called Max the Dutchman, who spoke of his wife Meg in New York, embraces his wife Sally in Liverpool.

Having light duties and short hours aboard ship, the sailors follow Jackson and board at Handsome Mary's Baltimore Clipper, at company expense. Riga stays at the Arms Hotel, attends the theater, entertains other captains aboard the *Highlander,* and drinks too much. Six weeks pass. Redburn tries to follow a "prosy old guide-book" his father bought in Liverpool in 1808, but cannot locate old landmarks with it, and therefore concludes that what guided the father does not always help the son. He admires the stone docks, sees some Germans seeking passage to the New World, talks with other sailors, attends a chapel ship, and visits a church on land. One day he finds a woman and her three children starving in a warehouse cellar. He cannot persuade authorities to aid, brings food and water to them himself, but a few days later discovers that they have died and been removed. Redburn observes beggars, maimed soldiers, immigrant laborers, proud-looking blacks, a Chartist, club members, and one afternoon three lovely girls who live with their parents in a country cottage. He is thrilled when they invite him in for tea and muffins.

Next day Redburn meets Harry Bolton, an effeminate young man who hints at an aristocratic past. He says that he is a Bury St. Edmunds orphan, has inherited money, was a midshipman for an East India company, and wants to be a seaman on the *Highlander*. With Harry financing a brief trip to London, the two visit an establishment which Redburn calls a "Palace of Aladdin" and in which Harry gambles and loses a large sum of money. The pair take a whirlwind train back to Liverpool. Harry signs up to work on Redburn's ship. With 500 emigrant passengers aboard in fetid conditions, the *Highlander* shoves off. A drunken sailor is slung onto the ship by a crimp for pay, is found dead in his bunk glowing phosphorescently, and is dumped overboard. Only Jackson is unmoved. A fifteen-year-old Sicilian passenger named Carlo thrills the crew by playing his hand organ. Dainty Harry disgusts the other sailors when, in spite of his boasts of nautical experience, he displays fear when ordered aloft in the rigging. Meanwhile, the dying Jackson sits idly by, smoking incessantly and cursing the world.

Redburn watches the emigrants. They have only one stove on which to cook. The Irish among them mistake Ireland for America. Two widowed Irish sisters have a set of triplets each. A famine develops. Riga refuses to provide aid. Cholera breaks out, and several die. Two babies are born aboard ship. A courageous mate and some crew members alleviate unspeakable conditions in steerage. When the *Highlander* is off Cape Cod, Jackson leaves his pallet and helps reef the sails, but he soon spouts blood from sin-ruined lungs and falls from the main-topsail-yard to his watery grave. After four months away from her home port, the *Highlander* is boarded by a pilot off the New Jersey coast. To avoid quarantine, the emigrants must jettison their bedding and scrub and fumigate their quarters. Cabin passengers are privately disembarked. Carlo sings himself ashore. Once the ship is docked, the men go to town, where Redburn and Harry buy food and ginger pop to share in the forecastle. Redburn picks up a message that he is required back home, tries without success to find Harry a job as a clerk in New York City, and is disgusted when Captain Riga tries to dock Redburn's pay because he dropped some hammers overboard. Riga hands Harry a dollar or two, but the proud fellow spurns it. Redburn and Harry bid each other farewell. While sailing on the Pacific Ocean years later, Redburn learns that Harry was crushed to death by a whale off Brazil.

Melville, distressed early in 1849 by the popular and critical failure of his novel *Mardi,* quickly composed two simpler and more superficially exciting narratives. They are *Redburn* and *White-Jacket.* He wrote the first in about three months; the second, in about two more. He was not pleased with either. He wrote the following to his father-in-law Lemuel Shaw*: "[N]o reputation that is gratifying to me, can possibly be achieved by either of these books. They are two *jobs,* which I have done for money—being forced to it, as other men are to sawing wood" (6 October 1849).

Redburn is partly autobiographical. Paralleling Redburn's case, Melville's father Allan Melvill* was an importer and visited Liverpool, his mother Maria Gansevoort Melville,* when widowed, moved to a small Hudson River town, his older brother Gansevoort Melville* was ill and preachy, and Melville's sisters Augusta Melville,* Catherine Gansevoort Melville (later Catherine Gansevoort Melville Hoadley*), Frances Priscilla Melville,* and Helen Maria Melville (later Helen Maria Melville Griggs*) echo Redburn's Jane, Martha, and Mary. The Manhattan friend of Redburn's brother is based on Alexander Warfield Bradford.* The *Highlander* is a copy of the *St. Lawrence,* aboard which Melville sailed from New York to Liverpool and back (1839), while several real-life crew members from the latter merchantman reappear in partly fictional form aboard the former. Redburn's progressive disappointments mirror those of his author's early manhood. A published source that Melville used is *The Picture of Liverpool; or Stranger's Guide* (1808), which is the equivalent of Redburn's "prosy old guide-book" and which Melville plundered when he has Redburn describe Liverpool sights. Sailors' yarns, published and otherwise, helped Melville, who also made up many of Redburn's adventures from his imagination. Reviews of *Redburn* in the United States and England were generally complimentary. How to define *Redburn* puzzled some reviewers because it was an amalgam of autobiography, romantic fiction, and social criticism. In addition, it is narrated from a shifting point of view—partly that of a callow participant, and partly that of a wiser man full of sad memories.

Richard Bentley* offered Melville £100 for the right to publish *Redburn* in England (September 1849), from proofs prepared by Harper & Brothers,* which published the American edition (November). By then, Melville was in England seeking a British publisher for *White-Jacket.* Meanwhile, sales of *Redburn* had begun to be disappointing. American royalties on 3,314 copies sold (through 1850) came to $300; slow sales later (to 1891) brought only an additional $384.

Bibliography: Gilman; Jonathan L. Hall, " 'Every Man of Them Almost Was a Volume of Voyages': Writing the Self in Melville's *Redburn,*" *American Transcendental Quarterly* n.s. 5 (December 1991): 259–71; NN 4.

Redburn, Jane. In *Redburn,* she is one of Wellingborough Redburn's three sisters. Melville had four sisters whom he left back home when, like his autobiographical hero Redburn, he sailed to Liverpool.

Redburn, Martha. In *Redburn,* she is another of Wellingborough Redburn's three sisters.

Redburn, Mary. In *Redburn,* she is another of Wellingborough Redburn's three sisters.

Redburn, Mrs. Walter. In *Redburn,* she is Wellingborough Redburn's affectionate mother. She is closely based on Melville's own mother Maria Gansevoort Melville.*

Redburn, Walter. In *Redburn,* he was Wellingborough Redburn's father, now a deceased bankrupt. Before his financial reverses, he was an importer on Broad Street, in New York, and he used to cross the Atlantic Ocean frequently. Redburn finds that his father's guidebook to Liverpool, purchased during the man's 1808 business and pleasure trip to this city, does not help the son. Walter Redburn is based on Melville's father Allan Melvill.*

Redburn, Wellingborough ("Boots," "Buttons," "Jack," "Jimmy Dux," "Pillgarlic"). In *Redburn,* he is the young man who leaves his home near the Hudson River, 180 miles north of New York City, to ship aboard the *Highlander.* She is commanded by Captain Riga and is bound for Liverpool. Once there, Redburn sees slum misery, meets Harry Bolton, and after a brief nocturnal visit with that friend to London boards the ship again for the voyage back home. He arrives much matured by his first voyage. Young Redburn is in many significant ways an autobiographical hero. The name Wellingborough is probably a reflection of Lansingborough, the New York town from which Melville departed for his first nautical adventure.

Red Hot Coal. In *White-Jacket,* he is mentioned in an anecdote as a murderous Native American on the Mississippi River. He collected scalps. His killing of Yellow Torch is compared to the naval habit of collecting enemy ships. Ben Browns painted hands on Red Hot Coal's blanket as symbols of victories.

Red Pepper. In *Billy Budd,* he is a red-haired forecastle mate of Billy's to whom Billy reports that the supercilious-acting afterguardsman was skulking around in their area.

Red Shirt, The. In "Marquis de Grandvin: Naples in the Time of Bomba . . ." *See* Garibaldi, Giuseppe.

Red Whiskers. In *Billy Budd,* he is a *Bellipotent* sailor whose insulting horseplay with Billy results in Billy's beating him up fast. Then he and Billy become good friends.

Rehoboam, King. In "Rammon," he is Solomon's arrogant, disdainful, ignorant son and successor. Rehoboam is depicted as Rammon's half-brother during whose reign troubles and disruption occur.

Reine. In *Omoo,* he is a French assistant, as is [Édouard Jules Gabrielle de] Carpegna, of [Armand-Joseph] Bruat, the governor of Tahiti. In real life, Édouard Dominique Reine was a lieutenant aboard the *Reine Blanche,* under the command of Abel Aubert Dupetit-Thouars.*
   Bibliography: George Pritchard,* *The Aggression of the French at Tahiti and Other*

Islands in the Pacific, ed. Paul De Deckker (Auckland, New Zealand: Auckland University Press, 1983).

"The Released Rebel Prisoner (June, 1865)" (1866). Poem, in *Battle-Pieces.* (Characters: [General Turner] Ashby, [General Ambrose Powell] Hill, [General James E. B.] Stuart.) The "disarmed" and "jail-worn" rebel, now seeing the massed might of the Union forces, is aware that his rebellion was deceitful, remembers his fallen leaders, and is reluctant to return home—because his home and his brothers are all gone.

Rembrandt (1606–1669). (Full name: Rembrandt Harmensz van Rijn.) Dutch painter, etcher, and illustrator. Rembrandt was born in Leiden, went to school and to the university there (through 1620), was trained in art (to 1623), moved to Amsterdam (1631), and married the wealthy Saskia Uylenburgh in 1634. After a son and two daughters died in infancy, she had a son, Titus (1641), who survived to adulthood. After Saskia's death (1642), Rembrandt had a mistress named Geertghe Dircx (to 1648), after which she successfully sued him for breach of promise (1649). By then he had a companion named Hendrickje Stoffels, who bore him a daughter, causing some scandal (1654), and who died of the plague (1663). Rembrandt had gone bankrupt (1656), suffered the loss at auction of his possessions (1657, 1658), and lived in poverty and seclusion. Titus, whose face he often painted, died of the plague a year before Rembrandt did. Rembrandt was a master at painting portraits, biblical, historical, and mythological scenes, landscapes, genre pictures, and still lifes. His best works are notable for sumptuous brush strokes, rich and somber colors, and startling chiaroscuro. His self-portraits repeatedly reveal his modesty and his compassionate, calmly searching gaze. Among his prominent works are *The Stoning of St. Stephen* (1625), *Music Lesson* (1626), *Christ at Emmaus* (c. 1628), *Andromeda* (c. 1630), *Anatomy Lesson of Dr. Nicolaes Tulp* (1632), *The Descent from the Cross* (c. 1633), *Saskia as Flora* (1634), *Belshazzar's Feast* (c. 1635), *The Sacrifice of Isaac* (1635), *Danaë* (1636), *Landscape with a Stone Bridge* (c. 1638), *The Night Watch* (1642—originally called *Militia Company of Captain Frans Banning Cocq*), *Christ Healing the Sick* (c. 1649), *Mill* (c. 1650), *Woman Bathing* (1655—perhaps Hendrickje), *Jacob Blessing the Sons of Joseph* (1656), *The Syndics of the Drapers' Guild* (1662), and *The Jewish Bride* (c. 1664).

Melville, of Dutch extraction himself, was predisposed to admire works by Rembrandt, a few of which he saw on his two trips abroad. According to his journals, he viewed a few Rembrandt portraits at Hampton Court and at the National Gallery in London (11 November, 17 December 1849) and, years later, *Night Watch* and *Syndics* in Amsterdam (24 April 1857). Melville does not note his impressions. Later, he valued a mezzotint of a picture by Rembrandt enough to have it framed for his home (1869). Melville called it *The Healing of the Blind,* but it may have been a copy of *Christ Healing the Sick,* easily Rembrandt's finest etching.

Bibliography: Kenneth Clark, *An Introduction to Rembrandt* (New York: Harper & Row, 1978); Leyda; Charles E. Mee, Jr., *Rembrandt's Portrait: A Biography* (New York: Simon and Schuster, 1988); NN 15; Shelley Karen Perlove, *Impressions of Faith: Rembrandt's Biblical Etchings* (Dearborn: University of Michigan–Dearborn, 1989).

"Report of the Committee on Agriculture" (1850). Article attributed in part to Melville. It was published, as by Melville's cousin Robert Melvill,* in the Pittsfield, Massachusetts, *Culturist and Gazette* (9 October 1850). (Characters: Morgan Lewis, Robert Melvill.) The committee appointed to award prizes for crops is happy to report that Berkshire County farms have improved: Grass and clover grow where swamps and quagmires once were, fruit trees and forest trees abound, barns have been built, and manure is properly collected and "renovates exhausted lands." It would be well, however, to cultivate corn with shorter stalks and more ears. Melville, who toured the county with his cousin (July 1850), probably accepted his request to write the committee report for him and deliberately made it verbose and flowery.

Bibliography: Jay Leyda, "White Elephant vs. White Whale," *Town and Country* 101 (August 1947): 68–69, 114d, 116–118; NN 9.

"A Requiem for Soldiers lost in Ocean Transports" (1866). Poem, in *Battle-Pieces.* After stormy weather abates, birds fly through the woodlands and fish frolic in ocean sprays. "All creatures" enjoy the new morning, "[s]ave," that is, those "from joyance torn" whose ships are smashed and who are washed away, never again to see "the light," the "long-sought land," or the bird flying near "the lone spar where mid-sea surges pour."

Bibliography: Glauco Cambon, *The Inclusive Flame: Studies in American Poetry* (Bloomington: Indiana University Press, 1963); NN 11.

"The Returned Volunteer to his Rifle" (1866). Poem, in *Battle-Pieces.* After the war, a humble soldier places his rifle over the hearth of his "haven" near the Hudson River. He often thought of this region, especially when he fought at Gettysburg, and he is grateful that "God kept it green."

"The Return of the Sire of Nesle A.D. 16—." *See* "L'Envoy: The Return of the Sire de Nesle, A.D. 16—" (under E).

Reynolds, Jeremiah N. (1799–1858). U.S. Naval officer. He participated in an official voyage around the world (1831–1834). He addressed members of the U.S. Congress on the subject of surveying and exploring the Pacific Ocean and the South Seas (3 April 1836), published a book on the subject (1836), and later published his correspondence on the subject (1837–1838). He must have been persuasive, since he participated in a voyage of surveying and exploration in the South Seas (1838–1842). His most significant books are *Voyage of the U.S. Frigate Potomac, under the Command of Commodore John Downes, during the*

Circumnavigation of the Globe, in the Years 1831, 1832, 1833, and 1834 . . .
(New York: Harper & Brothers,* 1834); ''Mocha Dick: Or the White Whale of
the Pacific: A Leaf from a Manuscript Journal'' (*Knickerbocker,* May 1839);
and *Pacific and Indian Oceans; or, The South Sea Surveying and Exploring
Expedition: Its Inception, Progress, and Objects* (New York: Harper, 1841). His
account of Mocha Dick, available to Melville while he was writing *Moby-Dick,*
tells of an enormous white bull whale, often harpooned, finally killed, but thereafter eerily sighted.
   Bibliography: Lowell LeRoy Balcom, ''Introduction'' to J. N. Reynolds, *Mocha Dick
or the White Whale of the Pacific* (New York: Charles Scribner's Sons, 1932); Leyda;
NN 6.

R.F.C. In ''The Paradise of Bachelors and the Tartarus of Maids.'' *See* Cooke,
Robert Francis.

Rhyming Ned. In ''Bridegroom-Dick,'' he is a sailor remembered by Bridegroom Dick.

Ribera, Jusepe de (1591–1652). (Nickname: Lo Spagnoletto.) Spanish painter.
He was baptized at Játiva, near Valencia. After working in various parts of
Spain, he went to Rome (1613) and then Naples (1616), and painted in both
regions later, in response to various church and private commissions. He married
Caterina Azzolino, the daughter of a well-to-do painter from Sicily, in 1616 (the
couple had three sons and three daughters). Influenced by Michelangelo da Ca-
ravaggio, Ribera soon produced dramatically lighted and shadowed paintings,
usually with dominant earth colors and dark backgrounds. Ribera combined all
of this with unique Spanish religious, mystical, and sensual elements. He produced etchings (from the 1620s). During the anti-Spanish insurrection led by
Masaniello* (1847), Ribera lived in the Royal Palace in Naples. Late in life, he
was ill and had financial problems. One of his pupils in Naples was Salvator
Rosa.* After Ribera's death, his widow had to mortgage the family's possessions. Among his best paintings are the following: *The Sense of Touch* (c. 1615),
Drunken Silenus (1626—ribald), *Saint Jerome and the Angel of Judgment*
(1626), *The Bearded Woman* (1631—one the most grotesque pictures ever
painted), *The Blind Beggar* (1632), *Apollo and Marsyas* (1637), *The Martyrdom
of Saint Bartholomew* (1639), *The Clubfooted Boy* (1642—touching) *Holy Family with Saint Catherine* (1648), and *Saint Sebastian* (1651).
   In ''Marquis de Grandvin: At the Hostelry,'' Melville describes Spagnoletto,
whom he also calls the Don, as a short, brawny Spanish artist who discusses
the picturesque with [Paolo] Veronese and argues splenetically with him. Spagnoletto is undoubtedly Jusepe de Ribera.
   Bibliography: Alfonso E. Pérez Sánchez and Nicola Spinosa, *Jusepe de Ribera 1591–
1652* (New York: Harry N. Abrams, 1992).

Ridendiabola. In *Mardi,* he is a fabulist, cited by Babbalanja. The name Ridendiabola is a combination of *ridens* (Latin for ''laughing'') and *diabolus* (Latin for ''devil'').

Riga, Captain. In *Redburn,* he is the vicious, hypocritical, Russian-born captain of the *Highlander.* A bachelor, he treats Redburn abusively during and at the end of the lad's first voyage. Riga may be partly based on Oliver P. Brown, captain of the *St. Lawrence,* a ship conveying goods and passengers on which Melville sailed to and from Liverpool. Brown is thought to have been from Stockholm but a long-time naturalized American citizen.
  Bibliography: Gilman, Leyda.

Rigadoon Joe. In ''Bridegroom-Dick,'' he is a sailor remembered by Bridegroom Dick.

Rigs. In *Redburn,* he is the second mate aboard the *Highlander.*

Ringbolt. In *White-Jacket,* he is a sailor who urges Jonathan to quit shouting insults at Don Pedro II, King of Brazil, for fear that all the main-royal-yard men will be punished. Ringbolt's name probably derives from ''Captain Ringbolt,'' the pen name John Codman* used when he published his *Sailors' Life and Sailors' Yarns* (New York, 1847), which Melville reviewed for the *Literary World* (6 March 1847).

Ringman, Goneril. In *The Confidence-Man. See* Goneril.

Ringman, John. In *The Confidence-Man,* he is the man with the weed, said by Black Guinea to be one of his character references. Ringman reminds Henry Roberts that they once met, blandly begs a bank note from him, and momentarily tempts him to purchase some Black Rapids Coal Company stock. Ringman surprises a scholar by lecturing against Tacitus for his cynicism and for his destruction of one's confidence in other people. Roberts relates the story of Ringman's wife Goneril to John Truman. Melville may be indirectly expressing sympathy for Pierce Butler, the long-suffering husband of the actress Frances Anne Kemble,* some of whose alleged traits Melville assigns to Goneril. Ringman may also be a satirical portrait of William Cullen Bryant, the celebrated poet, editor, and political writer; like Ringman, Bryant was melancholy and apparently cool, but seemingly had faith in humanity and hoped for progress.
  Bibliography: Egbert S. Oliver, ''Melville's Goneril and Fanny Kemble,'' *New England Quarterly* 18 (December 1945): 489–500; Trimpi.

Ringrope. In *White-Jacket,* he is an old sailor who as sailmaker helps Thrummings encase Shenly's body in canvas for burial at sea. Ringrope argues unsuccessfully in favor of taking the final stitch through the corpse's nose.

"Rip Van Winkle" (1924). *See* "Rip Van Winkle's Lilac."

"Rip Van Winkle's Lilac" (1924). Poem, as part of "Rip Van Winkle's Li-lac," in *Weeds and Wildings. See* "Rip Van Winkle's Lilac" below.

"Rip Van Winkle's Lilac" (1924). Prose and poetic narrative, in *Weeds and Wildings.* It contains introductory prose sections entitled "To a Happy Shade" and "Rip Van Winkle," followed by a poem entitled "Rip Van Winkle's Li-lac." (Characters: Washington Irving, [Joseph] Jefferson, Mrs. Rip Van Winkle, Rip Van Winkle.) In the first part, in prose, Rip Van Winkle is seen descending from "the Kattskills" at sunset in June, only to find a lilac tree in front of his door, where a willow used to be. Puzzled, he reminisces extensively. Earlier, a "Bohemian" artist regarded the pink lilac and the dilapidated house as more "picturesque" than the new church nearby, of which a passing parishioner is proud. In the second part, in poetry, Rip expresses his confusion. But then it is reported that later the lovely lilac, fragrantly duplicated by slips taken from it and planted throughout the region, immortalizes old Rip. In "Rip Van Winkle's Lilac," Melville may be suggesting that he is out of tune with his times but that his works may achieve immortality.
   Bibliography: Shurr, Stein.

Rob. In "Stockings in the Farm-House Chimney," he is depicted as waiting for the arrival of Santa Claus.

Roberts, Henry. In *The Confidence-Man,* he is a forwarding merchant from Wheeling, Pennsylvania, whose not remembering John Ringman that man gently attributes to brain fever. Ringman begs a bank note from Roberts and momen-tarily tempts him to buy some Black Rapids Coal Company stock. Roberts may be a satirical sketch, based on similarities in appearance and personality, of David Wilmot, the congressman from Pennsylvania famous for having intro-duced the abortive Wilmot Proviso (1846) forbidding slavery in territory ac-quired from Mexico.
   Bibliography: Trimpi.

Robins. In *Omoo,* he is apparently a London auctioneer. He is mentioned by the narrator when he is discussing Stubbs, a Sydney real-estate auctioneer.

Robles, Juan. In "Benito Cereno," he is Benito Cereno's *San Dominick* boat-swain. After being wounded during the slave revolt aboard ship, he was thrown into the sea with others by the slaves. Robles swam the longest, made the act of contrition in the water, and sank to his death.

Roddi. In *Mardi,* he is a reader of Lombardo's *Koztanza.* Roddi suggested that the work be burned, according to Babbalanja. Roddi is as harsh as one who does not spare the rod.

Rodney, George Brydges Rodney, Baron, Admiral (1718–1792). British naval officer. After attending school at Harrow (from c. 1725), he volunteered for the navy (1732), was promoted to lieutenant while on duty in the Mediterranean area (1739), was promoted to post-captain (1742), helped defeat the French off Ushant (1747), was governor and naval commander-in-chief in Newfoundland (1749), was in Parliament (from 1751), and served in American, European, and Caribbean waters during the French and Indian War (1755–1763). After shore duty at home, he was given the Jamaica command (1771–1774), gambled ruinously back home, was promoted to admiral (1778), and became the commander-in-chief of the Leeward Islands (1779–1782). He enjoyed successes against French and Spanish naval vessels but squabbled over booty, and commanded a controversial naval victory. He defeated Comte François Joseph Paul de Grasse, Marquis de Grassetilly,* the French admiral, in an engagement between Domenica and islets called the Saints, accepted his adversary's surrender and that of his flagship, almost unaccountably broke off the attack on De Grasse's half-demolished fleet (12 April 1782), and thus incurred the criticism of Sir Samuel Hood, Rodney's second-in-command. Rodney returned home, received a barony and a sizable pension, and in due time died in London. Rodney married Jane Compton in 1753. The couple had two sons and a daughter; then his wife died (1757), then the daughter (1758), and later the younger son at sea (1776). Rodney married Henrietta Clies in 1764 (the couple had two sons and four daughters).

In *Billy Budd,* Rodney is named as the British naval officer under whom [Captain the Honorable] Edward Fairfax Vere gallantly served in the West Indies as flag lieutenant, during which cruise Rodney defeated the French fleet under De Grasse's command. Vere was promoted to post captain.

Bibliography: David Spinney, *Rodney* (London: Unwin, 1969).

Roe. In *Mardi,* this is one of the twelve aristocratic Tapparian families on the isle of Pimminee, entertained by Nimni.

Rohon, Don Hannibal, De Aquaviva. In *Clarel. See* Hannibal, Rohon Del Aquaviva, Don.

Roi Mori. In *Mardi,* he is dead Karhownoo's deaf and grieving father.

Rolfe. In *Clarel,* he is a well-traveled American sailor and brilliant humanist. He mediates between the extremes of the other pilgrims. Rolfe is gracious, kind, tolerant, skeptical but honestly searching, sensitive, friendly and candid, earnest, and much admired. He espouses the best Hellenistic, Hebraic, and Christian values. Rolfe in a dozen ways is an autobiographical figure, with a past paralleling Melville's youth and early manhood. Rolfe refers to himself as "the Dead Man."

Bibliography: NN 12.

Rondo the Round, King. In *Mardi,* he is an ancient monarch who, according to Mohi, wanted his coffin lid to be made of amber. He had to settle for crystal. The word *rondo* is Italian for "round."

Roo. In *Mardi,* she is a rich old Tapparian widow who attends Nimni's party on the isle of Pimminee.

Roonoonoo. In *Mardi,* he is a rebel on the island of Juam. King Marjora defeated and executed Roonoonoo at Willamilla.

Ropey. In *Omoo. See* Rope Yarn.

Rope Yarn ("Ropey"). In *Omoo,* he is a landlubber aboard the *Julia.* Somewhere between twenty-five and forty years of age, he is a former London apprentice baker who has left his selfish wife back in Australia. When he dies at Papeetee, he is buried on the beach.

Rosa, Salvator (1615–1673). Painter. He was born in Arenella, near Naples, then under Spanish control. He reveled in the natural beauty of Naples and its environs, and studied art in Naples under Jusepe de Ribera,* the Spanish painter and etcher, and under the battle painter Aniello Falcone.* Rosa went to Rome to continue his studies (1635) but contracted malaria and returned home. Becoming famous, he went back to Rome (1639), where he gained added fame as a comic actor and musician, but also considerable notoriety as a poet and satirist. He made enemies by spoofing the famous and influential sculptor Gianlorenzo Bernini, participated in the abortive insurrection back in Naples led by Masaniello* (1647), escaped to Rome, and went to Florence at the invitation of Cardinal Giovanni Carlo de' Medici. Under his aegis, Rosa made his style of landscaping popular and attracted a variety of artists, musicians, and writers to his home, where he started what he called his Accademia dei Percossi ("the stricken ones"). Back for good in Rome (from 1649), he turned to religious and historical paintings. He also became a skillful etcher (from 1660), often sympathetically depicting common and suffering peasants and soldiers. His famous landscapes are broodingly romantic, with wild and dark skies, overhanging crags, and poetic ruins, and sometimes bandits, sailors, shepherds, and soldiers as well. From about 1650, Rosa kept Lucrezia Paolino, a beautiful Florentine, as his household *governante* and regarded himself as her husband. The couple had two sons, and during his last illness he may have married the faithful Lucrezia.

Rosa was one of Melville's favorite artists. During his first European trip,

Melville probably saw his famous painting entitled *Soldiers Gambling* in the Dulwich Gallery, London, which, according to his 1849 journal, he visited with George J. Adler* (17 November). Melville's descriptions of landscapes have been compared to the sometimes sublime and often savage landscapes of Rosa, with their fearsome mountains, forbidding crags, writhing trees, and wild-looking ruins. Melville was so familiar with Rosa landscapes that when, during his second European trip, he was in Messina and faced east, he noted the following in his journal: "Calabria's mountains in sight. Salvator Rosa look of them" (15 February 1857). In Melville's collection of engravings were some of works by Rosa. In his "Marquis de Grandvin: At the Hostelry," Melville describes Rosa as a proud, satirical painter. In "Marquis de Grandvin: Naples in the Time of Bomba . . . ," he mentions Rosa as linked with patriotic Neapolitan brigands.

Bibliography: Ottilie G. Boetzkes, *Salvator Rosa: Seventeenth-Century Italian Painter, Poet, and Patriot* (New York: Vantage Press, 1960); Sharon Furrow, "The Terrible Made Visible: Melville, Rosa, and [Giovanni Battista] Piranesi," *Emerson Society Quarterly* 19 (Fourth Quarter 1973): 237–53; Frank Jewett Mather, Jr., "Herman Melville," *New York Review* 1 (16 August 1919): 298–301; Lady Morgan, *The Life and Times of Salvator Rosa* (1823; new ed., London: David Bryce, 1855); NN 15; Leandro Ozzola, *Vita e opera di Salvator Rosa . . .* (Strassburg: J. H. Ed. Heitz), 1908).

Rosamond ("Moss-Rose," "Rose"). In "Amoroso," she is the poet's freshly blooming love.

"Rosary Beads" (1924). Group of three poems, in *Weeds and Wildings,* as part of the section entitled "As They Fell." In "The Accepted Time," the poet advises us to adore roses now and not wait until later. In "Without Price," he says that if we enjoy our roses now, our meat shall be red and our bread, white. In "Grain by Grain," we are advised to fence our roses against the encroachment of drifting desert sand and "ever-creeping Land."

Bibliography: Cohen, *Poems;* Shurr.

Roscoe, William (1753–1831). Historian, miscellaneous writer, and banker. Roscoe was born and lived in Liverpool, England. He attended school for only a few years (1759–1765), read voraciously in private, and helped his father, who was a market gardener. Roscoe wrote some poetry as a teenager, was apprenticed to a lawyer (1769–1774), and practiced law himself (1774–1796). He wrote an antislavery book entitled *Wrongs of Africa* (1787–1788). Adept in Italian, he wrote *The Life of Lorenzo de' Medici* (1796; with an appendix of illustrations, 1822) and *The Life and Pontificate of Leo the Tenth* (1805). Roscoe went into banking with a friend and also aided farmers near Liverpool (1793–1800). He published a translation of the sixteenth-century Italian poet Luigi Tansillo's *La Balia,* as *The Nurse: A Poem* (1798). Roscoe served as a member of parliament for Liverpool (1806–1807). He suffered severe banking reverses (beginning in

1816), sold his extensive collection of books and pictures to discharge part of his debts, and went into bankruptcy (1820). He published the biography of a self-taught linguist named Richard Robert Jones (1822), an edition of the works of Alexander Pope (1824), and a monograph entitled *Monandrian Plants* (1828). He married Jane Griffies in Liverpool in 1781 (the couple had seven sons and three daughters; his wife died in 1824). Henry Roscoe, one of his sons, published a two-volume biography of William Roscoe (1833). Melville identifies Roscoe in *Redburn* as the eminent historian, poet, and banker with whom Redburn's father dined in Liverpool back in 1808.

    Bibliography: Washington Irving,* ''Roscoe,'' pp. 16–21 in *The Sketch Book of Geoffrey Crayon, Gent.,* ed. Haskell Springer (Boston: Twayne Publishers, 1978).

Rose. In ''Amoroso.'' *See* Rosamond.

Rose, James (''Jimmy''). In ''Jimmy Rose,'' he is a gracious merchant of New York City who after sudden financial ruin disappears for twenty-five years. As suddenly, he reappears at the age of sixty-five to take tea and toast at the opulent homes of former friends. He retains the roses in his cheeks and also his fine aristocratic manners. Melville undoubtedly had his handsome, gracious, Frenchified, but ultimately impecunious uncle Thomas Melvill, Jr.,* in mind when he sketched Jimmy Rose's background and appearance. In a memoir of his uncle, Melville notes the aging man's fine complexion and ''the contrast between the man and his environment.''

Rosecrans, William Starke (1819–1898). Union Army officer. Born in Kingston, Ohio, he graduated from West Point (1842), was an army engineer in Virginia, taught engineering and natural philosophy at West Point (1843–1847), and after serving on army posts in New England resigned his first lieutenancy (1854). Rosecrans did engineering and architectural work in Cincinnati (1854–1855), undertook coal mining and river navigation work in the western part of Virginia (1855–1857), and was back in Cincinnati at the outbreak of the Civil War. He became a colonel of Ohio army engineers and of infantry volunteers, was appointed a brigadier general in the regular army, and served well under General George B. McClellan* at the battle of Rich Mountain (July 1861). Rosecrans commanded the Department of the Ohio and the part of Virginia that became West Virginia. Assigned to northern Mississippi under General Henry W. Halleck, Rosecrans soon replaced General John Pope* and served under General Ulysses S. Grant.* After the battle of Holly Springs, Mississippi (October 1862), the victorious Rosecrans became a major general of volunteers and commanded the Army of the Cumberland. He engaged Confederate General Braxton Bragg* at Stone River, Tennessee (December 1862–January 1863). After this decisive battle, Rosecrans maneuvered Bragg to Chattanooga (June 1863). Meanwhile, Halleck became controversial by stating that he would recommend promotion to regular-army major general for Grant or Rosecrans, depending on who won the next big battle. Rosecrans, whom Halleck could not persuade to advance prematurely, incurred the displeasure of officials in Washington, D.C., by an indiscreet letter. Rosecrans was outmaneuvered by Bragg, was defeated at Chickamauga (September 1863), and retreated to Chattanooga. When Grant took command of Union forces in the West, Rosecrans was relegated to command the enormous but less important Department of the Missouri (October 1863), declined to run as the vice presidential candidate with Abraham Lincoln* (November 1864), and was ordered to Cincinnati (December 1864), where he remained until after the war. Resigning from the army (1867), he became minister to Mexico (1868–1869), mined there and in California, served from that state in the House of Representatives (1881–1885), was register of the treasury (1885–1893), and retired to his ranch outside Los Angeles. Rosecrans was a competent and indefatigable strategist and a loyal friend of his men— who called him ''Old Rosy''—but was also an ill-tempered officer resentful of his peers and his superiors. He married Ann Eliza Hegeman in New York City in 1843 and was survived by three of their eight children.

In ''Battle of Stone River, Tennessee,'' Melville names Rosecrans as the Union officer whose men defeated the Confederate forces at Stone River.

Bibliography: William Mathias Lamers, *The Edge of Glory: A Biography of General William S. Rosecrans, U.S.A.* (New York: Harcourt, Brace, 1961).

''The Rose Farmer'' (1924). Poem, in *Weeds and Wildings,* as part of the section entitled ''As They Fell'' and including ''L'Envoi'' as a conclusion. (Characters: Amigo, the Parsee, the Persian.) A poet in retirement explains that he has inherited a farm located outside Damascus and ''consecrate[d] to roses.'' He is cultivating them now, but he has a problem. Should he sell thousands of his blooms for quick money or distill their attar laboriously for a greater but slower profit? When he asks a rich Persian florist for advice, he is told that there is ''[a]lways a market for . . . roses'' but attar is ''far from popular.'' A Parsee nearby, who also grows roses, is as thin ''as a rake with his distilling,'' is in debt, and has no friends. So the Persian advises the poet to enjoy his sequence of passing blooms, which he can sell and give to friends, instead of trying for rarefied attar, which might possibly be too expensive to attract customers. The poem is an allegory. Should a writer aim to please quickly or distill his thoughts into something essential and precious? Melville's rose farmer opts for no risk; Melville did not. Complicating ''The Rose Farmer'' is a subtext of sexual ribaldry, about ''ragged scrambles / Through . . . blessed thorns and brambles,'' with every ''rose / Bridling aloft the passionate head,'' ''husbanded'' and ''waxing . . . warm'' the while. In ''L'Envoi,'' the old man contends that he is ''young at core'' and offers this cryptic generalization: ''Wiser in relish, if sedate[,] / Come gray-beards to their roses late.''

Bibliography: Stein.

Rose-Water. In *White-Jacket,* he is an African-American assistant of Old Coffee, the ship's cook. Rose-Water has elegant reading tastes, once butts heads with May-Day, and is flogged for doing so by Captain Claret.
Bibliography: Grejda.

"Rose Window" (1924). Poem, in *Weeds and Wildings,* as part of the section entitled "As They Fell." While listening one "slumberous afternoon" to a preacher whose text is "The Rose of Sharon," the poet nods off and dreams that an angel with a lamp-like rose walks past, sheds "dappled down upon the dead," and turns their burial garments red. The poet awakens, looks at the rose window of the church, and sees that "sheafs of rays" passing through it transfigure the "dingy," "dusty" place.
Bibliography: Shurr, Stein.

Rotato. In *Mardi,* he is a fat, sagacious Mardian philosopher, mentioned by Mohi. In appearance, Rotato is *rotatus* (Latin for both "well-rounded" and "concise").

Rovenna, Don. In *Clarel,* he is a friend from Seville, mentioned with a sigh by the Lyonese.

Rowland. In *Pierre,* he is a manufacturer, along with his son, of a beard-growing product. It fails to produce results for young Pierre Glendinning.

Rowser. In *Israel Potter,* this is a sailor's name invented by Potter for himself when he alone boards the British frigate from the *Ariel.*

Roy, Jack. In "Jack Roy," he is praised as the zestful, gutsy captain of the maintop of the *Splendid.* He is gentlemanly, fun-loving, gallant, and heroic.

Rozas, Doctor Juan Martinez de. In "Benito Cereno," he is the royal councilor of Lima. He orders Benito Cereno to testify concerning the slave revolt aboard his ship the *San Dominick.*

Ruaruga. In *Typee,* he is Marheyo's next-door neighbor.

Rubens, Peter Paul (1577–1640). Flemish painter. He was born in Siegen, in Westphalia. (His Calvinist father had left Antwerp and had gone to Germany to avoid religious persecution.) When his father died (1587), young Rubens's mother returned to Antwerp, where she reared her gifted son as a Roman Catholic. He studied painting (1592–1598), at the end of which time he was officially judged to be a master. He journeyed to Italy, entered the court of the Duke of Mantua (1600–1608), and was sent on a diplomatic mission to Spain (1603–

1604), where he was inspired by the color and monumentality of Titian's paintings in Madrid. Rubens returned via Rome to Antwerp (1608), by this time famous and welcomed into the royal household. He married Isabella Brant in 1609 (the couple had one son and also two daughters, one of whom predeceased both parents), began to play a political role in the Spanish Netherlands, and displayed anti-Reformation tendencies in a stream of often enormous works. They exemplify his devotion to conservative Italian classical art, his Catholic beliefs, and his wild, energetic style. His twenty-one huge canvases depicting the life of Marie de' Medici (1622–1625) required his establishing workshops in which assistants, including Anthony Van Dyke,* helped him produce what ultimately amounted to more than 2,000 works. Rubens accomplished diplomatic missions for his patrons to help end war between the Spanish Netherlands and the Dutch Republic (1625) and to bring peace between Spain and England (1629–1630). Knighting Rubens, Charles I of England commissioned him to decorate the Whitehall Palace ceiling in London. The result was *The Allegory of War and Peace* (1630). Rubens turned partially to genre scenes, landscapes, and portraits. He did not let arthritis stop his flow of masterpieces.

Among his best paintings are *The Duke of Lerma on Horseback* (1603), *Veronica Spinola Doria* (c. 1607), *Samson and Delilah* (c. 1609), *Self-Portrait with Isabella Brant* (c. 1610), *The Raising of the Cross* (1611), *Descent from the Cross* (1614—perhaps his greatest work), *The Last Judgment* (1615), *The Miracles of Saint Loyola* (c. 1617), *Michael Ophovius* (c. 1618), *Ambrogio Spinola* (1625), *Assumption of the Virgin* (1626—dazzling), *The Three Graces* (c. 1635—Rubensesquely buxom), *Landscape with the Tower of Steen* (c. 1636—near his private chateau), *Moonlight Landscape* (c. 1637), and *Self-Portrait* (c. 1639). Four years after his first wife died, Rubens married the sixteen-year-old Helena Fourment, in 1630 (the couple had two sons and three daughters, the last being born eight months after the painter's death). Rubens's widow burned some of his nude paintings and was also in ligitation with her two stepchildren. Rubens was the most influential painter in northern Europe during his epoch and for years later. He was a knowledgeable collector of antique objets d'art.

When Melville was briefly in Cologne, he "saw the celebrated *Descent from the Cross* by Rubens," as he notes in his 1849 journal (9 December). During his second trip to Europe, Melville noted that a *Magdalen* by Rubens at the Palazzo Madama in Turin was "excellently true to nature, but very ugly" (10 April 1857). He also could have seen some Rubens works when he visited the Palazzo Rosso in Genoa a few days later (14 April). In Melville's collection of engravings were twelve of works by Rubens. In "Marquis de Grandvin: At the Hostelry," Melville mentions Rubens as a painter who prefers to paint Venus and swans rather than kitchen maids.

Bibliography: NN 15; Christopher White, *Peter Paul Rubens: Man & Artist* (New Haven, Conn.: Yale University Press, 1987); Wallace.

"Running the Batteries" (1866). (Full title: "Running the Batteries, as observed from the Anchorage above Vicksburgh [April, 1863].") Poem, in *Battle-Pieces*. (Characters: Hugh, Lot, Ned, [Commodore David Dixon] Porter, [Admiral David] Porter.) The narrator explains that on a moonless night four gunboats slide down the river, one after another. Rebel batteries open fire. A blaze from the town lights up the river traffic but also the forts ashore, allowing the gunboats to fire back with accuracy. A transport, set afire, provides still more light but soon burns out. The scene is frightful but also beautiful. The Union vessels make it safely past, and "Porter proves himself a brave man's son." On the night of 16 April 1863, David Dixon Porter,* son of the deceased David Porter,* ran a flotilla, composed of eight gunboats, three transports, and some barges and flatboats, past the Confederate batteries at Vicksburg, in support of his stepbrother David Glasgow Farragut.* On 22 April, Porter did the same thing again, this time with twelve barges, to supply the army of General Ulysses S. Grant* south of Vicksburg.

Bibliography: Boatner; Faust; Garner; Kenneth J. Hagan, *This People's Navy: The Making of American Sea Power* (New York: The Free Press, 1991); NN 11.

Russ, The. In *Clarel. See* the Russian.

Russell, William Clark (1844–1911). Sailor and man of letters. He was born in New York City to British parents, who placed him in private schools in Winchester and Boulogne, after which he joined the British merchant service (1858–1866), and went to India and Australia often. After he retired, Russell wrote a verse drama which failed, tried journalism and editing (1868–c. 1871), and began to turn out a stream of sea fiction. His first two novels—*John Holdsworth, Chief Mate* (1875) and *The Wreck of the "Grosvenor": An Account of the Mutiny of the Crew and the Loss of the Ship When Trying to Make the Bermudas* (1877)—were very popular. Some fifty-five volumes followed, including *In the Middle Watch: Sea Stories* (1885). Russell published biographies of three British nautical heroes—William Dampier (1889), Horatio Nelson* (1890), and Cuthbert Collingwood (1891). Russell urged the government to address the grievances of merchant seamen. Arthritis slowed but never stopped his literary activity. Russell married Alexandrina Henry (1868). She, their son, and their three daughters survived him.

Russell was a long-time admirer of Melville and his works. When to no avail he told an American short-story writer named Augustus Allen Hayes that someone ought to produce Melville's biography (1883), Russell wrote and published three pieces in England about Melville himself (1884, 1889) and one in the United States (1892). Melville dedicated his *John Marr* to Russell, identifying him only by initials in its "Inscription Epistolary to W.C.R." Russell in turn dedicated his novel *An Ocean Tragedy* (1890) to Melville. Melville made use of Russell's biography of Nelson for background material when he wrote *Billy Budd.*

Bibliography: Leyda, NN 11.

Russian, The ("The Russ"). In *Clarel,* he is a Russian pilgrim who temporarily leaves his Greek party to chat with Clarel at David's Well outside Bethlehem.

"The Rusty Man (by a Soured One)" (1924). Poem, in *The Works of Herman Melville.* (Character: [Don Quixote]). While the dusty-bearded man from La Mancha mopes and gropes in his "library fusty" and is determined to fight for the right, every serenely foolish "grocer green" "[t]hriveth apace."
   Bibliography: Cohen, *Poems;* Shurr.

Ruth. In *Clarel,* she is the innocent, beautiful, considerate daughter of Nathan and Agar. Ruth falls in love with Clarel. During a period of mourning after her father's murder by hostile Arabs, her house is closed to Clarel. Ruth and her mother die of grief while Clarel is away on his pilgrimage. Ruth is more a symbol of platonic love than she is a living woman.
   Bibliography: NN 12.

Ruyter, Mikiel Adriaanszoon de. In "Marquis de Grandvin: At the Hostelry." *See* De Ruyter, Mikiel Adriaanszoon.

S

St. Jago's Sailor. In *Moby-Dick,* he is a *Pequod* sailor who says that the Spanish sailor is insane to pick a fight with Daggoo during the midnight festivities in the forecastle.

Salem. In *Omoo,* he is a knife-wielding beachcomber sailor aboard the *Julia.* He fights Bembo and also signs the round-robin.

Sally. In *Redburn,* she is the wife of Max the Dutchman, who also has a wife named Meg in New York.

Salt, Henry S. (1851–1939). (Full name: Henry Stephens Salt.) Educator and man of letters. The son of a career colonel in the British artillery, he was born in India, went with his mother to England at age one, spent a happy childhood in Shrewsbury, attended Eton, and was a brilliant student in the classics at King's College, Cambridge (to 1875). He became a master at Eton but quit because he grew too liberal for the establishment. He devoted his life thereafter to writing. He became a vegetarian, socialist, pacifist, rationalist, humanist, and environmentalist. His publications include three books on his favorite thinker, Percy Bysshe Shelley,* *A Shelley Primer* (1887), *Percy Bysshe Shelley: A Monograph* (1888), and *Percy Bysshe Shelley: Poet and Pioneer* (1896), and also the following books: *The Life of James Thomson ("B.V.") with a Selection from His Letters and a Study of His Writings* (1889, rev. 1898), *The Life of Henry David Thoreau*[*] (1890, rev. 1896), *Tennyson as a Thinker* (1890—mostly negative), *De Quincey* (1904), and *Richard Jefferies: His Life & His Ideals* (1905—in praise of the poet-naturalist). Salt also published works on natural history, translations of Lucretius and Virgil, anthologies, and his own poetry, and he was an editor. His autobiographies are *Seventy Years among Savages* (1921—an attention- and respect-getting book about meat-eating Englishmen), *The Story of My Cousins* (1923, about his cats, dogs, and rook), *Memories of Bygone Eton* (1928), and *Company I Have Kept* (1930). Salt married Catherine Leigh Joynes of Cambridge in 1879. It has been reliably asserted that she was a lesbian and that their marriage was never consummated. She died in 1919. He married his longtime housekeeper Catherine Mandeville of Brighton in 1927.

Salt wrote to Melville late in 1889 to suggest republishing *Typee* in the Camelot Series of books he was editing and mentioned that he had published a complimentary essay entitled "Herman Melville" in the *Scottish Art Review* (November 1889). Melville wrote to John Murray,* the publisher of the British edition of *Typee,* to inquire about his giving permission; when Murray refused, Melville so informed Salt. Melville read Salt's life of Thomson and praised it— and Thomson—in a second letter to him. (Salt quoted two of Melville's comments on Thomson in the 1898 revision of his book on Thomson.) A transoceanic friendship ensued, and Salt became one of Melville's most solid British admirers. He wrote "Marquesan Melville" (*Gentleman's Magazine* [March 1892]). Ironically, after Melville's death Murray's son John Murray IV republished *Typee* and *Omoo,* with introductions by Salt (1893). Salt suggested to Murray (1910) a biography of Melville, collected information, but did nothing with it except to give it to John Freeman, who used it for his 1926 biography of Melville.

Bibliography: George Hendrick, *Henry Salt: Humanitarian Reformer and Man of Letters* (Urbana: University of Illinois Press, 1977); NN 14; Stephen Winsten, *Salt and His Circle* (London: Hutchinson, 1951).

Salvaterra ("The Tuscan"). In *Clarel,* he is a Franciscan from the Arno Valley in Tuscany. A fervid and ascetic proselytizer, he acts as a guide at the Latin Church of the Star of Bethlehem. While at this church in Bethlehem, Melville was guided into various caves by a Latin monk and noted the fact in his 1857 journal (26 January). Melville's description of Salvaterra may reflect the description of a Franciscan monk from Italy in *Incidents of Travel in Egypt, Arabia Petræa, and the Holy Land* (2 vols., 1837) by John Lloyd Stephens.

Bibliography: NN 12, NN 15.

Sambo. In "Authentic Anecdotes of 'Old Zack,' " he is General Zachary Taylor's confidential African-American servant. When an enemy shot bounces a hot pie onto the general's head, Sambo says that his boss is now armed "cap a pie." Rumor has it that Sambo is selling some of the general's personal items to Peter Tamerlane B— [that is, P. T. Barnum*].

"The Same" (1891). Poem, in *Timoleon.* In this quatrain, which is a continuation of "The Attic Landscape," Melville says that the scene casts a spell and has a charm that evokes Plato and "authenticates" his style.

Bibliography: NN 11, Stein.

Samoa. In *Mardi,* he is a one-armed Upoluan native. He is an oyster diver from the Samoan or Navigator Islands. The narrator finds Samoa aboard the *Parki.* Though otherwise fierce, he is submissive to his shrewish wife Annatoo. He accompanies Taji on his voyages through the islands of Mardi as far as King Borabolla's island of Moldoldo. Samoa surgically replaces a wounded part of Karhownoo's brain with part of a pig's brain. The patient dies. Later Taji learns that Samoa has been killed by three arrows, probably shot by Aleema's sons. Episodes aboard the *Parki* may derive in part from F. D. Bennett's *Narrative of a Whaling Voyage . . .* (London: Richard Bentley,* 1840). Some details of the brain surgery come from a passage in William Ellis's *Polynesian Researches* (4 vols., London, 1833).

   Bibliography: Davis; David Jaffé, "Some Sources of Melville's *Mardi,*" *American Literature* 9 (March 1937): 56–69; Merton M. Sealts, Jr., "Melville's 'Friend Atahalpa,' " *Notes and Queries* 194 (22 January 1949): 37–38; Smith.

Sampson. In *Redburn,* he is a partner in Sampson & Wilt, Liverpool, on whom Redburn's father called back in 1808.

Santa Anna, Antonio Lopez de (1794–1876). Mexican general and politician. He was born in Jalapa, became a cadet in the Spanish army (1810), and fought against Native Americans in northern Mexico (1811) and in engagements both against guerrillas and alongside rebels (to 1821). He joined independence forces under Augustin de Iturbide as a brigadier general (1822), helped cause Iturbide's overthrow (1823), and became governor of Yucatán (1824). Coming out of periodic retirement, Santa Anna participated in several military engagements against rebel and also Spanish forces (1828–1829, 1832–1835), meanwhile being elected president by Congress (1833–1836). The year 1836 was eventful: He fought against Texans, overran the Alamo (6 March), butchered American prisoners at Goliad (27 March), was defeated and captured at San Jacinto by Sam Houston and his men (April), and was freed upon promising (May) to recognize the independence of Texas; the Mexican government repudiated the agreement and suspended Santa Anna's dictatorship (July). Santa Anna gained the status of hero by losing a leg during his defense of Vera Cruz against a French naval attack (1838) and again became Mexico's intermittent dictator and president (1839–1845). Captured by rebels, he was exiled to Cuba (1845). At the outset of the Mexican War, he communicated with President James K. Polk, whose representatives arranged for his transportation to Mexico City to strive for peace (1846). Instead, as provisional president (1846–1847), he commanded Mexican troops against American army units until he was defeated by General Winfield Scott* (1847). He went into exile to Jamaica and New Granada (now Colombia) (1848–1853). Reelected president, he returned home for a one-year term (1853). He became despotic, was condemned for treason, forfeited his estates, and fled into exile to New Granada and the Danish West Indies (1858–1864). He returned to Mexico during the French occupation (1864), offered to work both for and against the French, was ordered to leave (1864), lived in New York City (1866–1867), failed in his bid to return to Mexico (1867), and went to Cuba, the Dominican Republic, and the Bahamas (1867–1874). Under 1874 amnesty terms, he was allowed to return home—nearly blind, senile, and in poverty. He died in Mexico City. Santa Anna married Doña Inés García, a Creole fourteen years of age, in 1825 (the couple had two daughters and two sons). His wife died in 1844. His marriage seven weeks later to Doña Delores de Tosta, age fifteen, angered his people. His memoirs, completed in 1874, are invaluable if often inaccurate.

In ''Authentic Anecdotes of 'Old Zack,' '' Melville mentions Santa Anna as the recipient of a sarcastic letter from General Zachary Taylor telling him to eat cannonballs like a man or cry ''Enough'' now. P. T. Barnum writes that he is attempting to buy Santa Anna for his museum. In ''Bridegroom Dick,'' Santa Anna is the Mexican general remembered by Bridegroom Dick from Vera Cruz days. In ''To Major John Gentian, Dean of the Burgundy Club,'' Santa Anna is mentioned as opposed by General Will Worth. In ''View of the Barnum Property,'' ''the great Santa-Anna boot'' is said to be exhibited.

Bibliography: Oakah L. Jones, Jr., *Santa Anna* (New York: Twayne Publishers 1968).

Sarpedon. In ''A Dirge for McPherson, Killed in front of Atlanta.'' *See* McPherson, James Birdseye.

Saturnina. In *Mardi,* he is a tall chief in the Temple of Freedom, in Vivenza. He is notable for his grand forehead, calm brow, and deep-set eyes. Saturnina is intended to be a depiction of Daniel Webster, who was decidedly visible and audible in the U.S. Senate at the time *Mardi* was published.

Bibliography: Davis.

Saveda, Miguel. In *Redburn,* he is the new crew member who is brought aboard the *Highlander* drunk. He dies soon thereafter and begins to exude flames.

Sawyer, Dr. In *White-Jacket,* he is the *Buccaneer* surgeon, who with others confers with Dr. Cadwallader Cuticle when that expert surgeon operates on the fatally wounded foretopman.

Scott, Winfield (1786–1866). (Nickname: ''Old Fuss and Feathers.'') Scott was born near Petersburg, Virginia, briefly attended the College of William and Mary (1807) and read for the law, joined a cavalry unit (1807), and returned to study law. His illustrious military career began when he accepted a commission as lieutenant colonel in the War of 1812 and emerged as a general (1814). He fought in military engagements and undertook pacification actions against Native Americans (1814, 1832, 1838), mediated in a Canadian–U.S. border dispute (1838), and was appointed general in chief of the U.S. Army (1841). At the outset of the Mexican War (1846–1848), Scott recommended Zachary Taylor* to be troop commander (1846) but criticized him for his apparent lack of progress and led the troops himself in the assault on Veracruz (1847) and elsewhere—culminating in the capture of Mexico City (1847). When Scott seemed insubordinate, President James K. Polk convened a board of inquiry (1848), but all charges were soon dropped (1848). Scott ran for the presidency as a Whig but was defeated by Franklin Pierce (1852), whereupon Congress voted him the rank of lieutenant general (1852), the first to hold such rank since George Washington.* Scott mediated a British–U.S. dispute over possession of San Juan Island in Puget Sound (1859). Serving in the first year of the Civil War, he predicted to President Abraham Lincoln* that the war would last years not months, suggested the "Anaconda Plan" of splitting and strangling the Confederacy, and was ridiculed for it—but only briefly. Scott retired to West Point (1861). He married Maria D. Mayo of Richmond, Virginia, in 1817 (the couple had five daughters and two sons). He and his wife were in Europe when he heard of the notorious *Trent* affair (late 1861). He hurried home to be available to Lincoln if needed, and Maria Scott then died in Rome (1862). Scott died at West Point.

In "Bridegroom-Dick," Scott is an American general remembered by Bridegroom Dick from old Vera Cruz days.

Bibliography: Charles Winslow Elliott, *Winfield Scott: The Soldier and the Man* (New York: Macmillan 1937).

"The Scout toward Aldie" (1866). Poem, in *Battle-Pieces.* (Characters: Archy, Belisent, Blake, the Chaplain, Corporal Chew, Captain Cloud, the Colonel, Garry Cuff, the Guide, Hair-Brains, [General Robert E.] Lee, Luke, the Major, Mink, Captain Morn, [Colonel John Singleton] Mosby, Pansy, Reb, Sergeant, Sir Slyboots, Steward, the Surgeon.) In this 798-line poem, mostly in odd-rhyming 7-line stanzas, Melville tells how the young Colonel, recently married and with his bride in a "bannered tent" at camp, leaves to pursue the elusive Mosby and his men, whose resourceful leader is imaged thus: "As glides in seas the shark, / Rides Mosby through green dark." The Colonel's men grow worried. They capture five Confederate prisoners, including one who seems hurt and cannot walk. They foolishly let the groaning man go. They detain a Southern girl and a man who appears to be her African-American servant. In reality, he is Garry Cuff, a Confederate soldier in disguise. The Colonel and his men are ambushed by the supposedly crippled soldier. The Colonel is killed, and several of his men are captured or wounded. Remnants carry their leader's body to camp, where they see his bride standing by their tent waving a handkerchief. Someone must tell her "the withering news."

This terrifying ballad was inspired by Melville's accompanying Major William H. Forbes, a Massachusetts cavalry officer under the command of Melville's cousin Henry Sanford Gansevoort,* a colonel in the Union army, on a scouting party toward Aldie, in Virginia (18–20 April 1864). While in the area, Melville probably met a young bride, Josephine Shaw Lowell, who was a nurse in the area, and her husband, Colonel Charles Russell Lowell, nephew of the author James Russell Lowell. Not long thereafter, Charles Lowell, then a brigadier general, was killed at the Battle of Cedar Creek (19 October 1864).

Bibliography: Joseph Fargnoli, "'Archetype and History in Melville's 'The Scout toward Aldie,' '" *Forum for Modern Language Studies* 27 (October 1991): 333–47; Garner; Edward W. Goggin, "Confusion and Resolution in 'The Scout toward Aldie,' '" *Melville Society Extracts* 92 (March 1993): 5–9; NN 11; Shurr; Stein; Warren; Wilson.

Scribe, Hiram. In "I and My Chimney," he is a master mason and a rough architect hired by the narrator's wife to persuade the narrator to tear down the chimney. The narrator dismisses him with a $50 bribe. Hiram Scribe is a sweetly satirical portrait of Melville's Pittsfield neighbor Oliver Wendell Holmes,* who in June 1855 examined Melville. Melville had sciatica and was mentally disturbed as well.

Bibliography: Leyda, Sealts.

Scriggs. In *White-Jacket,* he is a gallows-gaited, squint-eyed old marine. He cooks for the mess of the sergeant-at-arms Bland and also sells liquor smuggled aboard by Bland until their scheme is revealed by a customer when he is caught and flogged for drunkenness.

Scrimmage. In *White-Jacket,* he is a sheet-anchor man who argues with Bungs about buoys.

Seafull. In *White-Jacket,* he is the forecastleman who plays the part of the Mayor in the Fourth of July theatrical.

Sea voyages by Melville. Melville signed on the *Acushnet,* a whaling ship, at New Bedford, Massachusetts (Christmas 1840), and sailed from Fairhaven, Massachusetts (3 January 1841). He deserted her at Nukuhiva, in the Marquesas Islands (9 July 1842). He signed on the *Lucy Ann,* an Australian whaler (9 August), refused duty aboard her in Tahiti (September), and was imprisoned by the British consul there. Melville signed on the *Charles and Henry,* a Nantucket whaling ship (November), and was discharged at Lahaina, Hawaiian Islands (May 1843). He signed on the *United States,* a U.S. Navy frigate (August 1843), and was discharged in Boston (October 1844).

Melville was a passenger aboard the *Southampton,* a London liner, from New York (11 October 1849) to Deal, near Dover, England (6 November 1949). He took a Channel steamer from London Bridge to Boulogne, France (27 November 1949), returning via Ostend, Belgium, to Dover (13 December 1849). He took the *Independence* from Portsmouth (25 December 1849) to New York (30 January 1850).

Melville boarded the *Glasgow,* a screw-steamer, in New York (11 October 1856) for Glasgow (26 October). He left Liverpool on the *Egyptian* (18 November) and, via several ports, disembarked at Constantinople (12 December). He took the *Acadia,* possibly a paddle-wheel steamer (18 December), for Alexandria (28 December). He took a steamer to Jaffa (4–6 January 1857); an Austrian steamer *Acquile Imperiale* from Jaffa to Beirut (24–25 January); the Austrian steamer *Smirne* to Smyrna (1–6 February); and the Austrian steamer *Italia* to Pireus, near Athens (6–7 February). He took the fast steamer *Cydnus* (11 February) for Messina, Italy (13 February). He boarded a Neapolitan steamer (16 February) for Naples, arriving (18 February). He took the French steamer *Aventine* from Civita Vecchia, near Rome (21 March), for Leghorn, Italy (23 March). He took a Channel steamer from Rotterdam (25 April) to London (26 April). He boarded the iron screw-steamer *City of Manchester* in Liverpool (5 May) for the voyage home again, ending in New York (19 May 1857).

Melville boarded the clipper ship *Meteor,* captained by his brother Thomas Melville,* in Boston (30 May 1860), for San Francisco (12 October). He took the *Cortes* (20 October) and disembarked at Panama (4 November). After crossing the Isthmus, he took the steamer *North Star* (5 November) for New York (12 November 1860).

Melville (February 1888) sailed to Bermuda, returning aboard the *Trinidad* (late March)—his final sea voyage. His time at sea probably totaled about thirty-six months.

Bibliography: Howard; Leyda; NN 14 and 15.

Sebastian, Don. In *Moby-Dick,* he is a Spanish friend of Ishmael's who with Don Pedro heard Ishmael tell at the Golden Inn in Lima the thrilling story of Steelkilt and Radney of the *Town-Ho.*

Second Nantucket Sailor. In *Moby-Dick,* he is a *Pequod* sailor who participates in the midnight festivities in the forecastle.

Sedgwick, Catharine Maria (1789–1867). Woman of letters. She was a well-educated and socially active member of the prominent Sedgwick family in Stockbridge, Massachusetts, where she had been born. Never marrying, she lived near her brother Charles Sedgwick and his schoolteacher wife Elizabeth. Catharine Sedgwick was a philanthropist and a moderate feminist, wrote fiction combining romantic plots and homely settings (beginning 1822), went to Europe (1839–1840) and the American West (1854), but lived mostly in Stockbridge and New York. By 1855 she was the most popular authoress in the United States, publishing books for juvenile readers, biographies, moral tracts, novels, and travel letters. Among her friends in the Berkshires were the actress Frances Anne Kemble,* Nathaniel Hawthorne,* and members of his family. When Melville lived at Arrowhead, near Pittsfield, he was within the wide circle of the Sedgwicks. After the Berkshires picnic, during which Melville met Hawthorne (5 August 1850), members of the party had tea with their host, David Dudley Field,* a clergyman who had a home in Stockbridge and was the author of *A*

History of the County of Berkshire, Massachusetts (1829—later a source for Melville's *Israel Potter*). During teatime, Miss Sedgwick grilled Evert Duyckinck,* who had picnicked with the group, on *Hope Leslie; or, Early Times in the Massachusetts* (1827), one of her novels, and on Magawisca, a heroic Indian maiden in it. Melville evidently did not get himself involved. In fact, none of his extant letters so much as mentions the woman—or any other Sedgwick. He may have spoofed her popular novel *The Poor Rich Man and the Rich Poor Man* (1836) in "Poor Man's Pudding and Rich Man's Crumbs."

   Bibliography: Edward Halsey Foster, *Catharine Maria Sedgwick* (New York: Twayne Publishers, 1974).

"Seen Aloft from Afar." *See* "The Parthenon."

Seignioroni, Seignior. In *White-Jacket,* he is mentioned by Dr. Cadwallader Cuticle as a surgeon in Seville who recently invented a caliper-like substitute for the tourniquet.

Selkirk, The Countess of. In *Israel Potter,* she is the lovely wife of the Earl of Selkirk, whose seat at St. Mary's Isle John Paul Jones raids in the hope of taking Selkirk hostage. The historical Jones never talked with the countess, although his men did. In real life, she was the gracious, spirited Helen Hamilton. She married Dunbar Hamilton, later Douglas, the 4th Earl of Selkirk* in 1758. After bearing seven sons and six daughters, she was widowed (1799) and died three years later.

   Bibliography: John Morgan Gray, *Lord Selkirk of Red River* ([East Lansing]: Michigan State University Press, 1964).

Selkirk, The Earl of (1722–1799). He was Dunbar Hamilton, later Douglas, the 4th Earl of Selkirk, and Lord Lieutenant of Kirkcudbright, of Kirkcudbrightshire. He married Helen Hamilton in 1758 (the couple had seven sons and six daughters). His wife became the Countess of Selkirk.* When he died, their son, Thomas Douglas Selkirk, became the 5th Earl of Selkirk, since Thomas's six older brothers had all died. As the 5th earl, he founded settlements in Canada, gained control of the Hudson's Bay Company, was ruined by a rival fur company, and died of a broken heart. In *Israel Potter,* Melville erroneously states that Selkirk (the 4th earl) was a privy counsellor and a personal friend of King George III. In the novel, John Paul Jones wants to take Selkirk as a hostage, but learns from Countess Selkirk that Selkirk is in Edinburgh when Jones raids his seat at St. Mary's Isle. In reality, Jones never talked with the countess; moreover, her husband was at Buxton, Derbyshire, not Edinburgh. Jones allowed his men to seize the Selkirk family plate as booty but bought it back and returned it. Melville makes use of this incident in *Israel Potter.*

   Bibliography: Cohen, *Potter;* John Morgan Gray, *Lord Selkirk of Red River* ([East Lansing]: Michigan State University Press, 1964).

Selvagee, Lieutenant. In *White-Jacket,* he is a dainty, languid quarterdeck officer who never should have gone to sea. He is contrasted with Lieutenant Mad Jack. Selvagee is a hempen instrument used in heaving up the anchor. A lieutenant named Murray who served aboard the *United States* may have been the partial model of Selvagee of the *Neversink.*

Bibliography: Anderson; Charles R. Anderson, "A Reply to Herman Melville's *White-Jacket* by Rear-Admiral Thomas O. Selfridge, Sr.," *American Literature* 7 (May 1935): 123–44; NN 5.

Senior, The. In "The Scout toward Aldie." *See* the Major.

Sereno, Don. In *White-Jacket,* he is the captain of the Peruvian sloop of war aboard which Jack Chase served until he was arrested by Lieutenant Blink and returned to the *Neversink,* on orders from Captain Claret.

Sergeant. In *Pierre. See* Dates.

Sergeant. In "The Scout toward Aldie," he is a soldier under the command of the Colonel, who vainly leads a group of men in pursuit of [John Singleton] Mosby.

"Shadow at the Feast: Mrs. B— (1847)" (1924). Poem, in *The Works of Herman Melville.* (Character: Mrs. B—.) It is Christmas time, and in a valley under starry skies a loving family is gathered before a glowing hearth fire. Members pass the decanter. But one "kinswoman" glides by and "sits sadly," patiently, and by herself. She was a young bride in May but was widowed in June. Oh, "let her not hear" the happy Christmas wishes that ring out. Melville was married in 1847, the date of this enigmatic reminiscence. Mrs. B— has not been identified, and "B" may not be the initial of the person described.

Bibliography: Shurr.

Shakings. In *White-Jacket,* he is a former Sing-Sing convict. He is now a forehold sailor aboard the *Neversink,* which he calls a state prison afloat.

Shanks. In *White-Jacket,* he is a long, thin, pale sailor assigned as permanent cook of Mess No. 1, which is presided over by Jack Chase.

Sharp-Eyes. In "A Dutch Christmas up the Hudson in the Time of Patroons," this person is a young child who looks for Santa Claus.

Shaw, Elizabeth Knapp (1784–1822). The first wife of Melville's father-in-law, Lemuel Shaw,* whom she married in 1812. She was the mother of Elizabeth Knapp Shaw Melville,* Melville's wife. Her sister was Martha Bird Knapp Marett (1796–1878), who at her death willed $20,000 to Elizabeth Knapp

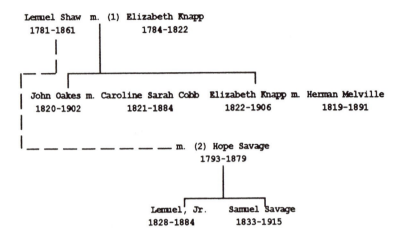

Shaw Family Tree

Shaw Melville. Martha Marett's daughter was Ellen Marett Gifford (?–1889), long a partial invalid and also a benefactress of the Melvilles, willing $10,000 to Melville's wife, $8,000 to Melville (1879), and later an additional $5,000 to him. The Gifford women must have experienced irrational guilt, among other emotions, when Philip Marett, Martha Marett's husband, was involved in bank embezzlement (1847).

Bibliography: NN 14.

Shaw, Hope Savage (1793–1879). Melville's stepmother-in-law. She became the second wife of the widowed Lemuel Shaw,* Melville's future father-in-law, in 1827. She was the daughter of Dr. Samuel Savage of Barnstable, Massachusetts. Melville took his wife Elizabeth Knapp Shaw Melville* to Boston a few weeks before their first child, Malcolm Melville,* was born in the Shaws' home (1849). Hope Shaw always made the Melvilles, together or separately, feel welcome in her home; however, she was privately critical of Melville for his improvident nature. Her diary is helpful in pinpointing his whereabouts and his activities and those of other Melvilles over the years, as are letters to her from Elizabeth Melville,* Augusta Melville,* and Stanwix Melville,* and members of her own immediate family.

Bibliography: NN 14.

Shaw, John Oakes (1820–1902). The only son of Lemuel Shaw* and Elizabeth Knapp Shaw,* his first wife. Called Oakes by the family, he married Caroline Sarah Cobb in 1844. They had two children, a daughter named Josephine ("Josie") MacC. Shaw (1848–1933) and a son named John Oakes ("Oakie") Shaw, Jr. (1850–1909). Oakie played with Melville's younger son, Stanwix Melville,* when both were little, and married a woman possibly named Anne. His father

John Oakes Shaw failed to find permanent work in Chicago and later was a Boston customhouse clerk (1849–c. 1857, c. 1861–c. 1881). Melville had little contact with Oakes Shaw, who described *Pierre* in a letter to his brother Lemuel Shaw, Jr.,* as "some *high faluting* romance which is spoken of with any thing but praise" (31 August 1852). Melville's granddaughter Eleanor Melville Metcalf calls Oakes Shaw "the least sympathetic (not to use a stronger term) of Herman's Boston brothers-in-law."

Bibliography: Garner, Leyda, Metcalf, NN 14.

Shaw, Lemuel (1781–1861). Jurist and Melville's father-in-law. Shaw was born in Barnstable, Massachusetts. His father, Oakes Shaw, was a Congregational minister for forty-seven years there. After being schooled largely at home by his father, young Shaw graduated from Harvard (1800), taught school in Boston (1800–1801), wrote and proofread for the Boston *Gazette* (1800–1801), and studied law in Boston and Amherst, New Hampshire (1801–1802), while being tutored in French. He published items in the Amherst *Farmers' Cabinet.* He was admitted to the bar in Hillsboro County, New Hampshire, and Plymouth County, Massachusetts (1804), after which he practiced law in Boston (1804–1830). Shaw knew Melville's father Allan Melvill* and was engaged to that man's sister Nancy Wroe Melvill,* but she died before the two could be married. He carried two love letters from her in his wallet for the rest of his life. Shaw married Elizabeth Knapp [Shaw*] in 1818. They had two children, John Oakes Shaw* and Elizabeth Knapp Shaw Melville.* Shaw's wife died during the year of the birth of her daughter. Shaw devoted himself to his children, his mother, and his work exclusively until he married Hope Savage in 1827. She thus became Hope Savage Shaw* and bore him two children: Lemuel Shaw, Jr.* and Samuel Savage Shaw.* Shaw provided for the high school education of his wife Hope Shaw's nephew Samuel Hay Savage (1827–1901), fatherless from 1839, and later Melville's walking and traveling companion, and still later trustee of Judge Shaw's estate.

Meanwhile, Shaw had been pursuing a distinguished career. He was a representative of the General Court of Massachusetts (1811–1814, 1820, 1829); a member of the Constitutional Convention (1820), where he associated with Levi Lincoln and Daniel Webster, among other political luminaries; and a state senator (1821–1822). Shaw prepared the first charter of the city of Boston (1822— it remained in force, but for a minor change [1856], until 1913). He argued sixty-two Supreme Judicial Court cases (1824–1830). Governor Levi Lincoln of Massachusetts appointed Shaw chief justice of Massachusetts (1830). By accepting the annual salary of $3,500, Shaw gave up a practice earning him from $15,000 to $20,000 annually. By 1830, however, he had substantial investments in banks and in insurance companies; in 1855, he paid $874 in personal estate and real estate taxes.

During his thirty-year tenure on the bench (to 1860), Shaw wrote 2,200 or so opinions, which were published in fifty-six volumes of the *Massachusetts*

Reports. Usually concerning commercial and constitutional law and written with clarity and logic rather than with rhetorical brilliance, they influenced litigation relating to labor, railroads, public utilities, and water power. His influence on American law is said to have been greater than that of any other state judge. Four cases were especially notable: that of anti-Catholic rioters who destroyed the Charlestown Ursuline convent (1834); that of the *Commonwealth v. Hunt,* in which Shaw repudiated criminal-conspiracy prosecutions of labor unions (1842); that of John White Webster for the murder of George Parkman, the uncle of the historian Francis Parkman (1850), in which Shaw sentenced Webster to hang; and that of the fugitive slave Thomas Sims, who was arrested in Boston and whom Shaw refused to release—his opinion being the first extensive sustention of the constitutionality of the 1850 Fugitive Slave Act. Shaw argued for political compromises to prevent the Civil War. He remained active in Harvard affairs, as an overseer of the college (1831–1853) and as a fellow of the college (1834–1861). A Federalist, he supported Webster's Whig policies. Shaw attended Unitarian church services.

Shaw became an even closer friend of the Melville family when in 1847 Melville married his daughter Elizabeth. At this time, Hope Savage Shaw obviously became Melville's stepmother-in-law. Earlier, Melville had dedicated *Typee* to Shaw (1845). Soon Shaw became Melville's puzzled friend and benefactor. He loaned—actually gave—Melville $2,000 to help him buy a house with his brother Allan Melville* in New York soon after both brothers got married (1847). Melville's first child, Malcolm Melville,* was born in Shaw's house in Boston (1849). Shaw "loaned" Melville $3,000 to help him buy Arrowhead, near Pittsfield, Massachusetts (1850), and another $500 soon thereafter. At this time, Shaw asked for and received notes from Melville, strictly for legal purposes, because the older man wanted his four children to be treated equitably. Shaw vacationed with Melville on Nantucket, during which time Melville learned about the Agatha story* (1852). Shaw vacationed in England and on the Continent with his son Lemuel Shaw, Jr. (1853). Melville's explanatory letter to Shaw about his worsening financial situation is embarrassing (12 May 1856). Allan Melville, in his capacity as a lawyer in New York City, drew up a mortgage on Arrowhead in Shaw's favor, to protect the generous man against persons to whom Melville might also owe money. Melville soon not only sold eighty wooded acres to a neighbor but also accepted a "loan" of $5,000 more from Shaw with which to regain solvency (1856). Shaw, who never recorded the mortgage, financed Melville's second trip to Europe and the Middle East to the tune of $1,400 or $1,500 (1856–1857), sent Melville $100 for winter supplies (8 November 1858), and offered moral support during his ventures as a lecturer (1857–1860). When Melville made plans to take a voyage with his sea-captain brother Thomas Melville,* Shaw wrote Melville a long, friendly, and candid letter about finances (15 May 1860), in which he proposed to cancel all debts, take over ownership of Arrowhead, and deed the place to Elizabeth Melville as her prospective inheritance (15 May 1860). Shaw persuaded his friend

Richard Henry Dana, Jr.,* to help Melville in his application for a consulship; Dana obliged by writing to a mutual friend, Charles Summer,* the influential senator from Massachusetts (1861). Melville, who obtained no consular appointment, was called home from his office-seeking activities in Washington by news of Shaw's mortal illness in Boston (1861). Weaving through these events was Shaw's unfailing concern for his son-in-law's health as well as his generosity and kindness to many relatives and friends of both Melville and his long-suffering wife.

Bibliography: Garner; Leonard Williams Levy, *The Law of the Commonwealth and Chief Justice Shaw* (New York: Oxford University Press, 1987); NN 14; Tom Quirk, "The Judge Dragged to the Bar: Melville, Shaw, and the Webster Murder Trial," *Melville Society Extracts* 84 (February 1991): 1–8.

Shaw, Lemuel ("Lem"), Jr. (1828–1884). The older son of Lemuel Shaw,* Melville's father-in-law, and of Hope Savage Shaw,* Melville's stepmother-in-law. He graduated from Harvard and was a member of the bar. When he was traveling in England, Melville wrote to his British publishers Richard Bentley* and John Murray* to ask them to befriend the young man (1852), who went on to the Continent, returned to England, was joined by his father, and went with him back to the Continent (1853). Having little comprehension of Melville's literary genius, Lemuel Shaw, Jr., wrote to his brother Samuel Savage Shaw* thus: "I have no great confidence in the success of his productions" (15 July 1856). In another letter to his brother, he categorized *The Confidence-Man* as belonging in "that horribly uninteresting class of nonsensical books he [Melville] is given to writing" (21 April 1857). Soon thereafter, Melville told Lemuel Shaw, Jr., that he did not plan "to write any more at present"—or so Lemuel wrote to his brother Samuel (2 June 1857). Melville did, however, write a great deal more. Both Lemuel Shaw, Jr., and his father sought political compromises to prevent the Civil War. Soon after peace was declared, Lemuel Shaw, Jr., visited Europe again (1865). He was kind and hospitable to his sister Elizabeth Knapp Shaw Melville* and her children; for example, he generously sent $75 to Stanwix Melville,* when the young man was seeking work near San Francisco (1877), and he also bequeathed a legacy to Elizabeth Melville* (1884). Lemuel Shaw, Jr., died of apoplexy at his club in Boston.

Bibliography: Garner, Leyda, NN 14.

Shaw, Samuel ("Sam") Savage (1833–1915). The younger son of Lemuel Shaw,* Melville's father-in-law, and of Hope Savage Shaw,* Melville's stepmother-in-law. As a teenager, he attended the 1847 wedding of his half-sister Elizabeth Knapp Shaw Melville* to Melville and wrote to her about "how disgusting wedding cake got to be!" (4 August 1856). He graduated from Harvard (1856) and went to Europe, mostly Berlin (1856). While in Rome, Melville rendezvoused with him for one brief day (21 March 1857). Samuel Shaw became a member of the bar. He socialized with Melville, hiked with him, and liked him greatly. When Melville had a road accident, Samuel Shaw impressed him by acts of kindness (November 1862), and he was considerate when Melville's son Malcolm Melville* committed suicide (1867). Samuel Shaw, who never married, attended Melville's funeral.

Bibliography: Garner, Leyda, NN 14.

Shaz Gold-beak. In "Under the Rose." *See* Gold-beak.

Sheba, The Princess of. In "Rammon," she is a learned, well-traveled Indian lady, who, it is said, brings Buddhistic beliefs to Solomon's Palestine.

Shelley, Percy Bysshe (1792–1822). Poet. Shelley was born at Warnham, near Horsham, West Sussex, studied with a local clergyman, was sent to a boarding school at Isleworth (1802–1804), and attended Eton (1804–1810) and then University College, Oxford (1810–1811). Expelled for writing *The Necessity of Atheism,* he eloped with and married Harriet Westbrook, age sixteen, in Edinburgh in 1811. The couple lived in various places and had a daughter (1813); then Shelley decamped with Mary Wollstonecraft Godwin, age seventeen, to France, accompanied by her stepsister Claire Clairmont (July 1814). Harriet had a son back in England (November 1814). Mary had a daughter who died weeks later (1815). The death of Shelley's grandfather Sir Bysshe Shelley (1815) made the young poet financially comfortable. He and Mary had a son (1816–1819), vacationed with Claire in Switzerland, associated with Lord Byron, and returned to England (1816). Harriet committed suicide in London, whereupon Shelley and Mary got married (1816). Denied custody of his children by Harriet, he and Mary had a daughter (1817–1818) and Mary published *Frankenstein; or, The Modern Prometheus* (1817). The couple, plus children, servants, and Claire, went to various cities in Italy (1818) and had another son (1819). Shelley drowned off Spezzia. During his brief period of creativity, he poured out writings. His major works are *Queen Mab* (1813, revolutionary poem), *Alastor* (1816, allegorical poem), *The Revolt of Islam* (1818, symbolic narrative poem), *The Cenci* (1819, poetic drama), *Prometheus Unbound* (1820, lyrical drama), and "A Defence of Poetry" (1821). His short poems include "Hymn to Intellectual Beauty" (1817), "Ozymandias" (1818), "Ode to the West Wind" (1820), "To a Skylark" (1820), and "Adonais" (1822). Shelley, a delicate, erotic, intense, skeptical, visionary poet of startling originality, remains controversial both because of his works and because of his personal conduct.

Melville's poet Yoomy in *Mardi* bears comparison with Shelley. In "Shelley's Vision," Melville suggests that Shelley is one who learns self-reverence.

Bibliography: Davis; Donald H. Reiman, *Percy Bysshe Shelley Updated Edition* (New York: Twayne Publishers, 1990).

"Shelley's Vision" (1891). Poem, in *Timoleon.* (Character: [Percy Bysshe] Shelley.) The poet wanders lonely, dejected, and bitter. Hate pelts him; so he "pelt[s] the pelted one" in return, by throwing a stone at his own shadow. Suddenly, however, "upon that sun-lit ground" he sees a crowned likeness of St. Stephen and begins to revere himself. St. Stephen was the first martyr, stoned to death for refusing to renounce his faith in Christ, but forgiving his enemies. While in Rome (February 1857), Melville visited the ruins of the Baths of Caracalla, where Shelley was inspired to write *Prometheus Unbound,* and also Shelley's grave. In his conduct if not in his writings, Shelley was anything but saintly; hence, Melville's intent may be partly to deride Shelley's unchristian conceit.

Bibliography: NN 11 and 15, Shurr, Stein.

Shenly. In *White-Jacket,* he is White Jacket's ill messmate, a topman from Portsmouth, New Hampshire. He dies of a pulmonary complaint and prostration aboard the *Neversink* and is buried at sea. Shenly is based on Edward Williams, the captain's cook aboard the *United States,* on which Melville served (1843–1844) and which is the prototype of the *Neversink.* Suffering from pulmonary disease, Williams was admitted to the sick bay (June 1844), where, though carefully treated, he died (August).

Bibliography: NN 5.

Shenly. In *White-Jacket,* he and or she is one of Shenly's two children.

Shenly, Mrs. In *White-Jacket,* she is the wife, in Portsmouth, New Hampshire, of White Jacket's messmate, Shenly, who dies aboard the *Neversink* and is buried at sea.

Shepherd, Daniel (?–1870). Lawyer and author. He was the law partner of Allan Melville,* Melville's brother. Melville met Shepherd through this professional connection. Shepherd cowitnessed a document assigning the copyright of *Typee* and *Omoo* to John Murray,* Melville's publisher in London (1850). Melville, his brother, and Shepherd vacationed together at Lake George, New York (August 1856). Shepherd anonymously published an historical novel *Saratoga: A Story of 1787* (1856). Soon thereafter, he entertained Melville, his brother, and their literary friend Evert Duyckinck* in his New York apartment (October 1856). Melville wrote Shepherd a letter (perhaps never mailed) in the form of a poem (6 July 1859). In "Epistle to Daniel Shepherd," he is identified as a Wall Street friend whom the poet invites to his country home for an Arcadian holiday. Whether Shepherd acted on any invitation to visit Arrowhead is not known.

Bibliography: NN 14.

Sheridan, Philip H. (1831–1888). (Full name: Philip Henry Sheridan; nickname: "Little Phil.") Union Army cavalry officer. Sheridan was born in Albany, New York, graduated from West Point (1853), served at frontier posts and elsewhere (to 1862), and became a colonel in the Michigan cavalry. He fought skillfully though outnumbered at Booneville, Mississippi (July 1862), was promoted to brigadier general, fought well defensively at Perryville, Kentucky (October), at Stone River, Tennessee (December–January 1863), and made major general. He was defeated at Chickamauga, Georgia (September), but attacked well at Missionary Ridge, south of Chattanooga, Tennessee (November). General Ulysses S. Grant* arranged for Sheridan to command the cavalry of the Army of the Potomac (beginning spring 1864). He did well during the Battle of the Wilderness (May), raided Confederate supplies near Richmond, Virginia, and attacked the cavalry of Confederate James E. B. Stuart,* who was killed at Yellow Tavern, Virginia (May). Sheridan commanded the Army of the Shenandoah (from August), burned the means of subsistence of the Confederates in the Shenandoah Valley, drove Confederate General Jubal A. Early* out of Virginia after the Battle of Cedar Creek (October), and was promoted to major general (October). Sheridan helped put Petersburg, Virginia, under siege (March 1865) and attacked the communication lines of Confederate General Robert E. Lee,* which hastened his surrender at Appomattox (April). Remaining in the army, Sheridan served along the shores of the Gulf of Mexico, in Texas, and in Louisiana (1869). His policies were so harsh during the early Reconstruction era that President Andrew Johnson removed him, after which he held commands in the West (to 1883), where he attacked Native Americans (1868–1869). Promoted to lieutenant general, he was named general-in-chief of the army (1883) and general of the army (1888). Sheridan married Irene Rucker of Chicago in 1875 (the couple had three daughters and a son). Sheridan completed *Personal Memoirs of P. H. Sheridan* three days before his death (2 vols., 1888). He was noted as a combat officer who took the offensive whenever possible and exploited every advantage he observed. He is unpopular because of his 1869 remark that the only good Indians he ever saw were dead ones.

Bibliography: Garner; Richard O'Connor, *Sheridan the Inevitable* (Indianapolis: Bobbs-Merrill, 1953).

"Sheridan at Cedar Creek (October, 1864)" (1866). Poem, in *Battle-Pieces*. (Characters: [General Jubal A.] Early, [General] Philip [H.] Sheridan.) It was published as "Philip" in *Harper's New Monthly Magazine** (April 1866) and reprinted in *Battle-Pieces*. The horse of "Philip, king of riders"—that is, General Philip H. Sheridan—should be shod with silver, clothed in ermine, wreathed, and shrouded in sable. The steed deserves silver shoes for carrying his rider forward to "retrieve the day." The ermine would match the "foam-flake" blowing about him in October. The horse deserves wreaths because "the charge he led / . . . turned the cypress / Into amaranths" for his rider. But a shroud is also appropriate because of the "mounds" of "nameless followers" of Philip who did not survive the battle. Confederate General Jubal A. Early's men were winning the Battle of Cedar Creek, Virginia (October 1864), until Sheridan led his famous "ride" down from Winchester fourteen miles to the north-northeast and counterattacked in the last major Shenandoah Valley engagement. Casualties at Cedar Creek were awesome: Union forces lost 5,665 (including 1,591 missing), while the Confederate losses were 2,910 (including 1,050 missing). Melville, who loved puns, somewhat spoils his poem by calling Early "belated" here.

Bibliography: Boatner; Cohen, *Poems*; Faust; Garner; NN 11.

Sherman, William Tecumseh (1820–1891). (Original name: Tecumseh Sherman; nickname: "Cump.") Union Army officer. He was born in Lancaster, Ohio. After his father died and young Sherman was adopted by the Thomas Ewing family, his foster mother added the name William to his original name. He graduated from West Point (1840), held assignments in Florida (1840–1841) and Fort Moultrie, South Carolina (1842), studied law in Georgia (1845), and during the Mexican War was in California (1846–1848). In 1850 he married Eleanor Boyle Ewing, the daughter of his foster father Thomas Ewing, whom President Zachary Taylor* had earlier named his secretary of the interior. Sherman bought cattle for the army in Kansas and Missouri (1852–1853) and resigned from the army to become a banker in San Francisco until the collapse of the boom occasioned by the Gold Rush (1857). Failing as a lawyer in Fort Leavenworth, Kansas, he became superintendent of the Louisiana State Seminary of Learning and Military Academy (now part of Louisiana State University) through the influence of his Southern friends Braxton Bragg* and P.G.T. Beauregard (1859–1861). When Louisiana seceded from the Union, Sherman became president of the St. Louis Fifth Street Railroad and soon thereafter was appointed a lieutenant colonel in the U.S. Army. After fighting unsuccessfully at the First Battle of Bull Run (July 1861), he was promoted to brigadier general (August) and commanded troops in Kentucky; however, he ordered so many reinforcements to face imagined enemy soldiers that hostile reporters called him insane. He was assigned under General Ulysses S. Grant,* was promoted to major general (May 1862), and did well under Grant at Vicksburg (November–July 1863). Sherman suggested the attack on Arkansas Post, which the gunboat flotilla of Commander David Dixon Porter* helped capture (early 1863). Sherman led units of three armies—the Cumberland, the Ohio, and the Tennessee, with 100,000 men at peak strength—in the march into Georgia (from May 1864), took Atlanta (September), went on toward the sea (November) with 62,000 men, occupied Savannah (December), turned north into South Carolina (February 1865), occupied Goldsboro (March) and Raleigh, North Carolina (April), and offered Confederate General Joseph E. Johnston liberal surrender terms (April). Soon after peace was declared, Sherman was named lieutenant general (July). President Grant appointed him a full general (1869), after which he served as the commanding general of the army (1869–1883). During that period, Sherman went on leave to Europe (1871–1872) and also established a war college at Leavenworth (1881). He lived as a civilian in St. Louis (1883–1886) and New York (from 1886). His wife died in 1888. Of their eight children, six survived him. Sherman published his *Memoirs* (2 vols., 1875). He was flinty-eyed and had a lightning-quick mind. Because he brought the horrors of war to civilians through the destruction of their goods and property, Sherman is regarded as the first modern general. He also has gone down in history for replying thus to suggestions that he run for president: "If nominated, I will not accept. If elected, I will not serve."

Melville mentions Sherman in several poems. In "The March to the Sea," he is described as the Union general leading the glorious, joyous, havoc-wreaking march to the sea. In "The Frenzy in the Wake: Sherman's advance through the Carolinas," he is mentioned. In "On Sherman's men who fell in the Assault of Kenesaw Mountain, Georgia," he is identified as the Union general whose men fell while attacking Kenesaw Mountain. In "Lee in the Capitol," Robert E. Lee, about to testify in Washington, D.C., remembers Sherman as victorious. In "Iris (1865)," Sherman and his march are mentioned.

Bibliography: Garner; R. D. Madison, "Melville's Sherman Poems: A Problem in Source Study," *Melville Society Extracts* 78 (September 1989): 8–11; Charles Royster, "Chronology," pp. 1085–1119 in *Memoirs of General W. T. Sherman* (New York: Library of America, 1984); Wilson.

"Shiloh: A Requiem (April, 1862)" (1866). Poem, in *Battle-Pieces.* In one long, nineteen-line sentence, Melville pictures the swallows flying low over the battlefield at Shiloh, where the parched wounded were rained on, and where the nearby log church echoed to the groans and prayers of the dying soldiers, who though "[f]oemen at morn" were "friends at eve." The poem contains one of Melville's most powerful lines: "What like a bullet can undeceive!" The circular motion of the "wheeling" swallows seems to hold the dead in a kind of natural embrace. Confederate General Albert Sidney Johnston attacked unprepared Union forces at Shiloh, near Pittsburg Landing, Tennessee (April 1862) and drove them back. Johnston's death prevented his men from exploiting their initial victory. Union reinforcements arrived under General Ulysses S. Grant* and, after a second day of fighting, forced a Confederate withdrawal. Casualties were terrifying: Union forces, 1,754 killed, 8,408 wounded, and 2,885 missing; Confederate, 1,723 killed, 8,012 wounded, and 959 missing.

Bibliography: Alder; Boatner; Cohen, *Poems*; Faust; Garner; Dennis Lloyd, " 'All is Hushed at Shiloh': A Reminiscence," *Border States* 8 (1991): 7–14; NN 11; Shurr; Warren.

Shippy. In *White-Jacket,* he is a pale young fellow whom "Happy-Jack" Landless advises to salute the officers, endure the floggings quietly, and drink grog.

Shirrer, Rev. Mr. In *Israel Potter,* Melville mentions him as the Scottish minister of Kirkaldy who, according to legend, interceded to evoke a squall that kept John Paul Jones from attacking the city. According to Edinburgh's 1778 annals, the prayer of Reverend Robert Shirra, who was a preacher living at

Kirkaldy on the Firth of Forth near Edinburgh, was followed by enemy vessels being driven out to sea.

Bibliography: Cohen, *Potter.*

"A Short Patent Sermon According to Blair, the Rhetorician: No. C.C.C.L.XXX.V.III" (1847). Article attributed to Melville, published anonymously in *Yankee Doodle** (10 July 1847). (Characters: [Hugh] Blair, Dow Jr.) Following Blair's suggested outline, the author introduces Dow Jr., divides his text into "wishy" and "washy," explains that Dow writes "clever" but long sermons, includes pathos by saying such sermons put his listeners to sleep, and concludes by saying that though sheeplike they will not consent to being beaten upon forever like sheepskin drumheads.

Bibliography: NN 9.

Shorty ("The Cockney"). In *Omoo,* he is the short Cockney partner of Zeke the Yankee in a farming venture at Martair. They employ Peter and Paul—that is, Dr. Long Ghost and the narrator. According to Lieutenant Henry A. Wise, who kept a journal of an 1846–1849 Pacific cruise aboard a U.S. naval vessel and visited Papeete in 1848, rumor had it that Shorty was still growing potatoes nearby some six years after Melville observed him, and that Shorty was shooting cattle owned by his neighbor. In reality, however, the cattle were wild and nominally belonged to Queen Pomare IV,* who gave farmers permission to shoot them as they wished.

Bibliography: Anderson.

Sicilian Sailor. In *Moby-Dick,* he is a *Pequod* sailor who dances during the midnight festivities in the forecastle and then lies down. He tries to warn Captain Ahab when the sea hawk is about to snatch off his hat.

Sid. In "Bridegroom-Dick," he is a frank cadet remembered by Bridegroom Dick.

Siddons, Sarah Kemble (1755–1831). Actress. Her parents, Roger and Sarah Ward Kemble, formed a traveling company in which some of their twelve children acted. Sarah Kemble was born in Brecon, Brecknockshire, Wales. Her brothers included the actors Charles Kemble* and John Philip Kemble.* She was well educated, married a handsome, insipid actor named William Siddons with her parents' reluctant consent (1773), and began a brilliant acting career, especially in tragedies. Her Lady Macbeth was astounding, which her brother John Philip Kemble capitalized on by playing opposite her. She tutored the royal children in elocution (from 1783) and retired from the public stage after a versatile career (1812). Her portraits were painted by Thomas Gainsborough, Thomas Lawrence, and Joshua Reynolds. In "The Fiddler," Siddons is the famous Drury Lane actress reputedly ousted from the public eye by Master Betty (*see* Betty, William Henry West).

Bibliography: Linda Kelly, *The Kemble Era: John Philip Kemble, Sarah Siddons and the London Stage* (New York: Random House, 1980).

Sidonia, Alonzo. In "Benito Cereno," he is an old Valparaiso resident who took passage aboard the *San Dominick* after he had been appointed to a civil office in Lima. When Sidonia saw Alexandro Aranda's mutilation, he jumped overboard and drowned.

Silva, The Marquis of. In *White-Jacket,* he is a Brazilian nobleman who, while attending Pedro II, king of Brazil, falls into the forepassage of the *Neversink.*

Silvio. In "Pausilippo (in the Time of Bomba)," he is a bent old harp player, described as formerly a political prisoner. In reality, he is a highly fictionalized Silvio Pellico,* the Italian man of letters.

Singles, Jenny. In *Israel Potter,* she is the Berkshire girl loved by Israel Potter but lost to Singles, who later became a sergeant in the American army.

Singles, Sergeant. In *Israel Potter,* he is the man who wins and marries Jenny, who was Israel Potter's childhood sweetheart. When Potter is in Falmouth, England, he sees his successful former rival again.

Sister Mary. In *Pierre. See* Glendinning, Mary.

Skrimshander. In *Moby-Dick,* this is Peter Coffin's nickname for Ishmael.

Skyeman, The. In *Mardi. See* Jarl.

Slim. In *White-Jacket,* he is a diffident midshipman rebuked in class by the Professor.

Slyboots, Sir. In "The Scout toward Aldie," he is a Confederate prisoner of the Colonel who leads a raid to capture [John Singleton] Mosby. Slyboots may be Mosby himself.

Smart, Purser. In "Bridegroom-Dick," he is the portly purser aboard the vessel commanded by Captain Turret.

Smith, Joe. In "The New Ancient of Days," he is a common man, dethroned by the new ancient.

Smith, Joseph Edward Adams (1822–1896). Editor, journalist, and poet. As editor of the *Berkshire County Eagle* and a literary personality in Pittsfield, Massachusetts, Smith published many complimentary notices of Melville's works and became his casual friend. Smith also knew Melville's Pittsfield friends John Rowland Morewood* and Sarah Huyler Morewood.* Using the pen name Godfrey Greylock, Smith wrote most of the sections in a guidebook of Berkshire County entitled *Taghconic; or, Letters and Legends about Our Summer Home* (1852; rev. ed., 1879), in which Melville is mentioned several times. Smith induced Melville to write a biographical sketch of his uncle, Thomas Melvill, Jr.,* which appeared anonymously in *The History of Pittsfield (Berkshire County), Mass., from the Year 1800 to the Year 1876, as Compiled and Written, under the General Direction of a Committee, by J.E.A. Smith* (1876). Smith also wrote *A History of Paper . . .* (1882), *History of Berkshire County, with Biographical Sketches of Its Prominent Men . . .* (1885), and *Pontoosuc Lake: The Railroad Ride to It, Its History, Topography and Romance* (1890). After Melville's death, Smith published a valuable, nine-installment *Biographical Sketch of Herman Melville* in the *Pittsfield Evening Journal* (27 October 1891–25 January 1892). Melville's widow Elizabeth Knapp Shaw Melville* published a rearranged, edited, and abridged version of this work as a pamphlet entitled *Biographical Sketch. Privately Printed for Mrs. Herman Melville* (1897). Late in his life, Smith wrote *The Poet among the Hills: Oliver Wendell Holmes[*] in Berkshire . . .* (1895) and *Souvenir Verse and Story . . .* (1896).

Bibliography: Leyda, NN 14.

Smyrniote, The. In *Clarel. See* Glaucon.

Smythe, Henry Augustus (1817–?). Merchant. Smythe worked in the Boston commission house of F. Skinner & Co. and then founded the house of Smythe, Sprague, & Cooper in New York (1857–1864). While traveling in a carriage from Berne to Basle, Switzerland, Melville met Smythe at Soleure (Solothurn) and traveled with him on to Heidelberg, Germany (April 1857). Smythe became president of the Central National Bank, in New York (1864–1866), was appointed Collector of the Port of New York (1866–1869), and processed some 5,000 applications for office. A few months after he assumed office, he appointed Melville, who had evidently renewed his friendship with Smythe, as inspector of customs at $4 per day (November 1866). Melville replaced a man named George S. Swackhammer. During his tenure, Smythe removed 830 employees, generally for incompetence. He was so honest that venal patronage dispensers often tried to discredit him.

Bibliography: Stanton Garner, "Surviving in the Gilded Age: Herman Melville in the Customs Service," *Essays in Arts and Sciences* 15 (June 1986): 1–13; Harrison Hayford and Merrell R. Davis, "Herman Melville as Office-Seeker," *Modern Language Quarterly* 10 (June, September 1949): 168–83, 377–88; NN 15.

Snarles. In *Moby-Dick,* he is a sign painter on the island of Nantucket. Mrs. Hosea Hussey would like him to paint a sign forbidding suicides in her Try Pots Inn.

Sneak. In *White-Jacket,* he is a hang-dog informer who replaces Bland when that man is temporarily suspended from his position as master-at-arms.

Snodhead, Dr. In *Moby-Dick,* he is a supposed authority, from the College of Santa Claus and St. Pott's, on the subject of Low Dutch and High German. He translates passages for the narrator from an ancient Dutch volume on whaling.

Snowser. In *Israel Potter,* this is a sailor's name invented by Israel Potter for himself when he alone boards the British frigate from the *Ariel.*

Sober Sides. In *Mardi,* he is an uninspired spectator of the war games held by King Hello and King Piko on the island of Diranda.

Socrates. In "The Paradise of Bachelors and the Tartarus of Maids," he is the head waiter at the sumptuous dinner of the latter-day Templars in London, attended by the narrator.

Soldier, The. In "An Epitaph," he is a dead soldier whose widow keeps the faith.

Soldier, The. In "A Scout toward Aldie." *See* the Colonel.

Solo. In *Mardi,* he is an avowed bachelor and a legatee mentioned in Bardianna's will. The aptly named Solo plans to go through life solitarily, so Bardianna wills him his one-person bed mat.

Solomon (?–922 B.C.). King of Israel. Solomon was the son of King David and Bathsheba. After his half-brother Adonijah failed in a coup to seize the throne, Solomon succeeded his father and became the third king of Israel (c. 961–922 B.C.). He made Israel a commercial power, eliminated those who threatened his rule, established alliances with Egypt and Phoenicia (among other foreign countries), built up his military forces, opened supply avenues, exploited forced labor, and created national stability and wealth sufficient to permit him to institute a large building program. One such structure was his famous Temple in Jerusalem. Solomon supported literary figures and was a writer himself, although "The Song of Solomon" and other works once attributed to him were composed by others. He was reputed to be wiser and more versatile than he really was. Toward the end of his reign, the people resented his imposition of high taxes, his harem of foreign princesses, and his several marriages. Foreign cults served his wives and traders and thus occasioned criticism by religious conservatives.

In "Magian Wine," Melville mentions Solomon in connection with certain charms. In "Rammon," Melville identifies him erroneously as the son of Jethro and the aging father of the unrobust Rammon. In Solomon's time, it is said, Buddhistic beliefs came through the Princess of Sheba to Palestine.

Bibliography: Martin Noth, *The History of Israel* (1958; New York: Harper & Row, rev. translation, 1960).

"The South Seas" (1858, 1859). Lecture. This was the second of three lectures given by Melville, the others being "Statues in Rome" and "Traveling: Its Pleasures, Pains, and Profits." He begins "The South Seas" by commenting on romantic connotations of their names, their extent, and early explorers (Vasco Nuñez de Balboa, Magellan, Captain Cook). He considers topics he might select from such a vast subject: sharks, swordfish, devil-fish, pelicans, penguins, man-of-war hawks, albatrosses, oceanic phosphorescence, islands. After touching on each, he decries the white man's treatment of the Polynesians: We have spread Christianity by military means, buccaneers have hidden on Pacific isles, and so did [Fletcher] Christian the *Bounty* mutineer. Melville once discouraged a reformer who sought advice on establishing a Fourierite colony among the Typees. Ohio Free Lovers and Salt Lake Mormons seeking to appropriate South Sea islands should beware. Melville describes two visionaries (Kamapiikai of Hawaii and Alvaro Mendaña) who failed to find a Polynesian paradise; tells about an American he saw on a remote island, in tatters though with three native wives; discusses types of lost seamen and beachcombers; talks about tattoos; is sorry he ever even whispered about "the mysterious rites of the 'taboo' ''; and discusses native newspapers, often run by foreigners, including the excellent Honolulu *Advertiser*. Admitting that the future of Polynesia is open to speculation, he hopes that Christians will forbid attempts to annex Hawaii and the Georgian Islands until our own civilization has produced more than "almshouses, prisons, and hospitals."

Bibliography: NN 9; Merton M. Sealts, Jr., *Melville as Lecturer* (1957; Folcroft, Pa.: Folcroft Press, 1970).

Spagnoletto ("The Don"). In "Marquis de Grandvin: At the Hostelry," Melville depicts him as a short and brawny artist who discusses the picturesque and argues splenetically with [Paolo] Veronese. Spagnoletto is undoubtedly Jusepe de Ribera,* who was nicknamed Lo Spagnoletto.

Spahi, The. In *Clarel. See* Belex.

Spanish Sailor. In *Moby-Dick,* he is a *Pequod* sailor who, during the midnight festivities in the forecastle, picks a fight with Daggoo by insulting him for being black. The storm interrupts them.

Spinoza, Baruch (1632–1677). Dutch-Jewish philosopher. He was born in Amsterdam into a Portuguese-Jewish family that had taken refuge in the Netherlands. His father was a well-to-do merchant. Spinoza's intellectual independence caused his excommunication from the Jewish community (1656), but he sought to remain friendly with synagogue authorities. Through tutors and colleagues, including Christian ones, and partly by himself, he studied Greek, Latin, and European languages, and came under the influence of the writings of René Descartes. Spinoza supported himself by grinding lenses and tutoring. He moved to Rijnsburg (1660), lodged with a surgeon, and wrote but did not publish treatises on God and man and on the understanding (1662). He published (1663) an exposition and criticism of Descartes's *Principles of Philosophy,* in which he opposed the French philosopher's belief in the transcendence of God, in the dualism of the mind and the body, and in his ascribing free will to God and human beings. Spinoza moved near the Hague (1664) and then to the Hague (1671). He anonymously published a treatise on theology and politics (1670). He declined a chair at the University of Heidelberg (1673). His posthumous works (1677) include a discussion of ethics geometrically presented—with propositions, demonstrations, and theorems, etc., and with biblical exegeses. In this book he also discusses the human mind as an extension of God's infinite mind and the human body as a mode of God's physical extension, and he reasons that mind-and-body parallelism permits an awareness of unifying correspondences.

In his poem "The Parthenon," Melville imagines Spinoza gazing on the magnificent Greek building and dreaming that the same architect designed both it and human beauty.

Bibliography: Roger Scruton, *Spinoza* (Oxford, England: Oxford University Press, 1986).

Spirit, A. In "A Spirit Appeared to Me," this is the creature that asked the poet to choose between living in a fool's paradise or in Solomon's hell.

"A Spirit Appeared to Me" (1924). Poem, in *The Works of Herman Melville.* (Character: a Spirit.) When a Spirit asked the poet whether he would prefer to live in "the Paradise of the Fool" or in "wise Solomon's hell," the poet readily chose the former.

Squaretoes, Squire. In "Cock-a-Doodle-Doo!," he is one of the narrator's rural neighbors. Squaretoes does not own the lusty cock.

Squeak. In *Billy Budd,* he is one of John Claggart's cunning corporals. He is an informer who lies about Billy Budd.

Standard. In "The Fiddler," he is the narrator Helmstone's friend. Standard explains that Hautboy is a former child prodigy who is now happier in his anonymity. The depiction of Standard may be Melville's mild parody of Evert Duyckinck.*

Bibliography: Donald Yannella, "Writing the 'Other Way,' " pp. 63–81 in Bryant, *Companion.*

Stanly, Glendinning ("Cousin Glen," "Glen"). In *Pierre,* he is Pierre Glendinning's once-cherished city cousin, a rich youth twenty-one years of age and recently returned from Europe. When Pierre needs housing in the city, Glen ignores him. Pierre's mother, Mary Glendinning, likes Glen, and after Pierre's departure from Saddle Meadows, she leaves Glen her property there. Stanly presses his courtship of Lucy Tartan and is so enraged when she moves in with Pierre and Isabel Banford that he whips Pierre with his cowhide. Pierre shoots Glen to death for his rashness.

Starbuck. In *Moby-Dick,* he is the *Pequod*'s chief mate's father, killed by a whale.

Starbuck. In *Moby-Dick,* he is the *Pequod*'s chief mate's brother, also killed by a whale.

Starbuck. In *Moby-Dick,* he serves as Captain Ahab's chief mate aboard the *Pequod.* Thirty years of age, Starbuck is a native of Nantucket, a Quaker by descent, and a tall, thin realist. Queequeg is his harpooner. Starbuck sees the Trinity in the doubloon nailed to the mast. He tries but fails to dissuade Ahab from pursuing Moby Dick, is tempted at one point to shoot his deranged captain but does not, and is lost at sea in the wreck of the *Pequod.* Starbuck may be based in part on Frederick R. Raymond, first mate under Valentine Pease, Jr.,* captain of the *Acushnet,* on which the *Pequod* is modeled to a degree. Raymond had a fight with his captain and went ashore at Payta.

Bibliography: Brian Higgins and Hershel Parker, eds., *Critical Essays on Herman Melville's Moby-Dick* (New York: G. K. Hall, 1992); Leyda.

Starbuck. In *Moby-Dick,* he is the small son of the *Pequod*'s chief mate and his young wife Mary Starbuck.

Starbuck, Mary. In *Moby-Dick,* she is the young Cape Cod wife of Starbuck, the chief mate aboard the *Pequod.* They have one small son.

Starr. In "Bridegroom-Dick," he is an officer chided because of his affection for the donnas.

Starry. In *Billy Budd,* this is one of the nicknames of Captain Vere.

Starry Banner. In "Bridegroom-Dick," he is evidently an officer remembered by Bridegroom Dick from old Vera Cruz days.

"Statues in Rome" (1857, 1858). Lecture. This was the first of three lectures by Melville, the others being "The South Seas" and "Traveling: Its Pleasures, Pains, and Profits." Melville begins "Statues in Rome" by asserting that non-artists can appreciate the beauty and grandeur of art, although they may not know the technical terms that artists and art critics use. He says that he will "paint the appearance of Roman statuary objectively" and "speculate on the emotions and pleasure" it evokes. He discusses statues on the St. John Lateran pediment ("colossal . . . , like storks") and statues and busts in the Vatican: Demosthenes ("muscular form," "face thin and haggard"), Titus Vespasian (not what "this outward seeming" would suggest), Socrates ("cool, sarcastic, ironical cast"), Julius Caesar ("businesslike cast"), Seneca ("like . . . a disappointed pawnbroker"), Plato ("fastidious . . . appearance"), Tiberius ("handsome, refined, and even pensive," "sinister . . . monster"), Apollo ("the crowning glory"), Laocoön ("great and powerful man writhing with the inevitable destiny"), and items in the Hall of Animals and "the sepulchral vaults." Melville comments on the statues in the Vatican Square and aloft at St. Peter's ("a vast and towering pile"). Statuary in Rome proper includes Monte Cavallo horses ("like those of Elijah"), a Castor and Pollux equestrian group ("untamed docility"), Moses by Michelangelo* ("stern, bullying genius of druidical superstition"), and the Farnese Hercules ("lazy ox, confident of his own strength"). Melville discusses the places where Vatican statues once stood (Coliseum, Forum, temples, villas). He concludes that most of these statues express tranquillity, and appeal to noble thoughts and tender feelings. Made by aspirers toward perfection, they endure and point toward the good. Together, they are "the index of the ancient world, just as the Washington Patent Office is of the modern," which is more practical and scientific. But the spirit of Rome still pervades our arts, laws, and philosophy; the Romans "live while these statues endure" and continue to inspire the world.

Bibliography: NN 9; Merton M. Sealts, Jr., *Melville as Lecturer* (1957; Folcroft, Pa.: Folcroft Press, 1970).

Stedman, Edmund Clarence (1833–1908). Poet, critic, editor, and stockbroker. Stedman was born in Hartford, Connecticut. When the boy was only two years old, his father died. Young Stedman moved with his mother and younger brother a year later to his maternal grandparents' home in New Jersey and was subsequently reared by a great-uncle in Norwich, Connecticut. His mother married William Burnett Kinney, who had been appointed minister to Sardinia (1841), went with him there, and published poetry and novels as Elizabeth Kinney. Stedman attended Yale (1849–1851), was expelled for running away with a theatrical company, but much later was given an honorary M.A. (1871). He edited the Norwich *Tribune* (1852–1853), eloped with and married Laura Hyde

Woodworth in 1853 (the couple had two sons and also a daughter who died in infancy). When Stedman turned twenty-one, he learned that he had been disinherited. He worked as a publisher, clock maker, real estate broker, and railroad clerk (to 1859); published *Poems, Lyrical and Idyllic* (1860); and became day editor of the New York *Evening World.* During the Civil War years, he was a Washington correspondent (1861–1863), a clerk in the attorney general's office and a banker (1863), and a broker (1864).

Stedman became a success as a Wall Street broker, a versatile man of letters, and a mentor to rebellious writers of more talent than he. Stedman was the associate editor and book reviewer of the new *Putnam's Magazine* (1867–1870), organized mainly by George Palmer Putnam.* In his *Poets of America* (2 vols., 1885), Stedman anticipates early twentieth-century critics by encouraging readers to focus on the text and by deploring literary didacticism. His conservative book on aesthetics entitled *The Nature and Elements of Poetry* (1892) is of less value. And his own *Poems, Now First Collected* (1897) are less important than his editing or coediting *A Library of American Literature* (11 vols., 1888–1890), *The Works of Edgar Allan Poe[*]* (10 vols., 1894–1895), *A Victorian Anthology* (1895), and *An American Anthology, 1787–1900* (1900). It may also be mentioned that an 1880 essay by Stedman in praise of Walt Whitman signaled the beginning of Whitman's acceptance by the establishment. Stedman also encouraged Edwin Arlington Robinson. Stedman's later years were marked by tragedy. His older son Frederick Stuart Stedman (1856–1906) embezzled from his father's firm (1883) and thus caused an estrangement lasting twenty-three years. Financial problems, which included payments to help the young man avoid indictment, ultimately forced Stedman to sell his Stock Exchange seat (1900). And his wife died in 1905, as did his reconciled son a year later. Laura Stedman, Stedman's granddaughter, helped George M. Gould prepare *Life and Letters of Edmund Clarence Stedman* (2 vols., 1910).

Stedman adversely reviewed *Clarel* in the *New-York Daily Tribune* (16 June 1876). When he cofounded the Authors Club (1882) and invited Melville to join, Melville accepted but then declined (1882). Stedman asked Melville (1888) for a poem in his own handwriting and an engraved portrait, for inclusion in his *Poets of America.* In a quick response, Melville copied out and sent him "Ditty of Aristippus" from *Clarel.* Melville agreed to let Stedman reprint "The Bell-Tower," "In the Prison Pen (1864)," "Sheridan at Cedar Creek (October, 1864)," and "The Stone Fleet: An Old Sailor's Lament (December, 1861)" in *A Library of American Literature.* By this time, the two had met, Melville received a few books on loan from Stedman, and Stedman began to regard Melville as a literary genius and an impressive personality. Stedman's *American Anthology* contains poems by Melville. Arthur Stedman, Stedman's younger son (1859–1908), attended Melville's funeral, became his literary executor, helped his widow Elizabeth Knapp Shaw Melville* in 1892 reissue four of his books (*Typee, Omoo, White-Jacket,* and *Moby-Dick,* for *Typee* providing a biographical and critical introduction), wrote other essays about Melville, and considered writing a biography of him.

Bibliography: Kathleen E. Kier, "Elizabeth Shaw Melville and the Stedmans: 1891–1894," *Melville Society Extracts* 45 (February 1981): 3–8; Leyda; NN 1 and 14; Robert J. Scholnick, *Edmund Clarence Stedman* (Boston: Twayne Publishers, 1977).

Steel. In *Pierre,* he is the publisher who, with partners Flint and Asbestos, rejects Pierre Glendinning's book. They intend to sue Pierre for costs and advances.

Steelkilt. In *Moby-Dick,* he is the proud Lakeman from Buffalo who is a sailor aboard the *Town-Ho.* The mate Radney threatens Steelkilt, who breaks his jaw and is flogged for the act. Steelkilt would have murdered Radney but for the timely appearance of Moby Dick, which both men chase and which savagely kills Radney. Steelkilt then deserts the *Town-Ho.* Did Steelkilt taunt Radney about homosexuality or transvestism? Steelkilt may be modeled in part on a man named Luther Fox, of Renselaerville, Albany County, New York. When Jenney, the first officer of the *Nassau,* a whaleship out of New Bedford, argued with Fox, Fox so severely cut Jenney's leg with a mincing knife that the man bled to death (April 1843). Fox was handed over to American consular authorities in Honolulu (June).

Bibliography: Thomas Ferel Hefferman, "Eonism on the *Town-Ho;* or, What *Did* Steelkilt Say?," *Melville Society Extracts* 83 (November 1990): 10–12; Leyda.

Steen, Jan Havickszoon (c. 1626–1679). Dutch painter. Born in Leyden, he studied art at Utrecht, Haarlem, the Hague, and Leyden (1640–1648). He entered the University of Leyden (1646) to avoid the military draft. He helped found the Leyden painters' guild (1648) and resided in the Hague (1649–c. 1654), Delft (c. 1654–1656), Warmond (1656–1661), and Haarlem (1661–1670). He ran a brewery in Delft (1654–1660) and a tavern in Leyden (1669–1679). In between times, he was a productive painter. Although his works include mythological, biblical, and historical narrative pictures, portraits (sometimes of himself in jovial disarray), and landscapes, Steen is most famous for his genre paintings. Earthy and often vulgar, they typically feature persons at religious festivities and enjoying holiday activities, people in kitchens and bedrooms, children and dogs, card players and actors, tavern and brothel frequenters, and scientists and physicians in laboratories and sickrooms. They demonstrate skillful draftsmanship, clarity of light, transparency of color, harmonious composition, and deft details and smooth surfaces. Although his tone is usually merry, his message can sometimes be cruel and satirical. His later production is more elegant. Of his 800 to 900 or so works, only 55 are dated or datable. The following are representative paintings: *The Doctor's Visit* (1660, physician attending woman); *The Morning Toilet* (1663, woman putting on stocking, with dog watching); *Feast of Saint Nicholas* (c. 1665, crowded domestic scene at Christmas time); *The Christening Feast* (1666, sixteen interconnected people in domestic setting, many at table, utensils on tile floor); *The Merry Family* (slovenly Dutch multigenerational group eating, drinking, making music but warned by written message near fireplace to set a good example to youth); and *The Quack* (charlatan showing "stone" taken from neck of gullible farmer to impressed rural crowd but also depicting dog, donkey, drunk man in wheelbarrow). Steen married Margaretha van Goyen, the daughter of a Haarlem painter, in 1649 (the couple had at least one son and one daughter); and he married Maria van Egmont of Leyden in 1673.

In "Marquis de Grandvin: At the Hostelry," Melville describes Jan Steen, nicknamed "Jan o' the Inn," as a realistic painter and a shabbily dressed spendthrift who, when he discusses the picturesque, especially with Paola [Veronese] of Verona, says merely, "For the Picturesque—suffice, suffice / The picture that fetches a picturesque price."

Bibliography: Baruch D. Kirschenbaum, *The Religious and Historical Paintings of Jan Steen* (New York: Allenheld & Schram, 1977).

Stetson. In *White-Jacket,* he is evidently an official at the New York Astor House, where Old Coffee was once employed.

Stevens, Henry (1819–1886). Bibliophile, bibliographer, bookseller, library developer, and scholar. Stevens was born in Barnet, Vermont, attended Middlebury College (1839), clerked in the Treasury Department and in the Senate in Washington, D.C. (1840), graduated from Yale (1843), and studied law at Harvard (1844). His long-standing love affair with books soon impelled him to London (1845), where he made the acquaintance of Sir Anthony Panizzi, who was then building up the book holdings of the British Museum. Stevens's initial purpose was to seek books for American libraries, at which he became successful and therefore remained. He became a book and manuscript dealer in London, and collected Americana for the British Museum—to the tune of 100,000 volumes (by 1865). He was an authority on the bibliographical history of the English Bible, on geographical and historical literature of the Western world, and on literature of voyages to it. He helped develop American collections concerning Benjamin Franklin,* and the Brown University library, the library of New York City, the Library of Congress, the Smithsonian Institution, and so on. He wrote books and prepared catalogues in his fields of specialization. His *Recollections of Mr. James Lenox of New York and the Formation of His Library* (1886) is partly autobiographical. Stevens was known as genial, hospitable, and crafty. He married Mary Newton Kuczynski in 1854. Their son continued the family book business. Henry Stevens's brother Benjamin Franklin Stevens was his partner for a time (1860–1864) and remained in London as a bookseller and a book agent. Their sister Sophie Stevens was the expatriate American painter William Page's third wife and lived with him in Rome (from 1857).

Stevens knew Melville's brother Gansevoort Melville* in London and attended his funeral there (1846). Soon after Melville first arrived in London,

Stevens called on him at his hotel. Melville described him in an 1849 journal entry as "a very fine fellow" (24 November), had dinner with him the following evening, and two days after that was shown by him through the British Museum library, possibly in the company of Panizzi. Upon returning from the Continent to London, Melville called on Stevens "& sat a while" chatting (17 December). Melville's love of old books may have been substantially reinforced by Stevens.

   Bibliography: NN 15; Wyman W. Parker, *Henry Stevens of Vermont: American Rare Book Dealer in London, 1845–1886* (Amsterdam: H. Israel, 1963).

Steward. In "The Scout toward Aldie," he is the hospital attendant who cares for the wounded after [John Singleton] Mosby has ambushed his Union pursuers led by the Colonel.

Stiggs. In *Moby-Dick,* he is a young sailor found harpooned to death in a back room of Hosea Hussey's Try Pots Inn on Nantucket. Stiggs had stopped there after a whaling voyage of more than four years.

Still, Bob. In *Redburn,* he is a portly drinking companion of Danby's in Liverpool.

"Stockings in the Farm-House Chimney" (1924). Poem, in *Weeds and Wildings,* as part of the section entitled "The Year." (Characters: May, Nellie, Rob, Willie.) "Willie and Rob and Nellie and May" are happy in the belief that Santa Claus, "a wight / More mortal than man," will stuff their stockings on Christmas Eve. Let truth delay, and let "these little ones . . . / . . . forever with fable play." This poem was probably written at Arrowhead. The four children in the poem probably represent his sons Malcolm Melville* and Stanwix Melville* and his daughters Elizabeth Melville* and Frances Melville (later Frances Melville Thomas*).
   Bibliography: Shurr, Stein.

Stockton, Cap[tain]. In "On the Chinese Junk," he is the owner of "the big shooter" which Cave Johnson may use to distribute the mails.

Stoddard, Richard Henry (1825–1903). Poet, critic, and editor. He was born in Hingham, Massachusetts, the son of a shipmaster lost at sea when the boy was about two years old. He and his mother moved about, to mill towns and Boston, until she remarried and took him along to New York City (1835). He left school in 1840 to earn money for the family and began to educate himself through voracious reading. He was an errand boy, an office boy, a scrivener, and an iron molder (1843); he published some poetry (1845) and became in New York a customs inspector (1853–1870); and he worked as a literary reviewer for newspapers (from 1861), a confidential secretary of ex–Civil War general George B. McClellan* (1870–1873), a secretary for the Department of Docks (1871–1874), a librarian in the office of municipal records (1877–1879), and a reviewer and miscellaneous editor. He married Elizabeth Drew Barstow in 1851 (the couple had three sons, all of whom, including Lorimer Stoddard, a talented playwright, predeceased them). Stoddard's wife, as Elizabeth Stoddard (1823–1902), published fine novels and fair poetry, and excelled her husband in profundity and significance. Her best novel is *The Morgesons* (1862), highly regarded for its naturalistic depiction of New England life. For decades, the Stoddards presided over an influential literary salon on East 15th Street in New York City (c. 1870–c. 1900). Two habitués were Edmund Clarence Stedman* and Bayard Taylor.* Stoddard's conservative tastes had a long-term influence on the American reading public, although in private Stoddard could be vigorous, salty, and profane. His first book of poems, *Foot-prints* (1849), he later regarded as so dreadful that he destroyed every copy but one (now in the Library of Congress). Later works include *Poems* (1851), *Songs of Summer* (1857), *The King's Bell* (1863), *The Book of the East, and Other Poems* (1867), *The Lion's Cub; with Other Verse* (1870), *Nathaniel Hawthorne[*]* (1879), *Poems* (1880), *Henry W. Longfellow: A Memoir* (1882), *Under the Evening Lamp* (1892), and *Recollections, Personal and Literary* (1903, with important reminiscences).

Given his sociable nature and his work as a customs inspector, it is surprising that he and Melville never became close friends. In December 1866 or so, an official wrote to Stoddard to announce that Melville was a new customs inspector, to ask Stoddard to be kind to him, and to tell—or remind—Stoddard that twenty-five years or so earlier Melville had been a widely known writer. When Stoddard prepared the 1873 edition of *The Poets and Poetry of America,* originally edited by Rufus W. Griswold (1842), he added seven poems from Melville's *Battle-Pieces,* including ''Sheridan at Cedar Creek (October, 1864),'' which Stoddard especially admired. The other six poems were ''Battle of Stone River, Tennessee,'' ''The Mound by the Lake,'' ''The Returned Volunteer to His Rifle,'' ''Shiloh: A Requiem (April, 1862)'' ''An Uninscribed Monument on One of the Battle-fields of the Wilderness,'' and ''The Victor of Antietam (1862).'' Stoddard may have been the unnamed author of the review of Melville's *Clarel* that appeared in the New York *World* (26 June 1876), and he certainly reviewed *John Marr* there (November? 1888). Stoddard wrote to Melville's widow Elizabeth Knapp Shaw Melville* that the two men had known each other ''at the receipt of customs, I at the cold stone building in Wall Street, and he on the river front,'' and added that their relationship was casual and that Melville was ''as reserved as a man of genius had a right to be'' (28 October 1892).

Bibliography: Leyda; NN 14; Merton M. Sealts, Jr., ''Melville and Richard Henry Stoddard,'' *American Literature* 43 (November 1971): 359–70; John Tomsich, *A Genteel Endeavor: American Culture and Politics in the Gilded Age* (Stanford, Calif.: Stanford University Press, 1971).

"The Stone Fleet: An Old Sailor's Lament (December, 1861)" (1866). Poem, in *Battle-Pieces.* The persona feels for those obsolete old ships, in one of which he "scudded round the Horn" on the India trade before "her wrinkles came" and she was converted into a whaler. Now several of them, some with such "patrician" names as the *Kensington* and the *Richmond,* are scuttled together— and "all for naught." "Nature is nobody's ally," and "[c]urrents will have their way"; so the harbor is now better than ever. This poem was inspired by the federal government's decision early in the Civil War (December 1861) to sink sixteen granite-loaded vessels in the harbor of Charleston to blockade the rebellious city, only to learn that the channel was ultimately improved by the act. Melville had personal connections with a few of the sixteen doomed vessels.

Bibliography: Garner; Mary Malloy, "The Old Sailor's Lament: Recontextualizing Melville's Reflections on the Sinking of 'The Stone Fleet,' " *New England Quarterly* 64 (December 1991): 633–42; NN 11; Warren.

"Stonewall Jackson (Ascribed to a Virginian)" (1866). Poem, in *Battle-Pieces.* (Character: [General Thomas J.] Stonewall Jackson.) The persona praises Jackson, who was charged with "the lightning's burning breath," was stoical, had an "iron will," was "as strong to inflict as to endure," and fatefully "followed his star" through various named battles. People will debate "the right and the wrong" of the war; "but the South had Stonewall's weight," and no Northerners "shall care to slur" his fame.

Bibliography: Garner.

"Stonewall Jackson Mortally Wounded at Chancellorsville (May, 1863)" (1866). Poem, in *Battle-Pieces.* (Character: [General Thomas J.] Stonewall Jackson.) "How can we praise" this man "[w]hose sword and prayer were long," who "stood for Wrong," and who "[v]ainly . . . died" for a dead cause? Because he was earnest, true to his beliefs, and relentless. So we can weep on his bier, to which "no wreath we owe."

Bibliography: Garner.

"Story of Daniel Orme." *See* "Daniel Orme."

Street, Alfred Billings (1811–1881). Lawyer, librarian, and poet. He was born in Poughkeepsie, New York, studied law with his father, moved to Albany (1839) to become editor of the *Northern Light* (1843–1844), and was appointed to be director of the New York State Library (1848–1862). Street published occasional verse, poetic narratives, and poetic descriptions of nature. Among his many works are *The Burning of Schenectady* (1842), *Frontenac; or, The Atotarho of the Iroquois, a Metrical Romance* (1849, retitled *A Poem of the Iroquois* [1866]), and sixteen poems to accompany a book of etchings called *Forest Pictures in the Adirondacks,* by John A. Hows (1864). *Poems* (2 vols., 1866) was a collection of Street's production. Richard Bentley,* who was one of Melville's British publishers, first published Street's *Frontenac* and reprinted some of his poetry in Bentley's *Miscellany.* Melville attended a reading of Street's poetry at the Pittsfield Young Ladies' Institute (1852) but failed to stay and talk with him afterward, although Street remained in Pittsfield for two days. Melville's uncle Peter Gansevoort (1788–1876),* who was Street's Albany neighbor, chided Melville for the slight. In a letter to Abraham Lansing* and his wife Catherine Gansevoort Lansing,* Melville says that Street's poem "The Old Garden" (published in *Frank Leslie's Illustrated Newspaper,* predated 18 August 1877) resembles "a flower-and-fruit piece by some mellow old Fleming" (14 August [1877]).

Bibliography: Leyda, NN 14.

Stribbles. In *White-Jacket,* he is a namby-pamby midshipman who lords it over Frank.

Stuart, James E. B. (1833–1864). (Full name: James Ewell Brown Stuart; nickname: "Jeb.") Confederate soldier. He was born in Patrick County, Virginia. His father was a lawyer and a Democratic congressman. Young Stuart attended Emory and Henry College (1848–1850) and West Point (1850–1854). Upon graduating, he served in Texas, New Mexico, and Kansas (1854–1859), became the aide-de-camp of Robert E. Lee* at Harpers Ferry (1859), and was promoted to captain (1861). At the outbreak of the Civil War, he resigned from the U.S. Army to join the Confederate Army as a lieutenant colonel (1861). Stuart, who was a religious temperance advocate, was a dashing combat officer. He fought well at the First Battle of Bull Run (July 1861), was promoted to brigadier general (September), conducted a daring ride all around the sprawling position of Union General George B. McClellan* (June 1862) just before the Seven Days' Battles (June–July), became a major general (July), and was placed in command of all cavalry units in the Army of North Virginia. Stuart fought superbly at the Second Battle of Bull Run (August), at Antietam (September), and at Fredericksburg (December). After General Thomas J. Jackson* was killed (May 1863), Stuart commanded the Second Army Corps, fought at Brandy Station, Virginia (June), but arrived late at Gettysburg (July). Stuart was killed at Yellow Tavern, Virginia, during the Battle of Cold Harbor against Union forces under General Philip H. Sheridan* (May 1864). Stuart married Flora Cooke, born in Missouri into an army family from Virginia, in 1851 (the couple had a son and a daughter). Flora's father, General Philip St. George Cooke, remained loyal to the Union cause during the Civil War; he was the uncle of John Esten Cooke, the Confederate cavalryman and the Southern novelist and biographer of General Thomas J. Jackson.

Melville mentions Jeb Stuart in two poems. In "The Released Rebel Prisoner," the released rebel prisoner thinks of Stuart as the dead Confederate general. In "Lee in the Capitol," the dead Stuart is remembered by Lee as he approaches the Capitol to testify before the Senate.

Bibliography: Burke Davis, *Jeb Stuart: The Last Cavalier* (New York: Rinehart, 1957).

Stubb. In *Moby-Dick,* he is the happy-go-lucky second mate of the *Pequod.* He is a reliable Cape-Codman and relishes smoking little black pipes. Tashtego is his harpooner. Stubb tricks the mate of the *Bouton de Rose,* a Guernseyman, out of an unsuspected treasure of ambergris. Stubb interprets the zodiacal arch on the doubloon nailed to the mainmast. He may be partially based on John Hall, the second mate of the *Acushnet,* which is to a degree a model for the *Pequod.* Hall reportedly returned home and then went to California.

   Bibliography: Leyda; Gordon Poole, "Stubb Diddles the *Rose-Bud:* Melville's Dirty Joke," *Melville Society Extracts* 92 (March 1993): 11–13.

Stubbs. In *Omoo,* he is a Sydney auctioneer whose rhetorical flourishes the narrator reads about in an Australian newspaper loaned to him by Dr. Long Ghost when both men are aboard the *Julia.*

Sub-Sub. In *Moby-Dick,* he is the grubbing sub-sub-librarian who supplies the prefatory extracts concerning whales.

Suffren de Saint Tropez, Pierre André de (1726–1788). French naval officer. He was born into a noble family at Saint-Cannat, in Provence. He entered the French navy as a cadet (1743), saw action at Toulon (1744), went to the West Indies and served at Martinique, and was shipwrecked off Cape Breton (1746). He was captured by the British in the Bay of Biscay and was imprisoned (1747–1748), went to Malta (1748), and served as a lieutenant during the French and Indian War (1754–1761). One engagement in which Suffren participated was off Minorca against British forces commanded by Admiral John Byng, who was court-martialed, convicted, and executed for poor maneuvering and slack follow-up (1757). Suffren was taken prisoner off Lagos (1757). After peace was declared (1763), he fought Barbary Coast pirates and did convoy duty in the Mediterranean (1767–1771). He was a daring part of a squadron led by Charles Hector, Comte d'Estaing* in American and West Indian waters (1778–1779). Suffren was captain of a vessel which with French and Spanish fleets captured an English convoy in the Atlantic Ocean (1780). D'Estaing recommended Suffren for duty in Indian waters, where he engaged Sir Edward Hughes* indecisively. Suffren did capture Tricomalee and accept the surrender of the British garrison (1782). Suffren's attacks would have gained more advantage but for poor support. Once peace was declared (1783), he returned to Toulon to many honors (1784), was promoted to vice admiral, and was ordered to command a fleet at Brest to attack the British once again; but he was killed in a duel with the Prince of Mirepoix which was occasioned by Suffren's refusal to reinstate two of the prince's relatives dismissed for misconduct. Suffren was energetic, resourceful, wrathful, and immensely fat.

   In *Israel Potter,* Melville identifies Admiral Suffrien as the commander of a fleet engaging an English squadron off Coromandel [Brazil]. Potter might have been involved in that engagement but for leaving the *Unprincipled* to join the depleted crew of a revenue cutter.

Bibliography: Louis-Édouard Chevalier, *Histoire de la marine française pendant la guerre de l'indépendence américaine* . . . (Paris: Hachette et Cie., 1877); Jonathan R. Dull, *The French Navy and American Independence: A Study of Arms and Diplomacy, 1774–1787* (Princeton, N.J.: Princeton University Press, 1975).

Sugar-Lips. In "Under the Rose." *See* Lugar-Lips.

"Suggested by the Ruins of a Mountain-Temple in Arcadia, One Built by the Architect of the Parthenon" (1947). (Character: [Ictinus].) Poem, in *Collected Poems of Herman Melville.* The poet compares the troubling "shattered marbles" to ice after freshets recede and also to something "[i]nterred alive" in "inexhaustion."

Sumner, Charles (1811–1874). Politician. Sumner was born in Boston and attended Harvard (1826–1830) and its law school (1831–1833). Although he practiced law for a while, he preferred writing reviews and revising law textbooks, and he enjoyed many literary friendships. Among his early such associates were Ralph Waldo Emerson* and Henry Wadsworth Longfellow. Sumner went to Europe (1837–1840), during which time he studied European politics and law and mastered French, German, and Italian. Returning to Boston, he practiced law, annotated several volumes of case reports (1844–1845), and became involved in liberal politics. He opposed the Mexican War (1846–1848), denounced the candidacy of Zachary Taylor* for president (1848), and favored pacificism (1849). Elected to the U.S. Senate as a Democratic–Free Soil candidate (1851), he evolved into a vituperative legislator of enormous influence (1851–1874). He helped found the Republican Party (1854), eloquently but tactlessly argued against any extension of slavery, and in his most famous speech—"The Crime against Kansas" (19, 20 May 1856)—called the Kansas-Nebraska Act "a swindle" and slavery "the harlot" of Senator Andrew P. Butler of South Carolina. Two days later, Butler's cousin Representative Preston S. Brooks of South Carolina approached Sumner from behind and so severely beat him with a cane that he had to seek medical treatment abroad and could not resume his senatorial duties until 1859. Up to the time of the Civil War, Sumner opposed proslavery and compromising elements alike and for the most part supported Abraham Lincoln.* Sumner's recommendations during the war included immediate emancipation, recruitment of African-Americans for the Union Army, confiscation of Southern property, abrogation of the constitutional rights of rebellious states, and no-nonsense diplomacy with England and France. After the war, his influence dwindled. In 1866, Sumner married Alice Mason Hooper, a widow half his age from Boston and with friends in Washington, D.C. They argued over money and social obligations, after which she left him (1867) and allowed him to divorce her for desertion (1873). Sumner, whose often eloquent speeches were published (15 vols., 1870–1883), was scholarly, high-principled, inflexible, and irascible.

Melville had contact with Sumner on at least two occasions. First, the two men met at the home of a cousin of Richard Henry Dana, Jr.* (1847). Second, when Melville sought a consular appointment in 1861, Dana, John Chipman Hoadley,* and Lemuel Shaw* asked Sumner to use his influence. Sumner received Melville graciously in his office in Washington, D.C., but was unable to be of any help. He helped Melville obtain a War Department pass to visit the Army of the Potomac with his brother Allan Melville* (April 1864). Here and there in *The Confidence-Man,* Melville indirectly satirizes Sumner's fancy latinate oratory; more specifically, the herb doctor in the same novel is thought to be based to a degree on Sumner, with regard to manners, personality traits, attitudes, and motives. Further, in "To Major John Gentian, Dean of the Burgundy Club," Melville mentions Sumner as Gentian's New England friend.

Bibliography: Edward Chalfant, *Better in Darkness: A Biography of Henry Adams—His Second Life, 1862–1891* ([Hamden, Conn.]: Archon Books, 1994); David Donald, *Charles Sumner and the Coming of the Civil War* (New York: Alfred A. Knopf, 1965); Donald, *Charles Sumner and the Rights of Man* (New York: Alfred A. Knopf, 1970); NN 14; Trimpi.

Sunshine. In *White-Jacket,* he is the hard-working, singing African-American assistant of Old Coffee, who is the cook of the *Neversink.*

Surgeon, The. In "Bridegroom-Dick," he is the grave physician who stands idly by before the ordered flogging of the Finn, according to Bridegroom Dick's reminiscences.

Surgeon, The ("Doc"). In "The Scout toward Aldie," he is a bluff, red-faced physician with the Colonel's men during their ill-fated pursuit of [John Singleton] Mosby. The Surgeon attends a Confederate prisoner, evidently Mosby himself, when that man feigns injury following a fall.

Surgeon of the Army in Mexico. In "Authentic Anecdotes of 'Old Zack,' " he is a physician who elaborately describes General Taylor's face, figure, and uniform.

"The Surrender at Appomattox (April, 1865)" (1866). Poem, in *Battle-Pieces.* (Characters: [General Ulysses S.] Grant, [General Robert E.] Lee.) Victory follows on victory like waves on waves. Richmond falls, and soon Lee hands his sword to Grant. Let us now sing about "Treason thrown, though a giant grown, / And Freedom's larger play."

Susan. In *Pierre,* she is a pretty girl in the Miss Pennies' sewing circle.

Swain, Nathan ("Nat"). In *Moby-Dick,* he is a whaler from Nantucket and Martha's Vineyard. Fifty years earlier, he killed fifteen whales in one day. His lance is on a wall in Peter Coffin's Spouter Inn. Captain Peleg remarks that Nat lost his daring as soon as he joined the church and became pious.

"The Swamp Angel" (1866). Poem, in *Battle-Pieces.* The poet lyrically describes the Swamp Angel as black, thick of lip, facing a city, and breathing doom from afar. At night it sends screaming stars that burst in the city, "age . . . the young," turn maidens pale, break down walls, and wreak havoc. Melville's subject is the Parrott cannon placed in the marshes of James Island outside Charleston and bombarding the rebel town during the Civil War. The Union gunners nicknamed the weapon "the Swamp Angel." The Parrott gun was named after its inventor Robert Parker Parrott, who graduated from West Point (1824), resigned from the U.S. Army (1836), developed his cannon in Cold Spring, New York, and patented both it and its shells (1861). It was a rifled, muzzled-loading cannon, fitted with a thick, heat-shrunk, wrought-iron band around the breech to help the barrel withstand pressure during firing. Different models fired from 10- to 250-pound shells, from 3 to 10 inches in diameter, with effective ranges of from 3,500 to 4,400 yards. Big Parrotts were useful in destroying masonry forts. Confederate forces also had Parrotts.

Bibliography: Boatner, Faust, Garner, NN 11, Warren.

Swanevelt, Herman van (c. 1600–1655). Dutch painter. He was probably born in Woerden, near Utrecht, where he probably trained. He went to Rome (1629–1641) and loved to look at old ruins and lonely places there and at nearby Tivoli. He was commissioned to paint Italian scenes in Vatican loggias and religious pictures at the Monte Cassino Monastery. With Nicolas Poussin,* he was commissioned to do religious and landscape paintings for a Madrid palace (late 1630s). After returning to Woerden (1642), Swanevelt moved back to Paris (from 1644), where he was appointed a court painter and later was elected to the Royal Academy (1651). He was considerably influenced by and at the same time slightly influenced Claude Lorrain.* Swanevelt produced a hundred or so etchings, some published in series. His innovative Arcadian-Baroque landscape style proved attractive. A beautiful and comprehensive example of his landscape technique is revealed in his *Landscape with Travelers* (early 1630s); it has central trees, silhouetted leaves and twigs, glowing blue sky with yellow clouds, peasants and animals, unimportant buildings at right and in middle distance. In "Marquis de Grandvin: At the Hostelry," Swanevelt is a good Dutchman who when he discusses the picturesque says, "Vain here to divide—/ The *Picturesque* has many a side."

Bibliography: Frederik J. Dupare and Linda L. Graif, *Italian Recollections: Dutch Painters of the Golden Age* ([Montreal]: Montreal Museum of Fine Arts, 1970).

Swede, The. In *Clarel. See* Mortmain.

Sweeny. In *Redburn,* he is the proprietor of the Turkey Cock, which is a restaurant on Fulton Street, in New York. Redburn takes Harry Bolton there for breakfast.

Sweet Wrinkles. In "Bridegroom-Dick." *See* Bonny Blue.

Sydney Ben ("the Ticket-of-Leave-Man"). In *Omoo,* he is a convict from New South Wales who is a sailor aboard the *Julia.* He does not sign the round-robin.

"Syra (A Transmitted Reminiscence)" (1891). Poem, in *Timoleon.* (Character: Pericles.) The persona remembers that he "saw it [Syra] in its earlier day." To escape bellicose Turks, a group of Greek refugees went to Syra (an island of the Cyclades), lived securely there, and when politically safe made "of the haven a mere mart." The "isled resort" became a place of "shanty-shop[s]" displaying various goods for sale but carelessly scattered "[l]ike plunder on a pirate's deck." Wine was available at "a tented inn," and "[a]rmed strangers . . . lounged" about. Fellows resembling "busy bees" chattered like children at play as they unloaded lighters from "anchored craft" offshore. Those "juvenile[s]" were "inapt for serious work" but remembered "[w]hen trade was not, nor toil nor stress," and "life was leisure, merriment, peace," money was unknown, and "love was righteousness." Melville visited Syra and noted impressions in his 1856 journal (2, 23, 25 December).
    Bibliography: Ekaterini Georgoudaki, "Herman Melville's Trip to Syra in 1856–57," *Melville Society Extracts* 74 (September 1988): 1–8; NN 11 and 15.

Syrian Monk, The. In *Clarel,* he is a thin, ascetic Dominican monk whom the pilgrims encounter at Quarantani while he is undergoing a forty-day temptation in imitation of Christ's.
    Bibliography: Shurr, Stein.

T

Taff the Welshman. In *Billy Budd,* he is a former shipmate whose burial at sea Billy Budd remembers, according to the poem "Billy in the Darbies," composed by Billy's friend.

Tahar, The King of. In *Omoo,* he is named as the father of Pot Belly, Queen Pomaree's first husband, whom she divorced. In reality, "Tahar" was Tapoa of Bora Bora, and his son was Tapoa, who in 1824 at the age of sixteen married Aimata, who was eleven and who became Pomare IV,* Queen of Tahiti. She repudiated her husband when he proved sterile (1829).
  Bibliography: Newbury.

Tahitian Sailor. In *Moby-Dick,* he is a golden-hued sailor who is reminded of his native land when he watches his mates dance during the midnight festivities in the forecastle. Later he and the grizzled Manxman heave the log, the weight of which breaks its rotten line.

Taji. In *Mardi,* he is the sailor who deserts the *Arcturion,* boards the *Parki,* kills Aleema and rescues Yillah, and then pursues her doggedly after she disappears from the isle of Odo. During his long and fruitless quest, Taji visits King Peepi of Valapee, King Donjalolo of Juam, the island of Nora Bamma, King Uhia of Ohonoo, King Borabolla of Moldoldo, the pontiff Hevohitee MDCCCXLVIII of Maramma, Nimni of Pimminee, King Hello and King Piko of Diranda, King Bello of Dominora, the country of Vivenza, the philosopher Doxodox of Hamora, King Yoky of Hooloomooloo, King Abrazza of Bonovona, the land of Serenia, and Queen Hautia of Flozella-a-Nina. Taji's companions include Jarl, Samoa, King Media of Odo, Babbalanja, Mohi, and Yoomy. At the end, Taji is still seeking Yillah, his lost love. The name Taji may be a modification of that of Tajo, who was a king of Tahiti whom Pomare I* conquered. *Taji* in Arabic means "my crown." Melville's characterization of Taji has Persian-literature overtones.

Bibliography: Davis; Finkelstein; Tyrus Hillway, "Taji's Abdication in Herman Melville's *Mardi,*" *American Literature* 16 (November 1944): 204–7; Julie M. Johnson, "Taji's Quest in Melville's *Moby-Dick:* A Psychological Allegory in the Mythic Mode," *Colby Library Quarterly* 18 (December 1982): 220–30; Lebowitz; Wright.

Talara. In *Mardi,* he is Donjalolo's friend, who comforts the young prince after his father has committed suicide to force him to become king of Juam.

Talbot, John. In *Moby-Dick,* he is a sailor lost at the age of eighteen off Patagonia, in 1836. His sister erected a tablet in his memory in the Whaleman's Chapel in New Bedford.

Talbot, Miss. In *Moby-Dick,* she is the drowned John Talbot's sister. She erected a tablet in his memory in the Whaleman's Chapel in New Bedford.

Talus. In "The Bell-Tower." *See* Haman.

Tamatoy, King. In *Omoo,* he is the king of Raiatair, one of the Society Islands, and the father of Tooboi.

Tammahamaha III. (Also spelled Tamehameha.) In *Omoo. See* Kamehameha III.

Tammaro, King. In *Mardi,* he is the king of Babbalanja's nursery story who rebuked the blind men for fancying that they could find a tree trunk which men with eyesight could not identify.

Tanee ("Pomaree-Tanee"). In *Omoo,* he is named as Queen Pomaree's henpecked second husband, from Imeeo. In reality, Pomare IV,* Queen of Tahiti, repudiated her first husband when he proved sterile (1829). She married Tenania, of the nearby island of Raiatea, in 1832. The couple had eight children. Two died as infants. A son died of syphilis at age twenty (1855). The next son, when his mother died (1877), became Pomare V. Their daughter was adopted by the queen's first husband and upon his death became the queen of Bora Bora (1860). Their last three children, all sons, distinguished themselves: One became King of Raiatea; another became a local chief; and another studied in France, returned to Tahiti, became a local chief, and was christened Prince Joinville in honor of one of the sons of Louis-Philippe* of France.

Bibliography: Newbury.

Taou Kwang. In "On the Chinese Junk." *See* Wang Taou.

Taquinoo, King. In *Mardi,* he was a fugitive king whose royalty was presaged by an eagle, according to the anonymous manuscript read in northern Vivenza. In due time, Taquinoo's son, Zooperbi, was driven into exile. The name Taquinoo derives from that of Lucius Tarquinius Priscus (616–578 B.C.), fifth king of Rome. Legend has it that when, as a fugitive from Etruria, he first arrived in Rome, an eagle snatched his cap, flew high in the air with it, and descended and put it back on his head—thus presaging royalty. During his monarchy, he subdued the Latins and the Sabines, drained the marshes, built several structures in Rome (including the Capitoline temple, the Circus Maximus, and the Forum), and introduced elements of Etruscan culture. He is supposed to have been assassinated by the sons of Ancus, Rome's fourth king, and was succeeded by Servius Tullius, sixth king of Rome (ruling from 578 to 534 B.C.), until—it is said—his son-in-law Lucius Tarquinius Superbus murdered him. In due time, Lucius Tarquinius Superbus was driven into exile.
   Bibliography: Charles Marie Franzero, *The Life and Times of Tarquin the Etruscan* (New York: John Day, 1961); Wright.

Tarnmoor, Salvator R. Pseudonym Melville used when he began to publish "The Encantadas."

Tartan. In *Pierre,* he is Lucy Tartan's deceased father, who was a friend of Pierre Glendinning's father.

Tartan. In *Pierre,* he is Lucy Tartan's second brother, two years her junior and a naval officer.

Tartan, Frederic ("Fred"). In *Pierre,* he is Lucy Tartan's brother, three years her senior and a naval officer. He tries with Glendinning Stanly to prevent Lucy from going to live with Pierre Glendinning and Isabel Banford, but without success. Tartan and Stanly challenge Pierre, who kills Stanly, after which Tartan tries to find his sister and does so, but only when she lies dead in Pierre's prison cell.

Tartan, Lucy. In *Pierre,* she is the beautiful, fair-haired, blue-eyed fiancée of Pierre Glendinning. When he abandons her to go to the city with Isabel Banford, who he pretends is his wife, Lucy follows and lives with the couple and their maid Delly Ulver. When Lucy learns—after Pierre has killed Glendinning Stanly, who wanted to marry her, and is in prison awaiting execution—that Isabel is Pierre's half-sister, she falls dead.

Tartan, Mrs. In *Pierre,* she is Lucy Tartan's mother, a well-to-do, purse-proud widow living in a seaport city with her only daughter. Mrs. Tartan is a matchmaker and initially approves of Pierre Glendinning for Lucy. After Lucy follows Pierre and Isabel Banford to the city, Mrs. Tartan visits them to urge her daughter to depart, but to no avail. She curses her daughter and sees her no more.

Tashtego ("Tash"). In *Moby-Dick,* he is a proud, pure-blooded Native American from Gay Head, in Martha's Vineyard, and the harpooner of Stubb aboard the *Pequod.* Tashtego sights the first sperm whale pursued. He is rescued by Queequeg when he falls into a whale head and it then drops from its hooks into the ocean. When Tashtego perishes in the wreck of the *Pequod,* he carries a sky hawk to its death with him.

Tati. In *Omoo,* he is one of the four recreant chiefs whom the French governor [Armand-Joseph] Bruat puts in charge of the four sections into which he divides Tahiti. The other sections are Kitoti, Utamai, and Paraita.

Tawney. In *White-Jacket,* he is an old African-American sheet-anchor man, who reminisces about being impressed off a New England merchantman during the War of 1812 aboard the British frigate *Macedonian* and being forced at gunpoint by Cardan [John S. Carden], her captain, to toil at guns aimed at the United States' man-of-war *Neversink,* which was then under the command of [Stephen] Decatur. Tawney is now old, sober, wise, frank, and capable. The source of his story of naval combat is Samuel Leech's *Thirty Years from Home; or, A Voice from the Main Deck . . .* (1843). Leech relates his service aboard the *United States* in combat against the *Macedonian* (October 1812).
   Bibliography: Grejda, NN 5.

Taylor, Bayard (1825–1878). (Full name: James Bayard Taylor.) Traveler, author, diplomat, and translator. He was born in Kennett Square, Pennsylvania, and moved with his family to a farm outside town (1829) and then to nearby West Chester (1837–1840). He studied French and Latin (1839) and Spanish soon thereafter, was apprenticed to a West Chester printer, and published a few juvenile pieces (1840, 1841). His formal education ended when he was seventeen. Encouraged by Rufus Griswold, the editor and betrayer of Edgar Allan Poe,* Taylor published his worthless *Ximena; or, The Battle of the Sierra Morena and Other Poems* (1844). With a never-ending itch to wander and write, Taylor arranged with various editors to go to Europe and send travel letters back to them (1844). Two years of movement from Scotland to Italy enabled him to learn German and Italian and to write his popular *Views Afoot; or, Europe Seen with Knapsack and Staff* (1846). Taylor bought and edited a newspaper in Phoenixville, Pennsylvania (1846), sold it (1847), and entered the New York literary world. In time, he knew almost every contemporary writer, whether respectable or "bohemian." One of his closest New York friends was Richard Henry Stoddard.* Taylor went to California to cover the Gold Rush (1849) and wrote it up in *Eldorado; or, Adventures in the Path of Empire* (2 vols., 1850).

In 1850 Taylor married his hometown sweetheart Mary S. Agnew, who died of tuberculosis two months later. Taylor found solace in travel to Egypt, Abyssinia, Turkey, India, China, and—with Commodore Matthew C. Perry—Japan (1851–1853). As a consequence, out came *A Journey to Central Africa; or, Life and Landscapes from Egypt to the Negro Kingdoms of the White Nile* (1854), *The Lands of the Saracen; or, Pictures of Palestine, Asia Minor, Sicily and Spain* (1854), and *A Visit to India, China, and Japan, in the Year 1853* (1855). Taylor edited a huge piece of hack work entitled *Cyclopaedia of Modern Travel . . .* (1856). Some of his other books, interspersed with his travel works at this time, are *Rhymes of Travel, Ballads and Poems* (1849), *A Book of Romances, Lyrics, and Songs* (1851), *A Handbook of Literature and the Fine Arts* (coauthored with George Ripley, the editor and critic, 1852), the moneymaking *Poems of the Orient* (1854), and *Poems of Home and Travel* (1855). Taylor became a lyceum lecturer and traveled some more, this time mostly in Scandinavia and Russia (1855–1857). He married Marie Hansen in 1857 in Germany (the couple had one daughter). Home again, Taylor published *Northern Travel: Summer and Winter Pictures: Sweden, Denmark and Lapland* (1857), *Travels in Greece and Russia, with an Excursion to Crete* (1859), *At Home and Abroad: A Sketch-Book of Life, Scenery and Men* (1859), *The Poet's Journal* (1862, including autobiographical poems), and *At Home and Abroad* (2d series, 1862). Although he had purchased farm land and had begun to build a home, he soon regarded his old neighborhood as less pastoral than dull, grew restless, and sought out new lands to visit.

Early in the Civil War, Taylor was appointed secretary of legation and then chargé d'affaires in St. Petersburg (1862), felt hurt when he was not promoted to minister (1863), returned home, and wrote three local-color novels: *Hannah Thurston: A Story of American Life* (1863, about social reform, including women's rights), *John Godfry's Fortunes, Related by Himself: A Story of American Life* (1864), and *The Story of Kennett* (1866). He published a brilliant translation of Johann Wolfgang von Goethe's *Faust, a Tragedy* (2 vols., 1870, 1871, in the original meters). As a consequence of his *Faust,* he became a nonresident professor of German literature at Cornell (1870–1877), during which time he published more volumes of poetry, including *Lars: A Pastoral of Norway* (1873), *Home Pastorals, Ballads and Lyrics* (1875), and *The Echo Club and Other Literary Diversions* (1876, parodying Walt Whitman and other liberal poets). Taylor was appointed minister to Germany, where he planned to find time and energy to write biographies of Goethe and Johann Christoph Friedrich von Schiller; however, he died in Berlin soon after his arrival there. His widow, as Marie Hansen-Taylor, coedited *Life and Letters of Bayard Taylor* (2 vols., 1884) and much later coauthored *On Two Continents: Memories of Half a Century* (1905).

Melville knew Taylor slightly, looked askance at his popular success, and could not have responded favorably to much of his prolific literary production. The two men met at a Valentine Day's party given by the New York reviewer

Anne G. Lynch (1848), but Melville evidently was not impressed. Taylor may have written the anonymous, partly laudatory review of *Mardi* that appeared in *Graham's Magazine* (June 1849). Evert Duyckinck* noted in his diary (2 October 1856) Melville's comment that just as the unhappy face of Charles I augured his bad fortune, so Taylor's good fortune was written all over his handsome visage. Taylor by courteous letter invited Melville to attend the Traveller's Club in New York (24 February 1865). It is not known whether Melville accepted. Melville's attitude toward Taylor may be reflected to a degree in his characterization of the cosmopolitan in *The Confidence-Man*. Melville enjoyed the company of Taylor's older cousin, Franklin Taylor, who was a fellow passenger when Melville voyaged from New York to London (1849), amused Melville when he mentioned his unsuccessful designs on two women passengers, and became a partial model of the narrator in "The Two Temples."

  Bibliography: Richard Cory, *The Genteel Circle: Bayard Taylor and His New York Friends* (Ithaca, N.Y.: Cornell University Press, 1952); Leyda; NN 9 and 14; Madeline B. Stern, "The House of Expanding Doors: Ann Lynch's Soirees, 1846," *New York History* 23 (January 1942): 42–51; Trimpi.

Taylor, Zachary (1784–1850). (Nicknames: "Old Rough and Ready," "Old Zack.") Soldier and president. Taylor was born in Montebello, Orange County, Virginia. He moved with his family to Louisville, Kentucky, where his entire formal schooling consisted of a brief period of time with a tutor. He became a soldier off and on (1806–1814) and then a regular army officer (from 1816). His victory over Seminole Indians in an engagement in Florida (1837) gained him promotion to brigadier general. Conflicts in Texas were the making of Taylor, who for years had been stationed there and in Arkansas. He was suddenly ordered by the War Department (1845) to be alert to a possible Mexican invasion of Texas, annexed the year before. He won two significant victories against Mexican forces and was promoted to major general even before war was declared (13 May 1846). In the fall, he captured Monterrey and granted a brief armistice, all of which caused his superiors, including General Winfield Scott,* commander-in-chief of the U.S. Army, to take steps to limit his dangerously growing popularity. But his victory at Buena Vista (22–23 February 1847) made him a hero eyed by the Whig Party as a presidential candidate. Scott won more victories himself, and peace followed (February 1848). Scott, among others, was bypassed at the Whig convention in Philadelphia (June), and Taylor was nominated, with the support of Abraham Lincoln* and other canny politicians. Taylor won the election (November), and the most ignorant and inexperienced president up to that time entered the White House. During his brief administration, Taylor upheld the union, urged California and New Mexico to seek admission as free states, threatened to lead the army himself against any efforts made by Southern states to secede, gave moral support to the Hungarian patriot Louis Kossuth (1849), was happy with the Clayton-Bulwer Treaty (1850) concerning a transisthmian canal in Nicaragua, and would have vetoed the controversial Compromise of 1850 if he had not suddenly died of gastroenteritis.

Taylor married Margaret Mackall Smith in 1810 (the couple had one son and five daughters). Two daughters died in childhood and one in early adulthood. The Taylors' son, Richard Taylor, received a good education in New England and abroad, managed the family plantation in Mississippi, and became a general in the Confederate Army during the Civil War. The Taylors' youngest daughter, Mary Elizabeth Taylor, married William Wallace Smith Bliss* in 1848. Bliss was General Taylor's chief of staff before, during, and after the Mexican War (1845–1849). While Taylor served as president, the Blisses lived in the White House and were extremely helpful to him.

In Melville's "Authentic Anecdotes of 'Old Zack,' " Taylor is satirized as the American Mexican War hero who defuses an enemy shell, washes and mends his own clothes, has his pants ripped by a nail put in his saddle as a joke, in a terse letter invites General Santa Anna to surrender, has a pie flung onto his head by a Mexican shot, and is the subject of various rumors. Major Bliss also figures in "Authentic Anecdotes of 'Old Zack.' "

Bibliography: Alfred Hoyt Bill, *Rehearsal for Conflict: The War with Mexico 1846–1848* (New York: Alfred A. Knopf, 1947); John S. D. Eisenhower, *So Far from God: The U.S. War with Mexico 1846–1848* (New York: Random House, 1989); Holman Hamilton, *Zachary Taylor: A Soldier of the Republic,* 2 vols. (Indianapolis: Bobbs-Merrill, 1941); *The Mexican War and Its Heroes* . . . (Philadelphia: Lippincott, Grambo, 1854).

Teamster, Squire. In "Poor Man's Pudding and Rich Man's Crumbs," he is the rich farmer who hires William Coulter at 75¢ a day and with watch in hand times him at his work.

Teei, King ("The Murdered"). In *Mardi,* he was the king of the island of Juam, whose brother Marjora killed him and set up his own residence at Willamilla. Teei was Donjalolo's nephew. In the Marquesan dialect, *teei* means, according to an 1843 Marquesan-French dictionary, "jeune homme de condition noble." Or the name Teei may derive from that of Keei, a cousin of Kamehameha I,* who defeated him in battle.

Bibliography: Anderson, Davis.

Teg. In "On the Sea Serpent," he is a dock fisherman whose friend Looney says he has caught the Nahant sea serpent.

"The Temeraire" (1866). (Full title: "The Temeraire [Supposed to have been suggested to an Englishman of the old order by the fight of the Monitor and Merrimac].") Poem, in *Battle-Pieces.* (Character: Admiral [Horatio Nelson].) When an Englishman thinks of modern ironclads, which prove that "oak, and iron, and man / Are tough in fibre yet," he recalls the "full-sailed fleets," especially the brave *Temeraire* advancing against the French and Spanish of old, and that noble Admiral's *Victory,* like an "angel in that sun." But now the *Temeraire,* her oak decaying, is tugged to the shore and dismantled, while sailors in modern warships "learn a deadlier lore." When Melville was in London in 1857, he saw several paintings by J.M.W. Turner,* including the *"Fighting Téméraire" Tugged to Her Last Berth to Be Broken Up, 1838* in the National Gallery, and may also have seen Turner's painting *The Angel in the Sun,* also in the gallery.

Bibliography: Cohen, *Poems;* Garner; NN 11 and 15; Warren.

Tempest, Captain Don. In "To Major John Gentian, Dean of the Burgundy Club," he is a navy friend of the Marquis de Grandvin.

Teniers, David, the Younger (1610–1690). Flemish painter and engraver. He was born in Antwerp into a family of painters. At first, he studied under his father, David Teniers the Elder, but soon grew more able. He became a member of the Master Antwerp Guild (1633). He painted indoor and outdoor peasant scenes, guard room and military scenes, religious and mythological pieces, portraits, and monkey pieces. He was also a well-paid copyist. He went to London as an art dealer to buy Italian paintings for a client (c. 1650). He moved to Brussels (1651) to become court painter, the curator of the art collection of Archduke Leopold Wilhelm (the Spanish regent), and a tapestry designer. Many of his pictures were sold in Spain as models for Spanish tapestries. He made 244 copies of the duke's holdings, which when engraved and published as *Theatrum Pictorium* (1660) became a resource of value to art historians. Teniers was retained as court painter when Don John of Austria replaced the archduke (1656). Teniers obtained the patronage of King Philip IV of Spain in founding the Antwerp Academy (1660–1665).

Some Teniers catalogues list more than 2,000 of his works. His best paintings, including *A Country Festival near Antwerp* (1643) and *Village Fête* (1646), are to be dated 1640–1650. They typically show geometrical positioning and combine soft and sharp touches. Teniers married Anna Brueghel, the daughter of the elder Pieter Breughel, in 1637. Their marriage contract was signed by Peter Paul Rubens.* Teniers and his wife Anna had at least one son and one daughter. Their son David, whose godmother was Helena Fourment, Rubens's second wife, became a painter. Teniers married a second time, in 1656. He and his second wife, Isabella de Fren, had at least one child.

In *Mardi,* Melville alludes to Teniers's *The Temptations of St. Anthony* (c. 1640). When he was in Turin in 1857, Melville viewed some tavern scenes by Teniers and noted the following in his journal: "The remarkable Teniers effect is produced by first dwarfing, then deforming humanity." In Amsterdam a week later, he encountered some "Dutch convivial scenes. Teniers and Breughel [the Elder?]" (10, 24 April). In "The Marquis de Grandvin: At the Hostelry," Melville has Dolce [Carlo Dolci] mention Teniers as a painter of inn signs.

Bibliography: R. H. Wilenski, *Flemish Paintings 1430–1830,* 2 vols. (London: Faber and Faber, 1960).

Theseus. In ''The Archipelago,'' he is the Athenian hero, mentioned as once roving through the Greek isles.

Third Nantucket Sailor. In *Moby-Dick,* he is a *Pequod* sailor who grows tired of dancing during the midnight festivities in the forecastle.

''This, That and the Other'' (1924). Part of *Weeds and Wildings,* containing ''The American Aloe on Exhibition,'' ''The Avatar,'' ''The Cuban Pirate,'' ''A Ground Vine Intercedes with the Queen of Flowers for the Merited Recognition of Clover,'' ''Inscription,'' ''Iris (1865),'' ''Profundity and Levity,'' and ''Time's Betrayal.''

Thomas, Frances (''Fanny'') Melville (1855–1938). Melville's younger daughter. She was born in Pittsfield, Massachusetts. She and her sister Elizabeth Melville* were closely supervised by their mother until Frances married a Philadelphian named Henry Besson Thomas (1855–1935) in New York City (1880). Before that escape, Frances lived with her parents in Pittsfield (until 1863) and in New York City. She resented being awakened and ordered to read proofs of *Clarel* with Melville (1876) at two in the morning. Frances and her husband lived in Orange, New Jersey, and had four daughters. Melville's granddaughters were Eleanor Melville Thomas Metcalf (1882–1964, wife of Henry K. Metcalf and mother of David Melville Metcalf [b. 1914] and Paul Cuthbert Metcalf [b. 1917]), Frances Cuthbert Thomas Osborne (1883–1980, wife of Abeel D. Osborne), Katherine Gansevoort Thomas Binnian (1890–1968, wife of Walter B. Binnian), and Jeannette Ogden Thomas Chappin (1892–1974, wife of Edward B. Chappin). Frances's daughter Eleanor Metcalf defined her mother as the only person in Melville's household capable of managing it in a practical manner. Eleanor's son Paul Metcalf has written that Frances Thomas (his grandmother) remembered Melville's irritating ways with the family with such resentment that she finally asked that his name not be mentioned again in her presence.

Bibliography: Leyda; Metcalf; Paul Metcalf, ed., *Enter Isabel: The Herman Melville Correspondence of Clare Spark and Paul Metcalf* (Albuquerque: University of New Mexico Press, 1991); NN 14.

Thomas, Richard (1777–1857). British naval officer. A native of Saltash, Cornwall, he joined the navy (1790), served in the West Indies and back home (to 1795), on Channel duty (1795–1796), and in the Mediterranean (1797–1801). He was promoted to lieutenant (1797) and commander (1803). He was shipwrecked off Newfoundland (1803) and spent more years in the Mediterranean (1805–1813), serving as the flag captain under Lord Cuthbert Collingwood until the latter's death (1810). Suffering occasional poor health, Thomas performed shore duties (1822–1825, 1834–1837). Promoted to rear admiral (1837), he was named commander-in-chief of the Pacific fleet (1841–1844). He became vice admiral (1848) and admiral (1854). He married Gratina Williams (1827), the daughter of a British marine lieutenant general.

Admiral Thomas was commander of the Pacific Station when relations between French and British interests in Tahiti and Hawaii were strained. He ordered a commodore under his command to refuse to recognize French control over Tahiti when it was granted by Queen Pomare IV* (1842). When Lord Captain George Paulet* exceeded his authority and briefly ruled Hawaii as a British protectorate, in accordance with a forced surrender by King Kamehameha III* (25 February 1843), Thomas, acting on his own authority, sailed from Valparaiso to Hawaii, conferred with King Kamehameha III, disavowed Paulet, and gained the king's acquiescence to concessions. Thomas made himself popular with the natives by reinstalling and saluting the Hawaiian flag (31 July). British subjects soon received favorable privileges. In *Typee,* Melville identifies Admiral Thomas as the commander-in-chief of the British Pacific Fleet in 1843. Melville explains that when he received Captain Charlton's report, Thomas dispatched Lord George Paulet to Hawaii, but then followed himself, restored the native flag, and caused "riotous rejoicing by the king and the principal chiefs."

Bibliography: Anderson; Kuykendall; W. P. Morrell, *Britain in the Pacific Islands* (Oxford, England: Clarendon Press, 1960).

Thompson ("The Doctor"). In *Redburn,* he is the slovenly, Bible-reading African-American cook aboard the *Highlander.* He is abstemious when he goes ashore at Liverpool and therefore is able to pocket seventy dollars in pay upon his return to New York.

Bibliography: Grejda.

Thoreau, Henry David (1817–1862). (Original name: David Henry Thoreau.) Naturalist, prose writer, poet, and journal keeper. Thoreau was born in Concord, Massachusetts, and moved with his family to Chelmsford (1818–1821), Boston (1821–1823), and Concord again. He entered Harvard (1833), taught during winter-term leave in Canton, Massachusetts, studied German with Orestes Brownson, and graduated from Harvard (1837). Thoreau joined the informal Transcendental Club organized by Frederic Henry Hedge and Ralph Waldo Emerson,* began his voluminous journal, taught school in Concord for only a few days (1837) and then in a school which he and his older brother John Thoreau conducted (1838–1841), began to lecture for the Concord Lyceum, and visited Maine (1838) for the first of several times. He and his brother fell in love with the same girl, Ellen Sewall of Scituate (1839), but she rejected both of them (1840). They enjoyed a two-week excursion on the Concord and Merrimack rivers in their homemade boat (1839). The literary result was *A Week on the Concord and Merrimack Rivers* (1849). Thoreau met Ellery Channing (1840), who became a close friend and his first biographer. Thoreau published poetry and essays in the *Dial* magazine (1840). He studied Oriental literature (from 1841), lived as handyman and gardener in Emerson's home (1841–1843), was grief-stricken when his brother died of lockjaw (1842), met Nathaniel Hawthorne,* and sold his boat to him for seven dollars (1842). Thoreau tutored Emerson's brother William Emerson's children on Staten Island (1843) and began informal contacts with New York abolitionists. Thoreau hiked through the Berkshires and the Catskills with Channing (1844) and began his experiment in plain living and high thinking at Walden Pond, near Concord (1845–1847). During this period, he was jailed overnight for refusing to pay his poll tax and also revisited Maine (1846). Leaving his hut by the pond, he was Emerson's live-in handyman again (1847–1848), after which he made his parents' home his residence. He gave a lecture at the Concord Lyceum entitled "The Rights and Duties of the Individual in Relation to Government" (1848), which after publication as "Resistance to Civil Government" (1849) was republished and became known as "Civil Disobedience." He went to Montreal and Quebec with Channing (1850). In poor health (from 1851), Thoreau published parts of *A Yankee in Canada* and vacationed in Maine (1853), lectured against slavery, published *Walden* (1854) and parts of *Cape Cod* (1855), did surveying work in New Jersey and met Walt Whitman in New York (1856), met John Brown* in Boston (1857), and after Brown's disastrous Harpers Ferry Raid gave and repeated a lecture entitled "A Plea for Captain John Brown" in Concord, Boston, and Worcester (1859). Hoping to improve his worsening respiratory system, Thoreau ventured as far west as Minnesota (1861) but soon returned home, where he revised many of his writings before he died of tuberculosis.

Egbert, who acts as a disciple to Mark Winsome in *The Confidence-Man*, looks and acts somewhat like Thoreau, and in several ways he resembles Thoreau in his relationship to Emerson. Melville may also have echoed other aspects of Thoreau in "The Apple-Tree Table," "Bartleby," and Cock-a-Doodle-Doo!," and other works. It is of interest that the British critic Henry S. Salt* admired both Melville and Thoreau.

Bibliography: Frank Davidson, "Melville, Thoreau, and 'The Apple-Tree Table,' " *American Literature* 25 (January 1954): 479–88; Leo Marx, "Melville's Parable of the Walls," *Sewanee Review* 61 (Autumn 1953): 602–26; Newman; Egbert S. Oliver, " 'Cock-a-Doodle-Doo!' and Transcendental Hocus-Pocus," *New England Quarterly* 21 (June 1948): 204–16; Oliver, "Melville's Picture of Emerson and Thoreau in *The Confidence-Man*," *College English* 8 (November 1946): 61–72; Oliver, "A Second Look at 'Bartleby,' " *College English* 6 (May 1945): 431–39; Trimpi.

Thouars, Admiral Du Petit. In *Typee. See* Dupetit-Thouars, Abel Aubert.

"A Thought on Book-Binding" (1850). Article published anonymously in the New York *Literary World* (16 March 1850). (Character: [George Palmer] Putnam.) The writer wishes that "Mr Putnam," the publisher of a new edition of *The Red Rover,* by J[ames]. Fenimore Cooper,* had bound the book not in "sober hued muslin" but in "flame-colored morrocco" or "jet black" with a red streak. The cover does have "mysterious cyphers," of appeal to pirates. Since books as well as people circulate in society, they should be dressed appropriately.

Bibliography: NN 9.

Thrummings. In *White-Jacket,* he is an old sailor who as sailmaker helps Ringrope encase Shenly's corpse for burial at sea. White Jacket persuades Thrummings not to take the last stitch through poor Shenly's nose.

Thule, The King of. In "The New Ancient of Days," he is mentioned as riding a sleigh drawn by reindeer from Pole to Wetterhorn in May.

Thumb, General Tom. In "Authentic Anecdotes of 'Old Zack,'" "The New Planet," and "View of the Barnum Property." *See* Tom Thumb.

"Thy Aim, Thy Aim?" (1947). Poem, *Collected Poems of Herman Melville.* The poet advises us to "strive bravely on," through "dust dearth and din," to "the goal"; however, we must expect any "guerdon," "repute," or "fame" to last only as long as a flower.

Bibliography: Shurr.

Ticket-of-Leave Man, The. In *Omoo. See* Sydney Ben.

Tidds. In *Israel Potter,* he is a midshipman aboard the British frigate which Israel Potter boards alone off the *Ariel.*

Tight, Tom. In "Bridegroom-Dick," he is a fine brig-o'-war officer, remembered by Bridegroom Dick as involved in trying and hanging a mutineer. Melville had his cousin Guert Gansevoort* in mind when he characterized both Tom Tight and Dainty Dave in this poem.

Tilly, Johann Tserclaes, Count of (1559–1632). Flemish field marshal. Born at the chateau of Tilly in Brabant, he was given a Jesuit education in preparation for the priesthood but preferred to become a soldier. He volunteered to join a Spanish infantry regiment (c. 1574), campaigned well, and became a company commander. When his unit was reduced, he reverted to the position of pikeman, fought at the siege of Antwerp, and was made governor of Dun and Villefranche (1590–1594). He joined the Austrian army to fight against Turkey, became a colonel (1602), formed a Walloon infantry regiment, and was wounded while assaulting Budapest. He became an artillery general (1604), was devoted to Catholicism and the emperor, and was promoted to field marshal (1605). He joined the army under Maximilian, Duke of Bavaria (head of the Catholic League), was made lieutenant general and commander-in-chief of field forces, and won at White Mountain (1620). Tilly was victorious in several battles during the Thirty Years' War (1618–1648), including those at Bélá Hora (1620), Höchst (1622), and Lutter (1626). After the resignation of Albrecht von Wallenstein (1630), Tilly (by now a count) stormed Magdeburg, could not prevent atrocities by his men—costing perhaps 25,000 deaths—but kept the cathedral, other religious buildings, and some civilians from destruction (1631). He was defeated by Gustavus Adolphus of Sweden at Breitenfeld (1631) and again at the Lech River (1632), where he was mortally wounded.

Melville mentions Tilly in *Clarel* as the commanding officer of one of Ungar's ancestors. The ancestor helped settle Maryland and later "in the Indian glade . . . wedded with a wigwam maid."

Bibliography: Francis Watson, *Wallenstein: Soldier under Saturn* (New York: D. Appleton-Century, 1938); C. V. Wedgwood, *The Thirty Years War* (1938; Garden City, N.Y.: Doubleday, 1961).

"Time's Betrayal" (1924). Poem, with an introduction in prose, in *Weeds and Wildings,* as part of the section entitled "This, That and the Other." (Character: King.) Melville explains that when young maple trees are ruthlessly poinarded for syrup, their leaves turn beautifully red earlier in autumn, thereby exposing the "murder." The poetic garland of Keats, who was "stabbed by the Muses," was also splendid.

Bibliography: Shurr, Stein.

"Time's Long Ago!" (1947). Poem, in *Collected Poems of Herman Melville.* Memories of time long gone have a serenity comparable to that of "unruffled" South Sea lagoons. The wreckage of ships may show on the shore, but each isle is green "[a]nd wins the heart that hope can lure no more."

Bibliography: Shurr.

Timoleon (c. 411–c. 337 B.C.). Greek general and statesman. As a resident of Corinth, he championed Greece against Carthage, acquiesced in the assassination of Timophanes, his initially courageous but ultimately tyrannical older brother, and was therefore exiled for twenty years. Then he was asked by Corinthian leaders to go to Syracuse, Sicily (c. 344), to defend Corinthian interests there against Carthaginians. He successfully invaded Taormina, demolished the opposition (to 338), and set up a constitutional, pro-Greek government in Syracuse. Declining to return home to Corinth, he retired in Sicily (337).

In Melville's poem "Timoleon (394 B.C.)," he is Timophanes's younger brother and is not favored by their mother. To preserve the rights of citizens in their native city of Corinth, Timoleon permits his tyrannical brother's assassination and is exiled for doing so. When he is appealed to by Corinth, Timoleon fights successfully in Sicily but decides thereafter to remain there in exile.

Bibliography: R.J.A. Talbert, *Timoleon and the Revival of Greek Sicily 344–317 B.C.* ([Cambridge, England]: Cambridge University Press, 1974; H. D. Westlake, *Timoleon and His Relation with Tyrants* (Manchester, England: Manchester University Press, 1952).

Timoleon (1891). (Full title: *Timoleon and Other Ventures in Minor Verse.*) Collection of poems, containing the following: "After the Pleasure Party," "The Age of the Antonines," "Art," "The Bench of Boors," "Buddha," "C—'s Lament," "The Enthusiast," "Fragments of a Lost Gnostic Poem of the 12th Century," "The Garden of Metrodorus," "Herba Santa," "In a Garret," "Lamia's Song," "Lone Founts," "Magian Wine," "The Marchioness of Brinvilliers," "The Margrave's Birth Night," "Monody," "The New Zealot to the Sun," "The Night-March," "The Ravaged Villa," "Shelley's Vision," and "The Weaver." In a subsection entitled "Fruit of Travel Long Ago" are the following poems: "The Apparition (The Parthenon Uplifted on Its Rock First Challenging the View on the Approach to Athens)," "The Attic Landscape" and "The Same," "Disinternment of the Hermes," "The Great Pyramid," "Greek Architecture," "Greek Masonry," "In a Bye Canal," "In a Church of Padua," "In the Desert," "Milan Cathedral," "Off Cape Colonna," "The Parthenon," "Pausilippo (in the Time of Bomba)," "Pisa's Leaning Tower," "Syra (A Transmitted Reminiscence)," and "Venice." "L'Envoy" is entitled "The Return of the Sire de Nesle. A.D. 16—" Melville dedicated *Timoleon* to the painter Elihu Vedder,* whose painting *Jane Jackson, Formerly a Slave* impressed him in 1865.

"Timoleon (394 B.C.)" (1891). Poem, in *Timoleon.* (Characters: Phocian, Plato, Timoleon, Timophanes.) Timoleon rescues his older brother, Timophanes, when Corinth is under attack. But their mother continues to favor Timophanes, "[h]er pride, her pet," who, however, becomes a tyrannical prince. Timoleon, who loves Corinth, tries to reason with his brother but fails and therefore permits him to be assassinated. His mother and the scorn of the "whispering" citizens drive him into a despairing exile, until, needing him, Corinth calls upon him to fight for it in Sicily. He does so, becomes a hero, and is regarded as "saviour of the state, Jove's soldier, and man divine." But he refuses to return home, "[a]nd never for Corinth left the adopted shore." Melville wonders whether "Providence, or Chance" accorded "glory" to Timoleon, who at the end queries the motives not of puny mortals but of "gods," who are the "Arch Principals" in the action. Melville's main literary source for "Timoleon" was Plutarch. Another source may be *The Two Brothers,* by Honoré de Balzac, which late in his life Melville read. In it, a mother wrongly favors her older son, who is neat, flashy, and full of bravado, over her younger son, who is unkempt, absent-minded, and eager to be artistic. Melville wove autobiographical threads into his "Timoleon": Melville's mother unfavorably compared him to Gansevoort Melville,* his flashier older brother; furthermore, in his final years, Melville regarded himself as having been assigned by the public and by critics to a would-be literary savior's undeserved exile.

Bibliography: Howard; NN 11; Vernon Shetley, "Melville's 'Timoleon,' " *Emerson Society Quarterly* 33 (2d quarter 1987): 83–93; Shurr; Stein.

Timoneer. In *Clarel. See* Agath.

Timophanes. In "Timoleon (394 B.C.)," he is Timoleon's older, tyrannical brother. To preserve the rights of citizens in their native city of Corinth, Timoleon permits Timophanes to be assassinated and is exiled for doing so. When appealed to by Corinth, Timoleon fights successfully in Sicily but remains in exile.

Tinor. In *Typee,* she is Kory-Kory's mother and Marheyo's wife. Tinor is a typical home-loving, bustling housewife.

Tintoretto (c. 1518–1594). Italian painter, born Jacopo Robusti in Venice and called Tintoretto because his father was a *tintore* (silk dyer). Tintoretto registered as an independent painter (1539), was on a jury with Paolo Veronese* to select mosaicists to decorate the San Marco basilica (1563), and became a member of the confraternity of San Rocco (1565), and an honorary member of the Accademia dell'Arte di Disegno of Florence with Titian* and others (1566). The art historian Giorgio Vasari visited Venice, admired Tintoretto's work, and called him "the most extraordinary brain that the art of painting has produced" (1566). With Veronese, Tintoretto designed decorations to celebrate the Venetian visit of King Henry III of France and painted the monarch's portrait (1574). Tintoretto's standing in the art world of Venice is suggested by his being voted a lifetime annual stipend by the confraternity for three paintings per year for the school and church of San Rocco (from 1577). A fire in the Doges' Palace in Venice destroyed some of his paintings (1577). He journeyed to Mantua to install several paintings for the duke there (1580) and painted under contract for King Philip II of Spain (1587).

Although he developed his own stupendous style, Tintoretto was at first influenced by Michelangelo* for design, Titian for use of colors, Schiavoni for rapidity of execution, and Paolo Veronese in general. Tintoretto painted oils and frescoes of mythological, biblical, allegorical, and historical scenes of great power, often with beautiful light effects, poetic coloration, and movement in multiplaned counterpoint. Tintoretto married Faustina de'Vescovi (sometimes written as Episcopi) in Venice in 1553. Her father was guardian of the Scuola Grande. (The couple had three sons and five daughters. Two sons and one daughter became painters.)

When Melville visited Venice, he jotted the following in his 1857 journal "To Gallery . . . St. Mark coming to rescue" (4 April). The reference is either to Tintoretto's *Miraculous Rescue of a Christian Slave by Saint Mark* (1548) or to his *Miraculous Rescue of a Shipwrecked Saracen by Saint Mark* (1566), both part of a series depicting events in the life of the patron saint of Venice. The former is far the better painting, showing a crowd of onlookers above the slave, nude and on his back as a radiant Saint Mark dive-bombs to save him; some thirty-three human figures, including three active torturers, are grouped geometrically and harmonize dramatically in their purple, dark pink, and orange-brown colors. The latter painting shows an acrobatic, radiant saint having descended feet first from the clouds and lifting the Saracen from waters swamping a boat and dooming others despite their mates' efforts. In "The Marquis de Grandvin: At the Hostelry," Melville presents Tintoretto as a lolling, leonine painter who discusses the picturesque with Franz [Frans] Hals and [Anthony] Van Dyke [Van Dyck], saying this: "This Picturesque is scarce my care. / But note it now in Nature's work."

   Bibliography: NN 15; Francesco Valcanover and Terisio Pignatti, *Tintoretto,* trans. Robert Erich Wolf (New York: Harry N. Abrams, 1985).

Tior, The King of. In *Typee,* he is the ruler of the valley of Tior, near Nukuheva, of the Typees and the Happars. Admiral [Abel Aubert Dupetit-] Thouars confers with this imposing monarch on occasion.

Tistig. In *Moby-Dick,* she is a Gay Head squaw who said that the name Ahab, which his widowed and crazed mother gave to him long ago, would prove prophetic.

Titian (c. 1490–1576). (Real name: Tiziano Vecellio.) Italian painter. Born in Pieve di Cadore, north of Venice, Titian studied under Gentile and Giovanni Bellini, worked with Giorgione of Castelfranco, executed religious and mythological paintings for churches and municipal buildings (from 1508), accepted commissions to cities near Venice, and went to Rome (1545–1546) and then Germany (1548, 1550–1551) to do portraits for Charles V. In Venice permanently thereafter, he enjoyed great professional success, phenomenal health, and considerable prosperity, was hospitable and generous, negotiated with Charles's son (the future King Philip II of Spain) for work, and painted on and on until he died of old age during the plague. Titian had two sons by a woman known as Cecilia, whom he then married, in 1525; she died in the year she gave birth to a daughter (1530; another daughter died in infancy). Titian was disconsolate and never remarried. When he died, his house was looted before authorities could take charge. Titian's sumptuous big scenes, his character-piercing seated and equestrian portraits, and his sensitively positioned nudes often became standard-setting prototypes. Melville, who saw several paintings by Titian, mentions him mainly in his journals. He saw what was probably a copy of a Titian *Venus* (Hampton Court, outside London, 11 November 1849); "A Lady by Titian . . . [and] Danae" (*La Bella Donna* [c. 1536] and perhaps *Danaë and the Shower of Gold* [1554], Rome, 7 March 1857); the nude *Venus of Urbino* of c. 1538 (she "charmed" Melville, Florence, 26 March 1857); perhaps *Death of St. Peter Martyr* ([by 1530], Venice, 3 April 1857—fire destroyed this masterpiece [1867]); the magnificent, three-tiered 1518 *Assumption of the Virgin* (''The great black heads and brown arms,'' Venice, 4 April 1857); ''Titians Virgin in the Temple'' (*Presentation of the Virgin in the Temple* [c. 1538], Venice, 4 April 1857); and some Titian portraits, perhaps including the more gently painted 1543 *Pope Paul III* (Turin, 10 April 1857). Melville adverts to ''Urbino's ducal mistress fair— / Titian's Venus, golden warm,'' in *Clarel.*

   Bibliography: NN 15; *Titian: Prince of Painters,* ed. Susanna Biadene (Munich: Prestel, 1990).

Titonti. In *Mardi,* he is a dead subject whose thriftiness King Peepi has inherited.

''To a Happy Shade'' (1924). *See* ''Rip Van Winkle's Lilac.''

Tobias. In ''To Major John Gentian, Dean of the Burgundy Club,'' he is a rosy-cheeked Burgundy Club waiter.

Toby. In *Typee,* he is an quick-tempered, athletic young sailor who deserts the *Dolly* with the narrator, spends some time with the Typees, goes to the beach for help, and disappears. In a sequel, the narrator explains that Toby went into debt to a native named Jimmy, was unable to obtain help, and had to ship as a sailor to New Zealand. Toby and the narrator met again, in 1846. The real-life Toby was Richard Tobias Greene.*

Tom. In *White-Jacket,* he was a sailor who, according to reminiscences of Tawney, was killed aboard the British frigate *Macedonian* in an engagement with the U.S. man-of-war *Neversink* during the War of 1812.

''To Major John Gentian, Dean of the Burgundy Club'' (1924). Poem, in *The Works of Herman Melville.* (Characters: Jerry Bland, Gentian, Major John Gentian, the Marquis de Grandvin, [Ulysses S.] Grant, Judge Myndert Van Groot, Nathaniel Hawthorne, Charlie [Charles] Fenno Hoffman, [Robert E.] Lee, [Antonio Lopez de] Santa Anna, Charles Sumner, Captain Don Tempest, Tobias, General Will[iam Jenkins] Worth, William.) The gallant and beribboned Gentian is praised by his admiring friends for his quiet valor in the Civil War, is encouraged to reminisce about persons he knew then, and is asked to write ''That Afternoon in Naples'' about his experiences as consul there.

Tomasita. In *White-Jacket,* she is a lovely Castillian belle of Tombez, Peru, who, says Jack Chase, used to caress his fine beard.

''Tom Deadlight (1810)'' (1888). Poem, with an introduction in prose, in *John Marr.* (Characters: Tom Deadlight, Holy Joe, Jock, Matt.) While dying in his hammock aboard the British *Dreadnought,* homeward bound from the Mediterranean, Tom Deadlight, a grizzled petty officer, bids farewell to his messmates Matt and Jock. Expressing the hope that he will see "you noble hearties" and "you ladies of Spain" in "the grand fleet" later, Tom asks Matt and Jock to give him a shot of liquor, put some tobacco in his dead mouth, and not "blubber like lubbers."

Bibliography: NN 11.

Tom, Happy. In *The Confidence-Man. See* Fry, Thomas.

Tom [Melville]. In "To Tom," he is the poet's brother, aboard his ship *Meteor* and therefore missed at home this Christmas. The captain of the *Meteor* at one time was Melville's brother Thomas Melville.*

Tommo. In *Typee,* he is the narrator who with Toby deserts the *Dolly* in the bay of Nukuheva, goes with Toby to the valley of the Typees, suffers pain in a leg, resides with Marheyo and Tinor for about four months, consorts with the lovely Fayaway, is saved by Kory-Kory, and escapes with the aid of Marnoo and Karakoee. Tommo's leg malady, if not psychosomatic, may have been caused by an infection, an insect or snake bite, an injury, or phlebitis. Tommo is also the unnamed narrator-hero of *Omoo.*

Bibliography: Lebowitz, Smith.

Tompkins. In "Hawthorne and His Mosses," he is an evidently imagined British author, to whom American authors should not be unflatteringly compared, as, for example, in saying that someone is merely an American Tompkins.

Tom Thumb (1838–1883). Midget and theatrical performer. (Real name: Charles Sherwood Stratton.) He was born in Bridgeport, Connecticut. As a well-proportioned midget, he was an example of ateliotic dwarfism, not achondroplastic (i.e., disproportionate), dwarfism. Even with three normal-sized siblings, he was under two feet in height and weighed less than sixteen pounds at age four. Overnight in Bridgeport in 1842, P. T. Barnum* heard of the midget and signed him up fast. His mother took him to Barnum's New York Museum, where he began to perform. Barnum, whom he always respected, taught him to dance, do impersonations, perform in tableaux vivants, recite, sing, and strut. He was graceful, vivacious, and witty. He went on a two-year tour, at first at $3 per week plus expenses, later at $50 per week. With his parents, Barnum, and a tutor, the midget made a tour abroad (1844), had three audiences with the intrigued Queen Victoria at Buckingham Palace, and toured in England, France, and Belgium. Returning home (1847), he toured in the United States and Cuba. He was advertised as General Tom Thumb (beginning 1849), retired briefly (1852), returned to England (1857), and toured on the Continent again. At maturity, he was forty inches tall and weighed seventy pounds. In a ceremony managed by Barnum, he married a midget named Mercy Lavinia Warren Bump in 1863. She was given the stage name Lavinia Warren when Barnum began to manage her too. One of Barnum's many hoaxes was that the couple had a daughter who died at the age of two. The couple formed the General Tom Thumb Company, which included Lavinia's midget sister Huldah Pierce Bump (stage name: Minnie Warren), a midget named "Commodore" George Washington Morrison Nutt, and their manager Sylvester Bleeker (formerly an actor and a Barnum aide), and they toured in the United States and Europe and went around the world (1869–1872). Barnum generously discontinued his commercial interest in the couple (1876). Tom Thumb, a successful business manager, accumulated a fortune, built a mansion in Middleboro, Massachusetts, his wife's hometown, and collected jewels and miniature furniture. He also speculated in property, indulged himself in cigars, horses, and yachts, grew fat, and at his death left only a small estate. His widow married an Italian midget named Count Primo Magri in 1885. She toured with him and also with his midget brother Baron Ernesto Magri. She died in 1919; Primo, in 1920.

In "Authentic Anecdotes of 'Old Zack,' " General Tom Thumb is P. T. Barnum's main feature. He is floored when General Zachary Taylor's tack-torn pants are put on exhibition. In "The New Planet," Tom Thumb is mentioned as having his fate controlled by the new planet. In "View of the Barnum Property," he is mentioned.

Bibliography: Countess M. Lavinia Magri, *The Autobiography of Mrs. Tom Thumb (Some of My Life Experiences)*, ed. and introduced by A. H. Saxon (Hamden, Conn.: Archon Books, 1979); NN 9.

Tom Tight, Lieutenant. In "Bridegroom-Dick." *See* Tight, Tom.

Tonans, Jupiter. In "The Lightning-Rod Man," he is the lightning-rod salesman whom the narrator tosses out of his house at the end of a wild thunderstorm.

"To Ned" (1888). Poem, in *John Marr.* (Characters: Adam, Ned Bunn, Paul Pry.) The poet asks his friend Ned Bunn where their old world is now. What will modern pleasure seekers, tired of commerce and ordinary vacations, find in those "Marquesas and glenned isles" such as he and Ned once knew? They were "Authentic Edens in a Pagan sea." The two friends, long ago, "breathed primeval balm / From Edens ere yet over-run." Ned's original is surely Melville's sailor-friend Richard Tobias Greene.*

Bibliography: Shurr, Stein, Warren.

Tongatona. In *Mardi,* he is a dead subject whose headlong valor King Peepi had inherited. His name may derive from that of Tongatabu Island, one of the Tonga Islands, west-southwest of the Marquesas. The British consul Charles Burnett Wilson* had a dispute with Tongatona natives (1840).

Bibliography: Anderson.

Tonoi. In *Omoo,* he is the chief of the fishermen and works sleepily for Shorty and Zeke at Martair.

Tooboi. In *Mardi,* he is a *Parki* sailor from Lahina, at Mowee, Hawaii. He is lost to sharks while he is bathing.

Tooboi. In *Omoo,* he is the heir of King Tamatoy of Raiatair. Poky introduces the narrator to a charming girl in Papeetee whom Tooboi is courting.

Tooke, John Horne (1736–1812). (Original name: John Horne.) Politician, clergyman, and philologist. John Horne was born in London, was blinded in his right eye during a school fight, graduated from Cambridge (1758, M.A. 1771), and became a vicar at Brentford (1760–1773). He traveled on the Continent (1763, 1765–1767), met Voltaire (1765), began to study philology, and associated with the radical politician John Wilkes (1769) but split with him to found the Constitutional Society to urge parliamentary reform and self-government for the American colonies (1771). He collected money to be sent to Benjamin Franklin* for the benefit of American patriots (1775) and was jailed for seditious libel (1778). He was soured by failing to be called to the bar (1779, 1782, 1794). By the 1780s, he had two illegitimate daughters, and later he had a son. Adopting the name Tooke to honor a benefactor named William Tooke of Purley, in Huntingdonshire (1782), John Horne Tooke supported William Pitt's efforts at reform (1782–1785), lost a lawsuit concerning electioneering conduct (1792), was tried for treason but was soon acquitted (1794) in the wake of conservativism sweeping England after the advent of the French Revolution, and obtained a seat in Parliament (1801). Instead of duelling his opponents, he challenged them to drinking bouts and regularly watched them slide under the table. He published radical essays but during his final illness burned all of his papers, including priceless correspondence. Tooke was one of the first philological scholars to see language as the product of historical evolution rather than as a rigid structure. His philological treatise is *The Diversions of Purley* (2 parts, 1786–1805). Some of Tooke's theorizing in this work made its way to Ralph Waldo Emerson* and, through him, to Henry David Thoreau,* among other American writers.

In *Israel Potter,* the Rev. Mr. Horne Tooke is the pro-American British clergyman who plots with Squire John Woodcock and James Bridges to use Israel Potter as a courier to Dr. Franklin in Paris. In reality, Tooke was in prison when Melville has his Potter inquire about him (1778).

Bibliography: Cohen, *Potter;* Minnie Clare Yarborough, *John Horne Tooke* (New York: Columbia University Press, 1926).

Tooroorooloo. In *Mardi,* he was an orator whose jawbones are now in Oh-Oh's museum.

Too-Too. In *Typee,* he is a young Typee native who has built a baby house in the branches of a coconut tree and who sings after he has climbed aloft.

Top-Gallant Harry. In ''Bridegroom-Dick,'' he is a sailor remembered by Bridegroom Dick.

Topo. In *Mardi,* he is a legatee mentioned in Bardianna's will.

Torf-Egill. In *Mardi,* he is mentioned as a Danish king who sailed a fine, swift, and blood-stained yacht.

''Tortoises and Tortoise Hunting.'' On 24 November 1853 Melville wrote to Harper & Brothers,* publishers, to say that his book mainly on tortoises and tortoise hunting would be completed the following January and to ask for an advance of $300. On 6 December 1853 he obtained the advance. Four days later, the publishing firm had a disastrous fire. On [20?] February 1854 Melville wrote to Harper & Brothers that the book was not ready and needed more work. He evidently converted whatever writing he had done on it into part of ''The Encantadas,'' was not asked to repay the advance, and never completed any book on tortoises and tortoise hunting, although in May and June 1854 he was still dickering with Harper & Brothers about it.
   Bibliography: NN 14.

Tot. In *Omoo. See* Old Mother Tot.

''To the Master of the *Meteor*'' (1888). Poem, in *John Marr.* (Character: [Captain Thomas Melville].) When he blows foam off his drink, the poet thinks of the lonesome sailor aboard the homeward-bound *Meteor* as he ''sweep[s] / Over monstrous waves that curl and comb.'' The captain of the *Meteor* at one time was Melville's brother Thomas Melville.

''To Tom'' (1947). Poem, in *Collected Poems of Herman Melville.* (Character: Tom [Melville].) The poet drinks and sheds tears on the glass, as he thinks of his brother aboard the *Meteor,* ''Lonesome on the torrid deep'' and missing Christmas at home. Melville's brother Thomas Melville* was master of the *Meteor.*

Toulib (''A Horror''). In *Clarel,* he is a crippled beggar whom Nehemiah befriends near the Gate of Zion in Jerusalem.

Towser. In *Israel Potter,* this is a sailor's name invented by Israel Potter for himself after he jumps aboard the British frigate from the *Ariel* and finds himself without allies.

Tranquo. In *Moby-Dick,* he is the king of Tranque, which is one of the Arsacides islands. Ishmael visited him once and saw there a glen decorated with carved whale bones.

"Traveling: Its Pleasures, Pains, and Profits" (1859, 1860). Lecture. This was the third of three lectures by Melville, the others being "Statues in Rome" and "The South Seas." He begins "Traveling" by saying that one who climbs out of a valley and up a mountain thrills when he see new objects in front of him. So it is with travel. Books about travel do not satisfy but merely stimulate. To enjoy travel, one must be young, free of care, genial, and imaginative. One must also be able to lounge, in order to appreciate art galleries, town squares, and churches slowly. Be prepared for such inconveniences as fleas, passport worries, and foreigners demanding bribes. Travel is profitable because it rids one of nationalistic and racial prejudices, liberalizes one's attitude toward clothes and beards, humbles one, and satisfies one's curiosity.
    Bibliography: NN 9; Merton M. Sealts, Jr., *Melville as Lecturer* (1957; Folcroft, Pa.: Folcroft Press, 1970).

Tribonnora, Prince. In *Mardi,* he is a mad prince of three islands near Mondoldo. He enjoys submerging small canoes by dashing over them with his large canoe.

Triton, A. In "Marquis de Grandvin: Naples in the Time of Bomba . . ." *See* Carlo.

Tromp, Cornelis Maartenszoon van (1621–1691). Dutch naval officer. He was born in Rotterdam, the son of Maarten Harpertszoon van Tromp, the distinguished Dutch admiral. Cornelis van Tromp commanded a squadron fighting Barbary pirates (1640), served with a fleet in the Mediterranean (1652–1653), and was promoted to vice admiral, the year his father was killed by the British in action in the English Channel (1653). Tromp's squadron was defeated by British naval units (1665). Tromp served under Admiral Mikiel Adriaanszoon De Ruyter* (1666). The two men were jealous of one another. When De Ruyter complained that Tromp behaved negligently, Tromp was relieved of his command (1666). The two soon became reconciled. Reinstated (1673), Tromp commanded skillfully in the North Sea against the Anglo-French fleet, partly in cooperation with De Ruyter (1673). Tromp visited England (1675), was promoted to lieutenant admiral of the United Provinces (1676), was named commander of the fleet against France (1691), but soon died.
    In "Marquis de Grandvin: At the Hostelry," Melville names Van Tromp (also Trump) as the captain of the *Dunderberg* who served with De Ruyter and is remembered by Van der [de] Velde.
    Bibliography: Charles Wilson, *Power and Profit: A Study of England and the Dutch Wars* (London: Longmans, Green, 1957).

"Trophies of Peace: Illinois in 1840" (1924). Poem, in *Weeds and Wildings,* as part of the section entitled "The Year." The poet compares the "hosts of spears" of growing Illinois maize, dancing in the sunlight, to the sunlit spears, plumes, and pennons of Asians marching against Greeks in times gone by. "Ceres' trophies" of stacked "golden grain" are better than any monuments to Mars.
   Bibliography: Stein.

Truman, John. In *The Confidence-Man,* he is the president and transfer agent of the Black Rapids Coal Company. He sells stock to the college man, to the merchant Henry Roberts, and to the coughing miser. The herb doctor tells the miser that Truman comes from Jones Street, in St. Louis. John Truman may be a partial caricature, with respect to personality, traits, style, and actions, of Thurlow Weed,* the New York editor and politician.
   Bibliography: Trimpi.

Truxill. In "The Encantadas," he is the brother of Hunilla. When he and his brother-in-law Felipe drowned while fishing, she became the wretched Chola widow of Norfolk Isle.

Tryon, Corporal. In "Lyon," he is a brave soldier from Iowa led with other soldiers by [Nathaniel] Lyon.

Tubbs. In *White-Jacket,* he is a sailor who was once a whaler. For this reason, Jack Chase abominates him and drives him from his chatty maintop.

"The Tuft of Kelp" (1888). Poem, in *John Marr.* The poet asks whether a fragment of kelp is "[b]itterer" as well as "purer" because it has been "[c]ast up by a lonely sea."
   Bibliography: Stein.

Turbans. In *Clarel,* this is the general name for Turks, among whom Nehemiah, called "the Hat," wanders with impunity.

Turkey. In "Bartleby," he is the Wall Street lawyer's short, British-born scrivener. Turkey is almost sixty years old and—unlike his fellow worker Nippers—is irritable only after the noon hour.
   Bibliography: Hans Bergmann, " 'Turkey on His Back': 'Bartleby' and New York Words," *Melville Society Extracts* 90 (September 1992): 16–19.

Turner, J.M.W. (1775–1851). (Full name: Joseph Mallord William Turner.) British painter and engraver. Turner was born in London. His mother died insane (1804). His father, who was a barber, taught him the rudiments of reading. Turner drew pictures as a child, studied at the Royal Academy, sketched on holidays in England and Scotland (from 1789), loved native scenery and atmospheric tones, exhibited *Fishermen at Sea* (1796) and *Buttermere Lake* (1798), had a liaison (1798–c. 1808, with the widowed Sarah Danby—the couple had two children), opened a studio in London (1800), and became a member of the Academy (1802). Turner made the first two of many trips to the Continent (1802, 1804), initially to France and Switzerland. His stormy *Calais Pier* (1803) and *Shipwreck* (1805), as well as several watercolors of Alpine scenes, were the result. He published seventy-one mezzotint plates in his *Liber Studiorum* (1807–1819); they present varied architectural, historical, marine, mountainous, and pastoral scenes, and were designed to challenge Claude Lorrain* and his *Liber Veritatis*. Turner provided magnificent illustrations for books by others. He taught perspective, off and on, at the Academy (1807–1838). His works in the 1810s stress atmospheric effects and floods of light. Many then (and later) depict human catastrophes in and under a potent, indifferent nature—for example, the turbulent *Shipwreck* (1805), *The Wreck of a Transport Ship* (1810), *The Burning of the Houses of Parliament* (1835), and *Peace—Burial at Sea* (1842; David Wilkie, a Royal Academy colleague of Turner's, died at sea and was buried off Gibraltar). Turner's visit to Italy (1819–1820) resulted in 1,500 sketches, filed for future use. In the 1820s, he toured England and Scotland again, returned to the Continent, and exhibited in Rome (1828). Shying away from publicity and combining more and more wealth with chronic stinginess, he bought a cottage in Chelsea (1839) and lived in it under a pseudonym, but often left it to sketch abroad. His watercolors of Swiss scenes reveal an increasing love of the abstract (1840–1846). In his last phase, Turner sacrificed detail and recognizable mass to blurry, colorful brushings, to suggest motion and space. Perhaps his most remarkable painting is *"Fighting Téméraire" Tugged to Her Last Berth to Be Broken Up* (1838); it shows the romantic old vessel, pale and angularly ghostlike, being removed by a dirty modern steam tug over glassy waters, with a fiery sunset in the eerie background. Toward the end of Turner's life, his eyesight and mental faculties deteriorated. Turner left nearly 300 paintings and some 19,000 drawings, many of which he bequeathed to England. Relatives fought over his estate of £140,000, some £20,000 of which he willed to the Academy.

Turner's influence on Melville was substantial, beginning in 1850 or 1851. Early evidence is found in *Moby-Dick,* in the description of the "boggy, soggy, squitchy picture" of "a Cape-Horner in a great hurricane," in Peter Coffin's Spouter Inn in *Moby-Dick.* Melville admired Turner's aesthetic of the indistinct. While in London, Melville visited the National Gallery at Trafalgar Square and examined several Turner paintings. In his 1857 journal, he notes the following: "Sunset scenes of Turner. 'Burial of Wilkie.' The Shipwreck. 'The Fighting— —taken to her last berth' " (1 May). His poem "The Temeraire" was inspired by Turner's painting of the vessel doomed by industrial "progress." Melville owned twenty-one engravings of works by Turner, including those of *Peace* and *The Téméraire.*

Bibliography: NN 15; Robert K. Wallace, *Melville & Turner: Spheres of Love and*

Fright (Athens: University of Georgia Press, 1992); Andrew Wilton, *Turner in His Time* (New York: Harry N. Abrams, 1987).

Turret, Captain (''Old Hemlock''). In ''Bridegroom-Dick,'' he is the Kentucky captain remembered by Bridegroom Dick as huge, fond of drink, and obliged once to come close to flogging the Finn.

Tuscan, The. In *Clarel. See* Salvaterra.

''The Two Temples'' (1924). Short story, in *Collected Works of Herman Melville.* (Character: [William Charles] Macready.) In ''Temple First,'' the narrator one Sunday morning walks from the Battery three miles up to a ''splendid, new-fashioned Gothic'' church, only to be turned away by a paunchy, beadle-faced man who says that there are no galleries. Rich-looking carriages standing outside attest to the wealth and comfort of the sinners within. With prayer book in hand, the narrator enters through a side door leading to the tower, and furtively climbs up some stone steps and then wooden ones. Finally he is standing at a hot ventilator which permits him to look through some gauzy wirework down upon the opulent congregation a hundred feet below and also at the glittering lights from the stained-glass windows. What he soon sees resembles a show, with the white-robed priest first intoning the hymn and then reappearing, clad in black, to deliver an eloquent if inaudible sermon, the text of which is ''Ye are the salt of the earth.'' After the benediction, the listeners flow out in three gilded freshets. When the narrator tries to leave, he finds the door locked. In desperation, he pulls some bell ropes hanging from his tower. The beadle-faced man unlocks the door, collars him, and hands him over to three policemen as a lawless violator of a place of public worship. He is fined and reprimanded by the judge.

In ''Temple Second,'' the narrator finds himself temporarily penniless in London one Saturday night. After his experience back in the church tower, he went to Philadelphia, obtained a job accompanying two women to England as their ''young physician,'' but was then discharged. The tide of humanity carries him between Fleet Street and Holborn and to a theater off the Strand. A placard announces Macready as Cardinal Richelieu. The narrator longs to refresh his spirits by attending the play but lacks money for a ticket. Suddenly a man gives him one, explaining that he has been summoned home and cannot use it. The narrator rationalizes that since we all live interdependently on charity in one form or another, he might as well go on in. Up, up he wanders, to the topmost gallery, reminded as he is doing so of the church tower back home. The orchestra reminds him of the church organ. A hundred feet below, glittering like coral through a sea of smoke, are bejeweled ladies. A ragged but handsome boy offers him a mug of ale, which he accepts so as to drink to the lad's father, who is in America seeking his fortune. Macready is stately on stage and reminds the narrator of the robed priest back home. The narrator leaves with the others, all borne forward on billows of music from the orchestra. It is strange, he muses when he is back in his lonely lodging: He was treated charitably in one temple in a foreign land but was thrust from another one at home.

While in London in 1849, Melville saw William Charles Macready* perform in the title role of *Othello* and recorded his dislike of the performance in his journal (19 November). At an earlier time, Melville may have seen Macready in *Richelieu; or, The Conspiracy,* by Edward Bulwer-Lytton, since the popular actor performed in it in Boston (1844) and New York (1849). The model for the person accompanying the ocean-crossing ladies was Franklin Taylor, an impoverished older cousin of Bayard Taylor.* Franklin Taylor, variously identified as a physician and as a schoolteacher, had unsuccessful "designs upon . . . two ladies" while in London, according to Melville's journal (14 November). Taylor later acted as the companion of a wealthy merchant's sick son on a voyage to Jerusalem, leaving Melville to go see Macready without him. "The Two Temples" was rejected by *Putnam's Monthly Magazine** on the grounds that it might offend religious readers—specifically members of the newly erected Grace Church on Broadway in New York City, who would easily recognize their temple and their sexton, Isaac Brown, as Melville's satirical targets. In two sadly contrasting parts, "The Two Temples" thus resembles two other stories that Melville also wrote: "The Paradise of Bachelors and Tartarus of Maids" and "Poor Man's Pudding and Rich Man's Crumbs."

Bibliography: Judith R. Hiltner, "Distortion from the Heights: Melville's Revisions of 'The Two Temples,' " *Studies in Short Fiction* 27 (Winter 1990): 73–79; Newman; NN 9 and 15; Beryl Rowland, "Grace Church and Melville's Story of 'The Two Temples,' " *Nineteenth-Century Fiction* 28 (December 1973): 339–46; Sealts.

Typee. In *Typee,* he is the hero and narrator. He rebels against Captain Guy of the *Julia,* instigates and signs the round-robin, and is imprisoned in the Calabooza Beretanee. When allowed to go free, he wanders with Dr. Long Ghost to Martair, Tamai, Imeeo, Loohooloo, Partoowye, and Taloo, and he finally ships aboard the *Leviathan.* At one point, Dr. Long Ghost calls him Paul.

Typee (1846). (Fuller title: *Typee: A Peep at Polynesian Life.*) Novel. (Characters: Captain [Richard] Charlton, the Commodore, Admiral [Abel Aubert] Du Petit Thouars, Fayaway, Jimmy, Dr. [Gerrit Parmele] Judd, Kalow, Queen Kammahammaha III, Karakoee, Karky, Karluna, Karnoonoo, General Kekuanoa, Kolory, Kory-Kory, Jack Lewis, Marheyo, Marnoo, Mehevi, Monoo, Moonoony, King Mowanna, Mow Mow, Mungo, Narmonee, Narnee, Ned, Lord George Paulet, Queen Pomare [IV], [George] Pritchard, Mrs. Pritchard, Ruaruga, Admiral [Richard] Thomas, Tinor, the King of Tior, Toby, Tommo, Too-Too, Captain Vangs, Wormoonoo.)

The narrator laments that, after six months at sea, their ship *Dolly* is a shambles. Their fresh food is also all gone, including Captain Vangs's pig and all the chickens except Pedro the rooster. So the captain plans to shift course for the Marquesas. Mowanna is now king of Nukuheva there. His jolly wife once startled the Frenchmen in the harbor by hoisting her skirts to compare her tattoos with those of a sailor. After a lazy period during which the narrator observes various fish and seafowls, the *Dolly* approaches Nukuheva, discovered in 1791. French warships are in port, the lovely island seeming a reproach to their guns. Natives bring coconuts to the ship, accompanied by beautiful maidens who swim alongside and climb aboard. Acts of debauchery follow. The white man's civilization is uniformly corrupting. The native fear and hate the French, with their shiny troops, curious forge, and strange horses. In 1842, a few weeks before the arrival of the *Dolly*, Admiral Du Petit Thouars named Mowanna king of the whole island to stir up unfriendly Typee natives and Happar natives to rebellion, which the French could then intervene to quell. Queen Pomare of nearby Tahiti, unable to resist French firepower, was obliged to desert her throne.

The narrator decides to jump ship. The captain is a tyrant, the crew pusillanimous, the food bad, and the future aboard a slow whaler uncertain. So he finds out what he can about the island—its harbor, native houses, inlets, mountains, valleys, and supposedly cannibalistic inhabitants. White occupation has been cruel, and the natives are often antagonistic. When the narrator goes ashore with a landing party, he plunges into the glen of Tior, where he sees a meeting between the king of Tior and Thouars. What a contrast! The savage appears happier. The narrator returns to the ship and asks Toby, a slight, quick-tempered, good-looking, intelligent, and likable fellow sailor, to jump ship with him. Toby agrees. When the captain fruitlessly warns his crew not to avail themselves of liberty ashore though granted, the pair go with their mates, who soon fall asleep in a canoe house. The escapees plunge into a grove and push through canes toward a mountain ridge, from which they hope to watch their ship leave later. At sunset they rest 3,000 feet above sea level. They gaze upon a scene of matchless loveliness. But a series of ridges and valleys puzzles them. Still, they refuse to retreat.

When they check their supplies, they find bits of tobacco mixed with sweat- and rain-soaked bread. They cut it into rations for six days. They take a path-like track until it stops by a ravine, where they fashion a hut that proves no defense against more rain. After a wretched night, the narrator awakens with chills and fever—and a mysteriously swollen leg. But beneath them unfolds a green paradise dotted with native huts. Toby thinks that they house Typee cannibals. To play it safe, they try to traverse rocky gorges toward the valley ahead of them, hoping that it will be fertile and unoccupied. The narrator burns with thirst, then turns icy cold. After a fruitless day, they quit that route, have a bite of food, build another little shelter, and rest. The narrator's leg still hurts, but Toby arises all refreshed, finds some soft bark, and eats it. He suggests that they follow the streams down to the huts, which are presumably in the Happar valley. They wade and crawl and, at night, build another hut. Next day they encounter a cataract a hundred feet down. They go down beside it by swinging on roots in rock fissures. They make another descent along ledges until the path ends.

They leap into palm trees and slide down their trunks. After another hut, another day, and another hut, they finally are safe in the gorgeous valley.

They feel that they must stay here openly and risk the possible enmity of the natives. While they are sampling the fruit of some little annue trees, they see a naked boy and girl and approach them, give them some cloth, and follow them to a village of attractive bamboo structures. It is evening. Several chiefs surround them. When it becomes clear that these natives are Typees, the narrator says, "Typee mortarkee," that is, Typees are good. In a trice, all is joyful. The narrator is dubbed Tommo. The leading chief, Mehevi, stares at his guests, whose white limbs the natives gather round to smell and feel. Everyone feasts on coconuts and poee-poee—a porridge made of breadfruit. They smoke, try to express their shared hatred of the French, and sleep.

After a night made restless by leg pains and fear, Tommo is aroused by a bevy of girls and a troop of boys. Mehevi enters in a war dress—head plumes, tusk necklace, whale teeth in ears, dark loincloth of tappa, anklets and bracelets of human hair, paddle spear, and pipe. He harangues a while, seeking information about the French. Noticing Tommo's swollen leg, he calls for a medicine man, who pounds the limb mercilessly and covers it with wet herbs. Tommo surveys the commodious, ventilated hut in which he is staying and takes note of the hideous features of Kory-Kory, the strong native assigned as his valet. He feeds Tommo and carries him to the stream for a bath. Tommo is delighted with Marheyo, Kory-Kory's senile father, and Tinor, his bustling mother. Best of all is gorgeous Fayaway, an olive-skinned, brown-haired, blue-eyed, slightly tatooed native girl—usually naked but for flowers in her ears.

One day, Tommo and Toby are escorted to the taboo groves, where they examine a temple called the Ti, 200 feet long. They spot some old muskets and a few dreadfully old men with tattoos which are turning green. That night, while beside the temple, they see flames and are fed tender pork. Tommo thinks that they are being fattened for the kill, but they are marched back to Marheyo's home. Uncertain of their future, Toby persuades Marheyo to lead him to the edge of Happar territory, which he hopes to cross to Nukuheva for medicine to treat his friend's leg. Toby is attacked by three Happars, is wounded in the temple, and is carried back to his friends. The white men grow despondent, despite Kory-Kory's lectures on Typee delights and despite Fayaway's ministrations. When boats are reported in the harbor nearby, Toby, promising to return with medicine, saunters to the beach under cover of the hubbub of natives carting coconuts to sell to the mariners. Conflicting accounts come back: Toby will return, he is missing, he has deserted. In any event, Tommo never sees him again in the lovely valley of the Typees, who redouble their efforts to please their melancholy invalid.

Tommo watches the natives as they prepare breadfruit in a variety of recipes. Three weeks or so pass. He goes native by wearing tappa robes, shows his hosts how he can sew, and shaves the head of a heroic-looking warrior named Narmonee. When his leg improves, Tommo feels happier and favorably compares this island paradise with civilization and its executions, wars, prisons, debts, strife, and illnesses. Suddenly word comes of a Happar attack. Mehevi and his allies repulse it. Tommo enjoys swimming with shoals of maidens in a lake a hundred yards across. He is permitted to break a long-standing taboo and take Fayaway in a boat. She stands up in it, converting herself into a fetching mast, and spreads out her robe for a sail.

Suddenly Marnoo enters. He is a handsome, curly-haired, bright-eyed native who is a sacred wanderer along all shores and through all valleys of the island. The Typees are thrilled by his eloquence. He astonishes Tommo by speaking English to him. But when Tommo persuades him to ask Mehevi to let him go back to Nukuheva, the attractive stranger refuses and decamps. Tommo, sad once more, determines not to flinch from fate. He whittles popguns out of bamboo and gives his shoes to Marheyo, who wears them around his neck. Tommo watches tappa manufacturing, samples horrible-tasting medicinal water, and inspects curious terraced masonry and house foundations called pi-pis. He watches the slaughter and baking of wild hogs and other preparations for a feast. This celebration takes place near the Ti and lasts three days and nights. Tommo dresses in a native way appreciated by his hosts, who feed him poee-poee and pork, share their tobacco with him, and treat him to a narcotic beverage called arva, useful in curing a certain disease introduced by white men. Tommo is puzzled by nude old women dancing stiffly, until Kory-Kory explains that the hags are bereaved widows of warriors. The pounding of sharkskin drums provides entertainment. Feeling certain that the banquet is religious, Tommo discusses native beliefs. In a hut near the lake, there is an effigy of a warrior paddling a canoe toward eternity. Natives offer food to their gods. One priest named Kolory has a religious doll which he whispers to and cuffs into giving proper answers. Tommo discusses the appearance of the natives, including their complexions and teeth. He discusses their customs regarding property; their sexual, familial, working (or nonworking) habits; and their burial rites. He explains that civilization has brought many Polynesians dreadful diseases, and missionaries have made some of the natives mere beasts of burden. Seemingly more virtuous than their ''superiors,'' the islanders are cooperative, happy, and without strife. He discusses the animals, insects, and birds of Typee, and taboos and tattoos. He resisted the art of Karky, master tattooer. He discusses the climbing and swimming abilities of the natives, and the weather, singing, hair oil, and cannibalism on the island.

One day Tommo sees three human heads, one that of a white man (not Toby), swung down from the ridgepole of Marheyo's hut. Embarrassed at the revelation, the inmates hustle the packages out of sight. Tommo's leg starts to hurt again. He fears that he will be beheaded and the rest of him cooked and eaten. He watches some fierce warriors, including one-eyed Mow Mow, return from a battle with the Happars and bring what seem to be three pole-slung bodies of defeated foes. Tommo is denied access to the Ti area, where a feast is held for chiefs and priests only. The following noon he is permitted to return to the taboo groves, where he spies a huge wooden vessel with a lid. Kory-Kory hustles him away, but not before he has glimpsed a fresh, flesh-garnished human skeleton. Kory-Kory calls it pig, and Tommo pretends to believe him. Ten days later, Marnoo returns but again refuses to intercede for Tommo, although he tells him to follow his path to Pueearka, his native valley. Tommo is intercepted by Kory-Kory, although his father Marheyo sympathizes with their gloomy guest. After what feels like about four months on the island, Tommo hears a rumor that Toby has returned. A boat stands offshore. Mehevi permits Tommo to be carried to a hut near the beach. Although Toby is not there, Tommo pretends to believe that he is, so that his enthusiasm will disarm the native guards while he tries to get to the water. Fayaway weeps at the possibility of his departure. Kory-Kory is sad too. But Marheyo, repeating the two English words he knows—''Home'' and ''Mother''—seems to understand. Karakoee, a tabooed renegade shanghaier of seamen, appears and tries to bribe the Typees with a musket, some powder, and some cloth to release Tommo to a tabooed crew waiting in a whaleboat outside the surf. Most of the Typees shake their javelins in anger. As Karakoee returns to the boat, Tommo embraces Fayaway a final time, rushes into the water, and is rescued. The boat pulls away. Several natives swim after it. Tommo thrusts a boat hook at Mow Mow's throat. An oarsman slashes another native's wrists at the gunwales. Soon the narrator tumbles aboard the *Julia,* an Australia vessel in need of additional crew members. It is three months before he is healthy again.

In an appendix, Melville explains details of the arrival from England of Lord George Paulet at Oahu. Captain Charlton, British consul-general, abused by anti-British authorities in the Hawaiian Islands, appealed to Admiral Thomas, who sent Paulet. This straightforward man accepted at face value a native subterfuge—the surrender of the island, designed to arouse world opinion against England. The first thing Paulet did when he began to govern the islands was to prohibit customary licentiousness. Five months later, Thomas landed at Honolulu, took down the British flag, and restored the islands to native rule. Riotous local rejoicing ensued, for which Paulet was again blamed, though wrongly. He deserved and received British and Hawaiian plaudits for his conduct. In a sequel, Melville explains what happened to Toby. When he left Tommo, he went to the beach near the Happar mountains and promised some money to an irresponsible and tabooed sailor named Jimmy, in the household of King Mowanna of Nukuheva, to lead him through Happar territory to Nukuheva. Once there, he signed as a sailor aboard a vessel to obtain money to pay Jimmy. Toby also asked that an armed boat be sent to Typee for his captive friend. But only Jimmy and some tabooed natives were permitted to go, and they returned without Tommo. After waiting for days, Toby shipped for New Zealand. In 1846 he and the author met again.

The derivation of the word ''Typee'' is puzzling. An 1843 Marquesan-French dictionary defines it as *peuple ennemi;* also *Teei* is said to mean *jeune homme de condition noble.*

Typee, a partly autobiographical novel, is based to a degree on Melville's experiences among the Typees for one month (9 July–9 August 1842). Melville wrote it while living in his mother's home in Lansingburgh, New York (probably from late 1844), and gave part of his manuscript to his brother Gansevoort Melville,* who was the newly appointed secretary of the American legation in London and whom Melville asked to negotiate for him there. Gansevoort interested John Murray,* the British publisher, in parts of it (October 1845). Murray momentarily doubted its authenticity, required a few changes in the interests of propriety, and soon (December) bought British rights to it for £100 and assurances that the American edition would not precede its appearance in England. While engaged in reading proof, Gansevoort shared parts of the book with Washington Irving,* then in London (January 1846). He also showed the book to George Palmer Putnam,* the American publisher then doing business in London. Putnam contracted for the publication of *Typee* in the United States by his firm, Wiley and Putnam. Gansevoort altered the text to some extent, and Murray's manuscript reader revised it further (and was paid just over £50 by Murray for his services). The British edition was published as *Narrative of a Four Months' Residence among the Natives of a Valley of the Marquesas Islands; or, A Peep at Polynesian Life* (27 February); the American edition was published as *Typee: A Peep at Polynesian Life. During a Four Months' Residence in a Valley of the Marquesas with Notices of the French Occupation of Tahiti and the Provisional Cession of the Sandwich Islands to Lord Paulet* (17 March). Melville dedicated *Typee* to Lemuel Shaw,* his future father-in-law. Gansevoort Melville died in May 1846. Richard Tobias Greene* turned up in Buffalo, New York, and published a notice that, as the original of Toby, he could vouch for the accuracy of Melville's narrative (July 1846). Melville published a sequel about Toby in revised editions of *Typee.* The British publisher George Routledge pirated it, as did Gibbs, another British firm (both 1850).

In addition to his own experiences for *Typee,* Melville read and drew on *Voyages and Travels in Various Parts of the World . . . 1803–1807,* by Georg H[einrich] von Langsdorff* (1813); *Journal of a Cruise Made to the Pacific Ocean in the U.S. Frigate Essex, in the Years 1812, 1813, and 1814,* by David Porter* (1815); *A Visit to the South Seas, in the U.S. Ship Vincennes, during the Years 1829 and 1830,* by Charles S. Stewart (1831); *Polynesian Researches,* by William Ellis (1833); *Voyages round the World,* by Edward Fanning (1833); and *Historical Account of the Circumnavigation of the Globe, and of the Progress of Discovery in the Pacific Ocean . . . ,* anonymously published (1836). Many reviewers of *Typee,* especially several in England, doubted its authenticity; others reviled its author for his criticism of the missionaries. Murray printed 5,000 copies of *Typee,* by the end of 1847 had sold 4,104, and printed 1,012 more copies (1848). Literary piracy slowed legitimate sales; still, Murray printed 758 more copies (1857), may have printed some more, but then watched sales dwindle into the 1870s. The British *Typee* went out of print (1876) and was brought back unprofitably a year later. Meanwhile, in America, Wiley and Putnam sold 5,958 copies and paid Melville $732 (through 1848). After complicated dealings, handled by Melville's brother Allan Melville,* Melville assigned rights to *Typee* to Harper & Brothers,* the New York publishers (1849). Their printings sold only 937 (1849–1851). Many copies of a new printing (1852) were burned in a disastrous six-house Harper fire (1853), and the American *Typee* soon went out of print (1854). In all, Melville perhaps realized about $2,000 from his first book; in addition, his identification as "a man who lived among the cannibals" prevented him from ever obtaining a coveted consular appointment.

Bibliography: Anderson; Bruce A. Harvey, " 'Precepts Graven on Every Breast': Melville's *Typee* and the Forms of the Law," *American Quarterly* 45 (September 1993): 394–424; Howard; Leyda; NN 1.

U

Uhia, King. In *Mardi,* he is the unnaturally ambitious monarch of Ohonoo, the Isle of Rogues. He worships the god Keevi in the valley of Monlova. Uhia once stood on a rock over the valley to prove his right to the throne. He envies bedridden Manta. In Uhia, Melville ridicules the imperialistic ambition of kings.

Ulver, Delly. In *Pierre,* she is one of Mary Glendinning's servants. Delly has evidently been seduced by Ned, another of the older woman's servants, and must therefore be dismissed. She passively accompanies Pierre Glendinning and Isabel Banford to the city, where she serves them as a maid in their cramped quarters among the Apostles.

Ulver, Mrs. Walter. In *Pierre,* she is Delly Ulver's old mother, who is grief-stricken when her daughter is evidently seduced by Ned and must leave the region.

Ulver, Walter. In *Pierre,* he is Delly Ulver's old father, who rents the red farmhouse by the lake where Isabel Banford lives for a short while.

Una. In "The Bell-Tower," this is the name of the garlanded hour of one on the clock bell, beneath which Bannadonna dies.

"Under the Ground" (1924). Poem, in *Weeds and Wildings,* as part of the section entitled "As They Fell." (Character: Master.) The poet asks the gardener's boy if he is actually bringing roses out of a nearby tomb. Saying yes, the boy explains that "the dank o' the vault" charms cut roses into blooming better.

Bibliography: Shurr, Stein.

"Under the Rose" (1924). Sketch, in *The Works of Herman Melville.* (Characters: My Lord the Ambassador, Azem, Geoffry, Gold-beak, the Great Duke, Lugar-Lips, My Lady.) A parenthetical note explains that this work is "an extract from an old MS. entitled 'Travels in Persia (Iran) by a servant of My Lord the Ambassador.' " Geoffry, the servant of My Lord the Ambassador from England to the Azem of Persia, says that one day the Azem's servant dropped roses of "divers hues" into a delicate amber vase for the Ambassador to enjoy. A few days later, Geoffry examined its relievos, formerly covered by the overhanging roses, and told the covetous Ambassador about them. The carvings were of angels, with a spade and a wine jar, walking, and squatting like Job. Stranger still were dead insects frozen in the amber. When the officials met, sat on green cushions, and smoked pleasantly, the Azem, fearful that he might be asked for the vase as a gift, said that it was worth more to him than a villa and showed his guest a poem by Lugar-Lips inspired by the anatomies in amber. Plying a Greek with wine later, the Ambassador got him to translate the poem, which said that amber walls are like windows revealing skeletons, that we are Death's open secret, and that the angel with the jar is coming. The Ambassador became gloomy, thinking that his death might be near. He was sixty-three years old, the age at which both his father and his grandfather died.

Ungar. In *Clarel,* he is a scarred former Confederate officer, descended from Maryland Catholics. Also part Native American, he is described as having "[a]n Anglo brain, but Indian heart." Now self-exiled, Ungar irregularly serves in the armies of Egypt and Turkey. He joins the pilgrims at Mar Saba and leaves them at Bethlehem. He is bitterly antidemocratic, admirably stoical, and deeply religious. He claims descent from [Johann Tserclaes, Count of] Tilly. Melville put several autobiographical touches in his characterization of Ungar.

Bibliography: NN 12.

"An uninscribed Monument on one of the Battle-fields of the Wilderness" (1866). Poem, in *Battle-Pieces.* The enigmatic monument says that silence, solitude, and rusted projectiles could merely "hint . . . [at what] here befell." Observers here should also "silent stand" and "lonesome."

Bibliography: Garner, NN 11, Warren.

Unknown, The. In *Clarel,* this is the first name by which Celio is referred to, at lower Gihon.

Urania. In "After the Pleasure Party," she is a Mediterranean woman who has devoted much of her life to astronomy—"O reaching ranging tube I placed /

Against yon skies.'' Suddenly she is annoyed when a man, whom she inexplicably longs for sexually, prefers a simple peasant girl. Urania feels incomplete, is tempted to join a nunnery, but instead prays—probably without effect—to the armed Virgin, which represents cold knowledge and art. Urania is based to a degree on Maria Mitchell, the celebrated astronomer whom Melville met in 1852 on Nantucket Island, Massachusetts, where she had been born into a big Quaker family. She was the daughter of William Mitchell, an astronomer, whom she assisted until he died (1869). During the devastating Boston fire of 1846, which destroyed some of their equipment and records, she burned her diaries and letters to prevent their being scattered and exposed to the public. She discovered a comet (1847), was the first woman to be elected to the American Academy of Arts and Sciences (1848) and to the Association for the Advancement of Science (1850), received other honors, photographed the sun, studied Jupiter and Saturn, and became America's first female professor of astronomy (Vassar, 1865–1888). She was evidently loved by a Boston astronomer who later married someone else. Mitchell, who never married, loved children, painted, and wrote for publication. Her sister, Phebe Mitchell Kendall, published *Maria Mitchell: Life, Letters, and Journals* (1896) but foolishly destroyed relevant papers she thought too private to be kept. Maria Mitchell had a Quaker uncle named Peleg Mitchell, who was a tinsmith, however, and not a sea captain like the Quaker Captain Peleg in *Moby-Dick.*

Bibliography: Nathaniel Philbrick, ''Hawthorne, Maria Mitchell, and Melville's 'After the Pleasure Party,' '' *Emerson Society Quarterly* 37 (4th quarter 1993): 291–308; Helen Wright, *Sweeper in the Sky: The Life of Maria Mitchell First Woman Astronomer in America* (New York: Macmillan, 1949).

Ushant, John. In *White-Jacket,* he is the brave, philosophical, well-traveled captain of the forecastle. He is about sixty years of age. When Ushant refuses to trim his magnificent, Neptune-like beard, he is put in the brig for the offense and undergoes a flogging by the order of Captain Claret; however, he retains his beard. The name Ushant may come from Ouessant (English: Ushant), the weather-defying, granitic island off the French coast.

Bibliography: Will Stephenson and Mimosa Stephenson, ''Melville's WHITE-JACKET,'' *Explicator* 51 (Summer 1993): 221–23.

Usher, The. In *Moby-Dick,* he is the fictitious grammar-school grammarian who supplies the prefatory etymology concerning whales.

Utamai. In *Omoo,* he is one of the four recreant chiefs whom the French governor [Armand-Joseph] Bruat puts in charge of one of the four sections into which he divided Tahiti. The others are Kitoti, Tati, and Paraita.

"A Utilitarian View of the Monitor's Fight" (1866). Poem, in *Battle-Pieces.* The poet explains that, since war is now conducted by mechanics and operatives plying cranks, pivots, and screws, and making "calculations of caloric," it should be placed where it belongs, "[a]mong the trades and artisans." Some of the grandeur of war has been lost, and "a singe runs through lace and feather." The *Monitor* was the first Union ironclad to see action during the Civil War. When the Union forces withdrew from Norfolk, Virginia, they sank the *Merrimac* in shallow water and burned her to the water's edge (April 1861). But the Confederates raised her, rebuilt her as an ironclad, and renamed her the *Virginia.* The *Monitor* challenged her at Hampton Roads, and the two vessels pounded each other to a draw and then disengaged (9 March 1962). The diction and meter of Melville's poem echo the relentless clash of combat.

Bibliography: Adler; Boatner; Cohen, *Poems;* Faust; Garner; Leo B. Levy, "Hawthorne, Melville, and the *Monitor," American Literature* 37 (March 1965): 33–40; NN 11; Warren.

V

V., L. A. In "Fragments from a Writing Desk," in No. 1, he is the author of a letter from the village of Lansingburgh to his friend M— in which he describes three lovely young women; in No. 2, he is the man who follows the bearer of a letter signed Inamorata, only to discover in a villa in the woods that the peerlessly beautiful woman is deaf and dumb.

Van. In *Omoo,* he is a quiet old Finnish sailor who, at one point, truthfully predicts that within three weeks few of his mates will remain aboard the *Julia.* He signs the round-robin.

Vanderbilt, Cornelius (1794–1877). Steamboat and railroad promoter and financier. Born in Port Richmond, Staten Island, New York, he quit school (1805), worked on boats in New York harbors, accepted $100 from his mother to buy a harbor sailboat (1810), started a freight and passenger service between New York City and Staten Island, made money (1813) supplying New York forts during the War of 1812, and built a commercial fleet for seaboard commerce (from 1814). Selling out at a profit (1818), he moved to New Brunswick, New Jersey; worked for a steamboat captain named Aaron Gibbons handling passengers, freight, and mail; sued would-be monopolistic competition and won in court (1824) and added to Gibbons's fleet; and moved to New York to enter the steamboat business for himself (1829). Vanderbilt defeated Hudson River competitors, added routes from Long Island to Providence and Boston (1830s), built up his fleet of "floating palaces," and enjoyed racing his best vessels (1840s and later). A millionaire by the 1840s, Vanderbilt responded to the Gold Rush by expanding his transportation lines via Nicaragua to California (1850), bought controlling interests in various New York railroads (beginning 1857), sold his Atlantic fleet for $3 million at the outbreak of the Civil War (1861), was defeated in a notorious struggle with the infamous Daniel Drew, James Fisk, and Jay Gould for control of the Erie Railroad (1868), regrouped, consolidated (1869), and extended his railroad lines as far as Chicago. Surviving the Panic of 1873, Vanderbilt financed the building of Grand Central Station in New York City (1875). He achieved financial preeminance in part through bribery and blackmail, stock manipulation and stock watering, and a flagrant disregard of an uninformed public. He married and began domineering his cousin Sophia Johnson in 1813. A year after she died (1868), he married a young woman named Frank Armstrong Crawford. Vanderbilt and his first wife had eight daughters and three sons who survived to maturity. He left an estate in excess of $100 million. William Henry Vanderbilt, his third and favorite son, inherited 95 percent of his father's wealth and became a powerful railroad man himself.

In ''On the Sea Serpent,'' Vanderbilt is mentioned as one who is owed money by [Cave] Johnson, the postmaster general, and it is hinted that persons employed on explosion-prone steamboats and railroads such as Vanderbilt owns need not apply to work for Johnson.

Bibliography: Wayne Andrews, *The Vanderbilt Legend: The Story of the Vanderbilt Family, 1794–1940* (New York: Harcourt, Brace and Company, 1941).

Van der Blumacher, Tuenis (''Van''). In ''A Dutch Christmas up the Hudson in the Time of Patroons,'' he is a Christmas caller who evidently likes Katrina.

Van de Velde. The name of a family of seventeenth-century Dutch artists. The most celebrated are Willem van de Velde the Elder (1611–1693) and his son Willem van de Velde the Younger (1633–1707). Van de Velde the Elder specialized in painting sea battles. He recorded contemporary events. He made on-the-spot sketches of ships and battles in ink on white panel or canvas—sometimes while under fire in a small boat—and used them to create paintings in his studio later. His works are of historical value because they accurately show the design, shape, and rigging of specific ships in actions between Dutch and British vessels. He taught his son much of what he knew about painting. When after a lull the Anglo-Dutch War resumed (1672), both Van de Veldes went to England, resided in Greenwich, became court painters for King Charles II, the Duke of York, and King James II, and depicted the continuing war—often from the British point of view. An excellent example of the elder painter's work is *The Council of War before the Four-Day Battle, 10 June 1666.* Van de Velde the Younger also went to sea with the fleet and sketched details useful in making paintings later. His work is also important for its documentary value. Two of his best works are *The Cannon Shot* (c. 1660), delineating a man-of-war saluting a small ship in the middle distance, and *The Harbor of Amsterdam* (1686), in which the central ship, in front of dozens in the distance, is the former flagship of Maarten Harpertszoon van Tromp, the father of Cornelis Maarten-szoon van Tromp.*

In ''Marquis de Grandvin: At the Hostelry,'' a ''Van der Velde''—without further designation—is described as a dreamy painter, formerly a sailor, who reminisces about dead Van Tromp and De Reyter [Mikiel Adriaanszoon De Ruyter]. Van der Velde is then joshed by Douw. Melville had a collection of prints and engravings of works by several artists, including Van de Velde the Younger. Henry Fothergill Chorley in his review of *White-Jacket* (*Athenaeum*, 2 February 1850) compares Melville's marine descriptions to those of ''the magnificent artist . . . Vendervelde.''

Bibliography: The Art of the Van de Veldes: Paintings and Drawings by the Great Dutch Marine Artists and Their English Followers (London: National Maritime Museum, 1982); Madlyn Millner Kahr, *Dutch Painting in the Seventeenth Century* (New York: Harper & Row, 1978); Jakob Rosenberg et al., *Dutch Art and Architecture, 1600–1800,* 2d ed., rev. (London: Penguin Books, 1972); Wallace.

Van Dyck, Anthony (1599–1641). (Alternate forms of name: Vandyck, Van Dyke.) Dutch painter. He was born into a wealthy, devout merchant family in Antwerp. His mother died when he was eight years old. He was apprenticed to a painter (1609), painted a fine portrait (1613), displayed evidence of genius, and entered an Antwerp guild as a master (1618). He painted models for tapestry cartoons (1618), was an assistant to Peter Paul Rubens* on ceiling paintings for a Jesuit church in Antwerp (1620), and then began to move about restlessly. He went to London (1620–1621) and Italy (1621–1625?), where he sketched works by old masters, including Titian. In Antwerp again (1627–1632), Van Dyck called himself the painter of the Infanta Isabella (1630). In London again (1632–1634), he was knighted (1632) and given the first of many commissions by King Charles I for portraits of members of the royal family (1632, 1635–1640). He negotiated with King Philip IV of Spain for work (1640). In Paris, he sought the commission to create historical paintings for the Louvre, but Nicolas Poussin* was named instead (1640?). Van Dyck, who was energetic, refined, grace-ful, and generous, was also ostentatious, arrogant, and luxury loving. He employed many studio assistants and servants, gave lavish parties, and suffered from the gout. Gravely ill, he went to Paris (1641), returned to London, and died there. His body was interred at St. Paul's, where his tomb and remains perished in the 1666 London fire. Van Dyck had a mistress named Margaret Lemon and an illegitimate daughter by her, and then married Mary Ruthven, one of the queen's noble ladies-in-waiting, in 1639 (the couple had one daughter).

Though overshadowed in his lifetime by Rubens, Van Dyck was and is second to none as a painter. He transformed portrait painting, as may be seen in his paired *Portrait of a Man* and *Portrait of a Woman* (1618), *Lucas van Uffel* (1622, crafty), *A Genoese Noblewoman and Her Son* (c. 1626, meticulously harmonized), *Henry Percy,* 9th Earl of Northumberland (1632, wearily self-

assured), *Sir Endymion Porter and Van Dyck* (c. 1635, contrasting amused nobleman and courteous artist), *Charles I in Three Positions* (1636, as a pattern
for Gianlorenzo Bernini's *Charles I* marble bust [1637] but independently startling), and *Queen Henrietta Maria* in profile (1637). Van Dyck also painted
religious subjects (*Samson and Delilah* [1620] and *Saint Augustine in Ecstasy*
[1628]), mythological subjects (*Venus at the Forge of Vulcan* [1632] and *Cupid
and Psyche* [1640]; the artist's mistress may have posed for the nude Psyche),
and—most beautifully—children (*Three Eldest Children of Charles I* [1635]).
Van Dyck's works are astonishingly expressive, strong and vigorous, tender and
poetic, noble and humane, and often melancholy.

Melville saw some Van Dyck paintings in 1849 at Hampton Court when he was
first in and near London but in his journal merely notes that the pictures there include ''Vandique's'' (11 November). During his 1857 trip to Europe, Melville
saw Van Dyck's *Children of Charles I* in the Palazzo Madama in Turin and could
also have seen other Van Dyck works when he visited the Palazzo Rosso in Genoa
(10, 14 April). In ''Marquis de Grandvin: At the Hostelry,'' Melville mentions
Van Dyke [Van Dyck] as a painter who urges Franz [Frans] Hals to come to England to paint there, and also discusses the picturesque with him.

   Bibliography: NN 15; Arthur K. Wheelock, Jr., et al., *Anthony van Dyck* (New York:
Harry N. Abrams, 1990).

Vangi. In *Mardi,* he is a promising young legatee mentioned in Bardianna's
will.

Vangs, Captain. In *Typee,* he is the tyrannical, neglectful captain of the *Dolly,*
from which the narrator escapes while she is in the harbor of Nukuheva.

Van Lord, Mrs. In *Pierre,* this is a fictitious, deceased widow's name in a
German prince's proclamation, as imagined by Pierre Glendinning.

Van Tromp. In ''Marquis de Grandvin: At the Hostelry.'' *See* Tromp, Cornelis
Maartenszoon van.

Van Winkle, Mrs. Rip. In ''Rip Van Winkle's Lilac,'' she was Rip's shrewish
wife, now deceased.

Van Winkle, Rip. In ''Rip Van Winkle's Lilac,'' he is the Kattskill loafer who
returns to his rickety house and is confused when he finds a big lilac in front
of the door where a willow used to be. The lovely lilac now immortalizes him.

Varnopi. In *Mardi,* he is an agent sent with Zuma to the Mardian island of
Rafona by Donjalolo to gain information.

Varvy. In *Omoo,* he is an old hermit who pretends to be deaf and dumb. He keeps contraband liquor in old sheds near Taloo.

Vavona. In *Mardi,* he is a blind, mystical Mardian poet, much celebrated but thought by some to be obscure. He is described as sublime by Babbalanja in his conversation with King Abrazza.

Vedder, Elihu (1836–1923). Painter and illustrator. He was born in New York City into a Dutch family from Schenectady. He showed an interest in drawing from the time he was twelve years old, studied in Paris (1856) and then Florence (to 1861), and returned to New York penniless. Unfit for military service because of a permanently injured left arm and living in poverty, he supported himself by making commercial drawings of various sorts until he finished and exhibited several paintings on melancholy, fantastic subjects (1865). After becoming a member of the National Academy and of the Society of American Artists (1865), he returned to France (1865–1867) and then made his permanent residence in Italy. He worked in Rome and Perugia and on Capri, and occasionally he visited the United States. His numerous works are more notable for power, grave simplicity, and imaginative and abstract qualities, than for management of color or technical finish. His finest production is a series of more than fifty black-and-white illustrations for an 1884 edition of *The Rubáiyát of Omar Khayyám.* Vedder also painted murals and ceiling decorations for the mansion of Collis P. Huntington in New York (1893), a Bowdoin College building (1894), and the Library of Congress in Washington, D.C (1896–1897). Two of Vedder's most bizarre pictures are *Questioner of the Sphinx* (1863), showing a bald, skinny Arab with an ear to the stone lips of the enormous monument, and *Memory* (c. 1870), revealing a bodiless head darkly floating above a nightmarish landscape. Vedder married Elizabeth Caroline Beach Rosekrans of Glens Falls, New York, in 1869. The couple had three sons and a daughter. One son died in infancy, another in childhood, and the third in early adulthood. The daughter survived Vedder.

While he was still a struggling artist in New York, Vedder often saw Jane Jackson,* an ex-slave from the South, selling peanuts on Broadway, near his studio. Her combination of meekness, patience, resignation, and endurance challenged him, and he persuaded her to sit for him and also had her photographed. The result was a painting called *Jane Jackson, Formerly a Slave.* Melville saw it when it was exhibited at the National Academy in New York (April 1865) and was inspired to write " 'Formerly a Slave': An Idealized Portrait, by E. Vedder." Whether Melville ever met Vedder is uncertain. Regardless, Melville dedicated his 1891 *Timoleon* "To my countryman, Elihu Vedder" but died shortly before Vedder's letter of thanks could be delivered. Vedder published two books of poetry: *Miscellaneous Moods in Verse* (1914) and *Doubt and Other Things* (1922). His autobiography, entitled *The Digressions of "V." Written for His Own Fun and That of His Friends* (1890), is accurate, rambling, and sardonic. In it, Vedder reports that *The Cumaean Sibyl,* another painting of his (c. 1876), was also inspired by Jane Jackson. Perhaps he named it as he did because Melville in his poem calls the ex-slave "Sibylline."

Bibliography: David Jaffé, " 'Sympathy with the Artist': Elizabeth Melville and Elihu Vedder," *Melville Society Extracts* 81 (May 1990): 10–11; Regina Soria, *Elihu Vedder: American Visionary Artist in Rome (1836–1923)* (Rutherford, N.J.: Fairleigh Dickinson University Press, 1970).

Vee-Vee. In *Mardi,* he is King Media's boy dwarf.

Velazquez, Diego Rodriguez de Silva y (1599–1660). Spanish painter. He was born in Seville, was apprenticed to a local painter (1611), and developed into a master (1617), especially adept in depicting groups of ordinary people in naturalistic detail and in balanced combinations of light and shadow. Velazquez went to Madrid (1622), where he became the court painter (1623) and much later the quartermaster general of the household of King Philip IV and Queen Mariana (1652). He met Peter Paul Rubens* in Madrid (1628). A visit by Velazquez to Italy (1629–1631) resulted in *The Forge of Vulcan* (1630) and other works experimenting in lighter colors and more motion. Back in Madrid, he painted *Philip IV in Brown and Silver* (c. 1631) and several equestrian portraits. He returned to Italy (1649–1651), during which time he painted his fabulous portrait of Pope Innocent X (1650). He painted religious and mythological works, historical scenes, genre pictures, and portraits of royalty, courtiers, court functionaries, and dwarfs. His greatest works include *The Waterseller of Seville* (c. 1620), *Los Borrachos* ("The Drinkers," c. 1628), *The Count-Duke of Olivares on Horseback* (1634), *The Surrender of Breda* (1635, with magnanimous Spanish victor and calm Dutch vanquished), a portrait of Velazquez's assistant Juan de Pareja (1650), *Queen Mariana* (1653), and *Las Meninas* ("The Maids of Honor," 1656), which features the Infanta Margarita, her attendants (including two dwarfs), a dog, and the artist himself erect before a large canvas and staring at the king and queen, who are seen only in a back-wall mirror reflection so bedimmed as to seem prophetic. Velazquez married Doña Juana de Miranda in 1618 (the couple had two daughters).

It is a pity that Melville never saw *Las Meninas,* a phenomenal masterpiece. It is remarkable that, although Melville when he was in Rome visited the Doria Pamfili palace and made a journal entry concerning several paintings in it, he did not comment on Velazquez's *Innocent X* there (10 March 1857). In his "Marquis de Grandvin: At the Hostelry," Melville mentions Velasques as a quiet and sedate painter.

Bibliography: Dale Brown, *The World of Velázquez* (Amsterdam: Time-Life Books, 1969); NN 15.

Velluvi, Queen. In *Mardi,* she is Donjalolo's third-night queen.

"Venice" (1891). Poem, in *Timoleon.* The poet suggests that the erection of Venice was accomplished by a combination of the "Pantheist energy" of coral, creating reefs, and of architects, creating with marble.

Bibliography: Cohen, *Poems;* NN 11; Shurr; Stein; Warren.

Ver. In "The Old Fashion," this is the eternally true spirit of spring and vital renewal.

Verbi. In *Mardi,* he is a critic who, according to Babbalanja, denounced Lombardo's *Koztanza* for having "a superfluous comma." Lombardo paid no attention to him. The name Verbi has to do with verbs and, by extension, the treatment of words.

Bibliography: Wright.

Vere, Captain. In *Billy Budd,* Captain Edward Fairfax Vere's distant senior relative, also a naval officer.

Vere, The Honorable Edward Fairfax, Captain ("Ed," "Starry"). In *Billy Budd,* Vere is the short, bookish, stern, courageous captain of the *Bellipotent.* Now about forty years old, Vere is experienced, disciplined, and learned, also refined and occasionally dreamy. When Billy Budd kills John Claggart, Captain Vere has him arrested and charged with murder, convenes a drum-head court, persuades its members to find Billy guilty, and hangs him. Mortally wounded in combat later, Vere dies with Billy's name on his lips. Captain Vere is one of the most enigmatic, ambiguously drawn characters in all of Melville's works.

Bibliography: Richard A. Hocks, "Melville and 'The Rise of Realism': The Dilemma of History in *Billy Budd," American Literary Realism 1870–1910* 26 (Winter 1994): 60–81; Edwin Haviland Miller, *Melville* (New York: George Braziller, 1975); Michael Paul Rogin, *Subversive Genealogy: The Politics and Art of Herman Melville* (New York: Alfred A. Knopf, 1983); Thomas J. Scorza, *In the Time before Steamships: Billy Budd, the Limits of Politics, and Modernity* (DeKalb: Northern Illinois University Press, 1979); Brook Thomas, "The Legal Fictions of Herman Melville and Lemuel Shaw," *Critical Inquiry* 11 (September 1984): 24–51.

Veronese, Paolo (1528–1588). (Real name: Paolo Calieri.) Italian painter. He was born in Verona. His father was a stonecutter. Young Calieri, soon called Il Veronese, studied painting (from 1541) under Antonio Badili, his uncle, won a competition in Mantua, and executed villa frescoes in Castelfranco (1551). He went to Venice (1553), where he was influenced by Titian* and Tintoretto.* Veronese obtained commissions for work in churches, government buildings, and villas (from 1555). He probably went to Rome for a time and thereafter was active back in Venice (from 1562), where he died, not long after having declined an invitation from King Philip II of Spain to help decorate the Escorial. Veronese's most striking paintings are enormous canvases crowded with richly colored figures, often almost magically foreshortened and set in front of and amid well-balanced classical architectural elements. His most memorable works, resembling dramatic tableaux, are *The Feast in the House of Simon the Pharisee* (c. 1560, oddly separated left and right by a dog and a vista into the distance), *The Pilgrims of Emmaus* (c. 1560), *The Marriage at Cana* (1563, 32 feet by 22 feet and containing more than a hundred figures), *The Family of Darius before Alexander* (c. 1570), and *Feast of the House of Levi* (1573, with superbly balanced groups beneath three precisely drawn arches). Veronese executed mythological scenes, Holy Family groups, pictures of saints, depictions of historical events, and portraits. He married his cousin, Badili's daughter Elena, in 1566. The couple had one daughter and four sons. Veronese was survived by two sons.

During his first European trip, Melville saw at Versailles what in his journal he called "Titan overthrown by thunderbolts etc." (6 December 1849). This painting was Veronese's retitled *Jupiter Smiting the Vices* (1554, now in the Louvre). During his second European trip, Melville could have seen some paintings by Veronese when he visited the Palazzo Rosso in Genoa (14 April 1857). In Melville's collection of engravings was one of a work by Veronese. In "Marquis de Grandvin: At the Hostelry," Melville describes Paola of Verona as a genial, richly arrayed painter who urges Douw to visit Venice.

Bibliography: Mrs. Arthur Bell, *Paolo Veronese* (London: George Newnes, 1904); NN 15; William R. Rearick, *The Art of Paolo Veronese, 1528–1588* (Washington, D.C.: National Gallery of Art, 1988); Wallace.

"The Vial of Attar" (1924). Poem, in *Weeds and Wildings,* as part of the section entitled "As They Fell." (Character: Lesbia.) The poet says that when Lesbia died, her "hopeless" lover wept hot tears into a vial. But when the poet's rose dies and goes to "the sepulchre of snows," the attar reminds him of the perished bloom. However, he admits, "There *is* nothing like the bloom."

Bibliography: Shurr, Stein.

Victor. In *Omoo,* he is a knavish adventurer from Marseilles on whose premises the outraged Tahitians find some liquor. Their confiscating it precipitates an incident which Admiral [Abel Aubert Dupetit] Thouars uses to his political advantage.

Victor, The. In "Magnanimity Baffled," he is a soldier who generously tries to shake the hand of his defeated enemy, only to find him dead.

"The Victor of Antietam (1862)" (1866). Poem, in *Battle-Pieces.* (Characters: [General Thomas J.] Stonewall [Jackson], [General Robert E.] Lee, [General George B.] McClellan, [General John] Pope.) When the government called on McClellan to lead, "plaudit[s] ran" through the ranks. But it is not always possible to distinguish between a delayed achiever and a "floundering ne'er-do-well";

so, after the Seven Days, a pall fell and McClellan was relieved of his command. Recalled again, he saved Pope and repulsed Lee at Antietam: "Only Antietam could atone." Assigned elsewhere yet again, McClellan was not supported at Alexandria. His soldiers still love him, and thinning ranks of his comrades drink to his health. Melville praises McClellan here for his accomplishments, does not criticize him for his alleged shortcomings, but uniquely censures the administration in Washington: "The leadsmen quarrelled in the bay; / Quills thwarted swords; divided sway."

　　Bibliography: Garner, NN 11, Shurr.

"View of the Barnum Property" (1847). Article attributed to Melville, published anonymously in *Yankee Doodle** (31 July 1847). (Characters: [P. T.] Barnum, [Antonio Lopez de] Santa-Anna, Tom Thumb, Yankee Doodle.) Thanks to Yankee Doodle's artist, who paid 25¢ to enter Barnum's American Museum and then made a stereotype on wood showing its monstrosities, we can see all by buying his picture for a mere sixpence.

Viking, The. In *Mardi. See* Jarl.

Vine. In *Clarel,* Vine is a curious, ambiguous, withdrawn pilgrim. He is evidently a writer or painter. He makes the acquaintance of Clarel and Nehemiah at the Sepulcher of Kings in Jerusalem. Vine, "a fountain sealed," is aesthetically sensitive and highly moral—if quietly so. Melville's portrayal of the middle-aged Vine as gifted, sensitive, jibing, reclusive, occasionally capricious, and seemingly serene but perhaps also frightened may owe much to his assessment of his friend Nathaniel Hawthorne.*

　　Bibliography: NN 12; Hershel Parker, "The Character of Vine in Melville's *Clarel,*" *Essays in Arts and Sciences* 15 (June 1986): 91–113.

Viner. In *Omoo,* he is a former shipmate of John Jermin. When after fifteen years the two meet again in the harbor of Papeetee, they become convivial. Viner signs as third mate aboard the *Julia,* of which Jermin is the first officer.

Vineyarder, The. In *Omoo,* he is the tall, robust captain of the *Leviathan.* He signs the narrator aboard at Taloo but refuses to take Dr. Long Ghost on as well.

Virginian, A. In "Hawthorne and His Mosses," this is the mask which Melville—saying that he is spending July in Vermont—assumes when he praises Nathaniel Hawthorne as a superb American author.

Viscaya, Manuel. In "Benito Cereno," he is a boatswain's mate thrown overboard alive with Roderigo Hurta from the *San Dominick* during the slave revolt.

Viscount. In *White-Jacket,* he is a dark-skinned courtier who dances attendance upon Pedro II aboard the *Neversink.*

Vivia. In *Pierre,* this is the name of the author-hero about whom Pierre Glendinning writes when he is at the Apostles.

Vivo. In *Mardi,* he is a sophist paraphrased by Babbalanja.

Voluto. In *Mardi,* he is an authority on amber cited by Mohi.

Volvoon, Professor Monsieur. In *Pierre,* he is a philosophical lecturer whom Charles Millthorpe accompanies.

Vondendo. In *Mardi,* he is an authority on amber cited by Mohi.

Voyages by Melville. *See* Sea voyages by Melville.

Voyo. In *Mardi,* he is a dead subject whose cunning King Peepi has inherited.

W

W—. In "Fragments from a Writing Desk," he is a mutual friend of L.A.V. and M—.

Wahabee, A. In *Clarel,* he is an evil Mohammedan whom Agath the Timoneer smuggled aboard *The Peace of God* so as to enable him to avoid the plague. But the Wahabee accidentally wrecked the ship because his sea chest contained blades that turned the compass.

Wallace, Lew (1827–1905). (Full name: Lewis Wallace.) Soldier, author, and diplomat. Wallace was born in Brookville, Indiana. When his widowed father was elected governor of Indiana (1837), he moved with his son to Indianapolis. Young Wallace reported Indiana House of Representatives news for the Indianapolis *Daily Journal* (1844–1845) and studied law in his father's office. He served as a lieutenant during the Mexican War (1846–1848), passed the bar (1849), practiced law, became a prosecuting attorney (1851–1853), worked in Crawfordsville (1853–1857), and served in the state senate (1857–1861). Because of earlier outstanding state militia work, he became a Union colonel at the onset of the Civil War. He saw action and was promoted to brigadier general (1861), fought on the second day at Shiloh (6 April 1862), and after commanding a division of 10,000 men during the successful attack on Fort Donelson (13–15 April) was promoted to major general. He displeased General Henry W. Halleck, his superior, but was defended by both President Abraham Lincoln* and General Ulysses S. Grant* (1862). Wallace helped defend Cincinnati (1863) and Washington, D.C., against Confederate General Jubal A. Early* (1864). After the war, Wallace sat on the courts-martial that tried Lincoln's alleged assassins and tried Henry Wirz, the Andersonville Prison commandant (1865).

Wallace, who vacillated in military, legal, and political work, was appointed governor of New Mexico territory (1878–1881; he is famous for negotiating with Billy the Kid) and was minister to Turkey (1881–1885). Meanwhile, Wallace had been developing his literary career. He published *The Fair God; or, the Last of the 'Tzins: A Tale of the Conquest of Mexico* (1873), *Ben-Hur: A Tale of the Christ* (1880), *The Prince of India; or, Why Constantinople Fell* (1893), and other works in prose and poetry; then came a posthumously issued autobiography (1906). Wallace married Susan Arnold Elston of Crawfordsville in 1852 (the couple had one surviving son).

In "Donelson (February, 1862)," Melville names Lew Wallace as a Union officer who participated in the siege of Donelson.

Bibliography: Irving McKee, *"Ben-Hur" Wallace: The Life of General Lew Wallace* (Berkeley: University of California Press, 1947).

Wang Taou. In "On the Chinese Junk," he is mentioned as the emperor of China. He writes to Doodle, king of the Yankees. (Wang Taou is also called Taou Kwang.)

Warbler, The. In *Mardi. See* Yoomy.

Washington, George (1732–1799). Revolutionary War general and first president of the United States. Washington was born in Westmoreland County, Virginia. He was privately educated, did surveying work (1748–1749), inherited Mount Vernon (1752), was involved in military actions against the French (1753–1758), married the widow Martha Custis (1759), and retired with her to Mount Vernon. Washington entered the Virginia political scene in opposition to the British colonial policy in America—first in the Virginia House of Burgesses (1759–1774) and then as a member of the First Continental Congress and the Second Continental Congress (1774–1775). He was selected to command the Continental armies during the American Revolution (1775–1783). Home again, he was asked to preside at a federal convention in Philadelphia (1787), where he was chosen president; he was reelected and continued to serve in that office (1789–1797).

In *Israel Potter,* General Washington is identified as the leader of the American Revolutionary forces whose taking of command in July 1775, after the Battle of Bunker Hill, Israel Potter witnesses. In "The Cincinnati," Melville mentions that Washington is the General-President of the Society of the Cincinnati.

Bibliography: James Thomas Flexner, *Washington: The Indispensable Man* (Boston: Little, Brown and Company, 1974).

Waterford, The Marquis of. In *Redburn,* he is presumably a madcap acquaintance of Harry Bolton in London.

Watteau, Antoine (1684–1721). French painter. He was born in Valenciennes. His father was a well-to-do but alcoholic tradesman and householder. Young Watteau took a few art lessons and then avoided military service by going afoot to Paris (c. 1702), where he copied paintings by others and developed his own creativity in his free time. Jean Mariette, an engraver and print dealer, became his first patron; Claude Gillot, a stage-set designer, his second (c. 1705). Through them, the sickly, shy, and lonely Watteau met literary and theatrical people. He worked with Claude Audrian, a designer of decorative ornaments (c. 1707–1709). Watteau gained popularity by painting exquisite war and camp scenes on copper. He exhibited at the Académie Royale and was made an academician (1712). Another patron, Pierre Crozat, gave fêtes where the artist could observe high society in all its hothouse finery and hypocrisy, which many of his paintings mirror. His restrained, mincing figures seem aware that their fancy days are numbered. After a trip to England, perhaps in search of medical treatment, Watteau returned to Paris, where he died of tuberculosis. His paintings are refined, sensitive, and sad, but never quite profound. His best ones include *Satire on Physicians* (1709, several doctors scaring one patient, in a theatrically painted outdoor setting), *The Bivouac* (c. 1710, pastoral setting), *Actors of the Comédie Française* (c. 1712, five quite different performers, mostly uneasy in appearance), *The Hardships of War* and *The Halt* (both 1715, showing weary, dreary soldiers and civilians, theatrically posed), *Savoyard with a Marmot* (1716, sadly grinning tramp), *An Embarrassing Proposal* (c. 1716, dramatically disagreeing couple with three attendants, all outdoors), *La Boudeuse* (c. 1718, high-eyebrowed, seated woman, evidently disliking what reclining man is saying), *Mezzetin* (1718, frustrated lover), *Rest on the Flight to Egypt* (1719, Holy Family with dove and swirling angel heads), and his masterpiece, *Gersaint Signboard* (1721, done as outdoor shop sign, showing interior of friend's gallery).

Melville had a collection of prints and engravings of works by several artists, including Watteau. In ''Marquis de Grandvin: At the Hostelry,'' Watteau is identified as a painter who is courteously addressed by [Paolo] Veronese.

Bibliography: Mikhail Guerman, *Antoine Watteau,* trans. Ian McGowan (New York: Harry N. Abrams, 1980); Donald Posner, *Antoine Watteau* (Ithaca, N.Y.: Cornell University Press, 1984); Wallace.

''The Way-Side Weed'' (1924). Poem, in *Weeds and Wildings,* as part of the section entitled ''The Year.'' The poet wonders whether the charioteer from the villa is aware that when he cuts goldenrods by the side of the road with his whip he is insulting the sceptre of ''October's god.''

Bibliography: Shurr, Stein.

Weaver. In *The Confidence-Man,* this is the name of a Virginia family that migrated with their cousins the Wrights to Kentucky but were treacherously killed with them by the perfidious Indian Mocmohoc.

"The Weaver" (1891). Poem, in *Timoleon*. The poet depicts a lonely, impoverished, pinch-faced artisan in "a mud-built room" relentlessly weaving a shawl "for Arva's shrine." Melville uses the word "Arva's" twice in the poem. Originally, his first "Arva's" was "Mecca's"; his second, "Mecca's" and then "Marva's." Merwa—sometimes spelled "Marva"—is a hill near Mecca. The poem has been subject to a variety of interpretations.

Bibliography: NN 11, Shurr, Stein.

Wedge, Dr. In *White-Jacket,* he is the *Malay* surgeon, who with others confers with Dr. Cadwallader Cuticle when that expert operates on the fatally wounded foretopman.

Weed, Thurlow (1797–1882). Journalist, lobbyist, and politician. He was born in Cairo, New York, but soon moved with his parents to Catskill (1799). After very little schooling, Weed worked in a blacksmith's shop, in a printing office, and on Hudson River boats (1806–1808). The family moved to Cortland (1808) and then Onondaga, and Weed worked for printers there and nearby (from 1811). During the War of 1812, he saw brief military service (1813), after which his career took off. He was foreman of the Albany *Register* (1817), did newspaper writing, failed as a newspaper publisher in both Norwich and Manlius (1818–1822), became an editorial writer for the Rochester *Telegraph* (1822–1824), was elected as a Whig to the New York Assembly (1825–1829), bought the *Telegraph* (1825), and sold it in order to publish the *Anti-Masonic Enquirer* (1826). While in Albany he published the influential Albany *Evening Journal* (1830–1863). Disruptions following the Panic of 1837 enabled Weed to help secure the elections of William H. Seward as New York governor (beginning 1839) and William Harrison as president (1841). Known as the "Dictator" and the "Whig oracle," Weed became a vote-getting and patronage-dispensing party manager, was sympathetic toward antislavery advocates, but grew critical of the tactics of some abolitionists. His support of Zachary Taylor* bore fruit after that man was elected president (1848); however, after Taylor's death, his successor Millard Fillmore's acceptance of the Compromise of 1850 caused the breakup of the Whig Party, and Weed took a rest abroad (1852). Home again, he joined the Republican Party (1854), supported John C. Frémont's unsuccessful bid for the presidency (1856), and failed in his own bid to be nominated for that office, which was won by Abraham Lincoln* (1860). Weed's management of Seward's campaign against Lincoln only helped Lincoln. During the Civil War, Lincoln accepted advice from Weed, sent him to England and France to improve relations after the *Trent* affair (1861–1862), and found him to be of help in defeating the bid by George B. McClellan* to become president (1864). By this time, Weed was less influential, had sold his *Evening Journal,* and had begun to reside in New York City (1863). He published *Letters from Europe and the West Indies* (1866) and edited the *Commercial Advertiser* (1867). Weed married Catherine Ostrander in 1818 (the couple had three daughters, one son, and an adopted orphaned daughter). Widowed since 1858, at his death he was survived by his own daughters, including Harriet Ann Weed, who edited and published his incomplete but useful autobiography (1883). Weed's grandson, Thurlow Weed Barnes, published *Memoir of Thurlow Weed* (1884).

Weed was a Melville family friend. His autobiography reports that Melville's distant cousin Hun Gansevoort* told him that Melville's first cousin Guert Gansevoort* told Hun in Philadelphia (1842) about his reluctance to render a guilty verdict in connection with the court-martial aboard the *Somers.* With a flat denial of Greene's veracity, Weed reprinted (*Evening Journal,* 3 July 1846) the statement by Richard Tobias Greene* (Buffalo *Commercial Advertiser,* 1 July 1846) that he was the true-life original of Toby in *Typee.* Evidently Melville met with Weed on 4 July and persuaded him to print an iffy retraction (6 July), after which Weed's *Journal* reprinted (13 July) Greene's longer comment (*Advertiser,* 11 July) on his experiences with Melville. Weed's enthusiastic review of *Redburn* (17 November 1849, *Journal*) helped its sales. John Truman in *The Confidence-Man* may be in part Melville's satirical portrait of Weed, who probably never read that novel and therefore did not see any ridicule of himself therein. Melville asked his uncle Peter Gansevoort (1788–1876),* who knew Weed and Seward, to use his influence with those two politicians when Melville was seeking a consular appointment (1861).

Bibliography: Leyda; NN 14; Trimpi; Glyndon G. Van Deusen, *Thurlow Weed: Wizard of the Lobby* (Boston: Little, Brown and Company, 1947).

Weeds and Wildings (1924). (Full title: *Weeds and Wildings with a Rose or Two.*) Collection of poems, to be found in *The Works of Herman Melville,* preceded by "Clover Dedication to Winnefred." In the dedication, the poet says that he and Winnie both like hardy red clover and white clover and that, although they have rarely found four-leaf clovers, he luckily found one on the fourth day of the first month of their marriage, forty-four years ago. Cows, farmers, and bees find clover pleasant. The poet used to bring clover to Winnie in their old farm home, during the summer, fall, and even winter seasons. He now dedicates these "aftergrowth" poems to her as he approaches his "terminating season." The poems then follow, with individual works grouped under the following titles: "As They Fell," "Rip Van Winkle's Lilac," "This, That and the Other," and "The Year."

Wellingborough, Senator. In *Redburn,* he is Wellingborough Redburn's great-uncle, who died while he was a member of the Congress in the days of the old Constitution.

Wellington, Arthur Wellesley, The First Duke of (1769–1852). British general and statesman. He was born in Dublin, entered the army (1787), was an Irish member of Parliament (1790–1795), was a division commander in the war against Tipu Sahib (1799), and was the supreme military and political commander in the Deccan (to 1805). Back in England, he became Irish secretary (1807–1809). He was successful as a lieutenant general in the Peninsular War

(1808–1814), was made a duke, was appointed ambassador to France (1814), and represented England at the Congress of Vienna (1814–1815). He was a central figure in the defeat of Napoleon* at Waterloo (1815), commanded the army of occupation in France (1815–1818), sat in the cabinet as ordnance general (1818–1827), represented England in Vienna again (1822), and was twice appointed commander in chief (1827–1828, 1842–1852), being prime minister in between (1828–1830). He supported the Catholic Emancipation Act only to avoid civil war in Ireland (1829), opposed the Reform Bill (1831–1832), and served under Prime Minister Sir Robert Peel (1834–1835, 1841–1846) as his foreign secretary (1834–1835) and as commander in chief (1841–1846). As a final service, Wellington organized the army to protect London from Chartist violence (1848). Wellington married Catherine Pakenham in 1806. The couple had two sons during a generally uncongenial marriage. His wife died in 1831.

Melville mentions the Duke of Wellington in two works. In *Redburn,* Redburn thinks Harry Bolton may take him to peep at the heroic Duke in Apsley House, in London's Hyde Park. In "Poor Man's Pudding and Rich Man's Crumbs," he is one of the aristocratic guests at the Guildhall Banquet in London following the Battle of Waterloo.

Bibliography: Elizabeth Longford, *Wellington: The Years of the Sword* (New York: Harper & Row, 1969).

Wen. In *Pierre,* he is an affected tailor turned publisher who, with his partner Wonder, offers to publish Pierre Glendinning's writings at Pierre's own expense.

"When Forth the Shepherd Leads the Flock" (1924). Poem, in *Weeds and Wildings,* as part of the section entitled "The Year."

White, Deacon. In "I and My Chimney," he is one of the neighbors of the narrator, who likes the deacon because he is old.

White Jacket. In *White-Jacket,* he is the narrator, a common seaman aboard the *Neversink,* commanded by Captain Claret. White Jacket joins Jack Chase's maintop crew and his mess; admires Lieutenant Mad Jack, Lemsford, Tawney, and John Ushant; goes ashore on liberty at Rio de Janeiro; despises Bland and fears the loathsome Articles of War; helps keep watch over the dying Shenly; falls from the weather topgallant yardarm and nearly drowns; and disembarks at Norfolk, Virginia. Many of White Jacket's experiences aboard the *Neversink* are fictional adaptations of Melville's own experiences as a sailor aboard the U.S. frigate *United States* (1843–1844).

White-Jacket (1850). (Full title: *White-Jacket; or, The World in a Man-of-War.*) Novel. (Characters: Marquis d'Acarty, Antone, Baldy, Dr. Bandage, Bill, Black Bet, Bland, Lieutenant Blink, Blue-Skin, Boat Plug, Bob, Baron [Waldemar] de Bodisco, Boombolt, Ned Brace, Lieutenant Bridewell, Broadbit, Tom Brown,

Ben Browns, Brush, Bungs, Joe Bunk, Candy, Captain [John S.] Cardan [Carden], Chase, Jack Chase, Claret, Claret, Captain Claret, Lord [Thomas] Cochrane, Admiral [Sir Edward] Codrington, Coffin, Corporal Colbrook, Coleman, the Commodore, Count, Dr. Cadwallader Cuticle, Cylinder, Dick Dash, Adolphus Dashman, Captain [Stephen] Decatur, Dick, Dobs, Patrick Flinegan, Flute, Frank, Gammon, Grummet, Guinea, Joe Hardy, Hodnose, Jack Jewel, Jim, John, King John VI, Jonathan, Frank Jones, Ned Knowles, "Happy Jack" Landless, Leggs, Lemsford, Long-locks, Lieutenant Mad Jack, Mandeville, Queen Maria [II], Mark, Marquis, May-Day, William Julius Mickle, Montgomery, Nord, Old Coffee, Old Combustibles, Old Revolver, Old Yarn, Chief Osceola, Paper Jack, Dr. Patella, Don Pedro II, the Pelican, Pert, Peter, Peter the Wild Boy, Pierre, Pills, Pounce, Priming, the Professor, Quoin, Captain Rash, Raveling, Red Hot Coal, Ringbolt, Ringrope, Rose-Water, Dr. Sawyer, Scriggs, Scrimmage, Seafull, Seignior Seignioroni, Lieutenant Selvagee, Don Sereno, Shakings, Shanks, Shenly, Shenly, Mrs. Shenly, Shippy, the Marquis of Silva, Slim, Sneak, Stetson, Stribbles, Sunshine, Tawney, Thrummings, Tom, Tomasita, Tubbs, John Ushant, Viscount, Dr. Wedge, White Jacket, Williams, Wooloo, Yellow Torch.)

The narrator, a sailor aboard the American naval vessel *Neversink,* needs a jacket; so he makes one out of white duck and is promptly dubbed White Jacket. He describes the activities of the various groups into which the 500-man crew are divided: starboard and larboard watches on three decks, sheet-anchor men, after-guardsmen, waisters, and holders. He discusses various ranks, from commodore and captain to other officers and so on down to helpless midshipmen. He admires Jack Chase, his "noble" first captain of the top who is much valued by Captain Claret. The quarterdeck officers are the dainty, languid Selvagee and Mad Jack, who is alcoholic and rough but admirably able. For friends, White Jacket has Lemsford, a nervous poet; Quoin, a wild gunner; Nord, an erudite but hermit-like fellow; Williams, a happy Yankee, once a peddler and teacher; Old Coffee, an African-American cook whose assistants are May-Day, Rose-Water, and Sunshine; Shanks, the skinny cook for Chase's rousing mess, which White Jacket is fortunately allowed to join; Wooloo, the Commodore's Polynesian servant; Mr. Pert, a disliked middy, unlike Boat Plug, a pleasant one; Old Revolver, the arms yeoman; and Old Combustibles, the man in charge of the gunpowder.

White Jacket laments the absence of grog, criticizes the dangers of maneuvers, praises the crew's collective skills, and describes their Fourth of July theatrical entitled *The Old Wagon Paid Off* and starring the histrionic Chase. As the *Neversink* approaches Cape Horn, the weather turns bad. The job of furling sails and hauling braces in snowy weather is difficult. The men are ordered on deck to witness the flogging of four seamen. A bully named John started a fight, and three others—Antone, Mark, and young Peter—joined in rather than report it as required. When Peter asks for mercy, Claret replies, "I would not forgive God Almighty!" The incident causes Melville to digress on the practice of flogging. He also digresses on the subjects of chaplains at sea, an anomaly because they preach over their audiences' heads and share in bounties paid for enemies killed. The ship snares some excellent port floating in barrels, which Claret commandeers but soon doles out to the happy crew.

When the *Neversink* anchors in the harbor of Rio de Janeiro, the ranking officers doll up in their fanciest uniforms and White Jacket whiles away his free time in the ship's library. He digresses on other diversions, which include tattooing, walking on deck, daydreaming and napping, polishing brass, playing checkers, and illicit gambling. He adverts to the subject of smuggling liquor aboard ship after shore leave. Sergeant-at-arms Bland did so in boxes ordered to his mess, sold bottles to sailors, flogged them when they were caught drunk by the officers, and was informed on and demoted; however, he took his punishment so bravely that he was soon reinstated. Ships in the squadron compete in sail-furling contests. During one such game, Baldy, a pleasant little Scot, falls to the deck and is crippled for life. White Jacket tries without success to auction his clumsy garment. Rumors of imminent combat cause the men to fear being killed or maimed, whereas some officers hope for war as a means of promotion. In the presence of the epauletted commodore, Chase eloquently pleads to Claret for liberty for the men. They get into Rio, go wild, and return worn out. One day Don Pedro II, the king of Brazil, visits the *Neversink,* resplendent in coat, pantaloons, chapeau, jewels, and feathers. More incidents follow. Mandeville, once an officer, is broken for habitual drunkenness, and a former fellow officer has him flogged for being drunk yet again. A common seaman named Frank averts his eyes when his brother, an officer, approaches the *Neversink* in a supply ship—this because differences in rank are so significant. A brawny foretopman, eager for liberty, violates orders, tries to swim ashore, and is shot in the thigh by a deck sentry. The ship's surgeon, Cadwallader Cuticle, amputates the wounded limb; the operation is brilliant, but the patient dies and is buried ashore.

The *Neversink* leaves port, races an English frigate and a French ship, but slips behind in the darkness. Chase recites the *Lusiads* and contends that he might have been another Homer but for circumstances. The men frolic on deck. Suddenly Claret accuses White Jacket of being absent during maneuvers and orders him flogged, but he is saved when Chase and a marine corporal named Colbrook defend him. On the first Sunday of every month, the men must listen as the deadly Articles of War are read aloud; also every Sunday they are ordered to worship God. The narrator relays the account of an old African-American sailor named Tawney, who was impressed off a merchantman and forced to man guns of the British *Macedonian* during the War of 1812. Chase tells of his experiences during the Battle of Navarino. When *Neversink* crew members are ailing, they go to the noisy, airless sick bay, where they are tended by Cuticle, Pelican, his assistant, and a steward nicknamed Pills. One patient, Shenly from New Hampshire, is hovered over by his mates but dies in the foul sick bay, is sewed inside a fragment of old sail, and is committed to the deep.

Near home now, Claret orders all beards shaven off or at least trimmed in a tidy manner. John Ushant, a philosophically bearded sailor sixty years of age, refuses, is chained in the brig overnight and flogged in the morning, but he is then allowed to keep his whiskers. This incident reminds the narrator of incidents involving floggings at sea, other punishments, and the fact that discipline is maintained because the seamen and the marines and the officers all hate each other. White Jacket digresses on impressment, slaves and foreigners aboard American vessels, and smoking and gossiping at sea. Off Virginia, White Jacket falls at midnight from the weather topgallant yardarm into the yeasty sea, cuts himself out of his white jacket, and is saved. He bids Chase farewell at Norfolk. The men scatter. Melville likes to remember his ship, still brooding at sea and plunging into the darkness. He concludes that life resembles a voyage in a vessel with sealed orders and bound for home.

Melville was distressed by the popular and critical failure of *Mardi;* he therefore quickly composed two simpler and more exciting narratives: *Redburn* and *White-Jacket.* He wrote the first in about three months; the second, in about two more. He was not pleased with either novel. He wrote to his father-in-law Lemuel Shaw* as follows: "[N]o reputation that is gratifying to me, can possibly be achieved by either of these books. They are two *jobs,* which I have done for money—being forced to it, as other men are to sawing wood. . . . So far as I am individually concerned, & independent of my pocket, it is my earnest desire to write those sort of books which are said to 'fail.'—pardon this egotism" (6 October 1849).

In composing *White-Jacket,* Melville made use of memories of service aboard the American frigate *United States,* his imagination, and many publications. Several characters are based on real-life sailors Melville knew or read about. These include Baldy, Bungs, Jack Chase, the Commodore, Lemsford, Nord, the Professor, Old Combustibles, Shenly, Tawney, and Williams. The celebrated episode of White-Jacket's fall from the yardarm into the ocean derives not from personal experience but from a passage in *A Marine's Sketches . . . ,* by Nathaniel Ames (Providence, 1830). Other sources include *The Life and Adventures of John Nicol, Mariner* (1822), by John Nicol; *Life on Board a Man-of-War; Including a Full Account of the Battle of Navarino . . .* (1829); *Evils and Abuses in the Naval and Merchant Service, Exposed . . .* (1839), by William McNally; *Life in a Man-of-War; or, Scenes in "Old Ironsides" during Her Cruise to the Pacific* (1841); and *Thirty Years from Home; or, A Voice from the Main Deck . . .* (1843), by Samuel Leech. The name *Neversink* may derive from the name of the Navesink or Neversink Hills or Highlands, on the New Jersey coast; these highlands are mentioned in *Mardi.*

While he was in London (November 1849), Melville negotiated with British publishers. Richard Bentley* published *White-Jacket* (January 1850) and paid the author £200. It sold fewer than 400 copies (by March 1852), and Bentley lost money. Harpers & Brothers,* who had advanced Melville $500 (September 1849), published it in the United States (March 1850), sold 3,714 copies (by April 1851), and paid the author another $112. The generally favorable reviews, especially in England, should have triggered better sales. Melville followed

White-Jacket with *Moby-Dick,* which failed in large part at first, and then with *Pierre,* which was a popular and critical disaster. These "failures" undoubtedly contributed to the poor later sales of *White-Jacket,* which earned Melville only an additional $357 in the more than three decades that followed (to 1887).

Bibliography: Charles R. Anderson, "A Reply to Herman Melville's *White-Jacket* by Rear-Admiral Thomas O. Selfridge, Sr.," *American Literature* 7 (May 1935): 123–44; Kathleen E. Kier, "*White-Jacket's* Classical Oration," *Studies in the Novel* 23 (Summer 1991): 237–44; NN 5; Howard P. Vincent, *The Tailoring of Melville's White-Jacket* (Evanston, Ill.: Northwestern University Press, 1970); Wright.

Wilkes. In *Billy Budd,* he is one of Captain Vere's midshipmen.

Will. In "Bridegroom-Dick," he is a sailor in the wardroom mess recalled by Bridegroom Dick. The *Cumberland,* which Will was aboard, was later sunk by the *Merrimac,* on which his former shipmate Hal served.

Willi. In *Mardi,* he is King Normo's fool in a story by Babbalanja. Willi was ordered to go to a tree but was free to walk there on his feet or on his hands. He chose his hands, to show his free will, but then continued on his feet because he pretty much had to. Willi represents free will, limited though Melville regarded it.

William. In *Omoo,* he is an ill sailor in the Calabooza to whom Dr. Johnson sends some liniment, which William promptly drinks. William may be Bill "Liverpool" Blunt, who signs the round-robin.

William ("Bill," "Willie"). In *Omoo,* he is a runaway ship's carpenter. This "rosy-cheeked Englishman" enjoys a great deal of work at Taloo, but his three-year love for Lullee is unconsummated because of a law preventing whites from marrying natives. In real life, William eventually married Lullee, according to Edward T. Perkins, who later visited the islands and published *Na Motu; or, Reef-Rovings in the South Seas: A Narrative of Adventures at the Hawaiian, Georgian, and Society Islands* (1854) about his observations there.

Bibliography: Anderson.

William. In "To Major John Gentian, Dean of the Burgundy Club," he is a waiter at the Burgundy Club.

Williams. In *White-Jacket,* he is a former Yankee peddler and pedagogue, from Maine. White Jacket esteems his wit and jolly philosophy. Williams tries unsuccessfully to stimulate the bidding at auction for White Jacket's jacket. The model for Williams is probably Griffith Williams, who shipped the same day (August 1843) Melville did aboard the *United States,* which becomes the fictitious *Neversink.*

Bibliography: Leyda, NN 5.

Williamson, Lieutenant. In *Israel Potter,* he is an officer who grows suspicious of Israel Potter when the latter boards the frigate alone off the *Ariel.*

Willie. in "Stockings in the Farm-House Chimney," he is a lad depicted as waiting for Santa Claus.

Wilson. In *Omoo,* Consul Wilson's old, white-haired, saintly father. He lives at Point Venus, in Papeetee.

Wilson, Charles Burnett (1770–1857). British missionary. He sailed from England as a member of the London Missionary Society (1798), but his vessel was captured by the French (1799). He was repatriated via Lisbon (1799) and in due time got to Tahiti (1801). He served at Moorea (from 1808), returned to his mission at Huahine (1812), and during a voyage with Queen Pomare IV* and members of her party was blown off course and landed at Raiatea (1816), where he established a Christian mission. Wilson was placed in charge of a mission at Matavai (1818–1842). After a brief retirement there (1842–1844), he moved to Samoa (1844), where he died. Wilson married twice. He took a trip to Sydney, Australia, married there (1810), and returned with his wife to Moorea (1812). She died at Matavai (1818). He returned to Sydney, married a second time (1821), and went back to Tahiti (1821). Wilson had several children. One son was his father's assistant at Tahiti, where he had been born (1811); another, named Charles Burnett like his father, replaced George Pritchard* at Papeete as acting British consul (1842).

In *Omoo,* Melville describes Wilson as the small, pug-nosed acting British consul at Papeetee and makes him the friend of the despicable Captain Guy of the *Julia.* Wilson heard charges and took depositions in connection with the trouble in 1842 aboard the *Lucy Ann,* captained by his friend Henry Ventom, who was the model of Melville's Guy. According to an 1848 journal kept by Henry Augustus Wise, a naval lieutenant, Melville's disparagement of Wilson was accurate.

Bibliography: Anderson, Leyda, NN 2, O'Reilly and Teissier.

Wilt. In *Redburn,* he is a partner in Sampson & Wilt, Liverpool, on whom Redburn's father called back in 1808.

Winnefred ("Madonna of the Trefoil," "Winnie"). In "Clover Dedication to Winnefred," in *Weeds and Wildings,* she is the poet's beloved, who loves clover as he does and to whom he dedicates his poems. Her being Melville's wife is proved by his having penciled "Lizzie" beside the word "Winnefred."

Bibliography: Shurr.

Winnie. In "Clover Dedication to Winnefred," in *Weeds and Wildings. See* Winnefred.

Winsome, Mark. In *The Confidence-Man,* he is a blue-eyed, red-cheeked, mystical-looking transcendentalist about forty-five years of age. To Francis Goodman, Winsome describes Charles Arnold Noble as a Mississippi operator. Mark Winsome in several ways may resemble Ralph Waldo Emerson* in his relationship to Egbert, who in the novel is portrayed as Winsome's disciple.
   Bibliography: Egbert S. Oliver, ''Melville's Picture of Emerson and Thoreau in *The Confidence-Man,''* *College English* 8 (November 1946): 61–72; Trimpi.

Winwood, Ralph. In *Pierre,* he is a cousin of Pierre Glendinning's father, whose portrait—the one showing the subject as young and rakish—Winwood secretly painted and then gave to Dorothea Glendinning.

''The Wise Virgins to Madam Mirror'' (1947). Poem, in *Collected Poems of Herman Melville.* Supposedly wise young females tell Madam Mirror, an old, forlorn resident of the garret, that they feel sorry for her but cannot console her, since they are able to skip about and enjoy immortal youth. They see brides and grooms, whereas, since ''the elderly only grow old,'' Madam Mirror is preoccupied with death. This glassy-eyed mirror has ''a horrible way / Of distorting all objects'' and even turns the virgins' ''symmetric'' figures witchlike. So the young ones do not give ''a fig for *Reflections* when crookedly false!'' This poem should be paired with Melville's ''Madam Mirror.'' Both owe their inspiration in part to ''Monsieur Miroir'' by Nathaniel Hawthorne,* which also puns on the word ''reflection.''
   Bibliography: Shurr, Stein.

''Without Price.'' *See* ''Rosary Beads.''

Womonoo. In *Typee. See* Wormoonoo.

Wonder. In *Pierre,* he is an affected tailor turned publisher, who, with his partner Wen, offers to publish Pierre Glendinning's writings at Pierre's expense.

Wood. In *Redburn,* he is the part-owner of the Parkins & Wood warehouse in Liverpool, where Betsy Jennings and her three children starve to death.

Woodcock, Mrs. In *Israel Potter,* she is Squire John Woodcock's widow, whom Israel Potter terrifies when he marches past her dressed in her late husband's finest clothes.

Woodcock, Squire John. In *Israel Potter,* he is the elderly, pro-American British squire who with Rev. Mr. [John] Horne Tooke and James Bridges plots to use Israel Potter as a courier to Dr. [Benjamin] Franklin in Paris. Woodcock hides Potter in a secret room behind his large stone chimney but then dies of apoplexy. The name Charles Woodcocke appears in late eighteenth-century records of Brentford, England, where action involving Melville's Squire Woodcock transpires; also, New Brentford tax records indicate that he and John Horne Tooke held property together. The name J. Woodcock and the name Squire Woodcock both appear in Henry Trumbull's *Life and Remarkable Adventures of Israel R. Potter...* (1824), Melville's principal source for his novel.

Bibliography: Cohen, *Potter.*

Woodcocke, Charles. *See* Woodcock, Squire John.

Wooloo. In *White-Jacket,* he is the Commodore's sedate and earnest Polynesian servant who thinks that snow is flour, hailstones are glass beads, and raisins are bugs.

Worden, John Lorimer (1818–1897). Union naval officer. He was born in Westchester County, New York, became a midshipman (1835), and served long and well at sea. At the outbreak of the Civil War, he was sent on a mission to deliver papers to a Union ship off Florida (1861). He was arrested while trying to return north by train, was imprisoned for several months, and was then released (1861). He saw dramatic action during the Battle of Hampton Roads. The Confederate ironclad *Virginia* (formerly the U.S.S. *Merrimac*) sank the wooden Union man-of-war *Cumberland* and burned the *Congress* (8 March 1862). Lieutenant Worden, in command of the Union ironclad *Monitor,* engaged the enemy vessel (9 March). Worden had himself confined in a revolving turret amidships and directed an indecisive but valiant exchange—the first such battle in naval history. During the fight, he was partially blinded and had to hand over his command to his lieutenant. Congress voted Worden official thanks and he was steadily promoted—to commander (1862) and captain (1863). He commanded the steam frigate *Montauk,* another ironclad, in the blockade of Georgia and saw later action. After the war, he was superintendent at Annapolis (1869–1874) and retired as a rear admiral (1886). Melville praises Worden for his "honest heart of duty" in the poem "In the Turret (March, 1862)."

Bibliography: Boatner, Faust.

Wormoonoo (also Womonoo). In *Typee,* he is mentioned as a native whose property, like that of all other Typees, is respected by all.

Worth, William Jenkins (1794–1849). Soldier. He was born in Hudson, New York. After routine schooling, he clerked in a store until the War of 1812 began. He enlisted as a private, was promoted to lieutenant, became the aide-de-camp of General Winfield Scott,* saw action, was promoted to captain, was crippled by a severe leg wound at Lundy's Lane (July 1814), and was promoted to major.

He remained in the army, partly as commandant of cadets and infantry instructor at West Point (1820–1828), served elsewhere, and became a colonel (1838). For his part in engagements against Seminole Indians in Florida, he was promoted to brigadier general (1838). Fame and trouble followed. Worth was assigned to the army of occupation in Texas as second in command under General Zachary Taylor* (1845). During the Mexican War (1846–1848), Worth was in an almost unbelievable number of battles—at Palo Alto, Resaca de la Palma, Monterrey, Vera Cruz, Cerro Gordo, Churubusco, Molino del Rey, Chapultepec, Perote, Puebla, and Mexico City (1846–1847). Though courageous, energetic, and daring, Worth was also egotistical, impatient, petulent, and ruinously ambitious. He favored Manifest Destiny, sought to annex Mexico, wrote to William L. Marcy,* secretary of war, to this effect (1847), and considered running for president. Worth joined a cabal of officers who were critical of Scott and filed charges against him. When Scott demanded an accounting, Worth grew defiant, was arrested, and had to appear before a court of inquiry (1847, 1848). Once the affair had blown over, Scott placed Worth in command of the Department of Texas (1848), where he died of cholera a few months later. Worth married Margaret Stafford of Albany, New York, in 1818 (the couple had three daughters and one son).

In "To Major Jack Gentian, Dean of the Burgundy Club," General Will Worth is identified as an American Mexican War general whom Gentian knew personally.

Bibliography: Edward S. Wallace, *General John Jenkins Worth: Monterey's Forgotten Hero* (Dallas: Southern Methodist University Press, 1953).

Wright. In *The Confidence-Man,* this is the name of a Virginia family that migrated with their cousins the Weavers to Kentucky but were treacherously killed with them by the perfidious Indian Mocmohoc.

Wrong. In "Timoleon (394 B.C.)," this is the name which Timophanes calls himself.

Wymontoo-Hee ("Luff"). In *Omoo,* he is a stalwart native of the island of Hannamanoo who ships aboard the *Julia.* He soon becomes seasick. He signs the round-robin but remains aboard the ship.

Wynodo. In *Mardi,* he is a neighbor of Bardianna, mentioned in the philosopher's will.

X

X—. In *Billy Budd,* he is a probably fictitious friend of the author. The personality and the intellectual makeup of X— were baffling.

Xiki. In *Mardi,* he is the god Doleema's butler, in a story by Mohi concerning the isle of Maramma. Xiki javelined to death a reluctant sacrificial victim to Doleema.

Yambaio. In "Benito Cereno," he is an Ashantee slave who polishes hatchets during Captain Amasa Delano's visit aboard the *San Dominick* and is killed during the attack led by Delano's chief mate.

Yamjamma. In *Mardi,* he is quoted by Babbalanja as a sage but ambiguously talking lawgiver.

Yamoyamee. In *Mardi,* this is one of the aristocratic Tapparian families on the isle of Pimminee, entertained by Nimni.

Yankee, The. In *Omoo. See* Zeke.

Yankee Doodle. In "Authentic Anecdotes of 'Old Zack,' " he is the boss of the newspaper *Yankee Doodle,* for whom the correspondent goes to General Zachary Taylor to obtain and report authentic anecdotes.

Yankee Doodle. In "On the Chinese Junk," he says that the Chinese junk is not "an unlicensed junk shop," suggests that the British should spike their guns rather than those of their Chinese hosts, and boards the junk with some friends to have a look at it and to talk to the captain. In "View of the Barnum Property," Yankee Doodle is mentioned as theorizing that nature produces monstrosities only for Barnum's museum.

Yankee Doodle. Magazine. It was one of several allegedly humorous magazines to appear before 1850. It was established in New York City in 1846, as a satirical spinoff from the *Literary World,* which was edited by Evert Duyckinck.* *Yankee*

Doodle was edited by the versatile Cornelius Mathews,* who was aided by George G. Foster and Richard Grant White. It published items by Horace Greeley and Nathaniel Parker Willis, among others. Charles Martin provided illustrations. After exactly one year, the magazine ceased publication. Melville published "Authentic Anecdotes of 'Old Zack' " in *Yankee Doodle* shortly before its demise. In addition, the following articles in *Yankee Doodle* have been attributed to him: "The New Planet," "On the Chinese Junk," "On the Sea Serpent," "A Short Patent Sermon According to Blair, the Rhetorician: No. C.C.C.C.L.XXX.V.III," and "View of the Barnum Property."

Bibliography: Edward E. Chielens, ed., *American Literary Magazines: The Eighteenth and Nineteenth Centuries* (Westport, Conn.: Greenwood Press, 1986); Leyda.

Yarn. In *White-Jacket. See* Old Yarn.

Yau. In "Benito Cereno," he is a vicious Ashantee slave who polishes hatchets during Captain Amasa Delano's visit aboard the *San Dominick.* He prepared Alexandro Aranda's skeleton for use as a warning figurehead.

"The Year" (1924). Part of *Weeds and Wildings,* containing "Always with Us!," "The Blue-Bird," "Butterfly Ditty," "The Chipmunk," "Clover," "The Dairyman's Child," "A Dutch Christmas up the Hudson in the Time of Patroons," "Field Asters," "In the Pauper's Turnip-Field," "The Little Good Fellows," "The Loiterer," "The Lover and the Syringa Bush," "Madcaps," "The Old Fashion," "Stockings in the Farm-House Chimney," "Trophies of Peace: Illinois in 1840," "The Way-Side Weed," and "When Forth the Shepherd Leads the Flock."

Yellow-hair. In *Israel Potter. See* Potter, Israel.

Yellow-mane. In *Israel Potter. See* Potter, Israel.

Yellow Torch. In *White-Jacket,* he is mentioned in an anecdote as the victim of Red Hot Coal, a murderous Native American on the Mississippi River who collected scalps.

Yillah. In *Mardi,* she is a beautiful, golden-haired, blue-eyed girl who was born at Amma and taken at an early age to Oroolia, where legend has it she became a flower. She was also enshrined as a goddess in the temple at Apo in the glen of Ardair. Her guardian is the priest Aleema, and he is taking her by ship toward Tedaidee for sacrifice, when Taji encounters them. To rescue her, Taji is obliged to kill Aleema, after which Yillah and Taji go to the isle of Odo and make love. She disappears, however, and Taji pursues her unavailingly. She may have drowned or may now be disguised as a maiden in Queen Hautia's court at Flozella-a-Nina. The name Yillah may be derived from the Arabic invocation of faith "La ilaha illa-llah" (There is no God but God); if so, her function in *Mardi* may be to symbolize the divine absolute. Yillah's name may also be related to that of the titular heroine of *Lalla Rookh,* which is a series of Oriental tales in verse by Thomas Moore. Yillah's physical attributes echo those of a native girl described in William Ellis's *Polynesian Researches* (4 vols., 1833). Yillah's relationship to a whirlpool may derive from that of the titular heroine of the novel *Undine,* by Friedrich Heinrich Karl Fouqué.

   Bibliography: Davis; Finkelstein; David Jaffé, "Some Sources of Melville's *Mardi,*" *American Literature* 9 (March 1937): 56–69; Lebowitz; Beverly Hume Thorne, "Taji's Yillah: Transcending the Fates in Melville's *Mardi,*" *Essays in Literature* 19 (Spring 1992): 61–72; Wright.

Yoky, King. In *Mardi,* he is the misshapen monarch of Hooloomooloo, the isle of Cripples. He gives Taji and his party a feast.

Yola. In "Benito Cereno," he is an African-born slave, a calker by trade, between sixty and seventy years old. He is killed during the attack on the *San Dominick* led by Captain Amasa Delano's chief mate.

Yoomy ("The Warbler"). In *Mardi,* he is the minstrel from the isle of Odo. He accompanies Taji, along with King Media of Odo, Babbalanja, and Mohi, on his long and fruitless search for Yillah. Yoomy and Mohi leave Taji on the isle of Flozella-a-Nina but return from Odo to try to rescue him from Queen Hautia of Flozella. Yoomy is a floral interpreter. His name may be Melville's variation on the name Jami (Nur ud-din 'Abd-ur-rahman ibn Ahmed), the fifteenth-century Persian classical poet and mystic. Yoomy bears comparison with the poet Percy Bysshe Shelley.* Ralph Waldo Emerson* mentions Jami in his poem "Saadi."

   Bibliography: Davis, Finkelstein.

Yorpy. In "The Happy Failure," he is the faithful old Dutch-African servant of the unsuccessful inventor-uncle of the young narrator.

Young Man, The. In "The Scout toward Aldie." *See* the Colonel.

Youth, The. In "The Scout toward Aldie." *See* the Colonel.

Z

Zack. In "Authentic Anecdotes of 'Old Zack.' " *See* Taylor, Zachary.

Zardi. In "Rammon," he is an urbane, well-traveled, but shallow and unthinking improvisator who visits the philosophically inquisitive Rammon in Jerusalem.

Zeke ("Keekee"). In *Omoo,* he is the tall Yankee partner of Shorty in a farming venture at Martair. They employ Peter and Paul—that is, Dr. Long Ghost and the narrator. In real life, the tall Yankee remained on the islands, took up with a native sweetheart, and turned lazy, according to Edward T. Perkins, who later visited the islands and published *Na Motu; or, Reef-Rovings in the South Seas: A Narrative of Adventures at the Hawaiian, Georgian, and Society Islands* (1854) about his observations there.
   Bibliography: Anderson.

Zenzi. In *Mardi,* he is a mercenary Mardian poet mentioned by Yoomy.

Zenzori. In *Mardi,* he is a reader who told Lombardo that his *Koztanza* was trash. Lombardo ignored him, according to Babbalanja. The name Zenzori derives from "censor."

Ziani. In *Mardi,* he is the conqueror of Barbarossa's fictitious son Otho, according to the historian Ghibelli, who writes that the Pope was pleased by Ziani's naval success.
   Bibliography: Wright.

Zmiglandi, Queen. In *Mardi,* she is a collateral ancestor of King Abrazza, according to Mohi.

Znobbi. In *Mardi,* he is "a runaway native" from Porpheero who is now an enthusiastic inhabitant of Vivenza. He says he helped a certain politician gain success. It may be that Melville has in mind here the 1844 politicking of his brother Gansevoort Melville* in support of the presidential campaign of James K. Polk.
   Bibliography: Wright.

Zonoree. In *Mardi,* he is a dead subject whose prodigality King Peepi has inherited.

Zooperbi. In *Mardi,* he was the son of King Taquinoo, according to the anonymous manuscript read in northern Vivenza. When he returned from camp, he found his country in arms against him. For 512 "moons," his expulsion was celebrated "annually." The name Zooperbi derives from that of Lucius Tarquinius Superbus (534–510 B.C.), the son of Lucius Tarquinius Priscus (616–578 B.C.), the fifth king of Rome. Legend has it that Lucius Tarquinius Superbus became the despotic seventh and last king of Rome (534 B.C.) by murdering Servius Tullius, who was the sixth king (from 578 to 534 B.C.) and who was also Superbus's father-in-law. While Superbus was away at war, his son Sextus Tarquinius in Rome raped Lucretia, who was his cousin Lucius Tarquinius Collatinus's wife. This act caused a revolt, which was headed by Lucretia's husband's cousin Lucius Junius Brutus and which led to the expulsion of Lucius Tarquinius Superbus and all other Tarquins and to the establishment of a republic (traditionally dated 509 B.C.). Failing to regain the throne, Lucius Tarquinius Superbus died in exile.
   Bibliography: Charles Marie Franzero, *The Life and Times of Tarquin the Etruscan* (New York: John Day, 1961); Wright.

Zozo. In *Mardi,* he was an enthusiast whose back tooth, which he knocked out in grief, is now in Oh-Oh's museum.

Zuma. In *Mardi,* he is an agent sent with Varnopi to the Mardian island of Rafona by Donjalolo for information.

General Bibliography

Arvin, Newton. *Herman Melville.* [New York]: William Sloane Associates, 1950.

Bellis, Peter J. *No Mysteries Out of Ourselves: Identity and Textual Form in the Novels of Herman Melville.* Philadelphia: University of Pennsylvania Press, 1990.

Berkow, Mary K. *Melville's Sources.* Evanston, Ill.: Northwestern University Press, 1987.

Bryant, John, ed. *A Companion to Melville Studies.* Westport, Conn.: Greenwood Press, 1986.

Cagidemetrio, Alide. *Fictions of the Past: Hawthorne and Melville.* Amherst: University of Massachusetts Press, 1993.

Chai, Leon. *Romantic Foundations.* Ithaca, N.Y.: Cornell University Press, 1987.

Coffler, Gail. *Melville's Classical Allusions: A Comprehensive Index and Glossary.* Westport, Conn.: Greenwood Press, 1985.

Dillingham, William B. *Melville's Later Novels.* Athens: University of Georgia Press, 1986.

Dimock, Wai-chee. *Empire for Liberty: Melville and the Poetics of Individualism.* Princeton, N.J.: Princeton University Press, 1989.

Gidmark, Jill B. *Melville Sea Dictionary: A Glossed Concordance and Analysis of the Sea Language in Melville's Nautical Novels.* Westport, Conn.: Greenwood Press, 1982.

Hayashi, Tetsumaro. *Herman Melville: Research Opportunities and Dissertation Abstracts.* Jefferson, N.C.: McFarland, 1987.

Hayford, Harrison, Hershel Parker, G. Thomas Tanselle, et al., eds. *The Writings of Herman Melville.* Evanston and Chicago: Northwestern University Press and the Newberry Library, 1968–. Vol. 1 (1968): *Typee: A Peep at Polynesian Life,* ed. Harrison Hayford, Hershel Parker, G. Thomas Tanselle. Vol. 2 (1968): *Omoo: A Narrative of Adventures in the South Seas,* ed. Harrison Hayford, Hershel Parker, G. Thomas Tanselle. Vol. 3 (1970): *Mardi and a Voyage Thither,* ed. Harrison Hayford, Hershel Parker, G. Thomas Tanselle. Vol. 4 (1969): *Redburn: His First Voyage . . . ,* ed. Harrison Hayford, Hershel Parker, G. Thomas Tanselle. Vol. 5

(1970): *White-Jacket or The World in a Man-of-War,* ed. Harrison Hayford, Hershel Parker, G. Thomas Tanselle. Vol. 6 (1988): *Moby-Dick or The Whale,* ed. Harrison Hayford, Hershel Parker, G. Thomas Tanselle. Vol. 7 (1971): *Pierre or The Ambiguities,* ed. Harrison Hayford, Hershel Parker, G. Thomas Tanselle. Vol. 8 (1982): *Israel Potter: His Fifty Years of Exile,* ed. Harrison Hayford, Hershel Parker, G. Thomas Tanselle. Vol. 9 (1987): *The Piazza Tales and Other Prose Pieces 1839–1860,* ed. Harrison Hayford, Alma A. MacDougall, G. Thomas Tanselle, et al. Vol. 10 (1984): *The Confidence-Man: His Masquerade,* ed. Harrison Hayford, Hershel Parker, G. Thomas Tanselle. Vol. 11 (forthcoming): *The Published Poems,* ed. Robert C. Ryan. Vol. 12 (1991): *Clarel: A Poem and Pilgrimage in the Holy Land,* ed. Harrison Hayford, Alma A. MacDougall, Hershel Parker, G. Thomas Tanselle. Vol. 14 (1993): *Correspondence,* ed. Lynn Horth. Vol. 15 (1989): *Journals,* ed. Howard C. Horsford with Lynn Horth.

Hayford, Harrison, and Merton M. Sealts, Jr., ed., *Billy Budd, Sailor (an Inside Narrative): Reading Text and Genetic Text.* Chicago: University of Chicago Press, 1962.

Herbert, T. Walter. *Marquesan Encounters: Melville and the Meaning of Civilization.* Cambridge, Mass.: Harvard University Press, 1980.

Higgins, Brian. *Herman Melville: A Reference Guide, 1931–1960.* Boston: G. K. Hall, 1987.

Howard, Leon. *Herman Melville: A Biography.* Berkeley: University of California Press, 1951.

Karcher, Carolyn L. *Shadow over the Promised Land: Slavery, Race, and Violence in Melville's America.* Baton Rouge: Louisiana State University Press, 1980.

Kier, Kathleen E. *A Melville Encyclopedia: The Novels.* 2 vols. New York: Whitston Publishing, 1990.

Kirby, David. *Herman Melville.* New York: Continuum, 1993.

Leyda, Jay. *The Melville Log: A Documentary Life of Herman Melville, 1819–1891.* 2 vols. New York: Harcourt, Brace, 1951; enl. ed., 2 vols., New York: Gordian Press, 1969.

McCarthy, Paul. *"The Twisted Mind": Madness in Herman Melville's Fiction.* Iowa City: University of Iowa Press, 1990.

Martin, Robert K. *Hero, Captain, and Stranger: Male Friendship, Social Critique, and Literary Form in the Sea Novels of Herman Melville.* Chapel Hill: University of North Carolina Press, 1986.

Matthiessen, F. O. *American Renaissance: Art and Expression in the Age of Emerson and Whitman.* New York: Oxford University Press, 1941.

Metcalf, Eleanor Melville. *Herman Melville: Cycle and Epicycle.* Cambridge, Mass.: Harvard University Press, 1953.

Mushabac, Jane. *Melville's Humor: A Critical Study.* Hamden, Conn.: Archon Books, 1981.

Newman, Lea Bertani Vozar. *A Reader's Guide to the Short Stories of Herman Melville.* New York: G. K. Hall, 1986.

Phelps, Leland R., and Kathleen McCullough. *Herman Melville's Foreign Reputation: A Research Guide.* Boston: G. K. Hall, 1983.

Reynolds, David S. *Beneath the American Renaissance: The Subversive Imagination in the Age of Emerson and Melville.* New York: Alfred A. Knopf, 1988.

Rogin, Michael Paul. *Subversive Genealogy: The Politics and Art of Herman Melville.* New York: Alfred A. Knopf, 1983.

Samson, John. *White Lies: Melville's Narrations of Facts.* Ithaca, N.Y.: Cornell University Press, 1989.

Sealts, Merton M., Jr. *Melville's Reading: A Check-List of Books Owned and Borrowed.* Madison: University of Wisconsin Press, 1966; new and enl. ed., [Columbia]: University of South Carolina Press, 1988.

Short, Bryan C. *Cast by Means of Figures: Herman Melville's Rhetorical Development.* Amherst: University of Massachusetts Press, 1993.

Shurr, William H. *The Mystery of Iniquity: Melville as Poet, 1857–1891.* Lexington: University Press of Kentucky, 1972.

Stein, William Bysshe. *The Poetry of Melville's Late Years: Time, History, Myth, and Religion.* Albany: State University of New York Press, 1970.

Sten, Christopher, ed. *Savage Eye: Melville and the Visual Arts.* Kent, Ohio: Kent State University Press, 1991.

Tolchin, Neal L. *Mourning, Gender, and Creativity in the Art of Herman Melville.* New Haven, Conn.: Yale University Press, 1988.

Warren, Robert Penn, ed. *Selected Poems of Herman Melville: A Reader's Edition.* New York: Random House, 1970.

Weaver, Raymond M., ed. *The Works of Herman Melville.* 16 vols. London: Constable, 1922–1924. Vol. 16 (1924): *Poems . . . Battle-Pieces, John Marr and Other Sailors, Timoleon, and Miscellaneous Poems.*

Weiner, Susan. *Law in Art: Melville's Major Fiction and Nineteenth-Century American Law.* New York: Peter Lang, 1992.

Wright, Nathalia. *Melville's Use of the Bible.* Durham, N.C.: Duke University Press, 1949.

———. "Herman Melville." In *Eight American Authors: A Review of Research and Criticism,* ed. James Woodress, pp. 173–224. Rev. ed., New York: W. W. Norton, 1971.

See also *American Literary Scholarship: An Annual / 1963* and later, ed. James Woodress et al., Durham, N.C.: Duke University Press; bibliographies published annually by the Modern Language Association of America; and standard dictionaries and encyclopedias, including *Academic American, Dictionary of American Biography, Dictionary of Literary Biography, Dictionary of National Biography, Encyclopedia Britannica, The Cyclopaedia of American Biography, Enciclopedia Italiana, Enciclopedia Universal Ilustrada: Euorpeo-Americana, Great Soviet Encyclopedia, Webster's Biographical Dictionary,* and *Webster's Guide to American History.*

Index

Long names of persons and long titles of works are usually given in short form, and titles of persons are omitted. Peripheral and incidental references, including non-substantive ones to spouses, as well as all alternate names and nicknames, are omitted. Page references to main entries are italicized.

A (*Mardi*), *1*
Abdon (*Clarel*), *1*
Abos and Padilla, José ("Benito Cereno"), *1*
Abrantes, Duchess d' (*Israel Potter*), *1*
Abrazza, King (*Mardi*), *1–2*
d'Acarty, Marquis (*White-Jacket*), *2*
An Account of the Arctic Regions (Scoresby), 302
Adam ("To Ned"), *2*
Adams, Hannah, *2*
Adeea (*Omoo*), *2*
"Adieu," *2*
Adler, George J., *2–3*, 27, 368, 392
"The Admiral of the White," *3*
Admiral of the White ("Haglets"), *3*
Adonais (Shelley), 4
Adondo (*Mardi*), *4*
The Adventures of Roderick Random (Smollett), 101
Adventures in the Pacific (Coulter), 129
Ady (*Mardi*), *4*
"The Aeolian Harp," *4*

"After-Piece," *4*
"After the Pleasure Party," *4–5*
Agar (*Clarel*), *5*
Agath (*Clarel*), *5*
Agatha Story, *5*, 84, 185, 410
"The Age of the Antonines," *6*
The Aggressions of the French at Tahiti (Pritchard), 370
Agrippina, *6*
Ahab, *6*, 302, 309, 344
Akim ("Benito Cereno"), *6*
Alanno (*Mardi*), *7*, 9
Albert (*Billy Budd*), *7*
Aldina (*Mardi*), *7*
Aleema (*Mardi*), *7*
Alexander I, *7*
Alla-Malolla (*Mardi*), *7*
All-a-Tanto, Commander, ("Bridegroom-Dick"), *7*
Allen, Ann, *7–8*, 25, 166, 167, 267, 281, 354
Allen, Bethuel, 8, 276
Allen, Ethan, *8–9*, 208, 232, 256

Allen, Martha Bent, 7–8
Allen, William, *7, 9*
Alma (*Mardi*), *9*
Alma (Prior), 9
Almanni (*Mardi*), *9*
"Always with Us!," *9*
Amabilia, Miss Angelica (*Pierre*), *9*
Ambassador, My Lord ("Under the Rose"), *9–10*
"The Ambuscade," *10*
Amelia, Princess, *10*
"America," *10*
"The American Aloe on Exhibition," *10–11*
American Antiquities (Bradford), 50
American Notebooks (Dickens), 92
An American Transport in the Crimean War (Codman), 86
Ames, Nathaniel, 491
Amigo ("L'Envoi"), *11*
Amor ("After the Pleasure Party"), *11*
Amoree (*Mardi*), *11*
Amores (Ovid), 11
"Amoroso," *11*
Ampudia, Pedro de, *11*
Anacreon, 98
Andrea ("Marquis de Grandvin: Naples"), *11–12*
Andrew of Hungary, 11–12
Angelico, Fra, *12*, 245
"Angel o' the Age!," *12*
Anna ("The Apple-Tree Table," "I and My Chimney"), *12*
Annatoo (*Mardi*), *12–13*
Anselm (*Clarel*), *13*
Anton, Charles, 287
Antone (*Omoo*), *13*
Antone (*White-Jacket*), *13*
Antonine [Antoninus Pius] ("The Age of the Antonines"), *13*
Antonine [Marcus Aurelius] ("The Age of the Antonines"), *13*
Antoninus Pius, *13*
"Apathy and Enthusiasm," *13*
Apollo ("Marquis de Grandvin: Naples"), *13*
Apostle (*Pierre*), *14*
"The Apparition (A Retrospect)," *14*

"The Apparition (The Parthenon)," *14*
"The Apple-Tree Table," *14–15*, 139, 290, 372, 374, 447
Aquella, Queen (*Mardi*), *15*
Aquovi (*Mardi*), *15*
Arabella ("Jimmy Rose"), *15*
Aranda, Alexandro ("Benito Cereno"), *15*
"The Archipelago," *15*
Architect of the Parthenon, *16*
Archy (*Moby-Dick*), *16*
Archy ("The Scout toward Aldie"), *16*
Arfretee (*Omoo*), *16*
Arheeto (*Omoo*), *16*
Arhinoo (*Mardi*), *16*
Aristippus, *16*, 236
"The Armies of the Wilderness," *16–17*
Armstrong, James, 83
Arnaut, *17*
Arrian (*Confidence-Man*), *17*
"Art," *17*
Asbestos (*Pierre*), *17*
Ashby, Turner, *17*
Aspasia, *17–18*, 347
"As They Fell," *18*
Astor, John Jacob, *18*, 26, 55, 121
Atahalpa (*Mardi*), *19*
Atama, Prince (*Mardi*), *19*
Atee Poee (*Omoo*), *19*
"At the Cannon's Mouth," *19*
"The Attic Landscape," *19*
Atufal ("Benito Cereno"), *19*
"Aurora Borealis," *19–20*
"Authentic Anecdotes of 'Old Zack,'" *20*
"Autobiography" (Boone), 49
Autograph Leaves of Our Country's Authors (Bliss and Kennedy), 202
"The Avatar," *20*
Avery, Latham, 258
Azem ("Under the Rose"), *20–21*
Azore Sailor (*Moby-Dick*), *21*
Azzageddi (*Mardi*), *21*
Azzolino, Queen, (*Mardi*), *21*

B—("Bartleby"), *23*
B—, Mrs. ("Shadow at the Feast"), *23*
Babbalanja (*Mardi*), *23*

Babeuf, Noël, 24
Babo ("Benito Cereno"), *23–24*
Baby ("The Chipmunk"), *24*
Bach, Old ("The Paradise of Bachelors"), *24*
Backus, John, 302, 355
Baker, Edward, 24
Baldy ("Donelson"), *24*
Baldy (*White-Jacket*), *24*
Ballad, Ned (*Mardi*), *24*
"Ball's Bluff," *24–25*
Baltimore (*Omoo*), *25*
Balzac, Honoré de, 450
Bandage, Dr. (*White-Jacket*), *25*
Banford, Isabel (*Pierre*), 8, *25*
Banker (*Clarel*), *25–26*
Bannadonna ("The Bell-Tower"), *26*
Bardianna (*Mardi*), *26*
Bargas, Lorenzo ("Benito Cereno"), *26*
Barlo, Bartholomew ("Benito Cereno"), *26*
Barnum, P. T., *26–27*, 268, 324, 454
"Bartleby," *27–29*, 100, 141, 283, 290, 309, 358, 447
Bartlett, William, 81
Bartlett, William Francis, *29*, 88, 89, 203, 307
Batho (*Mardi*), *30*
"The Battle for the Bay," *30*
"The Battle for the Mississippi," *30*
"Battle of Stone River, Tennessee," *30–31*, 429
"A Battle Picture," *31*
Battle-Pieces, 29, *31*, 39, 107, 181, 290, 429
Battle-Pieces of Herman Melville (ed. Cohen), 202
Beale, Thomas, 302
Beatrice (*Clarel*), *32*
Beauty (*White-Jacket*), *32*
Beecher, Henry Ward, 168
Belex (*Clarel*), *32*
Belfast Sailor (*Moby-Dick*), *32*
Belisent ("The Scout toward Aldie"), *32*
Bell (*Omoo*), *32*
Bell, Mrs. (*Omoo*), *32–33*
Bello, King (*Mardi*), *33*

"The Bell-Tower," *33*, 100, 290, 358, 372, 374, 425
Beltha (*Clarel*), *33*
Bembo (*Omoo*), *34*
"The Bench of Boors," *34*
Beneventano, Ferdinando, *34*, 85
Benignus Muscatel (*Clarel*), *34*
"Benito Cereno," *34–36*, 100, 290, 358, 372, 374
Bennet, George, 268
Bennett, Frederick Debell, 13, 182, 268, 302, 401
Bent, Ann, 8, 25
Bentley, Richard, *36–37*, 55, 267, 307, 383, 401, 411, 430,491
Benton, Thomas Hart, 356
"The Berg," *37*
Berzelli (*Mardi*), *37*
Berzilius, Jön Jakob, 37
Bettie (*Pierre*), *38*
Betty (*Moby-Dick*), *38*
Betty (*Omoo*), *38*
Betty (*Redburn*), *38*
Betty, William, *38*, 138, 228
Bey (*Clarel*), *38*
Biddy ("The Apple-Tree Table"), *38*
Biddy ("I and My Chimney"), *39*
Biddy ("Jimmy Rose"), *39*
Bidi Bidie (*Mardi*), *39*
Bidiri (*Mardi*), *39*
Bildad, Captain (*Moby-Dick*), *39*
Bill (*Israel Potter*), *39*
Bill (*Redburn*), *39*
Bill (*White-Jacket*), *39*
Billson, Charles James, *39–40*, 82
Billy (*Redburn*), *40*
Billy Budd, *40–44*, 291, 318
"Billy in the Darbies," *43*
Biographical Sketch of Herman Melville (Smith), 419
Biographical Sketch. Privately Printed for Mrs. Herman Melville (Smith), 419
Bishop (*Pierre*), *44*
Black, David, 60
Black Bet (*White-Jacket*), *44*
Black Dan (*Omoo*), *44*
Black Guinea (*The Confidence-Man*), *44*

Blair, Hugh (''A Short Patent Sermon''), *44*

Blake (''The Scout toward Aldie''), *45*

Bland (*White-Jacket*), *45*

Bland, Jerry (''To Major John Gentian''), *45*

Blandmour (''Poor Man's Pudding''), *45*

Blandoo (*Mardi*), *45*

Blattner, M., 1

Blink (*White-Jacket*), *45*

Bliss, Alexander, 202

Bliss, William Wallace Smith, *45–46*, 443

Blood, Asaph (''Daniel Orme''), *46*, 336. *See also* Orme, Daniel

''The Blue-Bird,'' *46*

Blue-Skin (*White-Jacket*), *46*

Blumacher, Tuenis Van der (''A Dutch Christmas''), *46*

Blunt, Bill (*Omoo*), *46*

Blunt, Jack (*Redburn*), *46–47*

Boat Plug (*White-Jacket*), *47*

Bob (*White-Jacket*), *47*

Boddo (*Mardi*), *47*

Bodisco, Waldemar de, *47*

Boerhaave, Herman, 49–50

Boldo (*Mardi*), *47*

Bolton, Harry (*Redburn*), *47–48*

Bomba (''Pausilippo,'' ''Marquis de Grandvin: Naples''), *48*

Bomblum (*Mardi*), *48*

Bondo (*Mardi*), *48*

Bonja (*Mardi*), *48*

Bonny Blue (''Bridegroom-Dick''), *48*

Boombolt (*White-Jacket*), *48*

Boomer (*Moby-Dick*), *48*

Boone, Daniel, *48–49*

Booth, Edwin Thomas, 23, *49*, 89, 165

Booth, John Wilkes, 49, 89

Borabolla (*Mardi*), *49*

Borhavo (*Mardi*), *49–50*

Botargo (*Mardi*), *50*

Bourbon-Draco (''Marquis de Grandvin: Naples''), *50*

Brace, Ned (*White-Jacket*), *50*

Brade (*The Confidence-Man*), *50*

Bradford, Alexander, *50–51*, 383

Bragg, Braxton, 31, *51*, 71, 248, 334, 393, 415

Brami (*Mardi*), *52*

Brandt (*Pierre*), *52*

Brandy-Nan (*Redburn*), *52*

Breckinridge, John, 31, *52*, 333

''Bridegroom-Dick,'' *52–53*, 152, 286

Bridenstoke (*Redburn*), *53*

Bridewell (*White-Jacket*), *53*

Bridges, James (*Israel Potter*), *53–54*

Bridges, John Edward, 54

Bridges, Molly (*Israel Potter*), *54*

Brief Memoirs (Field), 139

Bright Future (*The Confidence-Man*), *54*

Brinvilliers, Marchioness of, *54*

Bristol (*Redburn*), *54*

Bristol Molly (*Billy Budd*), *54*

Broadbit (*White-Jacket*), *54*

Brodhead, John, 55, 267, 330, 331

Brooks (''Authentic Anecdotes''), *55*

Brouwer, Adriaen, *55–56*

Brown (''Bridegroom-Dick''), *56*

Brown, B. Hobbema (''The Marquis de Grandvin''), *56*

Brown, John, 17, *56–57*, 210, 240, 290, 447

Brown, Martin, 302, 367

Brown, Mrs. (''The Apple-Tree Table''), *57*

Brown, Oliver, 388

Brown, Peter, 173

Brown, Tom (*White-Jacket*), *57*

Brown, William, 244

Browne, J. Ross, *57–58*, 86, 131, 302

Browns, Ben (*White-Jacket*), *58*

Bruat, Armand-Joseph, *58*, 66, 303, 361

Brun, Charles le, 263

Bruno, Giordano, 246

Brush (*White-Jacket*), *58*

Budd, William (*Billy Budd*), *58–59*

''Buddha,'' *59*

Bulkington (*Moby-Dick*), *59–60*

Bulwer-Lytton, Edward, 258, 462

Bunger, Dr. Jack (*Moby-Dick*), *60*

Bungs (*Omoo*), *60*

Bungs (*White-Jacket*), *60*

Bunk, Joe (*White-Jacket*), *60*

Bunkum, Colonel Josiah (''Major Gentian''), *60*

Bunn, Ned (''To Ned''), *60*

Burke, Joseph, 138
Burney, James, 129
"Butterfly Ditty," *60*
Byrne, Benbow, 34

Cabaco (*Moby-Dick*), *63*
Calends, Queen (*Mardi*), *63*
Calhoun, John C., 268, 321
The California and Oregon Trail (Parkman), 120, 289
Calvert, George, *63–64*
Camellus, George Joseph, 37
Camões [Camoëns], Luíz de, *64*, 69, 70, 297
Candy (*White-Jacket*), *64*
Canny, Walter (*Moby-Dick*), *64*
The Canterbury Tales (Chaucer), 93
"A Canticle," *65*
Captain ("The Death Craft"), *65*
Captain ("Marquis de Grandvin: Naples"), *65*
Captain (*Moby-Dick*), *65*
Captain Bob (*Omoo*), *65*
Captains ("The Admiral of the White"), *66*
Carden, John S., *66*, 107, 440
Carlo ("Marquis de Grandvin: Naples"), *66*
Carlo (*Redburn*), *66*
Carpégna, Éduoard, *66–67*
Casks (*Pierre*), *67*
Cavour, Camillo, *67*, 161
Celibate (*Clarel*), *67*
Celio (*Clarel*), *67*
Cellini, Benvenuto, 33
Cereno, Benito ("Benito Cereno"), *68*
Cervantes, Saavedra, Miguel de, 375
Chambers, Ephraim, 114
Chang Ching ("On the Chinese Junk"), *68*
Chang-foue ("On the Chinese Junk"), *68*
Chaplain ("The Scout toward Aldie"), *68*
Charity, Aunt (*Moby-Dick*), *68*
Charlemont (*The Confidence-Man*), *68–69*
Charles I, 228, 396
Charles II, 228
Charlton, Richard, *69*, 220, 222, 343

Chartres, Louis-Philippe-Joseph, *69*, 219. *See also* Orléans, Louis-Philippe-Joseph
Chase (*White-Jacket*), *69*
Chase, Jack (*White-Jacket*), *70*, 86, 210, 297
Chase, Owen, *70–71*, 302, 359
Chase, William Henry, 71
"Chattanooga," *71*
Chaucer, Geoffrey, 93
Cherry ("Hawthorne and His Mosses"), *71*, 279
Cherry ("Madcaps"), *72*
Cheever, Henry, 302
Chew ("The Scout toward Aldie"), *72*
China Aster (*The Confidence-Man*), *72*
China Sailor (*Moby-Dick*), *72*
"The Chipmunk," *72*
Chock-a-Block ("Bridegroom-Dick"), *72*
Chorley, Henry, 475
Chris, Cousin ("A Dutch Christmas"), *72*
Christodulus (*Clarel*), *73*
Christopher (*Pierre*), *73*
Chronological History of the Discoveries in the South Sea (Burney), 129
"The Cincinnati," *73*
The City of Dreadful Night (Thomson), 39
Claggart, John (*Billy Budd*), *73*
Clara (*Pierre*), *73*
Clarel (*Clarel*), 3, 39, 40, *73–82*, 107, 158, 159, 173, 185, 200, 284, 286, 291, 304, 359, 372, 425, 445
Claret (*White-Jacket*), *82*
Claret, Captain (*White-Jacket*), *82–83*
Clarissa (*Pierre*), *83*
Classical Dictionary (Anton), 276
Claude ("I and My Chimney"), *83*
Cleothemes the Argive ("The Fiddler"), *83*
Clerk of the Weather ("Peebles"), *83*
Clifford, John Henry, 5, *83–84*
Cloud, Captain ("The Scout toward Aldie"), *84*
"Clover," *84*
Cochrane, Lord, *84–85*, 86
"Cock-a-Doodle-Doo!," *85*, 290, 447

Codman, John, *85–86*, 132, 182, 388. *See also* Ringbolt
Codrington, Sir Edward, *86*
Coffin (*White-Jacket*), *87*
Coffin, Johnny (*Moby-Dick*), *87*
Coffin, Peter (*Moby-Dick*), *87*, 460
Coffin, Sal (*Moby-Dick*), *87*
Coffin, Sam (*Moby-Dick*), *87*
Cohen, Hennig, 202
Colbrook, Corporal (*White-Jacket*), *87*
Colburn, Henry, 36
Coleman (*White-Jacket*), *87*
Coleman, Deuteronomy (*Moby-Dick*), *87*
Coleman, John Brown, Jr., *87*, 88
Coleman, Nathan (*Moby-Dick*), *87*, 88
Coleman, Nathan (*Omoo*), *87–88*
Coleridge, Samuel Taylor, 88, 98, 125, 223
"The College Colonel," *88*, 290, 307
Colnett, James, 129
Colonel ("The College Colonel"), *89*
Colonel ("Iris"), *89*
Colonel ("The Scout toward Aldie"), *89*
" 'The Coming Storm,' " *89*, 165
The Coming Storm (Gifford), 89, 165
"Commemorative of a Naval Victory," *89*
Commodore ("Donelson"), *90*
Commodore (*Typee*), *90*
Commodore (*White-Jacket*), *90*
Compressed Narrative . . . of Sir Edward Codrington (Codrington), 86
A Condensed Geography and History of the Western States (Flint), 92
The Confidence-Man, *90–93*, 185, 284, 290, 291, 321, 354, 358, 411, 434, 442
"The Conflict of Convictions," *93–94*
Constable, John, *94*
Constantine I, *94–95*
Constantinople and Its Environs (Porter), 365
"The Continents," *95*
Cooke, Robert Francis, *95*, 312, 340
Cooke, William Henry, 95
Cooper, James Fenimore, 36, *96*, 120, 157, 208, 289, 372, 373, 447
"Cooper's New Novel," *96*
Coulter, John, 129

Coulter, Martha ("Poor Man's Pudding"), *96*
Coulter, William ("Poor Man's Pudding"), *97*
Count (*Pierre*), *97*
Count (*White-Jacket*), *97*
Craddock, James, 24
Cramer, William E., *97*
Cranz (*Pierre*), *97*
Crash (*Omoo*), *97*
Cream, William (*The Confidence-Man*), *97*
Creole ("The Encantadas"), *98*
Cresson, Warder, 316
Croesus ("Jack Gentian [omitted from the final sketch of him]"), *98*
Crokarky (*Israel Potter*), *98*
Cromwell, Samuel, 43
"Crossing the Tropics," *98*
Crowfoot, Widow ("Cock-a-Doodle-Doo!"), *98*
"C—'s Lament," 88, *98*
"The Cuban Pirate," *98*
Cuff, Garry ("The Scout toward Aldie"), *99*
"The Cumberland," *99*
Cupid ("The Paradise of Bachelors"), *99*
Curiosities of Literature (D'Israeli), 19
Curtis, Asa, 325
Curtis, George William, 33, *99–100*, 182, 184, 257, 371, 373
Cushing, William Barker, *100–101*
Cuticle, Cadwallader (*White-Jacket*), *101*
Cyclopedia of Wit and Humor (Burton), 244
Cyclopedia; or, An Universal Dictionary of Arts and Science (Chambers), 114
Cylinder (*White-Jacket*), 101
Cypriote (*Clarel*), *101*
Cyril (*Clarel*), *101*

Dacres, Julian ("I and My Chimney"), *103*
Daggoo (*Moby-Dick*), *103*
Dago ("Benito Cereno"), *103*
Dainty Dave ("Bridegroom-Dick"), *103*
"The Dairyman's Child," *103*
Dallabdoolmans (*Redburn*), *104*

Dana, Richard Henry, Jr., 57, *104*, 132, 181, 302, 411, 434
Danby (*Redburn*), *105*
Danby, Handsome Mary (*Redburn*), *105*
"Daniel Orme," *105*
Danish Sailor (*Moby-Dick*), *105*
Dansker (*Billy Budd*), *105*
Dante Alighieri, 81, 186
Darfi (*Mardi*), *105*
Darwin, Charles, 319
Dash, Dick (*White-Jacket*), *105*
Dashman, Adolphus (*White-Jacket*), *105*
Dates (*Pierre*), *105*
Deacon (*The Confidence-Man*), *106*
"The Deacon's Masterpiece" (Holmes), 192
Deadlight, Tom ("Tom Deadlight"), *106*
"The Death Craft," *106*
Decatur, Stephen, 66, *106–7*, 159, 220, 365, 440
Dedications, *107*
Dedidum (*Mardi*), *107*
Deer, Derick de (*Moby-Dick*), *108*
Delano, Captain Amasa ("Benito Cereno"), 10, 36, 68, *108*
Del Fonca ("The Bell-Tower"), *108*
Democratus, 108
Democritus, Mrs. ("The Apple-Tree Table"), *108*
Demorkriti (*Mardi*), *108*
Denton, Jack (*Billy Budd*), *108*
Dermoddi, Chief (*Mardi*), *109*
De Ruyter, Mikiel Adriaanszoon, *109*, 398, 458
Derwent (*Clarel*), *109*
The Descent of Man (Darwin), 318–19
Description of Greece (Pausanius), 198
Despairer (*Mardi*), *109*
De Squak (*Redburn*), *109*
Devonshire ("Poor Man's Pudding"), *110*
"The Devotion of the Flowers," *110*
Dewey, Chester, 15
Diamelo ("Benito Cereno"), *110*
Dick (*Omoo*), *110*
Dick (*White-Jacket*), *110*
Dickens, Charles, 92, 181, 237
Diddledee (*Mardi*), *110*

Diddler, Jeremy (*The Confidence-Man*), *110*
Dididi (*Mardi*), *110*
Didymus (*Clarel*), *110*
Digby (*Redburn*), *110*
The Digressions of "V" (Vedder), 477–78
Diloro (*Mardi*), *110*
Diogenes ("The Apparition [The Parthenon]"), *110*
"A Dirge for McPherson," *111*
Discovery, Settlement, and Present State of Kentucke (Filson), 49
"Disinterment of the Hermes," *111*
D'Israeli, Isaac, 19
"Ditty of Aristippus," *111*, 425
Dives ("The Piazza"), *111*
Divino (*Mardi*), *111*
Djalea (*Clarel*), *111*
Dobs (*White-Jacket*), *111*
Doc (*Pierre*), *112*
Documents Relating to the Colonial History of the State of New York (Brodhead), 55
Dodge, Mabel. *See* Hamilton, Gail
Dods, Daniel (*Redburn*), *112*
Dolci, Carlo, *112*
Doldrum (*Mardi*), *112*
Dominican (*Clarel*), *112*
Donald (*Billy Budd*), *112*
"Donelson," *112–15*
Donjalolo (*Mardi*), *113*
Donna ("Marquis de Grandvin: Naples"), *113*
Donno (*Mardi*), *113*
Doodle ("On the Chinese Junk"), *113*
Dou, Gerard, *113–14*
Dough-Boy (*Moby-Dick*), *114*
Douglas, Stephen A., 97, 244
Douw (*Pierre*), *114*
Dow Jr. ("A Short Patent Sermon"), *114*
Doxodox (*Mardi*), *114*
Dragoni, Prince(*Mardi*), *114*
Drinker, Tobias (*Redburn*), *114*
Drouon, Clement ("The Devotion of the Flowers"), *115*
Drouth, Daniel ("A Grave near Petersburg"), *115*

Dua ("The Bell-Tower"), *115*

Duke (*Redburn*), *115*

Dumdi (*Mardi*), *115*

Dundonald, Donald (*Pierre*), *115*

Dundonald, Thomas Cochrane, *115–16*

Dunk (*Omoo*), *116*

Dunker, Mrs. (*Pierre*), *116*

Dupetit-Thouars, Abel Aubert, 58, 66, *116–17*, 222, 303

Dupont, Samuel Francis, *117–18*, 360, 384

"Dupont's Round Fight," *118*

Durer, Agnes ("Marquis de Grandvin: At the Hostelry"), *118*

Dürer, Albrecht ("Marquis de Grandvin: At the Hostelry"), *118–19*

"The Dust-Layers," *119*

"A Dutch Christmas," *119*

Dutcher, Tom ("Jack Gentian [omitted from the final sketch of him]"), *119*

Dutch Sailor (*Moby-Dick*), *120*

Duyckinck, Evert, 3, 10, 20, 28, 86, 92, 96, *120–21*, 122, 126, 132, 156, 161, 184, 186, 190, 191, 192, 205, 229, 239, 245, 257, 267, 274, 282, 283, 290, 294, 307, 310, 354, 406, 413, 423, 442, 499

Duyckinck, George, 2, 28, 120, *121–22*, 161, 184, 267, 282, 284, 290, 307, 310

"The Eagle of the Blue," *123*

Early, Jubal A., *123–24*, 248, 414, 483

Eaton, Joseph Oriel, *124*

Edwards, Monroe ("Bartleby"), *124*

Egbert (*The Confidence-Man*), *124*

Eld ("The New Ancient of Days"), *125*

Elder (*Clarel*), *125*

Elementa Chemiae (Boerhaave), 50

Elijah (*Moby-Dick*), *125*

Ellery, Willis (*Moby-Dick*), *125*

Ellis, William, 188, 268, 330, 401, 467

Elsie ("A Dutch Christmas"), *125*

Elsie Venner (Holmes), 308

Emerson, Ralph Waldo, 57, 93, 124, *125–26*, 183, 184, 195, 257, 443, 446, 447, 456, 494, 501

Emir ("In the Desert"), *126*

Emir, The (*Clarel*), *127*

Emmons, Pop ("Hawthorne and His Mosses"), *127*

"The Encantadas," 100, *127–29*, 140, 290, 344, 358, 372, 374

Enderby, Samuel (*Moby-Dick*), *129*

English Sailor (*Moby-Dick*), *129*

An Enquiry into . . . the Wealth of Nations (Smith), 112

"The Enthusiast," *129*

"The Enviable Isles," *130*, 378

"L'Envoi," *130*

"L'Envoi: The Return," *130*

"Epistle to Daniel Shepherd," *130*, 413

"An Epitaph," *130*

Essay on the Principle of Population (Malthus), 187, 355

Estaing, Charles Hector, Comte d', *131*, 170, 432

Etchings of a Whaling Cruise (Browne), 57, 86, *131–32*, 302

Ethelward (*Clarel*), *132*

Eureka (Poe), 358

Eve ("The Lover"), *132*

Evils and Abuses in the Naval and Merchant Service Exposed (McNally), 45, 491

Excellency ("Marquis de Grandvin: Naples"), *132*

Excellenza ("The Bell-Tower"), *132*

The Faerie Queene (Spenser), 186, 267

Falcone, Aniello, *133*, 391

Falconer, William, *133–34*, 324

"The Fall of Richmond," *134*

Falsgrave (*Pierre*), *134*

Falsgrave, Mrs. (*Pierre*), *134*

Falsgrave, Rev. Mr. (*Pierre*), *134*

Falstaff, Sir John (Shakespeare), 203; Falstaff (in "Falstaff's Lament"), *134*, 203

Fanfum (*Mardi*), *135*

Fanna (*Mardi*), *135*

Farnoopoo (*Omoo*), *135*

Farnow (*Omoo*), *135*

Farnowar (*Omoo*), *135*

"Far Off-Shore," 135

Farragut, David Glasgow, 89, *135–36*, 150, 333, 365, 366

Fathers ("The Cincinnati"), *136*
Fayaway (*Typee*), *136*
Fedallah (*Moby-Dick*), *136–37*
Fee (*Mardi*), *137*
Feejee Mermaid ("The New Planet"), *137*
Felipe ("The Encantadas"), *137*
Fenn, Mrs. Curtis, 310
Ferdinand II, King of the Two Sicilies, *137*, 143–44
Fergus, Major (*Omoo*), *137*
Fernandez, Juan, *137–38*
Ferryman ("The Encantadas"), *138*
Fiddlefie (*Mardi*), *138*
"The Fiddler," 38, *138*, 182, 290
Fidi (*Mardi*), *139*
Field, David Dudley, *139*, 405
"Field Asters," *139*
Fifth Nantucket Sailor (*Moby-Dick*), *139*
"The Figure-Head," *139*
Filson, John, 49
Finfi (*Mardi*), *139*
Fingal (MacPherson), 212
Finn ("Bridegroom-Dick"), *140*
First Nantucket Sailor (*Moby-Dick*), *140*
Flagstaff, George (*Redburn*), *140*
Flash Jack (*Omoo*), *140*
Flask (*Moby-Dick*), *140*
Flavona (*Mardi*), *140*
Fleece (*Moby-Dick*), *140*
Fletz (*Pierre*), *140*
Flinegan, Patrick (*White-Jacket*), *140*
Flinnigan, Patrick (*Redburn*), *140*
Flint (*Pierre*), *140*
Flint, Timothy, 92
Flitz (*Pierre*), *141*
Flute (*White-Jacket*), 141
Fly, Eli, 27, 28, *141*, 158
Fofi (*Mardi*), *141*
Foni (*Mardi*), *141*
Foofoo (*Mardi*), *141*
Ford, Miss ("Jimmy Rose"), *142*
Ford, Mrs. William ("Jimmy Rose"), *142*
Ford, William "Jimmy Rose"), *142*
" 'Formerly a Slave,' " *142*, 210
"The Fortitude of the North," *142*
Forty Days in the Desert (Bartlett), 81

Fouqué, Friedrich, 501
Fourth Nantucket Sailor (*Moby-Dick*), *142*
Fox, Luther, 65, 377, 426
"Fragment," *142*
"Fragments from a Writing Desk," *142–43*
"Fragments of a Lost Gnostic Poem," *143*
France, King Louis XVI (*Israel Potter*). *See* Louis XVI
Frances ("Jimmy Rose"), *143*
Francesco ("Benito Cereno"), *143*
Francis II, King of the Two Sicilies, 1, 137 *143–44*
Frank (*White-Jacket*), *144*, 159
Franklin, Benjamin, *144–45*, 180, 219, 427, 456
Frederick William II, *145–46*
The French Metropolis (Gardner), 160
French Sailor (*Moby-Dick*), *146*
"The Frenzy in the Wake," *146*
Frithiof's Saga (Tégner), 212
"Fruit and Flower Painter," *146*
Fry, Mrs. (*The Confidence-Man*), *146*
Fry, Thomas (*The Confidence-Man*), *146–47*
Fulvi (*Mardi*), *147*

G— ("Jimmy Rose"), *149*
Gabriel (*Moby-Dick*), *149*
Gaddi (*Mardi*), *149*
Galgo, Luys ("Benito Cereno"), *149*
Galvan, George, 140, 302, 367
Gammon (*White-Jacket*), *149*
Gandix, Hermenegildo ("Benito Cereno"), *149*
Gansevoort, Catherine Van Schaick (maternal grandmother), *149–50*, 152, 154, 155, 156–57, 159, 292, 345
Gansevoort, Guert (cousin), 43, 89, 96, 103, 118, 136, *150*, 152, 153, 154, 159, 448, 487
Gansevoort, Henry (cousin), 43, 68, 89, *152*, 155, 157, 238, 239, 309, 334, 403
Gansevoort, Herman (uncle), 107, 160, *152–53*, 154, 155, 156, 157, 159, 287, 330

Gansevoort, Hun (distant cousin), 150, *153–54*, 289, 487

Gansevoort, John Wessel, 159

Gansevoort, Leonard Herman (uncle), 150, *154*, 156, 157, 158,159

Gansevoort, Leonard Herman, Jr. (cousin), *154*, 289

Gansevoort, Mary Ann Chandonette (aunt), *154–55*

Gansevoort, Mary Sanford (aunt), 152, *155*, 156, 157

Gansevoort, Peter (1749–1812) (maternal grandfather), 149, 152, 154, *155–56*, 158, 159, 166, 292, 293, 345

Gansevoort, Peter (1788–1876) (uncle), 82, 92, 107, 141, 150, 152, 153, 154, 155, *156–58*, 159, 189, 200, 238, 277, 282, 283, 284, 288, 292, 431, 487

Gansevoort, Peter L. (cousin), 154, *158*

Gansevoort, Stanwix (cousin), 144, 153–54, *158–59*, 289, 293

Gansevoort, Susan (aunt), 157, 158, *159*

Gansevoort, Wessel (uncle), 150, 154, 156, 157, *159*

"The Garden of Metrodorus," *159–60*

Gardiner (*Moby-Dick*), *160*

Gardiner, Captain (*Moby-Dick*), *160*

Gardner, Augustus Kinsley, *160–61*

Garibaldi, Giuseppe, 29, 67, 137, 144, *161–62*, 384

Gayete, Juan Bautista ("Benito Cereno"), *162*

"The 'Gees," *162*, 182, 290

Genteel, Jack ("Bridegroom-Dick"), *162*

Gentian ("To Major John Gentian"), *163*

Gentian, John ("The Marquis de Grandvin"), *163*

Geoffry ("Under the Rose"), *163*

Geological Evidence of the Antiquity of Man (Lyell), 318

George, Prince Regent of England ("Poor Man's Pudding"), *163*

George III, 8, 10, *163–64*, 193

Georiana, Theresa (*Redburn*), *164*

German (John James[?]), 213

"Gettysburg," *164*

Ghibelli (*Mardi*), *164*

Ghofan ("Benito Cereno"), *164*

Gibbon, Edward, 6, 190

Gibbs, 467

Gifford, Robert Swain, 89, *164–65*

Ginger Nut ("Bartleby"), *165*

"Give Me the Nerve," *165*

Glaucon (*Clarel*), *165*

Glaucon (*Republic* of Plato), 165

Gleig, Samuel (*Moby-Dick*), *166*

Glen ("Bridegroom-Dick"), *166*

Glendinning (*Pierre*), *166*

Glendinning, Dorothea (*Pierre*), *166*

Glendinning, General Pierre (*Pierre*), *166*

Glendinning, Mary (*Pierre*), *166*

Glendinning, Pierre [father] (*Pierre*), *166*

Glendinning, Pierre [son] (*Pierre*), 8, *166–67*

Gola, Martinez ("Benito Cereno"), *167*

Gold-beak ("Under the Rose"), *167*

"The Gold Bug" (Poe), 179

"Gold in the Mountains," *167*

Goneril (*The Confidence-Man*), *167*

"The Good Craft 'Snow-Bird,' " *167*

Goodman, Francis (*The Confidence-Man*), *167–68*

Goodwell (*Redburn*), *168*

Graceman, Mark (*Pierre*), *168*

Grand Duke of Florence ("Marquis de Grandvin: At the Hostelry"), *168*

Grandissimo (*Mardi*), *168*

Grando (*Mardi*), *168*

Grandvin ("The Marquis de Grandvin"), *168*

Grant, Ulysses S., 71, 121, *168–70*, 178, 240, 244, 257, 363, 366, 393, 414, 415, 416, 483

Grasse, François Joseph Paul de, *170*, 390

Grattan, H. P., 332

Graveairs, Don (*Clarel*), *170*

Graveling (*Billy Budd*), *170*

"A Grave near Petersburg," *171*

Gray-back ("Armies of the Wilderness"), *171*

Great Duke ("Under the Rose"), *171*

"The Great Pyramid," *171*

"Greek Architecture." *171*

"Greek Masonry," *171*

Green, (*The Confidence-Man*), *171*

Greene, Herman Melville, 172

Greene, John Wesley, 172

Greene, Richard Tobias, 60, *171–72*, 374, 453, 455, 467

Greenlander (*Redburn*), *173*

Griggs, Helen Maria Melville (sister), *173*, 277, 282, 285, 287, 289, 383

Griswold, Rufus, 96, 429, 440

Groot, Myndert Van ("To Major John Gentian"), *173*

"A Ground Vine Intercedes," *173*

Grummet (*White-Jacket*), *174*

Guernseyman (*Moby-Dick*), *174*

Guide ("The Scout toward Aldie"), *174*

Guinea (*White-Jacket*), *174*

Gun-Deck (*Redburn*), *174*

Guy (*Omoo*), *174*

Habbibi (*Clarel*), *175*

Hafiz (*Clarel*), *175*

"The Haglets," 3, *175–76*

Hair, Richard Melville, 172

Hair-Brains ("The Scout toward Aldie"), *176*

Hal ("Bridegroom-Dick"), *176*

Hall, James, 92, *176*, 306

Hall, John, 71, 302, 432

Hals, Frans, 55, *176–77*

Haman ("The Bell-Tower"), *177*

Hamilton, Gail (Mary Dodge), 43

Hancock, John, *177–78*

Hancock, Winfield Scott, 96, *178*, 334

A *Handbook for Travellers in Syria and Palestine* (Murray), 81, 101

Handsome Sailor (*Billy Budd*), *179*

Hannibal, Rohon Del Aquaviva (*Clarel*), *179*

Hans ("A Dutch Christmas"), *179*

"The Happy Failure," *179*, 182, 290

Happy Man (*The Confidence-Man*), *179–80*

Hardy, Ezekiel (*Moby-Dick*), *180*

Hardy, Joe (*White-Jacket*), *180*

Hardy, Lem (*Omoo*), *180*

Hardy, Mrs. Ezekiel (*Moby-Dick*), *180*

Harper & Brothers, 5, *180–81*, 200, 267, 330, 331, 383, 387, 457, 468, 491

Harper's New Monthly Magazine, 99, 138, 164, 179, 180, *181–82*, 215, 290, 350, 363, 414

Harry (*Moby-Dick*), *182*

Harry the Reefer ("The Death Craft"), *182*

Hartley, David, 115

Hatch, Agatha. *See* Robertson, Agatha Hatch

Hauser, 1

Hautboy ("The Fiddler"), *182*

Hautia (*Mardi*), *182–83*

Hauto (*Mardi*), *183*

Hawthorne, Julian, 185

Hawthorne, Nathaniel, 5, 33, 57, 71, 84, 92, 93, 107, 120, 121, 125, 139, *183–85*, 192, 195, 198, 205, 258, 283, 290, 301, 304, 307, 331, 351, 354, 358, 372, 373, 405, 429, 447, 481, 494

"Hawthorne and His Mosses," 120, 184, *185–86*, 279, 289

Hay-Seed (*Moby-Dick*), *186*

"Hearth-Roses," *186*

"Hearts-of-Gold," *186*

Heath, Joyce ("The New Planet"), *187*. *See also* Heth, Joyce

Hello (*Mardi*), *187*

Helmstone ("The Fiddler"), *187*

Henro (*Mardi*), *187*

Henry, 165

Henry V ("Falstaff's Lament"), *187*

Henry VIII, 187

Her ("Lyon"), *187*

"Herba Santa," *187*

"Herman Melville" (Salt), 400

He Sing ("On the Chinese Junk"), *187*

Heth, Joyce, 26

Hevaneva (*Mardi*), *187–88*

High-Chief (*Moby-Dick*), *188*

High Priest (*Moby-Dick*), *188*

Hilary ("Inscription Epistolary"), *188*

Hill, Ambrose Powell, *188*

Hines, Ephraim, 242

Hiram [I] ("Rammon"), *188*

Historical Account of the Circumnavigation of the Globe (anon.), 330, 467

A *History of Berkshire County* (Smith), 419

A History of the County of Berkshire (Field), 15, 139, 405–6

History of the Decline and Fall of the Roman Empire (Gibbon), 190

A History of the Navy of the United States (Cooper), 208

History of Pittsfield, 139, 281

History of Religious Sects (Adams), 2

History of the State of New York (Brodhead), 55

Hivohitee MCCCLVIII (*Mardi*), *188–89*

Hoadley, Catherine (sister), 27, 124, *189*, 190, 277, 282, 284, 285, 287, 289, 292, 383

Hoadley, John, 6, 124, 152, *189–90*, 284, 293, 294, 434

Hodnose (*White-Jacket*), *190*

Hoff, William, 326

Hoffman, Charles Fenno, *190–91*

Hohori (*Mardi*), *191*

Holmes, Oliver Wendell, 184, *191–92*, 198, 214, 280, 291, 307, 308, 404, 419

Holy Joe ("Tom Deadlight"), *192*

"Honor," *192*

"The House-top," *192–93*, 290–91

Howe, William, *193*, 231

Hugh ("Running the Batteries"), *193*

Hughes, Edward, *193–94*, 432

Hull, Isaac, *194–95*, 220

Hull, William, 194, *195*

Hummee Hum (*Mardi*), *196*

Humphreys, Charles, 68

Hunilla ("The Encantadas"), *196*

Hurta, Roderego ("Benito Cereno"), *196*

Hussey, Hosea (*Moby-Dick*), *196*

Hussey, Mrs. Hosea (*Moby-Dick*), *196*

Huysum, Jan van, *196*

I (*Mardi*), *197*

"I and My Chimney," 100, 192, *197–98*, 285, 290, 372, 374

Ibrahim Pasha, *198*

Iceland Sailor (*Moby-Dick*), *198*

Ictinus, *198–99*

Ideea (*Omoo*), *199*

Ides (*Mardi*), *199*

"Immolated," *199*

"In a Bye Canal," *199*

"In a Church in Padua," *199–200*

"In a Garret," *200*

Inamorata ("Fragments from a Writing Desk"), *200*

"In a Nutshell," *200*

Incidents of Travel (Stephens), 400

Income for Melville, *200–201*

India ("Honor"), *201*

Inez (*Clarel*), *201*

Infelez ("Benito Cereno"), *201*

"Inscription Epistolary to W.C.R.," 104, *201*, 397

"Inscription for the Graves at Pea Ridge," *201*

"Inscription for Marye's Heights," *201–2*

"Inscription for the Dead at Fredericksburgh," *202*

"In Shards the Sylvan Vases Lie," *202*

"In the Desert," *202*

"In the Hall of Marbles," *202*

"In the Jovial Age of Old," *203*

"In the Old Farm-House," *203*

"In the Pauper's Turnip-Field," *203*

"In the Prison Pen," *203*, 425

"In the Turret," *203*

"Iris," *204*

Irving, Washington, 96, 120, 121, 198, *204–5*, 212, 239, 257, 288, 372, 373, 467

Ishmael, *205*

The Isle of the Cross, 5

Israel Potter, 92, 107, 139, 145, 200, *205–8*, 290, 358, 372, 374

Jack (*Moby-Dick*), *209*

Jack (*Omoo*), *209*

"Jack Gentian (omitted from the final sketch of him)," *209*

"Jack Roy," *210*

Jackson (*Redburn*), *210*

Jackson, Jane, *210*, 477, 478

Jackson, Thomas J. (Stonewall), 17, *210–11*, 240, 247, 363,431

Jacobi, Cranz (*Pierre*), *211*

Jacobs, Thomas, 346

Jake ("Cock-a-Doodle-Doo!"), *211*

James IV, 187

Jami, 501

Jarl (*Mardi*), *211–12*

Jarmi (*Mardi*), *212*

Jefferson, Joseph, *212*

Jehu (''Poor Man's Pudding''), *213*

Jenney, 65, 377, 426

Jennie (*Pierre*), *213*

Jennings, Betsy (*Redburn*), *213*

Jenny (*Moby-Dick*), *213*

Jermin, John (*Omoo*), *213*

Jeroboam (''Rammon''), *213*

Jethro (''Rammon''), *213*

Jewboy, Jack, (*Israel Potter*), *213*

Jewel, Jack (*White-Jacket*), *213*

Jewsharp Jim (''Bridegroom-Dick''), *213*

Jiji (*Mardi*), *213*

Jim (*Israel Potter*), *213*

Jim (*Omoo*), *214*

Jim (*White-Jacket*), *214*

Jimmy (*Typee*), *214*

''Jimmy Rose,'' 182, *214–15*, 281, 290

Jingling Joe (*Omoo*), *215*

Jiromo (*Mardi*), *215*

Joan (*Omoo*), *215*

Joanna I, 12, *215*

Joaquin, Marques de Aramboalaza (''Benito Cereno''), *215*

Jock (''Tom Deadlight''), *215*

Joe (*Moby-Dick*), *215*

Joe (*Omoo*), *216*

John (*White-Jacket*), *216*

John VI, *216*

''John Marr,'' *216*

John Marr, 43, 104, 107, *217*, 291, 397, 429

Johnson, Cave, *217–18*

Johnson, Dr. (Omoo), *218*

Johnson, Guy, *218*

Johnson, James, 47

Johnson, Professor, *218*

Johnson, William, 101

Johnstone, Francis, 218, 247

Jonah, *219*

Jonathan (''On the Chinese Junk''), *219*

Jonathan (*White-Jacket*), *219*

Jones (*Redburn*), *219*

Jones, Frank (*White-Jacket*), *219*

Jones, John Paul, 8–9, 145, *219–20*, 335, 344

Jones, Jonathan (*Redburn*), *220*

Jones, Mrs. (''Jack Gentian [omitted from the final sketch of him]''), *220*

Jones, Mrs. (*Redburn*), *220*

Jones, Thomas ap Catesby, 90, 194, *220–21*, 225

Jones Three (''The New Ancient of Days''), *221*

Jo Portuguese. *See* Luis, Joseph

Jos (''The New Ancient of Days''), *221*

José (''Benito Cereno''), *221*

Josy (*Omoo*), *221*

Journal of a Cruise Made into the Pacific Ocean (Porter), 129, 365, 467

Journal of Francis Kemble Butler (Kemble), 229

Journal of a Residence on a Georgia Plantation (Kemble), 229

Journal of Voyages (Bennet and Tyerman), 268

Journal of a Voyage to the North Whale-Fishery (Scoresby), 302

Judd, Gerrit Parmele, 69, *222–23*, 343

Judy (*Redburn*), *223*

Julia (''The Apple-Tree Table''), *223*

Julia (''I and My Chimney''), *223*

Kaahumanu, *225–26*

Kalow (*Typee*), *226*

Kamehameha I, 113, 188, 225, *226*, 443

Kamehameha II, 225, *226*, 268

Kamehameha III, 116, 220, 222, 225, *226–27*, 228, 343, 438,446

Kandidee, King of (*Mardi*), *227*

Kannakoko (*Mardi*), *227*

Karakoee (*Typee*), *227*

Karhownoo (*Mardi*), *227*

Karkeke (*Mardi*), *227*

Karkie (*Typee*), *227*

Karky (*Typee*), *227*

Karluna (*Typee*), *227*

Karnoonoo (*Typee*), *227*

Karolus [I] (*Mardi*), *227–28*

Karolus [II] (*Mardi*), *228*

Karrolono (*Mardi*), *228*

Katrina (''A Dutch Christmas''), *228*

Kean, Hosea ("The 'Gees''), *228*
Keei, 443
Kekuanoa (*Typee*), *228*
Kemble, Charles, *228*, 229, 417
Kemble, Frances, 93, 167, 184, *228–29*, 388, 405
Kemble, John Philip, 228, *229*, 417
Kennedy, John P., 202
Keying ("On the Chinese Junk''), *230*
Killett, Capt. ("On the Chinese Junk''), *230*
Kilpatrick, Judson, *230*
King ("Time's Betrayal''), *230*
King Henry IV, Part I (Shakespeare), 134, 187
King Henry IV, Part II (Shakespeare), 134, 187
King Henry V (Shakespeare), 187
Kit (*Pierre*), *231*
Kitoti (*Omoo*), *231*
Klanko (*Mardi*), *231*
Knowles, Ned (*White-Jacket*), 231
Knyphausen, Wilhelm von, *231–32*
Ko-ka-poo ("On the Chinese Junk''), *232*
Kokovoko, King of (*Moby-Dick*), *232*
Kolory (*Typee*), *232*
Konno (*Mardi*), *232*
Kooloo (*Omoo*), *232*
Kory-Kory (*Typee*), *232*
Krako (*Mardi*), *233*
Kravi (*Mardi*), *233*
Kroko (*Mardi*), *233*
Kubla (*Mardi*), *233*
"Kubla Khan" (Coleridge), 233

L., B. (*Clarel*), *235*
L— (*Redburn*), *235*
Laced Cap ("Bridegroom-Dick''), *235*
Laffite, Jean, *235–36*
Lais ("The Parthenon''), *236*
Lakreemo (*Mardi*), *236*
Lalla Rookh (Moore), 501
Lamia (Lamia's Song), *236*
Lanbranka Hohinna (*Mardi*), *236*
Landless (*White-Jacket*), *237*
Langford, Joseph, *237*
Langsdorff, Georg Heinrich von, *237*, 330, 467

Lansing, Abraham, 155, 157, 159, *237–38*, 431
Lansing, Catherine, 82, 152, 155, 157, 159, *238*, 431
Larfee (*Mardi*), *238*
Larry (*Redburn*), *239*
Larry o' the Cannakin ("Jack Roy''), *239*
Lascar Sailor (*Moby-Dick*), *239*
"The Last Leaf" (Holmes), 192, 214, 280
The Last Supper (Leonardo), 242
Lathers, Richard, *239*
Lavender (*Redburn*), *239*
Law, George, 146–47
Lazarus (*Clarel*), *239*
Lazarus (*Moby-Dick*), *239*
Lear, King, 167
Lecbe ("Benito Cereno''), *240*
Lectures on Rhetoric (Blair), 44
Lee, Robert E., 57, 169, 202, 211, *240–41*, 244, 247, 255, 309, 334, 363, 414, 431
Leech, Samuel, 440, 491
"Lee in the Capitol," *241*
Le Fan ("Bridegroom-Dick''), *241*
Lefevre (*Omoo*), *241*
Legare, Tom (*Redburn*), *241*
Leggs (*White-Jacket*), *242*
Lehr der Chemie (Berzelius), 37
Lemsford (*White-Jacket*), *242*
Leonardo da Vinci, *242–43*, 378
Lesbia ("The Vial of Attar''), *243*
Lesbian (*Clarel*), *243*
The Letters of Madame de Sévigné (Sévigné), 263
Levi, Max (*Clarel*), *243*
Lewis, Jack, (*Typee*), *243*
Lewis, Morgan ("Report of the Committee''), *243*
The Life and Adventures of John Nicol, Mariner (Nicol), 491
The Life and Character of Chevalier John Paul Jones (Sherburne), 208
Life and Correspondence of John Paul Jones (Sands), 131, 208
Life and Remarkable Adventures of Israel R. Potter (Trumbull), 207, 297, 495
Life in a Man-of-War (anon.), 491

"The Lightning-Rod Man," 100, *243–44*, 272, 273, 290

Lily ("Madcaps"), *244*

Limeno, The (*Clarel*), *244*

Lincoln, Abraham, 24, 89, 97, 161, 212, 240, *244–45*, 255, 273, 320, 394, 403, 433, 442, 483, 486

Lippi, Fra Filippo, *245*

Literary World, 120, 184, 186, 267, 289–90, 310

"The Little Good Fellows," *245*

Livella (*Mardi*), *245–46*

Livy, 246

Llanyllan (*Pierre*), *246*

Lockwood, Henry, 370

Logodora (*Mardi*), *246*

"The Loiterer," *246*

Lol Lol (*Mardi*), *246*

Lombardo (*Mardi*), *246*

"Lone Founts," *246*

Longfellow, Henry Wadsworth, 36, 104, 120, 184, 358, 372, 373, 429, 433

Long Ghost, (*Omoo*), *246–47*

Long Island Sailor (*Moby-Dick*), *247*

Long Jim (*Omoo*), *247*

Long-locks (*White-Jacket*), *247*

Long Lumbago ("Bridegroom-Dick"), *247*

Longstreet, James, 202, 240, *247–48*, 334, 363

Loo (*Omoo*), *248*

"Look-out Mountain," *248*

Loon, Billy (*Omoo*), *248*

Looney ("On the Sea Serpent"), *248*

Lord Mayor of London ("Poor Man's Pudding"), *249*

Lorrain, Claude, *249*, 435, 460

Los Gringos (Wise), 330

Lot ("Running the Batteries"), *249*

Louis (Ludwig) I, 251

Louis (Ludwig) II, 251

Louis (Ludwig) V, 251

Louis (Ludwig) VI, 251

Louis (Ludwig) VII, 251

Louis (Ludwig) X, 251

Louis (Ludwig) XIV, 251

Louis-Philippe, *249–50*, 335, 361, 438

Louis XVI, *250*

Love ("Hearth Roses"), *250*

Lovely, Lord (*Redburn*), *250*

"The Lover and the Syringa Bush," *250*

Lowell, Charles Russell, 43, 89, 404

Lowell, James Russell, 43, 89, 120, 372, 373, 404

Lowell, Josephine, 89, 403–4

Lucree (*Mardi*), *251*

Ludwig the Debonnaire (*Mardi*), *251*

Ludwig the Do-Nothing (*Mardi*), *251*

Ludwig the Fat (*Mardi*), *251*

Ludwig the Great (*Mardi*), *251*

Ludwig the Juvenile (*Mardi*), *251*

Ludwig the Pious (*Mardi*), *251*

Ludwig the Quarreler (*Mardi*), *251*

Ludwig the Stammerer (*Mardi*), *251*

Luff (*Omoo*), *252*

Lugar-Lips ("Under the Rose"), *252*

Luis, Joseph (Jo Portuguese), 302, 367

Luke ("The Scout toward Aldie"), *252*

Lullee (*Omoo*), *252*

The Lusiads (Camões), 64, 69, 70, 297

Lyell, Charles, 318, 319

"Lyon," *252*

Lyon, Nathaniel, 187, *252–53*, 333

Lyonese (*Clarel*), *253*

M— ("Fragments from a Writing Desk"), *255*

McClellan, George B., 178, 211, 240, 244, *255–56*, 260, 309, 363, 393, 429, 431, 486

McClellan's Own Story (McClellan), 256

McCloud (*Israel Potter*), *256*

Macey, Harry (*Moby-Dick*), *256*

Macey, Mrs. Harry (*Moby-Dick*), *256*

McGee (*Omoo*), *256*

Mack (*Omoo*), *256*

McNally, William, 45, 491

MacPherson, James, 212

McPherson, James Birdseye, 111, *257*

Macready, William, 237, *257–58*, 462

Macy, Seth (*Moby-Dick*), *258*

"Madam Mirror," *258*

"Madcaps," *258*

Mad Jack (*White-Jacket*), *258*

"Magian Wine," *259*

Magnalia Christi Americana (Mather), 14

"Magnanimity Baffled," *259*
Mahine, 259
Mahinee (*Omoo*), *259*
Mahmud II (Mahmoud), 32, *259*
Mahone ("The New Ancient of Days"), *260*
Mai-Mai (*Omoo*), *260*
Major ("Bridegroom-Dick"), *260*
Major ("Fragments from a Writing Desk"), *260*
Major ("The Scout toward Aldie"), *260*
"Major Gentian," *260*
Makenzie, Alexander, 43, 73, 96, 107, 150
"The Maldive Shark," *260*
Maltese Sailor (*Moby-Dick*), *260*
Malthus, Thomas, 187, 335
"Malvern Hill," *260–61*, 291
Manco Capac, 261
Mandeville (*White-Jacket*), *261*
Manko (*Mardi*), *261*
Man of the Cave of Engihoul ("The New Ancient of Days"), *261*
"The Man-of-War Hawk," *261*
Manta (*Mardi*), *261*
Manutius, Aldus, 7
Manxman (*Moby-Dick*), *262*
Mapenda ("Benito Cereno"), *262*
Mapple (*Moby-Dick*), *262*
Marbonna (*Omoo*), *262*
"The March into Virginia," *262*, 291
"The Marchioness of Brinvilliers," *262–63*
"The March to the Sea," *263*
Marcus Aurelius, 13, *263*
Marcy, William L., 20, *263–64*, 496
Mardi, 276
Mardi, 36, 37, 55, 107, 181, 184, 200, 244, *264–69*, 282, 283, 285, 288, 289, 290, 291, 382, 491
Mardonna (*Mardi*), *269*
Margoth (*Clarel*), *269*
Margrave ("The Margrave's Birth Night"), *269*
Marhar-Rarrar (*Omoo*), *269*
Marharvai (*Omoo*), *269*
Marheyo (*Typee*), *269*
Maria II, 216, *270*, 345

Marianna (Millais, *Marianna*), 270
Marianna (Shakespeare, *Measure for Measure*), 270
Marianna (Tennyson, "Marianna"), 270
Marianna (Tennyson, "Marianna in the South"), 270
Marianna ("The Piazza"), *270*
Marie (*Pierre*), *270*
A Marine's Sketches (Ames), 491
Marjora (*Mardi*), *270*
Mark (*Mardi*), *270*
Mark (*White-Jacket*), *270*
Marko (*Mardi*), *271*
Marmonora (*Mardi*), *271*
Marnoo (*Typee*), *271*
"Marquesan Melville" (Salt), 400
Marquis (*White-Jacket*), *271*
"The Marquis de Grandvin," *271*
"The Marquis de Grandvin: At the Hostelry," *271–72*
"The Marquis de Grandvin: Naples," *272*
Marr ("John Marr"), *272*
Marr, Mrs. John ("John Marr"), *272*
Marrot ("Bridegroom-Dick"), *272*
Marten (*Pierre*), *273*
Martha (*Pierre*), *273*
Martin Chuzzlewit (Dickens), 92
Martindale (*Israel Potter*), *273*
"The Martyr," *273*
Marvel, Bill (*Mardi*), *273*
Mary (*Redburn*), *273*
Masa, Francisco ("Benito Cereno"), *273*
Masaniello, 133, *273*, 387, 391
Master ("Old Counsel"), *273*
Master ("Under the Ground"), *274*
Mate ("The Death Craft"), *274*
Mather, Cotton, 14
Mathews, Cornelius, 120, 182, 184, 192, *274*, 500
Matilda (*Redburn*), 274
Matinqui ("Benito Cereno"), *275*
Matt ("Tom Deadlight"), *275*
Max the Dutchman (*Redburn*), *275*
Maxwell, Mungo (*Israel Potter*), *275*
May ("Stockings"), *275*
May-Day (*White-Jacket*), *275*
Mayhew (*Moby-Dick*), *275*

May Queen (*The Confidence-Man*), *275*
"The Medallion in Villa Albina," *275*
Media (*Mardi*), 275, *276*
"A Meditation Attributed to a Northerner," *276*
Meditations (Marcus Aurelius), 263
Meg (*Redburn*), *276*
Mehevi (*Typee*), *276*
Melvill, Allan (father), 7–8, 25, 68, 156, 157, 166, 173, 189, 214, 237, *276–78*, 279, 280, 282, 283, 287, 289, 292, 293, 321, 354, 383, 384, 409
Melvill, Ann (cousin), 25, *278*, 281
Melvill, Françoise (aunt), *278*, 279, 280, 281, 354
Melvill, George (cousin), *278*, 280, 281
Melvill, Helen (cousin), *278*, 281
Melvill, Henry (cousin), *279*, 281
Melvill, Julia (cousin), *279*, 281
Melvill, Mary (aunt), 71, 278, *279*, 281
Melvill, Nancy (aunt), 276, *279*, 280, 409
Melvill, Priscilla (aunt), 200, 276, *279*, 280
Melvill, Priscilla Scollay (paternal grandmother), 280
Melvill, Robert (cousin), 278, *279–80*, 281, 386
Melvill, Thomas (paternal grandfather), 8, 214, 276, *280*
Melvill, Thomas, Jr. (uncle), 8, 25, 71, 72, 276, 278, 279, *280–81*, 354, 393, 419
Melvill, Thomas Wilson (cousin), 281–82
Melville, Allan (brother), 27, 51, 124, 157, 173, 185, 189, 208, 219, 238, 239, 277, 278, *282–83*, 285, 286, 287, 289, 292, 294, 307, 308, 410, 413, 434, 468
Melville, Augusta (sister), 153, 277, 282, 283–84, 285, 289, 292, 295, 383, 408
Melville, Catherine Eliza (sister-in-law), *284*, 294
Melville, Catherine Gansevoort (sister). *See* Hoadley, Catherine (sister)
Melville, Elizabeth (daughter), 40, 223, *284–85*, 286, 287, 289, 291, 408, 411, 428, 445
Melville, Elizabeth Knapp Shaw (wife),
12, 27, 48, 82, 107, 108, 185, 198, 200, 223, 278, *285–87*, 289, 291, 307, 310, 321, 407, 408, 409, 410, 411, 419, 425, 429, 492
Melville, Frances (daughter). *See* Thomas, Frances Melville
Melville, Frances Priscilla (sister), 153, 200, 238, 277, 282, 285, *287*, 289, 292, 293, 383
Melville, Gansevoort (brother), 51, 55, 68, 141, 156, 189, 205, 219, 277, 282, 283, *287–89*, 292, 294, 312, 330, 372, 380, 383, 427, 450, 467, 504
Melville, Helen (sister). *See* Griggs, Helen Maria Melville
Melville, Herman, *289–91*
Melville, Malcolm (son), 161, 239, 284, 285, 286, 289, *291–92*, 293, 408, 410, 412, 428
Melville, Maria Gansevoort (mother), 124, 143, 150, 153, 154, 155, 156, 157–58, 159, 173, 185, 189, 198, 238, 277, 282, 283, 285, 287, 289, *292–93*, 294, 345, 383, 450
Melville, Stanwix (son), 156, 285, 286, 289, 291, *293–94*, 295, 321, 408, 411, 428
Melville, Thomas (brother), 107, 124, 152, 199, 277, 280, 283, 284, 287, 289, 290, 292, 293, *294–95*, 407, 410, 454, 457
Memoirs (Abrantes), 1
Memorial of Henry Sanford Gansevoort (eds. Hoadley and Lansing), 152
Merry Andrews ("Marquis de Grandvin: Naples"), *295*
"Merry Ditty of the Sad Man," *295*
Merrymusk ("Cock-a-Doodle-Doo!"), *295*
Merrymusk, Mrs. ("Cock-a-Doodle-Doo!"), *295*
Metcalf, Eleanor (granddaughter), 284–85, 445
Methodist (*Clarel*), *295*
Methodist, The (*The Confidence-Man*), *295*
Metrodorus, *295–96*
Michelangelo, *296*, 424, 451

Mickle, William, 69, *296–97*

Midni (*Mardi*), *297*

"Milan Cathedral," *297*

Millais, John, 270

Millet, John (*Israel Potter*), *297*

Millthorpe (*Pierre*), *297*

Millthorpe, Charles (*Pierre*), *298*

Millthorpe, Miss (*Pierre*), *298*

Millthorpe, Mrs. (*Pierre*), *298*

Milton, John, 81

Mink ("The Scout toward Aldie"), *298*

Minta (*Mardi*), *298*

Miquel ("Benito Cereno"), *298*

Miriam ("Magian Wine"), *298*

"Misgivings," *298*, 290

The Missionary's Reward (Pritchard), 370

Mitchell, Maria, 471

Moby-Dick, 37, 57, 107, 181, 182, 185, 190, 200, 269, 290, 292, 293, *298– 303*, 307, 309, 344, 354, 357, 425, 460, 492

"Mocha Dick" (Reynolds), 302, 387

Mocmohoc (*The Confidence-Man*), *303*

Moerenhout, Jacques-Antoine, 116, 222, 250, *303–4*, 311, 343, 370

Mohi (*Mardi*), *304*

Mohijeddin Al-Arabi, 304

Molly (*Redburn*), *304*

Mondi (*Mardi*), *304*

Monee (*Omoo*), *304*

"Monody," *304*

Monoo (*Typee*), *304*

"Monsieur Miroir" (Hawthorne), 258, 494

Montaigne, Michel, *305*

"Montaigne and His Kitten," *305*

Montégut, Émile, 208

Montgomery (*White-Jacket*), *305*

Moonoony (*Typee*), *306*

Moore, Frank, 25

Moore, Thomas, 501

Morairi, José ("Benito Cereno"), *306*

Mordant (*Billy Budd*), *306*

Mordecai (*Omoo*), *306*

Moredock, John, 92; (*The Confidence-Man*), *306*

Moredock, Mrs. (*The Confidence-Man*), *306*

Morewood, John Rowland, 283, *307*, 419

Morewood, Sarah Huyler, 283, 288, *307– 8*, 310, 419

Morgan, Cadwallader, 101

Morille (*Redburn*), *308*

Morn ("The Scout toward Aldie"), *308*

Morrison, William, *308*

Mortmain (*Clarel*), *309*

Mosby, John, 43, 152, 238, *309–10*

Mosby's War Reminiscences (Mosby), 309

Mosses from an Old Manse (Hawthorne), 71, 186, 279, 351

Mother Moll (*Omoo*), *310*

"The Mound by the Lake," *310*, 429

Mounttop (*Moby-Dick*), *310*

Mowanna (*Typee*), *310*

Mow Mow (Mow-Mow) (*Typee*), *310*

Moyar (*Pierre*), *310*

"Mr. Parkman's Tour," *310–11*

Muhji ed-Din, 304

Mungo (*Typee*), *311*

"The Murder of Philip Spencer" (Hamilton), 43

Mure ("Benito Cereno"), *311*

Murphy, James, *311*

Murray, John, 36, 55, 81, 95, 101, 205, 232, 267, 283, 288, *312*, 330, 331, 340, 400, 407, 411, 413, 467

Mustapha (*Clarel*), *312*

"The Muster," *312–13*

"Mutiny on the 'Somers' " (Smith), 43

"My Jacket Old," *313*

Nacta ("Benito Cereno"), *315*

Na Motu; or, Reef-Rovings in South Seas (Perkins), 32, 33, 252, 492, 503

Namesakes. *See* Greene, Herman Melville; Hair, Richard Melville; Russ, Herman Melville

Napoleon, 145, 235, *315–16*, 488

Narmonee (*Typee*), 316

Narnee (*Typee*), 316

A Narrative of Colonel Ethan Allen's Captivity (Allen), 8, 208, 256

Narrative of a Four Months' Residence among the Natives of a Valley in the Marquesas (Melville), 467. *See also Typee*

Narrative of the . . . Shipwreck of the Whale-Ship Essex (Chase), 70, 302

Narrative of the United States Exploring Expedition (Wilkes), 6, 83, 136, 268, 302, 330, 375

A Narrative of Voyages and Travels (Delano), 36, 68

Narrative of a Whaling Voyage around the Globe (Bennett), 13, 182–83, 268, 302, 401

Nat (''Benito Cereno''), *316*

Nathan (*Clarel*), *316*

Nature, Dame (''The Encantadas''), *316*

The Naval History of the Civil War (Porter), 366

Navy Bob (*Omoo*), *316*

Ned (*Pierre*), *316*

Ned (*Redburn*), *316*

Ned (''Running the Batteries''), *316*

Ned (*Typee*), *317*

Nehemiah (*Clarel*), *317*

Nellie (*Pierre*), *317*

Nellie (''Stockings''), *317*

Nelson, Horatio, 40, *317–18*, 312, 315, 397

Nesle (''L'Envoy''), *318*

Nestors (''Marquis de Grandvin: Naples''), *318*

''The New Ancient of Days,'' *318–19*

''The New Planet,'' *319*

''The New Rosicrucians,'' *319*

''The New Zealot,'' *319–20*

Nichols, George, 263

Nicol, John, 491

''The Night-March,'' *320*

The Nile Boat (Barlett), 81

Nimni (*Mardi*), *320*

Nina (*Mardi*), *320*

Nippers (''Bartleby''), *320*

Noble, Charles (*The Confidence-Man*), *320*

Nones (*Mardi*), *320*

Nonno (*Mardi*), *320*

Noojoomo (*Mardi*), *320*

Noomai (*White-Jacket*), *321*

Nord (*White-Jacket*), *321*

Normo (*Mardi*), *321*

Nourse, Lucy (aunt), 276, 280, *321*

Nulli (*Mardi*), *321*

O (*Mardi*), *323*

Oberlus (''The Encantadas''), *323*

O'Brien (*Redburn*), *323*

O'Brien, Mrs. (*Redburn*), *323*

Observations on Man (Hartley), 115

An Ocean Tragedy (Russell), 397

O'Connell, Daniel, 232, *323–24*

''Ode on the Death of the Duke of Wellington'' (Tennyson), 318

''Ode to Dejection'' (Coleridge), 98

''Off Cape Colonna,'' *324*

Ohiro Moldona Fivona (*Mardi*), *324*

Oh-Oh (*Mardi*), *324*

''Old Age,'' (*Mardi*), *324*

Old Coffee (*White-Jacket*), *325*

Old Combustibles (*White-Jacket*), *325*

Old Conscience (*The Confidence-Man*), *325*

''Old Counsel,'' *325*

''The Old Fashion,'' *325*

Old Gamboge (*Omoo*), *325*

''The Old Garden'' (Street), 431

Old Gay-Head Indian (*Moby-Dick*), *325*

Old Honesty (*The Confidence-Man*), *325*

''Old Ironsides'' (Holmes), 192, 194

''The Old Manse'' (Hawthorne), 351

Old Mother Tot (*Omoo*), *326*

Old Plain Talk (*The Confidence-Man*), *326*

Old Prudence (*The Confidence-Man*), *326*

Old Revolver (*White-Jacket*), *326*

''The Old Shipmaster,'' *326*

Old Wine in New Bottles (Gardner), 160, 161

Old Yarn (*White-Jacket*), *326*

Omoo, 107, 153, 181, 200, 267, 268, 285, 289, 312, *326–31*, 400, 425

''On a Natural Monument,'' *331*

Ononna (*Mardi*), *331*

''On Sherman's men who fell,'' *331–32*

''On the Chinese Junk,'' *332–33*

''On the Grave of a young Cavalry Officer,'' *333*

''On the Home Guards who perished,'' *333*

"On the Men of Maine killed," *333*
"On the Photograph of a Corps Commander," *334*
"On the Sea Serpent," *334*
"On the Slain at Chickamauga," *334*
"On the Slain Collegians," *335*
Oram (*Mardi*), *335*
Orchis (*The Confidence-Man*), *335*
Orchis, Mrs. (*The Confidence-Man*), *335*
Orléans, Louis-Philippe-Joseph, *335–36*.
    See also Chartres, Louis-Philippe-Joseph
Ormulum (Orm), 336
O'Regan, Mike (*Redburn*), *335*
O'Regan, Mrs. (*Redburn*), *335*
O'Regan, Pat (*Redburn*), *335*
O'Regan, Teddy (*Redburn*), *335*
Orlop Bob ("Bridegroom-Dick"), *336*
Orm, *336*
Orme, Daniel ("Daniel Orme"), *336*
Ormsby, William, 43
Osceola, *336–37*
Othello (Shakespeare), 237, 258, 462
Otho (*Mardi*), *337*
Ottimo (*Mardi*), *337*
Ovid, 11
Ozonna (*Mardi*), *337*

Pacific and Indian Oceans (Reynolds), 387
Paige, Elbridge, 114
Paivai (*Mardi*), *339*
Paki, 341
Palaverer (*The Confidence-Man*), *339*
Palmer (*Clarel*), *339*
Palmer ("The Encantadas"), *339*
Pani (*Mardi*), *339*
Pansy ("The Scout toward Aldie"), *339*
Paola of Verona. *See* Veronese, Paolo
Paper Jack (*White-Jacket*), *340*
"The Paradise of Bachelors and the Tartarus of Maids," 182, 290, 312, *340*, 363, 462
Paraita (*Omoo*), *340*
Parker (*Israel Potter*), *341*
Parki (*Mardi*), *341*
Parkins (*Redburn*), *341*
Parkman, Francis, 120, 289, 410

Parkman, George, 83, 410
Parmelee, Mary, 143
Parrott, Robert, 435
Parsee ("The Rose Farmer"), *341*
"The Parthenon," *341*
Pat (*Omoo*), *341*
Pat (*Redburn*), *341*
Patella (*White-Jacket*), *341*
Paterson, John, 342
Patriarch (*Clarel*), *342*
Paul (*Omoo*), *342*
Paulet, George, 69, 222, *342–43*, 446
Paul Pry ("To Ned"), *343*
Pausanius, 198
"Pausilippo," *343*, 347
Pazzi, Madame ("The Apple-Tree Table"), *343*
Pearson, Richard, *343–44*
Pease, Valentine, Jr., 6, 302, *344*, 423
"Pebbles," *344*
Pedro, Don (*Moby-Dick*), *344*
Pedro II, 216, 270, *345*
Peebles, Maria, 143, *345*
Peenee (*Mardi*), *345*
Peepe, 345
Peepi (*Mardi*), *345–46*
Peggy (*Redburn*), *346*
Peleg (*Moby-Dick*), *346*
Pelican (*White-Jacket*), *346*
Pellico, Silvio, 343, *346–47*, 418
Pence, Peter (*Pierre*), *347*
Pendiddi (*Mardi*), *347*
Pennie (*Pierre*), *347*
Peri ("Marquis de Grandvin: Naples"), *347*
Pericles, 17–18, 198, *347*, 356
Pericles ("Syra"), *348*
Perkins, Edward, 32–33, 252, 492, 503
Perkins, Peter (*Israel Potter*), *348*
Perry, Oliver Hazard, 107, *348*
Persian ("The Rose Farmer"), *348*
Personal Memoirs (Grant), 169, 178
Personal Memoirs (Sheridan), 414
Pert (*White-Jacket*), *349*
Perth (*Moby-Dick*), *349*
Perth, Mrs. (*Moby-Dick*), *349*
Pesti (*Mardi*), *349*
Peter (*White-Jacket*), *349*

Peter the Wild Boy (*White-Jacket*), *349*
Peterson, T. B., 208, 372
Phidias, 198
Phil ("Bridegroom-Dick"), *349*
Phil (*Israel Potter*), *349*
Phillis ("Marquis de Grandvin: At the Hostelry"), *350*
Philo (*Mardi*), *350*
Philosophical Intelligence Office Man (*The Confidence-Man*), *350*
Phipora (*Mardi*), *350*
Phocian, *350*
"The Piazza," 290, *350–51*
The Piazza Tales, 92, 290, 291, *351*, 354
The Picture of Liverpool, 383
Pierre (*White-Jacket*), *351*
Pierre, 37, 92, 107, 156, 173, 181, 278, 285, 290, 291, 292, *351–55*, 358, 492
Piko (*Mardi*), *355*
Pills (*White-Jacket*), *355*
Pip (*Moby-Dick*), *355*
Pipes (*White-Jacket*), *355*
"Pisa's Leaning Tower," *355*
Pitch (*The Confidence-Man*), *355–56*
Pius IX, *356*
Placido, *356*
Plato, 350, *356–57*, 400
Platoff ("Poor Man's Pudding"), *357*
Plinlimmon, Plotinus (*Pierre*), *357*
Plunkett, Henry Willoughby Grattan. *See* Grattan, H. P.
Plunkett ("On the Chinese Junk"), *357–58*. *See also* Grattan, H. P.
Plutarch, 450
Poe, Edgar Allan, 93, 120, 179, *358*, 372, 373, 425, 440
Poky (*Omoo*), *359*
Polk, James K., 9, 20, 217, 288, 401, 403, 504
Pollard, George, 70, *359*
Pollo (*Mardi*), *359*
Pond, Rachel, 204
Polynesia (Russell), 330
Polynesian Researches (Ellis), 188, 268, 330, 401, 467, 501
Pomare I, *359–60*, 438
Pomare II, *359*, 360
Pomare III, *360*

Pomare IV, 116, 117, 250, 303, 311, 343, *360–61*, 367, 370, 417, 437, 438, 446, 493
Ponce ("Benito Cereno"), 36, *361*
Pondo (*Mardi*), *362*
"Pontoosuce," *362*
Poofai (*Mardi*), *362*
"Poor Man's Pudding and Rich Man's Crumbs," 182, 290, 340, *362–63*, 406, 452
The Poor Rich Man and the Rich Poor Man (Sedgwick), 406
Pope, John, 255, *363–64*, 393
Pope, The ("The New Ancient of Days"), *364*
Po-Po, Emeemear (*Omoo*), *364*
"The Portent," 290, *364*
Porter, David, 106, 129, 135, 220, *364–66*, 467
Porter, David Dixon, 135, 365, *366–67*, 415
"Portrait of a Gentleman," *367*
Portuguese Sailor (*Moby-Dick*), *367*
Potter (*Israel Potter*), *367*
Potter, Israel R., 145
Potter Mrs. (*Israel Potter*), *368*
Pounce (*White-Jacket*), *368*
Poussin, Nicolas, 249, *368–69*, 435, 475
Praxiteles, 111
The Prelude (Wordsworth), 109
Prescott, Richard, *256*
"Presentation to the Authorities," *369*
Priming (*White-Jacket*), *369*
Primo (*Mardi*), *369*
Prince — ("Rammon"), *369*
Prince of Golconda ("The Marquis de Grandvin"), *369*
Principles of Geology (Lyell), 319
Prior, Matthew, 9
Pritchard, George, 58, 116, 311, 360, *369–70*, 493
Pritchard, Mrs. (*Typee*), *370*
Professor (*White-Jacket*), *370*
"Profundity and Levity," *371*
Punchinello ("Marquis de Grandvin: Naples"), *371*
Purser (*Billy Budd*), *371*
Putnam, George, 31, 120, 206, 208, 288,

358, *371–72*, 373, 425, 467–68
Putnam, Israel, *372–73*
Putnam's Monthly Magazine, 28, 33, 99,
    100, 172, 197, 206, 208, 244, 290,
    373–74, 371, 425, 462
"Puzzlement as to a Figure," *374*

Queequeg (*Moby-Dick*), *375*
Quiddi (*Mardi*), *375*
Quixote, Don, *375–76*
Quoin (*White-Jacket*), *376*

Rabbi (*Clarel*), *377*
Rabeelee, (*Mardi*), *377*
Rabelais, François, 377
Radney (*Moby-Dick*), *377*
Radney, Mrs. (*Moby-Dick*), *377*
"A Rail Road Cutting near Alexandria,"
    377–78
"Rammon," *378*
Raneds ("Benito Cereno"), *378*
Rani (*Mardi*), *378*
Raphael, *378–79*
Rartoo (*Omoo*), *379*
Rash (*White-Jacket*), *379*
Ratcliffe (*Billy Budd*), *379*
"The Ravaged Villa," *379*
Raveling (*White-Jacket*), *379*
Ravoo (*Mardi*), *379*
Raymond, Frederick, 302
Raymonda (*Mardi*), *379*
Rea (*Mardi*), *380*
"A Reasonable Constitution," *380*
Reason the Only Oracle of Man (Allen),
    8
Reb ("The Scout toward Aldie"), *380*
"Rebel Color-Bearers at Shiloh," *380*
Rebellion Record (Moore), 24–25, 372
Redburn, 36, 37, 51, 107, 154, 161, 181,
    184, 200, 237, 267, 278, 285, 294,
    380–83, 321, 382, 491
Redburn, Jane (*Redburn*), *383*
Redburn, Martha (*Redburn*), *383*
Redburn, Mary (*Redburn*), *383*
Redburn, Mrs. Walter (*Redburn*), *383*
Redburn, Walter (*Redburn*), *384*
Redburn, Wellingborough (*Redburn*), *384*
Red Hot Coal (*White-Jacket*), *384*

Red Pepper (*Billy Budd*), *384*
The Red Rover (Cooper), 96, 372, 447
Red Whiskers (*Billy Budd*), *384*
The Refugee (Melville), 208, 372. *See
    also Israel Potter*
Rehoboam ("Rammon"), *384*
Reine (*Omoo*), *384–85*
"The Released Rebel Prisoner," *385*
Rembrandt, 113, *385–86*
Reminiscences of Richard Lathers (Lath-
    ers), 239
"Report of the Committee on Agricul-
    ture," 280, *386*
*Reports of Cases . . . in the Surrogate's
    Court of the County of New York*
    (Bradford), 50
Representative Selections (Melville, ed.
    Thorp), 130
The Republic (Plato), 165
"A Requiem for Soldiers lost in Ocean
    Transports," *386*
"The Returned Volunteer to his Rifle,"
    386, 429
"The Return of the Sire of Nisle," *396*
Reynolds, Jeremiah, 302, *386–87*
R.F.C. *See* Cooke, Robert Francis
Rhyming Ned ("Bridegroom-Dick"), *387*
Ribera, Jusepe de, 133, *387*, 391
Richelieu (Bulwer-Lytton), 258, 462
Ridendiabola (*Mardi*), *388*
Riga (*Redburn*), *388*
Rigadoon Joe ("Bridegroom-Dick"), *388*
Rigs (*Redburn*), *388*
Ringbolt, 131, 132, 388. *See also* Cod-
    man, John
Ringbolt (*White-Jacket*), *388. See also*
    Codman, John
Ringman, John (*The Confidence-Man*),
    388
Ringrope (*White-Jacket*), *388*
"Rip Van Winkle" (Irving), 205, 212
"Rip Van Winkle's Lilac," *389*
Rob ("Stockings"), *389*
Roberts, Henry (*The Confidence-Man*),
    389
Robertson, Agatha Hatch, 5, 86
Robertson, James, 5, 86
Robins (*Omoo*), *389*

Robles, Juan ("Benito Cereno"), *389*
Roddi (*Mardi*), *390*
Rodney, George, 170, *390*
Roe (*Mardi*), *390*
Roi Mori (*Mardi*), *390*
Rolfe (*Clarel*), *390–91*
Rondo the Round (*Mardi*), *391*
Roo (*Mardi*), *391*
Roonoonoo (*Mardi*), *391*
Rope Yarn (*Omoo*), *391*
Rosa Salvator, 133, *391–92*
Rosamond ("Amoroso"), *392*
"Rosary Beads," *392*
Roscoe, William, *392–93*
Rose, James ("Jimmy Rose"), *393*
Rosecrans, William, 31, 334, *393–94*
"The Rose Farmer," *394*
Rose-Water (*White-Jacket*), *395*
"Rose Window," *395*
Rosman, James, 302
Rotato (*Mardi*), *395*
The Round Trip (Codman), 86
Routledge, George, 331, 467
Rovenna (*Clarel*), *395*
Rowland (*Pierre*), *395*
Rowser (*Israel Potter*), *395*
Roy, Jack ("Jack Roy"), *395*
Rozas, Juan ("Benito Cereno"), *395*
Ruaruga (*Typee*), *395*
Rubens, Peter Paul, *395–96*, 444, 475, 478
"Running the Batteries," *397*
Russ, Herman Melville, 172, 321
Russell, William Clark, 104, 107, 188, 217, *397*
Russian (*Clarel*), *398*
"The Rusty Man," 376, *398*
Rutn, (*Clarel*), 398

"Saadi" (Emerson), 501
Sailors' Life and Sailors' Yarns (Ringbolt), 86, 131, 388
St. Jago's Sailor (*Moby-Dick*), *399*
Salem (*Omoo*), *399*
Sally (*Redburn*), *399*
Salt, Henry, *399–400*, 447
Salvaterra (*Clarel*), *400*
Sambo ("Authentic Anecdotes"), *400*

"The Same," *400*
Samoa (*Mardi*), *401*
Sampson (*Redburn*), *401*
Sands, Robert, 131, 208
Sanford, Nathan, 155, 157
Santa Anna, Antonio Lopez de, 11, *401–2*
Saturnina (*Mardi*), *402*
Saveda, Miguel (*Redburn*), *402*
Sawyer (*White-Jacket*), *402*
The Scarlet Letter (Hawthorne), 186
Scenes, Incidents, and Adventures in the Pacific Ocean (Jacobs), 346
Schiller, Johann Christoph Friedrich von, 200
Schmerling, Philippe, 261, 319
Scoresby, William, Jr., 302
Scott, Winfield, 169, 178, 240, 247, 255, 401, *402–3*, 442, 495, 496
"The Scout toward Aldie," 152, *403–4*
Scribe, Hiram ("I and My Chimney"), *404*
Scriggs (*White-Jacket*), *404*
Scrimmage (*White-Jacket*), *404*
Seafull (*White-Jacket*), *404*
Sea voyages by Melville, *404–5*
Sebastian (*Moby-Dick*), *405*
Second Nantucket Sailor (*Moby-Dick*), *405*
Sedgwick, Catharine Maria, *405–6*
Seignioroni (*White-Jacket*), *406*
Selkirk, Countess of (*Israel Potter*), *406*
Selkirk, Earl of, *406*
Selvagee (*White-Jacket*), *407*
Sereno (*White-Jacket*), *407*
Sereno, Bonito, 68
Sergeant ("The Scout toward Aldie"), *407*
"Several Days in the Berkshire" (Mathews), 307
Sévigné, Madame de, 263
"Shadow at the Feast," *407*
Shakespeare, William, 81, 134, 167, 186, 187, 203, 237, 258, 270
Shakings (*White-Jacket*), *407*
Shanks (*White-Jacket*), *407*
Sharp-Eyes ("A Dutch Christmas"), *407*
Shaw, Elizabeth Knapp, 285, *407–8*, 409

Shaw, Hope (stepmother-in-law), 82, 267, 284, 285, *408*, 409,411
Shaw, John (brother-in-law), *408–9*
Shaw, Lemuel (father-in-law), 5, 28, 71, 83, 92, 104, 107, 173, 190, 200, 279, 280, 281, 282, 285–86, 289, 290, 292, 321, 359, 382, 411, 407, 408, *409–11*, 434, 467, 491
Shaw, Lemuel, Jr. (brother-in-law), 200, 286, 293, 409, 410, *411*
Shaw, Samuel (brother-in-law), 409, *411–12*
Sheba, Princess of ("Rammon"), *412*
Shelley, Mary, 33
Shelley, Percy Bysshe, 4, 399, 401, *412*
"Shelley's Vision," *412–13*
Shenly (*White-Jacket*), *413*
Shenly, Mrs. (*White-Jacket*), *413*
Shepherd, Daniel, 282, *413*
Sherburne, John, 208
Sheridan, Philip, 123, *413–14*, 431
"Sheridan at Cedar Creek," 291, 309, *414–15*, 425
Sherman, William Tecumseh, 71, 123, 230, 248, 263, 313,*415–16*
"Shiloh," 291, *416*, 429
Shippy (*White-Jacket*), *416*
"The Shipwreck" (Falconer), 133–34, 324
Shirrer (*Israel Potter*), *416–17*
"A Short Patent Sermon," *417*
"Short Patent Sermons" (Dow), 114
Shorty (*Omoo*), *417*
Sicilian Sailor (*Moby-Dick*), *417*
Sid ("Bridegroom-Dick"), *417*
Siddons, Sarah, 38, 228, 229, *417–18*
Sidonia, Alonzo ("Benito Cereno"), *418*
Silva, Marquis of (*White-Jacket*), *418*
Silvio ("Pausilippo"), *418*
Simonides, 98
Sinai and Palestine (Stanley), 81, 101
Singles, Jenny (*Israel Potter*), *418*
Singles, Sergeant (*Israel Potter*), *418*
Sketches of History, Life, and Manners, in the West (Hall), 92, 306
"Sketch of Major Thomas Melville Junior" (Melville), 281
Slim (*White-Jacket*), *418*

Slyboots, Sir ("The Scout toward Aldie"), *418*
Small, Elisha, 43
Smart (*Billy Budd*), *418*
Smith, Adam, 112
Smith, Edward, 281
Smith, H. D., 43
Smith, Joe ("The New Ancient of Days"), *418*
Smith, Joseph, 307, 308, *419*
Smollett, Tobias, 101
Smythe, Henry, *419*
Snarles (*Moby-Dick*), *420*
Sneak (*White-Jacket*), *420*
Snodhead (*Moby-Dick*), *420*
Sober Sides (*Mardi*), *420*
Socrates, 165
Socrates ("The Paradise of Bachelors"), *420*
Soldier ("An Epitaph"), *420*
Solo (*Mardi*), *420*
Solomon, *420–21*
"The South Seas," 97, 290, *421*
Spagnoletto ("Marquis de Grandvin: At the Hostelry"), *421*
Spanish Sailor (*Moby-Dick*), *421*
Spencer, John, 43
Spencer, Philip, 43
Spenser, Edmund, 33, 186, 267
Spinoza, Baruch, *422*
Spirit ("A Spirit Appeared to Me"), *422*
"A Spirit Appeared to Me," *422*
Squaretoes, Squire ("Cock-a-Doodle-Doo!"), *422*
Squeak (*Billy Budd*), *422*
Standard ("The Fiddler"), *422–23*
Stanley, Arthur, 81, 101
Stanly, Glendinning (*Pierre*), *423*
Starbuck (chief mate in *Moby-Dick*), 302, *423*
Starbuck (*Moby-Dick*), *423*
Starbuck, Mary (*Moby-Dick*), *423*
Starr ("Bridegroom-Dick"), *423*
Starry Banner ("Bridegroom-Dick"), *424*
"Statues in Rome," 290, *424*
Stedman, Edmund Clarence, 111, 284, *424–26*, 429
Steel (*Pierre*), *426*

Steelkilt (*Moby-Dick*), *426*
Steen, Jan, *426–27*
Stephens, John, 400
Stetson (*White-Jacket*), *427*
Stevens, Henry, *427–28*
Steward ("The Scout toward Aldie"), *428*
Stewart, Charles, 330, 467
Stiggs (*Moby-Dick*), *428*
Still, Bob (*Redburn*), *428*
"Stockings in the Farm-House Chimney," *428*
Stockton ("On the Chinese Junk"), *428*
Stoddard, Richard Henry, *428–29*, 440
"The Stone Fleet," 425, *430*
"Stonewall Jackson (Ascribed to a Virginian)," *430*
"Stonewall Jackson Mortally Wounded," *430*
The Story of the Great March (Nichols), 263
The Stranger's Grave (Plunkett), 357–58
Street, Alfred, 36, *430–31*
Stribbles (*White-Jacket*), *431*
Stuart, James E. B., 240, 309, 414, *431*
Stuart's Cavalry Campaign (Mosby), 309
Stubb (*Moby-Dick*), *432*
Stubbs (*Omoo*), *432*
Sub-Sub (*Moby-Dick*), *432*
Suffren de Saint Tropez, Pierre André de, 194, *432–33*
Sugar-Lips ("Under the Rose"). *See* Lugar-Lips
"Suggested by the Ruins of a Mountain-Temple," *433*
Sultan of Sulus, 136
Sumner, Charles, 411, *433–34*
Sunshine (*White-Jacket*), *434*
Surgeon ("Bridegroom-Dick"), *434*
Surgeon ("The Scout toward Aldie"), *434*
Surgeon of the Army in Mexico ("Authentic Tales"), *434*
"The Surrender at Appomattox," *434*
Susan (*Pierre*), *434*
Swain, Nathan (*Moby-Dick*), *435*
"The Swamp Angel," *435*
Swanevelt, Herman van, *435*

Sweeny (*Redburn*), *436*
Sydney Ben (*Omoo*), *436*
"Syra," *436*
Syrian Monk (*Clarel*), *436*

Taff the Welshman (*Billy Budd*), *437*
Taghconic (Smith), 308, 319
Tahar, King of (*Omoo*), *437*
Tahitian Sailor (*Moby-Dick*), *437*
Taji (*Mardi*), *437–38*
Tajo, 438
Talara (*Mardi*), *438*
Talbot, John (*Moby-Dick*), *438*
Talbot, Miss (*Moby-Dick*), *438*
Tamatoy (*Omoo*), *438*
Tammaro (*Mardi*), *438*
Tanee (*Mardi*), *438*
Taquinoo (*Mardi*), *439*
Tarnmoor, Salvator R., 127, *439*
Tarquinius (Lucius Tarquinius Priscus), *439*, 504
Tarquinius (Lucius Tarquinius Superbus), *439*, 504
Tartan (*Pierre*), *439*
Tartan, Frederic (*Pierre*), *439*
Tartan, Lucy (*Pierre*), *439*
Tartan, Mrs. (*Pierre*), *439–40*
Tashtego (*Moby-Dick*), *440*
Tati (*Omoo*), *440*
Tawney (*White-Jacket*), *440*
Taylor, Bayard, 120, 168, 372, 373, 429, *440–42*, 462
Taylor, Zachary, 11, 27, 45–46, 51, 169, 244, 247, 308, 326, 363, 402, 415, 433, *442–43*, 496
Teamster ("Poor Man's Pudding"), *443*
Teei (*Mardi*), *443*
Teg ("On the Sea Serpent"), *443*
Tégner, Esais, 212
"The Temeraire," *443–44*
Tempest, Don ("To Major John Gentian"), *444*
Teniers, David, the Younger, 34, *444–45*
Ten Months in Brazil (Codman), 86
Tennyson, Alfred, Lord, 270, 318, 399
Theseus ("The Archipelago"), *445*
Third Nantucket Sailor (*Moby-Dick*), *445*
Thirty Years from Home (Leech), 440

"This, That and the Other," *445*

Thomas, Frances Melville (daughter), 12, 153, 223, 284, 285, 287, 289, 291, 428, *445*

Thomas, Richard, 69, 221, 343, *445–46*

Thompson (*Redburn*), 446

Thompson, William, 92

Thomson, James, 39, 40, 399, 400

Thoreau, Henry David, 15, 28, 57, 93, 124, 125, 183, 373, 399, *446–47*, 456

Thorp, Willard, 130

"A Thought on Book-Binding," 372, *447–48*

Thrummings (*White-Jacket*), 448

Thule ("The New Ancient of Days"), *448*

Thumb, Tom. *See* Tom Thumb

Thutmose III, 119

"Thy Aim, Thy Aim?," *448*

Tidds (*Israel Potter*), 448

Tight, Tom ("Bridegroom-Dick"), *448*

Tilly, Johann, *448–49*

"Time's Betrayal," *449*

"Time's Long Ago!," *449*

Timoleon, *449–50*

Timoleon, 107, 286, 291, *450*, 477

"Timoleon," 288, 350, *450–51*

Timophanes ("Timoleon"), 451

Tinor (*Typee*), *451*

Tintoretto, *451–52*, 479

Tior (*Typee*), *452*

Tistig (*Moby-Dick*), 452

Titian, *452–53*, 479

Titonti (*Mardi*), 453

Tobias ("To Major John Gentian"), *453*

Toby (*Typee*), 453

"Toby's Own Story" (Greene), 172

To Cuba and Back (Dana), 104

Tom [Melville], 454

Tom (*White-Jacket*), 453

"To Major John Gentian," *453*

Tomasita (*White-Jacket*), 453

"Tom Deadlight (1810)," *453–54*

Tommo (*Typee*), *454*

Tompkins ("Hawthorne and His Mosses"), 454

Tom Thumb, 26, *454–55*

Tonans, Jupiter ("The Lightning-Rod Man"), *455*

"To Ned," *455*

Tongatona (*Mardi*), *455*

Tonoi (*Omoo*), *456*

Tooboi (*Mardi*), *456*

Tooboi (*Omoo*), *456*

Tooke, John Horne, 53, 145, *456*

Tooroorooloo (*Mardi*), *456*

Too-Too (*Typee*), *457*

Top-Gallant Harry ("Bridegroom-Dick"), *457*

Topo (*Mardi*), *457*

Torf-Egill (*Mardi*), *457*

Torriano, Juanelo, 33

"Tortoises and Tortoise Hunting," *457*

"To the Master of the *Meteor*," *457*

"To Tom," *457*

Toulib (*Clarel*), *457*

"The Town-Ho's Story", 182

Tracy, Nathaniel, 8

Tranquo (*Moby-Dick*), *458*

"Traveling," 290, *458*

Tribonnora (*Mardi*), *458*

Tromp, Cornelis van, 109, *458*

"Trophies of Peace," *459*

Truman, John (*The Confidence-Man*), *459*

Trumbull, Henry, 207, 297

Truxill ("The Encantadas"), *459*

Tryon ("Lyon"), *459*

Tubbs (*White-Jacket*), *459*

"The Tuft of Kelp," *459*

Turbans (*Clarel*), *459*

Turkey ("Bartleby"), *459*

Turner, J.M.W., 444, *459–61*

Turret ("Bridegroom-Dick"), *461*

Twice-Told Tales (Hawthorne), 186

The Two Brothers (Balzac), 450

"The Two Temples," 290, 340, 363, 372, 374, 442, *461–62*

Two Years before the Mast (Dana), 57, 104, 181, 302

Tyerman, Daniel, 268

Tyler, John, 43

Typee, 51, 107, 172, 181, 191, 200, 232, 237, 267, 285, 288, 312, 330, 374, 410, 413, 425, *462–68*, 487

"Typee" (Greene), 172

Uhia (*Mardi*), *469*
Ulver, Delly (*Pierre*), *469*
Ulver, Mrs. Walter (*Pierre*), *469*
Ulver, Walter (*Pierre*), *469*
Una ("The Bell-Tower"), *469*
"Under the Ground," *469–70*
"Under the Rose," *470*
Undine (Fouqué), 501
Ungar (*Clarel*), *470*
"An uninscribed Monument," 429, *470*
Urania ("After the Pleasure Party"), *470–71*
Ushant, John (*White-Jacket*), *471*
Usher (*Moby-Dick*), *471*
Utamai (*Omoo*), *471*
"A Utilitarian View of the Monitor's Fight," *471–72*

V., L. A. ("Fragments from a Writing Desk"), *473*
Van (*Omoo*), *473*
Vanderbilt, Cornelius, 217, *473–74*
Van der Blumacher, Tuenis ("A Dutch Christmas"), *474*
Van de Velde, *474–75*
Van Dyck, Anthony, 176, 396, *475–76*
Vane's Story (Thomson), 39
Vangi (*Mardi*), *476*
Vangs (*Typee*), *476*
Van Lord, Mrs. (*Pierre*), *476*
Van Winkle, Mrs. Rip ("Rip Van Winkle's Lilac"), *476*
Van Winkle, Rip (Irving), 198
Van Winkle, Rip ("Rip Van Winkle's Lilac"), *476*
Varnopi (*Mardi*), *476*
Varvy (*Omoo*), *477*
Vavona (*Mardi*), *477*
Vedder, Elihu, 107, 142, 210, *477–78*
Vee-Vee (*Mardi*), *478*
Velazquez, Diego, *478*
Velluvi (*Mardi*), *478*
Veloso, Fernão (*The Lusiads*), 70
"Venice," *479*
Ventom, Henry, 174, 247, 493
Ver ("The Old Fashion"), *479*
Verbi (*Mardi*), *479*

Vere, Honorable Edward Fairfax, Captain (*Billy Budd*), *479*
Veronese, Paolo, *479–80*, 451
"The Vial of Attar," *480*
Victor ("Magnanimity Baffled"), *480*
Victor (*Omoo*), *480*
"The Victor of Antietam," 429, *480–81*
"View of the Barnum Property," *481*
Vine (*Clarel*), 185, *481*
Viner (*Omoo*), *481*
Vineyarder (*Omoo*), *481*
Virginian ("Hawthorne and His Mosses"), *481*
Viscaya, Manuel ("Benito Cereno"), *481*
Viscount (*White-Jacket*), *482*
A Visit to the South Seas, in the U.S. Ship Vincennes (Stewart), 330, 467
Vivia (*Pierre*), *482*
Vivo (*Mardi*), *482*
Voluto (*Mardi*), *482*
Volvoon (*Pierre*), *482*
Voyage of the U.S. Frigate Potomac (Reynolds), 386–87
Voyages and Travels in Various Parts of the World (Langsdorff), 237, 330, 467
Voyages aux îles du Grand Océan (Morenhout), 303
Voyage to the South Atlantic (Colnett), 129
Voyo (*Mardi*), *482*

Wahabee (*Clarel*), *483*
"Wakefield" (Hawthorne), 5
Walcott, Ephraim, 302, 349
Walden (Thoreau), 15
Walks about . . . Jerusalem (Bartlett), 81
Wallace, George, 242
Wallace, Lew, *483–84*
Wang Taou ("On the Chinese Junk"), *484*
Washington, George, 8, 26, 121, 177, 195, 204, 240, 280, 373, 403, *484*
Waterford (*Redburn*), 484
Watteau, Antoine, *485*
"The Way-Side Weed," *485*
Weaver (*The Confidence-Man*), *485*
"The Weaver," *486*
Webster, Daniel, 268, 402, 409

Webster, John, 245, 410
Webster, John White, 83
Wedge (*White-Jacket*), *486*
Weed, Thurlow, 150, 153, *486–87*, 459
Weeds and Wildings, 107, 286, *487*
Weeks, Hiram, 65
Wellingborough (*Redburn*), *487*
Wellington, Arthur, Duke of, *487–88*
Wen (*Pierre*), *488*
The Whale, 37. *See also Moby-Dick*
The Whale and His Captors (Cheever), 302
''When Forth the Shepherd Leads the Flock,'' *488*
White (''I and My Chimney''), *488*
The White Devil (Webster), 245
White-Jacket, 36, 37, 39, 47, 64, 104, 181, 200, 267, 285, 290, 312, 382, 383, 425, *488–92*, 475
Wilkes (*Billy Budd*), *492*
Wilkes, Charles, 6, 83, 136, 268, 302, 330, 375
Will (''Bridegroom-Dick''), *492*
Willi (*Mardi*), *492*
William (*Omoo*), *492*
William (''To Major Gentian''), *492*
Williams (*White-Jacket*), *492–93*
Williams, Edward, 413
Williams, Griffith, 492–93
Williamson (*Israel Potter*), *493*
Willie (''Stockings''), *493*
Wilmot, David, 389
Wilson (*Omoo*), *493*
Wilson, Charles, 455, *493*
Wilt (*Redburn*), *493*
Winnefred (''Clover Dedication''), *493*
Winsome, Mark (*The Confidence-Man*), *494*
Winter Sketches from the Saddle (Codman), 86
Winwood, Ralph (*Pierre*), *494*
Wise, Henry, 32, 65, 330, 493
''The Wise Virgins,'' *494*
Wonder (*Pierre*), *494*
Wood (*Redburn*), *494*
Woodcock, John (*Israel Potter*), 53–54, 145, *494–95*

Woodcock, Mrs. (*Israel Potter*), *494*
Woodcocke, Charles, *495. See also* Woodcock, John
Wooloo (*White-Jacket*), *495*
Worden, John, *495*
Wordsworth, William, 109
Wormoonoo (*Typee*), *495*
Worth, William, *495–96*
The Wreck of the Grosvenor (Russell), 188, 397
Wright (*The Confidence-Man*), *496*
Wymontoo-Hee (*Omoo*), *496*
Wynodo (*Mardi*), *496*

X— (*Billy Budd*), *497*
Xiki (*Mardi*), *497*

Yambaio (''Benito Cereno''), *499*
Yamjamma (*Mardi*), *499*
Yamoyamee (*Mardi*), *499*
Yancey, William, 320
Yankee Doodle, 20, 120, 274, 319, 332, 334, 417, 481,*499–500*
Yankee Doodle (''Authentic Tales''), *499*
Yankee Doodle (''On the Chinese Junk''), *499*
Yau (''Benito Cereno''), *500*
''The Year,'' *500*
Yellow Torch (*White-Jacket*), *500*
Yillah (*Mardi*), *500–501*
Yoky (*Mardi*), *501*
Yola (''Benito Cereno''), *501*
Yoomy (*Mardi*), *501*
Yorpy (''The Happy Failure''), *501*

Zardi (''Rammon''), *503*
Zeke (*Omoo*), *503*
Zenzi (*Mardi*), *503*
Zenzori (*Mardi*), *503*
Ziani (*Mardi*), *503*
Zmiglandi (*Mardi*), *504*
Znobbi (*Mardi*), *504*
Zonoree (*Mardi*), *504*
Zooperbi (*Mardi*), *504*
Zozo (*Mardi*), *504*
Zuma (*Mardi*), *504*

About the Author

ROBERT L. GALE is Professor Emeritus of American Literature at the University of Pittsburgh. His other books include *A Henry James Encyclopedia* (1991), *The Gay Nineties in America: A Cultural Dictionary of the 1890s* (1992), and *A Cultural Encyclopedia of the 1850s in America* (1993), all published by Greenwood Press.